CHINA

GUIDE

YOUR PASSPORT TO GREAT TRAVEL!

CRITICAL ACCLAIM FOR RUTH LOR MALLOY'S *CHINA GUIDE*
– *New, revised, 9th edition!!!* –

"The most comprehensive and practical of the many recent books I've seen. An up-to-date, informative guide to China travel."

Loren Fessler, author of *China* and *Chinese in America*

"This hefty book is packed with facts, maps, and terrific tips on everything from accidents to earthquakes, toilets to tipping. (A) first-rate history of the awakening giant, Malloy answers most questions a novice traveler might have."

Paul King, *The Toronto Star*

"This guide may be the best once-over-lightly look at China ... it not only covers destinations, restaurants, hotels and shopping, but also gives you a passing acquaintance with useful aspects of Chinese culture."

Keith Graham, *The Atlanta Journal/The Atlanta Constitution*

"For my money, this is the best book on the market. Malloy has put together a comprehensive book which calls it like it is, but at the same time explains why it is like it is! You won't be able to put this book down, so loaded is it with ancedotes, tips, and down-to-earth common sense. If it sounds like I'm raving, it's because this book definitely deserves it!"

Lorraine Williams, *The Budget Traveler*

ABOUT THE AUTHOR

Ruth Lor Malloy is a Canadian of Chinese ancestry. She has been a veteran travel writer, conference organizer, social worker, freelance photographer, wife and mother, and author of guide books to China since 1975, including Fielding's People's Republic of China, now an Open Road travel guide. She travels frequently to China, has lectured on a Yangtze River cruise ship, and leads tour groups there.

She has also published a novel and, with her daughter Linda, is the author of Open Road Publishing's *Hong Kong and Macau Guide*. Her home is in Toronto, but she has recently been living in Kazakhstan and India.

HIT THE OPEN ROAD - WITH OPEN ROAD PUBLISHING!

Open Road Publishing now has guide books to exciting, fun destinations on four continents. As veteran travelers, our goal is to bring you the best travel guides available anywhere!

No small task, but here's what we offer:

• All Open Road travel guides are written by authors with a distinct, opinionated point of view – not some sterile committee or team of writers. Our authors are experts in the areas covered and are polished writers.

• Our guides are geared to people who want great vacations, great value, and great tips for both standard tourist sights *and* fun, unique alternatives.

• We're strong on the basics, but we also provide terrific choices for those looking to get off the beaten path and *experience* the country or city – not just *see* it or pass through it.

• We give you the best, but we also tell you about the worst and what to avoid. Nobody should waste their time and money on their hard-earned vacation because of bad or inadequate travel advice.

• Our guides assume nothing. We tell you everything you need to know to have the trip of a lifetime – presented in a fun, literate, no-nonsense style.

• And, above all, we welcome your input, ideas, and suggestions to help us put out the best travel guides possible.

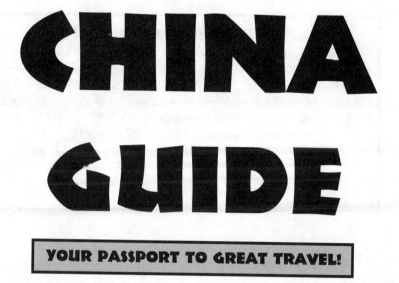

CHINA GUIDE

GUIDE

YOUR PASSPORT TO GREAT TRAVEL!

RUTH LOR MALLOY

OPEN ROAD PUBLISHING

9th Edition

Copyright ©1996 by Ruth Lor Malloy
Library of Congress Catalog Number 96-67031
ISBN 1-883323-29-0

Photo credits: front cover photo by James Nelson; back cover photo of Great Wall by Rich Monastersky and Cheri Wiggs; back cover photo of little boy by Jack Hollingsworth. Photos on pages 21, 45, 245, 563, and 610 courtesy of Rich Monastersky and Cheri Wiggs; page 477 courtesy of Michael and Rachel Lostumbo.

Maps by Rob Perry, except those on page 12 and pages 24-25.

TABLE OF CONTENTS

ACKNOWLEDGMENTS   13

1. INTRODUCTION   15

2. EXCITING CHINA! - OVERVIEW   16
How To Use This Book   20

3. SUGGESTED ITINERARIES   26

4. A SHORT HISTORY   28

5. LAND & PEOPLE   44

6. PLANNING YOUR TRIP   61
Before You Go   61
    When To Go?   61
    Other Things To Consider When Planning   62
    What to Pack   62
    China National Tourist Offices   68
    Check Your Own Customs Regulations   68
    Health Precautions   69
    Formalities   70
    Chinese Missions Abroad   71
    Hotel Reservations   72
Getting There   73
    How Should You Go?   73
    Using Travel Specialists   81
    Making Reservations   88
    Entering China   88
Arriving in China   96
    Border Formalities   96
    Changing Money   96

CONTENTS

Getting to Your Hotel   96
Making Connecting Flights   97
Leaving China   97

7. BASIC INFORMATION   99

8. GETTING AROUND CHINA   146
Flying in China   146
Trains   150
Bicycles   153
Getting Around Cities & Towns   154

9. SHOPPING   158

10. SPORTS & RECREATION   166

11. FOOD & DRINK   169

12. ACCOMMODATIONS IN CHINA   180

13. CHINA'S BEST HOTELS   190

14. BEIJING & THE GREAT WALL   193
Beijing   193
    Arrivals & Departures   193
    Orientation   195
    Getting Around Town   196
    Where to Stay   198
    Where to Eat   211
    A Proposed Itinerary   218
    Seeing the Sights   220
    Nightlife & Entertainment   236
    Shopping   238
    Practical Information   241
The Great Wall   243

15. SHANGHAI   246
Arrivals & Departures   247
Orientation   248
Getting Around Town   249
Where to Stay   250

CONTENTS

Where to Eat   260
A Proposed Itinerary   262
Seeing the Sights   263
Nightlife & Entertainment   269
Shopping   270
Excursions From Shanghai   274
Practical Information   275

16. EAST CHINA   278

Fuzhou   278
Grand Canal   281
Hangzhou   281
Hefei   290
Huangshan Scenic Area   294
Nanjing   297
Ningbo   308
Quanzhou   311
Shaoxing   315
Suzhou   317
Wuxi   326
Xiamen   329
Yangzhou   333
Zhenjiang   336

17. NORTH CHINA   342

Chengde   342
Datong   347
Hohhot   350
Jinan   355
Qingdao   359
Qinhuangdao   365
Beidaihe   367
Qufu   369
Shijiazhuang   373
Tai'an   375
Taiyuan   377
Tianjin   381
Weifang   387
Weihai   389
Yantai   390
Zunhua   395

CONTENTS

18. NORTHEAST CHINA   397

Changchun   397
Harbin   401
Shenyang   404
   Excursions from Shenyang   406
     Anshan   407
     Dalian   407
     Dandong   409
     Fushun   409

19. NORTHWEST & CENTRAL CHINA   411

Northwest China   411
   Dunhuang   411
   Jiayuguan   414
   Kashi   416
   Lanzhou   418
   Silk Road   422
   Turpan   426
   Urumqi   429
   Xi'an   434
   Yinchuan   453
   Xining   456
Central China   459
   Kaifeng   459
   Zhengzhou   463
     Excursions from Zhengzhou   465
     Anyang   465
     Cave Temples & Tombs   467
     Dengfeng County Area   468
   Luoyang   470

20. TIBET   476

Lhasa   476
   Excursions from Lhasa   489
     Shigatse & Gyantse   489
     Royal Tibetan Tombs   491
     Ganden Monastery   491
     Elsewhere in Tibet   491
     Treks   491

CONTENTS

21. SOUTH CHINA 493

Changsha 493
Guangzhou 497
  Excursions from Guangzhou 512
    Foshan 512
    Jiangman 514
    Shantou 514
    Shaoguan 515
    Taishan 516
    Xinhui 518
    Xiqiao Mountain 519
    Zhaoqing 519
    Zhongshan 521
    Zhuhai 523
Guilin 525
Haikou, Hainan Island 537
Jingdezhen 540
Jiujiang 541
Lushan 542
Nanning 544
Shenzhen 548

22. SOUTHWEST CHINA 556

Chengdu 556
  Excursions from Chengdu 561
    Wildlife Preserve 561
    Emei Shan Mountain 561
    Jiuzhaigou 562
    Leshan 563
    Sansu Shrine 564
    Tibet 564
    Wolong Nature Preserve 565
    Xichang 565
    Zigong 565
Chongqing 566
  Excursions from Chongqing 571
    Stone Buddhist Sculptures at Dazu 571
    Fengdu 572
    Diaoyu Castle 573
Guiyang 573
  Excursions from Guiyang 576
    Anshun 576
    Ethnic Villages 577

CONTENTS

Kunming   579
   Excursions from Kunming   585
     Jing Hong   585
     Xiaguan & Dali   587
     Lijiang & Zhongdian to Tibet   589
Wuhan   591
Yangtze Gorges   597

23. RECOMMENDED READING   611

24. CHINESE CHARACTERS   615

INDEX   638

MAPS

China & Neighbors   12
People's Republic of China   24-25
Beijing Subway   197
Beijing   219
Shanghai   251
Hangzhou   283
Nanjing   301
Qingdao   361
The Silk Road   425
Xi'an Terracotta Army Museum   442
Kaifeng   460
Tibet & Central Lhasa   479
Guangzhou   507
Guilin   531
Li River Cruise   534
Yangtze Gorges   603

CONTENTS

SIDEBARS

The Best, The Largest, The Most ...
19

*Abbreviations & Shorthand Used
in This Book* 23

Essential Up-to-Date Information
62

*Chinese Yuan/U.S. Dollar
Exchange Rate* 67

Movies to Get You Ready for China!
68

*Western Hotels in China & Their
Toll-Free Numbers* 73

Get It In Writing! 82

1997 And All That 92

*Now That You've Arrived, Don't
Forget To ...* 97

Books in English 100

Medical Emergencies 104

A Phonetic Guide to Chinese 114

Save on Airfare! 129

*Calling Card Access Numbers &
Country Codes* 143

Flying China's Friendly Skies 148

Approximate Flight Times 149

All Aboard the Iron Rooster! 150

*Checklist for Travelers
on Their Own* 157

Join a Camel Trek! 167

Try Chinese Wine 173

Here's the Best Way to Eat ... 177

U.S. Dollar Prices 181

Room Problems? 183

Two Unique Dining Experiences!
212

The Hutong Tour 235

Beijing's Jazz & Classical Hotspot!
237

*Some Good Books to Get You in
the Mood for Shanghai* 248

Pudong 249

Grand Canal Boat Tours 322

Pearl S. Buck, Friend of China 338

The Snake Story & Chinese Opera
340

The Philosophy of Confucius 371

Visit a Factory 385

Kite Heaven! 387

If You're a Bird Watcher 403

Eating & Drinking on the Silk Road
424

The Uygurs 432

Tourist Sights in Xi'an By Location
436

The Jewish Community of Kaifeng
462

*Searching for China's Oldest
Dynasty* 469

How to Arrange Travel to Tibet
481

Wanted – Dalai Lama Photos 483

*Guangdong's Gift to the World:
Her People* 500

*Beware the Karaoke Craze
in Guangzhou!* 505

The Museum of the Nanyue King
506

By Bus to Hong Kong 513

Discounts in Guilin Hotels 527

Going to Vietnam 547

Traditional Medicine At Work!
570

The Burma Road 590

The Dam 599

"Li Sao" by the poet Quyuan 610

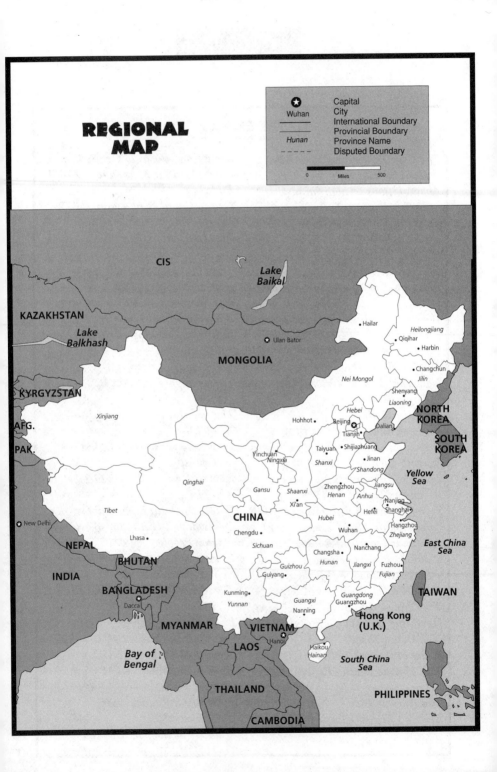

REGIONAL MAP

★	Capital
Wuhan	City
—	International Boundary
—	Provincial Boundary
Hunan	Province Name
– – –	Disputed Boundary

0 Miles 500

CIS

KAZAKHSTAN

Lake Baikal

Lake Balkhash

MONGOLIA

Ulan Bator

Hailar

Heilongjiang

Qiqihar

Harbin

Changchun

Jilin

Nei Mongol

Shenyang

Liaoning

NORTH KOREA

KYRGYZSTAN

AFG.

PAK.

Xinjiang

Hohhot

Hebei

Beijing

Tianjin

Dalian

SOUTH KOREA

Taiyuan

Shijiazhuang

Yinchuan

Ningxia

Shanxi

Jinan

Shandong

Yellow Sea

Qinghai

Gansu

Shaanxi

Zhengzhou

Henan

Jiangsu

Anhui

Nanjing

Shanghai

Tibet

Xi'an

CHINA

Hubei

Hefei

New Delhi

Chengdu

Wuhan

Hangzhou

Zhejiang

NEPAL

Lhasa

Sichuan

Changsha

Nanchang

East China Sea

BHUTAN

Guizhou

Hunan

Jiangxi

Fuzhou

Fujian

INDIA

Guiyang

BANGLADESH

Dacca

Kunming

Yunnan

Guangxi

Nanning

Guangdong

Guangzhou

TAIWAN

MYANMAR

VIETNAM

Hanoi

Hong Kong (U.K.)

Bay of Bengal

LAOS

Haikou

Hainan

South China Sea

PHILIPPINES

THAILAND

CAMBODIA

ACKNOWLEDGMENTS

Many people are responsible for this book: travelers who took the time to share their experiences and impressions, hotel officials who talked not just of their work but of the problems and joys of living in China, business travelers on airplanes, and fellow tourists in hotel elevators, trains, and mountain tops. I am particularly grateful to friends who traveled with me on tours from Kazakstan, to the Yangtze Gorges, on the China Travel Service (H.K.) four-day Guangdong tour, and with Distant Horizons (Boston). A special thank-you to Cathy Thomas who shared my passion for 6 am taiji sessions, and to Joan Ahrens whose knowledge of the value of Chinese antiques and curios helped open my eyes to the bargains available in China. Your reactions were particularly valuable.

I also appreciated the time taken to share their experiences by Loren Fessler, Elaine Freedman, Alison Hardie, Violet Ho, Leu Siew Ying and her friends from the French Consulate in Shanghai, Rob Maddock, Melvin S. Merzon, Elaine Nicholson, Linda Rose, Al and Gloria Shapiro, Catherine Smith, John Stonham, and old China-hands S.J. Chan, Caroline Walker, Andrew and Judy Wark.

A special thank-you goes to the China National Tourism Administration in Beijing, the China Tourist Office in New York, Cynthia McLean of the Canadian Council of Churches, the Canadian Embassy (Beijing), Canadian Consulate (Shanghai), and the United States Consulate (Shanghai). What could I have done without the input of seasoned professionals like Marion Darby of Shangri-La International, Carole Goldsmith of the Portman Shangri-La, Linda Ho of Holiday Inns Asia-Pacific, Trinity Travel (Toronto), Guo Yimei of China Travel Service (Hong Kong), Bonnie Yang of China International Travel Service (Qingdao), Cheng Mei Hong of the Shanghai Tourism Administration, Ren Li of CITS, Graeme Allen of the Holiday Inn Urumqi and the Shangri-La Hangzhou, and Yang Yi of China Travel Service (Urumqi).

There were also Great Escapes Trekking (Kathmandu) on whom I've grown dependant, Hirokazu Maruhasi of Japan Air System (Guangzhou), the incomparable Michael Sun of the Guangzhou Tourist Corporation, the Guangdong Tourism Administration, Shenzhen Tourism Administration, Sichuan Tourism Administration, Zhejiang Tourism Administration, and the Ningbo Tourism Bureau. Thanks also to guides Zhang Jian, Lincoln Cui and Mary Wei in Xinjiang, the Henan Tourism Administration, Zhou Shi Zhi of CITS (Chongqing), the subscribers of the Travel China Newsletter, Folke and Christina von Knobloch of Central Asia Travel (Almaty), and the many people who answered my questionaires.

Especially helpful were Beijing's Capital, China World, Great Wall Sheraton, Hilton International, Holiday Inn Lido, Holiday Inn Crowne Plaza, Movenpick, Palace and Shangri-La Hotels; Chengdu's Jin Jiang and Chengdu Hotels; Guangzhou's Dong Fang, Garden and China Hotels; Guilin's Fubo and Royal Garden Hotels, and Kunming's Green Lake Hotel. Thanks also to Shanghai's Holiday Inn Crowne Plaza, JC Mandarin, Portman Shangri-La, Sofitel Hyland, Sheraton Hua Ting and Westin Tai Ping Yang Hotels, The Gap Restaurant, and the Jia Jia Le Restaurant. Among my biggest sources of information were the International Travel Exposition (ITE) in Hong Kong and leads from China Daily and Travel China. My gratitude also goes to Bob Orchard, publisher of the Travel China Newsletter for his optimism and encouragement, and to my editor Jonathan Stein for his guidance and support.

Most of all, this book would not have been possible without the cooperation of my family, especially my husband Michael Malloy (who did go along on two China trips), and my daughter Linda who helped to edit this book. To all go my thanks, and the thanks of our readers.

1. INTRODUCTION

China is a fascinating place, a historically and culturally rich country. A visit to China is an incredible experience. In this 9th edition of my China guides, I've updated this book to again bring you the real China. I'll take you to all the great destinations you've heard so much about, plus hundreds more you may not know. I'll show you terrific hotels and guest houses, restaurants and temples and recommend hundreds of fun and exciting things to do.

I'll take you along the length of the Great Wall, steer you to a fun camel ride along the romantic Silk Road, show you where to bicycle among the beautiful mountains of Guilin, guide you along China's great rivers and incomparable gorges. I'll take you strolling through the backstreets and alleys of Beijing, Shanghai, and Kunming, and steer you to my favorite bird-watching spots. For sheer beauty, China is hard to beat, with some of the world's most spectacular and little known natural scenery.

In Beijing, wander the Forbidden City and marvel at the majestic Summer Palace and the intriguing Temple of Heaven. In Shanghai, stroll along the Bund and visit the Yu Yuan Gardens. In Xi'an, take in the incomparable terracotta army (nearly 2,200 years old) and the magnificent city wall. And sleep in world-class hotels and dine on China's famous banquet food — where else can you get culinary delights shaped like phoenixes, swans, and rabbits?

You'll also find hundreds of pages of travel advice, trip planning ideas, local customs. food, hotels, detailed descriptions of where to go and what to do, and special advice for business people and Overseas Chinese. You'll need important place names and foods in both Chinese and English. I've even got advice on finding a job there.

So go west – across the Pacific to China for the trip of a lifetime!

2. EXCITING CHINA! - OVERVIEW

Yes, you must visit China. You've got to see what it has to offer. It's too big a country to ignore. It has the world's largest population and one of the oldest civilizations. It has had thousands of years to develop a variety of multi-splendored cultures.

For the sightseer, China has fantastic international-class attractions. There's something here for the history nut, the archaeology freak, the nature lover, the photographer, the adventurer and the vacationer. I hope you have the time and means. Visit ancient monuments, palaces, tombs and temples, river gorges and mountains. Hike through primitive forests, past varieties of trees once eaten by dinosaurs. Enjoy festivals of sweet and juicy lichis and dancing dragons; worship at smoky temples with burning incense and prostrating pilgrims. Meet China's different peoples, many of whose ornate embroidered hand-made costumes differ from village to village. Take photos of curved temple roofs silhouetted against golden red sunsets. Capture on film the misty look of mountain paintings seen on aged scrolls.

Shop or just enjoy looking at antiques, carved gilded beds, inlaid chests, porcelain, jades, cloisonne, carpets, cashmere and silk. Consider everything from up-to-date stainless steel cutlery to suitcases to gowns covered with beads and sequins. I'll show you how you can save half or more of the price you'd pay at home.

Sample China's great food with its endless variety and styles of cooking, from bland to fiery hot, its chicken and prawns, camel humps and scorpions! I'll take away the mystery and teach you how to order — and how to eat the Chinese way.

See where people lived 6000 years ago, where they made pottery and buried their dead. Puff your way up the Great Wall that 2200 years ago was linked together for over 6000 kilometers, or meditate in China's classical gardens or mountain tops. Search for traces of foreign influence - Marco

Polo, Jesuit missionaries, Jewish refugees, Muslim traders and Mongol invaders. I'll show you the development of Buddhist art.

Say "Wow!" at the camels, sand dunes, wild elephants, and the Chinese people who write in Arabic. Feel wonder at the functioning mountain-top monasteries, fighting monks, cities full of 19th-century European architecture, creepy tombs and eerie caves. Get a tan on a beach or be pampered by China's growing number of international class resorts. Get treated with some Chinese herbal medicines, acupuncture or qigong. They just might work for you.

Discover terraced mountains, gothic cathedrals, pagodas, and 100 scarlet and gold-robed "monks" marching as one with lighted lanterns on their heads. Look for the world's highest mountains, jeep through the desert, hot-air balloon over the Yellow River or fly an ultra-lite plane over the Li River. Gallop horses on China's prairies. Make friends with the hospitable natives.

Find out about one of the world's fastest growing economies, China's rite of passage as she resists yet tries to join the world community, as she moves from feudal thinking beyond communist quotas to free-market capitalism. Look for surviving pockets of the primitive and exotic. Look for the soul of the great cities with their new modern buildings, palatial hotels, subways and superhighways. Relax at nightclubs, discos, karaoke bars, in jacuzzis and on beaches, and enjoy the convenience of international direct-dial telephones, credit cards, cellular-phones, and fiber optics.

In **East China**, look for traces of the old maritime trade, the hybrid temples with fancy eaves and the great adventurers who sailed to Africa, saved Taiwan from the Dutch, and fought the pirates. Look for the schools and hospitals, monuments from successful migrants to Southeast Asia, and evidence of the Muslim traders and their mosques. Go to the silk cities with their museums, to the tranquil beauty of West Lake and discover the legacy of the Song dynasty.

Search for traces of Chiang Kai-shek and first president Sun Yat-sen in the Nationalist capital of Nanjing. Consider charming Yangzhou where Marco Polo was an official. Enjoy the old garden cities and Huangshan, the favorite of landscape mountain painters. Find the China of American author Pearl S. Buck and read her beautifully-written novels.

In **North China**, explore Beijing, the national capital, and enjoy the magnificence of the 15th-century Forbidden City palace. Walk where emperors and their families rode bicycles and played badminton. Go to the Ming and Qing imperial tombs, summer palaces, and fly a kite in Tiananmen Square. Further north, see the great Yungang Cave Temple and the incredible Hanging Temple. Hike around the temples of Wutai Mountain, Tai Mountain, and Chengde.

Follow the Great Wall by road from Badaling to the Bohai Sea and relax in Beidaihe. Hike or ride through the Mongolian grasslands with their vast vistas and horse herds. Plan your trip to include a re-enactment of an emperor's ritual worship at the temple of Confucius.

Marvel at the huge kites in the kite museum or take in the annual kite festival in Weifang. And enjoy bustling Shanghai with its European architecture, its shopping and one of the best museums in the country. If you can, visit the **Great Wall** at both ends and also in between for a better conception of its immense length and the centuries it still spans.

In **Northwest China**, follow Marco Polo from oasis to oasis along the Silk Road, thrill at the vibrant Sunday market and question the veiled women in the Uygur city of Kashi. Admire the Buddhist murals in Dunhuang's famous caves where the oldest existing printed book in the world was found. In **Central China**, bask in the refined culture of the Song dynasty in old Kaifeng, gasp at a martial arts display at the Shaolin Temple, and applaud the giant buddhas in the Longmen caves. Try to conceive of life in the Shang dynasty (16th to 11th century B.C.) when they made those incredible bronzes and sacrificed humans to the gods. And don't miss the Terracotta Warriors, the Tang and Han tombs, the temples, dance shows, and museums of Xi'an.

In **Northeast China**, ride behind one of the endangered steam locomotives and look for signs of Japanese and Russian occupation. Spy on great flocks of red-crested cranes and appreciate the sparkling ice sculpture festival. Follow in the footsteps of Puyi, the last emperor, his Manchurian palace and Communist prison.

In **South China**, pay respect to a 2000-year old noblewoman and her beautiful lacquerware and silks, and inspect the ancestral homeland of many Chinese migrants to North America, Britain and Australia. Visit the hyper-active trading port of Guangzhou with its museums, pagodas, and family temples. Enjoy the miniatures of China's main tourist attractions and the theme park of China's minorities. Cruise the lovely mountain-lined Li River in Guilin, visit minority villages, and botanical gardens.

In **Southwest China**, join a tour to visit Miao, Bouyei, Bai, Dong and Tibetan villages. Get water-splashed in the traditional way and look for former headhunters. Relax as dramatic scenery floats by on a Yangtze River cruise, and race a dragon boat in the hometown of its inspiration. Examine the fine sculptures of Buddha and ancient life in Dazu, trek in the forests of Jiuzhaigou, and look for endangered pandas in or outside of Chengdu. Climb sacred Emei Mountain or make a less stenuous visit to the great Buddha at Leshan. Find the dinosaurs and the equally giant lanterns. Go south and up to **Tibet** for one of the world's unique, isolated, thriving cultures.

Keep reading and I'll help get you to all of these and more!

THE BEST ...

Beach: Zalong Bay, Hainan (in the process of development)
City walls: Xi'an and Nanjing
Confucian experience: Qufu
Cruises: Yangtze Gorges and the Li River, Guilin
Gardens (Classical): Beijing, Suzhou, Hangzhou
Gardens: (miniature landscapes): Yangzhou
Imperial palaces: Forbidden City; Summer Palace (Beijing); Shenyang
Imperial tombs: Ming (Beijing), Qing (Zunhua) and Tang (Xi'an)
Mosques: Xi'an and Kashi
Mountain for scenery: Huangshan
Mountain for climbing: Qomolangma (Everest, in Tibet)
Museums: Beijing, Shanghai, Xi'an
Museum (dinosaurs): Zigong (Chengdu)
Museum (neolithic): Xi'an
Museum (kite): Weifang
Nature Reserves: Jiuzhaigou (Chengdu) and Wulingyuan (see Changsha)
for **wilderness;** Wolong near Chengdu and the Baishuijiang in Gansu province
for **pandas;** Bird Island near Xining, Poyang Lake near Jiujiang, and Qiqihar
near Harbin for **birds;** Jing Hong for **wild elephants;** Wuhan for **dolphins;**
Yichang for **sturgeon;** Hefei for **alligators**
Shopping (general, arts and crafts): Shanghai, then Beijing
Shopping in street markets for antiques (Sundays only): Tianjin, Shanghai
and Beijing
Shopping (Tibetan artifacts outside Tibet): Chengdu
Temples (Buddhist): Tibet, Suzhou, Hangzhou, Chengde, and Beijing
Temples (caves): Dunhuang, Datong and Luoyang
Temple (kung fu): Shaolin (Zhengzhou)
Tomb figures: Xi'an
Zoo for pandas: Chengdu, Chongqing and Beijing

THE LARGEST ...

Monument: the Great Wall
Buddha: Wuxi, then Leshan

THE MOST ...

Romantic cities: Hangzhou, Suzhou, and Guilin
Exotic experiences (with comfort): Tibet in March
Important Buddhist sights: Xi'an, Luoyang, and Dunhuang; the   Sacred
Mountains with many temples: Putuo Shan (Ningbo), Jiuhua Shan (Hefei), Wutai
Shan (Datong), and Emei Shan
Interesting small cities: Chengde, Dali, Guilin, Kaifeng, Kashi, Lhasa,
Quanzhou, Qufu, Suzhou, Taishan, Turfan, Xigaze, Yangzhou, Zhaoqing
Last Emperor sites: Puyi lived in Beijing, Changchun, Fushun, and Tianjin.
Manchu dynasty palace and tombs in Shenyang
Steam locomotives locations: Northeast China

HOW TO USE THIS BOOK

More than 1000 destinations are open to foreign visitors. Listed here are the most important destinations. Mentioned under these headings, especially those of the provincial capitals, are minor destinations that you might also like. The list here is grouped by regions along traditional Chinese lines so you will know what else is close by to see.

China is so large that you might prefer to fly. To go from Urumqi to Kashgar within Xinjiang Autonomous Region by land takes three days, by air one hour.

Where the Chinese characters or pinyin for tourist sites and restaurants have been available, they are listed in Appendix A. You can point to the characters or attempt to say the pinyin.

The words "Guest House" and "Hotel" are interchangeable and do not imply quality. The words "monastery" and "temple" are also interchangeable.

For shoppers, I have listed items produced locally which tend to be cheaper. Don't jump to the conclusion that a temple founded in 1250 A.D. means the buildings are over 700 years old. The buildings may have been rebuilt recently. In a country that has had many upheavals, air raids, and revolutions, it's amazing that so many great monuments have survived to this day.

No other country has as many historic sites or as varied offerings as China. Chinese governments on all levels and UNESCO have selected some of the most important ones for protection and renovation.

Hours given for stores and tourist sites are approximate and subject to change. Those in summer are about an hour later than those in winter. Telephone first if in doubt. Schools, villages, and factories are basically the same in the whole of China, and these are not mentioned in every destination unless there is something special about them. Please visit schools, villages, and factories wherever possible to give your trip more depth about China.

China is now producing a great deal of travel literature of its own. I encourage you to supplement the information here with what is available in China, especially more detailed maps. And consider hotels as friends, especially the ones in which you are staying. They should give you lots of free local advice.

Some of the tours mentioned, especially those away from the main cities, are available only to tour groups booking in advance, not to individuals on the spot.

Do not consider any guidebook as your only source of information about a country. A guidebook should stimulate your interest, give you good background, and give you a lot of essential facts. So ask many questions while you are in China. Only then will you learn.

AT WORK IN WESTERN CHINA

Names

There is some redundancy in names, such as Lu Shan Mountain, (*shan* means mountain) but they are for people who don't know Chinese, and such names are commonly used in English. It may appear cumbersome to put in the pinyin, the English, and the Chinese characters for place names, but in China some people will use the Chinese names and others will use the English, so Chinese characters should help avoid confusion.

Sources differ sometimes as to historical dates and events, and English translations of site names. Please be flexible. Names like Han, Song, Ming, and Qing refer to dynasty, as 'in the Ming,' with Mongol the same as Yuan, and Manchu the same as Qing.

Spellings

In 1979, China adopted the pinyin system of romanizing its language based on the Beijing pronunciation. Thus "Peking" became Beijing. The old spellings can still be found in old books and are still used occasionally in China. I have tried to use the pinyin spelling and on some occasions the old Wade-Giles. The old and new names of major cities and dynasties are in Chapter Seven.

Another confusing area has been whether words like Hong Qiao should be together as one or separated into two words. The tendency now is to combine place names into one word even though they can be very long. Shijiazhuang, for example, would be easier to pronounce if separated into Shi Jia Zhuang, but is found written both ways.

Avoid confusing the provinces Hunan and Henan, Jiangxi and Jiangsu, Shaanxi and Shanxi, Hubei and Hebei, and the cities Jilin and Jinan.

There is still no standard translation for important place names; for example, Lingyan Si in Jinan has been translated Magic Cliff or Intelligent Rock Temple in different pieces of Jinan tourist literature.

Correct telephone numbers have also been difficult to obtain. In some places more than one is listed because sources differed. Try both. Failing that, ask an English-speaking source like **CITS** (China International Travel Service), your hotel telephone operator, business center, or an embassy for an up- to-date telephone number.

Miscellaneous

The imperial dating system has always been used in China. For example, 'in the fifth year of the Emperor Hongwu.' I have compromised here by giving specific dates and/or the dynasty name. Dynastic identification is important because it puts events into context. Some dynasties are more important than others and I hope you will gradually learn them.

I have tried to make the information in this book as accurate as possible at press time. The situation in China is so fluid that changes will have taken place by the time you visit. When in doubt, ask. And should you find things different, please let me know so I can make changes for future editions.

The travel agencies, hotels, restaurants, and other enterprises listed here should be able to help you. As far as I can see they are reliable, but a mention in this book is not necessarily a recommendation. You should know your options.

Finally, to avoid having to carry a book as heavy as this, you might want to cut out the pages you think you'll need in China, and staple each section. Carrying 'Beijing' is a lot easier than carrying the whole book around Beijing.

Have a great trip!

ABBREVIATIONS & SHORTHAND
USED IN THIS BOOK

* – *National, historical or revolutionary monument protected by the State Council*

– *State-designated cultural relics shops for certified antiques*

B.C. – *Business center or hotel office capable of sending faxes, and offering a secretary for hire, photocopying, and typewriter rentals*

CAAC – *Collective word for China's domestic airlines*

Credit Cards – *Credit cards accepted: American Express, Visa, MasterCard, and sometimes Diners*

CITS – *China International Travel Service*

CTS – *China Travel Service*

CYTS – *China Youth Travel Service Tours*

Dist.A.P. – *Distance from airport*

Dist.R.W – *Distance from main railway station*

executive floor - *usually including complimentary continental breakfast, a lounge, concierge service, and sometimes drycleaning.*

HK – *Hong Kong*

HKTV – *English-language broadcasts sometimes with CNN from Hong Kong*

IDD – *International Direct Dial*

JV – *Joint Venture*

Post Office – *Most hotels can sell you stamps. Post Office means a genuine post office that can weigh packages and letters*

Ren. – *Renovated. Only major improvements mentioned*

USTV – *Satellite television reception from outside China usually of Star TV (Hong Kong) channels. Some hotels get The Bold and the Beautiful, sports, entertainment, and/or music channels. Some hotels get CNN, NHK, ABC, or NBC too*

Wide twin – *twin beds at least 53" wide each*

Y – *Yuan (Chinese currency; a number of hotels only accept payment in yuan)*

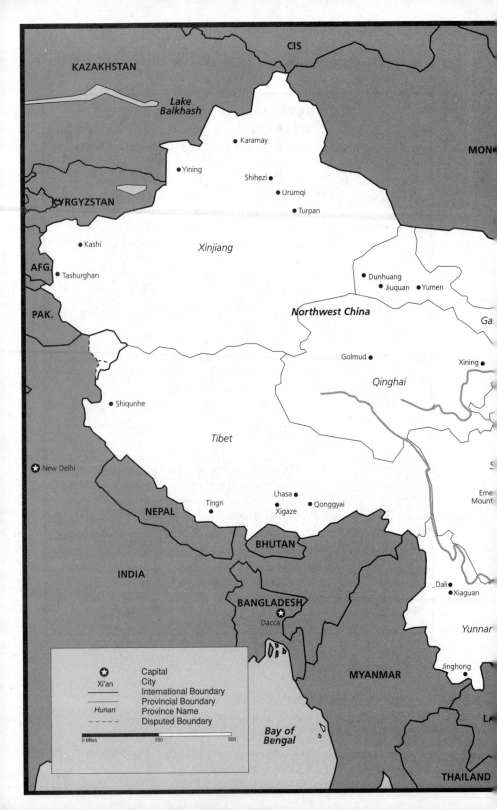

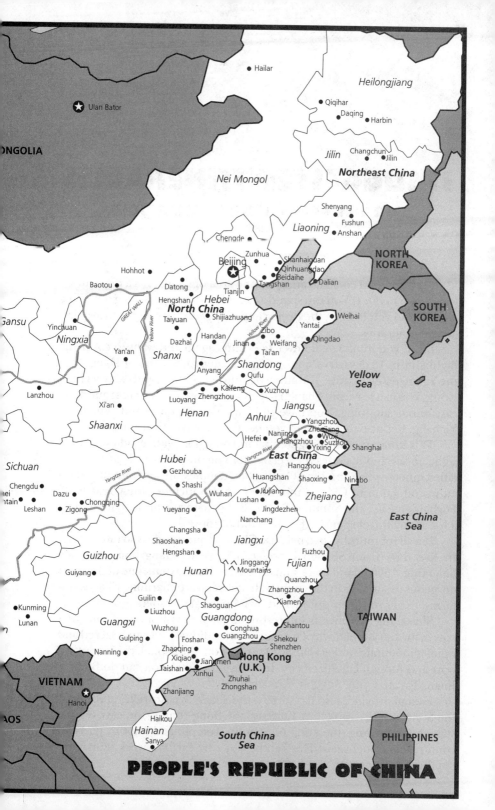

26

3. SUGGESTED ITINERARIES
FOR THE PERFECT CHINA VACATION!

I recommend concentrating on one area of China. It's a big country with much to offer! You can spend at least five days sightseeing in Beijing alone – and you'll see in the *Beijing* and *Shanghai* chapters extensive day--to-day itineraries.

But if you think you'll never see China again and want to cover the highlights in 18 days, try Beijing, Xi'an, Shanghai, Suzhou or Hangzhou, the Yangtze River cruise, Kunming or Guiyang, Guilin, and exit via Hong Kong. You can leave out Shanghai if you want to avoid big cities anddon't care about shopping. You have to include Chongqing, and Wuhan or Yichang, because that's where you get the Yangtze River cruise boat.

This itinerary is an enlightening introduction with a wide variety of sights to see and includes the Terracotta Warriors, classical gardens, big cities, quiet towns, the Grand Canal, good temples, ancient mummies and an introduction to China's minorities. It also includes the Great Wall, Forbidden City, and Summer Palace. But you go at a hectic pace and fly a lot. Many travel agents offer this kind of tour.

I'm all for tours by road because China's countryside is so interesting. In five days from Shanghai, you can drive to **Hangzhou**, then see **Shaoxing**, **1000 Island Lake**, and onward to **Huangshan**, one of the most gorgeous mountains in the country. In between are charming villages and farms, as yet relatively untouched by modern skyscrapers.

Shandong province is interesting and some visitors do a tour that covers the tiny hometown of Confucius, a medium-sized city, a sacred and unique mountain under UNESCO protection, the capital, the largest sea port and foreign colonized city. In 8 days, 7 nights, you can do Beijing, Jinan, Tai'an, Qufu, Suzhou, Shanghai.

Henan province also has variety: the Shang dynasty relics at **Anyang**, the Song dynasty capital of **Kaifeng**, the **Song tombs**, the cave-temple statues at **Luoyang**, the kung fu **Shaolin Temple** and a lot of pleasant countryside in between. This can be done by car in a week. For more details, see *Zhengzhou*.

People fly on long weekends out of Hong Kong for a relaxing holiday in **Guilin**, or shopping in Shanghai, Tianjin or Beijing. From Shanghai, you can visit the temples of **Ningbo**, or do a pilgrimage to **Putuoshan** in two days. From Beijing, you can take the train and spend a weekend visiting **Buddhist temples** and summer palace in **Chengde**.

In the cooler weather, I would also head out of Macau or Hong Kong for **Guangdong** province, nothing spectacular but interesting and enlightening: **Zhongshan** for the delta countryside and Dr. Sun Yat-sen's home, **Taishan** because it's the home of early Chinese- American immigrants, **Foshan** for the Ancestral Temple, **Zhaoqing** for charming mountain scenery, **Guangzhou** for the Cantonese food, and **Shenzhen** for the theme parks. China Travel Service offers four-day tours to some of these destinations, and you can stay longer in Shenzhen and do the theme parks on your own before returning to Hong Kong.

Most of the above suggestions tend to concentrate on South, East and North China. One of my favorite tours especially for people interested in textiles, China's minorities, and great scenery is in the Southwest: from Shanghai and Suzhou or Hangzhou, you fly to **Guiyang**, **Kaili**, and **Anshun**. The hotels in the Southwest are not as nice but you can visit minority villages and meet real weavers and embroiderers. **Suzhou** has a good silk museum. An itinerary like this can take ten days. If you want to see **Tibet**, an ancient culture clinging to the roof of the world, that's another four to six days at least.

For the adventurous and more minorities, there's the **Burma Road** of World War II fame and **Dali**, **Lijiang**, and **Zhongdian**, and then south to the Burmese (Myanmar) border. You need a week to ten days.

And don't forget the **Silk Road**, especially for people who have already done classic China. You can spend more time in imperial **Xi'an**. Don't miss **Jiayuguan** with its fortress at the western end of the Great Wall, the best of the cave temples in **Dunhuang**, the earthen ruins in **Turpan** and the Sunday market in **Kashi**. Forget Urumqi except to go in and out, and to enjoy the lovely Holiday Inn. In 12 to 14 days you can cover Beijing, Urumqi, Kashi, Turpan, Dunhuang, Jiayuguan, Xi'an and Shanghai.

4. A SHORT HISTORY

EARLIEST TIMES

The ancestors of human beings have lived in China for 8,000,000 years. Archaeologists found the remains of Ramapithecus man in Lufeng in Yunnan province. Yuanmou Man lived 1,000,000 years ago and Lantian Man, 600,000 to 700,000 years ago.

The famous **Peking Man** is a mere youngster. He's only 400,000 to 500,000 years old. About 20,000 to 30,000 years ago, Liuchiang Man lived in Guangxi, near Guilin. Hotao Man lived in Inner Mongolia, and Upper Cave Man back in Zhoukoudian. Other milestones are the **Lungshan Culture** and **Yangshao Culture** in Henan of 5,000 to 7,000 years ago. (See Xi'an's Banpo Museum.)

Dynasties date from about 2000 B.C. and overlap because different dynasties controlled different parts of China at the same time. Eastern and Western usually refer to periods of the same dynasty with different capitals.

The **Xia** dynasty usually dates from about the 21st to 16th centuries B.C. and marks the beginning of the slave system. It is known for irrigation and flood control work, a rudimentary calendar, the earliest form of writing (about 2300 B.C.) and the earliest bronzes. Some archaeologist place its capital in Henan province.

The **Shang** (16th to 11th centuries B.C.) had the earliest glazes, wine, and silk. It developed ritual bronze casting to a high art and even had carved jade handles on swords and spears. A famous Shang relic is an ivory cup inlaid with jade. It had iron and used cowry shells for money. It traded outside of China and developed writing and ancestor worship. It communicated with the gods by cracking tortoise shells and began the first cities: Zhengzhou and Anyang.

The **Western Zhou** (11th century to 771 B.C.) and the **Eastern Zhou** (770 to 249 B.C.) welded bronze and produced the first lacquer. It used copper coins and crossbows and lived in walled cities. It developed elaborate rituals and music using jade instruments, and further developed ritual bronze vessels in profusion.

Confucius lived in the **Spring And Autumn Period** (770 to 476 B.C.). This was a time of warring states fighting for power. Confucius preached a return to the Zhou rituals and tried to stabilize society by insisting on obedience to emperors, fathers, husbands, and older brothers. This was the beginning of feudalism. This period had cylindrical tile sewer pipes, iron implements and oxen for plowing, and a form of steel. It used metal spade-shaped coins, and had a knowledge of mathematics, astronomy and medicine.

The **Warring States** (47 to 221 B.C.) was a transitional period to feudalism. **Master Sun** produced his famous book *The Art of War*, praised as recently as a few years ago by General Norman Schwartzkof. During this period, **Mencius** promoted Taoism. The silent Mohists flourished. The first large scale irrigation and dams included erosion control. People used iron farm tools and manure for fertilizer. They mined and produced salt. Doctors first diagnosed diseases through feeling the pulse. Scientists wrote the first books on astronomy, and used magnets.

Emperor **Qin** (221 to 206 B.C.) unified China for the first time, and started building the **Great Wall** and the **Terracotta Army**. He standardized weights, measures, writing, and currency. He developed a strict legal code. His dynasty had the first clay burial figures, highly developed medicine and agriculture. But he is infamous for burning most historical records except those dealing with the Qin, and he executed scholars.

The **Eastern and Western Han** (206-B.C. to 220 A.D.) had the water wheel, windmill and the first seismograph. It produced the first plant-fiber paper and a water-powered bellows for smelting. It had the first important Chinese medical text, and used general anesthesia in surgical operations, acupuncture and moxibustion. Its astrologers produced the first armillary sphere and discovered that moonlight comes from the sun. During its reign, Szuma Chien wrote China's first history book. And burying rich people in jade suits was fashionable. Emperor Han Ming-ti order the first Buddhist temple built in Luoyang in 68 A.D.

The **Silk Road** (2nd century B.C. to 14th century A.D) connected China to India, West Asia and even Rome with trade routes. The Chinese exported silk, tea, iron and steel, peach and pear trees, and the knowledge of paper making and deep-well digging. They received grapes, pomegranate and walnut trees, sesame, coriander, spinach, the Fergana horse, alfalfa, Buddhism, Nestorianism, and Islam. The main stops in China west from Xi'an were Lanzhou, Wuwei, Dunhuang, then north through Turpan or south through Ruoqiang. Arab and Persian traders settled in Xi'an and Yangzhou.

During the **Three Kingdoms** (220 to 265) people managed to develop a water pump, celadon, and ships big enough to carry 3000 men, in spite of the fighting.

The **Western and Eastern Jin** (265 to 420) followed, then the **Southern** and **Northern Dynasties** (420 to 589). During these periods the Chinese developed the first arched stone bridge, the widespread use of celadon, and two crops a year. The Northern Wei dynasty started the Buddhist cave statues at Luoyang and Datong.

The **Sui** (581 to 618) built the 2,000 kilometer-long Grand Canal, ships up to 70 meters long, and an arched stone bridge still in use today in Zhaoxian county, Hebei.

CHINESE CIVILIZATION FLOURISHES

The **Tang** (618 to 907) was one of China's most prosperous and culturally developed dynasties. From this era we have three-color and snow-white porcelains, inlaid mother-of-pearl, gold and silver, wood-block printing, fine silk, and woven feathers. It used an adjustable curved-shaft plow and made an attempt at land reform. The Tang was the most prosperous period of the Silk Road but it also traded by sea. It opened a special office for foreign trade in Guangzhou, where Arab traders built a mosque. A Tang princess took Buddhism to Tibet. Chinese monks took Buddhism to Japan and Korea. (Kyoto is modeled on Xi'an). Chinese monk Hsuan Tsang went to India (629-645) to obtain the Buddhist sutras. Chinese travelers also went to Persia, Arabia, and Byzantium. Tang poets are still the most respected. Look for fat faces in paintings and sculptures. They are most likely Tang.

The **Five Dynasties** (907 to 960) was a transitional warring period. The Liao (916 to 1125) controlled Inner Mongolia and part of southern Manchuria. It invaded China and occupied Beijing and built an extant 66.6-meter wooden pagoda in Ying Xian, Shaanxi.

The **Northern and Southern Song** (960 to 1279) was a prosperous and culturally-developed period. It had the first paper money, moveable type, compass, gunpowder, and rocket-propelled spears. It made fine porcelains and red lacquer and improved on the use of acupuncture and moxibustion. It made progress in mining and metallurgy. Hangzhou, then known as Qinsai, was the largest, richest city in the world according to Marco Polo.

The **Western Xia** (1038-1277) controlled today's Gansu and western Inner Mongolia. During the Jin (1115 to 1234) the first western missionaries were recorded. Franciscan friars arrived in Inner Mongolia. The Jin captured Beijing and controlled Kaifeng, the Wei River valley, Inner Mongolia, and northwestern China.

The **Yuan** or Mongols (1271 to 1368) had a water clock and improved cotton spinning and weaving. They gave us the famous blue-and- white, the underglaze red porcelain, and cloisonne. They controlled all of today's China and areas north and east including Moscow, Kiev, Damascus, Baghdad, and Afghanistan. From 1275-92, **Marco Polo** visited and served in the court of **Kublai Khan**.

The **Ming** (1368 to 1644) imported corn, potato, tobacco, peanuts, sunflower, and tomatoes from America. It refined the blue-and-white porcelain and added colors. It had sea links with Malacca, Java, Ceylon, and East Africa. The Chinese lent Macau to the Portuguese, and the first Christian missionary, **Matteo Ricci** of the Society of Jesus, lived in Macau and then in Beijing. The Dutch colonized "Formosa" (Taiwan) until 1662.

The **Qing** (1644 to 1911) is noted for some of the best porcelains. It had to cope with foreign incursions. **Cheng Chengkung**, or Koxinga, drove the Dutch from Taiwan. Qing forces expanded into Russia, Korea, Vietnam, Burma, and Sikkim, but later lost a great deal of territory. The British introduced most of the opium as a narcotic. During this dynasty, the first U.S. trading ship, Empress of China arrived in Guangzhou, the first British mission met the emperor (at Chengde) and the first Protestant missionary, Robert Morrison of Britain, arrived. U.S. missionary work started in 1830.

In 1839, China attempted to stop the opium trade. It burned 20,000 chests near Guangzhou, more than half a year's trade. This resulted in the Opium War (1840 to 1842). Britain needed to sell China opium to balance trade. British forces with French help seized a few cities along the coast and threatened Nanjing. The Chinese gave in, ceding Hong Kong island to Britain and opening to foreign trade Guangzhou, Xiamen, Fuzhou, Ningbo, and Shanghai. This was the beginning of the foreign exploitation of China. Also involved were Germany, Italy, Japan, Belgium, Russia and the United States. In 1848 Chinese emigration to America and Australia started.

THE DECLINE OF THE DYNASTIES

The **Taiping Heavenly Kingdom** (1851 to 1864) was a rebellion against the Manchus led by a Christianity-inspired Cantonese who believed himself the younger brother of Jesus Christ. Starting in 1851 in Guangxi, this became the largest peasant movement in Chinese history. At one time or another it occupied most of China. It established a capital at Nanjing for eleven years. It was defeated in part by a foreign mercenary army led by British officer **Charles Gordon**, known as Chinese Gordon, who was later killed in the Sudan.

The **Second Anglo-Chinese War** (1856 to 1860) was also known as the Arrow War. It ended after the sacking of Beijing, the burning down of the Summer Palace and more unequal treaties for China, including the ceding of Kowloon to the British. In 1870, China started to send thirty students a year to the United States to study. Students also went to Britain and France.

During the latter half of the 19th century, the French took Vietnam (then a tributary state of China) and Japan seized Taiwan, the Pescadores, and the Liaoning peninsula from China. In 1898, Britain leased the area north of Kowloon and about 235 islands around Hong Kong for 99 years. The Chinese reacted with unhappy incidents like the Tientsin Massacre of French missionaries. It was during this turn-of-the century period that the **Empress Dowager Tzu Hsi** kept the **Kuang Hsu Emperor** under house arrest for defying her (he passed various reforms to modernize China.

In 1899, the United States declared that foreign powers should not cut up China into colonies and all nations should be free to trade with China. Only Britain bothered to reply, but for a while China looked to the United States as its only foreign friend. Then in 1900 came the **Boxer Rebellion**, also known as the Rebellion of the Society of the Righteous and Harmonious Fists, a reaction, at times encouraged by the Empress Dowager, against increasing foreign domination. The Boxers attacked foreigners and Chinese Christians.

Foreign powers, including the Americans, responded by capturing Beijing, sacking it, and forcing another humiliating treaty on China. Then the Japanese invaded southern Manchuria. The Empress Dowager died in 1908 and was succeeded by two-year- old **Pu-yi**, the last emperor of China.

THE REPUBLIC

On October 10, 1911, the first victory of **Dr. Sun Yat-sen's** republican revolutionaries followed an accidental explosion in one of their bomb factories in Hankou. Dr. Sun became president of the Chinese republic with its capital at Nanjing. But the new country suffered a lot of growing pains and external problems. Outer Mongolia, with Russian help, declared independence from China. In 1913, Yuan Shih-kai was elected president. Then Japanese troops took over the naval base at Qingdao and won its infamous Twenty-one Demands. Many Chinese protested. They protested more after Yuan proclaimed himself emperor.

The republic was saved when Yuan died of a heart attack, and warlords gained control of the country. World War I ended with the Japanese keeping its gains in China and western powers retaining their pre-war concessions.

The May 4, 1919 student demonstrations against the Versailles Treaty marked the beginning of the nationalistic and cultural upsurge known as the May Fourth Movement, the training ground for many Communist revolutionaries.

On July 1, 1921, the Chinese Communist Party was founded in Shanghai with Russian Communist help, although the Soviets preferred to support Sun Yat-sen. Dr. Sun agreed to cooperate with Russian and Chinese Communists and sent Chiang Kai-shek to Moscow for military training. Mikhail Borodin and General Vassily Blucher arrived as advisers. Dr. Sun could not be sure of help from Britain and America. On March 12, 1925, he died of cancer in Beijing.

In 1926, **Generalissimo Chiang Kai-shek** and officers with Soviet supplies, led the Northern Expedition in a successful attempt to unify China, wrest control from the warlords, and fight the unequal treaties. In 1927, the **Northern Expedition** took Nanjing and Chiang tried to purge Communists in Shanghai. Chou En-lai escaped and went on to found the Chinese Red Army which attempted to take Changsha. Ill-prepared, it withdrew to Jiangxi where the Communists established the first Chinese soviet, distributing land to the peasants in the area. The next year the Nationalists took Beijing and renamed it **Peiping** (*Northern Peace*).

In 1931, the Japanese invaded Manchuria and set up a puppet government under Pu-yi called **Manchukuo**. Chiang accepted a humiliating truce in 1933 while continuing to attack the Communists on Jinggang Shan with a 'scorched earth' policy. On October 16, 1934, the Communists, aware they could no longer hold their base on Jinggang Shan, started out with 80,000 troops on the Long March. They arrived three months later in Xunyi, Guizhou. **Mao Tse-tung** took over as leader of the March and they decided on northern Shaanxi as their goal, the only Communist base big enough. In addition, they could fight the Japanese invaders in that area.

From Xunyi, the march continued in spite of Nationalist bombs and troops. The major battles were fought at Loushan Pass (February 1935) and Luting suspension bridge over the Tatu River. Edgar Snow gives a good account of the march in his book, *Red Star Over China*. Some of the important battles have been immortalized in ivory or porcelain. The **Long March** was joined by other Communist armies and ended in northern Shaanxi in 1935, a journey of 12,500 kilometers. The original marchers were reduced to 8,000, including 30 women. The Communists moved to Yan'an in 1937.

The Communists fought against the Japanese while the Nationalists tried to eliminate the Communists. In 1936 Chiang was kidnapped by one of his own officers at Huaqing Hot Spring and forced into a wartime coalition with the Communists against the Japanese, in what is known as the **Xi'an Incident**.

THE JAPANESE WAR & CIVIL WAR

On July 7, 1937, the killing of Japanese soldiers near Beijing set off the 1937-45 war between Japan and China, during which Japan occupied most of urban China. Chiang moved his capital to Hankou and finally to

Chongqing while the western powers remained neutral. Many warlords with their private armies rallied to fight the Japanese but were destroyed.

Although the Nationalists blocked supply routes, the Communist armies waged guerrilla warfare against the Japanese, engaged in political and economic work among peasants, and developed strategy, discipline, and plans for the takeover of the rest of China.

In 1938 the Canadian surgeon **Dr. Norman Bethune** joined the Communist Eighth Route Army and died the following year of blood poisoning while operating without antiseptics. Because of his skills at improvisation and selfless devotion to duty, Bethune later became a Chinese national hero. (See *Shijiazhuang*.)

The United States entered the war after Japan's attack on Pearl Harbor in 1941. It increased aid to Chiang and tried to reconcile Mao and Chiang against the Japanese.

The war ended in 1945. China got most of her territory back, including Taiwan and the Pescadores. Outer Mongolia and Manchuria were placed under the Russian sphere of influence. The Chinese **civil war** continued though, especially in Manchuria. US President Harry Truman ended aid to the Nationalists to avoid American involvement in the civil war.

The Communists advanced and eventually won because of severe inflation, Nationalist corruption, the breakdown of law and order, mass Nationalist troop defections, and the Communists' success in winning the hearts and minds of the peasants.

THE MAO YEARS

On October 1, 1949, known as Liberation Day, **Chairman Mao** proclaimed the birth of the **People's Republic of China** from the Gate of Heavenly Peace, Tiananmen, in Beijing. Later Chiang and loyal troops and officials fled to **Taiwan**. Refugees flooded Hong Kong. The Communists tried but failed to take the offshore islands of Matsu and Quemoy across from Taiwan.

For the next decade the Communists, with Russian help, tried to rebuild the nation and put their ideals into practice. They started trials by peasants of landlords and executed about two million people. They attempted to "remold" intellectuals. They divided the land among the peasants, 0.15 to 0.45 acres each.

In 1950, the Korean War began and North Korea invaded South Korea. Chinese forces joined the North after the United Nations and South Koreans counterattacked north of the 38th parallel border and China felt threatened. The Chinese jailed and expelled many foreign missionaries, teachers, and scholars as imperialist spies. China accused the United States of using poison gas and germ warfare and circulated maps showing American bases surrounding China. The Americans began an embargo which ended in the 1970s.

China started to use Hong Kong and Macau as trading centers and sources of foreign exchange. In 1950, Britain recognized China. In 1951, China took Tibet. In 1955, the Chinese suppressed a rebellion there and in 1959, the Dalai Lama fled to India.

During 1956-57, Mao, in an effort to incorporate intellectuals into the revolution, began the **Hundred Flowers Movement**: "Let a hundred flowers bloom together, let the hundred schools of thought contend." Mao believed the overwhelming majority of intellectuals supported the revolution and communism, and encouraged intellectuals to speak freely about the bureaucracy. Intellectuals did not respond and about a year later the Communist Party began its own efforts to clean-up the bureaucracy. Once started, the intellectuals participated fully. However, the attacks were so severe that within five weeks the Movement ended and the **Anti-Rightest Campaign** began, aimed at the intellectuals.

The **Great Leap Forward** (1958-60) was a failed economic plan that led to the death of millions of people. Mao was convinced that food production could be substantially increased by reorganizing people into communes. Unfortunately, the communes were reporting increases in production when production was decreasing. Initial efforts to report the bad news were not well received by Mao, and the devastating program continued until 1960.

In 1961, Mao accused the Russians of being revisionists, giving in to capitalism and to "nuclear blackmail." China rejected Russia's offer of nuclear weapons in exchange for bases in China. China and Russia divorced in 1960 when Nikita Khrushchev ordered the end of all Soviet aid. Russian advisers left and the Chinese insisted on repaying Russian military aid immediately.

These years, 1959 to 1962, were a difficult period for China. In addition to the repayments, the country endured 'natural calamities.' Liu Shao-chi became president while Mao continued as Communist Party Chairman. India asserted control of disputed border territory. China sent a punitive invasion force into India and then announced a ceasefire and withdrew.

In 1963, China started to supply Hong Kong with fresh water. In 1964, it exploded a nuclear bomb at the Lop Nor testing grounds in Xinjiang. In 1964, Chiang Ching, Mao's wife started a campaign to make culture serve the revolution and abolished traditional Peking opera. Later she allowed only eight operas to be performed, all written by revolutionary committees. In 1965, an article instigated by Mao in a Shanghai newspaper introduced the **Great Proletarian Cultural Revolution** to the public for the first time. The next year, activists put up the first important

'Big Character Poster' at Beijing University and Chairman Mao felt that people were forgetting the aims of the revolution. He swam the Yangtze River at Wuhan (nine miles) to show he was still powerful and in charge.

Mao taught that workers and peasants were the basis of the Chinese revolution. Many party cadres were re-educated in 'correct' political thinking by learning to respect and love physical labor. Doctors swept floors to help them identify with the masses and understand their problems. Corruption was punished harshly.

The first of many Red Guard rallies in Tiananmen Square in support of Chairman Mao was held August 18, 1966. Schools closed so that students, really **Red Guards**, could travel and learn to make revolution. Red Guards, riding free on trains and sleeping in school dormitories were fed by municipalities. They traveled the country taking part in revolutionary movements against the **Four Olds**: the elimination of old ideas, culture, customs, and habits. They destroyed religious statues, buildings and ancestral tablets. Many Tibetan and other monasteries were destroyed during this period.

They changed the names of streets and parks from old dynastic names to 'The East Is Red' (*Dong Fang*) and 'Liberation' (*Jiefang*), stripped some women of their tight western trousers and cut off long 'bourgeois' hair. They also attacked elements of foreign influence, and any obstacles to completing the course of the revolution.

They denounced Deng Xiaoping and in 1968 deposed President Liu, who died shortly afterward (but was officially rehabilitated in 1979). The Cultural Revolution became very violent and led to riots in Hong Kong and Macau. The schools reopened in 1969. Fellow peasants and workers chose which student should study in university. They based eligibility on the completion of at least two years of manual labor, how well you knew Maoist theory, and how enthusiastic and selfless you were in serving the people.

The next year, China launched its first satellite. In 1971, the United States table tennis team and U.S.Secretary of State Henry Kissinger visited China and paved the way for American recognition of China and the visit of President Richard Nixon in 1972. China took the United Nations seat occupied by Taiwan, and Canada resumed diplomatic relations.

Deng Xiaoping was rehabilitated in 1973, and became vice-premier in charge of planning. In 1974 China asserted control of the Paracel Islands as one million Soviet troops ringed its northern border. In January 1976, **Premier Chou En-lai** died and Deng Xiao-Ping became acting premier. Chou supporters put wreaths in Tiananmen Square in his honor. Chiang Ching, Mao's wife, ordered the removal of the wreaths. A clash ensued and Mao blamed Deng, who once again fell into disfavor.

Not long after, a massive earthquake shook North China centering on the city of Tangshan and was believed by many to foretell the death of Mao Tse-tung a few months later. **Hua Guo-feng** succeeded him and arrested the **Gang of Four** who were blamed for many of the country's ills. The Four were **Chiang Ching**, Mao's widow, and three leaders from Shanghai. Deng was rehabilitated again and resumed his previous posts. The following year, posters advocating personal freedoms and democracy appeared on **Democracy Wall**, but this experiment didn't last very long at all.

In 1979, the U.S. and China resumed full diplomatic relations. Tensions between China and Vietnam were worsening in the late 1970s, and China went to war in 1979 owing to what Beijing termed Vietnamese 'armed incursions' into China.

THE DENG XIAO-PING ERA

In 1980, **Zhao Ziyang** became premier. Leaders tried to improve living standards and eliminate "left deviation, that is, the over- rigid and excess control of the economic system, the rejection of commodity production, and the mistaken attempt to transfer prematurely the ownership of all enterprises to the state."

Under the orders of **Deng Xiao-ping**, they began an economic reassessment and encouraged foreign investment. They banned Democracy Walls and sentenced **Wei Jingsheng**, one of the leaders of the movement, to 15 years in prison for subversion. (He was jailed again for another 14 years in 1995.)

By 1980, Chinese officials had stated that Mao's contribution to China outweighed his mistakes. China modified the commune system, making the family the basic economic unit and diminished the role of the Communist Party. They gave the Gang of Four suspended death sentences. **Hu Yao-bang** replaced Hua Guo-feng, Mao's chosen successor as Chairman of the Communist Party. China announced gradual price changes based on market forces. The following year United States Defense Secretary Casper Weinberger visited, and permitted the sale of some U.S. military technology to China. The campaign against 'spiritual pollution' (immoral foreign influences) was vigorously pursued for a while but gradually declined.

The leadership denounced the Cultural Revolution and the Communist Party booted out thousands of leftists. They started encouraging intellectuals to contribute to modernization.

Record harvests and an increase in cash crops encouraged the new economic policies. The leadership ordered all state-owned companies to make a profit and pay taxes. Foreign exchange reserves hit a record high, and China went on an importing spree. Factories became independent and made their own production and marketing decisions. President Ronald Reagan visited, and US-China relations warmed. Britain and China agreed that Hong Kong would revert back to China in 1997. Deng proclaimed a one-country, two-systems policy in dealing with Taiwan and Hong Kong.

The Communist Party spelled out its plan for the next three to five years and explained 'socialism with Chinese characteristics.' In 1985 the leadership reduced two-hour lunch breaks to one hour for factory workers. Sweden became the first customer for China's satellite launching service in 1986. Queen Elizabeth II visited. China joined the Asian Development Bank. Some government-owned factories were allowed to issue stock. For the first time since Liberation (1949), a factory declared bankruptcy and a stock market opened (in Shanghai). The government announced that all new factory workers would be under limited instead of life-time assignments. The government also started a federal unemployment insurance and pension scheme.

In 1987, student demonstrations for more freedom led to the resignation of leaders advocating 'bourgeois liberalization.' This included the Communist Party general secretary. University students were forced to take courses in Marxist-Leninist theories, trips to the countryside and factories, and military training.

As a result of independence demonstrations by Tibetans in Lhasa, China closed Tibet to all foreign tourists except for prepaid tours. It expelled some foreigners from the region for "interfering." Taiwan permitted its citizens to visit the mainland. Many tearful reunions took place between family members who had not seen each other since 1949. Mail, telegram, and telephone service also resumed. China opened the rostrum on the Gate of Heavenly Peace to tourists in 1988. China's foreign debt grew to $35 billion. Ugly demonstrations against African students occurred, especially in Nanjing.

In the late 1980s, previously suppressed individualism surfaced. The press printed real news, not just government-approved news. For students, the new attitudes extended to politics, and demonstrations. The leadership, once benevolent on many levels, became nepotistic and corrupt with lavish state spending on banquets, foreign cars, and overseas trips. If Mao were alive, he would have started another Cultural Revolution. Inflation started getting out of control.

The 40th anniversary of the founding of the People's Republic of China occurred in 1989. The **Panchen Lama**, the second highest Tibetan Buddhist leader, died and more demonstrations for independance took place in Lhasa. The Dalai Lama offered a compromise: China could oversee its foreign affairs and keep troops in Tibet in exchange for religious and cultural autonomy. He was awarded the Nobel Peace Prize.

In Beijing, the death of Hu Yao-bang set off student demonstrations and hunger strikes that continued relatively unopposed for a month and a half. The students asked for the end of government corruption and a say in student government. They shouted defiant foreign slogans. Demonstrations centered in **Tiananmen Square** in Beijing, but took place in other towns and cities as well. Plans for the historic visit of Soviet President Mikhail Gorbachev were thwarted because of the students. The leadership was divided on how to react.

What emerged was a reversion to old ways. Like a traditional, autocratic Chinese father who 'lost face' in front of a guest and realized his authority was disintegrating, the Chinese leadership regressed to brute force. An estimated 300 to 3000 people were killed in Tiananmen Square on June 4 ' innocent bystanders, unarmed demonstrators, civilians, soldiers and some rioters. Over 450 military, police, and public vehicles were alleged by the government to be destroyed. Student leaders were arrested.

The government said those killed were 'ruffians and criminal elements taking advantage of the turmoil.' It said the students needed political education and sent some to the army. It set students and workers to studying the government's version of the 'counter-revolutionary rebellion' and arrested student leaders. Shanghai and Beijing executed rioters. It arrested a youth for trying to place a wreath in the square and jailed a debated number of people for 'counter-revolutionary crimes'.

Around the world, thousands of protesters marched, especially in Hong Kong. Some foreign governments imposed economic sanctions. Some of the student leaders took refuge in foreign missions. The most prominent was astrophysicist **Fang Lizhi**, who lived for almost a year in the United States Embassy before being allowed to leave for the U.S.

Tourism almost stopped. The World Bank suspended all loans (it has since resumed them). Some foreign businesses withdrew. Countries abroad gave preferential treatment to Chinese refugees and made it easier for Chinese students to stay. Because of these actions and the awarding of the Nobel Peace Prize to the Dalai Lama, China accused foreign governments of interfering in its internal affairs. Amnesty International said at least 500 people were executed for offenses related to the demonstrations and for counter-revolutionary activities.

By late 1990, China was relatively back to normal, the press dull and obedient. Foreign businesses came back. International sanctions were lifted. The economy continued to grow, especially in the countryside, and China soon had an international trade surplus. Martial law was lifted in Beijing and Lhasa. Inflation was held down to 2%, compared to 17% in 1989. Twelve Catholic bishops were arrested because of secret Vatican ties. Beijing's **Asian Games** was an organizational success, but did not attract the large numbers hoped for. Taiwan and other Asian tour groups helped to bring up 1990 tourism figures to about 95% of 1988 levels.

In 1991, China's first nuclear power plant started operating in Zhejiang province. China counted eight AIDS victims since 1985 and 607 HIV positive people, mainly in Yunnan. China implemented a five-day work week and cut back on free health care and subsidies to state corporations.

The United States accused China of using forced prison labor for exports anddemanded the protection of intellectual property rights. Still, China achieved an international trade surplus including a $10 billion surplus with the United States.

In 1992 the **Euro-Asia Railway Bridge** from Rotterdam to Lianyungang was completed. Hong Kong Governor Chris Patten and Chinese officials clashed over giving more political power to the Hong Kong people and the construction of the new Hong Kong airport. And the nation had a 12% economic growth rate.

DEMOCRACY & HUMAN RIGHTS

Democracy movements are not new. Writing criticisms and complaints in public places has occurred in China for centuries and especially during the Cultural Revolution, when they were used to attack capitalist roaders (but not to criticize the government).

Late in 1978, the writing of big character posters on Democracy Walls flourished unhindered. Four months later, this right was restricted. Taboo were criticisms of socialism, the dictatorship of the proletariat, party leadership, and the ideas of Marx, Lenin, and Mao.

In 1979, foreigners could visit Democracy Walls, talk with anyone and accept leaflets. But then some Chinese were arrested and charged with passing state secrets to foreigners. In December 1979, however, wall posters were curtailed. In September 1980, these rights were deleted from the constitution.

In 1989, a million people supported student demonstrations for democracy in Beijing, and more elsewhere in the country. They were brutally suppressed. If you want more information on this subject, and on political rights in general, contact Amnesty International, Asia Watch, the US State Department.

TODAY

In the mid-1990s, the country is booming. China continued to buy airplanes and cars from the United States and its overheated economy triggered inflation and subsequent economic controls. The government announced a staff cutback of 25% within the next three years and kept trying to get rid of highly subsidized state enterprises.

The collapse of the **Gouhou Dam** in Xinjiang region killed 242 people and president Jiang Zemin ordered the Chinese press to print positive news. The government forbade officials from going into business or practicing nepotism. They were forbidden from trading in stocks or accepting gifts of money. But as they have for thousands of years, many officials bypassed the rules. The government announced that over 60% of China's 500 cities was short of water.

In the mid-1990s, China arrested, sentenced, and then released Chinese-American Harry Wu, a former prisoner who was determined to enlighten the world about conditions in China's prisons. The deportation instead of imprisonment permitted U.S. First Lady Hilary Clinton to attend the United Nation's Women's Conference in Beijing along with about 30,000 other women.

China strongly protested visits of the Taiwan president to the United States, even though these were private. It felt threatened by the Taiwan elections. The United States continued to object to the violation of intellectual property rights and human rights. Some Chinese think that the United States wants to hold China's progress back and are again turning to Russia for support. A conflict between the government and the Dalai Lama about the reincarnation of the Panchen Lama threatened even more any reconciliation on Tibet.

Work on the controversial Yangtze Gorges Dam continued in earnest. China bought American cars, factories, electric generators, subway and railway cars and airplanes. It hired Canadians to design shopping malls.

What is China's future? In China, there's the euphoria of Hong Kong's return on July 1, 1997 and Macau's return on December 20, 1999. 1997 is Visit China Year. But there's also the uncertainty of the succession and the threat of runaway inflation and corruption. China has come a long way, but still has a long way to go.

CHINA'S DYNASTIES

The names of the dynasties below are given two ways: the first word is spelled using Pinyin transliteration; the word in parentheses is the old spelling.

Xia (Hsia)	c. 21st-16th century B.C.
Shang (Shang)	c. 16th-11th century B.C.
Western Zhou (Chou)	c. 11th century-771 B.C.
Spring & Autumn Period	770-476 B.C.
Warring States Period	475-221 B.C.
Qin (Chin)	221-206 B.C.
Western Han (Han)	206 B.C. - A.D. 24

Eastern Han (Han)	25-220
The Three Kingdoms	220-265
Wei (Wei)	220-265
Shu (Shu)	221-263
Wu (Wu)	222-280
Western Jin (Tsin)	265-316
Eastern Jin (Tsin)	317-420
Southern/Northern Dynasties	420-589
Southern Dynasties	420-589
Song (Sung)	420-479
Qi (Chi)	479-502
Liang (Liang)	502-557
Chen (Chen)	557-589
Northern Dynasties	386-581
Northern Wei (Wei)	386-534
Eastern Wei	534-550
Western Wei	535-556
Northern Qi (Chi)	550-577
Northern Zhou (Chou)	557-581
Su (Sui)	581-618
Tang (Tang)	618-907
Five Dynasties	907-960
Liao (Liao)	916-1125
Song (Sung)	960-1279
Northern Song (Sung)	960-1127
Southern Song (Sung)	1127-1279
Western Xia (Hsia)	1038-1227
Jin (Kin)	1115-1234
Yuan (Yuan)	1271-1368
Ming (Ming)	1368-1644
Hongwu (Hung Wu)	1368-1399
Jianwen (Chien Wen)	1399-1403
Yongle (Yung Lo)	1403-1425
Hongxi (Hung Hsi)	1425-1426
Xuande (Hsuan Teh)	1426-1436
Zhengtong (Cheng Tung)	1436-1450
Jingtai (Ching Tai)	1450-1457
Tianshun (Tien Shun)	1457-1465
Cheng Hua (Cheng Hua)	1465-1488
Hongzhi (Hung Chih)	1488-1506
Zhengde (Cheng Teh)	1506-1522
Jiajing (Chia Ching)	1522-1567
Longqing (Lung Ching)	1567-1573

Wanli (Wan Li)	1573-1620
Taichang (Tai Chang)	1620-1621
Tianqi (Tien Chi)	1621-1628
Chongzhen (Chung Chen)	1628-1644
Qing (Ching)	1644-1911
Shunzhi (Shun Chih)	1644-1662
Kangxi (Kang Hsi)	1662-1723
Yongzhen (Yung Cheng)	1723-1736
Qianlong (Chien Lung)	1736-1796
Jiaqing (Chia Ching)	1796-1821
Daoguang (Tao Kuang)	1821-1851
Xianfeng (Hsien Feng)	1851-1862
Tongzhi (Tung Chih)	1862-1875
Guangxu (Kuang Hsu)	1875-1908
Xuantong (Hsuan Tung)	1908-1911

44

5. LAND & PEOPLE

THE LAND

China extends from Mongolia and Siberia on the north and to Central Asia, Afghanistan, Pakistan, India and Nepal on the west. On the south it borders Bhutan, Bangladesh, Myanmar, Laos and Vietnam. And on the east, it touches only North Korea and until they become part of China again, onto Hong Kong and Macau. Its east coast is washed by the Yellow Sea, the East China Sea and the South China Sea. It also considers Taiwan and the Paracel Islands part of China. It is 9.6 million square kilometers, the world's third largest country.

If you keep in mind that Beijing is the same latitude as Philadelphia, Guangzhou the same as Havana, and Urumqi in the far west is a four-hour flight to Beijing in the east, you get a feeling for the vastness of the country. Its northern-most tip is as far north as James Bay.

China extends upwards too, with the highest mountains in the world, and downwards to the second lowest body of water. It has vast deserts and fertile valleys, great prairies, evergreen forests and rubber plantations. It is big and varied.

THE PEOPLE

China has 1.2 billion people, 22% of the earth's population living on 7% of the earth's arable land. That she has done so much with so little is a credit to Chinese pragmatism and ingenuity. The official language is Mandarin Chinese or *putonghua*. This is taught in the schools. You will also hear the distinctive Shanghai, Fujian, and Guangdong (Cantonese) languages, and hundreds of dialects. Most people however use a common written language.

China has 56 different ethnic groups. The majority are Han. Eight percent of the population are members of 55 other nationalities. These 91 million people live in areas totaling half of China, including strategic areas near its borders. Yunnan province for example has 26 different nationalities. Although they are usually less educated and poorer, the varied cultures of these minorities are rich, meaningful and fascinating.

GOOD FRIENDS!

A nationality doesn't necessarily settle in one location. Often sub-branches are spread over several provinces, with different costumes and dialects; for example, the **Miao** are found in Guizhou, Hunan, Yunnan, Guangdong, Guangzi, and Sichuan. Miao women in Guizhou wear pleated shirts and in Hunan wear trousers. The color and designs of their headdress also varies.

During festivals and market days, most minorities, especially women, wear their distinctive costumes, which many decorate with fine embroidery, and, sometimes, heavy silver jewelry. Hairstyles could indicate marital status.

The festivals of the nationalities are worth experiencing. The **Dai** celebrate a water-splashing festival similar to that in neighboring Thailand and Burma. The **Kazakhs** have a horse racing festival, the **Yi** a torch festival, the **Tibetans** celebrate the Great Prayer Festival, and so on. **Mongolians** have colorful sporting meets, with distinctive wrestling, horses, and archery. Facilities for tourists in minority areas are still modest but not impossible.

The Chinese Psyche

China is a country that has infuriated yet tantalized the world for centuries. China's arrogant indifference, the wealth and 'divine right' of its emperors have intrigued generations of curious people everywhere.

In recent years, its fanatical adherence to communism has continued to mystify. People around the world are asking, 'Is it becoming capitalist?' Before the terrible 1989 events at Tiananmen Square, people asked: 'Is it becoming democratic?'

Before 1949

China became a nation over 2200 years ago. Thousands of years of relative isolation allowed the Chinese to develop their unique Confucian-based culture until the 19th century. At that time, more advanced technology and greed led many European countries and Japan to grab power and territory in China. The Chinese reacted with bewilderment, anti-foreign rebellions, and in 1911 with a republican revolution. After a period of embarrassing national disintegration, first under the warlords and then during the civil war and the Japanese invasion, the country was finally reunited in 1949 under the Communists.

The Chinese people until very recently, have been 80% agricultural. Attachment to land has colored their behavior. Their religion, loyalties, and efforts have always been based on pragmatism, family, and ancestral lineage. They subordinated the wishes of the individual to the system and in most cases still do. This is changing, unless one considers 'getting rich' a part of the system too. After all, the acquisition of money is now another government-approved campaign.

Before 1950, China's economy stemmed primarily from a feudal system, land rented to peasants in return for a percentage of the crops. Landlords ideally had responsibility for the welfare of their serfs, on whom they were largely dependent for their wealth.

After 1949

After taking over China, the **Communist** leaders embarked on a series of programs following religiously the theories of **Mao Zedong** (Mao Tse-tung), the man who had led them to power. But the Chinese leaders were pragmatists first. When one approach didn't work, they tried another.

The Communists started out with a land-to-the-peasants program, then collectivization, communes, and finally private plots. The upheavals of the Cultural Revolution cost millions their lives. This troubled period ended with Mao's death in 1976.

During the Cultural Revolution, begun in earnest in 1966, they abolished private plots, then reinstated and encouraged them later. In the

1970s, it was apparent that even that system was not meeting the needs of the people.

THE NEW ECONOMIC POLICIES

In the early 1980s, an economy largely based on the family replaced the communes. Most counties adopted the Responsibility System, whereby rural inhabitants rent land or machines. The government receives an agreed share of the produce while villagers keep or sell the surplus. Anybody can also work on projects such as handicrafts, livestock, and vegetables for their own gain. These you will see in 'free markets.' Families and collectives have opened hotels, restaurants, and factories. It would seem that China has almost come around full circle, with the government replacing the feudal landlords. But has it?

Under the new economic system, the government no longer determines all that is grown or produced, nor does it mandate quantities; the market affects most production directly. Many peasants have been working furiously and are making more money then ever before. China is undergoing another revolution. For the first time, rural China is earning less than 50% of its income from agriculture and many rural inhabitants are making more than salaried city dwellers.

The revolutionary slogans of nationalistic self-sufficiency and personal sacrifice of the nineteen fifties and sixties have given way to international cooperation and modernization and some people are getting richer faster than others. The new economic policies also include opening to foreign investment. The leadership has successfully attracted foreign capital, especially to its coastal areas, with a series of regional development zones extending from Dalian in the north to Beihai city in the south, and especially in Shenzhen, Guangzhou, Shanghai, Dalian, and Tianjin. Other areas are following: parts of Guangdong, Fujian, the Yangtze valley (from Pudong in Shanghai to Chongqing) and Hainan Island.

In these zones, the government has given tax breaks and has built harbors, roads, and improved telecommunications. Factories, office blocks and hotels have spread everywhere. Many areas have or will soon have IDD telephones and international airports. Beijing, Hangzhou, and Shanghai have video telephone services. In early 1993, China had over 200,000 mobile telephone subscribers. By mid-decade, it had four million pagers. The progress is uneven; Some previously booming cities have lost their steam because of poor leadership.

New Freedoms & Affluence?

The effects of the new economic policies are apparent everywhere, as you can see by the many construction cranes, satellite dishes, and traffic jams. Groups of former peasants have built hotels, roads, libraries, and schools in their own villages. In many areas, you can see a great deal of new peasant housing, most of luxury size. You can find American clothing like Victoria's Secret and L.L. Bean in fashionable street markets and hotel stores.

You can see the relaxing of the puritanical Maoist ethic in the new freedom to enjoy life more than they have in the past. People are eating out in restaurants and families are ordering more elaborate wedding feasts. People are buying video machines, color televisions, washing machines, refrigerators, and mopeds. Many private citizens can afford cars and trucks, and rooms in fancy hotels.

In many ways, life is much easier and more fun. Check out the dancing and exercises at six in the morning and the outdoor evening dance parties in every city. Note the people wearing high-heels and sunglasses. The women are adding glamour to their lives with permanent waves, lipstick, and colorful dresses. Notice the billiard halls, discos, and state lotteries. Chinese tourists flock everywhere, especially on their two-day weekends. Many even travel outside the country. None of this was permitted ten years ago.

Ten years ago, anything foreign was considered counterrevolutionary. Now, Paul Simon, John Denver, foreign orchestras, dance groups, and artists like Robert Rauschenberg have performed in China. The country is becoming more permissive and you may even find nude paintings in art galleries. New also is the more mature approach to history. The mainlanders are giving credit to the Nationalists for their help in fighting the Japanese invaders.

After decades of drabness, China is looking more cheerful and prosperous. It is a nice change.

The Flip Side

But the new economic policies have had other results. People became aware of what was going on in the outside world. Students and government officials traveled abroad. Thousands of foreign teachers spread democracy along with new languages. Young people working in tourism or selling in free markets make more money than their parents, especially if the parents worked for the government.

The importation of luxury goods like television sets, video machines, and Mercedes Benzes depleted foreign exchange. The attitude that nothing Chinese was good and everything foreign was desirable began to permeate people's thinking.

New classes of wealthy farmers and merchants, and on the other extreme, large numbers of poor people have developed. A 'floating population,' tied by registration to rural communities, has moved to the cities hoping for lucrative work. Beijing's floating population is about three million, and *The Wall Street Journal* estimated 100 million nationwide, with an annual increase of seven million. The children of these floaters are not getting adequate schooling or immunization. Nor are they being overseen by work units and villages for birth control and criminal behavior. Municipal governments are trying to regulate them.

China's Economy Today

In the early 1990s, China's industrial output grew 20% annually, investment over 40%, foreign trade over 22% and the GNP over 12%. The gross domestic product, now about one-tenth of the United States, is expected to increase to about two-thirds of that of the United States in the next ten years. China's growth rate is among the highest in the world, leaving North America's rate far behind. In the mid-1990s, the government had to launch an austerity program to try to control inflation. China is also trying to cut down on government subsidies for some food items and health care. It is trying to eliminate the many unprofitable government enterprises that take up one-third of the national budget. But *guanxi* is still important, and bribery exists on all levels.

China is developing infrastructure such as electric railways, the trans-China superhighways, nuclear power plants, airports and ship quays. It is going ahead full swing with the controversial Three Gorges Dam across the Yangtze River.

The growing middle and upper classes have an increasing appetite for consumer goods from abroad. There are opportunities to sell foreign-made products to the Chinese. Just find yourself a good Chinese partner. There are many new private schools and clinics that need up-to-date equipment from North America and just think of the millions eager and able to travel abroad.

China is attempting to develop better relations with all its neighbors: both Koreas, Vietnam, India, Laos, the new Central Asian nations, and especially Russia. It has rebuilt the train and trade links with Hanoi, for example.

China's government is communist. **Jiang Zemin** is president. Officially at the top is the **National People's Congress**. The **State Council** is the executive organ accountable to this congress and is similar to a cabinet. The **Communist Party** now is trying to re-enter almost every facet of life, after pulling back in the mid-to-late 1980s. It blamed the 1989 student demonstrations on the lack of political education of the people.

But many Communist Party members seem to be afflicted now with money fever too – at least until the next campaign against corruption. At press time, people seemed very casual about politics.

CURRENT ATMOSPHERE & QUESTIONS

Now is a crucial time to visit because what happens in the coming years will determine China's future direction. The 1990 census revealed that China has 1,160,017,381 people, a lot more than it had expected and planned for. Many intellectuals are afraid of another suppression and are trying to leave the country. Young people with little faith in their government still dream of making a fortune in richer countries abroad. Conversely, a growing number of North Americans are setting up businesses, getting jobs and establishing homes in China.

Many people speak freely with foreigners now. I suggest you use discretion in talking politics, human rights, and the western point of view, unless you want to be booted out of the country.

With care, there are many questions for you to ask: What about social security? Free health care? What is being done about AIDS, and illegal drugs? Legal rights? What is the effect of satellite television? email and the internet? Fax machines? Can the government regulate these sources of new information?

What are they doing about the air pollution? What do the Chinese feel about the fall of Communism and the disintegration of the Soviet Union? To whom besides Myanmar (Burma) and Pakistan is China selling arms now? Is China really killing baby girls? Is China ready for democracy? How do mainlanders feel about the 1996 Taiwan elections? And the war games at the same time? Perhaps you can find the answers.

RELIGION

At first, the Communists discouraged religion and the Cultural Revolution destroyed many religious buildings and symbols. Since the late-1970s the government again has allowed religion to openly exist and has been helping reconstruct religious buildings. Today you will see worshippers in most temples, mosques and churches. There is a revival of religions and superstitions. Although the Chinese constitution says that all Chinese citizens have freedom of belief, implementation remains uneven. Today in some provinces, there is still interference in Christian church affairs by 'leftist cadres.'

China's great traditional religions are Taoism, Buddhism, and Confucianism, although in some sense, Confucianism is more of an ideology or philosophy. Taoism and Confucianism are uniquely Chinese. Buddhism came later. Islam and Christianity are more recent imports. Ancestor worship and animism are ancient folk religions.

Chinese people are pragmatic, worshipping whatever gods might answer their prayers. They want to cover all the bases. If a friend prayed successfully to one god for a baby boy, then other barren women try that god too. It is not unusual for the same person to have his children baptized as Christians, burn incense to a deceased grandfather, and then retire to contemplate in a Taoist or Buddhist monastery. The same person may support several different temples and churches at the same time and worship his or her ancestors.

Religions have been encouraged, tolerated, and persecuted. In the early Tang, some emperors ordered the killing of Buddhists, while other emperors encouraged Buddhism. Additionally, emperors financed many religious buildings.

Ancestor Worship

Ancestor Worship involves praying to departed ancestors as you would pray to Buddha or a saint. You take care of them with incense and offerings and they take care of you. You worship your ancestors in gratitude for your life.

There used to be at least one ancestral temple, or **miao**, for every village, since each village was comprised of people with a common ancestor. Some temples were very elaborate and were used as the village school. If people moved away from the village, they might set up shrines in their homes where they informed the ancestors of important family events like births and marriages. Many families kept a family history book. The Red Guards destroyed many of these books and family tablets during the Cultural Revolution. When you go to a village, ask about the ancestral temple. In ancestral temples, tablets with the names of the ancestors were kept in neat rows and worshipped with burning incense, gifts of food, and ceremonial bowing at least twice a year.

Animism & Other Religions

There are temples to city gods. Fishermen worship the Goddess of Heaven, **Tian Hou**, who bears some resemblance to the goddess **Guanyin**. In villages, you will see incense burned at the foot of sacred trees and in tiny shrines. See *Quanzhou* for **Manicheanism**, and *Xi'an* and *Quanzhou* for **Nestorianism**.

Buddhism

Buddhism arrived in China from India. **Gautama**, the founder, was an Indian prince, born in the sixth century B.C., who was brought up confined to a palace. When he was 29, he saw the suffering of the outside world and forsook his wealth and family. For six years, he traveled in search of life's meaning. He found it and then preached his ideas for 45 years: the **Four Noble Truths** and the **Noble Eightfold Path to Nirvana**. The circles on top of Buddhist stupas and pagodas are in the same numbers: four and eight.

Buddha taught that the source of all suffering is selfish desire, and one must stop all desire. Some sects believe in asceticism. The Chinese, Mongolians, and Tibetans generally follow the **Mahayana** school of faith and good works, and believe Buddha is divine and can answer prayers. You will see people in temples, smoking incense in hand, nodding to the statues or kowtowing on the floor, asking for favors, without regard for the extinction of all desire. Achieving **Nirvana** is the aim of all forms of Buddhism, accomplished by ending the continuous cycle of reincarnation through the extinction of the self. Today, China has more than 3,600 Buddhist temples open for worship with over 30,000 monks and nuns.

Buddhist temples come in two basic varieties, of which there are infinite variations. First are **Chinese Buddhist temples**, surrounded by windowless walls, which frequently have four fierce-looking, larger than life-size, human- type guardians after the first gate. Each temple might have different names for these. Inside the first hall, visitors are greeted by the fat, laughing Buddha, **Maitreya**, or in Chinese, *Mi Lo Fu*. He is the Buddha still-to-come. Behind him is **Wei Tou**, the military bodhisattva, the armed warrior who guards the Buddhist scriptures. Wei Tou is probably comparable to the Indian god Indra.

Central in the main hall is the Buddha, known also as the Enlightened One, **Sakyamuni**, or **Prince Siddhartha Gautama**. Also in this hall are usually statues or paintings of **bodhisattvas**, known in Chinese as *pusas*. These are saints who have gained Enlightenment but have come back to the world to help other people attain it too. A favorite bodhisattva is **Avalokita**, known in China as *Guanyin* (Kwan Yin, Kuan Yin), or the Goddess of Mercy, who may have several heads and arms and may be carrying a vase or a child. She is usually behind Sakyamuni, facing north.

BODHISATTVA

a.

b.

c.

d.

e.

f.

g.

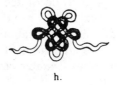

h.

THE EIGHT BUDDHIST EMBLEMS OF HAPPY AUGURY

a. The wheel of the law   e. The lotus flower
b. The conch shell   f. The covered vase
c. The state umbrella   g. The pair of fishes
d. The canopy   h. The endless knot

Guanyin started out as a male god in China until about the 12th century, when his followers preferred to worship him as a woman. He is still sometimes depicted as male. Said one guide, 'Men believe he is male and women believe she is female.'

Other bodhisattvas are **Amitabha**, in charge of the souls of the dead, **Manjusri**, in charge of Wisdom, usually with a sword in his right hand and a lotus in his left, and the bodhisattvas of Pharmacy, Universal Benevolence, and the Earth.

Arhats, known in Chinese as *lohan,* are people who have achieved Nirvana. They are usually depicted in groupings of 16, 18, or 500, and are based on real Indian holy men. These are frequently seen in paintings or as statues. Devout Buddhists should know each of them by name.

The swastika is a Buddhist symbol of good luck, of Indian origin, later inverted and used by the Nazis. Most temples have live fish and turtles. Full-time Buddhists are vegetarians. Some Buddhist monks had pieces of incense burned into their skulls at their initiation, but this is no longer required.

An interesting study to make as you sightsee is of the clothing carved on buddhas. Some wear the plain, draped robes of Indian holy men, others the fancy, feminine Chinese court dress with jewelry. Buddhism arrived in China from India, but Buddhist art in China became distinctly Chinese. Can you date a statue from its clothes? The fatness of its face?

You will probably see many more Buddhist temples than Taoist and Confucian. You can also see the robed monks chanting prayers if your timing is right. Do you find the rituals mechanical or mystical?

The second kind of Buddhist temple you'll see are called **Lama Temples** in China, and are different from other Chinese Buddhist temples not only in their statues, but also in their architecture. Usually built on mountainsides, they have tall, narrow windows, flatter less ornate roofs, and are usually decorated over the main door with a gilded wheel of Buddhist doctrine and two deer. Statues inside are frequently decorated with turquoise and coral, and many of the statues wear pointed caps, or are of couples copulating. The best-known of these temples are in **Tibet**, but important examples are also in Beijing, Chengde, Qinghai, and Inner Mongolia.

Lama temples are expressions of the Tibetan and Mongolian form of Buddhism, into which have been injected elements of the early Tibetan religion called **Bon**.

Many Tibetan Buddhists believe that the **Dalai Lama**, who is considered both the temporal and religious head of Tibetan Buddhism, is a reincarnation of Avalokita or Guanyin, or the god Chenrezi. The religion's peaceful and wrathful aspects are reflected in the murals and statues of these temples. Tibetan Buddhism is also divided into sects, the main ones being the meditative **Yellow Hats** and the sensual **Red Hats**.

Note: The Chinese government refers to Tibetan Buddhism as 'Lamaism' and their temples as 'Lama' temples, but the Tibetans themselves do not. See also *Lhasa* and *Chengde*.

Cave Temples with frescoes and Buddhist statues were first built in India and spread with the Silk Road into China. Caves have always been conducive to meditation. There, one gets a feeling of security, like being back in a mother's womb. **Dunhuang** is the greatest for its paintings. The two at Lanzhou are noted for their strikingly dramatic sites and the richness of their sculpture. Important for carvings are also **Datong** and **Luoyang**.

Other cave temples listed as protected historical monuments by the State Council are at Anxi and Linxia in Gansu; Handan in Hebei; Turpan, Baichen, and Kuqu in Xinjiang; Guangyuan, Leshan, and Dazu in Sichuan; Jianchuan in Yunnan; Gongxian in Henan; Guyuan in Ningxia; and Hangzhou in Zhejiang.

Christianity

Christianity arrived in full force with Christian missionaries in the latter part of the 19th century. The unequal treaties after the Opium War in 1842 forced China to accept missionaries. Because of backing by foreign powers, Chinese Christians tended to be an elite group, at times successfully appealing to their foreign protectors if they got in trouble with Chinese law. This caused much resentment.

Some foreign missionaries closed their eyes to ancestor worship to make converts. Many Chinese questioned the exclusivity of Christianity.

Dr. Sun Yat-sen, the father of the Chinese republic, was a Christian, but as a Chinese nationalist he criticized missionaries as lackeys of foreign imperialists. Many Chinese misunderstood the missionary motives. Some of these fears led to such incidents as the Tientsin Massacre (see *Tianjin*). The Chinese attacked missionaries more because of nationalism than religion.

Missionary schools influenced some Chinese Communist leaders. Mao Zedong once edited the Christian-sponsored *Yale-in-China Review*. Zhou Enlai admired the ideals and the work of the YMCA and YWCA.

In 1950, the hysteria of the Korean War led the Chinese to consider westerners, including many missionaries, as 'enemy aliens.' They accused them of spying and sabatoge and jailed some. After all, Americans and Canadians were killing Chinese soldiers in Korea. (This hysteria was similiar to the incarceration of Japanese people on our west coasts.)

The Communists felt that foreign imperialism was linked to the Chinese Christian dependence on foreign missionaries. After 1949, the Communists encouraged Christian churches to cut their ties with their foreign mentors and Protestants set up the **Three-Self Patriotic Movement**. The Catholic Church, however, officially opposed the rulers of new China. Most of the bishops not jailed fled. When those Catholic leaders who remained nominated new bishops to meet the pastoral needs of more than 100 vacant dioceses, the Vatican ignored these nominations. When Chinese leaders went ahead with consecrations, Rome regarded them as irregular.

The situation has begun to improve now. Having missed Vatican II, some priests still celebrate the Mass in Latin for older Catholics, but young priests are being trained to celebrate in Chinese. Many consecrations are now recognized (unofficially) by Rome.

During the **Cultural Revolution**, the Red Guards destroyed and closed churches and temples as part of the movement against the Four Olds. Many church buildings became apartments, factories and warehouses. The Catholic Cathedral in Guangzhou was used for storage.

In 1978-79 after the Cultural Revolution, the government encouraged the rebuilding of temples and churches, returned deeds to congregations and paid overdue rents. It had to relocate the people and factories who had taken over the buildings. Some Christians had actually continued to tithe even while the churches were closed and later brought these treasures to their newly-opened gathering places.

Over 8000 Protestant churches and over 20,000 meeting points across China are flourishing with over 12 million Protestant Christians and 15 to 25 million enquirers. Thirteen seminaries and Bible Schools are open. A few churches have to open Saturdays as well as Sundays to accommodate worshippers. Some Christians worship corporately in their homes.

While some foreigners have questioned the authenticity of the 'state-recognized' versus the 'house' Christian, most Chinese believers do not think they are different. It may be a matter of convenience. Some Christians attend both the small family fellowships and the large general congregations. Leadership training is the major challenge for the burgeoning congregations of often semi-literate Christians in the countryside. In 1988, two Protestant bishops were installed. It was the first such event since 1955.

Foreigners wanting to contact Protestant groups should ask for the **China Christian Council** or **Three-Self Patriotic Movement**. Catholics should ask for the **Chinese Catholic Patriotic Association**. Don't let the word Patriotic bother you. It doesn't sound as chauvinistic in Chinese. You should also consult your own church or national church organizations. When you get to China, worship with the Chinese and please do not disturb the service with a camera, or by being late or leaving early.

Chinese Christians, particularly those in isolated places, will probably be delighted to have you join. Please don't be overly generous. The Chinese want to be self-reliant. Donations with no strings attached can be made to the **Amity Foundation**, a Christian-inspired people's organization devoted to health, education, and welfare projects for all Chinese, not just Christians.

Recently, a group of foreigners was arrested and deported for proselytizing. You can ask Christians in China if they want missionaries.

As for smuggling in Bibles, those days are over. The United Bible Society has given a modern press to the Amity Foundation, which is helping the Protestant churches publish their own literature. Since 1981, the China Christian Council has printed over 10 million Bibles.

There are also about 4.5 million Catholic Christians, 1000 large Catholic churches, and 10,000 chapels. Between 1980 and 1985, about 130,000 adults were baptized. Eleven seminaries are now open and about 12 convents with 200 women under formation. In 1990, several Roman Catholic clergymen with ties to the Vatican were arrested.

Christian Churches were most frequently built in western architecture with gothic windows, and many Roman Catholic churches look like transplants from Europe.

Confucianism

Confucian temples used to be in every sizable community in China, at one time about 2,680 of them, now dwindled in number down to about 300. For a history and description of Confucianism, see *Qufu*.

Confucius was worshipped because his teachings supported the stratification of society, with the emperor and elder males on top. He was officially worshipped during the spring and autumn equinoxes. Try to imagine the burning incense and the muffled clang of gongs, as slow, rhythmic processions of officials in long red gowns and caps arrived, each man to kowtow, head to the ground, in deepest reverence. They left offerings of food and wine on the altar. Musicians played ritual bells. Such ceremonies still take place in Qufu and in Taiwan.

Confucian temples did not usually have statues, but simply tablets with the names of ancestors written on them. The walls were red. The south gate was usually left unbuilt until a son from the town passed the difficult examinations and became a Senior Scholar. Only a Senior Scholar and the Emperor could enter by the south gate. No women were considered for the examinations, but if Chinese opera plots are to be believed, some did successfully take them disguised as men.

Was Confucianism a religion or a philosophy? This question is frequently debated. While Confucius himself skeptically rejected the supernatural, Chinese people did and, in some cases, still do consider him a god. He is among the Taoist deities too. But he was primarily a teacher of ethics, of 'right conduct,' and good, stable government. Many Confucian temples now are only museums because Confucianism no longer has imperial patronage. The largest temples are in Beijing and Qufu.

Taoism

Taoism (Daoism) was founded 1800 years ago by a sage named **Lao Zi** (Lao Tzu), whose message was conveyed to the world by a disciple named Mencius. It preaches that everything exists through the interplay of two opposite forces: male-female; positive-negative; hot-cold; light-dark; heaven-earth; yang-yin, etc.

Taoists try to achieve harmony out of the conflict of these forces through the Tao or the Way. Taoism is closer to nature than other religions, its saints have found enlightenment by spending years meditating in caves. Over the years, it has been diluted by superstitions like charms, spells, ghosts, nature spirits, and supernatural beings. Taoism was most popular in the Tang and Song, but declined in the Ming. Its most famous monasteries are in Beijing, Chengdu, Shenyang, and Suzhou.

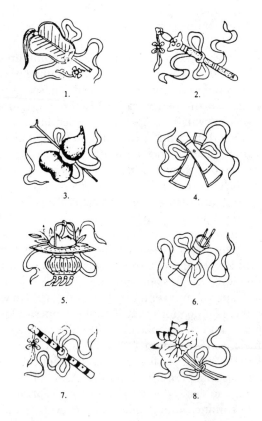

THE ATTRIBUTES OF THE EIGHT TAOIST GENII

1. The fan
2. The sword
3. The pilgrims' staff & gourd
4. The castanets
5. The flower baskets
6. The tube and rods
7. The flute
8. The lotus flower

Taoist temples are identified by Taoist gods, among whom are **Guanyin** and **Confucius**. You can identify other gods and saints by the symbols they carry.

The **Eight Taoist Genii** (Immortals or Fairies) were originally eight humans who discovered the secrets of nature. They lived alone in remote mountains (one of them in a cave at Lushan), had magic powers and could revive the dead. They are usually found together on a vase or in one painting, or as a set of eight porcelain pieces. Chung Li-chuan carries the fan to revive the spirits of the dead, Lu Tung-in the supernatural sword, Li Tieh-kuai the staff, Tsao Kuo-chiu the castanets, Lan Tsai-ho the flower basket, Chang Kuo the bamboo tube, Han Hsiangtzu the flute, and Ho Hsien-ku the lotus flower. Two are women.

In the center of the dual **Yin-Yang**, the principles of being are surrounded by the eight **Trigrams of Divination**. The Eight Trigrams represent eight animals and eight directions. At eleven o'clock are the three unbroken lines of heaven; then clockwise, clouds, thunder, mountains, water, fire, earth, and wind. These are used in fortune telling. You may have heard of the **I Ching**, which uses these trigrams.

Feng Shui

Geomancy is making a comeback, influenced by its success in Hong Kong. *Feng* means wind and *shui* means water. It is geomancy, the placing of graves, dwellings, doors and furniture in harmony with the forces of nature. **Feng shui** is related to Taoism. It is more an art or pseudo-science than a religion. In some cases it makes practical sense since it prefers that dwellings face south with mountains behind them to protect people from cold northern winds.

Good luck comes from dragons who live in mountains, and it is best to site a structure or village so that good luck goes into it. If you don't have mountains, you plant trees where the dragons can reside.

Spirits only travel in straight lines, so windows and doors should not be in line with each other as the good luck will go in one side of a building and out the other. Buildings must not interfere with the flow of chi, the cosmic breath which brings harmony and health.

It is preferable for a structure to be surrounded on three sides by running water. If it isn't, the geomancer may suggest a fountain. He might tell you to hinge a door in another direction or to get gold fish for good luck with one black one to absorb the bad luck.

One Chinese-Canadian attributes his success to moving his brother's grave to a site with better feng shui. He smuggled the bones out of Hong Kong to the ancestral home in China on the advice of a fortune teller, and was careful to consult a geomancer.

Islam

Moslems are followers of the Prophet Mohammed, who was born in 570 A.D. This religion gives a different emphasis to the god of Judaism and Christianity. Old Testament prophets and Jesus Christ are considered honored prophets, but Mohammed was the last and the greatest. The holy book is the Koran, which teaches a strict code of behavior (no pork, alcohol, idols, etc.), and the universal brotherhood of all believers. During the holy month of Ramadan, they fast during the day.

Islam arrived in China in 652 A.D. during the Tang Dynasty, with Arab and Persian traders who settled in Guangzhou, Quanzhou, Hangzhou, and Yangzhou. During the 13th century, Kublai Khan brought Moslem soldiers, artisans, and officials to China to work for him. Approximately 10 million Chinese Moslems are known today as **Hui**, but Uygurs, Kazaks, Kirgiz, Uzbeks, etc., are also Moslems, a total of about 17 million followers of Mohammed. Mosques are always open afternoons on Friday, the holy day.

Islamic mosques are architecturally of two varieties. Those with rounded, onion-like domes and minarets, are mainly in northwest China. Other mosques look like Chinese temples, with curved roofs and ornate dragons and phoenixes (in spite of the prophet's teachings against making images).

In either style, visitors always remove their shoes inside the great halls. There is a place for washing hands and feet before prayers. The main building is the Great Hall, which is decorated with Arabic writing, arches, and flower motifs. Moslems pray five times a day, facing the holy city of Mecca in Saudi Arabia.

Moslems can pray anywhere, but the devout usually pray in a mosque if they can. Note the prayer rugs with designs woven into them indicating the direction in which to kneel. Carpets made in Moslem areas deliberately do not have images of animals or objects on them. Note also the disproportionate number of women worshippers, and in some mosques, separate sections for women.

6. PLANNING YOUR TRIP

BEFORE YOU GO

WHEN TO GO

The best time weather-wise is **May-June** or **September-October**, but you could run into crowds and delays. You could also try late April or early November and hope for good weather. In November, plan to go to Beijing first and then move south.

Definitely avoid the lunar new year (around late January or early February), especially in Guangzhou and Fujian, as hotels and trains are full of Overseas Chinese visitors, prices are at their highest, and some tourist attractions are closed. Avoid Guangzhou during the trade fairs and any other cities with big events. Do go to Lhasa in March when the days are warm, the nomads are pilgrimaging, and few other tourists are around. (Avoid Lhasa in the summer when tourists outnumber costumed Tibetans.)

The **hottest time** of the year is usually July and early August. Almost all hotels, most tourist buses and some taxis are air- conditioned. Put mountain or seaside resorts at the end of a hot tour. During April–May and through the summer, rain and high humidity make south China (including Guangzhou and Guilin) quite oppressive, but the greenery is lush and beautiful. Inner Mongolia and the Silk Road have a problem with sandstorms in spring and autumn. Avoid mountain areas, the Yangtze Gorges and any other place with outdoor sights in the rainy season because of floods or landslides that could disrupt sightseeing and photography.

Roughly, China extends from the same latitudes as James Bay in Canada to Cuba. Beijing is at almost the same latitude as Philadelphia, and Guangzhou as Havana. Take altitude into account: the higher, the colder, especially at night.

Winter in North China begins in mid-November and extends to late February and the air is very dry. The Spring Festival is frequently the coldest time of the year. Industrial pollution is particularly bad in winter too. But most tour agencies and hotels give discounts.

Wise tourists who are healthy and not afraid of the cold could plan trips in the winter even in the north. New-fallen snow transforms any city into a wonderland and makes red pavilions and curved gold roofs intensely beautiful. It also makes roads slippery and traffic slow-moving. Hotels are not crowded (except for conventions.)

It is important to remember that the Chinese do not heat their buildings (like museums and palaces) as warmly as foreigners do even though it can be cold. South of the Yangtze there is no heat at all. But most tourist hotels three stars and up are heated. Some low-price hotels do not have any heat at all. If the cold bothers you, go only to the tropics to Hainan and south Yunnan in winter. Even in Guangzhou, you could need a top coat and a sweater at that time of year.

OTHER THINGS TO CONSIDER WHEN PLANNING

If you are interested in visiting schools, factories, and offices, avoid vacations, holidays and weekends. If you want to see a festival consider those dates.

Now that China has a five-day work week, the business hotels in cities accessible by air with Hong Kong are not full on Friday and Saturdays nights and prices are softer as Hong Kong residents go home then. Cheaper tourist hotels and popular tourist attractions however are busier on weekends with China's growing number of domestic tourists. Avoid the Forbidden City and Great Wall on weekends.

ESSENTIAL UP-TO-DATE INFORMATION

*If you're worried about civil unrest, floods, whatever, phone the **U.S. State Department** in Washington, D.C. (202) 647-5225; or consult any American consulate abroad (American Citizens' Services). In Canada, phone **External Affairs**, 1-800-267-6788.*

*For information from the **China National Tourist Office**, try their internet address at **http://www.travelfile.com/get?chinanto**.*

WHAT TO PACK
Clothing & Luggage

Sightseers should dress for comfort with good walking shoes. Sneakers are ideal. White is the color of mourning, so brighten it up with colored ribbons or something. Bring sunscreen and a sun hat or buy one there.

You might feel compelled to dress up for dinner in five-star hotels and for a captain's banquet on Yangtze cruise ships. But you don't have to.

Chinese people are generally informal. While top class international hotel restaurants would like men to wear jackets and ties, they will not send you away if you don't have these.

From mid-November to late March, north China, including Beijing, is bitterly cold. I even froze in Beijing one May; two sweaters and a top coat were barely enough. Many of the cheaper hotels are not heated.

A jogging suit is ideal for lounging and sleeping on trains. Take along a coat, long underwear, heavy slacks, thermal socks, and warm boots. A hot water bottle will help keep you warm in cheaper hotels.

Do as the natives do: plan for layers of warm clothing and a lightweight top. If you have to, you can buy down coats and wool and silk long underwear in China for half the price you'd pay at home. If you are also traveling to warmer climes or need room in your luggage for purchases, you could take clothes you can discard when no longer useful.

The rainy season is March to May in the south, with rain or drizzle almost every day. After it starts getting hot, a trench coat will feel like a sauna. You can buy cheap umbrellas there.

All of lowland China is hot in July, so bring cotton clothing. Sundresses and shorts on foreign women are common now in big cities. In smaller towns, especially if you are alone, women should dress more modestly.

Most Chinese women wear trousers and loose-fitting blouses, and, increasingly, skirts or long shorts. Men wear slacks and white shirts even in offices. In winter, they wear layers of sweaters and Western-style or Mao jackets. Everyone wears padded coats. Trench coats are in style for office workers. The new, with-it generation has been dressing more colorfully. Jeans are in style. Modern young women in China wear tights and even miniskirts.

Women should dress modestly. Chinese women don't dress elegantly except in the highest levels of society. Please don't upstage your hostess. The Chinese like to see foreign women wearing Chinese dress, but try not to look like restaurant staff.

If you are invited to dinner, you can ask your host if what you have on is all right. Should men wear ties? Women should not overdo makeup or you'll have other people wondering if your eyelashes and hair are real. Does everyone in Australia have blue eyelids? Some younger Chinese women wear makeup. Sure, take your heels but go easy on the jewelry.

At less formal banquets, many Chinese men and women wear loose-fitting shirts and trousers. Some might be coming from work or arriving by bicycle. Chinese officials do not usually bring their spouses to banquets, but this is changing slowly at upper levels.

Wearing cosmetics, jewelry, and bright colors (except for children) was considered self-indulgent, bourgeois, and counter-revolutionary from 1949 until recently. Doing so led to assault, hours of interrogation and even imprisonment during the Cultural Revolution. It is understandable why the older generation hesitates about changes. For business, dress as you would in your own country to show respect.

Laundry is done in one day at most hotels if in by 8 am. All hotels three stars and up in big cities have dry cleaning. The Chinese do an adequate job, but if your dress is special, they could ruin it. It would be wise to wash delicate clothes like silk underwear yourself. Some hotels provide clothes lines in bathrooms.

Your **luggage** should be locked and will probably have to endure a lot of punishment. Some bags have been left out in the rain. Your bags should have your name, telephone number, and address outside and inside.

If you're going in a tour group, you're usually allowed one or two suitcases. You should also have a carry-on bag for overnight train rides (your big bag may not be accessible) and airplanes (in case your luggage is delayed or lost).

Individual travelers should know that China's domestic airlines are strict about their limit on checked bags. (First class 30 kilograms, economy 20 kilograms.) Discounted fares have an allowance of 20 kilograms (first class) and 15 kilograms (economy). Economy carry-on bags should not exceed a total length, width, and height of 115 centimeters (or 45 inches). Air China allows two pieces of luggage on trans-Pacific flights, each not exceeding 32 kilograms and the sum of the height, width and length no more than 158 centimeters (or 62"). A weight limit of 35 kilograms usually applies on trains but is rarely enforced.

Porters and trolleys are available in some but not all train stations and airports. Independent travelers should be prepared to carry their own luggage in some train stations, perhaps up and down a flight of steps, to a taxi. Consider a set of luggage wheels.

Toiletries

In the joint-venture hotels you will receive at least North American quality shampoo, conditioner, and soap. The Chinese- managed hotels will probably give you toothbrush, soap, and a few other goodies like combs and Chinese shampoo.

If you're adventurous, experiment with Chinese brands. The lemon shampoo is acceptable. The ginseng toothpaste is weird, but it might improve your sex life. Handy-wipes for cleaning hands are good. Take sanitary napkins or tampons if needed. They can be hard to find.

Short-wave Transistor Radios

During the 1989 turmoil, in the days following June 4, *China Daily* mentioned nothing of the tanks and killings. And shortly afterwards,

CNN and foreign newspapers were stopped. They have resumed, but one never knows. Many hotels have news in English and/or CNN. Hotels are supposed to do their own censoring. But as China owns part of the satellite, if you want to keep abreast, do take a short-wave radio.

Photography

You can buy Kodak and Fuji print film but usually only 100 A.S.A. Ektachrome is getting more common but don't count on it. It is best to bring your own. Be sure to take extra batteries, flash cubes, video tapes, and Polariod film.

Personal video cameras are allowed. Use of commercial video cameras requires permission at tourist sites. Video cassettes might be erased by airport x-ray machines, so pack them in lead pouches. If declared, your cassettes may be seized and screened with a charge of about Y5 each. Officials are looking for pornography and religious materials. If you don't have any, your tapes should be returned in hours or weeks.

Photographic film and computer diskettes should not be x-rayed at airport security. Ask for a hand-inspection. Multiple exposures to x-rays can adversely affect them.

Maps & Books

You can usually buy a detailed map in English in each city. For wandering around on your own without a guide, take a Chinese-English phrase book.

Medicines, Vitamins, & Goodies

Take what you need. Exact equivalents may be hard to find. Chinese traditional medicines are frequently effective, so if you're adventurous, you might try them. Many hotels and cruise ships have doctors. With Chinese painkillers, you might experience strange mood changes. A few pharmacists in big cities can fill Western prescriptions, but don't count on it except in Beijing.

Take Pepto-Bismol tablets (mild) and Immodium (serious) in case of diarrhea or upset stomach. Ask your doctor about Diamox for altitude sickness for Tibet. If you're bothered by pollution or dust, take a nose mask (or buy a cheap silk scarf in China).

Please consult a knowledgeable doctor about malaria. The danger is only in Hainan and the tropics close to the Laotian border. For these infected areas, take long sleeves and trousers for after dark (when these mosquitoes bite) and a good repellent. If you have flu-like symptoms after being bitten, tell your doctor to check for malaria. It can be fatal.

Take a few snacks and if you need more, buy them in China. Mineral water is available but boiled water is free.

Gifts

Gifts are not essential, but you may want to give them to friends or exceptional service people. Cash is becoming the norm. What are good gifts? Anything not made in China is usually acceptable. Some people give novelties like refrigerator magnets or unusual ball-point pens. You can give candy, postcards, Italian silk ties, cosmetics, souvenir playing cards, baseball caps, t-shirts, pins, or picture books with scenes of your country. Or something for their children like coloring books or books in English. For breaking the ice with children, take a bag of balloons or tiny cars.

You don't have to take gifts to schools, and certainly not to factories and communes. But schools do not usually receive any compensation for the disruption caused by visitors. If you want to leave a souvenir of your visit, give general gifts like books, frisbees, and pictures that everyone can enjoy. Giving to a few individuals may upset the others.

Since people everywhere are studying English and other foreign languages, books are a great idea. Books about your country are good. China is short of teaching materials in English. Guides, of course, would prefer cash, but you might also want to leave them copies of magazines such as Vogue or People, your used guide book, music tapes, or cartons of cigarettes (Marlboro Lights is a favorite). If you are going to Lhasa, Tibetans appreciate photos of the Dalai Lama, but passing these out may be construed as interference in an internal dispute by the Chinese authorities. If you are visiting foreign residents in China, ask what gifts they would like.

Packing for Business

Business cards are essential for business people, preferably in Chinese on the back. It is good to take a one page introduction in Chinese of your company (if possible). A few hotels print cards within 24 hours.

Officials dealing with Japan and Hong Kong have been accepting television sets and condos (!) Some have asked shamelessly for computers and 'Benzes.' There is no guarantee that an expensive gift will get you what you want. The danger is that from time to time, campaigns rage against corrupt officials who use their positions for personal gain. Chinese jails aren't nice. Chinese legal rights aren't the same. The government has executed people for accepting bribes. Usually, inviting an official to a banquet to celebrate a deal, or to thank especially helpful people, is sufficient. Modest corporate gifts like agenda books and lighters are fine. Some Chinese appreciate hard liquor, like Chivas Regal.

Money & the Cost of Travel

First, it's a good idea to take a money belt and neck safe to hold valuables. Take mainly travelers' checks as a precaution against theft.

If you're on a prepaid tour you only have to worry about incidentals like airport taxes (Y50 for domestic and Y90 for international), bicycle rentals, shopping, overweight luggage, a massage, barber or hairdresser, a round of drinks at a bar, postage stamps, long-distance telephone calls home, laundry, and unexpected emergencies. If you're not on a prepaid trip, take your credit card (most hotels three stars and up accept Visa, MasterCard and American Express), travelers checks, and cash in small denominated United States currency for shopping (you get slightly better prices). The bills should not be old, worn nor torn. Most travel agents and Chinese airlines do not accept credit cards.

Prices differ. Hotels in big, busy cities like Beijing and Shanghai are just as expensive as New York City. Hotels in smaller towns like Guilin and Suzhou are much cheaper. Food in restaurants outside of hotels is cheaper. In street markets you can eat well for less than Y10 a meal if you have to and want to.

CHINESE YUAN/U.S. DOLLAR EXCHANGE RATE

You'll note that prices in this book, as in China, are listed with a "Y" before the number, as in Y100 – which tells you that the cost is 100 yuan. The 1996 rate of exchange is 8.3 yuan to one U.S. dollar.

Laundry prices and quality depend on the quality of the hotel. At Guangzhou's five star Garden Hotel, a two-piece track suit cost Y45, a shirt Y40, trousers Y40, undershirt or underpants Y12, a pair of socks Y11. The coffee shop at the Holiday Inn in Guilin: Appetizers Y26-Y42; Soups Y17-Y24; Salads Y16-Y32; Sandwiches Y28-Y42; Entrees Y38-Y80. The evening dance show at the Guishan Hotel or Royal Garden Hotel in Guilin costs Y60. Taxis range from Y1, but mostly Y1.60, to Y2 a kilometer. Mass transit subways cost Y2. Public buses are cheaper. Entrance fees to tourist attractions are cheaper than at home.

Booking plane tickets through a travel agency can cost $10 service fee. Guides can cost $40 a day for one guest. Airport transfers can cost $20. A one-day city tour or the Li River Cruise in Guilin with lunch and bus can cost $50. The entrance to the Forbidden City in Beijing has been Y60.

Telephone calls from hotels are expensive; telecommunication offices or card telephones are much cheaper. The above prices will change and are offered to help you budget your money. There are ways of doing some of these activities more cheaply, but you should prepare yourself for high prices or you may have to do without. Take a generous supply of money. It will cost you time and money if your bank has to send you more.

MOVIES TO GET YOU READY FOR CHINA!

You can borrow videos of tourist attractions from Chinese missions, and film festivals do show Chinese films occasionally. Check your neighborhood video store. Look for Academy Award nominees **Ju Dou** *and* **Raise the Red Lantern,** *by director Zhang Yimou. Then there's* **Farewell My Concubine** *and* **Red Sorghum.** **The Horse Thief,** *set in Tibet, and* **The Ballad of the Yellow River** *are tragic. Other good movies are* **The Day the Sun Turned Cold, The Puppetmaster, Good Men, Good Women, Yellow Earth, In the Heat of the Sun, To Live** *and* **The Blue Kite.**

The only foreign-made movies I can recommend are **The Sand Pebbles** *(although filmed in Taiwan),* **The Last Emperor** *(with great shots of the Forbidden City),* **A Great Wall,** *and* **Bethune, The Making of a Hero.** **The First Emperor** *(shown on the museum circuit), is short but excellent, especially if you're going to Xi'an.*

CHINA NATIONAL TOURIST OFFICES

You can get brochures and questions answered from the **China National Tourist Offices**. Their addresses in various countries include:
• **Australia**: *19/F, 44 Market Street, Sydney NSW 2000, Tel. (02) 2994956, 2994057. Fax (02)2901958*
• **England**: *4 Glentworth Street, London NW1, Tel. (071) 9359427, 9359787. Fax (071)4875842*
• **Israel**: *Post Office Box 3281, Tel-Aviv, 61030, Tel. (00972) 3- 5226272, 3-5240891. Fax 3-5226281*
• **Japan**; *6/F Hamamatsu Cho Building, 1-27-13, Hamamatsu-cho, Minato- ku, Tokyo, Tel. (0081)03-34331461. Fax 03-34338653*
• **Singapore 0106**: *1 Shenton Way, #17-05, Ribina House, Tel. (0065) 2218681/82. Fax (0065) 2219267*
• **United States**: *Empire State Building, 350 Fifth Avenue, Suite 6413, New York, NY 10118, Tel. (212) 7608218. Fax (212) 7608809*; and *333 West Broadway, Suite 201, Glendale, CA 91204*

CHECK YOUR OWN CUSTOMS REGULATIONS

It is easier to get customs information before you leave. Find out what you cannot take back. Customs have confiscated dried beef and pork. The U.S. allows no fruit unless canned or dried, but Agriculture Canada allows tropical fruit like fresh mangoes, that are not grown in Canada. Dried medicinal herbs are okay. Certain animal products are forbidden or restricted. For example, both Canada and the U.S. allow no ivory, crocodile, alligator, leopard, or tiger products, as these are endangered. For more detailed information, contact your local customs office.

Many countries allow duty free coin and stamp collections, antiques (over 100 years old), and 'works of art' (one of a kind-not factory-made copies). Be sure to get a certificate of proof when you buy. The red wax seal on an antique is China's proof that the item is allowed out of the country.

Before you leave, register valuable items you will be bringing back with your own Customs, especially if they look new. You will need serial numbers, or you could carry an appraisal report for jewelry with photo, bill of sale, or Customs receipt (if applicable). This is to avoid hassles on your return. You don't want to pay duty on possesions you've had for years.

In the **United States**, you can obtain a booklet from the **U.S. Customs Service**. Americans are allowed a duty-free exemption of $400 on accompanied baggage every 30 days after a 48 hours absence. You pay 10% on the next $1000 worth of goods. This includes a maximum of 200 cigarettes (one carton) and one liter (33.8 fl.oz.) of alcohol. Tax rates vary. For example, the tax rate on carvings from Hong Kong is lower than on carvings from China. You can mail gifts worth US$50 or less, but the receiver cannot accept more than one duty- free parcel in one day. You should tell U.S. Customs if you are carrying over $10,000 in cash. I was once checked boarding a plane by U.S. marshalls for this.

Canada has a duty and tax-free personal exemption on CDN$50 worth of goods after 24 hours, $200 after 48 hours, and $500 after seven days absence. Over that, you pay about 15%. You may send duty-free gifts from abroad. Each gift must be valued at $60 or less and, Revenue Canada says it should have a gift card or letter or be gift wrapped. These must not be alcoholic beverages, tobacco, or advertising matter. Contact a Revenue Canada customs office for more information. **Certificates of Origin**, obtained at some Friendship Stores and factories, could mean a much lower duty rate on silk, for example.

HEALTH PRECAUTIONS

Consult a travel clinic for updating your shots especially tetanus. You are not required to have any immunizations as a requirement for entering China, unless you've been in an African yellow fever area six days prior to your arrival in China. Long-term travelers should ask about Encephalitis B and Hepatitis B.

Some North American cities are recommending immunization against typhoid, tetanus, polio, and Hepatitis A. A health certificate is required for people residing in China for over a year and includes an AIDS test. Get one before you leave home. In south China, malaria pills are recommended for malarial areas. Most tourists do not have to worry about this, but those going off-the-beaten-track to Hainan Island or areas of China bordering Laos, Burma, and Vietnam should check. Consult U.S. travel advisories and when you get to China.

Be warned about the poisonous lead level in some glazes. Do not eat or drink regularly out of Chinese ceramics, especially yellows, until you have them checked.

For more details, see Chapter 7, *Basic Information.*

FORMALITIES

Passports & Visas

You will, of course, need a valid **passport**. Give yourself plenty of time to get a copy of your birth certificate, photos, and sponsors.

You can get a **tourist visa** from any Chinese consulate in five working days. If you're in a hurry, it can be done in less. You can also get a visa in one working day (or in less if you pay more) at the Chinese visa office in Hong Kong. Your travel agent can also get a visa for you for a fee. A frequent traveler should try for a multiple-entry visa.

For a prepaid group tour of nine or more, travel agents can obtain one visa but you have to enter and leave China together. (You can should ask for a separate visa if you want to leave on your own.)

Transit visas are not necessary if you stay less than 24 hours inside the transit lounge of the airport. You must have a visa for your next stop, and a confirmed plane reservation out. In an emergency, visas can be obtained at some ports in China.

A Chinese passport holder living abroad does not need an entry visa, but may have difficulty leaving China.

Travelers to Tibet need to be part of a prepaid tour, and travel agents can arrange this. If you want to book this in China after you get there, do not mention Tibet on your Chinese visa application form, because the consulate will then insist that you need a permit for Tibet before you go.

A **Visa Application Form** requires one photo, the usual information and the host unit in China. The host can be CITS, the Chinese agency organizing your trip, the hotel where you have a confirmed reservation, or a friend in China who has invited you. If you are visiting relatives or friends you will need their names(s), nationality, occupation, place of work, and relationship to applicant.

Sometimes, especially if booking by mail, a photocopy of the first essential pages of your passport is required. In case of unexpected delays, give yourself a few more days in China than you think you need.

Your visa will admit you to any international airport or seaport in China and to any of the cities currently open to foreign visitors without a travel permit within the time limit mentioned. A one-month visa for example is good for one month from the day you enter China, not from the day you get a visa.

Visas are good for most of China. You may need an alien travel permit later to go to some off-the-beaten track places even if just traveling by road between open cities. Some provinces like Fujian, Guangdong, and Shandong have no restrictions. Jilin is 99% open, and Liaoning is lmostly open.

If your visa has expired, you will probably be detained and fined when you try to leave the country. See Emergencies in the *Basic Information* chapter for this and for what to do about restricted areas.

You may need visas for other countries in which you will be traveling, such as train travel through Germany, Poland, Russia and Mongolia. All these have missions in Beijing. It can be difficult getting a Mongolian visa because its embassy keeps irregular hours. It is faster and cheaper to go to a country's mission yourself. It can be done by mail or courier; otherwise, consult your travel agent. Get as many visas as you can before you leave home.

CHINESE MISSIONS ABROAD
Australia
• **Embassy of the People's Republic of China**, *75 Corinthian Drive. Tel. (06) 2734780, Yarralumla, Canberra, A.C.T. 2600.* Consulates General in Sydney and Melbourne.

Canada
• **Embassy of the People's Republic of China**, *515 St. Patrick St. Tel. (613) 234-2706 or 234-2682, Ottawa, Ont., K1N 5H3*
• **Consulate General of the People's Republic of China**, *240 St. George St., Tel. (416)964-7260. Toronto, Ont., M5R 2P4*
• **Consulate General of the People's Republic of China**, *3380 Granville St., Tel. (604) 736-3910, Vancouver, B.C. V6H 3K3*

England
• **Embassy of the People's Republic of China**, *49-51 Portland Place, Tel. (01) 636-5726, London, WIN 3AG.*

Japan
• **Embassy of the People's Republic of China**, *4-33, Tel. (03) 403-3389 or 403-3380, Moto-Azabu 3-chome, Minato-ku, Tokyo*

Nepal
• **Embassy of the People's Republic of China**, *Baluwatar, Kathmandu, Tel. 411740 or 412589*

US

- **Embassy of the People's Republic of China**, *2300 Connecticut Ave., N.W., Tel. (202) 328-2517 or (202) 328-2500; Fax (202)328-2564, Washington, DC 20008*
- **Consulate General of the People's Republic of China**, *100 West Erie St., Tel. (312) 803-0095 or (312) 803-0122, Chicago, IL 60610*
- **Consulate General of the People's Republic China**, *3417 Montrose Blvd., (713) 524-4311; Fax (713)524-7656, Houston, TX 77066*
- **Consulate General of the People's Republic of China**, *443 Shatto Place, (213) 380-2506-7; Fax (213) 380-1961, Los Angeles, CA 90020*
- **Consulate General of the People's Republic of China**, *520 12th Ave., (212) 330-7409; Fax (212) 502-0245, New York, NY 10036*
- **Consulate General of the People's Republic of China**, *1450 Laguna St., (415) 563-4857 or (415) 563-4885; Fax (415)563-0494, San Francisco, CA 94115*

HOTEL RESERVATIONS

Reservations are recommended during high tourist season, festivals, or trade fairs. Definitely have a hotel booked at least for your first night then. Your travel agent can reserve rooms or you can do it yourself. Phone your airline or the relevant hotel reservation system. For example, for the Sheraton Hotel in Beijing, phone Sheraton's toll-free number below or the Sheraton nearest you. You can also fax hotels directly. Hotels should give you a confirmation if asked.

You can also use hotel toll-free numbers to get an idea of prices and specials and then compare these with what travel agents have to offer. Cheaper hotels do not usually accept reservations. If you are traveling prepaid without a guide, make sure you are carrying vouchers for these and the telephone number of your travel agent in case something goes wrong.

Some of the major cities like Beijing and Shanghai have direct telephone connections with the international airport. You can try to make a reservation immediately upon arrival. Many hotels have representatives at airports.

Some travel agents in North America or China have booked blocks of rooms in many Chinese hotels at group rates. You can usually get cheaper rooms at these hotels if you book through these travel agents. Only about two per cent of guests pay published hotel rates in China. Save your money for something else.

WESTERN HOTELS IN CHINA & THEIR TOLL-FREE NUMBERS

Caesar Park Hotels and Resorts: (212)681-9455
Forum Hotels International: 1-800-327-0200
Hilton International: 1-800-445-8667
Holiday Inns Worldwide: 1-800-HOLIDAY, internet http:// www.holiday-inn.com
Hyatt International Corporation: 1-800-233-1234
Intercontinental: 1-800-327-0200
Leading Hotels of the World: 1-800-223-6800
New World Hotels International: 1-800-637-7200 or 1-800-44UTELL
Radisson Hotels: 1-800-333-3333
Nikko: 1-800-645-5687
Novotel/Sofitel/Mercure: 1-800-221-4542
Omni: 1-800-THE OMNI
Orient Hotel Reservations: Sino-American Tours, 1-800-221-7982
Pan Pacific: 1-800-538-4040
Preferred Hotels: 1-800-323-7500
Ramada Worldwide Reservations: 1-800-854-7854, 1-800-228-9898
SAS: 1-800-223-5652 or SAS office
Shangri-La International: 1-800-942-5050
Sheraton International: 1-800-325-3535
Steigenberger: 1-800-223-5652
Summit: (201) 902-7704
Swiss-Belhotel: 1-800-553-3638
Swissôtel: 1-800-637-9477
Westin: 1-800-228-3000

GETTING THERE

HOW SHOULD YOU GO?

Take your pick. The group tour is not the only way to go, but it could be cheaper and has less hassles for all but the tour guide.

Package Tour or Going Solo?

A prepaid group tour is the easiest way to go but individual travel is becoming a lot easier, more popular, sometimes cheaper and tailored to your own pace. Individual travel can be time-consuming and frustrating if you make your own bookings but it also more interesting.

Prepaid Tours

Just book with a good travel agent and most of your problems are solved. You can choose a set tour with other people (cheaper) or have one custom-made. The average size is 20 people or less. The fewer people you have the more expensive the rate per person will be. It is probably cheaper to book a hotel through a travel agent well established with China than to book on the spot after arrival.

China prefers prepaid tours. They use scarce staff interpreters more efficiently and are given preference. Even groups of four pay-as-you-go individuals run the risk of being downgraded or having their reservations canceled in favor of a tour group.

If you just want to see China, a general-interest tour is ideal. Figure out what areas interest you and call a lot of travel agents. If you want to visit schools, factories, or hospitals, take a special-interest or Friendship Association tour. Or make sure schools, factories, or hospitals are included in your tour.

Prepaid tours are treated the same in China except for the quality of the hotel and food. You can choose between a standard or a more expensive 'deluxe' room. If the price of a tour differs from one agency to another, it could be because (1) all meals or better meals are included; (2) there is an orientation session, and perhaps a full-time, knowledgeable international guide; (3) one agent is getting a bigger commission; (4) the tour operator has better connections in China or flies Air China.

Most group tours are flexible, so you can avoid most of the group activities or stay in another hotel (at your own expense). However, deviation means more money. If you get sick and spend another night in the same hotel, the hotel probably charges individual not group rates.

Tour groups can be fun if you have the right people. But a tendency does develop to regard the Chinese as 'them' as opposed to 'us.' As soon as group members start joking about the 'natives,' you've crossed the line and become a group tourist. If you are visiting China to meet the people and learn about the country, make an effort to break free. Venture out into the streets alone. Lounge in parks, especially on Sundays. A lot of students are waiting to practice their English on you. You might even be invited to someone's home.

Questions for Prepaid Tours with Set Itineraries

How many of your desired destinations are offered? How many days will you have in each place? How many people are in the group? How old? Sexes? Will you be asked for tips for guides and drivers in each city? Airport taxes? Do you have an international guide? National guide? What happens if your plane is canceled or your guide doesn't meet you? Ask about refunds if you are stuck in an airport for a day.

What is the price? Why is it different from another organizer with the same cities and number of days? Usually the price includes visa fee, group transportation (from your home airport or your first point in China?), hotel accommodation (double or single occupancy?), one, two or three meals a day, sightseeing, group transfers and admission tickets to tourist attractions and cultural events. Does the price include taxes and service charges? Will you be traveling with a guide or interpreter? Are the hotel rooms 'standard' or 'deluxe'? Are the trains soft or hard class? Are the airplanes first or economy class?

Price quotes do not usually include passport fees, excess baggage, medical, and other personal expenses. Nor do they include expenses for itinerary changes or prolonged tours 'due to unforeseen circumstances.' Ask about those 'unforeseen circumstances.' These could include plane cancellations, overbooking, arriving at the airport after the plane leaves, illness, or accident. Who pays for these inconveniences? Will you be expected to pay on the spot? Ask about health, evacuation and cancellation insurance. What are the benefits? What language will the guide speak? What refund do you get if the tour is partly canceled? What hotels do you get? (Check the hotels in this book to see if those are what you want.) What happens if the tour operator goes out of business?

On the Yangtze cruise, are shore excursions included in the price?

All tours are subject to changes in itinerary by the Chinese, so don't blame your travel agent entirely. Prices, too, are subject to change.

Cruising to China

Cruise lines include **Cunard**, **EuroLloyd**, **Pearl Cruises**, **Princess** and **Royal Viking**. You usually pay extra if you want a guided tour at ports of call. See also *Yangtze Gorges*.

Minipackages

Travel agents offer packages that could include only travel tickets, hotel accommodations, and breakfast. You sightsee on your own or book sightseeing tours locally. It is an ideal compromise for business people and those who want to do their own thing. In some but not all cities, you can join a relatively inexpensive local tour but times are not necessarily at your convenience.

Independent Traveling

Many foreigners have traveled in China happily and successfully on their own. Some backpackers have loved it, not minding dormitory accommodations and delays. Travelers with bigger budgets have an easier time. Your hotel can meet your plane or train if requested. Most hotels have travel desks. You can join a group tour or hire a taxi for sightseeing.

On-your-own traveling is not as easy in China as in Europe. If you can't speak Chinese, however, you can get around with this guide book. The Chinese are usually sympathetic and helpful to lost and bewildered foreigners.

Special Tours

Chinese travel agents are willing and eager to accommodate you, but they are not always able to. Put your special request to several travel agents at home and in China. Give them plenty of time. You can write an organization in China directly with a pretty good chance of getting a reply. The best way to communicate is by fax. Letters can take up to three weeks from North America. They arrive faster if addressed in Chinese with the postal number (code). They are answered more quickly if written in Chinese. If you telephone China, it helps to have a Mandarin-speaking person with you.

Scientists can contact the Foreign Affairs Department of the **Chinese Academy of Sciences**. Mountain climbers should contact the **Chinese Mountaineering Association**. School groups contact **CYTS**. Sports teams wanting to play Chinese teams, or individuals wanting a ski package or parachuting should try **China International Sports Travel Service**. For factory, farm and school visits as well as monuments, try **China Friendship tours**. For religious groups, consult your own organizations.

Travelers of Chinese Ancestry

An **Overseas Chinese** is anyone with a Chinese surname, face, or the address of a relative and/or an ancestral village in China. There are no special discounts now for Overseas Chinese. **CTS** is the most experienced agency for Overseas Chinese. They can help find your relatives and tell you what gifts you can take them duty-free.

It is permissible to live with relatives in China or have relatives stay with you in your hotel. You can take part in special camps and seminars offered by the Overseas Chinese Association in some counties in Guangdong province. Xinhui county has been giving free or cheaper room, board, and travel in the county, and courses for two weeks, mostly for young people with roots in the county. Taishan gives courses, but it charges. These are great introductions to China and the area. Courses could be on language, painting, medicine, music, dance - and are in English.

You could write the **Overseas Chinese Association** or travel agent in your county for information or try a Chinatown travel agent, a family association, or a county association. You can probably find these in any large Chinatown in America. A Chinese consulate or travel agent might have information.

If you enter China on a Chinese passport, you are considered Chinese and subject to Chinese laws, not the laws of your country of citizenship.

Before you go, Overseas Chinese should start collecting the names of relatives, particularly of ancestors, born in China. The name of your ancestral village is essential is you want to visit it. Be aware that many villages have changed their names, but in China, you might find an older person who remembers it. Usually you refer only to your father's family. No one cares about maternal lines! The names should help people in your village place you. The welcome is better if they can establish a connection than if they can't. The names, of course, should be written in Chinese.

Take as much documentation as you can; a letter in Chinese from your family association, your father's or grandfather's old passport, and a map of where they lived in the village. If you don't have a Chinese name, get one. It doesn't have to be legal, but it will make things easier for you as you travel around China. Just be sure you know how it is pronounced in both your family dialect and pu tong hua.

Traveling with China Friendship & Other Associations

These associations the world over can give information on China and sponsor their own study tours. Some entertain visiting Chinese delegations, teach English, collect books for China, show movies, and provide lecturers on China. They can give you an idea of organizations who send people to China.

The Cultural Affairs Office at a Chinese mission can usually give addresses. The **Chefoo Schools Association** organizes tours for alumni back to the old school in Yantai and Lushan. Their address is: *Post Office Box 147, 260 Adelaide Street East, Toronto, Ontario, M5A 1N0. Tel. (416) 467-4820.*

Traveling On Business

The usual procedure is to communicate with a trade or commercial office at a Chinese mission abroad, your mission in China, or your government's department of trade. These will all probably tell you to contact a Chinese trading corporation, some of whom have representatives in North America. If the Chinese are interested they will send you an invitation that will give you a visa or you could get a tourist visa and investigate business possibilities directly. No one has ever asked to see my passport for doing business except at some trade shows.

If you want to sell goods retail through Chinese stores, look for a Chinese joint-venture partner. Your hotel business center, trade council, sister city offices, trade shows, and your country's trade office in China might be able to introduce you to potential partners.

If you have a host organization make your travel arrangements, you should tell your host the quality of the hotel you want because s/he might assume you want to save money. It may not be up to your standards. It is embarrassing for a host to make changes after you arrive.

Do take business cards, and some description of your company, preferably in Chinese. See also Business in the *Basic Information* chapter.

Study Tours, Language Learning & Jobs

For students exchanges, in the United States contact the **Council on International Exchange of Scholars**. In Canada, contact the **Chinese Embassy**. Some universities, colleges, states, provinces, and cities organize exchanges. Ask around. Contact the **American Institute for Foreign Study** for Chinese language study (see below).

'Self-supporting' foreign students are accepted at some schools in China. You can apply directly. Academic credits may not be equivalent. Tuition depends on the school and has been about $1600 to $2500 for a Masters program, with living expenses at $1.50 to $6.00 a day. Living conditions can be hard.

Graduate students and research scholars can contact the **Committee on Scholarly Communication with the People's Republic of China**. Contact also the **Center for International Education**, and the **United Board for Christian Higher Education in Asia**. The British counterpart is the **British Academy**.

Some helpful contacts include:
- **Academic Travel Abroad, Inc.**, *3210 Grace Street, NW, Washington, D.C. 20007. Tel. (202)3333355, (800) 5567896*
- **American Institute for Foreign Study**, *102 Greenwich Avenue, Greenwich, CT 06830. Tel. 1-800-727-AIFS or (203) 869-9090. Fax (203) 869-9615. E-mail: ChinaEdEx@aol.com*
- **CET**, *Academic Programs, 3210 Grace Street, NW, Washington, DC 20007. Tel.(800) 2254262*
- **Center for International Education**, *U.S. Department of Education, 600 Independence Avenue, SW, Washington, D.C., 20202-5332. Tel. (202) 4019772. Fax (202) 2059489*
- **China Educational Exchange**, *1251 Virginia Avenue, Harrisonburg, VA 22801. Tel. (540) 432-6983. Fax (540) 434-5556. E-mail ChinaEdEx@aol.com*
- **China Teaching Program**, *Western Washington University, Old Main 530, Bellingham, WA 98225-9047. Tel. (360) 650-3753. Fax (360) 6502847. E-mail:work@cc.wwu.edu*
- **Committee on Scholarly Communication with China**, *Suite 2013, 1055 Thomas Jefferson Street, NW, Washington, D.C. 20007. Tel. (202) 3371250. Fax (202) 3373109. E-mail:China@NAS.edu*

- **International Executive Service Corporation**, *Post Office Box 10005, Stamford, Conn., 06913-0437. Tel. (203) 967-6000*
- **United Board for Christian Higher Education**, *475 Riverside Drive, New York, 10115 Tel. (212) 870-2608.*
- **WorldTeach**, *Harvard Institute for International Development, One Eliot Street, Cambridge, MA 02138-5705. Tel. (800) 4TEACH-0. Fax 4951599*

Traveling As a Casual Student

Many provincial travel and tourism offices offer courses in cooking, martial arts, acupuncture, and other Chinese arts, but primarily for groups. Several colleges and universities offer six-to-eight-week Chinese language courses. It's best to start learning before you go to China, and expect polishing from a short course.

Visiting as a Foreign Expert

Specialists and professionals can give lectures or demonstrations to their Chinese counterparts if invited to do so. Don't expect anything more than a 'thank you' and maybe a tax write-off for part of your expenses.

Teaching in China

China hires foreign language teachers for one to two year contracts. The great need is for English language teachers and also teachers of middle-level technology and managerial skills. There have been more than 9000 foreign teachers a year working in China.

Long-term experts usually have at least a Masters and three years' teaching experience. They should receive a contract, transportation and home leave. The stipend ranges from Y1000 to Y1200 a month. 30 to 50% of your salary can be taken out of China in foreign currency. Some experts receive free accommodation, medical care, etc. Their salary is frequently ten times that of local teachers, so no complaints, please.

Foreign teachers (not experts) are usually locally hired and do not get the same benefits. Some money-strapped colleges have hired native English-speakers without any teaching qualifications who just drop by. They give only room and board and try to help find financing through North American organizations. Some teach and study part-time. In Guilin, one American student was teaching English six hours a week for Y30 RMB an hour plus a meal.

Foreigners should know how to say 'no,' if the Chinese pile work on them. I would also suggest getting advice from someone who has taught in China and bring as many teaching materials as possible. Ask a China Friendship Association. A commitment about sufficient heat and hot water is essential. Some foreign experts have had a terrible time with the cold.

If you'd like to teach in China, a helpful publication is *China Bound: A Guide to Academic Life and Work in the PRC* by Karen Turner-Gottschang.

Working as a Volunteer or Paid Consultant

Yes, there are jobs available in China and your chances increase if you know the language. Try **United Nations Volunteers**, and teachers' organizations. The **China Educational Exchange** wants physicians and agricultural specialists. Foreign commercial companies offer the highest salaries and usually the best living conditions. Get a list of North American companies with offices in China and contact them before you leave home. You can find some of these in *China Daily*, China-related economic periodicals and some North American newspapers. The **Canadian Executive Service Organization** in Toronto sends retired Canadians as volunteer consultants. Its American counterpart is the **International Executive Service Corps** based in Connecticut.

You can also contact the **Chinese Educational Association for International Exchange**, *37 Damucang Hutong, Beijing* or the **Foreign Experts Bureau**, *Friendship Hotel Beijing, 100873 or P.O. Box 300, Beijing, 100086.* It is quicker to write directly to the Office of the President or the Foreign Affairs Office of the school where you wish to teach, as the Foreign Experts Bureau is primarily a central clearing house. The Bureau is looking for people to work in universities, newspapers, publishing houses and other cultural institutes.

To become a United Nations Volunteers, write: **Palais des Nations**, *CH-1211 Geneva 10, Switzerland. Fax (41 22) 798 85 70.*

To volunteer from Canada, contact the China Desk of the **Canadian Council of Churches**, *129 St. Clair Avenue West, Toronto, Ontario, M4T 1N5, Tel. (416) 921-1923. Fax (416) 9213843*; the **Canadian Executive Service Organization**, *Operations Center, Suite 2000, 415 Yonge Street, Toronto, Ont. M5B 2E7. Tel. (416) 596-2376*; the **China Educational Exchange**, *c/o Mennonite Central Committee, 134 Plaza Drive, Winnipeg, MB R3T 5K9. Tel. (204) 261-6381* or **Academic Relations**, *Department of External Affairs, 125 Sussex Drive, Ottawa, K1A OG2. Tel. (613) 992-6668. Fax (613) 992-5965.*

Traveling to China As a Job Hunter

Tourists can try to pick up jobs while traveling in China, but don't count on it. If you are an experienced teacher, ask around, a travel agent, a hotel, or any college or university. If you speak English and have any idea about teaching, you could ask any about-to-be-opened hotel or a tourism school if it wants an English teacher or other staff.

Talk with business people about job possibilities. Good English-speaking secretaries are in short supply. But check out work regulations and income tax first. Local hires might be paid Chinese-level salaries. See *Fuzhou*.

Traveling to China For Medical Treatment

Some provincial travel and tourism agencies, for example in Wuxi, offer tour packages for treatment in Chinese sanitariums or you can book directly with the sanitariums. Do not expect North American standards. Some hotels have qigong, acupuncture, or non-smoking clinics, at prices cheaper than North America. See *Chongqing*.

Traveling to China As a Guest

Lucky you. Do be aware that local residents and even government corporations may not know all the attractions you want to see. One visitor to Shenyang desperately wanted to find the locomotive museum, but local friends had never heard of it. Tell your hosts what you want to see and what kind of accommodations you would like. Give them plenty of time to make arrangements. And don't expect them to be as efficient as a travel agency. Expect delays and time wasted with formalities.

USING TRAVEL SPECIALISTS

The easy way is to get a good travel agent. The hard way is to attempt this all yourself. The first way, believe it or not, could be cheaper for you.

Choosing a Travel Agent

You should consult an agent experienced with China. In dealing with North American travel agents, consider the following. How long have they been sending people to China? How many people did they send last year? If the answer is more than three years, and in the hundreds, you should be okay. The Chinese do their best for people they know and trust.

It's best to book everything in advance in high tourist season. Many tours from North America are cheaper than flying to Hong Kong or China and booking tours from there. The cheapest flights are probably through Chinatown agencies.

Contact all convenient China-bound airlines, get a quote from its major **consolidators**, and see if your own travel agent can match it. These are agents who buy large groups of tickets at cheaper rates and sell them at cheaper rates. There may be restrictions of various sorts with them.

For individual travelers, can the agent advise you what to do if your guide doesn't meet you at the airport? Would the agent know the prices and quality of cheaper hotels? Does the city have tour groups you can join on the spot? The cost of taxis?

You should be able to find a knowledgeable travel agent through the China Master Agents program, which trains and certifies travel agents as specialists in China travel. Contact: **Creative Concepts Marketing**, *P.O. Box 2881, Reston, VA 22090. Tel. (703) 391-2129; Fax (703) 391-2178.*

You can also call a Chinese consulate for an agent. Or you can use any of the experienced agents below.

Sometimes a travel agent will discount, especially if you buy packages. And yes, you might save money organizing your own tour group but it's not easy. The more people you have, the cheaper it is if you know what to do. But there are also a lot of headaches as flight schedules and prices change without warning.

GET IT IN WRITING!

If you are traveling without a guide, and your travel agent at home says you can pick up your plane ticket in China, or that your hotel room has been paid, just be sure you get it in writing. I have gone to CITS in China to pick up tickets and they never heard of me. The tickets were later found under the code number of the tour group I was leading, or my nationality. I have seen guests arguing in hotels because the hotels had no record of payment. The traveler has to pay and then collect refunds from travel agents at home.

Travel Agents

Some of the following agencies, especially **China Travel Service** in the United States and Canada, and **China International Travel Service** in the U.S., can book Chinese domestic flights, ferry, and train tickets. They can confirm and ticket charter flights between Hong Kong and China. They can confirm hotels in China with discounted rates in major cities.

These agencies and those listed below can book tours, mini-packages, join-in tours, and special interest tours for individuals or groups. A few can book the trans-Siberian train. All tour agents can probably book international tours like China and Vietnam, or China and Hong Kong. Phone them and compare services and prices.

Prepaid travelers booking through a travel agent usually have to pay the full price of the tour prior to their arrival in China. You may have to pay extra at the end of your trip. If there are to be additional expenses, you are usually consulted during the trip. For example, flights delayed by weather might mean an option of paying for an additional day or cutting out another part of the tour.

Many travel agencies cover small additional costs themselves rather than antagonize their clients. On the other hand, you might get some money back.

You might ask if the tour operator is a member of **USTOA**, which provides consumer protection if a travel company goes bankrupt. Top of the line is **Abercrombie and Kent**. Among the the big operators are **Orient Flexi-Pax Tours** (tours and hotel bookings) and **Pacific Delight**, which can do both individual travel and groups. Smaller travel agents are **Partners In Travel, Ltd.** of Minneapolis.

CET specializes tours for academic groups. **Distant Horizons** has high quality tours with lecturers.

In the US, contact:

• **Abercrombie & Kent International, Inc.**, *1520 Kensington Road, Oak Brook, IL 60521-2141, Tel. 1-800-323-7308, (708) 954-2944. Fax (708) 954-3324.* This is among the top of the line.

• **American-International Homestays, Inc.**, *Post Office Box 7178, Boulder, CO 80306-7178. Tel. 1-800-876-2048*

• **Asian Pacific Adventures**, *826 South Sierra Bonita Avenue, Los Angeles, CA 90036-4704. Tel. (213) 935-3156, Fax 935-2691.* This has had bicycle tours in southwest China and Inner Mongolia.

• **Avia Travel**, *5429 Geary Boulevard, San Francisco, CA, 94121. Tel. (415) 668-0964, 1-800-950-2842. Fax (415) 386-8519.* Their specialty is cheaper airfares.

• **Backroads Bicycle Touring**, *1516 5th Street, Berkeley, CA 94710-1740. Tel. (510)527-1555. Fax (510) 527-1444*

• **China for the Connoisseur**, *345 East 56th Street, Suite 6F, New York 10022, Tel. 1-800-827-2808, or (212) 753-2862, Fax (212) 832-0433.* Can arrange scuba diving and water skiing tours.

• **China International Travel Service** *(GD), 138B, World Trade Center, San Francisco, CA 94111. Tel.(415) 362-7477, 1-800-362-3839. Fax (415) 989-3838*

• **Distant Horizons**, *619 Tremont Street, Boston, MA 02118. Tel. (617) 267-5343, 1-800-3331240, Email: disthoriz@aol.com.* They offer high quality tours with lecturers.

• **Elderhostel**, *75 Federal Street, Boston, MA 02110-1941. Tel. (617) 426-8056*

• **Euro-Asia Express**, *475 El Camino Real, #206, Millbrae, CA 94030. Tel. 1-800-782-9624, 1-800-782-9625. Fax (415) 692-7450.* Offering cheaper airfares.

• **Journey to the East, Inc.**, *P.O.Box 1334, Flushing, New York, 11352-1334. Tel. 1-800-366-4034 or (718) 358-4034. Fax (718) 358-4065.* Knows Tibet, southwest China, and the Yangtze.

• **Mountain Travel-Sobek**, *6420 Fairmount Avenue, El Cerrito, CA 94530-3606. Tel. 1-800-227-2384; (510) 527-8100. Fax (510) 525-7710.* They offer trips to Tibet and Pakistan.

• **Orient Flexi-Pax Tours**, *630 Third Avenue, New York, 10017. Tel. 1-800-545-5540 or (212) 692-9550. Fax (212) 661-1618, 661-1193*

- **Pacific Delight Tours, Inc.**, *132 Madison Avenue, New York, New York, 10016. Tel. 1-800-221-7179 or (212) 684-7707. Fax (212) 532-3406.* They have offices also in Los Angeles, and Minneapolis) .
- **Partners in Travel, Ltd.**, *825 On the Mall, Minneapolis, MN, 55402-2606. Tel. 612-338-0004.* This is a small but experienced agency.
- **Rahim Tours**, *12 South Dixie Highway, Lake Worth, Florida, 33460, Tel. (407) 585-5305 or 1-800-556-5305; Fax (407) 582-1353.* China via Russia.
- **U.S. China Travel Service, Inc.**, *Main Office, 212 Sutter Street, Second Floor, San Francisco, CA 94108. Tel. (415) 398-6627, 1-800-332-2831, 1-800-553-8764.* Also *223E, Garvey Avenue, Suite 138, Monterey Park, CA 91754. Tel. (818) 288-8222*

Some experienced Canadian travel agencies are:
- **Bestway Tours and Safaris**, *3526 West 41st Avenie, Vancouver, B.C., V6N 3E6. Tel. (604) 264-7378, 1-800-663-0844. Fax (604) 264-7774.* Specializes in travel between Pakistan, China, and Central Asia).
- **China Travel Service (Canada) Inc.**, *438 University Avenue, Suite 306, Toronto, Ontario, M5S2K8. Tel.(416) 979-8993. Fax (416) 979-8220; 556 West Broadway, Vancouver, B.C., V5Z 1E9. Tel. (604) 872-8787, 1-800-663-1126. Fax (604) 873-2823*
- **Chinapac International**, *Suite 301, 1195 West Broadway, Vancouver, B.C.V6H3X5. Tel. (604) 731-1693, 1-800-661-8182. Fax (604) 731-1694*
- **Conference Travel and Tours**, *4141 Yonge Street, Suite 402, North York, Ontario, M2P 2A8. Tel. (416) 221-6411, 1-800-387-1488. Fax (416) 225-7334.* This is the agent for the fancy China Orient Express railway train.
- **Goway/Pacesetter Travel**, *3284 Yonge Street, Suite 300, Toronto, M4N 3M7. Tel. (416) 322-1034; 1-800-387-8850. Fax (416) 3221109, 1-800-665-4432*
- **Intours Corporation**, *2150 Bloor Street West, Suite 308, Toronto, Ontario, M6S 1M8. Tel. (416) 766-4720. Fax (416) 7668507.* They can book Trans-Russian trains to China.
- **Tour East Holidays**, *1033 Bay Street, Suite 302, Toronto, M5S 3A5. Tel. (416) 929-0888, (800) 667-3951. Fax (416) 929-8295*

Knowledgeable travel agents in other countries:
- **Helen Wong's Tours**, *Level 18, Town Hall House, 456 Kent Street, Sydney, N.S.W.2000, Australia. Tel. (02) 2677833. Fax (02) 2677717*
- **Folke and Christina von Knobloch**, *Central Asia Tourism Corporation, 52 Amangeldi, Almaty, 480012, Kazakhstan. Tel. 7-3272-639017, Fax 327-5811451. E-mail 77202.60001. COMPUSERVE 177000.1511*
- **Great Escapes Trekking**, *Post Office Box 9523, Baluwatar, Kathmandu,*

Nepal. Tel. 977-1-418951 or fax 977-1-411533. E-mail GRT@GREATPC.MOS.COM.NP. Great Escapes address in the U.S. is *c/o Sonam Gyalpo Lama, Myths and Mountains Inc., 976 Tee Court, Incline Village, Nevada 89451. Tel. 1-800-670-6984, fax (702) 832-4454.* They can arrange trips to Tibet from Nepal.

- **Pacific Discovery Tours**, *P.O.Box 6145, 2/F, 109 Queen Street, Auckland, New Zealand. Tel. 64-9-3660379. Fax 3773735*
- **Thomas Cook (N.Z.)**, *10-12 Commerce Street, P.O.Box 2223, DX2102, Auckland 1, New Zealand. Tel. 0-9-3793924. Fax 0-9-3089041*
- **Sitara Travel Consultants (Pvt) Ltd.**, *Sitara House, 232 Khadim Hussain Rd., Post Office Box 63, Rawalpindi, Pakistan. Tel. (92) 51-564750. Fax (92) 51 584958.* Tours from Pakistan into China.

Travel Agents in China

If you want to deal directly with China, the headquarters of the main competing travel agencies follow. Branches of some of these agencies are also listed under each destination:

- **China Travel Service**, *Head Office is at 2 Bei San Huan Dong Road, Beijing, 100028. Tel. (010) 4612599, 4622288. Fax 4612599*
- **China International Travel Service**, *103 Fuxingmenei Avenue, Beijing, 100800. Tel. (010) 6012044, 6039331. Fax 6012013*
- **CYTS Tours Corporation**, *23C Dong Jiao Min Xiang, Beijing, 100006. Tel. (010) 5135122 and 5243388. Fax 5135137, 5249809*
- **China Rail Express Travel Service Group**, *Block 3, Multiple Service Building, Beifengwo Road, Haidian District, Beijing, 100038. Tel. (010) 3272532, 3225152. Fax 3261824*
- **China International Sports Travel Company**, *4, Tiyuguan Road, Beijing 100061. Tel. (010) 7117367. Fax 7117370*

Some travelers have booked directly with the local branches of these agencies listed under each city. Only Class A travel agencies can deal directly with clients from abroad before they arrive in China. But you can go to local agencies after you arrive.

Some provincial agencies like Hebei (Shijiazhuang), Jiangsu (Nanjing), Shandong (Jinan), Tianjin, and Zhejiang (Hangzhou) are very good. There are also the new national travel agencies organized by the airlines with a travel agency partner. There should be no problem with air tickets and cancellation of confirmed flights with these agencies.

Prices are not always the same. Each Chinese travel agency has different connections and tries to underprice each other, so it's good to telephone the several agencies listed under each destination. They should be able to meet you at airports, sell you plane and train tickets, reserve hotel rooms and tours, confirm flights, obtain travel permits, etc. They should provide guide-interpreters. Tour prices for one or two people are high, but some travelers have found that going four to a taxi is cheaper than taking city tours. Ask also about CITS' **Panda Tours**, or existing tours you can join. Ask about booking hotels; it might be cheaper than booking them yourself.

You can usually be confident of a travel agency in a good hotel. If the travel agency doesnt measure up, complain to the hotel's general manager.

Quality of service is uneven. Top guides and duds are in every agency. Branches in one city might be excellent but terrible in another. Agencies compete with each other, steering you toward their own hotels and tours. Some travel agencies have become decentralized and are almost like franchises. Local and provincial governments tend to have more control over local branches than head offices in Beijing which are now trying to regain control.

Foreign travel agents usually buy tours organized by Chinese travel agents and adapt them for their own groups. Frequently the local schedule is left to the local guide. Tourists should know what they want to see and insist on going there before their time runs out. Tourists should never let themselves be at the mercy of tour guides.

Hong Kong Travel Agents

As transportation and other services are continually being improved, you can ask travel agents here for up-to-date information. **Hong Kong Tourist Association** (H.K.T.A.) can give you addresses and telephone numbers. It has offices conveniently located in the Buffer Hall (incoming passengers only) of Hong Kong's Kai Tak airport, at the Star Ferry pier in Tsimshatsui, Kowloon, and in the basement, Jardine House, 1 Connaught Place, Central on Hong Kong island.

Most travel agents listed here should be able to book the Trans-Siberian train and domestic Chinese flights. Most can book group tours with English-speaking guides. They can make arrangements for individual travelers, get visas, and book tickets by mail before you arrive. Phone around for quotes. Cheap airfare is advertised in local newspapers, but at your own risk. CITS and CTS and about four other agencies are able to get you to Shenzhen for 72 hours without a visa.

A few travel agents, but not those listed here, have given the industry a bad name because of unreliable service. Worse are the ones who take your money and disappear. The following have been in business for years, and I have used some of them myself.

If any of them fail you, please let me know and I will take them off the list. Abercrombie and Kent, and American Express, are good and easy to find. Tell me also if you have found other reliable agencies.

- **China International Travel Service (H.K.)**, *6/F, Tower II, South Seas Center, 75 Mody Road, Tsimshatsui, Kowloon. Tel. 27325888; 1018 Swire House, 11 Chater Road Central, Tel. 28104282. Fax 27217204*
- **China Travel Service (H.K.)**, *Head Office. C.T.S. House, 78-83 Connaught Road Central, Hong Kong. Tel. 25252284. Fax 28684970.* Branches at: *77, Queen's Road Central, Hong Kong. Tel. 25220450, 25236222 (department for individual travelers second floor; 27-33, Nathan Road, 1/F (entrance on Peking Road), Kowloon. Tel. 23157188. Fax 27217757. (Open Sundays and holidays); railway station, Kowloon. Tel.3330660.* Branches also in Bangkok, Frankfurt, Jakarta, Los Angeles, London, Manila, Paris, San Francisco, Singapore, Sydney, Tokyo, Toronto and Vancouver.
- **China Youth Travel**, *11/F, Energy Plaza, 92 Granville Road, Tsimshatsui East, Kowloon. Tel. 27212398. Fax 27217596.* Tied to CYTS in China. Good for budget travel.
- **Moonsky Star**, *Chungking Mansion, Nathan Road 36-44, E-block, 4/F, Flat 6, Tsimshatsui, Kowloon. Tel.2723 1376. Fax 2723 6653. E-mail: CompuServe.100267.2570*
- **Time Travel Services**, Block A, 16/F, Chung King Mansion, Nathan Road, Tsimshatsui, Kowloon. Tel.23666222. Fax 27395413. Branch in the Hyatt Regency. These can book the trans-Siberian trains.
- **Travel Advisers Ltd.**, *Room 1006, 10/F, Silvercord, Tower One, 30 Canton Road, Tsimshatsui, Kowloon, (across from the Marco Polo Hotel), Tel. 23758321, 23753173. Fax 23751078.* In business since 1932. Also cargo handling.

If you try a travel agency on your own, make sure it is a member of the Hong Kong Tourist Association. If it does anything questionable, then the association can help. Always telephone first for information and tell the agency where you got its name. Having learned of it through this book, it is answerable for any mistakes to me. You in turn are adding to my influence with them. This is a lesson in Chinese *guanxi*.

Since the price of visas, tours, and train tickets can vary, ask around. You should book long group tours one to three months in advance, but you still might be able to get a tour after your arrival in Hong Kong. Agents need two passport photos, one or two application forms, and your passport for a China visa. Send a photocopy of the passport if done by mail.

You can get a visa in one working day or less at the **Visa Office**, *Ministry of Foreign Affairs, 5/F, China Resources Building, 27 Harbour Road, Wanchai at Gloucester Road on Hong Kong Island, 24-hour telephone information service at 2827-1881.* It's located near the New World Harbour View Hotel and Hong Kong Convention Centre. Open Monday to Friday 9 am to 12 noon; 2 to 5 pm and Saturday 9 to 12. Closed Sunday and public holidays. You need one photograph. A photo service is available.

MAKING RESERVATIONS

Book as much of your itinerary as possible beforehand. Generally in high season, it might take two months or more in advance to get the flight you want. You pay nothing to make a reservation and can always cancel later. Flight schedules are difficult to obtain in China. They do exist in English but it is easier to get them from a Chinese airline abroad.

If you want one of the cheaper seats set aside on some flights for discounted prices (not Chinese airlines), you should book at least six months in advance. If you can't get the flight you want, you can always take a chance and try 'stand-by.' I was 16th in line for stand-by once out of Shanghai and managed to get on my desired flight, but you never know.

For big events like the United Nations Women's Conference, held in 1995, you should try to book six months to a year in advance, even if you're not attending these.

Complex international bookings are not as easy to make in China as elsewhere. Hong Kong travel agents can book some Chinese trains and ferries especially for groups. It is harder for individuals. You can book bus tours from Pakistan, ferries from Japan and Korea, and trains from Europe. As for the trans-Siberian railway, you should start asking travel agents about these at least four months in advancex.

ENTERING CHINA

By Air

In some cases, you pay less through an agent because a good one should know about cheaper flights, excursion fares, off-season discounts, and charter airlines. But shop around and check both airlines and agents.

Airlines do not fly all routes daily; some fly once a week, so plan your schedule carefully. Give your agent a list of stops you want to make before and after China, and how long you want to spend in each place. Suggest several options.

You can fly direct, with one or two stops from many countries and to many cities in China. You can fly to Beijing and Shanghai from Brussels, Los Angeles, New York, Paris, San Francisco, Seattle, Tokyo, Vancouver, etc. There are flights to Beijing from Helsinki (Finnair only), Karachi, Kuwait, London, Pyongyang, Rome, Stockholm, Tel Aviv, Ulan Bator, Vientiane, Zurich, etc. You can fly to Guangzhou from Ho Chi Minh (Saigon), Penang, Surabaya, Melbourne, etc. You can also enter at Urumqi, Harbin and Kunming.

Ask your agent if the international flights are nonstop. Is there an extra charge for stopovers? A day in Paris? You've always wanted to see

Kyoto! Is going via Hong Kong or Macau really the cheapest? Maybe it's better via Karachi, Singapore, or Bangkok. How about going on to Australia? How about around-the-world fares?

Airlines

There is a lot of choice. **Finnair** claims the shortest time from the U.S. east coast to Beijing: less than 16 hours in two shifts. **Cathay Pacific** is considering offering leg rests in Economy and BBC news. **Northwest** necessitates a change in Tokyo. **CAIL** has been talking about flying directly to Guangzhou from Vancouver without a change in Hong Kong.

Airlines flying into China include Air China, Air France, Aeroflot, All Nippon Airways, CAIL, China Eastern, China Southern, Dragonair, Finnair, Japan Airlines, JAS, LOT, Lufthansa, Malaysia, Northwest Airlines, Pakistan International Airlines, SAS, Silkair, Singapore Airlines, Swissair, Thai International and United.

Chinese airlines like China Southern, China Eastern, and Dragonair fly regularly to many cities in China. In addition, there are regular charter flights organized by China Travel Service and China International Travel Service (see below). These are "charters" because of a technicality in aviation regulations. They fly regularly and are okay, but travel agents abroad aside from CTS and CITS abroad cannot usually book them.

Together these companies fly from Hong Kong to Beijing, Changchun, Changsha, Chengdu, Chongqing, Dalian, Fuzhou, Guangzhou, Guilin, Guiyang, Haikou, Hangzhou, Harbin, Hefei, Jinan, Kunming, Lanzhou, Luoyang, Meixian, Nanchang, Nanjing, Nanning, Ningbo, Qingdao, Shanghai, Shantou, Shenyang, Tianjin, Wuhan, Xiamen, Xi'an, Zhanjiang and Zhengzhou. Airlines keep adding new cities so do ask.

Via Central Asia

Travel from Kazakhstan, Kirghizstan, and Uzbekistan is possible but the rules keep changing. The Chinese embassy in Almaty has refused for a while to give tourist visas, but tourists have managed to go with business visas through Central Asia Travel there. Sometimes the border is closed. The Kazair flight from Almaty to Beijing is not reliable. China Northwest Airlines flies from Almaty to Urumqi but it's hard to find the ticket office open. When you get to Urumqi, officials give you forms in Chinese and Russian. Just ask for one in English.

Road travel is only available to tour groups and hitchhiking is not advisable, especially through Kirghizstan where the border area is not really populated. Adventurers who have done it have gone for six hours in summer and only seen two vehicles and one horseman.

From Bishkek it takes two days to the Chinese border at Torugart which closes by 4 pm local time. You are also at the mercy of Kirghiz border guards asking for WHO (World Health Organization) cholera shots as a ploy to get a bribe. Public transportation is available on the Chinese side. Contact **Bestway Tours and Safaris** (Vancouver), and **Central Asia Travel** (Almaty) above.

There are daily trains from Moscow to Almaty. Then trains from Almaty leave Kazakhstan on Wednesdays at 7:45 pm, and arrive at Urumqi at 7:10 am on day two, about 36 hours in total of which 10 hours is spent at the border changing wheels. Rahim, Intours, and Bestway can make train reservations, but cannot sell a train ticket alone without the preceding land (hotel) package in Russia and Kazakhstan. Central Asia Travel (Almaty) can usually book just about anything. Tashkent also has flights to Beijing.

Via Europe

The **Euro-Asia Land Bridge** is a railway line that runs from Rotterdam to Lianyungang on China's east coast. You enter China from Almaty (Kazakhstan) close to Urumqi. You change trains in Moscow, Almaty and Urumqi. Contact Rahim Tours (Florida) and Intours (Canada). Check with the China Railexpress Travel Service above.

Via Hong Kong

Many travelers enter China through Hong Kong. Tours and flights bought together in North America could be less expensive than buying a flight in North America and then a tour in Hong Kong. Do check.

Hundreds of thousands of Hong Kong Chinese and many foreign residents travel to China yearly from Hong Kong. Travel agents here have a high degree of expertise and many have direct connections with individual tourism officials in China. Hong Kong is also loaded with professional China watchers, China-related banks, and experienced business people who can give advice.

It is a good place to stock up on camera film, books in English on China (if published in Hong Kong), and it has one of the best selections of pre-Qing Chinese antiques for sale (which cannot be exported legally from China.) Read my *Hong Kong & Macau Guide*, Open Road Publishing.

For bus, ferry and flight schedules and prices, ask China Travel Service or China International Travel Service in Hong Kong to fax you a copy.

By Ship to Guangzhou

From Hong Kong to Guangzhou daily, there's one **hovercraft** to Huangpu and one catamaran to Zhoutouzui in 3 1/2 hours. These leave in the early morning and you can't see much of the scenery.

Overnight ferries leave Hong Kong and Guangzhou nightly and arrive in the morning. No sailings on the 31st of any month. This slow boat to China is comfortable in air-conditioned deluxe cabins (two to four passengers). Some people have found the cabins stuffy and the bathrooms badly maintained. No announcements are in English.

All ships and hoverferries leave from the new China Ferry Terminal in China Hong Kong City, *on Canton Road in Tsimshatsui*. Ferries dock at Zhoutouzui or in Huangpu (Whampoa) on Guangzhou's south shore. Customs and immigration sometimes takes over an hour for the large ship. Because the ships are on a river, stability is good except during typhoons. Seasickness is not usually a problem.

By Ferry to Other Parts of China

Ferries go to Guanghai in Taishan (3 1/2 hours), Haikou (about 18 hours), Jiangmen (about four hours), Ningbo (about 55 hours), Sanya, Shanghai (2 1/2-days), Shantou, Shekou (about one hour), Xiamen (22 hours), Zhaoqing (12 hours), Zhongshan (less than two hours), and Zhuhai (about one hour). Depending on the class, going by ship could be the cheapest and most direct way to get to these cities from Hong Kong. Avoiding Guangzhou saves time and hassles too.

Services are basic. No regard for sexes is made in the assignment of cabins on ships, but you can protest. Meals are usually very early. On the bigger ships, the pools may be unswimmable.

By Train

To Guangzhou, at least four air-conditioned through-trains leave Kowloon Railway Station *in Hung Hom* (near Tsimshatsui East hotels). It is usually a 3 1/2 hour ride to the Tianhe Railway Station but there is a faster high-speed train too. It's best to buy tickets in advance, but you can also buy them at the train station on the day of departure - if any are left.

To Shenzhen, frequent electric trains zip to the border at Lo Wu from the Kowloon Railway Station or Kowloon Tong MTR Station. In the border points of Lo Wu and Shenzhen, passengers line up to walk through two customs buildings. Passengers going on to Guangzhou can make easy connections. This way is cheaper than the through express train to Guangzhou, but not recommended unless you like waiting in lines. No toilets are on these Hong Kong trains. See *Shenzhen*.

To the Shenzhen Airport

There is no direct bus service from the Hong Kong airport to the Shenzhen Airport, where you can take flights to Chinese cities cheaper than from Hong Kong. A Hong Kong city bus goes to downtown Shenzhen where you can take a bus or taxi to the airport. There is a ferry service from the Hong Kong City Ferry Terminal (above) departing daily about six times a day to the airport. It takes one hour and includes a short bus ride.

By Public Bus
Express buses regularly go to such cities as Foshan, Fuzhou, Guangzhou, Haikou, Quanzhou, Shantou, Xiamen, Zhaoqing and Zhanjiang Some of the longer routes may have an overnight hotel stop. A double-decker city bus goes from the Admiralty MTR station on Hong Kong island (see posted signs for schedules) to hotels and Splendid China in Shenzhen, and to hotels in Guangzhou. Buses go from China Hong Kong City (above) and the pier in Tsimshatsui East (but no signs) to hotels like the Garden Hotel in Guangzhou. CTS organizes regular buses so telephone. Taking these buses means lugging your own baggage at the two border-crossing points (no carts). Do avoid leaving Hong Kong during rush hours and arriving in the Chinese cities during rush hours.

1997 AND ALL THAT
At first, the change-over to the Chinese administration of Hong Kong from the British administration of Hong Kong should only affect visas to Hong Kong, and probably eliminate visas to China from Hong Kong. Commonwealth and American citizens for example will have to get visas to Hong Kong. (Before July, 1997, they don't.) The Hong Kong Tourist Association will remain as is. Flight schedules will remain.

However, Hong Kong should be opening a new airport on Lantau Island in 1998 and logistics from there to China will probably be changed and greatly improved. After the changeover, you probably won't be able to buy pre-Qing antiques legally here. Other changes should be gradual.

Via South Korea
There are flights but there's also a 480-passenger ship which leaves Inchon on Wednesdays and Saturdays at 16:00 and arrives in Weihai the next morning at 9:00. A 640-passenger ship sails every five days between Inchon and Tianjin (758 kilometers in about 28 hours). Do not expect a fancy cruise ship. These are cargo/passenger ferries.

Via Macau
Macau has a new international airport and flight connections with a growing number of Chinese cities. You can also reach this Portuguese territory on the south side of the Pearl River delta after a 50-minute jetfoil or 20-minute helicopter ride from Hong Kong. It is also a free port. Its prices are lower than Hong Kong's, but its shopping selection is not as vast. Macau is famous for gambling casinos, good Portuguese food and

charming Iberian architecture. It has old temples and a small, but excellent traditional Chinese garden. It will revert back to China in 1999.

Currently, citizens of U.S., Canada, New Zealand, Australia and the EEC do not need a visa for Macau if you stay less than 20 days. Travel agencies in Macau can arrange tours to China, and day tours to Zhongshan and Zhuhai, within 24 hours.

You can walk across the border to China next to the Barrier Gate. It is open from 7 am to midnight daily. You can get buses and taxis, on the China side. Boats go only to Guangzhou. The international airport is linked with one of Asia's longest bridges so that eventually China-bound passengers won't need to go through Macau immigration.

China Travel Service is at *Hotel Beverly Plaza, 2/F, Avenida Dr. Rodrigo Rodrigues, Macau. Tel. (853) 782331, 782211. Fax 550032.* In the US, the **Macau Tourist Information Bureau** is at *3133 Lake Hollywood Drive, Los Angeles, CA 90068. Tel. 800-331-7150. Fax (213) 851-3684.*

Via Mongolia

According to press reports, there is a bus on the 30th of each month from Bulgan, Mongolia to Qinghe county in Xinjiang, and vice versa on the 20th of each month. There are highway, rail, and flight connections between Mongolia and Inner Mongolia but we have heard nothing about foreigners entering by land except by the international train from Ulan Bator.

Via Nepal

You can get Nepalese visas easily at the border or at the airport on arrival for $15 for 15 days or $25 for one month. August is usually the busiest month and should be avoided if possible. You won't get the best guides or hotel rooms. The Chinese embassy is open Mondays, Wednesdays and Fridays only.

China Southwest Airlines flies new 757's. Flights have been pretty reliable and are scheduled on Tuesdays and Saturdays from April first to the end of November. For views of Everest, sit on the left side from Kathmandu.

You can also go by road to Tibet, but because of rains between June 15 and September 15, there are landslides. Most happen before Barabise at the 52 and 54-kilometer marks (from Kathmandu), and the 100 kilometer mark. On the China side, landslides are common 13 kilometers from the border. Porters on the Nepal side can carry luggage over the slides for about US$10 each. They have been known to disappear around corners, so keep up with them. Be prepared to hike several hours yourself.

From Kathmandu to the border is 114 kilometers (four hours or more). From Zhangmu at the border, travelers switch to landcruisers and buses. The most expensive tours usually get the best. Although the two governments have signed an agreement allowing buses from each side to cross the border, no scheduled bus service has started yet so it is still necessary to switch to Chinese-owned vehicles. From here to Lhasa can take three days if you sight-see.

Travel agents like **Great Escapes** in Kathmandu can also arrange for you to enter northwest Tibet and drive to Lake Manasarvovar and Mt. Kailash.

Via Pakistan

Pakistan and China both have had flights to Beijing and Urumqi from Islamabad and Karachi. You can also go by land. My best source of information on this spectacular Himalayan route has been **Bestway Tours & Safaris** (Vancouver). See also **Sitara Travel** in Pakistan, addresses above under *Using Travel Specialists*. You can get China visas in Islamabad in three working days.

The **Karakorum Highway** and border posts at Sust (Pakistan) and Tashkurgan (China) are usually open May 1 to October 31 for foreign tour groups but the rains in July and early August frequently set off landslides.

From Islamabad, you can try to fly to Gilgit (Pakistan). Be prepared for delays of one or two days because of weather. The alternative is road for 14 to 16 hours from Islamabad to Gilgit. Sitara Travel in Pakistan above can help you arrange transportation. The weather is most reliable in September and October.

From Gilgit, a public bus leaves about 9 am taking about six hours (189 miles) to the border. You can also get a car. There should be Chinese buses on the other side for the six-hour drive to Taxkorgan. If you want to pay more to be sure of transportation, CITS can meet you with a vehicle at the border.

Public minibuses are available at the border and individual travel is possible but not easy. Individuals have successfully hitchhiked. Motion sickness might be a problem. Women have traveled alone on this route safely, though I wouldn't recommend it.

Two small, cheap guest houses are in **Taxkorgan: the PAMIRS** (80 beds, the better of the two) and the **TRAFFIC**. The altitude is about 3200 meters or over 9000 feet. From Taxkorgan to Kashgar is 175 miles and takes nine hours, public buses only budge when full. You could try to hitchhike. Do not expect express highways.

The highest point on the road is about 16,000 feet at Khunjerab/Kunjirap Pass. The temperature ranges from minus four degrees centigrade to 30 degrees in summer. I suggest you read William Dalrymple's *In Xanadu, A Quest*, about his 1986 visit before the road was finished, and Diana Shipton's *The Antique Land* about her life in Kashgar in 1946-48.

Besides the scenery, the advantage of this route is its proximity to what used to be Gandhara, the area between today's Peshawar and Taxila, where Chinese pilgrims came in the Tang dynasty to learn about Buddhism. There are ruins of monasteries, the influence of Alexander the Great, and superb collections of Greco-Indo art in museums.

Via Southeast Asia

The **Vietnam-China border** is open and you can take a train right into China. See below. The Lao and Myanmar borders are not generally open to foreigners, but Kunming travel agents should be able to arrange tours. Consulates are in Beijing and Guangzhou. See *Nanning*.

Foreigners can fly from Hanoi to Nanning, Guangzhou, and Beijing. You can also go by train or bus to Nanning which has flight connections with other parts of China and Hong Kong and is joined to Guilin by a fast tourist train. You should take advantage of being in this remote area of Guangxi to see its ethnic minorities. Tours can be picked up at the border.

You can also go by passenger ship from Haiphong in Vietnam to Fangcheng in Guangxi province, 131 miles and about 10 hours away.

Via Russia

From Moscow, the Chinese train to Beijing has been leaving Tuesdays at 11:50 pm and goes through Irkutsk, Ulan Bator, Erlian and Datong, before arriving in Beijing on Mondays. The Russian train leaves Saturdays at 1 am and goes through Irkutsk, Manzhouli, Harbin, Shenyang to Beijing. The routes are the same for both trains to Ulan-Ude near Lake Baikal, but the Russian one continues for 12 hours via Harbin to Beijing.

Moonsky Star Ltd. (Hong Kong, with a sister travel agency called Monkey Business Infocenter in Beijing) can give you detailed information and copies of *The Trans-Siberian Handbook* by Bryn Thomas. They say that there are four- and two-bed sleepers. The Chinese hard-class is very dirty. Take your own food, especially for the Mongolian sector.

Because of the difficulties and popularity of the Trans-Siberian train route start researching four months before you go. You will need visas through most countries on the route. You can book through Moonsky Star (Hong Kong), InterPacific (New York City), Rahim Tours (U.S.), CITS (Guangdong branch in San Francisco) or Intours (Canada). See also 'Beijing.'

Russian Railways say that the Chinese train is 'irresponsibly' overbooked and 'does not allow any mid-trip interruptions or boardings during May-September... If you wish to stop enroute, you should plan your trip using local trains...'

It also says that the Chinese trains have downgraded confirmed reservations, allowed too many people into the compartments, and passengers pass the time drinking. Some cars do not have heat in winter. I have heard the same about the Russian trains. U.S. sources say the Chinese soft-class train is better.

Via Taiwan

At press time, there were no official passenger services between Taiwan and China. Travelers from Taiwan usually go to China via Hong Kong or Macau. This could change any day.

ARRIVING IN CHINA

BORDER FORMALITIES

Have your passport, Health Declaration, and entry forms ready for inspection. You get these from your plane or look for them upon arrival at Immigration. You have to present your passport, pick up your luggage, and pass through Customs in your first Chinese city. Give yourself plenty of time between planes. If you are taking in any large duty-free gifts to China, necessitating a stamp on a receipt, have that ready too and a completed Customs form.

People with nothing to declare do not have to fill a Customs form (except in Urumqi). If you declare recorded videotapes upon entry, you may be delayed as Customs officials screen them.

Keep your Baggage Declaration (if any) and your Departure Card in a safe place. You might need them on the way out.

You are allowed duty-free items for your own personal use. Forbidden are fire arms, ammunition and explosives, materials like books and video tapes "detrimental" to China's politics, economy, culture and ethics, poisonous drugs, narcotics and opium, morphia, heroin, etc., diseased animals, plants and their products, unsanitary foodstuffs and Renminbi over Y6000.

CHANGING MONEY

Every arrival hall and every hotel three stars and over and some two stars have a place to buy Chinese currency.

GETTING TO YOUR HOTEL

Top hotels have vehicles that can meet you upon arrival if you let them know when and on what you are arriving with train or flight number. In some cities, aggressive touts might compete for your fare and grab your bags. Usually there is a cheaper taxi stand outside. Insist on using the meter or settle on a price before you get in. Take down the odometer reading. No taxi should charge more than Y2 per kilometer. Consult the distance from the airport to the hotel as listed in this book. Most taxi drivers are honest, but...

There is also an airport bus to the downtown office of the CAAC-affiliated airline from which you can get a taxi. It is cheap.

If you neglected to make hotel reservations, or otherwise need help, look first to see if there is a CITS branch or hotel representative wherever you are. If not, telephone the tourist hotline, CITS, CTS, or one of the hotels listed in this book.

NOW THAT YOU'VE ARRIVED, DON'T FORGET TO ...

• *Keep your passport handy for registering at hotels, buying travel tickets, checking in at airports, applying for an alien travel permit, and sometimes changing money. Otherwise keep it locked up in a safe deposit box or in a pouch around your neck. You have to show some identification if you are involved in an automobile accident, for example. If you are staying in China a long time or there is reason for an evacuation or worried parents, register with your embassy or consulate.*

• *Adjust your watch. All of China is in the same time zone.*

MAKING CONNECTING FLIGHTS

Consult your cabin crew before you arrive. There should be signs to the transit lounge and connecting flights. Ask the information desk. International passengers do have to go through immigration and customs formalities before boarding domestic flights.

LEAVING CHINA

Reconfirm your flight at least 72 hours before departure. You can telephone the airline yourself unless you are flying a Chinese airline. While Air China says you can reconfirm international flights by telephone, my own experience has been different.

If you telephone, get a reservation number so that you can locate your reservation later. It is easiest to ask your hotel or travel agent to reconfirm for a small fee.

Make sure your visa has not expired or you will be detained and fined Y5000.

If your flight is early in the morning, book transport and breakfast the night before. Some airports have restaurants that open about 7 am. Be prepared to pay the airport tax required for all international flights, including those to Hong Kong.

You can buy foreign currency back before or after Customs clearance if you have your foreign exchange receipts. You need your departure form completed for immigration when you leave China. If you are leaving by land, the rules might be different; for example, you might clear Customs at the Qinibah Hotel in Kashgar if you leave for Pakistan by bus.

Your next big hurdle is Customs in your own country. Have your list of purchases and receipts handy. If you know the rate of duty, list the goods with the highest rate first on your declaration form. Report unaccompanied luggage so they will be exempted too. Show your Certificates of Origin if you have any. The onus of proof that an article is an 'antique' or 'work of art' and therefore free of duty, is on the owner of the goods. A Customs officer might not accept your certificate or receipts.

Depending on the country, you probably have the right to appeal any decision.

7. BASIC INFORMATION

BARBERS & HAIRDRESSERS

The best are in hotels. The quality of work, even in a three-star is not bad but you might wonder about the hygiene at that level.

BEGGARS

Yes, there are a few. Use your own discretion. As I would in New York City, ask them why they have to beg, and then decide whether to give. Or take them to the closest restaurant and give them a meal. Or ignore them.

BOOKSTORES

Stores with a wide selection of books in English are usually in major hotels (like the **Jin Jiang** in Shanghai or the **Dong Fang** in Guangzhou.) They are also in a few Friendship Stores (like Beijing's) or foreign languages book stores (a good one in Shanghai on Fuzhou Street, and in Beijing (Wangfujing Avenue). They should have many books in English and published in China, including children's books, picture books, tourism literature, and western novels. These are cheaper than in North America. See sidebar on next page. Don't expect much in smaller cities.

Bookstores in hotels should also have the *International Herald Tribune, Asian Wall Street Journal, Time,* and *Newsweek,* and Hong Kong's *South China Morning Post.*

BUSINESS

Trading with China is not like trading with other countries. As one trade official put it, "If you want to play in the Chinese sand pile, you have to play by Chinese rules."

These rules are much too complicated to put into a travel guide. There are lots of books, business guides, and experienced people to give advice. But to get you started: trading with China is done primarily through foreign trading corporations, a list of which you can obtain from a Chinese mission. Joint ventures are negotiated through the **Ministry of**

BOOKS IN ENGLISH

*To help get immersed in old (and new) China, read **Romance of the Three Kingdoms** while sitting on a cliff at Zhenjiang, overlooking the Yangtze, at the place where the widow of Liu Pei pined for her husband. Read **A Dream of the Red Chamber** while relaxing in the courtyard of one of the reproductions of the setting. Read **Pilgrimage to the West** on a trip along the Silk Road. Translations of these books are cheaper in China, and if you have the time, will add immeasurably to your experiences there.*

* **A Dream of the Red Chamber** (also known as **Dream of Red Mansions**) is one of the most popular novels because it paints a vivid and convincing picture of how the rich (and their servants) lived during feudal times. Any Chinese over 35 years of age should know it. It is the story of a wealthy family, connected with the imperial court, who lived and declined during the Qing dynasty. The plot might move too slowly for Western readers, who probably will have trouble also remembering the Chinese names. (Make notes as you read it.) However, for details of lifestyles it is excellent, with descriptions of a funeral, impertinent bond servants, the visit home of daughter and imperial concubine Yuan-chun, etc. The sexual encounters are mentioned, and some are surprising, but they are not fully described.*

* Attendants dressed as the characters inhabit the Red Chamber reproductions, known also as Daguan Yuan (Grand View Garden) in Beijing and Shanghai.*

Foreign and Economic Cooperation (MOFTEC). An increasing amount of business is now done with private companies.

Do not expect decisions to be made as quickly as elsewhere. You may need two or three visits as an introduction to show the sincerity of your interest. In one factory I was taken to, the managers dawdled long enough to take me and several of their buddies to lunch at company expense, more a treat for themselves than for me.

Do take a pile of your business cards preferably with a Chinese translation on the flip side. It would also be helpful to take a one-page introduction of your company in Chinese. Exchanging cards with both hands is now part of the ritual when people meet for business.

Business Hours

Office hours are usually 8:30 am to 4:30 or 5:30 pm with lunch 11:30 or 12 to 1:30 or 2 pm. China has a five day work week. Store hours vary with each city and are usually open Sundays and holidays.

CHILDREN - TAKING THE KIDS

I took my five-year-old for a five-week visit, my seven-year old to visit relatives, and my nine-year-old on a group tour. I even took a reluctant teenager on an eight-destination tour. I was glad I did, but then, this depends on the child. A year later, the teenager went back to China on her own with her school to work on a commune!

I did not use a baby-sitter because the children accompanied me to evening movies and theatrical performances. Chinese dance dramas are easy for a child to understand, and acrobats and puppets are fun for all ages. The younger children did find the traditional operas boring.

I would not take a child just to be left with a Chinese-speaking baby-sitter unless the child understood Chinese. On one trip, at communes and factories, many willing hands kept them amused while grown-ups talked. The children were interested in seeing how things were made. Guilin, with its caves, mountains, and boat trip was ideal.

The Chinese love children and are intrigued by those different from their own. You may have to protect children with blond hair and blue eyes, for instance, from being overly fondled. Tour-bus drivers bought mine popsicles and pinched cheeks. In restaurants they disappeared with waiters to be shown off to the cooks.

Two of them became sick with bad colds, but doctors took care of them. They were well in a couple of days, missing only one day of the tour. Two lived with relatives. The seven-year-old had a ball learning how to bring up water from an open well, washing his own clothes by hand, and tending a wood-cooking fire. It took awhile to adjust to the smelly outhouses, but he managed. The neighborhoods where we lived with family were full of other children, and in spite of initial shyness and the language barrier, they made friends. Strangers on the street and in buses would stop and try to talk to them. Barriers of formality melted right away, and I'm not the only one who has gotten a room in an overcrowded hotel because my child was very tired.

Food was a problem. The young ones lived only on scrambled eggs and *cha siu bow* (barbecued pork buns). Hamburgers and milk are now easier to find. Baby food in jars for infants and disposable diapers are in Friendship Stores, but may not always be available. Most hotels do not charge for children sharing their parent's room. Most hotels can arrange for babysitters.

CIVIL DISTURBANCES

If there is any possibility of unrest in China, check with your country's mission for advice. They should have up-to-date advisories. You might send a copy of your itinerary to your mission so they will know where to contact you.

COMMERCIAL DISPUTES

In cases of commercial disputes, the authorities have seized the passports of the foreigners involved, especially those of Chinese origin, until the dispute is settled. A commercial dispute could be the non-payment of a hotel bill by your credit card company. Try to resolve the dispute before arriving in China.

COMPLAINTS

The **China National Tourism Administration** is directly under the State Council, China's cabinet. It oversees tourism in China, regulating prices and quality of hotels, restaurants, guides, and some travel agencies. For complaints regarding travel agencies organizing tours from abroad, write directly to: *Room 6040, Beijing International Hotel, 9 Jianguomenwai Dajie, 100005. Tel. 5126688. Fax 5129972.* You should also send a copy to the city which prompted the complaint. You stand a good chance of getting a refund if warranted.

For other complaints, you should contact the provincial and city tourism administrations. Addresses are in the destination sections in this book. They have the power to punish or take away licenses. This authority may not work perfectly, but they should help you.

Complaints should be in writing and addressed to the **Quality Supervisory Bureau** at the tourism corporation or administration in the province concerned. Give venue, date, people involved and amount of refund requested.

ELECTRICITY

Chinese appliances are 220 volts and have either two, or more commonly, three-pronged plugs (with straight or slanted prongs). Many hotels have transformers for electric razors for North American two-prong plugs. Power outages are not common in hotels three stars and up, many of which have their own generators.

EMBASSIES & CONSULATES

Foreign embassies are in Beijing; consulates are in Chengdu, Guangzhou, Shanghai, and Shenyang.

EMERGENCIES

Chances are these things won't happen, but just in case, here are some things to do. In case of earthquakes, flood, plane crashes, and other such events reported by the media at home, do contact your friends and family at home that you are all right. They could be bothering your country's mission in China about your safety.

Credit cards: if lost, telephone your credit card company collect as soon as possible or you'll be charged for any purchases after date of loss. Hopefully, you will have made a photocopy of the number.

Deaths: someone should contact the relevant embassy or consulate, which in turn tries to get in touch with next-of-kin and take charge. The mission can make arrangements for the repatriation of remains. Goods belonging to the deceased and death certificates might be released to next-of-kin only after the bills are paid.

Demonstrations: Dont be afraid of them. They are usually orderly except in Tibet, where demonstrators and bystanders have been shot without warning by police. If a policeman asks you to move on and not take photos, please obey or accept the consequences. Recent demonstrations against African students should not discourage other black people from visiting. I have never heard of any other unpleasantness against blacks. Chinese people stare and occasionally titter at all foreigners. Please let me know if you find anything different. During the 1989 democracy demonstrations, foreigners were treated with respect by the students and caution by the military. I don't know of any foreigners hurt.

Earthquakes: The main danger is collapsing buildings. If you can't get outside into the open, away from falling debris, dive under a desk, table, or bed, or take shelter in a doorway. As soon as the shaking stops, which is usually after a few seconds, rush outside by the stairway (not the elevator).

Expired visas: You can get an extension from the Foreign Affairs Department of the Security Police in one or two days in any city.

Hostile Crowds: The May 1985 soccer riot in Beijing proved that this could happen. Anyone looking like the victorious Hong Kong Chinese were threatened and abused. If you think you're surrounded by hostile people, try smiling. Chances are theyre just curious or even jealous. Ignore them or try to make friends. Speak to individuals quietly, in English if you don't know Chinese. Someone may understand. Above all, act friendly and cool. Shouting obscenities is counterproductive. Call for the police. Apologize if you need to. If someone is drunk, just leave.

Law-breaking: if you are accused of breaking a Chinese law, contact your country's mission. Do not expect the rights that you would have in your own country, like bail, but you might see a lawyer. Minor violations could mean detention and deportation. An American once fell asleep while smoking and set fire to a hotel. Ten people died and he was sentenced to 18 months imprisonment and ordered to pay compensation. Some foreign travelers have wandered into a restricted area and were detained by the police, sometimes questioned most impolitely, and put on the next bus out. You might be put in jail and deported or nothing might happen.

Just don't do anything illegal! China has relations with Interpol. Illegal possession of drugs could mean seven years imprisonment. Journalists must get permits before interviewing students and reporting on activities in universities. If in doubt, ask.

MEDICAL EMERGENCIES

Generally for medical emergencies, taxis are quicker to get than ambulances. In Beijing, however, if you telephone 120 and inform the despatcher that the patient has had a heart attack, the ambulance should arrive with a defibrillator. 120 is also used for ambulances in many other cities.

For a medical problem while in your hotel, try "Reception," "Assistant Manager," or the attendant on your floor. Some attendants sleep in a room close to the service desk. Many hotels have doctors during the day or on call. As a precaution, always get the room number of your guides.

Facilities for treating emergencies in China are not as sophisticated as in many other countries but Beijing has clinics with western doctors. Do not expect elaborate life-support equipment, or to be up walking the day after a broken hip.

The Chinese do not store O-negative blood in their blood banks because Chinese people do not have it. In case of very serious ailments, contact your country's mission for help and advice. A medical evacuation by air even from nearby Guangzhou to Hong Kong could cost about $25,000. There are no western doctors in Guangzhou.

Money Problems: If you run out, ask your embassy to cable home for some, or telephone collect. It usually takes five banking days or you can try Western Union. Borrow if you can from fellow travelers. Your credit card can get you cash advances with a 4% or so service charge, or some cards can get you free check cashing from the Bank of China or American Express. Away from big cities, cash advances might take hours to clear with questions like, "What is your mother-in-law's first name?" Some airlines take credit cards. You can ask your hotel for a cash advance to be paid for with your bill on your credit card. The U.S. embassy gives small emergency loans, but very reluctantly.

Passports: if lost, talk to your guide or hotel. Get a certificate from the Security Bureau saying it's been lost, and contact your country's mission. This document acts as a temporary identification that will get you to a city with your consulate. You should have a photocopy of your passport number. If you are staying in China a long time (U.S. citizens over six months, Canadians over three months), it is always good to register with your country's mission. You will be able to get a new passport a lot easier if yours is lost.

If you are traveling with a guide, your escort might have your passport number and can obtain a document so you can travel to other cities in China to get a new passport. CITS should be able to help you if you are on your own. You need a passport to travel in China, leave China, and get a hotel room.

For a new passport, you need evidence of citizenship, like a birth certificate and passport photos. Some but not all U.S. consulates have instant passport photo machines. Your embassy could give you a temporary passport within one or two hours. With this document you can get a Chinese visa so you can leave China.

Losing a passport creates a lot of trouble and additional expense. It could mean staying a couple of extra days or leaving your tour group. Guard yours carefully.

Police: in most cities, the emergency number is "110."

Theft: pickpockets operate even in daytime. Do not leave purses or brief cases unattended. Hotels have safe deposit boxes. Cheaper hotels have more chance of theft. Always use the peephole in your hotel room door before opening it to strangers. If in doubt, phone Reception. If something is missing from your hotel, notify the management. If you need a police report so you can claim insurance, go to the Public Security Bureau. Recent travelers in Xian found it took them 3 1/2 hours at Public Security to register the loss of a walkman. Did you declare it to Chinese Customs coming in? Lost property might turn up later if you inform enough people.

Traffic Accidents: If your car accidentally injures anyone, do what you should in your own country. Attend to the injured. Otherwise, stay where you are. Do not get involved in arguments. Wait for the police to arrive. The police will take statements, and if you are found to be in any way responsible as the driver or even as a passenger (were you distracting the driver?), you may be liable for a fine or payment for damages. The fine would remunerate the family of the injured, or deceased for the rest of his productive years. There is a standard formula. If the accident is serious, contact your country's mission.

Travelers Checks: if lost, take your receipts to the Bank of China. For American Express, contact their offices in China. It has courier refunds. For phone numbers, *Tel. Hong Kong (852) 8859332.* 24-hour refund service for American Express has been also available at Sheraton Hotels in Tianjin and Beijing, or at the Holiday Inn Lido (Beijing).

Typhoons: This Cantonese word meaning big wind denotes a hurricane or tropical cyclone. These may hit China anywhere along the Pacific coast from April to November. They usually last for a maximum of three days and you should stay inside substantial buildings on high ground. The danger is falling debris, as well as strong winds, rain and floods. Airports will probably be closed.

ENDANGERED SPECIES

China and many other countries are parties to the **Convention on International Trade in Endangered Species of Wild Fauna and Flora** (CITES). Any species or products of a species on its lists could be seized by the Customs Department of the signatories, unless you have a permit. Get details from your government wildlife service. The much-publicized **Save the Panda** campaign is an expression of this concern. It means that even while you pass through Hong Kong, you risk confiscation of garments and ornaments made of parts of certain animals, like some turtles.

Locally, however, Chinese officials are relaxed about restricting the sale and eating of some endangered or threatened species, like the giant salamander. Coats of spotted cats have been found for sale in Friendship Stores. But China has executed the killers of pandas.

The problem is knowing what is or is not on the list, and what is fake. When in doubt, don't eat or buy products made from any wild animals, especially spotted cats, alligators, and birds. But some deer, game, birds, bears, and snakes for example, are grown commercially and can be eaten.

Among the other Chinese species listed by the Convention are: Himalayan argali, Tibetan brown bear, golden cat, dhole (wild dog), gibbons, Przewalskis horse, langur, macaque, and wild yak. Among the birds are the relict gull, crested ibis, and some varieties of cranes, storks, pheasant, and egrets. Avoid parts of elephants, crocodiles, tortoises, and marine turtles. You will need a permit for live specimens of all parrots, monkeys, cats (except domestic), hawks, eagles, falcons, tortoises, boas, pythons, and iguanas, and some song birds, cobras, lizards, fish, butterflies, corals and mollusks. Also all orchids and all cacti and many other flora are protected.

There are rules about traveling with exotic pets, and permits must be obtained prior to departure.

Contact the U.S. Federal Wildlife Permit Office or the Canadian Wildlife Service if you have any questions.

The authority allowed to issue CITES permits in China is: **The Peoples Republic of China Endangered Species of Wild Fauna and Flora Import and Export Administrative Office**, *Ministry of Forestry, Hepingli, P.O. Box 100714, Beijing, Tel. 4214180 or 4229944.* Branches also in Chengdu, Guangzhou, Shanghai, and Tianjin.

For animal lovers wanting to see 300 Pere David Deer and 12 Prezewalski Horses, try to contact Prof. Wang in Beijing, *Tel. 6841773, ext. 191.*

GARDENS & PARKS

Relaxing in a Chinese garden is different from rushing through on a guided tour. Go back to one you especially like and just sit and absorb. A Chinese garden is not just a park or something attached to a building. It is an art form, the world in miniature, with mountains, water, plants, and buildings - a three-dimensional Chinese painting you can enter to try to experience infinity.

Gardens were built for a leisurely lifestyle in which poetry, philosophical contemplation, and the beauty of nature were of the utmost importance. Imagine living here! The ugly world of poverty and injustice was kept outside the high walls.

Take your time exploring. Look at the integration of the buildings with nature, the pinpointing of places of particular beauty by unusually-shaped windows and moon gates. Absorb the tranquillity of the water. Look at the reflections. Think of poetry. The meaning of life. A garden takes time - infinite time.

GAMBLING

Gambling has been illegal in Communist China, but it's gradually coming back. There have been state lotteries for decades. In the last few years, horse races have started again, at first with prizes like cartons of cigarettes, but lately, with real cash.

Casinos are planned. Members of the **Hong Kong Jockey Club** have been able to place bets on Hong Kong horse races in Beijing's **Hong Kong-Macao Centre**.

GLOSSARY OF TERMS & ABBREVIATIONS

arhats - Buddhists who have attained Nirvana.

bodhisattvas - Buddhist saints who attained Nirvana but returned to help others. See What Is There to See and Do?

CAAC - formerly Chinas only airline and now it oversees all Chinese airlines. It is used here collectively for former CAAC regional airlines.

cadre - in Chinese kanpu, meaning core element. Any person who plays a leadership role in the Party.

CITS - China International Travel Service.

CTS - China Travel Service

dagoba - similar to an Indian stupa, a bell-shaped tower under which is buried a Buddhist relic or the ashes of a monk.

Dist.A.P. - distance from airport.

Dist.R.W. - distance from railway station.

feng-shui - also known as geomancy, it is the placing of graves, dwellings, doors and furniture in harmony with the forces of nature

Food Street - term usually used for Chinese fast food or snack restaurant.

guanxi - connections

HK - Hong Kong

JV - joint venture; a business arrangement involving several parties.

lohan - the Chinese word for arhat, or Buddhist saint

Manchu - the group from northeast China who ruled China under the dynasty name Qing.

Mongol - the group from north China who ruled China under the dynasty name Yuan.

neolithic - pertaining to the Stone-Age period in which man developed pottery, weaving, and agriculture, and worked with polished stone and metal tools.

penjing - the art of growing miniature trees and plants. Similar to Japanese bonsai.

PLA - Peoples Liberation Army

pinyin - the official system of romanizing the Chinese language now adopted as official.

pusa - the Chinese word for bodhisattva or Buddhist saint, who is on a higher level than lohan.

qigong - Chinese yoga. Health and healing through breathing exercises, massage, and magnetism.

ren. - renovated

RMB - *ren min bi* - peoples money, one of the terms used to refer to Chinese currency.

stele - a large stone tablet used to commemorate an event, a life, or an important piece of writing.

taiji or **taichi** - Chinese shadow boxing

TGIF - Thank God It's Friday.

Wade-Giles - The most commonly used of the old systems of romanizing the Chinese language.

WC - water closet. Toilet.

wok - a large, round pan for cooking.

work unit - Every salaried worker belongs to one of these.

X - telephone extension

GUIDES

The people who escort foreign visitors are guide-interpreters, "guides" for short. Training is on the job, usually learned by accompanying an experienced guide for several months. But some agencies have been so short-handed that guides with little English and training have been used. The Department of Education is responsible for staff training, and prospective guides spend four years learning a language, Chinese history, geography, and art history. Guides must pass an exam before they can wear an official badge with their photo.

If you are on a group tour of several cities, you might get a national guide who stays with you during your whole stay. At each city you also get a local guide and, at some attractions, an on-the-spot guide. If there is a shortage, you may not get a national guide.

For most visitors, your Chinese escorts will be the only Chinese people you can get to know well. Ask them lots of questions about life in China. Guides are open about discussing their salaries and training, especially if they like you. Some might tell you they get no salaries and depend on tips. It might not be true.

Please be patient when a guide is speaking English. If it is painful to listen to, keep it to yourself. It is better than nothing. Confusion over numbers is a common translation problems. The Chinese think in terms of ten thousands rather than thousands. Do not mistake sixteen for sixty or seventeen for seventy. Ask your guide to write down important figures for you. When you are using an interpreter, speak slowly and simply.

Remember that guides are not scholars. Their knowledge of traditional Chinese culture is frequently limited to the few books they read. Take this book with you for background information.

Guides do not usually eat with you unless invited. At mealtimes, they can be found in a staff dining room. Most also stay in your hotel overnight. It is a good to know where they can be reached.

If any of them greets you with "It's my birthday today but I wanted to help you out so I came" or some such, don't believe it. One guide broke into tears and said she would lose her job if she didn't take our group to two factories a day to buy things! But why should tourists have to go along with this shortsighted policy, the result of the fierce competition between agencies? Each agency is trying to lower prices to compete. But at the expense of guide professionalism? Do raise your objections!

HEALTH & MEDICAL CONCERNS

China is among the healthiest and cleanest countries in Asia but there have been reports of typhoid, malaria, plague, and rabies, usually in isolated rural areas far off the tourist routes (though a few cases of rabies have shown up in Shanghai). Venereal diseases are back after an absence of decades and HIV positives are growing in number, but these are still rare compared to other Asian countries. One hears occasionally of encephalitis, hepatitis, cholera, and intestinal parasites. Avoid wading in lakes and rivers in central China's Yangtze River area because of schistosomiasis.

You can find out about these and malaria areas from the World Health Organization or your travel clinic. Malaria only occurs in Hainan and the tropical parts of Yunnan province and you should ask about prevention. It is spread by mosquitos, usually after dark. If you are bothered by mosquitoes there, use the net above your bed, or ask for one. You should use mosquito repellents after dark, and wear long sleeves and pants when you go out at night. Check for malaria if you have flu-like symptoms within a year afterwards.

Chinese medical facilities are good for common ailments. Many Overseas Chinese go to China for acupuncture, qigong, and even western medical treatment. If you are sick, you will probably be given a choice of western or traditional Chinese medicine, or both. Chinese herbal medicines are frequently effective, but my kid had to be bribed with lots of candy to drink his herbal tea, because it tasted so awful.

Outside of a few clinics in Beijing and Shanghai, Chinese medical facilities might look grubbier than those in the West. An examination with medicines at a hotel clinic is cheap.

Chinese guides are usually concerned about the health of their guests. They frequently check whether you have enough clothing on. If you complain about your health too much, you might get a doctor even if you don't request one. Most tour organizers state emphatically that tours to China are rugged. They are not for invalids or people with respiratory or heart conditions because of the climbing, the dust and air pollution. The Chinese are especially nice to older people, but older or frail people should take precautions.

Some North American prescriptions can now be filled in China especially at western clinics in Beijing. Some Chinese pharmacies might have patent medicines. But don't count on it. If you are hospitalized, you might have to take your own mug, plate, towel, soap, and a friend. The staff and other patients may not speak English. Standards are not the same as in America. In one of the best hospitals in Beijing, beds were only changed once a week.

Remember, a prepaid group tour is usually strenuous with a packed schedule, unless the group agrees to a slower pace. Most hotels but not restaurants have elevators. Things can be easier for pay-as-you-go individual travelers who can do things at their own speed. If you're not in good health, don't travel alone.

Chinese hospitals are adequate, and some doctors have western training and excellent western standards especially in Beijing and Shanghai. But most facilities are at least 30 years behind what you're used to.

HOLIDAYS, FAIRS, & FESTIVALS:
OFFICIAL CHINESE HOLIDAYS

January 1	(offices closed)
Spring Festival/New Year	the date depends on the lunar calendar around the end of January or early February (offices closed for three days).
May 1	Labor Day
October 1- 2	National Day, celebrating the founding of the People's Republic of China in 1949

In addition, the following are celebrated with special programs, but offices and schools are open:

March 8	International Working Womens Day
March 12	Tree-planting day, south China April (first Sunday) Tree-planting day, north China
May 4	Youth Day (May 4th Movement)
June 1	Childrens Day
July 1	Founding Day of The Communist Party of China
August 1	Founding Day of the Peoples Liberation Army
September 10	Teachers Day
September 27	World Tourism Day; Celebrated by different cities in turn.

The Chinese also celebrate several other traditional holidays. The **Lantern Festival** starts the last day of the Spring Festival. The **Dragon Boat races** commemorate the untimely death of an upright official. (See *Zigui* and *Yueyang*) The **Mid-Autumn Festival** celebrates the most beautiful full moon of the year.

Check with travel agents about the dates of festivals around the time of your visit like Weifang (for the **kite festival**), Kunming (for the **Water-splashing Festival** and **Third Moon Market**), and Guiyang for **festivals of**

the nationalities. Be aware that the dates for some festivals might not be decided until the last minute, especially in Tibet. On the other hand, festivals might be canceled without much warning.

Some festivals are just an excuse to sell something, but most are colorful and exotic. Bring lots of film. People dress in their best. Many festivals are punctuated with fireworks, dragon dances, competitions, courtship rituals, parades, pageants, thousands of dancing school children, and special banquets. Some are genuine folk festivals, religious celebrations, and horse and camel markets and, as such, are not organized for tourists. Organizers might decide the dates one or two days before, or make last-minute changes. Arrangements for tourists should improve with experience and time.

Some festivals are so well organized, tourists travel with police escorts quickly from place to place, without a chance to stop and take photographs.

I suggest booking a tour for a festival with a travel agency because festivals attract tens of thousands of people. As one of the crowd, you won't see much unless you're well over six feet tall. If a travel agency has organized something, you should be able to get a good seat and at least a place to sleep.

INFORMATION FOR TOURISTS

Beijing and Shanghai have tourist handouts distributed in hotels. Especially helpful are *Welcome to China – Beijing* and *Beijing This Month*. Beijing also has had *Beijing Scene* available free from the San Wei Bookstore and Mexican Wave Cafe. In Shanghai, you should be able to get a free booklet from the Shanghai Information Booth in the east end of the People's Square mass transit station one floor down below ground level.

Several cities and all provinces and regions have tourist offices and travel agents where free literature is available.

Consider your hotel your friend. The better quality the hotel, the more information it can give you. Hotels, four stars and up, are usually the best sources. Try assistant managers, concierges or public relations. Some hotels organize their own tours. Hotel telephone operators and business centers can usually find telephone numbers for you.

Contact travel agents at their local head offices, especially North American Sales Managers. Branches in hotels only want to sell tours and clerks might not even speak English.

China has been producing a large number of maps, guidebooks in English, and a twice-a-month tourism newspaper. The Cartographic Department maps are helpful if up to date. They are very detailed. Jinans, for example, shows Taishan Mountain and diagrams of the Confucian

Family Mansion and Confucian temple. These maps list major hotels, tourist attractions, restaurants, stores, and important telephone numbers. Tourism information is becoming easier to obtain. Information desks have opened at some airports.

Many tourist attractions have inexpensive, knowledgeable on-site guides paid by the hour. A few have English-speaking guides. Some tourist attractions also have unofficial freelance guides, who may know very little and speak poor English. Test their knowledge first and decide on a price beforehand. Try Y20 an hour for your group, not per person. You could also eavesdrop on someone else's guide.

Some diplomatic missions have libraries with books about China. The U.S. consulates have current travel advisories with up-to-date information on travel risks. Consulates should also have important addresses like those of doctors and pharmacies.

Fellow travelers are great. Most love to share their experiences. You can find them everywhere. They can tell you what was worthwhile to visit and what was not. Dont be shy about asking.

Foreign residents are also great. Foreign students and experts may look down on tourists, but if you invite them to dinner they should be able to give you a lot of good tips, such as where you can buy cheap name brands. Contact these people at the expat hangouts listed in major cities.

LANGUAGES OF CHINA

In Shanghai they speak Shanghainese; in Shantou, Hainan, and Taishan, they speak dialects of Cantonese; in Fujian, they speak Fukienese. Most of the 55 national minorities have their own distinctive languages or dialects. But the whole country knows **putonghua** or **Mandarin**, based on Beijing pronunciation. Many of the older officials speak Russian. Younger ones might speak English. A few people speak French.

Chinese is not all that hard to understand. Listen carefully as it is spoken because tones are very important and a wrong tone could change the meaning of a word. Some words recur frequently. Ask what these mean. You probably know some Chinese already. *Shanghai* means above the sea – *Shang* is above. When you get to Beijing, you will hear about Beihai Park, North Sea Park. *Hai* again is sea. As for *Bei*, also found in Beijing, it means north. Beijing is Northern Capital. *Jing* is the same jing as in Nanjing, Southern Capital.

Other words that you will probably encounter:
ang = nunnery
binguan = guesthouse
can guan = restaurant
ci = temple
da lu = avenue

A PHONETIC GUIDE TO CHINESE

To pronounce Chinese letters, learn the following phonetic alphabet showing pronunciation with approximate English equivalents. Letters in the Wade-Giles system are in parentheses. The following is in **putonghua***:*

a (a), a vowel, as in far;

b (p), a consonant, as in be;

c (ts), a consonant, as in ts in its; and

ch (ch), a consonant, as in ch in church, strongly aspirated;

d (t), a consonant, as in do;

e (e), a vowel, as er in her, the r being silent; but ie, a diphthong, as in yes and ei, a diphthong, as in way;

f (f), a consonant, as in foot;

g (k), a consonant, as in go;

h (h), a consonant, as in her, strongly aspirated;

i (i), a vowel, two pronunciations:

1) as in eat

2) as in sir in syllables with the consonants c, ch, r, s, sh, z and zh;

j (ch), a consonant, as in jeep;

k (k), a consonant, as in kind, strongly aspirated;

l (l), a consonant, as in land;

m (m), a consonant, as in me;

n (n), a consonant, as in no;

o (o), a vowel, as in aw in-law;

p (p), a consonant, as in par, strongly aspirated;

q (ch), a consonant, as ch in cheek;

r (j), a consonant pronounced as r but not rolled, or like z in azure;

s (s, ss, sz), a consonant, as in sister; and sh (sh), a consonant, as sh in shore;

t (t), a consonant, as in top, strongly aspirated;

u (u), a vowel, as in too, also as in the French u in tu or the German umlauted u in Muenchen;

v (v), is used only to produce foreign and national minority words, and local dialects;

w (w), used as a semi-vowel in syllables beginning with u when not preceded by consonants, pronounced as in want;

x (hs), a consonant, as sh in she;

y used as a semi-vowel in syllables beginning with i or u when not preceded by consonants, pronounced as in yet;

z (ts, tz), a consonant, as in suds and zh (ch), a consonant, as j in jump.

dong = east
fan dian = hotel or restaurant
ge = small pavilion
guan = pass
he = river
hu = lake
jiang = river
jie = street
ling = tomb
lou = multi-storied pavilion big enough for people to live in
lu = road
men = gate
miao = temple, usually ancestral or Confucian
quan = spring (of water)
sha = sand
shan = mountain
si = temple
ta = pagoda
tang = temple
ting = tiny pavilion usually in rural areas in which people can rest
xi = west
xian = county
yuan = garden
zhong = middle or central
zhou = city state (smaller than a province; larger than a city)

If you can, ask someone to teach you numbers because you need to hear the tones. Reading numbers will help in museums. You only have to learn ten; the rest are combinations. Learn the polite things first: good morning, please, Thank you, and good-bye. When someone asks you to help with English, ask to be helped with your Chinese. Exchange lessons with people you meet at English Corners, which are found in many cities in a designated park on Sundays. Ask at a university English department.

LAUNDRY

Most hotels three stars and above will do your laundry and drying cleaning if you get it to them by 8 am. It should be done the same day by 6 pm. Many also have express service.

LEARN ABOUT CHINA

To get the most out of your trip, read before you go. There is a dizzying list of good books on China. The more you know, the more you'll learn and enjoy. A statue may be striking, but it is more meaningful if you know it's the 'warrior woman,' made famous in American literature by Maxine Hong Kingston. A building in a park in Lhasa becomes the movie theater built by Heinrich Herrar where the German refugee showed the young Dalai Lama his first movies. Many books are listed with individual cities throughout this guide.

LECTURES

China Friendship Associations and universities can recommend lecturers and some have copies of Chinese periodicals. Talk to old China hands, recently returned schoolteachers as well as travelers contacted through these groups.

Some addresses:
• **Australia China Friendship Society**, *Ross House 4/F, 247 Flinders Lane, Melbourne 3000. Tel. 96548099, 95837255. Fax 95842107*
• **Great Britain-China Centre**, *15 Belgrave Square, London SW1X 8PS. Tel. (0171)2356696. Fax (0171)2456885. E-mail:gbcc@gn.apc.org*
• **Federation of Canada-China Friendship Associations**, *2948 Scott Street, Victoria, B.C.,V8R 4J6. Tel. (604)5985962. Fax (604)5985959*
• **New Zealand China Friendship Society**, *Tel.0-4-3848464.* Tours: David Blanshard, *40 Edgecumbe Road, Tauranga. Tel. (07)5786470*

LEARN SOME CHINESE

If nothing else, learn to read numbers. Then you will know dates in museums and street numbers. It is best to learn Mandarin which is understood all over China. But if you're visiting relatives, they could speak a local dialect in their home. They should however understand Mandarin.

The same Chinese characters are understood throughout China. The characters used today have been simplified since 1950. Make sure that your teacher gives you the new script and the pinyin romanization.

The level of English is improving daily, but is still poor. Take a phrase book. I don't speak much Chinese and sometimes travel alone and have a good time even without an interpreter. The Chinese try very hard to understand attempts to communicate. Draw pictures and try charades. Make friends with potential interpreters. And remember the more you try to speak Chinese, the more friends you'll make, and the more you'll enjoy China.

Some key phrases are:

hello!	*ni hao?*
how are you?	*ni hao?*
goodbye	*zai jian*
thank you	*xie xie*
I'm sorry	*dui bu qi*

how much?	*duo shao qian?*
good	*hao*
no good	*bu hao*
restaurant	*canting*, or *fandian*
hotel	*binguan, fandian*, or *dajiudian*
toilet	*cesuo*
east	*dong*
south	*nan*
west	*xi*
north	*bei*
middle	*zhong*
street	*jie*
avenue	*dajie*
road	*lu*

LEAVING PURCHASES IN ONE CITY WHILE YOU TRAVEL AROUND CHINA

How do you cope with purchases in China? Is there an alternative to lugging them around the country and paying excess baggage if you are reluctant to ship them home directly?

This is no problem if you are going to be in the same city twice. Leave purchases with friends, hotels or airport baggage checkrooms (big cities only) to be picked up later. If you did a lot of shopping in Shanghai and are leaving from Guangzhou in a week, one possibility is sending a package EMS (Express Mail Service) from a post office to your hotel in Guangzhou. It should arrive on time. Just don't count on the regular mail service.

LIFE IN CHINA

Like any developing country, China is going through a lot of growing pains. Air pollution has been bad, but China is doing something about it: no-smoking areas, no coal-burning areas downtown, no polluting factories downtown, and compulsory car washing in some cities. And there will be more measures at this rate. Shanghai was showing signs in 1996 of emerging as a world-class city with expressways, fancy stores, and newly refurbished buildings. It and Beijing now have world class restaurants with a wide variety of good Thai, Japanese, continental and American restaurants. Of course development means a lot of construction noises, and you should avoid hotels in the process of renovating if you expect to spend time there during the day.

Traffic jams and vehicle exhaust fumes are still bad in most cities. Insist on air-conditioned vehicles if this bothers you a lot. You might have to start to tour early (like 7:30 or 8 am) to avoid the rush hour. Some large tour groups (such as convoys of five tour buses all from ocean cruise ships), have moved around with police car escorts. You can visit small cities and the countryside, which are interesting and have much cleaner air.

China's cities are crowded especially in downtown shopping areas and on the roads at rush hours. People in cities generally live in small apartments. But the very poor could sleep in railway stations. Salaries are very low by North American standards even for doctors, though rents are low. People in cities look well dressed; no one is in rags. The young look very stylish indeed.

In the countryside, rich farmers have an incredible amount of space in comparison. But the growing numbers of poor people is very apparent there.

LOOKING UP SPECIFIC CHINESE CITIZENS

Yes, you can visit friends and relatives in China, even while on a group tour or business trip. Give yourself at least 30 days for an answer by mail. Ask for their telephone and fax numbers so you can call when you arrive. Chinese friends and relatives should also be able to take time off with pay to visit and even sightsee with you. As a courtesy to your hosts or sponsors, inform them if you want to take time off from the planned schedule. You might ask when the best time would be. Local Chinese can go to your hotel without any problem except late at night.

Some local people may feel uneasy about entering a hotel, particularly a fancy one. Many are glad to see inside and brag to their friends that they ate there or at least had a photograph taken inside. If they are reluctant, you could arrange to meet in a restaurant, a park, or their home. You could take them on sightseeing trips with your tour group (for a fee). This will give you time to visit without missing the attractions.

Your chances of going to the home of a friend will depend on the political climate at the time. It could also depend on how embarrassed some Chinese are about the modesty of their lodgings or whether they can afford a taxi or elaborate meal for you. So do not insist if local Chinese friends hesitate.

Overseas Chinese have a freer time talking with Chinese citizens. Chinese people generally are not open to discussing their deepest feelings, problems or sex life. It took six months of living together before one Chinese roommate confided to me how unhappy she was about her parents.

China does go through occasional xenophobic periods and your Chinese friends might get into difficulty if they meet you. Immediately after the 1989 Tiananmen troubles, many Chinese intellectuals were fearful of contacting foreign friends.

BASIC INFORMATION 119

Warning: never give a dog as a gift. In Beijing, registering one costs Y5,000 for the first year, and Y2,000 each subsequent year.

LUNAR CALENDAR

This is uniquely Chinese with the year consisting of 12 months of 29 or 30 days each. Every three or so years, an extra month is added. The year starts on the second new moon following the winter solstice, which could be any time between January 21 and February 20 on the western calendar. In 1997, it starts on February 8.

MARRIAGE

It could take about one month but it is possible for a foreigner to marry a Chinese citizen. Permission has to be given by the work unit of the Chinese spouse and in some cases compensation paid before permission is granted to leave the country. The government might want to be repaid for education in return for a contracted number of years of work. Consult your country's mission about the implications.

METRIC CONVERSIONS
Celsius-Fahrenheit Conversion Table, in Degrees

Centigrade (Celsius)		Fahrenheit
-40		-40
-20		-4
0	Freezing Point	32
10		50
20		68
30		86
40		104
50		122
60		140
70		158
80		176
90		194
100	Boiling Point	212

To convert Fahrenheit to Celsius subtract 32, multiply by five, and divide by nine. To convert Celsius to Fahrenheit multiply by nine, divide by five, and add 32.

Weights & Measures

China uses both the metric system and the Chinese system.
1 gong-jin (kilogram) = 2.2 pounds

1 jin or gun (catty)	= 1.33 pounds = .604 kg
1 dan (picul)	= 100 catties = 133 pounds or 60.47kg
1 mi (meter)	= 39.37 inches
1 gong li (kilometer)	= .6 mile = 1 km.
1 li (Chinese mile)	= .3106 mile = 1/2 km.
1 mu	= .1647 acres
1 hectare	= 2.471 acres
	= 10,000 square meters
100 hectares	= 247.1 acre = 1 sq. km.
259 hectares	= 1 sq. mile

Kilometer-Mile Conversion Tables

To convert kilometers to miles, multiply by 6 and divide by 10.

Miles	Kilometers	Miles	Kilometers
1	1.6093	1	.621
2	3.2186	2	1.242
3	4.8279	3	1.863
4	6.4372	4	2.484
5	8.0465	5	3.105
6	9.6558	6	3.726
7	11.2651	7	4.347
8	12.8744	8	4.968
9	14.4837	9	5.589
10	16.093	10	6.21
20	32.186	20	12.42
30	48.279	30	18.63
40	64.372	40	24.84
50	80.465	50	31.05
60	96.558	60	37.26
70	112.651	70	43.47
80	128.744	80	49.68
90	144.837	90	55.89
100	160.93	100	62.1
200	321.86	200	124.2
300	482.79	300	186.3
400	643.72	400	248.4
500	804.65	500	310.5
600	965.58	600	372.6
700	1126.51	700	434.7
800	1287.44	800	496.8
900	1448.37	900	558.9
1000	1609.3	1000	621

(Prepared by Linda Malloy)

MONEY & BANKING

Major credit cards are accepted at top hotels, many of the medium-priced hotels in big cities, some top restaurants, and many tourist stores. American Express seems to be the most useful, with its free emergency check-cashing service and its ability to pay for Chinese airplane tickets. You can buy other airplane tickets with a credit card from only a few foreign airlines, like some Dragonair offices, CAIL, Finnair, JAL, Northwest, United and Lufthansa. With an American Express card, you can purchase travelers checks at the Bank of China.

Be aware that:
• Cash advances cost about 4% and could take hours to get. You might be able to convince your hotel to charge a cash advance as well as your hotel expenses to your credit card.
• Personal checks are not generally accepted, but some can be cashed at the Bank of China with some credit cards. You could also try your embassy or hotel.
• It takes five banking days to cable money to China, assuming everyone knows his job and has your passport number.
• Payment can also be made with Renminbi Travelers Letter of Credit bought with foreign currencies and issued by Bank of China branches overseas.
• A few ATM machines have opened for international credit cards but you shouldn't count on it. Shanghai has two and they have a high service charge.
• Cash brings a slightly lower foreign exchange rate than travelers checks.

The Hong Kong Bank, Royal Bank of Canada, and Bank of America have branches in China but not always for retail business. This is changing, so check with your bank before you go. Most foreign bank branches are in Shanghai or Special Economic Zones.

Foreign Currencies and Exchanging Money

In early 1996, the U.S. dollar was worth about 8.3 Chinese yuan, the Canadian six, and the Hong Kong dollar almost at par.

It is best to take U.S. dollars. Among the foreign currencies also accepted are: Australian, Austrian, Belgian, British, Canadian, Danish, French, German, Hong Kong, Japanese, Malaysian, Dutch, Norwegian, Singaporean, Swedish, and Swiss.

You can change money at border points, government tourist stores, the Bank of China, and major hotels. You can buy back 50% of the foreign currency you originally sold if you can present your exchange receipts.

Before you go to isolated places like Xigaze, Jing Hong and Kaili, ask about money changing. Frequently, this is only done there in banks, not open on Sundays, early mornings, or evenings. Get enough changed before you go. Four and five-star hotels can change money most of the time. There is a small service charge every time you exchange money, and there's not much difference between the rates at the Bank of China and the hotels. You will probably need your passport number or hotel room number to change money at the hotels.

In Guangzhou, especially in Shenzhen, Hong Kong cash has been accepted in stores and by street peddlers. However, using foreign currency is illegal, and there are periodic crackdowns. Local Chinese value Hong Kong and U.S. dollars because of inflation and because some people are going abroad and need it. Peddlars everywhere, even in far-off Tibet, accept U.S. dollars eagerly.

Remember, foreign exchange rates fluctuate. Please consult your bank, the Bank of China, hotel, or the *China Daily*.

Local Currency is called **Renminbi** (RMB) - peoples money. The Chinese dollar, known as the **yuan** (or **kuai**) equals 10 **jiao** or 100 **fen**. Yuan notes are in denominations of 100, 50, 20, 10, 5, 2, and 1. The smaller jiao notes are 5, 2, and 1. The coins are 5, 2, 1 fen and Y1.

Although prices are quoted in foreign currencies, you must pay for tourist hotels in renminbis.

MUSEUMS

These can be deadly dull if you don't do it right. I have seen people hurrying past pieces without batting an eyelash that set my heart pounding.

You will get much more out of a Chinese museum: (1) if you read something about Chinese history first (for a quick course see Chapter 4, *A Short History)*; (2) if you take a knowledgeable guide; and (3) if you are eager to learn things like the date of the earliest pottery, weaving, writing, money, etc. It might excite you even more to compare these with the earliest in your civilization. Try to figure out how and why things were made. Trace their development.

China is so rich in archaeology that most cities have good collections. These are lessons in history. The problem for foreigners is that most museums do not have titles in English. If you don't have a guide and have learned your Chinese numbers, at least you could look up the dates on pages 41-43 and get a general idea of the period and what the relic might be. Each gallery is usually labeled with a dynasty name and/or a date and is usually set up chronologically from primitive to revolutionary times.

Some museums have booklets in English. Some museums have been built over archaeological sites, a most exciting idea. You stand where you know people stood 6,000 years ago and look at the remains of their children. The skeletons are still there, excavated and protected by glass. If you are at all psychic, you might feel some ancient vibes in a situation like this.

Bronzes are not as well known abroad as Chinese porcelains or paintings. The museums in China are full of these ceremonial vessels, easily dismissed as uninteresting. They are, in fact, very exciting and the product of a highly developed technology with no peer anywhere else in the world at that time. Where else has anyone cast 800 kilograms of molten bronze into a one-piece bell over 3000 years ago? Just think of the logistics of doing it. Did they use cranes? How many finished bells were discarded when they did not produce the correct tone? Did anyone get beheaded for the mistake?

And then to bury the result! The economy must have been pretty solid to support this kind of extravagance. Or did the masses have to suffer for it? Confucius, who seems to have been sensitive to the needs of common people, looked back to the Zhou dynasty as a golden age of order and prosperity. Something about the bronze era must have been right.

Bronzes are uncensored history books cast in metal said one enthusiastic scientist. The earliest script was inscribed on them, like a family Bible, recording family names and important dates. Later, historical events were recorded on them.

The shapes of ritual bronzes were based originally on everyday utensils like two-level steamers and cooking pots. From bronzes, archaeologists have concluded that weapons and agricultural tools were basically of the same designs. No one seems to know if the bronzes themselves were used in daily life. They were usually found in tombs buried with the dead for the use of the spirits.

The Chinese cast this alloy of tin and copper from molds. Emperor Yu of the Xia Dynasty (about 21st-16th century B.C.) is believed to have ordered some vessels made by vassal states as tribute. Unfortunately, these bronzes were lost by the end of the Zhou dynasty and have yet to surface.

The oldest surviving bronzes are from the Shang dynasty, and one can trace the development of the art in China's well-stocked museums; the shapes of the legs, the decorations, the type of script. Even if you cant read Chinese, at least you can see the differences in style from dynasty to dynasty.

As you study them, note that the early thin-walled Shang pieces were relatively crude, with two-dimensional patterns and stylized bogeyman figures. Look for ogres, serpents, dragons, and nipples (bosses) in bands. Later, the patterns covered the whole vessel in increasingly elaborate ways. Can you recognize cowrie shells, cicadas, birds, and braided rope motifs? Animal heads became three-dimensional and realistic. Animal statues like elephants and tigers started appearing. Bosses became coiled serpents. (Castings of human figures were rare except among the Ba people of the Yangtze.) Walls became thicker. The shapes of the legs developed from blades to dowels. Then gold or silver inlay came into being. More and different shapes appeared.

Bronzes were fashionable until the Han, after which the art died out. (See Provincial Museum under *Wuhan*.)

Some guides are steering tourists away from the revolutionary sections of museums, thinking they may not be interested. Do tell them if you are. It is good to see China's version of historic events. It may differ from what you have always heard. For this reason, Chinese history from 1840 on should be of tremendous interest. Did British soldiers really sack and rape in every city they captured? Was the British ship Amethyst acting cowardly or heroically? Did the missionaries deserve to be thrown out of China? Why do the Communists glorify the Christian-inspired Taipings and the fanatical Boxers? Was the Long March a cowardly or heroic act? Was the Great Leap Forward a mistake? Was the Cultural Revolution a mistake without any redeeming features?

MUSIC & CHINESE OPERA

Music lovers can find classical Western and contemporary Chinese and Western music. Among the best Chinese orchestras are the Shanghai Chinese Orchestra, Hong Kong Chinese Orchestra, Peking Central Folk Orchestra, Beijing Central Philharmonic Orchestra, and China Broad-casting Symphony Orchestra.

Among the most famous contemporary Chinese composers are Chou Wen-Chung (USA), Luo Jing-jing (Shanghai), Tan Dun (Beijing), Ma Sitson (USA), and Ju Hsiaosong (Beijing).

Also look for programs or cassettes that include popular compositions like the erhu concerto *Manjianghong*; *The Butterfly Lovers* for orchestra and violin; *Reflections of the Moon on Two Lakes*, an erhu concerto; *Lady General Mu Kweiying*, an orchestral work converted from Chinese opera.

The erhu, banhu, gaohu, and zhonghu are stringed instruments held upright and played with a bow. The pipa and liuqin look and sound like mandolins, the ruan more like a banjo. The yangqin is like a dulcimer played with bamboo mallets. Other Chinese instruments are the guqin, sheng, bamboo flute, and zheng.

Cui Jian is China's top pop singer.

Traditional **Chinese Opera** should be experienced at least once. It is very popular with older people and is sung in its own classical language. Your guide might not understand it except for the subtitles for the songs. The jabbering in the audience is usually a discussion of what is going on.

Some cities have shorter performances for foreigners in comfortable theaters, occasionally with subtitles in English. To the uninitiated, traditional Chinese opera can be dull, with its many long monologues, high-pitched singing, and sluggish action. The villain is always known at the beginning. The chairs are frequently hard, and there may not be heat or air-conditioning. The performance usually takes three hours, and the percussion instruments especially are loud, as if to elevate the audience to a higher level of consciousness - but not as high as at a rock concert.

Chinese opera dates from the Yuan and blossomed into one of the most popular entertainment forms during the Ming. For a largely illiterate population, operas were courses in history. They were performed at major festivals, weddings, funerals, birthdays, promotions, etc. for human and ghostly guests.

China has many forms of traditional opera. The most popular are Beijing and Qunqi. Qunqi has more dancing movements and more melodic, mellow tunes. During a performance, one sees either a whole story or excerpts from several operas.

In the old days, operas were social events. As some went on for weeks, people came and left as they pleased, chatted with friends, ate and drank. The crack of watermelon seeds and the sipping of tea blended with the music, which spectators also sang if the tune was familiar. In addition to shouting approval and clapping, one also growled and swore when actors were less than perfect. In the old days, performers were considered little better than beggars and prostitutes in spite of many years of training and practice. Today, performers are considered cultural workers and are respected as artists.

The stories are usually ancient, so a knowledge of history helps. They are also based on classic literature, like *The Dream of the Red Chamber* or *Pilgrimage to the West*. Some are based on modern history. Two books, published in China, should be helpful: *Latsch's Peking Opera as a European Sees It* and *Wu's Peking Opera and Mei Lanfang*.

Mei Lanfang was one of the greatest female impersonators. It is common to have a man play a woman's role. The Shaoxing opera company has only female players. The makeup might throw you, but much goes into it: the temples taped to slant the eyes, paste-on hair pieces to reshape faces, and many colors to indicate character, a white face shows a treacherous but dignified person and a white patch on the nose indicates a villain. Red is for loyalty and sincerity, black, honesty and all-around goodness, yellow, impulsiveness, gold and silver for demons and gods.

It is always fun to watch the actresses in love scenes expressing themselves with delicate and reserved gestures. Note how they excitedly carry their tune to a higher and higher pitch within one breath.

Usually the staging, the costumes, and the acting are outstanding. The fighting scenes, if any, are breathtaking and graceful, like ballet. Cymbals and hollow wooden knockers punctuate the action. The audience frequently applauds a musician, especially the one playing the stringed erhu. Usually a good opera singer tries to keep his own erhu player for life. The costumes are handmade and artfully embroidered, depending on the character played.

The singing takes some getting used to. It can sound like screeching and whining. But it takes many years of training to achieve such perfection. Settings are usually simple and symbolic. The acting, too, is symbolic, and Chinese audiences know what every gesture, every move of the eyebrow means. Among the symbols: an old man and a girl with an oar are on a boat; a man lifting up his foot as he exits is stepping over the high threshold of a door; crossed eyes mean anger; walking with hands extended in front means it's dark; a man holding a riding crop means hes riding a horse, or sometimes he is a horse. You should be able to tell the difference! A particularly well-executed swing of long hair (anguish) or prolonged trembling (fear) will elicit gasps of appreciation and applause.

Two bamboo poles with some cloth attached represent a city wall or gate. A chariot is two yellow flags with a wheel drawn on each. A couple of poles on either side of an actor is a sedan chair. A hat with two long, dangling pheasant or peacock feathers is worn by a high military officer, usually a marshal; a hat with wobbling wings out to the sides just above the ears belongs to a magistrate. Generals have flags matching their costumes and are mounted like wings on their backs. The flags are distributed to identify imperial messengers.

After the performance, you may want to go backstage to see everything up close, and possibly makeup being removed.

NURSERY SCHOOLS

Many tours schedule visits to nursery schools, which are always entertaining and charming. Count on half a day. In some nursery schools, visitors are involved in some of the childrens games. In all nursery schools you will tour the classrooms, have a performance of songs and dances, and get a briefing with an opportunity to ask questions.

Nursery-school songs are a good indicator of the current political atmosphere. At one time the children were singing songs about shooting down American planes. Recently, we found a five-year-old girl doing a sexy dance (of course we voiced objections to her teachers!). In more advanced schools, you may be expected to read an English lesson. Suggest that your reading be recorded so the children can hear it again so they memorize your accent and inflections.

PHOTOGRAPHY

China is now like most other countries regarding photographs. At one time I couldn't even take a photo of my five-year-old on a public boat. Today you can take pictures everywhere except inside police stations and prisons, military installations, and certain museums. Flash photography damages relics. Museums charge a fee or confiscate your film. Out of courtesy, please ask people if you can photograph them close up. Would you like someone to stick a camera in your face without permission?

If your camera breaks down, look for a Kodak agent, who might be able to repair it for you. China has lots of camera stores. If you want to buy film in China, there's Kodak and Fuji. Some of the Kodak boxes for 100 ASA are entirely in Chinese. Do not buy from peddlars who leave the film in the sun. Aim for air-conditioned stores. It is not easy to buy film with speeds higher than 100. Try the Beijing Friendship Stores, or specialized photo stores.

SAVING MONEY

Those who want to save money need more time, and shouldn't care about the highest available standards of cleanliness and comfort. The more expensive the hotel, the higher the cost of other services like laundry and food. Chinese-managed hotels with the same star ratings as joint ventures are usually cheaper. Spend time comparing prices and quality. Avoid services offered by hotels, especially tempting mini-bars. But ask your hotel about reconfirming or booking flights. They just might do it for free.

All Holiday Inns discount 20% off the published rate for persons 65 years and over. It also gives 10% off food and beverage. Sheraton gives seniors' discounts, and cheaper room prices if booked in advance. Look into special hotel packages, especially in winter.

At each hotel ask to look at the cheaper rooms. They could be all right. Reception clerks tend to think all foreigners want the top quality rooms. Rooms on the uppermost floors and with the best views are usually more expensive. Tell the clerk you're a student (if you have your card), or a foreign expert (even if you've just given one lecture). Ask if the hotel has CAA, AAA or seniors' discounts. Anything! Ask for the Sales Manager who is in a position to give the biggest discounts. Many hotels have dorms with up to 30 or 40 beds in a room for about Y25 a bed and up. Try hostels. Share rooms with friends, as most rooms cost the same for one or two guests. Hotels in big cities are more expensive, so stay away from the center of the city. Find a room in small town hotels and commute. Or take anything you can get for the first night, and then look around.

On telephone calls home, use a phonecard telephone and ask your family to call you in your hotel room at the cheapest North American rates.

Book hard-class train or take buses or ferries between cities. You might not mind it. Avoid travel agents. If you have to use them, use travel agents associated with hotels that cater to backpackers. Their services are usually cheaper.

Do not assume that the Chinese are giving you anything free. Always ask, "What is the charge?"

Eat in bun or noodle shops or at market stalls. These cost less than hotel restaurants and some are clean. One backpacker spent two and a half months eating cheaply at market stalls and never got sick. But others arent so lucky, so stick to well-cooked food and avoid tap water and raw vegetables. China has a lot of food stores now with cheap, decent looking cooked foods on sale.

Travel with Chinese friends. Avoid tourist restaurants. Invite one of the young people trying to practice English on you to take you to a restaurant where ordinary people eat. Foreign hitchhikers have traveled around China successfully, sleeping in hostels for local Chinese (after much persistent pleading), sometimes for less than Y2 a night. (Take your own bedding and you won't be surprised by bedbugs.)

Some New World Hotels International offer a "Hungry Hour" where for the price of one drink, you can eat all the snacks you want. It's a good deal.

Stay with friends or relatives. Courtesy demands you take them presents, but this could be anything from cookies to a refrigerator.

Travel during low tourist season. The south is pleasant in the wintertime.

Backpackers should be able to manage on $20–$25 a day for a bed in a dorm, food, and local transportation.

Take public transportation, or bicycle rickshaws for short trips instead of taxis, or rent a bicycle.

Ask your hotel service desk or CITS if there is a tour you can join. Try to round up other individual travellers to go with you on the same tour. This lowers the rate you have to pay. If you are one or two people, this may be cheaper than taking taxis. But four people sharing a taxi might be cheaper than taking a bus tour.

You might try to hitch free rides with tour groups. While you're at a tourist attraction or hotel, make friends with other foreigners, and ask if you can get a ride with them. They usually don't mind if it's FROM the tourist attraction.

Do your own laundry or take it outside your hotel. At the Holiday Inn Lido in Beijing, you don't pay a service charge if you leave your laundry at a store in the building. If laundry is too expensive, buy underwear and tee shirts, and dress shirts at street markets instead.

SAVE ON AIRFARE!

Save before you go to China: Look for bargain airfares. Haggle with managers in travel agencies and airline offices (especially Air China, CAIL, KAL, PAL, SIA, and CAL). You have nothing to lose but your pride. Read the youth travel columns in newspapers. Talk to backpackers about cutting costs. Find out about flying as a courier. Check out travel agents in local Chinatowns. What about the train from London to Beijing via Moscow? Check out Euro-Asia Express or Avia Travel (See Chapter 6, Planning Your Trip). If the Canadian dollar remains low, U.S.-based travelers might consider buying plane tickets and tours from a Canadian travel agent. It's worth your while to investigate.

Look into the special air rates between London and Hong Kong for British citizens, or excursion fares. How about PAL via Manila? CITS and CAAC discount from December 1 to March 31 on some routes and tours. Hotels too.

Let the Chinese pay your way, or at least part of it. Go as a teacher or foreign expert.

Organize your own tour group. You could get free airfare and hotel rooms, but expect a lot of work. You need about 15 people.

OVERSEAS CHINESE

Do not hesitate to look up relatives (if you have any) in China. You can learn more about China from your relatives than from any tour. It won't be the same but it will be a deeper kind of experience. I'm third generation Canadian. The first time I met my family in China, they pointed out a long-forgotten photograph on the wall of my Canadian family taken 20 years before. My aunt knew everyone by name. Until I started planning a trip to China, I didn't know she existed. In her home, I saw how a six-course meal could be cooked in one wok in one hour. I learned how politeness smoothes over a multitude of sins, all ignoring my embarrassing encounter with a naked grown-up nephew who was bathing behind a screen in the kitchen (there was nowhere else to bathe). On the streets they pointed to the strange-looking foreigners, my fellow North Americans who had then just started to invade Xinhui. I didn't learn much about the history of the city, but I sure learned a lot about Chinese people and myself.

I think people of Chinese ancestry in particular should visit China. If you feel this bicultural conflict as many of us do, it would be good to explore the Chinese part of your roots. If nothing else, it will help you understand your parents, your grandparents, or your great-grandparents. It might even help you understand things about yourself.

In my father's village in Taishan, I was shocked to learn he had been born in a mud house. I found the watch towers where he used to look out for bandits, and imagined him riding the water buffalos. My grandfathers grave was a simple mound. I had expected something more elaborate, considering the money my father sent back to the village.

I highly recommend a visit to your ancestral village, if you can find it. Even if you have no relatives there, at least you can look around and see how you would have lived if your ancestors had not emigrated. If you do find relatives, you might find your name, if you're male, in a family history book.

Don't be concerned if you don't have money to take expensive presents. People outside China send back presents to family partly to show off. They also send them because they feel a strong family obligation. People in China ask for expensive luxury presents like Omega watches because they want to keep up with the Wongs. Remittances have supported a few idlers. If you don't want to contribute to idleness and foolish pride, don't give expensive gifts.

Sure they'll ask you to pay for schooling and to help your cousin emigrate to the U.S. If you can help them, do. If you can't, don't. Getting to know your relatives and learning about China are much more important than a few dollars. You might just want to treat them to dinner at a restaurant, a nice gesture, especially if you're staying with them.

Usually, Chinese relatives just want the use of your foreign passport. It will cost you nothing but time. Only Overseas Chinese with foreign passports can import or buy certain desirable goods duty-free. They should pay you back.

NIGHTLIFE

Just about anything you might want to do can be found in China. This runs the gamut from typically western activities, such as the symphony and discos, to more uniquely Chinese activities like acrobats and opera. Most movies are in Chinese, some with English subtitles. Look for historical dramas so you can see costumes and architecture, like *The Three Kingdoms* and *The Dream of the Red Chamber*. The *China Daily* has notices about cultural events in Beijing and on national television.

Chinese **television** consists primarily of documentaries, travelogues, kung fu action thrillers, and tearjerkers. It also has news, sports, boring political speeches, and educational broadcasts, such as language lessons.

The Chinese **acrobats** are usually very entertaining. Also offered are song and dance troupes and sports competitions. I highly recommend exhibitions of *wushu*, a traditional martial art.

Most tour groups will be taken to one or two cultural presentations. If you want to go to more, you can on your own. They are very cheap - usually less than four yuan. Tickets should be booked in advance through your hotel.

In Beijing, there are good **movies**, usually with English subtitles. Take advantage of cheaper prices for western performers too. In almost every city, batches of seats for various kinds of performances are reserved for foreigners. You might be able to get some of these at your hotel service desk. China has ticket scalpers too.

Dance parties and **discos** are more fun if you get up and dance, and so are karaoke bars if you get up and sing. Dances are organized at hotels or in parks out of doors (at 6 am to after dark). Because people are shy, you will find men dancing with other men and women dancing with each other. But many couples dance too. The music is a melange of fox trots, waltzes, tangos, cha-cha, and rock. In some places, you can take your own cassettes.

Night markets are opening up all over where weather permits, for clothes and for some great cheap food. Many hotels provide microphones for guests in karaoke bars along with high-tech monitors, a Japanese tradition.

Nightclubs and North American-type **bars** have opened, some with live entertainment in the big cities. The best bars are in hotels but many small decent bars have opened. Just be wary of bars where hostesses sit down and drink with you and then bill you excessively for their drinks. Many hotels now have gyms, bowling alleys, and lighted tennis courts. On Friday evenings, many local foreign residents get together to celebrate TGIF. They are good sources of information. Contact your consulate for locations. Hotel coffee shops, bars, and many stores stay open late. Massages are great and serious. Men message men; women massage women. Beijing, Guilin, and Xi'an are among the cities with dinner theatres.

The days of going to bed at 9 pm because there's nothing to do have disappeared in the big cities.

POSTAL SERVICE

Postal Services are generally reliable and airmail post cards and letters take seven to ten days to North America. Hotels can provide stamps but for mailing packages you need a real post office. Only international post offices can despatch parcels overseas. Some hotels can send packages for you but you have to pay a service charge and the taxi fare to and from the international post office. In addition, you probably have to have your package sewn up in white cloth or sealed in regulation boxes *after* Customs inspection. You have to fill out forms in triplicate. A few post offices provide boxes. Customs inspect all packages, even those sent inside China. Registration and insurance are cheap and recommended - if you have someone in the city to follow up should packages get lost.

Surface mail to North America can take six weeks to three months. Letters mailed in China to Chinese addresses must have an envelope with red squares at the top for the postal code. It must also be a regulation size and addressed in Chinese. Consult your hotel's business center if you have a problem.

Post offices in Beijing are open 8:30 am to 6 pm on weekdays, and some are closed Saturday afternoons. All are closed on Sundays.

Express Mail Service (EMS) from post offices takes three days to the United States and cost at least Y147 for up to 500 grams. You can book courier services through hotel business centers or directly with DHL, UPS, TNT, or OCS. These have very strict rules about sending goods.

Letters could take up to 15 days to reach you. You can be reached more quickly by telephone or fax to your hotel. You could also schedule a mail pick-up at your embassy. American Express has client mail service in several cities like Beijing and Guangzhou.

Telexes are still being used, but most people fax. You can save money by typing your own telexes. Hotel business centers are convenient for sending these, but are more expensive than Post and Telecommunications offices. If you expect to receive telexes or faxes in your hotel, give your room number as part of your address to correspondents. And keep looking for incoming messages at the front desk or at the business center. Cable is cheaper, but slower and might not be reliable. You usually book them at post offices.

PUBLIC SAFETY

Chinese safety standards are casual except where a lot of foreign tourists are concerned. We urge you to avoid amusement park rides since these are primarily for locals and we have heard of accidents. I have heard of no serious mechanical cable car failures up mountains where foreign tourists go.

SOCIAL SITUATIONS

Does Yes Mean YES? Well, usually. Cultural differences do create misunderstandings. For example, a memorandum of understanding in trade means that negotiations can begin in earnest. It does not mean, as many foreigners have sadly discovered, that a contract has been signed. See *Business* above.

If a Chinese nods and says yes, yes, he could be just trying to please you. He may not understand a word you are saying. So be wary. Ask a question that needs a full sentence in answer. For the same reason, a Chinese might give you dates and spellings and swear they are right. But what he means is that it is the best information he has and if you press him, he will check.

Chinese people are very polite in their personal relationships with friends or business acquaintances. They try not to hurt feelings. If you make a mistake, the very polite ones will not point it out to you. If you do something they do not like, they might ask someone senior to you to talk to you about it.

But Chinese people may not seem polite at times, especially in crowds, or clerks in government stores. But if someone introduces you properly, most Chinese will prove to be extremely hospitable and helpful. The shop girl who ignores you is probably afraid of you or is unfulfilled by her job. Don't take it personally.

Once I caught my knee in the door of a crowded bus and got a bad bruise. At the time, my cousins laughed while I felt like crying. It was their way of reacting to embarrassment. Just don't feel offended.

Does No Mean NO? Well, sometimes. You will have to judge for yourself as to when a negative decision can be challenged.

You might hear *mei you*. It means "there isn't any." It basically means please disappear, but when you don't, something has to be done. Some foreigners have challenged it at airline offices by standing firm, smiling, asking for the manager, and refusing to budge until they got a ticket.

By protesting to a hotel clerk who said there was no room, I did get a bed in a dorm. This does not mean you should try to argue every time you are told it is not possible, or that your safety cannot be guaranteed. It could mean: (1) language is a problem and they do not understand your request; (2) they don't want to be bothered trying; (3) they don't want too many people going there, but if you insist, they'll let you go; (4) there is genuine concern for your safety; (5) you really aren't allowed to go.

Arguing is an art too. Do not lose your temper or youve lost the battle. Suggest an alternative.

Note: Sometimes a no answer is a no. Sometimes no should be answered with "How much will it cost?" or "Would Y10 help?"

Ask Questions: an official of the Overseas Chinese Travel Service once told me the only advice he had for visitors was, "ask questions." It is good advice. The Chinese do not volunteer much information. So when in doubt, ask!

Applause: you could be greeted by applause as a sign of welcome at institutions and cultural performances. It might even happen on the streets. Applaud back.

Criticisms and Suggestions: you may be asked for these. If you have any, do give them. It will help improve services. Mention that the bathroom floor is filthy. Ask the attendant to clean it. If an attendant has been particularly helpful, write it down. She may get a bonus.

Good Manners: while it may be fashionable to be late elsewhere in Asia, this is not so in China, where groups of children may be outside in the rain waiting for your car so they can applaud as you arrive. Traditionally, Chinese conversations, even business conversations, start out with something innocuous: a discussion of the weather or a painting on the wall. A friendy mood is set first. Then comes the business.

Chinese people may not be polite in crowds. They may surround your bus and stare at you. But it is their country. Also, when using an interpreter, don't forget to look at the person with whom you are actually conversing.

Chinese Hospitality: this can be very lavish and people may go into debt to show how happy they are to see you. It is always appropriate to take a gift when you go to a Chinese home. Presents or money for the children are fine (about Y20 each) if you are a relative or a close friend. Otherwise, it is insulting. If you have time for a return banquet, that would be the easy way out.

If you are accompanied by a Chinese friend or relative, avoid buying anything in a store because they may want to pay for it. The salary range for most people is quite low. Chinese don't have to pay exorbitant medical bills when sick, most pay no income tax. and rent is low. Butpeople have to save a long time to buy what you wouldn't think twice about buying. Hospitality may demand that you be given a gift. Suggest something inexpensive if you are asked.

I have visited many homes - of peasants, officials, workers, and professional people. By western standards, most are crowded. Poorer families might share a kitchen and bathroom with several other families. In only rare cases will there be room for overnight guests especially in the cities. Toilets may be the squatting kind. In smaller communities you may find a container of earth or a bucket of water for covering or flushing.

In rural areas, you might have to sightsee on foot or on the hard back ends of bicycles if your hosts cannot afford any other means of transportation. It is a real adventure!

If Youre Invited to A Wedding: in old China, a gift of money in a red packet was the accepted thing to give. Money is still much appreciated. But gifts to help set up a new household are more frequently given now: porcelain tea sets, videos, and bed covers (preferably red, for happiness). In some places, giving a clock is bad luck. It implies a time limit on the marriage.

Wedding invitations usually mean a banquet, but do ask. You can say something like: "I've never been to a Chinese wedding before. Tell me what to expect." Budget Y200 for casual acquaintances.

Names and Forms of Address: "attendant" is the best translation for all service personnel like waiters, room boys, and chambermaids. If you have to get their attention, you can call them *fu wu yuan*. Ask people what they want to be called. Some have English names.

Relatives are referred to and called by their relationship to you, like Second Aunt Older Than My Father, or Fifth Maternal Uncle of My Grandfathers Generation. Your relatives will tell you what to call them.

Chinese put surnames first. Chou En-lai would be Premier Chou. You rarely address a person by his given name, except children or relatives.

Guanxi: this is relationships, influence, pull, and connections and are an important part of Chinese life. Schoolmates, teachers, relatives, workmates - people who know each other well have a stronger and longer hold on each other than in the West. Guanxi is related to merit and to helping each other. Strangers are politely accepted, but with reservation, until they have proved themselves trustworthy, friendly, and useful. But this isnt fair to capable people without connections.

Flirting: you will probably be considered uncivilized if you indulge in too much display of affection in public, even with your own spouse. Older Chinese will be embarrassed. Friendly embraces are unusual even upon greeting a Chinese friend of long standing. The younger generation is more understanding.

Warning: If a young Chinese woman is walking with a Caucasian man, many Chinese assume she is a prostitute. Prostitution is illegal and the police have been known to wait and watch so they can catch couples in bed. It is illegal to be a customer.

Joking about Politics and Sex: many visitors are warned not to joke about sex or politics, particularly Chinese politics. With the older generation, to joke about sex is considered crude. To joke about politics or even to argue about it is to show lack of sensitivity. Politics is taken very seriously in China. People are put into jail because of it, lose their jobs, and spend long hours in meetings discussing political implications. Some young people, however, might find such humor refreshing and I have heard some tell hilarious (and perhaps dangerous) political jokes in public.

Ask Political Questions: don't be afraid. If it is done in the right spirit, both the Chinese and you can learn a lot. Political discussions can get heated. Remain calm. If you succeed in convincing them, it wont be because of shouting and red faces.

If they look uncomfortable with the question, don't pursue it. They may be under a lot of pressure to give the correct political answer and they may not know it. The better you know a person, the franker an answer you will get. And no answer is also an answer, if you know what I mean.

SECURITY

Pilfering in hotel rooms is on the increase, so lock your valuables away. Strong padlocks and fancy luggage tags have disappeared between hotels on flights, though usually nothing else is missing. You should watch your purse and wallet in crowded areas. Like elsewhere in the world, take the usual precautions.

Double lock doors at night. Memorize the fire escape map on the door. Do not allow strangers into your hotel room. Check with the front desk by telephone if the person at your door has no key and claims to be hotel maintenance. But generally, do not worry. You can go out safely at night.

China is safer than many places in the U.S. If political disturbances erupt again, please feel confident that in 1989, tour guides acted professionally. They avoided danger and got their guests out of China safely. No tourists were injured. Some hotels acted admirably, the Palace in particular, checking people out and in to make sure they were safe.

U.S. Citizens Services in Guangzhou which covers southern China says there is very little crime, except for pickpocketing, mostly around the Guangzhou railway station, and in Yangshuo at the end of the Li River trip from Guilin.

SMOKING

There seems to be more awareness of the hazards of cigarette smoking. A handful of joint-venture hotels have no smoking areas in restaurants, elevators, and some floors. Smoking is forbidden in airport waiting rooms and on certain train coaches and domestic flights. But smoking is still very common. China has the most smokers in the world and 4.4 million Chinese die of smoking-related illnesses a year.

SPELLINGS: NAMES OF PEOPLE

Pinyin	Wade-Giles
Bainqen Lama	Panchen Lama
Cixi	Tzu Hsi (Tsu-hsi, Qing Empress Dowager)
Deng Xiaoping	Teng Hsiao-ping
Feng Yuxiang	Feng Yu-hsiang (general)
Guan Yu	Kuan Yu (Three Kingdoms)
Guo Moruo	Kuo Mo Ruo
Hua Kuofeng	Hua Guo-feng (former Party chairman)
Jiang Jieshi	Chiang Kai-shek
Jiang Qing	Chiang Ching (widow of Mao Tse-tung)
Lin Biao	Lin Piao
Liu Shaoqi	Liu Shao-chi (former president)

Pinyin	*Wade-Giles*
Mao Zedong	Mao Tse-tung
Sun Yixian	Sun Yat-sen (father of republican China)
Xuan Zhang	Hsuan-tsang (Tang dynasty monk)
Yuan Shikai	Yuan Shih-kai (2nd president of China)
Zhong Shan	Chung Shan (honorific name of Sun Yat-sen)
Zhou Enlai	Chou En-lai (former premier of China)
Zhu Yanzhang	Chu Yuan-chuan (first Ming Emperor)

SPITTING

Campaigns in some cities have taken place against the unhealthy and disgusting habit of spitting in public. It is a reflection of rural society. Fines in Beijing have averaged Y42 and have been successful in curtailing, but not eliminating, spitting. The Chinese believe that swallowing phlegm is unhealthy.

SYMBOLS

You will see these everywhere; in palaces, temples, pagodas, museums, fancy restaurants, gardens, parks, on dishes, windows, and screens. Knowing what they are will help you recognize bits of Chinese culture even in North America in Chinese restaurants.

The **Chinese Dragon** is said to have the head of a camel, the horns of a deer, the eyes of a rabbit, the ears of a cow, the neck of a snake, the belly of a frog, the scales of a carp, the claws of a hawk, and the palm of a tiger. It has whiskers and a beard and is deaf. It is generally regarded as benevolent but is also the source of thunder and lightning. The five-clawed variation was once reserved exclusively for the emperor. The flaming ball represents thunder and lightning, the sun or the moon, or the pearl of potentiality. It is frequently surrounded by clouds.

THE DRAGON OF HEAVEN

The **cloud design** is most frequently blue and depicted in the lower border of a rich man's gown in a traditional opera costume or in a painted antique portrait.

The **scepter** is frequently about half a meter long and made of metal, stone, bone, or wood. It is like a magic wand and is frequently given as a gift, a symbol of good wishes for the prosperity and longevity of the recipient. The larger ones are found in museums.

The **lion** is not native to China. The design is unique to China because the craftsmen never saw a real one. Lions are frequently seen in front of buildings as protectors either playing with a ball (male) or a kitten (female). They are considered benevolent. The **ball** is said by some to represent the imperial treasury or peace. Others say it is the sun, a precious stone, or the Yin-yang. Seen also on festive occasions as a costume for dancers, the lion is sometimes confused with the **Fo dog**, which is usually blue with longer ears.

The **phoenix** is said to resemble a swan in front, a unicorn behind, with the throat of a swallow, the bill of a fowl, the neck of a snake, the tail of a peacock, the forehead of a crane, the crown of a Mandarin duck, the stripes of a dragon, and the back of a tortoise. Its appearance is said to mean an era of peace and prosperity. It was the symbol used by the empresses of China and is often combined in designs with the dragon.

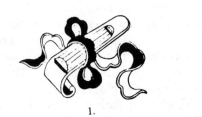

1.

2.

3.

4.

The intellectual elite was associated
with these four symbols in ancient times with:
1. The harp; 2. The chess board; 3. The books; 4. The paintings.

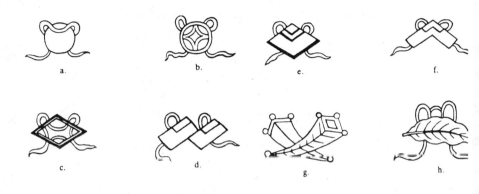

THE EIGHT PRECIOUS THINGS:

a. the pearl; b. the coin; c. the rhombus (victory); d. the books;
e. the paintings; f. the musical stone of jade (blessing);
g. the rhinoceros-horn cups; h. the artemisia leaf (dignity)

These are only two of the many variations frequently seen.
There is even a teapot in the Shou design.
1. the round Shou; 2. the long Shou, both meaning long life

Below is one of the many variations of the character for happiness.
Sometimes it is circular and doubled, especially prominent at weddings.

THE FU, MEANING HAPPINESS

The word for **bat** in Chinese is *fu*. So is the word for happiness. A bat
is thus a symbol of happiness. These are everywhere: on the walls and

ceilings of the Forbidden City, on the ceiling of the restaurant of the Peace Hotel in Shanghai. The peach is a symbol of longevity.

The bat   Bat and peach

FIVE BATS, SURROUNDING THE CHARACTER SHOU

When five bats are combined with the longevity character, they mean they give great blessings: happiness, wealth, peace, virtue, and longevity.

SCEPTER, WRITING BRUSH, AND UNCOINED SILVER.
Together, these are a symbol of success.

THE THREE FRUITS
The three fruits are fragrant fingers of Buddha, peach, and pomegranate. Together they mean happiness, longevity, and male children.

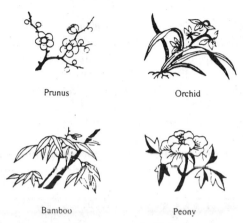

Prunus

Orchid

Bamboo

Peony

The prunus or plum blossom symbolizes beauty; the orchid, fragrance; bamboo is an emblem of longevity, and the peony means wealth and respectability.

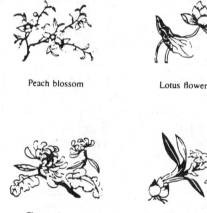

Peach blossom

Lotus flower

Chrysanthemum

Narcissus

These are featured singly or combined in a set of four: the peach blossom represents spring, the lotus flower is summer, chrysanthemum is autumn, and narcissus is winter. Frequently there are only one of each of these on a four-panel screen.

Other common symbols are the **crane** (longevity), the **stag** (longevity and prosperity), and the **lotus** (purity and perfection). The Buddha is usually seated on a lotus.

Among the many strange beings are the two at the top two corners of many temple roofs, tails pointing to the sky. This is a carp turning into a dragon, symbolic of a scholar turning into a magistrate. There is also the **unicorn**, known as *qi-lin*, with the body of the musk deer, the tail of an ox, the forehead of a wolf, and the hoofs of a horse. The male has a horn, the female does not. It is a good, gentle, and benevolent creature.

The **wooden fish**, a red object found in most Buddhist temples, is a clapper, used for beating time while the monks chant the sutras. Some say that the monks dropped the sutras in water as the holy scriptures were being brought from India. A fish ate the sutras, so it was beaten to force it to regurgitate. Others say if you don't beat the fish, there will be an earthquake.

The **tortoise**, usually seen with a giant stele on its back, is one of the four supernatural animals, the others being the phoenix, the dragon, and the unicorn. Real ones are frequently kept at Buddhist temples, for they are sacred, an emblem of longevity, strength, and endurance.

TELEPHONE & TELECOMMUNICATIONS

You should be aware that telephone, fax, and e-mail communications could be government-monitored. E-mail providers have had to sign agreements stating they are not sending anything illegal.

Most local telephone calls from hotels have been free, but top hotels in the big cities, are charging Y1 to Y2 a call. A few hotels, like the JC Mandarin (Shanghai) have a complimentry telephone just off the lobby. Complimentary telephones are also in most restaurants or on the assistant manager's desk. Most hotels prefer you use their business center and charge Y2 a call. Public telephones range from Y0.05 to Y2.00.

Many local Chinese now have private telephones. Those that don't might share a telephone with everyone else in their building. You need a Chinese-speaker to reach them. Each village has at least one telephone in the village office. You can leave a message asking your friends to telephone you at your hotel. Be sure to give your room number.

Over 500 cities have **International Direct Dial** (IDD). Direct dial is much faster (20 seconds) than operator-assisted calls, which might take from three minutes to a couple of days (in remote towns). Dialing direct from your hotel room is the easiest but one of the most expensive way to communicate abroad from China. Just ask the hotel operator what numbers to dial to access your country. The operator can also give you country and city codes. You pay a three-minute minimum and a service charge.

Some hotels, especially in Beijing, have card phones in their lobbies. These telephones are also on the streets, in shopping centers, railway stations, and in telecommunications offices in over 50 cities. This is the cheapest way to call. There is no service charge and no minimum. You can buy phone cards from the hotels or more cheaply from the telecommunications offices in set denominations. You use the card until you no longer have a balance. The cost of the call is automatically deducted.

You can also telephone abroad by dialing a local number, and connecting immediately with an American or Canadian operator for example. You can then charge the call to your own telephone calling card, or "collect." The hotel does charge a service fee if you call this way from your room, but if you call from a public telephone, it is cheaper.

CALLING CARD ACCESS NUMBERS & COUNTRY CODES

*For the U.S., **AT&T** is 108-11, **MCI** is 108-12, and **Sprint** is 108-13; For **Bell Canada**, dial 108-186.   AT&T also has "USA Direct" or "Canada Direct" telephones in some hotel lobbies and airports.*

*China's code is **86**. Some other country codes are:*

Australia - 61	*Malaysia - 60*
Canada - 1	*Philippines - 63*
Hong Kong - 852	*Singapore - 65*
India - 91	*Thailand - 66*
Japan - 81	*United Kingdom - 44*
Macau - 853	*United States - 1*

Don'-t forget the time difference. China has forbidden "Call-Back" telephone calls, but you can telephone your own family and have them phone you. Make sure you give them your hotel room number.

A few hotels and business centers like the Portman in the Shanghai Center (Shanghai) have call forwarding and conference call facilities. You can lease cellular phones through business centers in some hotels.

Faxes sent overseas are expensive from both hotels and government telecommunication offices because they charge a three-minute minimum. It is best to find a friend with a fax machine so you only pay for the amount of time you use. One page usually takes less than one minute. Some hotels have "special packages" for faxes and phone calls. It would be cheaper to send a fax to China from your home (before 8 am and after 11 pm) in North America than to send one from a hotel in China.

If you are touring during the day and want to leave a message with someone in the same city during office hours, send a fax from your hotel. Local faxes are reasonably priced and shouldn't have a three-minute minimum.

E-mail and Internet services are starting to be available, but so far not through hotels or in English. But things are changing.

Some cities have **videophones**. Try the telecommunications office on East Nanjing Road, near the Peace Hotel in Shanghai.

TIME ZONES

All of China is in the same time zone. Beijing is 13 hours ahead of New York and Toronto. Please make adjustments for standard and daylight savings time.

TIPPING

This is officially forbidden. However, service people do accept tips and make more money than doctors, university professors, and government officials. Tipping is an area of transition and new rules are developing. We suggest you tip in hotels only for services above the call of duty. Do not tip the attendant who fixes your broken toilet. That is his duty. Avoid tipping in hotels that add a percentage for service. While staff may not necessarily get the service charge, you have paid for their services. In some hotels, tips are accepted as a token of friendship and shared among the staff.

A suggested tip for a bell man is Y5 to Y10 a load and for a porter at the train station Y2 to Y10. As for tour guides and drivers, tip only those who have been exceptionally good, and no more than US$2 per day per client for each. Victoria Cruises suggests you put US$5.00 per day per guest into a box on top of a 15% surcharge on services. The $5 tip is split among all Chinese service staff including cooks, and other behind-the-scene personnel. Victoria encourages its guests to tip individual service people as well if they want.

The Holiday Inns Lido and Crowne Plaza said tipping is not expected nor encouraged. Miserable hours have been wasted in tour groups arguing about tips and gifts.

Asking for tips is strictly forbidden. A few attendants in newly opened hotels will refuse tips. Please thank them profusely. Such purity of spirit should be encouraged. You could perhaps give them a modest souvenir instead and send a letter of commendation to the tourism administration praising them. As for guides, they expect tips and recently have had to share them. A few have had to give a set amount to their travel agencies whether they receive money or not. But this is not your problem.

TOILETS

You are out shopping. Nature calls. What do you do? The best is to head for the closest tourist hotel, barge in as if you are staying there, and use its facilities. Dont expect western toilets except in tourist hotels or on the well-beaten foreign tourist path. The Chinese toilet is the squatting kind – over a hole in the ground. These are difficult for people with poor knees. There is usually no place to hang up purses. Toilets are best in your own hotel room.

Some public toilets, especially those in less developed areas, stink unbearably. Foreigners could dab perfume or Tiger Balm under their noses. Sometimes it is better for people traveling by road to stop behind a bush to fertilize the fields. This is certainly better than sharing toilets with writhing maggots.

TOURISM REALITIES

Going on a group tour doesn't eliminate all problems. But it does mean someone else has to deal with them, and that someone else should also be able to find you a clean toilet. Shortages of trained, experienced staff with a good command of English plague all sectors of the industry because it has expanded too quickly. Recent group tourists have complained of inexperienced guides, although most are excellent. It is very important to take a list of what you want to do and see. Otherwise, some guides will just take you shopping.

I still hear stories like the one about the hotel that charged more for a single room than a larger double or about the Canadian who rode a public bus from Kunming to Dali packed like sardines. Her neighbor kept reaching over her and throwing up out the window, refusing to change seats.

Most of the horror stories happen to individual travelers trying to save money.

Recently, China's travel agencies have been hit hard by inflation. Because they tend to book tours six months to a year in advance, their profit margins have shrunk by the time the groups arrive with payment. In order to break even, they have been taking a share of the tips given to guides and drivers, making contracts with tourist stores and taking a percentage of sales. They have had to downgrade the restaurants to which they take their groups. The competition between Chinese agencies is so severe that agencies try to keep prices down at the expense of quality. If you want better service, you have to pay for it. Talk it over with your travel agent at home or head for upmarket tours like Abercrombie and Kent.

There are illegal tour buses that overcharge. (Always agree on a price beforehand.) A problem on CTS' Guangdong tour from Hong Kong was luggage. The tour brochure said the price included the handling of one piece of luggage but the service was not offered. Guests had to carry their own, up and down flights of stairs and long corridors. No one told them to leave it at their Hong Kong hotel until they returned. Also, in spite of the rainy season, CTS did not have enough umbrellas for our group. And it poured at times.

8. GETTING AROUND CHINA

Whenever you go anywhere alone, carry the name of your hotel in Chinese. If you are traveling between cities, take the telephone number of your travel agent in both places. If your flight is canceled, at least you can telephone for help.

Note: A cancellation fee is always charged when you make changes in travel arrangements.

Always carry lots of small change for shopping and expenses.

Among your highest priorities upon arriving in a new place is to arrange your out-bound travel.

If you are traveling overnight by train or by ferry (not a luxury tourist ship), take your own mug, soap, chopsticks, and towel.

Always carry toilet tissue with you.

FLYING IN CHINA

China's air safety record and service have improved considerably since the early 1990s. Northwest Airlines has been helping to train Chinese pilots and the United States Federal Aviation Administration has been helping China overhaul the industry, from installing radars to training personnel. On routes between main cities, your flights will probably be on new planes and on time (except in bad weather).

If you have a choice of flights, choose the shortest flying time. You are more likely to get a newer plane with bigger seats. Aim for the earliest flights. Delays become compounded as the day progresses. Tickets have to be paid for by noon, the day before departure. Only American Express credit cards and cash are accepted to pay for Chinese airline tickets. Some airline ticket offices have facilities for cash advances from a credit card, but it costs 4% more.

All domestic reservations have to be reconfirmed before noon two days before the flight. Your ticket probably has to be stamped and your passport seen. Travel agencies should be able to do this for a fee. If there is any doubt, reconfirm. When you reconfirm, ask for the check-in time.

Some airlines say that confirmation is not necessary if you are in the city of departure for less than 72 hours. But I have heard of passengers being dropped off overbooked flights for not reconfirming.

It is best to arrive at the airport early in case of overbooking, one and a half hours for domestic flights and two hours for international flights. Check-in ends 30 minutes before flight time. Prepare to pay either a domestic or an international airport tax. You might also be asked to pay personal accident or baggage insurance. It is very difficult to get accurate flight departure information over the telephone or even after you arrive at the airport. If a flight is late, insist on a progress report; if very late, free food. Give yourself extra time to get to the airport in rain or snow. Be sure to confirm delays with more than one official before you go back into town.

Most planes are booked from the front. There may not be room for all the carry-on bags. Planes have been known to leave early and of course sometimes late. Do not expect luggage carts (except at international airports) or porters. Be prepared to carry your own bags.

Carry some snacks and a good book. Airport waiting rooms have an information desk with a clerk who might know some English. Some have electronic monitors showing flight numbers. Because boarding announcements are not always audible or in English, check frequently. You could look out the window for your plane. The plane number is painted on the fuselage and should be mentioned on your boarding pass. You could also look for other people with the same color boarding pass and try out your few words of Mandarin. Some people take a friendly interest in foreign travelers and will tell you when to board the flight.

Some airports have a room for smokers. Meal announcements are usually not in English, so keep your eyes on fellow passengers. Be prepared to walk to your plane no matter what weather, and to be pushed by other travelers.

Until recently, **CAAC** was the only airline operating domestically in China. It is now broken up into regional subsidiaries of CAAC, and are run by former CAAC personnel with CAAC planes and facilities. China Southern, China Eastern and Air China are the largest.

Their IATA codes are:
- **Air China** (Beijing) – CA
- **Northeast Airlines** (Shenyang) – CJ
- **Northwest China Airways** (X'ian) – WH
- **China Southern Airlines** (Guangzhou) – CZ
- **Southwest Airlines** (Chengdu) – SZ
- **China Eastern** (Shanghai) – MU
- **Xiamen Airlines** (Xiamen) – MF
- **Xinjiang Airlines** (Urumqi) – XO

There are other domestic airlines including the small GP China General Aviation Corp., 3U Sichuan Airlines, WU Wuhan Airlines, 3Q Yunnan Airlines and ZY Zhongyuan Airlines.

CAAC continues to manage civil aviation, including safety standards, airports, licensing and international relations.

In terms of market share, tops is Air China, second is China Southern and third, China Eastern. Of the non-CAAC affiliates, Shanghai Airlines is the best. China United (CUA) flies old military aircraft.

One schedule for all CAAC affiliates is available. It comes out twice a year, in November and April and has been found on sale in some airports. It is easier to get at Chinese airline offices abroad than in China.

CAAC affiliates have booking offices in major tourist hotels. If you are flying with a Chinese airline, you should be able to make domestic reservations through Air China or China Eastern in North America. You should be able to make reservations 15 days to three months before a flight.

Most flights have only economy class. Hot food has been served on some flights, but food is usually cold, edible and unconventional: for example, Southwest Airlines' box lunch was shrimp chips, sponge cake, plain roll, spicy beef jerky and sausage in pastry which would have been better hot but it was okay; Xinjiang Airlines has served cold, smoked fish, chicken and corned beef, a hot rice dish, three kinds of pastry and an apple. If any domestic airline is responsible for unscheduled overnight stopovers, hotel accommodation will be arranged by the carrier free of charge. (But you might have to insist.)

Buying airline tickets is not always easy and you may have to fly stand-by. Because many travelers book more than one flight in order to insure a seat, keep trying. Rumor has it that seats are saved until the last minute for VIPs.

FLYING CHINA'S FRIENDLY SKIES

China is buying many new planes, opening convenient booking offices, and building or expanding airports.

Some planes are small and uncomfortable (especially for big foreigners). Some have broken seat belts and luggage bins that fall open. Cabin crews are not always careful about safety checks, but safety is improving. The domestic airlines also need to learn a lot about public relations and computers. You can book return flights and a whole itinerary now to major cities. Aviation has expanded so quickly there is a shortage of trained crews. It has had 30% increases in passenger volume yearly and flies over 30 million passengers a year.

If any domestic airline cancels a flight, you get a full **refund**. If a passenger asks for a refund 24 hours before flight departure, the cancellation fee is 10%. If you fail to cancel before flight time there is a 50% refund. Refunds can only be made at the place of purchase or a place approved by CAAC. Full refunds on international tickets are made if you cancel before check-in time.

Foreign airlines also fly to China but have no domestic services. Not all can sell seats in China, not even on their own planes. Only some like

APPROXIMATE FLIGHT TIMES FROM BEIJING

Flying time depends on the type of aircraft used and routing.
Beijing to:

Baotou	80 minutes
Beihai	three hours, 10 minutes
Changsha	two hours
Changzhou	one hour, 50 minutes
Chongqing	two hours, 10 minutes
Dalian	one hour
Fuzhou	two hours, 30 minutes
Guangzhou	three hours
Guilin	two hours, 25 minutes
Haikou	three hours, 25 minutes
Hangzhou	one hour, 40 minutes
Harbin	one hour, 40 minutes
Hohhot	one hour, 10 minutes
Hong Kong	three hours
Huangshan	two hours, five minutes
Kunming	three hours, 10 minutes
Luoyang	one hour, 35 minutes
Nanchang	two hour
Nanjing	one hour, 35 minutes
Nanning	three hours, five minutes
Ningbo	two hours, five minutes
Shanghai	one hour, 40 minutes
Shantou	two hours, 30 minutes
Shenzhen	two hours, 45 minutes
Tianjin	25 minutes
Urumqi	three hours, 25 minutes
Wuhan	one hour, 45 minutes
Xiamen	two hours, 25 minutes
Xi'an	one hour, 45 minutes

United Airlines and Lufthansa will accept credit card payments for tickets. It is difficult or impossible to endorse a plane ticket from one airline to another.

Airline Miscellany

No babies under 10 days of age and no pregnant women almost due are allowed to fly. An infant under two not occupying a separate seat and accompanied by an adult is charged 10% of the adult fare. Children two to 12 are charged 50% of the adult fare.

If a checked bag is lost, the compensation will not exceed Y40 per kilogram. If you want more, you can buy luggage insurance.

Some Chinese airlines operate international flights similar to other international airlines, but with minimal services. Flights have cheap headsets, unenthusiastic cabin crews, alcoholic drinks in first class, beer in economy, and movies.

No smoking is allowed on all international flights and flights under six hours.

Passengers holding international tickets with confirmed space on the first connecting flight should get free meals and hotel accommodations provided by CAAC within 24 hours after their arrival at the connecting points.

Helicopter service is available in some cities depending on demand.

TRAINS

China has a vast network of railways, linking every provincial and regional capital (except Lhasa and Haikou) to Beijing. Railway lines have been burgeoning and many are being electrified. Diesel is replacing steam. Service has improved, with air-conditioned express tourist trains between Nanjing and Shanghai, Hangzhou and Wuxi, Shenyang and Dalian, Jinan and Qingdao, Shenzhen and Shaoguan, Beijing and Chengde, Guizhou and Anshun, etc.

ALL ABOARD THE IRON ROOSTER!

*China is buying better passenger trains, and improvements have started to show. Some travel agents have chartered air-conditioned coaches for their clients. A **luxury train trip** along the Silk Road is organized by Conference Travel of Canada and China Express Railway Service.*

Train tickets can be obtained through hotels or travel agencies (usually for a service fee) or at the railway station. When the price of railway tickets is cheaper than airplanes, it is difficult to get a ticket. In some big cities, special ticket windows are provided for foreigners, but be prepared for frustration and arguing. Lineups can be long, especially for hard class.

Try to buy your tickets at least six days in advance. Travel agencies can usually reserve soft class train tickets a week in advance. It is cheaper but riskier to buy tickets for the current or next day at train stations. There might not be seats left, especially for overnight rides and on holidays. Seasoned travelers say the best time to queue for day train tickets is just before lunch. When the clerks return half an hour later, you'll be first in line.

Scalpers around train stations and in some coffee shops can buy tickets for you with a big markup. While this is illegal, everybody does it; but some scalpers might not be seen again. You pay upon receipt. Some foreign travelers have been successful using cheaper tickets bought by Chinese friends because conductors don't care. Travelers have boarded trains using platform tickets and then bought tickets from the conductor on the train. This, however, is risky, as space may not be available.

Hard & Soft Class

Trains are classified as special express, regular, and suburban. Passengers usually have a choice of hard and soft-class seats or berths. The most comfortable are in the middle of a coach, away from noise and wheel vibrations. State your preference when you buy.

Prepaid tourists usually travel **soft-class berth**, which can be almost the same price as going by plane. The berths are the height of bourgeois comfort if you have air conditioning. Compartments usually have lace curtains, a table with lamp, an overhead fan, and sleeping spaces with bedding and towels for four people on two upper and two lower bunks. An overhead loft stores large suitcases.

It is best to take a small overnight bag if you are sleeping on the train. Most group luggage is stored at one end of the car and may not be accessible.

Ask the conductor to lock your door when you go to the dining car. The plug for the fan (if you have one) and the switch for the loudspeaker are frequently under the table. Dining-car food is edible and, on some trains, surprisingly good, but simple. Passengers usually give their orders to a steward beforehand and are notified when their food is ready.

Six people share one compartment of **hard-class** berths in the same amount of space as soft class. Berths are padded and tiered in threes, the middle berth being the best.

Hard class is noisy and dirty, with other passengers smoking, frequently clearing throats and spitting on the floor. You cannot turn off the loudspeaker, which starts at six am. Sheets and warm blankets are provided, but if you get on between terminals, these may have been used.

Passengers can eat in the dining car, but can also buy food from vendors on the train itself before the train departs. Don't expect gourmet fare! Food from vendors can be downright unappetizing, like a box of rice with pork (including the skin and hair). Bring your own cups of instant noodles. Steaming hot water is available in each car. Hard-class seats are very crowded. Accommodations can be upgraded after the train is underway if space is available. The conductor is usually in the middle coach.

Train Basics

Train schedules should be available in three-star hotels, or at foreigners counters in railway stations. Give yourself plenty of time to find your train. Platforms are not marked in English, but the train number is posted. The destination of each coach should be marked on its side. Expect train stations to be very crowded with people sleeping on the floors overnight. Expect people to push and shove. Do protect small children.

Like travel on overnight ferries, men and women are assigned compartments without regard to sex, even in soft class. If this arrangement bothers you, ask for another compartment. The Chinese are used to such travel. Tourist groups usually sort themselves out. I have never heard of sexual harassment on a train in China, so don't feel nervous.

To protect valuables, do not use your purse as a pillow. Things have been stolen that way. Put your valuables in a money belt around your waist or around your neck under your clothes. Tie your camera to your arm.

Toilets look like they've been hosed down and not scrubbed. You might want to use a disinfectant. On coaches reserved for foreign tourists, you can be sure of toilet paper and soap (in a common soap dish). Soft-class travelers on some trains now have a choice of western toilet seats or a squat.

A washroom in each car offers several sinks with running water. Many prepaid tourists wait until they arrive at their hotels before washing. However, sometimes on arrival early in the morning, hotel rooms have not been vacated, and tourists are taken sightseeing instead.

Some coaches on express trains are air-conditioned. No smoking is allowed in some coaches but this is not enforced unless you complain. Baggage might be checked for inflammable and dangerous articles. Luggage is frequently pushed in and out of train windows to a waiting guide because it's easier than hauling it.

On some trains, the dining car becomes a disco or karaoke bar at night.

Do not discard your ticket. You might be asked for it again at the exit gate of your arrival station, but then again you might not. That's the way China is. Regulations keep changing.

Round trip train tickets cannot be booked. So consider booking the next leg of your journey immediately upon arrival.

Long-Distance Buses

Air-conditioned buses and mini-buses speed along many routes, some of them two-tier for almost horizontal sleeping. Ask about the kind of bus you will be taking because some buses are small, hard- seated, and very crowded, with little luggage space except on the roof. They can be uncomfortable for big foreigners, especially if you have to stand. I have heard horror stories of windows impossible to close in freezing weather, and carbon monoxide poisoning because of bad maintenance. So check your bus before you commit yourself.

The main problem with buses are traffic jams getting in and out of cities and onto highways. It is usually better to take a train although China has built many good expressways. Still, buses are good for seeing the countryside and meeting people – but you have to be strong and adventurous. You should book your trip ahead of time at a bus station, Overseas Chinese hotels, or at travel agencies. I strongly urge you to take your own food. These buses stop at dumpy restaurants with a busload of travelers and you can't expect service immediately. As soon as the driver is finished, the bus leaves. Toilets are usually primitive.

Some youth travel agencies have tours by tourist bus in Fujian and Guangdong, a great way to see the country.

Hitchhiking

Backpackers have hitched rides with truck drivers. On-your-own tourists in isolated spots have been able to get rides on tour buses (sometimes free). Its a matter of luck. If you have connections with foreign experts, etc., you might be able to use staff cars.

One way to hitchhike is to wait at the door of your hotel. Stop anyone getting into a vehicle and ask for a ride. Or you can go out to the main road and try to wave vehicles down. You could have a note in Chinese asking for a free ride or you could offer to pay for the ride. Always ask beforehand for the price. Hitchhikers have been treated to meals by hospitable drivers, but should offer to pay. I was once picked up by the police and treated to a banquet. They even refused my cigarettes.

As a precaution, hitchhikers should make a record of the vehicles license number. And avoid drunk or suspicious-looking drivers as you would in North America.

BICYCLES

These can be rented from hotels and bicycle-rental shops. Some rented bicycles have fallen apart. Check everything at the shop. You will probably have to leave a deposit or some identification, butdo not leave a passport. Clerks have accepted old student cards, expired drivers licenses, anything with a photo. Guard your receipt.

Always park in a supervised parking lot, otherwise your bicycle may disappear. Make a note of the license number and where you left it. Put on some colored tape or a tag so you can find it quickly again among hundreds of identical bicycles. Most cities have bicycle lanes, and some have streets forbidden to bicycles.

If you are staying for any length of time, you might want to buy a bicycle and sell it when you leave.

Officially all bicycles should have bicycle licenses, but most foreigners have had no trouble without one. Some people have taken their own bicycles into China. (To ship a bicycle by train means having to go to the train station a day ahead of time and, at the other end, spending time finding it.) Spare parts for foreign makes are a problem.

You can take a group tour by motorcycle or bicycle, but these tours are not cheap. A truck carrying spare parts follows behind and picks up tired bikers.

Some adventurous bikers have traveled from town to town on their own. Please be aware of the problems. Roads might not be paved. If you get into an accident, you might not be able to communicate. You might secure only substandard accommodations. You might need alien travel permits for some areas. Check about licenses if you want to travel by motorcycle. Police hassle motorcyclists.

For safety's sake, do not travel alone. If you do, let me know of your experiences.

GETTING AROUND CITIES & TOWNS
Walking
Something has to be said about walking because of all the bicycles and cars: crossing streets can be dangerous! Try to let a native upstream run interference. Cross at lights. Some cities have overpasses, so use them.

Motorscooter Rickshaws
For two people or more, these are cheaper than taxis and can take lots of luggage, but they're not comfortable, with much swerving and bouncing. Prices are often fixed and paid in advance.

Bicycle Rickshaws
Built for two, these cost very little or a lot in tourist areas, but you can only go short distances. Please consider the driver and get off and walk up steep slopes. Bicycle rickshaws are ideal for leisurely sightseeing in places like Hangzhou. They are on the increase even in Beijing, but taxis might

be cheaper. Please don't ride them in heavy motorized traffic since they can be dangerous. Agree on a price in advance, especially in tourist towns. Make sure the price is for the ride, not for each person.

Be careful about your belongings as thieves on bicycles have been known to grab purses and cameras from these *san-lien che*.

Taxis

Taxis are normally outside tourist hotels, railway stations, airports, passenger-ship quays and places frequented by visitors. You can ask someone to telephone for a taxi, and you can also flag down a taxi on the street in many cities.

If taxis are not easy to find and you have several stops to make, it's better to hire one by the half-day or full day. You can also pay by the meter (or odometer) with a charge for waiting. Always agree on the price before you go. Usually you need not pay for a meal for a driver if you are near his home base, but you might invite him to a meal if you are a long way from his home base. Restaurants and hotels have sections for staff if you don't want to eat together.

If you need a taxi early in the morning or for a full or half day, it is best to make a reservation at a taxi stand the night before. Taxi companies also have buses for larger groups.

Not all taxis have meters, but hotels should know prices. While most drivers are honest, a few have added imaginary waiting time in Chinese to the receipts, or charged higher rates. If you feel cheated, don't pay, and ask cheerfully for someone to call a policeman. If you have already paid, get a receipt, take the drivers name and license number, and complain to the manager or dispatcher at his/her taxi stand or to the local tourism administration. Ask your consulate for advice. Some cities have a taxi complaint office. Letters to China Daily have resulted in penalties for the driver and apologies from the taxi company.

Another ploy is to pay what you consider the proper fare, get out, and leave. If the driver follows you, negotiate a settlement. Some drivers charge extra because they have to pay the touts who bring them customers. Try to avoid the middle man.

Some travelers have been greeted at railway stations and airports by a pack of touts grabbing at their bags, a frightening experience indeed, especially if you don't know what these strangers are doing. If you need help with bags and don't mind paying more than a regular taxi, settle on a price, and go along with them, but do not stray too far from your luggage. There is usually a line of legitimate taxis with meters waiting outside.

You can hire a taxi to take you from city to city, but you have to pay the fare back to the driver's base. Ask ahead of time for the approximate fare and distance and if you need an alien travel permit. The problem is military zones.

Public Tourist Buses

These are available in a few cities around railway stations. They go to some tourist attractions with a detailed commentary in Chinese. They are a good bargain if you take along a guide book. It's best to take your own lunch to save time eating in restaurants, and make sure you know how long your bus is staying at each stop. Write down the bus number so you can find it again. Make sure you agree on a price before you hop in, and be aware that some drivers have threatened to leave their passengers behind at tourist attractions unless they pay more.

Shuttle Buses

Shuttles are available at a few hotels. Take them to airports, Friendship Stores, and a few tourist attractions.

Public City Buses

These are usually oppressively overcrowded, especially during rush hour and Sundays. But they are cheap and often your only means of transportation. Hotel personnel can tell you which bus to take. Some cities have bus maps in English, or you can take a map with you and point. Fellow passengers are usually friendly and helpful. Some public mini-buses have set routes. They are more expensive than city buses but cheaper than taxis and you do get a seat. As in all crowded places, beware of pickpockets.

Subways

You can use subways in Beijing, Shanghai and Tianjin and maps are available. Other cities are building them. Walk down the stairs, pay about Y2, and choose your platform. Signs are in pin-yin; in Shanghai, they're also in English. If you avoid rush hour, they are a great way to get around.

Public Ferries & Tour Boats

China has some real antiques crossing harbors and rivers. They are cheap, but avoid them if they look too crowded and tippy. Fatal accidents with boats have recently been blamed on overloading and drunken crews.

Self-drive Cars

You have to be a Chinese resident to get a driver's license in China. You need a medical certificate and your own drivers license translated into Chinese. There is a written test and you are allowed to bring your own translator. You cant use an international license to drive in China.

You can however make arrangements to drive your own car into China but it coss you about $1,000. China Sports Travel organizes car rallies from Paris to Beijing.

Most roads are open to foreigners. Four-to-six-lane highways are being built: #107 goes from Beijing south to Shenzhen, #312 from Shanghai west to Yining (Xinjiang.) Travel agents can arrange groups of self-drive jeeps and cars on the Silk Road and in Tibet.

Wheelchair-confined Travelers

Only a few hotels have been set up for people in wheelchairs, with wider bathroom doors and bars near toilets. A lot of helpful hands are available, however, and many hotels have ramps. Most of those are in top-of-the-line hotels. If these facilities are crucial to your visit, contact these hotels to make sure a room is available for you.

Among the hotels with lower sinks, bathtub bars, etc., for wheelchair-confined travelers: in Beijing, the Capital, China World, Guangdong Regency, Hilton, Holiday Inns, Kempinski, Shangri-La, Swissotel; in Chongqing, the Holiday Inn; in Dalian, the Holiday Inn; in Fuzhou, the Lakeside; in Guangzhou, the Garden, Holiday Inn, and International; in Guilin, the Sheraton; in Kunming, the Green Lake Hotel and Holiday Inn; in Shanghai, the Garden, Hilton, Holiday Inn and Westin; in Shenzhen, the Forum and Shangri-La; in Tianjin, the Hyatt; in Xiamen, the Holiday Inn; in Xian, the Garden, Holiday Inn, Hyatt, Lee Garden, and Sheraton.

CHECKLIST FOR TRAVELERS ON THEIR OWN

• *Fax your hotel before you arrive to arrange transport; give them your flight number or train and coach numbers. Someone at your destination should hold up a sign with your name or the hotel's name on it. Most hotels charge for picking you up. If you have less than a day, you could also ask the hotel or a travel agency to reconfirm or book the next stages of your travel.*

• *Consult your hotel travel service or a travel agency about the next leg of your trip, reconfirming plane tickets or booking train tickets.*

• *For your day of departure, book a taxi and if there are no porters, ask if the driver can carry your luggage to the train platform or check-in counter. If the driver cannot and you have loads of luggage, ask the hotel to help you. The hotel might send a bellman with you and you might only need to pay a tip.*

9. SHOPPING

China is noted for its unique handicrafts. In an increasingly mechanized world, it is refreshing to find that it is still producing good arts and crafts in its time-honored tradition like hand-knotted carpets, paintings, embroidery, porcelain, cloisonne, stone carvings, and feather paintings. It is a good place to buy Chinese antiques too, little pieces of history. Lower grades of silk might be cheaper in North America but higher grades are cheaper in China.

The most important things to remember about shopping in China are:

• Always say, "That's too expensive. Can you give me a better price?" Haggling is expected.

• For the best prices, always check prices in several shops and markets.

• Your guide will want to take you shopping to specific stores. The travel agency gets commissions or else owns the store. You will not get the best prices and I have found some items nine times the price of a government arts and crafts store. Try to go to the stores in this book. I don't get a commission.

• As a general rule, the more Chinese shoppers there are in a shop, the better the prices probably are. If foreign tourists are the only customers, beware.

• Shop where there are many other stores or stalls of the same kind. You can move on to competitors if you can't get the prices you want.

• Government stores are guaranteed, with reasonable prices fixed by the local tourism bureau or administration. If customers have solid evidence of misrepresentations, you should be able to get your money back. You can also try to appeal to the tourism bureau for mediation and a copy of their list of approved stores. Even in some of these shops, you can get a five percent discount if you ask.

• At government stores, clerks tend to ignore you. At private stores, clerks are more aggressive and ask you to offer a price. Some private merchants are so aggressive, theyve scared customers away. One of the worst places is at the Terracotta Army in Xi'an, where little children charm tourists out of their money, and women hard sell beautiful jackets with tears in their eyes and grab you by the arm. In Xi'an, I bargained one merchant down to ten and then he insisted it was ten U.S. dollars!

- There are fakes and misrepresentations, plastic pearls passed off as real, substitutes called "jade," and counterfeit U.S. cigarettes and antiques. Your approved stores should be okay. Elsewhere, do not believe labels. Check the quality carefully yourself.

- An American "size nine" doesn't mean a thing in China. If you are buying for yourself, you should try on clothes for size. If you are buying clothes for someone else, you should have their measurements. Wool and cotton products will probably shrink if washed in hot water.

- Check everything carefully for flaws.

- With street peddlers who carry their wares with them, go off on a side street or to some less crowded place so you can shop and think at the same time, if possible. Even peddlers with stalls might take you into their homes and show you things. You can haggle better this way, without people screaming at you. But take precautions. Tell others where you're going. Though I've heard of nothing adverse happening in China, you should never go off with strangers alone anywhere in the world.

- International name brands are probably more expensive in China unless the goods are made there. They are aimed at the fashionable Chinese consumer.

- Do not expect exchanges except in government stores and department stores.

- Consider possible laundering problems before you buy. Some ethnic skirts could lose their pleats, and the paper lining of jackets and baby blankets from Xi'an might disintegrate if washed.

- The export of antiques from Tibet is forbidden. Your purchases there, if detected, could be seized.

- Not all stores can crate and ship goods outside of China. Ask before you buy. In some cases, the local U.S. consulate might be able to help you if the goods shipped to you are not what you ordered.

- Save your sales slips so you can argue with Customs officials in your own country. Receipts are in Chinese with English numerals, so make a note of what each refers to. Put on tags of your own at the time of purchase to remind you where you bought, how much you paid, and what it is.

- Clothing and other items imported from elsewhere for sale in China are, of course, cheaper in the country of origin. Some of what you see may have been made in Hong Kong or Taiwan.

• When comparing Chinese prices with those elsewhere, don't forget to include the sales tax at home and the rate of duty. China doesn't add a sales tax.
• Prices are cheapest in the city of manufacture.

ANTIQUES

Quality antiques are not cheap, but Chinese antiques are usually cheaper here than in your own country or Hong Kong. Officially, antiques made between 1795 and 1949 are not allowed out of China unless they have a red wax seal on them. Only a few stores are allowed to sell anything for export made before 1795.

In practice Customs officials rarely search the bags of departing visitors. Customs did catch one foreigner trying to take out old porcelain and confiscated the pieces until she could take them to the **Arts Objects Clearance Office** on her return to Beijing (which she later did). These offices are in the Beijing Friendship Store and in Shanghai, unfortunately with very inconvenient hours and only open two days a week.

The usual rule is, if you like it, and want to pay the price, then buy it.

The best antique shopping are the Sunday morning street markets in Tianjin, Shanghai and Beijing: old clocks, watches, cricket boxes, porcelains, porcelain bird feeders, curtain holders, porcelain soap dishes, jewelery, embroidery, and even Qing army boots.

You can usually tell reproductions because they're mass-produced and sold in almost every stall, for about the same price. These reproductions could make good gifts too — if the prices are low enough. But there are also one-of-a-kind treasures.

Daily markets with fixed stalls are in Beijing, Guangzhou, Guilin, Shanghai, Tianjin, Tunxi, Xian and elsewhere. Bird and fish markets are fun, and could have some interesting and cheap curios and crafts too.

Antiques and crafts are also found for sale in some museums.

Some antique stores might look like government antique stores but are actually contracted to private dealers. You can haggle and in fact you should start at a quarter of the first asking price. To prove to your own Customs people that what you have bought is a duty-free antique, you have to get a receipt stating its age. Only antiques in government stores are guaranteed.

FACTORY STORES

Every arts and crafts factory has a showroom where visitors can buy but prices could be higher than elsewhere. Some showrooms are open all the time, others are open by appointment only. Aim for factories that have overruns from export orders. They should have western styles, possibly more to your liking. Group tours sometimes get discounts.

FRIENDSHIP STORES

Friendship Stores are government stores set up for foreigners but now anyone can shop there and most are like any other modern department store. At least one Friendship Store serves every city. Prices are about the same or slightly higher than other Chinese stores, but the goods are of better quality and some items are unavailable elsewhere. Government stores have a reputation for honesty. If they know something is fake, clerks usually tell you.

In addition to arts and crafts, the larger Friendship Stores have textiles, television sets, watches, bicycles, sewing machines, lace, silk jewelry bags, cosmetics, herbal medicines, food, jewelry, thermos bottles, camera film, cameras, jackknives, flashlights, cashmere sweaters, and silk blouses - just about anything. Friendship Stores have locally-made goods for sale too.

The best Friendship Stores are in Guangzhou, Beijing, and Shanghai. The Beijing Friendship Store delivers goods to your hotel, takes telephone orders, and ships. Some privately-run stores are using the "Friendship" name and reputation, but they are not government run with guarantees.

Department Stores (*shang chang*) frequently have arts and crafts, too. Look for good buys in clothing, gloves, sneakers, down, furs, novelties, etc. Some styles and qualities are better than in the Friendship stores.

PEDDLERS OF MINORITY HANDICRAFTS

It is usually more meaningful to buy handicrafts (usually embroidery) direct from the maker in her village. Walk into any minority village, and someone will probably show up with something to sell. Prices are best here. A good embroidered jacket from the Miao nationality costing $60 in a Kaili village would probably sell in New York City for a couple of hundred dollars. If you can't get to the village, look for a peddler. They usually hover around the entrances to hotels in Kaili and Guilin.

HOTEL STORES

Stores in fancy joint-venture hotels are not cheap, but you can find some of the best clothing styles, fabrics, and antiques. In three-star hotels, you might also be able to find a few pieces with name brands like Oleg Cassini, L.L. Bean, Victoria's Secret, and Land's End. Some styles have not yet reached North America. But sizes and color ranges are limited.

Hotels aimed at Japanese tourists like the Garden in Shanghai or the Friendship in Hangzhou have excellent quality and high priced goods. The Sheraton Hua Ting has had some of the best prices for cloisonne.

MARKETS

Markets with lots of similiar shops or stalls, either indoors or out, have the cheapest prices and are sometimes good quality. You have to be extremely careful and haggle. They might have genuine name brands and real jade carvings. Markets sell everything: fruit and vegetables, clothes, antiques, curios, pets, flowers and handicrafts. With no changing rooms, people buying jeans have to try them on over their own trousers.

Wholesale Markets are also a good place to purchase gifts. Groups of silk factories have banded together to form one such market outside Hangzhou. Groups of sweater manufacturers have done the same outside of Ningbo. Other factories have probably done the same elsewhere. Prices and selection are generally good.

HAGGLING

The chance of bargaining down prices is better in China than in Hong Kong. Haggling is imperative in privately-run stores and markets unless you want to pay three or four times the going rate. Check government Friendship Stores for current prices and try to beat them. Dont expect guides to be on your side; some have been scolded or beaten for telling tourists the price is too high. Prices might fall quicker if you offer U.S. cash.

The secret is to know prices, not to show any enthusiasm for the thing you want to buy, and not to buy the first thing you see. At markets, many stalls sell the same things. If you are asked what you want to pay, suggest a ridiculously low amount - a quarter of the price. Then walk away pretending you are not interested. The seller might counter with hand motions for you to give a higher bid and you could come up a bit. Start to move away again and look at the same thing in the next stall. It is a guessing game - the seller trying to decide how badly you want it, and you trying to decide the bottom line for the seller.

The most successful time to haggle is when you're the first customer of the day, no other customers are around, when the weather is bad, and the merchant wants to go home.

Shopping with U.S. dollars in cash could bring prices down if the difference between the official and black market rates is wide. In the mid-1990s, it didn't matter in Beijing, but in Shanghai and Hangzhou, street markets and some small private stores were giving at least a two per cent discount on such purchases.

I usually set myself a limit, like Y60. Peddlers laugh but occasionally I get something good at that price.

HOW TO CHOOSE

Before you go to China, learn about quality in museums and stores. If you are a serious shopper, plan your trip so you can see how a favorite craft is made. Locally-made crafts are listed under each destination in this book.

In the factory, you can study how the pieces are made andwhat makes a good piece. Will the wood or lacquer crack in dry, centrally heated houses? You should handle some of the best pieces. Feel the weight and the surface texture. Compare these with ordinary quality goods. For reproductions, study the originals in nearby museums. Remember also that handmade articles are different - of course! So before you buy, check carefully, not just for flaws, but for the rendering that you like best.

Generally speaking, consider (1) the amount of work involved in the production - the finer and more intricate something is, the better; (2) good proportions, lines, balance, and color; (3) how closely it represents what it is supposed to represent: (4) the quality of the material - will it chip? and (5) whether it will be a joy forever, or will you easily tire of it? Primitive art doesnt have to be well proportioned or intricate.

Crafts can also be made-to-order, but most Chinese factories are not set up for easy ordering. The cross-stitch factory in Yantai can make good replicas of photographs, for example. These of course take a lot of time. The most difficult part of such an exercise is getting the craftsman to understand just what you're looking for.

Most general tours include at least one handicraft factory and always one Friendship or Arts and Crafts store. Many cities also have handicraft institutes where new crafts are developed and craftspeople are trained.

If you are more interested in handicrafts than temples, it is best to take an individual or special-interest tour. On a regular tour, the average tourist will be back on the bus waiting while you're still talking about the iron content in glazes.

MYTHOLOGICAL & HISTORICAL SUBJECTS IN ARTS & CRAFTS

• Poet Shi Yung of the late Spring and Autumn Period has a knot on top of his head and a sword at his back.
• Wei Tou is the guardian of Buddhism and of the Goddess of Mercy.
• Guan Yin was originally a god, but in recent sculpture, always the Goddess of Mercy. She is depicted with children, or carrying a cloud duster (like a horsetail whip), or with many heads and arms, or with a vase.
• Princess Wen Chen was the Chinese princess who married a Tibetan king and took Buddhism to Tibet.

• Li Shi-zen was the Ming dynasty author of the classic book on medicinal herbs. He is shown carrying herbs in a basket and a hoe.
• God of Longevity is an old man with a peach.
• God of Wealth is a well-dressed man with a scepter.
• Laughing Buddha or Maitreya is fat and jolly and sometimes is surrounded by children or standing alone with raised hands.
• Eight Taoist Genii - see pages 57-58.
• Fa Mu-lan is the famous woman general who inspired Maxine Hong Kingston's *The Woman Warrior.*
• Characters from classical Chinese novels: *Water Margin, The Dream of the Red Chamber, Pilgrimage to the West.*

BUYING SOMETHING UNIQUELY CHINESE

China has a good variety of novelties, things distinctively Chinese to take back to your nieces and nephews and bridge buddies. Porcelain shards made into small pendants or boxes that can be stood up for display are good. We found shard pendants for Y20 each in the government antique store in Hangzhou, a good way to recycle broken pottery.

There are cute tea pots in unusual shapes, hand-painted scrolls, curved daggers for paper openers, and hand-stitched quilts (in American styles). Cork carvings are traditional and pretty: some are tiny but some are as big as three by six feet. Look for finely embroidered pictures, horn or root carvings, carvings of whimsical animals, silk bags shaped like little children, multi-fabric pictures, and balls within balls.

There's all kinds of lacquerware, bamboo, and feather craft. Zhejiang province has some great screens with stone pictures.

Acupuncture dolls are about ten inches high with genuine acupuncture needles and an instruction booklet (in Chinese) for your medical friends. If these are too expensive, try acupuncture posters, found in bookstores are cheap. Health balls to improve blood circulation and avoid arthritis are good for older people.

Posters, postcards, and comic books are fun and cheap, and so is a map of the world showing China in the center, or of Canada and the U.S. in Chinese characters. There are childrens story books in English or showing Chinese characters like our ABCs. If you're in a foreign language bookstore, youll find a great many books in English (cheap), all printed in China. Book lovers must visit Liulichang in Beijing to look at samples of fine Chinese printing.

Some museum reproductions are quite good and not too expensive. Check out the retail store in any museum you visit.

You can buy T-shirts hand-painted to order and chops with rubber stamps both made by artists in hotel lobbies. There are lots of cheap souvenir pins with pandas or names of tourist sites. Consider Chinese kites, traditional baby bonnets of silk or rayon trimmed with fur ears to make a baby look like a tiger kitten, Mao caps, folding scissors, and battery-operated toys.

Avoid stuffed animals unless you know what's inside.

Bottles for snuff, and usually with an ivory spoon, is a 250-year old artistic medium. Old ones are collectors items, the most valuable made of carved pink coral and amber decorated with lacquer and pearl. Many are made of Peking glass. Since early in the 19th century, they were painted on the inside surface, an art that continues to this day. Obviously, these pieces are meant for show, not use. These, along with the round balls also painted inside, exhibit a great deal of skill as the painter must adjust the perspective to the shape of the medium.

Cloth wall hangings of Chinese zodiac animals are best from Beijing and Lanzhou. Xi'an's are not as good. Cheap tiger slippers for babies are good buys in X'ian.

Cloisonne comes in lovely ladies, beads, bracelets, vases, thimbles, scissors, jack-knives, nail clippers, and pill boxes. Silk is made into ties, cute, cheap panties and boxer shorts.

There are fancy gold-trimmed chopsticks from Fuzhou, and stone chops with rubber stamps of your name. Hong Kong visitors take back Chinese wines, vodka and Chinese teas.

Vests with appliques have been a hit with tourists in Xi'an, where they are cheaper than elsewhere in China.

Tailors are not as good as in other places in Asia, like Hong Kong, and clothes take longer to make. But they are cheap! Don't bother having clothes tailored here unless a tailor is recommended by Western friends and you have a picture or sample of what you want made. Even Shanghai tailors have lost the art.

Furs, cashmere sweaters, down coats, and leather jackets are bargains, but please, please, don't buy any endangered species. A Hong Kong furrier said the quality of the tanning of a lot of Chinese skins is not very good and might later stink when wet, so check items carefully.

Live plants, birds, and animals: Check with your embassy. Usually these are not allowed into your country without specific certificates, not easily obtainable outside your country.

China has some fine musicians, and music lovers might like their recordings. Pirated compact discs, many of questionable quality, can be purchased in street markets, under the counter, for about Y15 each. If you're caught with these at Customs, however, they will be confiscated.

Movies and slides of Chinese tourist attractions are available. Film in 16 and 35 millimeter sizes, as well as video cassettes, can be purchased.

If you know you're going to buy something fragile, you should bring your own bubble wrap for packing fragile porcelains and crafts.

10. SPORTS & RECREATION

China, which tried very hard to host the 2000 Olympics, is sports-crazy. The favorite spectator sport is **soccer** and probably the most popular participatory sport is **billiards**, which you see everywhere. Soccer is a passion and like elsewhere has deteriorated into fights. The season in Beijing is May to October; in the south the season is all year round. In Shanghai it's played at **Hong Kou Stadium**; in Beijing it's at **Workers' Stadium** near City Hotel. Just follow the cheering.

The favorite traditional sport at which the Chinese excel is **ping-pong**. It is less popular than billiards, and the national tournament is usually in May. Another traditional sport is **kung fu**, which has been practised since the Tang dynasty at Shaolin Temple outside of Zhengzhou. For Chinese **martial arts**, look for announcements of demonstrations in tourism materials. In Beijing, try the **Beijing Wuyi Diyuan Theater** and the **Huaxia Cultural and Martial Arts Center**. The most important place is of course **Shaolin Temple** itself, which gives demonstration and courses. See *Zhengzhou*.

The sport taking the most space in recent years has been **golf**, but few Chinese actually play; the courses are mainly for foreigners especially Japanese. You can make arrangements to play through the top hotels. Zhongshan has hosted World Cup golf. Good courses are also in Zhuhai, Tianjin, Shenzhen, Shanghai, Beijing and a growing number of cities.

Many sports now emerging are new to China. There's **hot-air ballooning** and **gliding** in Anyang, and gliding in Jiayuguan. Chinese **climbers** and others can attack over 60 peaks, including Qomolangma (Everest). **Skiing** has been slow in developing but there are now four public resorts and one training resort (Jilin province). The best is at **Yabuli** in Heilongjiang province, which hosted the 1996 Asian Winter Games. It has a 2,496-meter cable car and a five kilometer run, with bars and international telephones on the slopes, restaurants, rentals, and an inn with a swimming pool. For more information, contact the **Heilongjiang Season Travel Service**, *Tel. (0451) 2626594 or fax 2627844*. A year-round ski facility is the

Yulong Alpine Skiing Slope in Yunnan province. Heilongjiang and Jilin provinces have **ice hockey teams**.

American **football** has not developed much of a following. The Agricultural University has a team. A full-time high school for baseball players has started in Fengtai, a Beijing suburb, and there are 2,000 little leagues in China. **Baseball stadiums** are in Chengdu, Lanzhou, Shanghai and Guangzhou. **Rugby** has been developing so well that a team could be participating in Hong Kong's prestigeous Rugby Sevens soon. Beijing has an annual **Cricket Sixes** in the autumn with Chinese and expatriate teams. Salem Cigarettes sponsors international **tennis** and brings in Michael Chang. The **Beijing marathon** is run during the Spring Festival and there's nothing to stop you from running with it.

Participatory sports are few and far between. **Sailboarding** is in Qingdao, Xiamen, and Qinhuangdao. Sanya, Dalian and Qingdao have **scuba diving**. These water sports will increase with the development of resorts in the next two or three years. **White water rafting** is in the upper reaches of the Yangtze River in Sichuan and Qinghai, and in Dalian and Shaoguan. Many groups bring their own rafts, but China Sports can supply tents and bags.

The **Shanghai Acrobats** have a school for professionals with students from all over the country. If you have the right guanxi or connections, you might be able to wrangle a visit. Start with the manager at the Shanghai Centre, Shanghai, *Tel. 62798600*.

Horse racing is increasing. Events at the **Beijing Country Horse Racing Club** is not comfortable, however, because you sit on concrete steps. The minimum bet is five yuan. A board does display the odds and the same eight or ten horses race each time.

JOIN A CAMEL TREK!

*Travel agents like **China Sports Travel** can organize one-week **camel treks** in the Taklamakan Desert or take you riding with those most famous of horsemen, the Mongols.*

For those who want to play against Chinese teams, and many foreigners do, contact the China Sports Travel Service (see address in Using Travel Agents in Chapter 6, *Planning Your Trip*). On a less formal basis, contact your embassy or consulates, or the sports departments of international schools in China. Some foreigners who live in China organize their own sports teams and sometimes look for volunteers to join them. Ask the British Chamber of Commerce in Beijing.

The bulletin boards of supermarkets frequented by foreigners like **Welcome at the China World** or the **Holiday Inn Lido** in Beijing could have notices about the **Hash House Harriers** ("a drinking club with a running problem") orother sports programs.

For **gym machines**, your best bet is a good hotel. In Shanghai the Portman has a good health club. The Hilton's isn't bad at all.

Beijing has the **China North International Shooting Range** where you can shoot off weapons from pistols to bazookas for a price. It's near Badaling and the Ming tombs (*Tel. 9971368. 8:30 am to 5:30 pm daily*).

A tip for **hunters**: always ask for prices beforehand. If you kill something, it could be very, very expensive — thousands of dollars! There also isn't much wild game left. You can look into this yourself at the **Miyun Hunting Ground**, *Yaoxiang Valley, Xinchengzi Township, Miyun County, Tel. 9944472*, featuring hunting for hare, pheasant, and deer. This is just outside of Beijing. Hunting tours are arranged by China Sports Travel in Heilongjiang and Qinghai.

11. FOOD & DRINK

BACKGROUND

The infinite number of Chinese dishes, flavors, textures, and methods of cooking meals makes eating exciting. The most famous cooking styles are Beijing, Cantonese, Shanghai, and Sichuan. There are also vegetarian and minority foods. Try the local food. Cantonese is best in Guangdong; Sichuan in Sichuan.

Chinese food is usually chopped up in thin, bite-size pieces, making knives unnecessary at the dinner table. The thinness is for quick cooking, using a minimum of fuel. Chinese food can also appear whole, like fish or pork hocks, but these can be easily separated by chopsticks. When poultry is cooked whole, it is chopped up before appearing at the table. Sometimes the bones are splintered so the food inside the bones can be reached. Do be careful.

HOW TO USE CHOPSTICKS

The bottom stick is held firmly by the base of the thumb and the knuckle of the ring finger. The top stick is the ONLY one that is moved and is held by the thumb and the index and middle fingers. The tip of the top stick should be brought toward the tip of the bottom one. Keep the tips even.

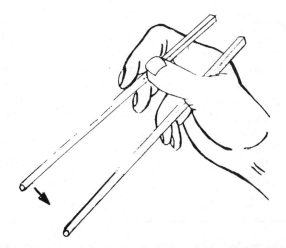

Chinese ingredients reflect the many periods of famine in Chinese history. Everything possible is eaten; nothing is wasted, not even chicken feet, duck tongues, jellyfish, and sea slugs – all famous delicacies.

The Chinese food served to most prepaid groups is usually adequate. If you want to eat better, you can pay more for better restaurants. If food is important, take a gourmet tour.

THINGS TO REMEMBER ABOUT RESTAURANTS IN CHINA

Until recently, restaurants were generally dumpy and tacky, a reflection of revolutionary attitudes. The new economic policies mean many new or renovated eating places, some very striking joint ventures in the gaudy Hong Kong style, and you can even find Starbuck's coffee. International-class hotels import ingredients and executive chefs. Some families and factories have also started restaurants with better food and service than state-run establishments.

The current make-a-profit-or-quit policy has forced improvements everywhere. Provincial and city-state tourism administrations are regulating restaurants. They should have a list of those fit for foreign tourists and if you have a complaint, contact the local tourism administration. Each restaurant should have a plaque that says it's been approved.

You might be put into private dining rooms in restaurants. These are less colorful but cleaner than eating with the masses, and usually cost more. However, you won't be stared at and can make a reservation.

Many state-run restaurants receive guests at 6 pm and then rush you out at 8:30 or 9 pm so the staff can go home. If you want to linger, choose a privately-owned restaurant or hotel coffee shop.

The days are long gone when you could trust waitresses to give you a correct bill. Hold on to the menu. Check the items, prices, and total.

ORDERING

Menus in restaurants for foreign visitors are usually in English and Chinese and a la carte. Some restaurants have a fixed menu too which you don't usually see. You have to ask. The fixed menu is served to tour groups, who need not worry about ordering. Individuals can order this too for an easy way out. Food on the fixed menu is relatively inexpensive and you get more variety for one or two people. Just say *feng fan* or *bao chan*. Menus change every day.

Gourmets avoid fixed menus and buffets because the food is not freshly cooked. But buffets, with their large number of different dishes, are good introductions. If you like a particular dish, ask the name so you can order it again.

Every restaurant has its specialties. These are probably more expensive but are sometimes not worth it. In Ningbo, they included red blood-raw clams! Aim also for local or regional dishes like fresh seafood if you're near an ocean. (Top-quality restaurants and hotels everywhere get seafood flown in and charge a lot more.) Meals in the countryside are usually excellent because the vegetables go from the garden to the wok.

It is best to eat with a large group of people to get a greater number of courses. Ten is ideal for a table, and you may get a private room thrown in. When ordering, two people should order three courses plus a starch; five people should order six courses plus a starch or two. Choose only one of poultry, fish, beef, pork, or vegetable. This will give you variety and abundance. If you find you are getting too much, order less next time.

If you need more courses, start the rounds again. If you've already chosen chicken, choose duck or goose. Vary tastes and textures: sweet, pepper-hot, salty, steamed, deep-fried, poached, boiled, roasted, baked in mud – the choice is endless.

Don't feel that every meal should be a banquet. The danger in China is overeating.

For popular restaurants, it is always best to reserve a table and even order meals ahead by telephone, especially for banquets. Restaurants for the masses won't take reservations. Ask your hotel's service desk to make reservations for you, telling the restaurant how much you want to pay but also approving the dishes suggested. One restaurant suggested bears' paws, a local delicacy and an endangered species, which no one ate. Most of the cost went into that one dish!

ELABORATE BANQUET DISHES

These should be ordered at least 24 hours ahead of time and a hefty charge is levied if you cancel.

Don't look for chop suey, chow mein with crispy noodles, or fortune cookies – those are Chinese-American dishes. China has fried noodles, but they are not the same. But with the new economic policies, anything could show up! And be aware that some wild animals used by the Chinese as food are, or may soon be, on the endangered species list. Please avoid them. Tell your host in advance that you don't want them.

SPECIAL DIETS

If you have special food preferences, let your guide know. For an upset stomach, order rice congee, which is rice cooked to a gruel consistency and flavored with salted egg, fermented bean curd, or whatever. Congee is easy on the stomach. Avoid fried dishes, spices, and dairy products. Eat dry crackers, arrowroot biscuits, and apple sauce.

If you have cankers in the mouth, try *hung pean* (chrysanthemum tea). It comes already sweetened in one-cup packages and is an old Chinese remedy.

People on general-interest tours should not expect special diets. Salt-free and diabetic diets are impossible. Chinese cooking uses more salt than western cooking. You could, however, go on a special tour for people with the same restrictions. Vegetarians usually manage on a general tour if you don't mind meat sauces. Vegetarian restaurants exist, but are not on the daily tourist route. Muslim restaurants also exist but so far no kosher cooking.

DESSERTS

Foreigners on tours will be offered fresh or canned fruits. If you're in Guangdong in May or June, ask for fresh **lichees** – or buy them in markets. Look for **pomelo**, especially in Guilin or Sichuan. It's a sweet grapefruit with a thick rind. Try **Hami melon** on the Silk Road. China also has ice cream, sweet red beans, sweet almond paste, and deep-fried crystallized apples and bananas. Aside from fruit, the Chinese do not have much of a tradition for desserts.

To be absolutely safe, eat only imported ice creams like Bud's, Wall's, and Movenpick's.

BEVERAGES

Most prepaid meals for foreigners include soft drinks, beer, and tea. Canned fruit juice, foreign-brand soft drinks, and liquor cost extra. Coca-Cola and Pepsi have bottling plants in China. The dreaded orange soda has been replaced in some cities by good, fresh, or reconstituted juices. **Laoshan** is the most famous mineral water but others are good.

Tsingdao beer is the favorite. It is made with barley, spring water, and hops from a German recipe. Five Star Beer has been designated by the government for state banquets. Local beers are usually good. Locally-brewed foreign beers are increasingly available. Moslem restaurants don't serve alcohol.

The Chinese consider the following three liquors to be the best: **Mao tai**, made from sorghum and wheat yeast, aged five or six years in Guizhou province, very potent and usually served in tiny goblets; **Fenjiu**, mellow and delicate flavor from Shanxi province; **Wuliangye**, five-grain spirit from southern Sichuan, with a fragrant and invigorating flavor.

The best Chinese wines are: **Yantai** red wine from Shandong, Chinese red wine from Beijing, **Shaoxing** red wine from Zhejiang, and **Longyan** rice wine from Fujian.

TRY CHINESE WINE

Foreign wines are very expensive; the Chinese version is cheaper. **Dynasty's White Riesling** *is tolerable.* **Qingdao Chardonay** *(the product of an Australian joint venture) and* **Dragon Seal's Cabernet Sauvignon** *(a French joint venture) are popular. You can get foreign wines mainly in the top hotels.*

Dairies are beginning to open up, but outside big cities, you only get **UHT**, powdered or canned milk. If you're uncertain of the pasteurization, order milk hot. It'll probably arrive sweetened. In Tibet you can get **yak butter tea** and in Yunnan, there's crispy fried goat's cheese.

Drinking tea is an art in China. Some springs are famous for their tea-making qualities. If you go to Hangzhou, try **long jing tea** there. A favorite tea in hot weather is **po li**. **Keemun** is good in the wintertime and when you've had greasy food. **Lu an** should help you sleep. **Oolong** is the most common tea in south China, while most foreigners like **jasmine**. Jasmine is said to heat the blood and should be balanced at the same meal with po li.

Every Chinese has a personal list of the four most famous green teas. **Long jing** (dragon well), **yun wu** (mist of the clouds), **mao hong** (red straw), and **bi lu chuen** (green spring) are probably among the most popular.

BREAKFASTS

Foreign tour groups in one- and two-star hotels usually receive western breakfast with greasy eggs. You also get lightly toasted bread, coffee, and fruit or canned juice. Four-star-and-up hotels now have western buffets or mixed western and Chinese buffets.

You can opt for Chinese breakfasts if enough people in the group want them. Chinese breakfasts differ regionally: **dim sum** or **rice congee** with peanuts, pickles, salt, or 1000-year-old eggs in south China; in the north, you could get lots of different **buns**, or 'oil sticks,' which are like foot-long doughnuts, deep-fried and delicious but hard to digest. You dip these in hot soy milk. In Shanghai, you might get gelatinous **rice balls** with sugar inside, or baked buns with sweet bean paste inside. They are great!

WESTERN FOOD

Most tourist hotels seerve western food, but it is rarely as good as Chinese. Bread is cut thick and is usually white. Sometimes it is one Chinese meat-and-vegetable course with bread instead of rice. Excellent western food is available in four-star and up joint-venture hotels and restaurants, especially in Beijing, Shanghai and Guangzhou. Some of these hotels also have delicatessens where you can buy cold cuts. Some restaurants in Northeast China have Russian food.

Local Chinese prefer Chinese food and have rejected invitations to western meals 'because of too much meat' ' or the lack of familiarity with knives, forks, and western table manners.

COURTESIES

Group tours should be punctual at meals as the food is usually ready on time. Meals are served family style and the dishes may be sitting on the table getting (ugh!) cold.

Guests of honor are traditionally given seats where they face the door. Left-handed people should sit where they can avoid clashes with right-handed chopsticks.

Many restaurants distribute damp towels at the beginning of meals to refresh guests as well as to clean. You can wipe faces, backs of necks and hands with them. Sometimes towels are distributed during the meal and always at the end.

If you pass tea or bowls or calling cards, to be polite, use both hands and bow.

Chinese food is usually served on large platters, which ideally arrive one at a time. The food comes hot off the wok at the peak of perfection to be eaten immediately.

In families, diners pick what they want with chopsticks which are great for reaching across tables, keeping fingers clean, and hitting naughty children. Outside of families, use serving spoons. After guests express admiration for the beauty of the food, Chinese hosts put the best morsels on the plates of the people around them. You could do this, too, after the first round. Since you put your own chopsticks into your mouth, you should use the other end for serving. The host usually invites guests to start eating. Groups of friends can declare a moratorium on such formalities and have everybody dig in. *He fai* means 'Raise chopsticks!'

Slurping or even burping indicates that you are rude. If you don't have enough room on your dish for bones and other discards, just leave them neatly on the table itself. Less-polished Chinese will spit them onto the floor!

GOOD RESTAURANTS

In very fancy restaurants, an attendant distributes every course and guests do not help themselves. Individual plates are removed and re-placed with clean ones after most courses. The host usually invites guests to start eating.

GIVING A BANQUET

Hosting a feast is the accepted and most important way to return hospitality or to show gratitude for a favor. If your guide persists in refusing your invitation to eat with you, he may relent and join you the day before you leave as a farewell gesture.

You may want to throw a banquet for some of your Chinese colleagues and people who have been helpful. Discuss your guest list with one of the Chinese involved so you won't offend anybody important by leaving them out. Discuss spouses and times and seating arrangements, but don't be offended if spouses don't show up. The venue is important because some restaurants are more prestigious than others.

Even-numbered days are more auspicious than odd-numbered days. Restaurants may be busier with wedding parties then.

TOASTING & BANQUETS

Chinese people do not like to drink alone. Toasting at banquets is a complicated art, and you are not expected to know the finer points. Just do what you do at home. Stand up, give one or two sentences, make sure everybody is joining you, and drink. *Gan bei!* means 'Empty your glass!'

The first toaster is usually the host, who gets the ball rolling. A frequent toast is to the friendship of the people of your country and China, and the health of friends and comrades present. You can tell a funny story and then talk about your sadness about leaving China and the new friends you have made, and meeting again in your country.

Toasts might continue all evening, and so might the meal, or at least until the restaurant turns out the lights. If the banquet is extremely large, the host might circulate to all the tables, drinking toasts at each one. On smaller, less formal occasions, the Chinese may want to drink you under the table. Be alert; they may be putting tea in their own glasses. You may want to try that yourself after awhile.

I have been to banquets where I haven't didn't touch a drop of liquor. I can't get *mao tai* past my nose – it's so strong. Chinese hosts are not usually offended if you toast with tea or soft drinks. If you don't want to drink liquor, mumble something about a medical problem, like an allergy. Try to divert your fellow diners. Try exchanging songs – but no drinking ones. It may be the only occasion when you'll hear the national anthem of China. You can turn your cup or glass upside down to signal to the waiter that you've had enough.

If you want to stop eating and your host keeps piling food onto your plate, just lay down your chopsticks. Thank him politely but don't eat anymore. Your host shouldn't feel insulted.

Recently, as an austerity measure, the lavishness of top-level state banquets was curtailed officially to four courses and a soup, and the length limited to one and a half hours. This might be the beginning of a trend, but then again, it might not. Banquets are part of the culture.

EATING WITH THE LOCALS

You can eat quite well for comparatively little money if you're willing to try food stalls and restaurants for the masses. The standard of cleanliness and speed of service are not generally as high as in restaurants for tourists. The cigarette smoke may be suffocating. It is customary to share tables with other diners in busy restaurants.

Payment is made when you order (so you can't stomp out impatiently). Some finicky eaters take their own chopsticks and spoons to places like this, but as far as I can see the dishes are scalded, and if the food is freshly cooked, there should be no problems. The soup sterilizes the untensils (you hope), but you can also scald them yourself with tea. I highly recommend James D. McCauley's *The Eater's Guide to Chinese Characters* if you are eating off the tourist track.

FAST FOOD STALL, MOBILE CANTEENS, & CAFETERIAS

These are recent innovations and are multiplying quickly. Some serve instant noodles. A knowledge of Chinese isn't necessary; you can point.

Outdoor night markets are an adventurous attraction for gourmet as well as budget travelers. Make sure the food is steaming hot and the utensils are scalded or eat directly from the cooking container. Avoid uncooked sauces and condiments.

FOOD STREETS

Food streets are usually managed by hotels so are cleaner and more foreigner-oriented. The food is usually light and prices are reasonable: noodles, fried rice, side orders of barbecued duck, cuttle-fish, etc.

EATING PRECAUTIONS

To avoid an upset stomach and intestinal parasites, do not drink water out of faucets. Most bottled drinks are fine, but make sure the seal isn't broken. Steer clear of ice, popsicles, ice cream (except for foreign brands), watermelon, and other fruit. Don't eat anything raw unless it's imported, or carefully washed and peeled. Animal and human manure is used in China as fertilizer. Local people have developed immunities.

Be careful on ferries and small boats. Dishes are frequently washed in river water and are not always scalded carefully afterward. Some people take disinfectants like tincture of iodine. Two drops in a liter of water kills all germs in 20 minutes. When cooking your own food, as in Mongolian

Hot Pot, be careful that the untensils you use on raw meat or fish are not the same utensils you put into your own mouth. Sterilize utensils in the hot pot.

HERE'S THE BEST WAY TO EAT ...

*Mantou: the plain steamed roll. Either take bites while holding with chopsticks or fingers, or break apart and stuff pieces with bits of meat. You can also dip it in sauces. **Jiao zi** are small stuffed ravioli-like pastries, steamed or fried; **bao zi** are steamed dumplings and may have beans or meat and vegetables inside. The names get confusing.*

__White rice:__ served in bowls. Put the bowl up to your mouth and shove the rice in with chopsticks. More genteel people might want to pick up chunks with chopsticks.

__1000-year-old eggs:__ you usually have to either acquire a taste or close your eyes and think of something else; they are best eaten with pickles and are delicious.

__Shrimp with shell left on:__ take a bite of half, then, with your teeth and chopsticks, squeeze out the meat. You could use your fingers to shell them. Cooking shrimp in their shells retains most of the yummy flavor.

__Two–and three-foot long noodles:__ lean over your bowl and pick up a few noodles with chopsticks. Put the noodles in your mouth, biting off pieces and leaving the rest temporarily in your bowl. Don't worry about slurping. The Chinese enjoy long noodles because they symbolize longevity.

__Ice cream:__ ask for a spoon.

OTHER TIPS

The secret of eating a Chinese meal is finding out first how many **courses** you will be getting. Banquet meals usually have a copy of the menu on the table. If there are 12 courses, take no more than one-twelfth of what you would usually eat in a meal from each plate; otherwise, you will be too full to eat the later dishes. Also take your time. You can't rush through a big meal. Some famous banquets have taken days.

Fish is the last formal course in some places. If you happen to be eating with superstitious fishermen, don't turn a fish over to get at the flesh on the other side. It means their boat will turn over!

Do not worry about 'Chinese restaurant syndrome.' Its symptoms are an increased pulse and a tight feeling around the sinuses. This 'syndrome' is a result of the large amount of Monosodium Glutamate (MSG) in Chinese food in America. Cooks in China use a little, but not as much. You can ask them to leave out MSG (*wei jing* or *Ajinomoto*), salt, chilis or anything else.

Among the beauties of a Chinese meal is the variety. If you don't like one thing, you might like something else. On prepaid tours, you might want to talk with your escort about the overabundance of food when meat for the common man is so limited – if this bothers you.

Menus in English are by translators, not public relations people. Some dishes may sound absolutely terrible, but are really very good. Don't let a name like 'frog oil soup' throw you.

Preserved fruit is delicious, but do not eat too many at a sitting. They are full of preservatives.

Another new development are the health restaurants, with dishes made from Chinese herbal medicines with lots of ginseng, sea horses, deer antlers, and things best left unmentioned. Some foods are known to combat high blood pressure; other foods are good for pregnant women. These are indeed for the adventurous eater because of their unusual flavors, and they can be very delicious.

If you invite average Chinese people to dinner, be sensitive that a meal in a tourist restaurant is a real treat. Normally, they cannot afford it. Since they get little meat, do order more for them. Do encourage them to take the leftovers home. They may be too polite to ask.

REGIONAL CUISINES

For specific dishes, see my chapter on *Chinese Characters*.

Beijing or Peking or Northern cooking is light and salty with few sauces but lots of garlic, leeks, and scallions. It has flour-made buns, rolls and meat dumplings. Food is baked, steamed, roasted, fried, or boiled in soup. In winter, be sure to try hot pot.

Cantonese or Guangdong or Southern style has crisp vegetables quickly fried in peanut oil and is somewhat sweet with starch in the sauces. It uses a lot of oyster sauce or fish sauce in cooking or poured over boiled vegetables. A few dishes are dog, monkey, and snake. (Please, no pangolin and other endangered species!) **Dim Sum** are those small fried or steamed Cantonese pastries served at breakfast or lunch and are ordered from a menu (classier), or chosen from a trolley brought to your table. The trolley attendant can take off any cover for you to see inside. The most famous dim sum restaurant is the Panxi Restaurant in Guangzhou. But it's great in most restaurants in that province. Chicken feet, known as Phoenix feet, are delicious! Honest!

Fujian cooking has lots of seafood and light soups, suckling pig, and nonfat spring rolls. You may recognize Filipino dishes like lumpia and lechon, originally from this province.

Shanghai cooking from Eastern China is similiar to that of Suzhou, Yangzhou, and Wuxi. It is cooked longer in sesame oil, neither sweet nor salty. It can be very ornamental. Borscht is on the menu of most of

Shanghai's restaurants because of all the White Russians who once lived in Shanghai. Look for crab in November.

Some **Sichuan** (Szechuan) dishes are highly spiced, peppery hot, and oily. Formal banquet cooking is more bland. Smoked duck with camphor and tea flavor is not spicy hot.

Vegetarian cooking has had a long tradition in China and was first documented 2000 years ago. It developed with Buddhism, which forbids its adherents from killing animals and restaurants are frequently found near Buddhist temples. Distinctively Chinese are dishes that imitate meat in taste, texture, and looks. While this does not encourage reverence for life as taught by Buddha, it does make it easier for some Buddhists to become vegetarian. Many of the dishes are made of soy bean and use a lot of monosodium glutamate.

The following are some suggested dishes from the **Ju De Lin Restaurant** near the Lama Temple in Beijing and should give you an idea of what is available: Water chestnuts and bean curd; Mushrooms and bamboo shoots; Shrimp (actually carrots, cucumber, bamboo shoots, mushrooms, radish); Black and white fungi; Sea crab (actually potato, radish, mushroom, bamboo shoots); Roast duck (actually bean curd); Sweet and sour pork (actually locust seed); and Fish ball soup (tomato and celery).

12. ACCOMMODATIONS IN CHINA

ABBREVIATIONS & HOTEL JARGON

Before we begin, here are the abbreviations relevant to hotels and accommodations from Chapter 2, *Overview*, in our How to Use This Book section:

- **B.C.** – Business center or hotel office capable of sending faxes, and offering a secretary for hire, photocopying, and typewriter rentals
- **CITS** – China International Travel Service
- **Credit Cards** – These are the credit cards accepted by the hotel: American Express, Visa, MasterCard, and sometimes Diners
- **CTS** – China Travel Service
- **CYTS** – China Youth Travel Service tours
- **Dist.A.P.** – Distance from airport
- **Dist.R.W** – Distance from main railway station
- **executive floor** - usually including complimentary continental breakfast, a lounge, concierge service, and sometimes drycleaning.
- **HKTV** – English-language broadcasts sometimes with CNN from Hong Kong
- **IDD** – International Direct Dial
- **JV** – Joint Venture
- **Ren.** – Renovated. Only major improvements mentioned
- **USTV** – Satellite television reception from outside China, usually Star TV (Hong Kong) channels. Some hotels get The Bold and the Beautiful, sports, entertainment, and/or music channels. Some hotels get CNN, NHK, ABC, or NBC.
- **Wide twin** – twin beds at least 53" wide each
- **Y** – Yuan (Chinese currency; a number of hotels only accept payment in yuan)

US DOLLAR PRICES

All dollar prices given in this book, unless otherwise noted, are in US dollars.

SOME GENERALITIES

The hotels mentioned here are the top hotels in each city and the best hotels in each price category, also chosen for location. Hotel ratings such as 'three-star,' 'four-star,' etc., indicate the government's rating system, with five the highest quality. Most hotels have singles, doubles, and suites. Those of the lowest stars might have dormitories of three or more beds to a room. Most hotels of three-stars and higher will respond with a fax to a request for a reservation if so asked. Those listed here are up to international standards except where noted and you can be sure all have western private baths, coffee shops, a bar, a Chinese restaurant, air conditioning (except in the cooler regions), money changingfacilities, televisions, and telephones in rooms. Most have hair dryers, karaoke, business centers and gyms. Many have facilities for conventions. Some have in-room safes and satellite television.

In a few cases, the "best" hotels in a city may not be very good.

The quality of most facilities four stars and up is usually very good. Those of three stars might be a little worn with dirty carpets but they are usually acceptable for all but the most fussy foreign tourists. English-language capability has improved but still leaves much to be desired.

SERVICE WITH A SMILE?

A shortage of staff with international experience means that service is not usually up to Bangkok's cheerful or Hong Kong's efficient standards. Chinese hotels are training staff and are attempting to fire the hopeless. They are fining workers or giving bonuses, depending on performance and volume of business. Some cities have started Tourist Hotlines to help with any problems, emergency translating, or complaints.

But many tours still cannot guarantee their hotels. In far-off Tibet, except for the Holiday Inn, it's first come, first served.

The furious pace of hotel construction is slowing down. The range spans from huge palaces fit for visiting heads of state to tiny temple hostels for pilgrims. New Chinese-managed hotels might be very beautiful, but they can deteriorate quickly. I have tried to grade hotels, but six months later the quality might be completely different.

In the Chinese-managed hotels, total renovations are made every three to four years, but in the meantime, soft drinks and spit get hopelessly ground into beautiful wool carpets. Foreign-managed hotels try to practice perpetual maintenance.

The top joint-venture hotels have raised the level of expectations for all hotels. Tourists used to be happy with a tacky room and private bath, and then, later, an air-conditioner and television set. Today's visitors expect a refrigerator, spotless rugs, non-smoking rooms, and an in-room safe.

BACKGROUND

In 1978, the hotels of China were run by bureaucrats to provide only a place to bathe, sleep and eat. Many were subsidized. One managers said then that he preferred Chinese guests because foreigners were too fussy: 'Americans should learn from the Japanese not to complain!'

In some cities, especially during high tourist seasons, the demand for rooms exceeded supply. In the early 1980s, tour groups for Beijing slept 50 kilometers away in Hubei province. Some business people attending the Canton Trade Fair in 1979 slept in hotel lobbies. Yet other cities had a surplus of rooms.

HOTELS TODAY

Chinese tourism officials now want to attract tourists. While most hotels are still owned by a government agency, the dramatic increase in hotels has resulted in good old-fashioned capitalistic competition. Pleasing visitors has become important! Standards have risen! Chinese guests sometimes get displaced to make room for foreigners!

Joint ventures both in the construction and in the management of some hotels have given China many hotels of international deluxe standard. A few hotels are being built solely by foreign interests. Big hotel chains are involved.

Some staff members have been sent on training programs outside China, and regular training programs take place on the job. Many hotels have also imported foreign executives and managers.

But not all joint ventures are of international standard. Some have deteriorated because of poor management. In the 1990s, foreign tourists are usually billeted in a standard Chinese hotel room, or, if they choose to pay more, in a better one. They can also choose, as backpackers will tell you, to live cheaply in a shared dormitory. But most travel agents won't book those!

Hotel rooms are frequently classified from standard/moderate, to superior, and up to deluxe. 'First class' is usually below superior and might even be the same as standard. Hotels with standards deemed unacceptable to foreigners are being phased out.

Brand-new hotels may not have their act together in regard to services, but at least the rooms will be in pristine condition. There is a tendency for Chinese partners to insist on a 'soft' opening before all facilities are ready. A lot of hammering and the hint of better things to come after the 'hard' or 'grand' opening may be annoying to you.

ROOM PROBLEMS!

*Many hotels now have **Public Relations Departments**. Should you have problems in a hotel three stars and above, try the **Gong Guan Xi** during office hours. Almost all tourist hotels have someone on duty somewhere who speaks English. Ask to see a hotel room before you commit yourself to it.*

HOTEL STAR RATINGS

Government assessments are a good indication of design, equipment, hygiene, maintenance, management, service quality, and facilities (but not location). To qualify for a rating, hotels must also receive letters from satisfied guests. Write and offer your opinions, good or bad. Star ratings are sometimes given for political reasons.

Each of the following items begets a certain number of points. Each star rating has a minimum number of points. Three stars does not mean that every hotel so graded has special guestrooms for wheelchaired people, for example. (They might only have one wheelchair.)

Local or provincial governments hand out one to three star ratings but the national government must approve the three stars. Four and five stars are determined by the national government.

Only hotels fully opened for one year are formally rated, and a plaque should be prominently displayed. Each successively higher rating incorporates the best criteria of the ratings below it.

Foreigners are not supposed to stay in a hotel with less than one star because the standards are terrible – but many do.

Among the criteria:

One Star hotels must have air conditioning, coffee shop, dining room, and at least 20 guest rooms, cleaned daily. Of these, 75% must have private baths. It must have central heating, a lobby with information and reception desk, postal service, and 12-hour a day cold and hot running water.

Two Star hotels must have at least 20 guest rooms, 95% with private baths, 50% with telephones and 16 hours of cold and hot running water. Western and Chinese breakfast must be offered.

Three Star hotels must have at least 50 beautifully-decorated guest rooms with dressing table, desk, drawers, closet; carpet or wood floor; bedside panel; 24-hour cold and hot water; 110/220V outlet; telephones in every room with international direct dial (IDD); mini-bar and refrigerator; color television sets, in-house movies, music; writing materials; sunproof curtains; and bed turn-down service.

They must have single rooms and suites, western and Chinese dining rooms (with English-speaking attendants and the last order no earlier than 8:30 pm), 16-hour coffee shop, banquet hall or function room, buffet breakfast and bar service (until midnight), and 18-hour room service.

They must also have elevator service, public telephone and washroom, equipment and service for disabled people, disco or karaoke, massage, beauty parlor, barber, bookstore, reading room, 12-hour a day foreign exchange, safe deposit boxes, store, camera film developing, fax and telex services, luggage storage, 24-hour laundry and drycleaning, wake-up calls, shoe polishing, and taxis. They should be able to mend articles of everyday use for guests. They should accept major credit cards. They must have an emergency electricity supply for public areas, medical services, 16-hour a day doorman, and message service. On duty 24-hours a day should be a luggage porter, checkroom service, guest reception, and managers on call. An assistant manager should be in the lobby 18 hours a day. There should be a price list, tourist map (English-Chinese), flight and railroad timetables available. *China Daily* and *China Tourism News* should be on sale (or free).

Four Star hotels should have luxurious and spacious sound-proof rooms, low-noise toilets, and hair dryers. They should have guest and service elevators, background music, health club, swimming pool, sauna, business center, greenhouse, 24-hour doorman, reservations accepted through fax/telex, 24-hour room service, and onward reservations in China for guests. Guest reception and assistant manager should be available in the lobby 24 hours.Laundry should be returned by next day.

The restaurants in four-star hotels should provide two kinds of Chinese food with the last order no earlier than 9 pm. Bar service should be available to one am. There should be a 24-hour coffee shop and a breakfast and dinner buffet. A clinic should be on-site. A business center with photocopying, typing and translation services should be available, as should a ticketing agency with city tours and babysitting services.

Five star hotels are usually palatial with huge lobbies, their standards not quite matching the best of Paris or New York, but very close. Service should be better than the four-star hotels described above. See *Top Hotels* section below.

No-Star Hotels

These can be very dirty, with public hole-in-the-floor toilets, no English, heat or air conditioning. A few might have rats, bedbugs and cockroaches. They might have mosquito nets.

Don't be surprised if attendants snarl at guests, are reluctant to carry luggage, answer bells, or give any type of service. A few might be fire traps with stairways locked or blocked. Few have good bedside reading lamps. One Canadian woman was interrupted at 2 am by the attendant with a male friend who wanted to sell her souvenirs. But there are no-star hotels where the staff is sweet and helpful.

One & Two Star Hotels

These can be acceptable sometimes. The English and service are not very good, but you might be surprised. An attendant can go to the bank for money changing, or take cables to the post office. Most can get plane or theater tickets, or hail a taxi. You can frequently borrow adapters (for electric razors), portable electric heaters, fans, hair-dryers, and irons. Some also have in-house television (in Chinese) and you can request special programs.

Most have shower curtains, hand or low shower heads, and one day laundry service. The air conditioning and heat might not be adequate. Many have good bedside reading lamps. But the carpets will be stained and badly laid.

Sometimes gates are locked after 11 pm. While most hotels over three stories have elevators, sometimes these are turned off at night. In either case, bang and wake someone up.

Western breakfast selections might be limited to greasy fried eggs, orange juice, toast, and coffee. The Chinese breakfast would probably be better.

Attempts to make reservations by telex or letter might just end up in a pile of unclaimed mail. Few staff, if any, can read English. Just take a chance and show up, or telephone on arrival. Some hotels charge the guest if the hotel has to telex back. This is understandable, considering the cost of telexes and the low room rate.

A few of these hotels might have roaches, but I have never experienced bed bugs. A few might also have smelly and clogged public toilets, and poor plumbing in the rooms.

In some of these hotels, standards might differ according to floors. Foreigners are usually given the best and most expensive rooms. In areas recently opened to foreigners, the local people are not used to western standards of hygiene. If a room is mostly used by local people, the hotel won't bother to do more than mop up.

Top Hotels

Many hotels have a video library with old movies in English. Top hotels like the Shanghai Hilton can do things like hire, clean, and cater a railway car from Shanghai to Suzhou.

There are now a few hotels of five-star international standard. Lack of fluent English and the inability to anticipate the needs of world-class travelers are the main problems with most. This should change.

Some hotels have their own fleets of Mercedes limousines or Toyota vans that make regular runs to the airport or city center. At least two hotels have Rolls Royces. Some hotels have been inviting guests to cocktail parties once a month, upgrading frequent guests, or giving the 6th night free. Many have executive floors with concierges, free continental breakfasts, and fast check-in.

The danger of a luxury hotel, in China as elsewhere, is its great economic disparity with the life of the ordinary citizen. The cost of one night in such a hotel could be the equivalent of several months income. If you go to learn about China, you'll have to make a great effort to do so if you stay in a luxury hotel.

HOTEL BASICS

Air-conditioning and heat: All starred tourist hotels have these, but the quality varies according to cost. Once the heat is turned on for the winter, it takes three days in some hotels to switch back to air-conditioning. If there is a sudden heatwave, you might find your hotel too hot. Ask the attendant to open the windows, if you can't do it yourself.

Beds: These are usually firm and good. Rooms for standard groups usually have twin-size beds, too small for couples. Some beds are too short and narrow for tall foreigners. Be sure you have an extra blanket before the attendant goes off for the night.

Check-out time: usually noon with 50% of the room rate charged if you stay until six pm.

Chinese customs: While some hotels may look like North American hotels, don't be surprised to find staff sleeping in the lobby, and occasionally on the dining room tables.

Discounts: You should always try for one, especially if occupancy is down. Sample dialogue: 'Look, I'll tell all my friends to come here.' 'I'm booked at another hotel but I heard you were cheaper.' 'I'm an Overseas Chinese,' and 'Okay, but how about including breakfast?' 'Can I speak with the sales manager, please?'

Keys: There are different systems. In the lower ranks, you might not get a key at all. An attendant will open and lock your door for you Soviet-style. At the other end of the scale, you might get a customized key card. In many hotels, the key card also activates the electricity. If there are two people in a room and one wants to read and then sleep while the other goes bar-hopping, there might be a problem with the lights. Stick a comb or folded paper in the light slot.

Locks: Even some three-star hotels do not have double locks on their guestroom doors. An attendant could barge in on you at any time after a token knock. A rubber doorstopper helps.

Prostitution: yes, it does exist, even in the best of hotels. You might get strange telephone calls from women at night. It is of course illegal, and cities like Guangzhou werefree of them in the mid-1990s, but one never knows when it will return. You can complain to the management if you see or experience this and find it troublesome.

Restaurants: Those in hotels are usually the best in town, especially for western food.

Security: Most top hotels have excellent security. You don't usually see anyone but hotel guests and staff on guest room floors. No unregistered guests can stay in rooms after 10 or 11 pm. (This is not always enforced in poorly-managed hotels.) Hotel thefts are rare, especially in the three stars and up range, but don't leave tempting valuables unlocked and in sight. Use the safe deposit boxes. Pilfering by hotel staff is rare but on the increase. Items taken recently have included perfume, sweaters, shoes, flashlights, cigarettes, and film. If you are on a lower floor, make sure your windows are locked.

Smoke alarms are usually in every room. Fire extinguishers should be on every floor, and fire hoses on higher floors. Most rooms have fire exit maps in English on their doors.

Sports: Hotels at all levels could have bicycles for rent, ping pong, badminton, and billiards. Attendants at swimming pools are not necessarily trained lifeguards, and you should supervise your own children. Also personally check the cleanliness of a pool. Many hotels have imported fitness equipment. And you can ask about taiji groups you can join at 6 am in the parks. Some hotels have aerobics, morning bicycle tours, and jogging maps.

State Guest Houses: These can be palatial, some suites fit for queens with large gardens and lots of privacy. Rooms are frequently big, with high ceilings. The service, service facilities, and maintenance, however, are poor.

Suites: Some of the top hotels have fancy two-story duplexes, or studios (which can be an office by day). Even medium-range hotels might have incredible luxury suites with gold-plated fixtures, antiques, and jacuzzis. Three people traveling together should ask about a suite. They could be less expensive than you think.

Surcharges: At the higher levels, even Chinese-managed hotels add a surcharge of five to 20% on rooms, telephone calls and meals. Part of this is a municipal tax.

Telephones: In most hotels, there's a telephone in every room. You can make local calls by first dialing '0' or '9'. If it is not a dial phone, tell the operator what number you want. To reach an outside line, say *wai xian* (why she-an). To ask for the service desk, where there just might be someone who speaks English, say *fu wu tai* (foo woo tie). To get other rooms in most hotels, just dial the room number unless otherwise notified.

Not all hotels will have IDD capability in every guest room. You might have to call the operator or go to a desk in the lobby. If there is no IDD, you can still call from your room. You might have to book the call at the service desk, and pay a service charge beforehand. Or an attendant might come knocking on your door afterwards. It could take hours.

There is usually a service charge, even for collect calls not completed. You might want to ask the rate first. For more information, see Chapter 7, *Basic Information*.

Tipping: see Chapter 7, *Basic Information*.

Water for Drinking: Hot, boiled water is available in thermoses in all hotels, either in the room, or free on request. Sometimes, there is a flask for cooling. I strongly suggest you do not drink water out of the tap, not even in the top hotels.

Some hotels have electric kettles that turn themselves off upon boiling. This does not give enough time to kill all the bacteria. Do not use the non-potable water in these devices. Many hotels also provide ice cubes, hopefully made of boiled water.

Workmanship: This could be bad. You can't expect people who have never seen a western hotel to know that paint shouldn't be slopped on top of marble nor bare holes left in bathroom floors.

Hotel Chains: The top chains are the Hilton, Holiday Inn Crowne Plaza, Kempinski, Okura, Shangri-La, Sheraton, Singapore Mandarin and Westin. I would also recommend the Forum, Holiday Inn, Hyatt, KYZ, Lee Gardens, New World, Nikko, New Otani, Novotel, Ramada, SAS, Sofitel and Swiss-Belhotel. Of the cheaper chains, Chains City hotels are good, but we have found dirty carpets and grubby walls.

Of the Chinese-managed groups, the Jin Jiang runs the gamut from the pretentious Jin Jiang Tower (Shanghai) and to the very good Kunlun (Beijing) down to modest hotels with peeling wallpaper and poor service. The China Friendship Tourist Hotel Group ranges from one or two good properties down to poor ones.

HOTEL PRICES

Many hotels give discounts if their occupancy rate is low at the time you want to go. 'Walk-in' discounts can range from 10 to 40% of the published price. Corporate discounts have been up to 60% if your company has signed a contract guaranteeing a minimum number of rooms per year Sheraton hotels give 'Suresavers' with 30% saving if booked 30 days in advance. It also has weekend specials. Also see Saving Money in Chapter 7, *Basic Information*.

It is almost meaningless to print published prices because they keep changing and are negotiable. For the latest prices for hotels belonging to international chains, use the North American toll-free numbers in Chapter 6, *Planning Your Trip*. But prices for rooms booked by travel agents might be cheaper.

China's system of awarding stars to hotels gives some indication of price, but a four star in Beijing is much more expensive than a four star in Guilin.

Again, bear in mind that published prices for many hotels vary by season and, frankly, are often not reliable. Your best bet to find out prices for Chinese hotels – even sometimes for those accommodations where prices are given in this guide – is to check with the local tourist bureau or CITS branch in the destination you intend to visit.

13. CHINA'S BEST HOTELS

In Beijing
HOLIDAY INN LIDO
(Lido Fandian)
Jichang Rd., Jiang Tai Rd., 100004. Four Stars. Tel. 64376688.
Fax 64376237, 64376540.
$160 to $180. In US, Tel. 1-800-HOLIDAY.

The **Holiday Inn Lido** in Beijing is really exotic for China because it's more like an American hotel. It looks like a sprawling American suburban establishment. But it's actually better than an American hotel of the same chain because it has everything you could possibly need if you've just spent two weeks in far-off Guizhou province or jeeping across the Gobi Desert. It's like being back in North America with all kinds of North American services at your fingertips – well, almost.

It beats other hotels in China because the English is good — among the best in Beijing. It has a real post office, a real bank, a real "drug store," and a real supermarket under the same roof. It has a cheap Chinese restaurant where you don't have to worry about hygiene. And it only charges one yuan for telephone calls.

The rooms are big, unpretentious and comfortable; the twin beds are actually double beds. Each room has thermoses of hot and of cold drinking water and a bucket of ice. There're a minibar, jasmine tea bags, and good quality stationery.

And if you happen to be there for Thanksgiving or Christmas, you can get a turkey dinner. You can get a hamburger any time and the best Thai food in Beijing in a luxurious Thai setting. Its Cantonese restaurant has live fish in a tank, but you can't have everything. Its Tex-Mex food has been, well, weird.

From its business center you can send faxes and make photocopies any time of the day or night, with great service: a nice lady re-addressed sixty letters for me into Chinese for mailing locally – without charge.

You can catch up with the world through its 25 television channels including CNBC, C-SPAN, several Japanese channels, Cartoons-TNT, and CNN. You can get Neighbours on Star TV. Every guest gets a copy of the *Herald Tribune* as well as *China Daily*. It also has a book shop with current foreign newspapers and some books in English, a deli, and a laundry shop. If you use the laundry outlet at the back of the hotel, you don't pay the 15% service charge. If you book at its air ticket office, you don't have to pay travel agent's booking fees.

Its video store has 1,400 titles at Y12 per tape and you can get a temporary five-day membership for Y10 and rent a machine for Y70. The hotel has ice cream you don't have to worry about eating and a real American breakfast.

A night market across the street has cheap clothes, hand-made quilts, and a few curios. The market is not as good as those downtown, but if you're going back to the interior, you can pick up what you need then. It is a long way from downtown, but the free hourly shuttle bus is handy or a taxi can take you along the new express road to the Friendship Store in 15 to 20 minutes. It is easy to remember the Chinese name "Lido Fandian" for taxi drivers.

There always seems to be a Lido representative at Beijing airport. The Holiday Inn's bellmen there hauled our luggage to the shuttle, avoiding what could have been a long wait with luggage in the airport taxi line. After a couple of nights at the Lido, you feel recharged and ready to go back to places with no international news, no weather reports, and no decent food.

In Beijing
CHINA WORLD HOTEL
(Zhong Guo Da Fan Dian)
1 Jianguomenwai Dajie, Da Bei Yao, 100004.
Five Stars. Tel. 65052266. Fax 65050828.
In US, Tel. 1-800-942-5050. $280 and $300.
Presidential suites $2,000 and $2,500.

I will always remember the **China World Hotel** in Beijing that cold, dry January when I arrived with a raw throat from a cold with eyelids heavy from fatigue. As I walked through its huge concert-hall-sized lounge, a symphony orchestra was playing Mozart under a giant Chinese landscape painting. As I entered my room, the attendants were setting up exactly what I needed, a humidifier. Downstairs there was a steam bath – much needed moisture for my dried-out body. The orchestra was food for my soul.

The China World, like the Holiday Inn Lido, is a self-contained world. It too has a good supermarket, a good bakery, a deli, a gym, and several places to reconfirm plane tickets. It has a wide range of restaurants in the complex including one where you can get a quick, cheap lunch. You really don't have to go outside at all. It has more stores than the Lido and is a quick drive to Tiananmen Square, but it's a lot more expensive. You're paying for a very luxurious and palacial hotel, a marvellous lobby lounge, good rooms and service. You're paying for a downtown location, and a very spacious and private hotel driveway, within walking distance of offices, markets and department stores.

In Hangzhou, East China
SHANGRI-LA HOTEL HANGZHOU
(Shang Gorilla Fandian)
78 Beishan Road, 310007. Tel. 7977951. Fax 7073545, 7996637.
Five Stars. In US, Tel. 1-800-942-5050.
$100 to $140 booked through Hangzhou Overseas Tourist Company.

I've liked the **Shangri-La Hotel Hangzhou**, even before it was taken over by the Shangri-La people. You can just walk out the door, past the trees, cross the road, and you are at lovely West Lake, *Sai Woo* in Cantonese, the name of a favorite Toronto Chinatown restaurant. The name is well-chosen because the lake, especially at dawn, has a magic quality about it. As you walk out onto the causeway with water on either side, you can see the morning sun, a rosy one on my last trip, peeking out from behind strings of falling willow branches, bare in winter. And if you stand in the right spot, you can frame the sun under the deeply-curved Song-dynasty pavilion roof while the mist hides the line of modern skycrapers on the tranquil horizon. You breath deeply as everything seems to blend together in a living, classical Chinese painting.

The hotel itself is romantic, old in a nice way, quiet, warm, not marred by glitz. The rooms are bigger than its rival, the Dragon; the atmosphere is more classy but simple and not pretentious. The lake is an extension of the hotel garden.

14. BEIJING & THE GREAT WALL

BEIJING

(Peking; Northern Capital)

Surrounded by Hebei province on the northern fringe of the North China plain, **Beijing** is 183 kilometers west of the seacoast and about 44 meters above sea level, with mountains to the north, west, and east. The population is 11 million (five million urban), with an estimated five million bicycles.

The best time to visit is autumn. The hottest days are in July and August, up to 38 degrees centigrade: the coldest are in January and February, down to minus 20 degrees centigrade. Dust storms occasionally blow from December to late March, and sometimes into May. The winter air is heavily polluted and very dry; hopefully your hotel will supply humidifiers. The annual precipitation is 683 millimeters, usually from June to August. There's a chronic water shortage, which should be alleviated in the future by diverting water from the Yellow River.

ARRIVALS & DEPARTURES

By Air

On almost the same latitude as Philadelphia, Beijing is about four hours west of Tokyo, three hours north of Guangzhou or Hong Kong, and two hours northwest of Shanghai. It has air links with 100 other cities.

If you're flying into Beijing, be aware that fog might delay flights. The booking offices for all Chinese airlines are at: *15 Changan Xi Ave., west of telegraph building (clock tower) and Zhongnanhai gate. Tel.6017755.* Bookings can also be arranged at the Beijing, Beijing International, Kunlun, Great Wall, Holiday Inn Lido and Xiyuan hotels.

If you have **general airport inquiries**, *call 64563604 for international flights and 64562233 for domestic flights.* For your convenience, here are the airlines servicing Beijing with their local phone numbers:

- **Aeroflot**, *Tel. 65002412*
- **Air China**, *domestic Tel. 66013336; international Tel. 66016667; adminis-trative offices Tel. 66017755 X 2317. Fax 64011027*
- **Air France**, *Tel. 65051818, 65051431*
- **All Nippon Airways**, *Tel. 65053311*
- **American Airlines**, *Tel. 65004837*
- **Austrian Airlines**, *Tel. 65917861*
- **British Airways**, *Tel. 65124070, 65124075*
- **Canadian Airlines International**, *Tel. 64637901*
- **China Eastern**, *Tel. 66024071, airport 64564089*
- **China Northern**, *Tel. 66024078, airport 64562170*
- **China Northwest**, *Tel. 66017594, airport 64562368*
- **China Southern**, *Tel. 66016899; airport 64564089*
- **China Southwest**, *Tel. 65016828, airport 64562870*
- **Dragonair**, *Tel. 65051252, 65054343. Fax 65054347*
- **Ethiopian Airlines**, *Tel. 65050314*
- **Finnair**, *Tel. 65127180. Fax 65127182*
- **Japan Airlines**, *Tel. 65130888*
- **Korean Airlines**, *Tel. 65051047*
- **Lufthansa**, *Lufthansa Center, Tel. 64654488. Fax 64653223*
- **Malaysian Airlines**, *Tel. 65052681-3*
- **Mongolian Airlines**, *Tel. 64561225*
- **Northwest**, *Tel. 65053505. Fax 65051855*
- **PIA**, *Tel. 65051681-4. Fax 65052257*
- **Qantas**, *Tel. 64674794, 64673337. Fax 64669494*
- **SAS**, *Tel. 65120575-77*
- **SIA**, *Tel. 65052233. Fax 65051178*
- **Swissair**, *Tel. 65123555, 65123556. Fax 65127481*
- **Thai International**, *Tel. 65123881-3*
- **United Airlines**, *Tel. 64631111, 65128888*
- **Xinjiang Airlines**, *Tel. 66024083; airport 64562803*

By Train

Beijing is 36 hours north of Guangzhou and 19 hours northwest of Shanghai, and can also be reached by train from Ulan Bator (Mongolia), and, beyond that, from Moscow.

The new **Xi** or **West Beijing Railway Station** building is in southwest Beijing on *Jianguomenwai Avenue, 6.7 kilometers from Tiananmen Square*. It services all trains going through the city of Zhengzhou, including the Beijing-Guangzhou line. The old station near the Beijing International Hotel is the terminal for three international lines (Trans-Siberian, Mongolia, and North Korea) and trains from Shanghai and Inner Mongolia. This division might change, however, so ask when you book your tickets.

For **train inquiries**, *call 6554866, 65776851, 65129525*. To **purchase tickets for foreigners**, *call 65581032*.

If you're planning on traveling to **Russia** by train, check first with the U.S. Embassy for tips regarding travel through Russia. The better train is the Chinese one, leaving on Wednesdays via Datong. The Russian train leaves on Saturdays via Shenyang and Harbin. They take seven days to reach Moscow. You can buy tickets at **China International Travel Service** *(Beijing International Hotel)*, and at the **Monkey Business Infocenter**, *Beijing Commercial Business Complex, Number One Building Yu Lin Li, Room 106, 1th floor, Youanmenwai, 100054. Tel.63292244 X 4406, fax extension 2532. E-mail CompuServe 100267.2567.*

I have heard that the train is fully booked in high season from Moscow to Beijing in both directions by East Europeans who get return tickets before they go. Give yourself at least two weeks in Beijing to get all the visas. You have to get a visa for your farthest point first, before you can get the others.

CITS Offices

The **CITS Beijing Branch** can get you information on prices, schedules, etc, for international trains, domestic flights, Yangtze cruise, the ferry between Tianjin and Korea and Japan. Offices and hours are: **Beijing International Hotel**, *Tel. 65120509. Fax 65120503*; also **Beijing Tourism Tower**, *ground floor, 8:30 to 11 am; 1:30 to 4:30 pm. Saturday 8:30 am to 12 noon. Tel. 65158844, 65158587. Fax 65158251, 65158602.*

For individual travelers, *Tel. 65158566* or look for the booth at the Jianguo, Beijing, and Tianlun Dynasty, as well as other hotels.

ORIENTATION

Beijing is the most important place to visit in China, not just because it is the capital but because it has a 3,000-year history, beginning in the Western Zhou, when it was known as **Ji** (Chi). Its most impressive historical monuments date from the 13th century. The museums here are the best in China, the temples among the most impressive. The palaces are the biggest and most elaborate. For most Chinese people, visiting Beijing has been and still is a lifetime ambition and many are now able to do it.

The **Liao** (916-1125) were the first to build a capital here. They called it Nanjing, Southern Capital, as distinct from their old capital farther north in Manchuria. The name was changed again to **Yanjing** (Yen Ching) in 1013. In 1125, the Jin, a Tartar dynasty, overthrew the Liao and enlarged the city, calling it **Zhongdu**, Central Capital. The Mongols (Yuan) under Kublai Khan overthrew the Jin and built a new capital called **Dadu** (Ta Tu). In 1368 the Ming drove out the Yuan and established its capital at Nanjing in 1409, with Beijing, then called **Peiping Fu**, as an auxiliary capital.

Beijing became the main capital again in 1421 (Ming) and continued as the Qing capital into the early 1900s. In 1860, it was invaded by foreign, mainly English and French, troops. The foreigners completely destroyed the Yuanmingyuan Palace. The Boxers took over in 1900 and laid siege to the Foreign Legation section, but were repelled by an international military force while the Qing Empress Dowager fled temporarily to Xian. In 1928, the Nationalist government moved its capital to today's **Nanjing**, and Beijing became **Peiping** (Northern Peace). The Japanese held it from 1937 to 1945. When the Communists took over in 1949, it regained its old name and former position as capital of the nation.

During imperial times, no structures taller than the Forbidden City were allowed. Fortunately, the buildings of Beijing escaped the Pacific War relatively intact. In 1959, ten massive buildings were completed for the tenth anniversary of the founding of the People's Republic. Built in the heavy, plain Soviet style, these included the Great Hall of the People, the Museums of History and the Revolution, and the Palace of the Minorities. They are period pieces now.

Beijing is centered around the **Forbidden City** and **Tiananmen Square**. The old foreign legation area was southeast of these, between the Beijing, Xiqiao, and Capital Hotels. The few remaining European buildings there reflect that period of its history. The Chinese city was south of the **Qianmen Gate** on the southern edge of Tiananmen Square.

Beijing now consists of ten districts and nine counties. Rural villages raise the famous force-fed Beijing ducks. Over 2000 factories, mainly in the suburbs, produce iron and steel, mine coal, make machines, basic chemicals and petroleum, electronics, and textiles.

The people of Beijing speak **Mandarin** (*putong hua*), the official national language, but they twirl their tongues more. They are predominantly **Han**, but you will see flat, wide Mongolian and Manchu faces too. Beijing people tend to be reserved compared to other Chinese. Don't be put off by this, for they are warm and friendly once they get to know you.

GETTING AROUND TOWN

You need at least six days to cover the important attractions in Beijing. Many individual travelers use **public buses** successfully if they have plenty of time. Just avoid rush hours. These operate from 5 am to 11 pm. Bus tickets are about five jiao or half a yuan no matter what the distance.

Bus and **subway** maps are available in many hotels. Subway trains operate every three to eight minutes from early morning to late evening.

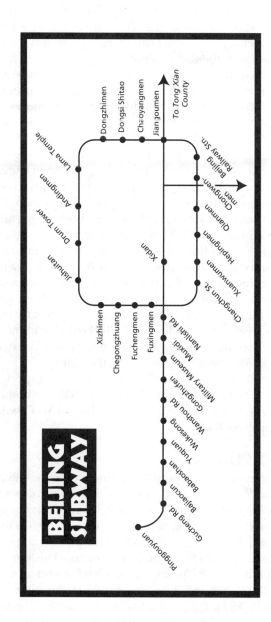

BEIJING SUBWAY

Dongzhimen
Dongsi Shitao
Chaoyangmen
Jianguomen
To Tong Xian County
Lama Temple
Andingmen
Drum Tower
Jishuitan
Xizhimen
Chegongzhuang
Fuchengmen
Fuxingmen
Nanlishi Rd.
Muxidi
Military Museum
Gongzhufen
Wanshou Rd
Wukesong
Yuquan
Baboashan
Bajiaocun
Gucheng Rd.
Pingguoyuan
Xidan
Changchun St.
Xuanwumen
Hepingmen
Qianmen
Chongwen men
Beijing Railway Stn.

The east-west subway line is 24 kilometers long with 10 more kilometers to be added in 1997. The subway west along Jianguomenwai Dajie from the World Trade Centre along Chang'an Avenue should now be operating. Tickets are about Y2. The circle subway, a 16-kilometer loop, makes a rectangle around Tiananmen Square and the Forbidden City and reaches near the Beijing Zoo.

Taxis are plentiful and available 24 hours. The cheapest are those marked with Y1.00. Do be aware that all taxis using the expressway to and from the airport have to charge an additional Y10 toll. **Bicycle rickshaws** should be cheap for short distances but decide on a price before you hop aboard.

Most hotels can offer **city tours** with English-speaking guides and lunch in the Y270 and Y320 range. These are not offered daily, however. A relatively inexpensive tourist bus service for Y60 a day is recommended for those with some Chinese and a good guidebook or map. This can be booked at the Guanghua Hotel, the Tian Tan Sports Hotel, and some of the cheaper hotels for the Great Wall and Forbidden City. The human guides only give short introductions. Basically, you're on your own.

Regular tours go to the Great Wall, Ming Tombs, Fragrant Hills, Summer Palace, Tanzhe Temple, Yunshui Cave, Qing tombs, and Chengde (Jehol). These out-of-town tours can be booked through any travel agent. Some cheaper tours leave from south of Tiananmen Square on the same street as the Qianmen Kentucky Fried Chicken Restaurant, but some minibus tours have been known to cheat guests and threaten to leave them stranded unless more payment is forthcoming.

Tourist handouts are distributed in Beijing hotels. Especially helpful are *Welcome to China – Beijing* and *Beijing This Month*. Another publication, *Beijing Scene,* is also available free from the **San Wei Bookstore** and at the **Mexican Wave Cafe.**

WHERE TO STAY

There are plenty of hotel rooms in the low season (roughly November 15 or December 1 until March 1. The Palace Hotel considers Christmas to the end of February its low season.) During this period you can get good discounts or packages with breakfasts. In winter 1995-1996, the well-located three-star Novotel charged $60 net for a single and the four-star Holiday Inn Lido charged $99 including breakfast. The four-star Xiyuan charged $65 for a room including buffet breakfast and an upgrade.

Booking through travel agencies abroad at the same time, some visitors paid only $50 a night for a five star-room. So haggle for lower prices if you think the hotels are not full.

Most hotels now have a direct telephone line from the airport's international arrivals terminal, and many have airport shuttle buses which we recommend because queues for regular taxis can be long. For those on budgets, there are cheap CAAC buses. From the airport to downtown Beijing, taxis should cost between Y60 and Y100.

Beijing has so many good hotels now. Below are those I recommend because of quality and location. I also want to show you a wide price range including cheaper ones for budget travelers. You need not stay away from Beijing because of high hotel prices if you're willing to put up with grubby hotels and poor English.

The most luxurious and classy hotels, with good services, are the **China World** and **Shangri-La**, followed by the **Palace** and the **Kempinski**. This order will probably change as these hotels are redecorated. The late 1990's is a good time to visit as many hotels are being refurbished.

The best of the four-star hotels is the **Holiday Inn Lido** and the better-located **Jianguo**. The best of the three-star hotels is the **Novotel** because of its central location and good standards. Also good is the **Zhaolong**. The best of the cheapest hotels is the **Tian Tan Sports**, but don't expect much.

The **Grand Hotel** is the only hotel with beautiful Chinese decor in all its rooms. I wonder, though, about its service.English is spoken poorly here. It's the closest hotel to the Forbidden City/Tiananmen and lies along the northern edge of the old Legation quarter. It has the best location, and a great atrium lounge. For a view of the Forbidden City, try the 10th floor bar at sunset on a clear day.

The second-best location for tourists and some business people is on and near **Wangfujing Avenue** (and its mix of modern chrome-plated shopping malls and tiny old stores with latticed wooden fronts). Also within walking distance of the Forbidden City are the Palace, Holiday Inn Crowne Plaza, Guangdong Regency, Novotel, Peace, Tianlun Dynasty, and Taiwan hotels, roughly in order of quality with the Palace the best. This area is also near Beijing municipal government offices, and good restaurants, and is about 10 kilometers from the new railway station.

The **Haoyuan** is in a special category. It makes you feel you're really in old Beijing. It has few services and no English. The **Wangfujing Grand** is too new to rate, but it looks good.

The third-best location, especially for business people but also for shoppers, is about four kilometers east on **Jianguomenwai Dajie**, which is actually on the same street as Tiananmen Square and the Forbidden City. On the south side of this broad avenue from west to east bunched together are the Gloria Plaza and Chang Fu Gong Hotels, the Beijing Tourism Tower, CVIK Building, S.C.I.T.E. Tower, and the CVIK Hotel. On the north side spread out west to east are the International Club, C.I.T.I.C. Building, Friendship Store, Silk Street, Gui You Department

Store, Jianguo (good value for the money) and Beijing-Toronto Hotels, and China World and Traders Hotels in the China World Trade Centre (CWTC). The dumpy Guanghua is beyond the China World and Traders. The western part of this less crowded, two kilometer-long area is also within walking distance of the United States embassy, Ritan Park, and the International post office. The old railway station is close by and the new West Beijing Railway Station is about 12 kilometers west of the China World and takes about 30 minutes by taxi.

The **China World Trade Centre** (CWTC) is a city in itself with hotels, apartments, offices and shops. It also has exhibition and conference centers, and the offices of Dragonair, Ethiopian, Northwest and Singapore airlines, CITS, Bank of China, DHL and American Express. The Guanghua Hotel is across the road to the east.

The **Beijing International Hotel** is between these two areas, and walking distance to the old railway station. It is a nice compromise but Tiananmen is still a half-hour walk away. A little closer to Tiananmen Square is the **Capital Hotel**, within walking distance of the south end. A little further from Tiananmen Square and more modest is the Xinqiao Hotel in a more crowded Chinese neighborhood to the southeast. It is along the southeast edge of the Old Legation Quarter. The **Minzu** is well located west of Tiananmen Square near the CAAC office, the airport bus terminal, the Cultural Palace, and busy Xidan Street.

The **Jing Guang Hotel** is about two kilometers due north of the CWTC. A little further out near Beijing Workers Stadium, the San Li Tun markets, and lots of bars and restaurants, are the **City** and the **Zhaolong** hotels. Farther out still are the **Kempinski**, **Sheraton Great Wall**, **Kunlun**, **Landmark Towers**, and **Huadu** hotels in descending order of quality. This group is relatively close to two diplomatic areas, including the Australian and Canadian embassies, and the Agricultural Exhibition Centre. The **Beijing Hilton** is north of this area, and all are within walking distance of each other, about 15 kilometers from the new West Beijing railway station.

The most convenient major hotel to the airport is the fancy **Beijing Movenpick Hotel**, now being promoted as a resort. The **Holiday Inn Lido/Grace/Yanxiang** cluster (in descending order of quality) is in a residential area, about 30 minutes from Tiananmen, the next closest to the airport, and within walking distance of each other's services.

The **Radisson SAS Hotel** is adjacent to the **China International Exhibition Center** (CIEC) in the north of the city. It is not near anything else except for Carrefour, one of the cheaper stores with imported goods, a McDonald's, and a couple of small restaurants. One of these restaurants is Yunnanese with a Yunnan Dance and Song troupe. The lobster brunch makes up for the location of the SAS.

The **Exhibition Center Hotel** is closest to the Beijing Exhibition Center but the **Debao, Xiyuan**, and **Shangri-La** are in the same neighborhood and are of better quality. They are near the zoo, paleozoological museum, the Negotiations Building, a Pizza Hut and Xinjiang Cun (Village) moslem food markets. These are about 36 kilometers from the airport and about 10 kilometers from the new railway station. Along with the Shangri-La, Holiday Inn Downtown, Friendship Hotels and high-tech district of Zhong Guan Zhun, these are in the northwestern part of the city. Also in the northwest is the new Beijing Experimental Zone, 16 kilometers from Tiananmen and 7.7 kilometers from the new railway station. The Third Ring Road (Xisanhuanbei Lu) express highway has made these hotels, especially the Shangri-La and Friendship Hotels, quickly accessible from the city center (15 minute drive) and the airport. Beijing and Qinghua Universities are further northwest and beyond them, the Summer Palace and Western Hills.

I cannot recommend the **Diaoyutai State Guest House** (Diaoyutai Guo Binguan) at 2 Fu Cheng Road because of the tight security. While the spacious grounds are beautiful, guests have recently complained about the long distance they have to and from the gate and the limited number of services. I'd like to recommend the **Fragrant Hill Hotel** because of its good convention setting isolated in the Western Hills, but it is now very run down. Until it gets a complete overhaul, I'm leaving it out. And forget also about the **Jin Lang Hotel** in spite of its good central location. It is very badly managed.

Prices listed here are in US dollars or Chinese yuan, and are subject to change, negotiations, and a 10 to 15% surcharge. Beijing imposes an additional tax of about Y6 per room per day. Local telephone calls range from free to two yuan. The Movenpick charges five fen a minute. Some hotels have in-room safes only in suites or executive floors; I have listed those that have them in every room.

Again, *Dist.A.P.* is distance from airport; *Dist.R.W.* is distance from the railway station.

CAPITAL HOTEL (*So Du Dajiudian*), *3 Qianmen Dong Jie, 100006. Currently about four-star standard aiming for five stars, Tel. 65129988. Fax 65120321, 65120309. $180 to $240. Presidential suite $2,500.*
Built 1989. Major renovations 1993 to mid-1996. 22 stories, 326 large rooms. In-room safes. Executive floor. USTV. Four bowling lanes. Gym. Indoor pool and gym. Seafood, Sichuan and Japanese restaurants. 24-hour room service. Singapore Mandarin International Management.
BEIJING GRACE HOTEL (*Xin Wan Shou Binguan*), *Jiang Tai Xi Road, Chao Yang District, 100016. Four stars, Tel. 64362288. Fax 64361818. $110-$170. Presidential suite $500.*

Built 1990. Major renovations 1996. 17 stories. 479 small rooms. Japanese, Continental, Shanghai and Cantonese food. USTV. Acupuncture clinic. Singapore J.V. with mainly Asian guests.

BEIJING HILTON INTERNATIONAL *(Xi Er Dun Fandian), 4 Dong Sanhuan Bei Road, 1 Dongfang Road, 100027. Five stars, Tel. 64662288, 4674754. Fax 64653052, 64672970. In US, Tel. 1-800-445-8667. $230 to $310. Presidential suite $1500. Dist.A.P. 20 kilometers. Dist.R.W. eight kilometers.*

Built 1993. 25 stories, 363 rooms. Executive floors. USTV. In-room safes and in-house movies. 24-hour room service and business center. Cantonese, Japanese and American fusion cuisine. Indoor pool, squash, tennis, and gym. Bicycles. Non-smoking floors. Clinic. Trying to be environmentally friendly. Breakfast buffet Y125.

BEIJING HOTEL *(Fandian), 33 Changan Dong St., 100004. Five stars, awarded only because of its long history and special status. Tel. 65137766. Fax 65137703 (sales), 65137307. East Building $160 to $300; Middle Building $160; West Building $110. Dist.A.P. 30 kilometers. Dist.R.W. two kilometers.*

Three connecting buildings with a total of 876 rooms. USTV. Cantonese, Sichuan, Japanese and Huaiyang food. Famous acupuncturist. Gym. Poor English and socialist management are problems. Spotted carpets. AT&T. Middle Wing (1917), renovated 1993. It has large rooms with high ceilings. West Wing (1954 with renovations in 1994) has 300 small rooms. The East Wing is best. 1974. 7th and 14th VIP floors renovated 1991. 583 large rooms with 3.6 meter-high ceilings, some with balconies. Dim reading lights but bathroom heat lamp. Mouldy grouting. USTV. In-room safes. Lots of good shopping, a real post office, and a Bank of China branch. Breakfast buffet Y45.

BEIJING LANDMARK TOWERS *(Liangmahe Fandian), 8 Dong San Huan Bei Rd., Chao Yang Dist. 100004. In same compound as Great Wall Sheraton. Three stars, Tel. 65016688 Fax 65013513. $100 to $120.*

Built 1990. Renovations 1996. 15 stories. 488 small rooms. 240 apartments. Small soft beds. Charming decor. Cantonese, Sichuan, Chaozhou, Huaiyang, and Korean restaurants. USTV. Small indoor pool. Gym. Sauna.

BEIJING MOVENPICK HOTEL *(Guo Du Dafandian), Xiao Tianzhu Village, Shunyi County. P.O. Box 6913, 100621. Four stars, Tel. 64565588. Fax 64565678, 64561234. North American Tel. 1-800-34HOTEL. $120 to $165. Dist.A.P. three kilometers. Dist.R.W. 25 kilometers.*

The Movenpick is isolated from everything except a small village off the main airport road. Built in 1990 with renovations in 1995. 12 stories, 427 rooms, the cheapest ones with wooden floors. Non-smoking floors. USTV. Cantonese, Mongolian, and Swiss/European restaurants (with cheese fondue) and good Sunday brunch. Good hardware but small elevators. Acupressure and therapeutic massages and qigong. Good health club with one of Beijing's largest swimming pools, squash, aerobics and tennis. It can organize water skiing, bicycle tours and horseback riding, and it has a golf-putting range. It has activities for children on weekends, a children's menu and a camel name Ueli. Breakfast buffet $12. Chinese breakfast $6.

BEIJING INTERNATIONAL HOTEL *(Beijing Guoji Fandian), 9 Jianguomenwai Dajie, 100005. Four stars, Tel. 65126688. Fax 65129972. $85 to $120. Dist.A.P. 28 kilometers. Dist.R.W. 0.5 kilometers.*

This is mainly a hotel for tour groups. Built 1987. Renovations 1995, 1996. 29 stories, 1049 large rooms. Italian, Korean, Shandong, Sichuan, and Chaozhou food. Revolving restaurant. 24-hour room service. USTV and inhouse movies. CITS offices. Tennis. 10 bowling lanes. Gym. Heated indoor pool and sauna. Supermarket. Florist.

BEIJING-TORONTO HOTEL *(Jinglun Fandian), 3 Jianguomenwai Dajie, 100020. Four stars, Tel. 65002266. Fax 65002022. Tel. 1-800-NIKKO-US (645-5687). $170 to $180. Dist.A.P. 30 kilometers. Dist.R.W. three kilometers.*

Built 1984, renovated yearly. 12-story glitzy hotel. 659 rooms. Small bathrooms. Wide twins. Aeroflot and Qantas offices. Indoor pool, gym and bicycles. Clinic. Japanese, Cantonese and snake restaurants. Well maintained and managed by Nikko Hotels International.

BEI WEI *(Binguan), Xi Jing Rd., Xuan Wu District, 100073. Two stars. Tel. 63012266. Fax 63011366. Y272.*

In southeast Beijing a few blocks south of the Temple of Heaven next to the better known Rainbow Hotel (Hongqiao Fandian). Built 1954. 5 stories, 200 rooms. Only western breakfast. I can recommend this modest hotel for desperate backpackers only. The standards and English are problems.

CHINA TRAVEL SERVICE TOWER, *2 Beisanhuan East Road. 100028. Four stars. Tel. 64612412, 4622288. $160 to $180.*

Good location on Third Ring Road and the Capital Airport Expressway, it is however, isolated because of these two conveniences. It is difficult to get to and there is nothing of interest around it. Gold-domed pagoda-like roofs. 1994. 160 small rooms. Korean and Chao Zhou restaurants. Cheaper if booked through China Travel Service.

CHINA WORLD HOTEL *(Zhong Guo Da Fan Dian), 1 Jianguomenwai Dajie, Da Bei Yao, 100004. Five stars, Tel. 65052266. Fax 65050828. In US, Tel. 1-800-942-5050. $280 and $300. Presidential suites $2,000 and $2,500. Dist.A.P. 27 kilometers. Dist.R.W. five kilometers.*

Built 1990. 21 stories. 743 large rooms. Large desk with telephone. Non-smoking floor. Executive floors. Business Center should have Internet soon. AT&T. USTV. Deli. Bake shop. 12 bars and restaurants including

Cantonese, French, Japanese and Express food (with Y35 lunch) in complex. Facilities include gym, squash, tennis, pool, bowling, disco, and a drugstore. Managed by Shangri-La International.

CITY HOTEL BEIJING *(Cheng Shi Binguan), 4 Gongti Dong Rd., Chaoyang District, 100027. Three stars, Tel. 65007799. Fax 65008228, 65007668. About $100 to $120.*

In San Li Tun close to the clothes and fruit markets, and innumerable restaurants and bars. 1989. 85 big rooms with in- room safes. 135 studios and apartments. USTV. Shuttle bus. Small gym. Cantonese and hot pot restaurant. Managed by Chains International (HK). Bit scruffy but comfortable.

CVIK HOTEL, *23 Jianguomenwai Dajie, 100004. Four stars, Tel. 65123388. Fax 65123542, 65123543. $125 and $160.*

Built 1991. 15 stories, 320 rooms with small bathrooms and beds and in-room safes. Eighth floor and up renovated in 1996. Cantonese Hong Kong joint-venture restaurant. 24-hour room service and business center. USTV. Gym, indoor pool and tennis.

DEBAO HOTEL, *Building 22 Debao Xinyan, West District, 100044. Three to four star standard. Tel. 68318866, 68334571. Fax 68334571. $135 and $145.*

Close to the Si Zhi Men subway station on busy street near the zoo, post office, and Exhibition Centre. 11 stories, over 300 rooms. USTV. Currently new and good-looking, but the service here has yet to be tried. Chaozhou Restaurant. Pool. Gym. Sauna and steam bath.

EXHIBITION CENTRE HOTEL *(Zhan Lan Guan Binguan), 135 Xi Zhi Men Wai St., 100044. Three stars, Tel. 68316633. Fax 68347450. $55 and $80, but $100 in high season. Dist.A.P. 33 kilometers. Dist.R.W. 12 kilometers.*

Quiet setting on own small lake with a large garden. 1988. Seven stories, 250 rooms. USTV. Pub. Chaozhou and Shandong food. Small gym. Bicycles. Small, friendly hotel with quite good English but getting very run down.

FRIENDSHIP HOTEL *(Youyi Binguan), 3 Baishiqiao Rd., 100873. Tel. 68498888. Fax 68498866. $150 in Number One during peak season. Dist.A.P. 33 kilometers. Dist. R.W.16 kilometers.*

In residential suburbs at a good location close to a Third Ring Road (Bei San Huan) exit. Can walk to Bai Shi Qiao (high tech area). Built in 1954 for Soviet experts, this is currently home also for many foreign teachers. Five and six-story buildings. Large gardens. Russian-style, Cantonese, Shandong, Huaiyang and Sichuan food. Cheap shuttle bus downtown. Indoor and outdoor pools, gym and tennis. Bowling due now. Buildings One, Two, Three and Five should now be four stars, with Number One the best. The rooms are small, though, with a total of 1300 rooms, each with kettles, minibars, in-room safes, and USTV.

GLORIA PLAZA HOTEL *(Kai Lai Dajiudian), 2 Jianguomennan Avenue, 100022. Four stars, Tel. 65158855. Fax 65158533. $160 and $190. Presidential Suite $1,200.*

Built 1992 with major renovations 1995. 423 large rooms and suites. Executive floors. USTV. 24-hour business center and room service. Good Vietnamese food and Korean barbecue, European and good Cantonese seafood. Pub. Gym with a view, indoor pool and sauna. H.K.J.V.

GRAND HOTEL BEIJING *(Gui Bin Lou Fan Dian), 35 Changan Dong Ave. 100006. Five stars, Tel. 65137788. Fax 65130048. Book through Leading Hotels of the World 1-800-223-6800. $260 and $280.*

This is the most beautiful part of the Beijing Hotel complex. Built 1989-90. 10 stories. 218 large rooms. 24-hour business center. USTV. Indoor pool, gym and sauna. In-room safes. Small dark lobby but beautiful five-story atrium with zodiac reproductions from the old Summer Palace. Cantonese, especially good Sichuan, and French food. English could be a problem. Looks a little worn. Good breakfast buffet $12 and $14.

GREAT WALL SHERATON HOTEL *(Changcheng Fandian), Donghuan Bei Rd., Chaoyang Dist., 100026. Five stars, Tel. 65005566, 65004555. Fax 65003398, 65001919. In US, Tel. 1-800-325-3535. $275 amd $325. Presidential suite $2,500. Dist.A.P. 25 kilometers. Dist.R.W. nine kilometers.*

Built 1985, with complete refurbishment 1996-1997. 21 stories. 1007 rooms. Wide twins. 24-hour business center, Air China, CITS. Executive floors. USTV. 24-hour coffee shop. Cantonese, Sichuan and French restaurants. Pub. Indoor pool, Clark Hatch health club, and tennis court. Architecture patterned after glitzy Dallas hotel.

GUANGDONG REGENCY HOTEL BEIJING *(Hua Qiao Da Sha), 2 Wangfujing Avenue, 100006. Five stars, Tel. 65136666. Fax 65134248. $140 to $190. Dist.A.P. 35 kilometers. Dist.R.W. four kilometers.*

Close to the back gate of the Forbidden City. 1991-92. Eleven stories. 400 rooms, said to be largest in town. USTV. VCR players. Non-smoking rooms. Scandinavian grill room and imperial Chinese, Tex-Mex and Cantonese food. Deli. Gym, indoor pool. I found this hotel uncertain about its future, so I hesitate about recommending it. It's a good place, but needs a bit of sprucing up.

GUANGHUA HOTEL *(Guang Hua Fandian), 38 Donghuan Bei Rd., 100020. Two stars, Tel. 65018866. Fax 65016516. Y292. Dist.A.P. 33 kilometers. Dist.R.W. five kilometers.*

Built 1967. I cannot recommend this hotel until it's scheduled renovation occurs sometime in 1996 or 1997. Four stories. 100 rooms. No credit cards, no IDD nor elevators. Spacious rooms but only for desperate budget travelers who want a good location.

HAOYUAN BINGUAN, *53 Shijia Huton (Lane), Dengshikou St., 100010. Tel. 65125557, 65253179.*

On lane east of the Tianlun Dynasty Hotel, 164 steps east of the Hitrade Clothing Store (on Dong Dan Nan Da Jie). Look for two white lions outside a rust-colored gate. Built 1984. 17 rooms. Mostly long-term residents. Clean but maintenance needs work. Few services. No English, not even on the gate. But it's charming, and cheap in traditional Chinese style. Operated by the All-China Womens Federation.

HOLIDAY INN CROWNE PLAZA *(Wang Guan Jia Re Jiu Dian), 48 Wangfujing Ave., 100006. Five stars, Tel. 65133388. Fax 65132513. Tel. 1-800-HOLIDAY. $200 to $290. Presidential suite $600. Dist.A.P. 35 kilometers. Dist.R.W .three kilometers.*

Built 1991. Nine stories, 385 rooms. Wide twins. In-room safes. Executive floors. Non-smoking floor. USTV. 24-hour business center with packing and mailing service. Grill room/fine dining. Cantonese food with live crabs in a tank, and spacy eight-storey, atrium coffee shop. Bicycles. Health club with steam bath and view of Forbidden City. Tanning machine. Fancy karaoke. Art gallery.

HOLIDAY INN LIDO *(Lido Fandian), Jichang Rd., Jiang Tai Rd., 100004. Four stars, Tel. 64376688. Fax 64376237, 64376540. In US, Tel. 1-800-HOLIDAY. $160 to $180. Dist.A.P. 17 kilometers. Dist.R.W. 15 kilometers.*

Across from Lido Park with fish pond, and childrens playground. 1984-85. Renovations 1995 and later. Five stories. 1000 spacious, attractive rooms. Wide twins. Executive floor. USTV with HBO. 24-hour business center. Post office. Bank of China. Air China. CTS, United and Lufthansa counters. AT&T. 24-hour clinic. Good pizzeria, deli and pub. Cantonese, good German farmhouse, Indonesian, great Thai but terrible Tex-Mex restaurants. Non-smoking areas. Video rentals. Bicycles. 20 lanes of bowling, gym, indoor pool. Hi-tech disco/karaoke. Cyclone-fun pub. Japanese, German and international schools on premises. Good supermarket and Hong Kong "drug store" (no pharmacist). This hotel also has the distinction of being the world's largest Holiday Inn. Seniors' discount. Buffet breakfast Y110.

HOTEL NEW OTANI CHANG FU GONG HOTEL *(Chang Fu Gong Fandian), 26 Jianguomenwai Dajie, 100022. Five stars, Tel. 65125555, 65125711 (Sales). Fax 65139810-11. In US, Tel. 1-800-4218795; in Canada 1-800-2732294. $180. Dist.A.P. 28 kilometers. Dist.R.W. two kilometers.*

Managed by New Otani International. Built 1990, partially renovated 1995. 24 stories. 500 rooms. Hand showers. Low bathroom ceilings. Molded plastic sinks. USTV. Japanese restaurant with good lunch. Narrow indoor pool, tennis, gym. Some notices in Japanese only. Japan Air Lines office with free airport shuttle for own passengers.

HUADU HOTEL *(Fandian) 8 Xinyuan Nan Rd., Chaoyang Dist., 100027. Three stars, Tel. 65001166, 65001754. Fax 65001615. $75 to $85. Dist.A.P. 25 kilometers. Dist. R.W. nine kilometers.*

Built 1982. Renovating soon. Six stories, 522 rooms with in-room safes. Air China. Post office. Grubby but adequate for budget travelers. Badly managed. Don't expect it to honor reservations nor pass on messages.

JIANGUO HOTEL *(Fandian), 5 Jianguomenwai Dajie, 100020. Four stars, Tel. 65002233. Fax 65002871. In US, Tel. 1-800-553-3638. $170 to $190. Dist.A.P. 27 kilometers. Dist.R.W. three kilometers.*

Built 1982. Good standards. Mediterranean style architecture. Four stories with nine-story tower. 457 rooms with wide twins. 24-hour business center. USTV. Adding executive floor. Asiana and Alitalia airline offices. French and Cantonese food. Gourmet food/bake shop. Video rental. Indoor all-year pool. Gym. Carpets could be cleaner. Little worn but okay. Clinic. Swiss-Belhotel, management consultants. Breakfast buffet Y119.60.

JING GUANG NEW WORLD HOTEL *(Jing Guang Zhong Xin), Jing Guang Centre, Hu Jia Lou, Chao Yang Qu, 100020. Five stars, Tel. 65018888. Fax 65013333. In US, Tel. 1-800-5388882. $190 to $230.*

Built 1990. Good standards. 52 stories (not all hotel). 492 guest rooms. Jacuzzis in suites. Non-smoking floor. Executive floors. USTV and pay movies. Food Street. Cantonese and Korean food. 24-hour room service. Indoor pool. Gym. Deli. Managed by New World Hotels International.

KEMPINSKI HOTEL *(Yan Sha Zhong Xin, Kai Bin Si Ji), Beijing Lufthansa Centre, 50 Liangmaqiao Rd., Chaoyang District, 100016. Five stars, Tel. 64653388. Fax 64653366. In US, Tel. 1-800-426-3135. $275 to $320. Presidential suite $2,500. Dist.A.P. 25 kilometers. Dist.R.W. seven kilometers.*

In large complex with office building, apartments and department store. Built 1992. 18 stories, 530 rooms. In-room safes. Executive and non-smoking floors. Bavarian, Vietnamese, and Italian restaurants. Brewery. USTV but no CNN. Indoor pool, sauna, solarium, gym, tennis. Service good. A Lufthansa hotel.

KUNLUN HOTEL *(Fandian), 2 Xin Yuan Nan Rd., Chaoyang District, 100004. Five stars, Tel. 65003388. Fax 65003228. $200 to $230. Presidential suite $2,000. Dist.A.P. 25 kilometers. Dist.R.W. nine kilometers.*

Managed by Jin Jiang Group. Built 1986-88. Renovations 1995 and 1996. 29 stories, 900 rooms and office suites with in-room safes. Air China. USTV. Revolving restaurant. Japanese, Italian, Pizza, Korean, Vietnamese, Shanghai, and Cantonese restaurants. Indoor pool, gym, and tennis. Shuttle bus. Staff friendly, lively and helpful. Good, dependable hotel with play room for children.

LONG TAN HOTEL, *15 Panjiayuan Nan Lu, Chaoyang District, 100021. Tel. 67763008, 67712244 extension 5895. Three stars. Y286 to Y352.*

Near Long Tan Hou Park, the Long Tan is a blue, 12-story building next to expressway in southeast Beijing. 251 rooms. Recommended for desperate backpackers only.

LU SONG YUAN HOTEL *(Binguan), 22 Banchang Hutong, Kuan Jie, East District, 100009. Two stars, Tel. 64040436, 64011116. Fax 64030418. About Y298. No credit cards.*

North of Art Gallery and near hospital. Buses #104, 108, 113, 2. 31 rooms. Garden style. Only hostel affiliated with World Youth Hostel Federation in China. If staff doesn't give 10% discount to World Youth Hostel Federation members, complain to the Federation. Two dorms with six beds each.

MINZU HOTEL *(Fandian), 51 Fuxingmennei St., 100031. Three stars. Tel. 66014466. Fax 66014849, 66022120. Y645.*

The Minzu has 600 rooms. Rooms are clean in renovated sections. Built 1959. Renovated 1996. Maintenance a problem. Nine stories. 615 rooms. Seafood, Japanese, Chouzhou, Sichuan, Huaiyang food. Bicycles. No USTV.

NOVOTEL BEIJING WANGFUJING *(Song He Dajiudian), 88 Dengshikou, Dongcheng Dist. 100006. Three stars, Tel. 65138822. Fax 65139088. Novotel and Accor reservation systems, in US Tel. 1-800- 2214542. $110 to $124.*

Built 1992. Good standards. 310 rooms. USTV. Thai and Cantonese restaurants. Low hall ceilings. Modest, attractive and well maintained. No pool. Breakfast buffet $11.50.

PEACE HOTEL *(Heping Binguan), 3 Jinyu Hutong, Wangfujing Avenue, 100004. Across from Palace Hotel. Tel. 65128833. Fax 65126863. $120 to $180. West building is three stars and cheaper ($90) with smaller rooms. Presidential suite $1,000.*

Built 1952. All rooms should be redecorated in 1996. 307-room tower. 22 stories. USTV. Post Office. Small indoor pool and gym. East Building has four stars and executive floors. Acupuncture and qigong clinic. H.K.J.V. Breakfast buffet $7.

RADISSON SAS HOTEL *(Huang Jia Fandian), 6A Beisanhuan Road, Chaoyang Dist., 100028. Four-star standard. Tel. 64663388. Fax 64653186, 646531183. In US, Tel. 1-800-854-7854. $180 to $210. Presidential suite $800.Dist.A.P. 20 kilometers. Dist.Tiananmen 10 kilometers.*

Built 1992-93. 15 stories. 374 smallish rooms with kettles. Choice of different decors, some with unusual colors like black leather and light yellow walls. The least radical is the art-deco. Some desks have no drawers. In-room safes and trouser press. Executive floors. Non-smoking rooms. Narrow twin beds. USTV with a speaker in the bathroom. Scandinavian

Grill room. Sichuan and Cantonese food. Deli and bake shop. Indoor pool. Tennis. Squash. Gym. Express three-hour laundry. This hotel is very clean, bright and cheerful. Seniors' rate available. Breakfast buffet Y125.

SHANGRI-LA HOTEL *(Shang Gorilla Fandian), 29 Zizhuyuan Rd., 100081. Five stars, Tel. 68412211. Fax 68418006. In US, Tel. 1-800-942-5050. $215 to $235. Presidential suite $1,200. Dist.A.P. 38 kilometers. Dist.R.W. 15 kilometers.*

Managed by Shangri-LaInternational. 1986-87 with renovations in 1996. 24 stories. 783 rooms. Offices. Executive floor. Non-smoking floor. USTV. Cantonese, Continental and Italian cuisine. Indoor tennis, indoor pool, gym and squash. Shuttle bus. Breakfast buffet Y128.

SUMMER PALACE GUEST HOUSE *(Yiheyuan Binguan), Summer Palace, 100091. Tel. 62581144 X 462. Rate varies.*

It is very difficult to get a room here because of its long-staying guests, but it's worth a try for the incredible setting and antique furniture. The guest house is a long walk from the main gate and there is no English at its gate. Even people in neighboring stores do not know it and travel agents will not book it. But this is real traditional China. Start looking for it a few meters before the west end of the Long Corridor, before the stores, under the three-story pagoda on the hill. Look on the right, the north side, for a red wall with grey around the entrance with white trim and green-and-red framed windows in front painted with flowers. There's gold trim on its red door and vines cover its entranceway. Look for the sign on a tree that reads BO9446, or on a cypress BO8552. It only has six suites with beds for 20 people. Some mahogany beds are carved with imperial dragons. It also has thick carpets, antique plumbing and poor English. Pay whatever they ask. How many foreigners can say they slept at the Summer Palace?

THE PALACE HOTEL *(Wangfu Fandian), 8 Goldfish Lane (Jinyu Hutung), Wangfujing St., 100006. Five stars, Tel. 65128899. Fax 65129050, 65127118. $260 to $340. Dist.A.P. 27 kilometers. Dist.R.W. two kilometers. Tel. 1-800-223-6800 or 1-800-262-9467.*

The Palace is a member of the Leading Hotels of the World and Preferred Hotels. Built 1989. Renovations 1996 and 1997. 17 stories. 530 classy rooms most with in-room safes. Duplex suites. Bathroom panic button. Non-smoking floor. Executive floors. Room service, business center and pressing service — all 24 hours. Bank of China. USTV. French, Sichuan, and Chaozhou food. Especially good are its Italian, Bavarian and Cantonese restaurants. Good Sunday brunch. Year-round indoor pool. Gym. Rolls Royces. Acupuncture. Bicycles. Florist. AT&T. Partially owned by the People's Liberation Army. Managed by Peninsula Group.

TIANLUN DYNASTY HOTEL *(Tianlun Fandian), 50 Wangfujing St., 100006. Four stars, Tel. 65138888. Fax 65137866. In North America, reserve* *through 1-800-44UTELL. Y900 to Y1280. Dist.A.P. 35 kilometers. Dist.R.W. three kilometers.*

Built 1991-92 and deteriorating. Nine stories, 408 rooms. In-room safes. USTV. Bake shop. Cantonese and Vietnamese cuisine. Food Street. Gym. Indoor pool. Bowling. Tennis. Huge 2500-square meter, seven story-high European-style atrium with fountain and "sidewalk" restaurant. Antique shop. This hotel looks like it's going to seed.

TIAN TAN SPORT HOTEL, *10 Tiyuguan Road, 100061. Two stars, Tel. 67113388, 67117366. Fax 671115388. Y291 to Y328.*

Half a block east of the east gate of the Temple of Heaven. IDD. B.C. Money exchange. Dirty and badly-laid carpets. Indonesian restaurant. Ticketing service.

TRADERS HOTEL *(Gu Mao Fandian), 1 Jianguomenwai Dajie, 100004. Four stars, Tel. 65052277. Fax 6505818. In US, Tel. 1-800-942-5050. $190 and $210.*

Built 1989. 298 rooms. Non-smoking rooms. In-room safes. USTV. Guests can use facilities like the gym and pool at sister China World Hotel next door. Comfortable, small, intimate hotel with good service and high standards, currently expanding to 590 rooms and adding a fitness center. Shangri-La International Management.

WANGFUJING GRAND HOTEL *(Wangfujing Dafandian), 57 Wangfujing Ave., 100006. Aiming for five stars. Currently too new to be rated. Tel. 65221188, 65138912. Fax 65138920. $180 to $230. Presidential suite $1,800.*

Second best hotel view of the Forbidden City. 1996. 14 stories, 227 rooms, USTV, and in-room safe. Executive floor. Sichuan and Cantonese restaurants. Gym. 20-meter indoor pool, sauna, gym, and joint-venture Japanese night club. Breakfast buffet Y85.

XIN QIAO HOTEL *(Fandian), 2 Dong Jiao Min Xiang St., 100004. Three stars, Tel. 65133366. Fax 65125126, 65128902. Y704. Dist.A.P.35 kilometers. Dist.R.W. 0.75 kilometers.*

Night food market outside. Big clothes shopping market attached. Built 1954. Renovated 1990-91. Six stories, 320 rooms. Small bathrooms. Carpets could be cleaner. USTV but no CNN. In-room safes. Cantonese, Shandong and Japanese food. Natural hot spring water. Bicycles. Generally good. Problem with maintenance and English. H.K.J.V.

XIYUAN, *1 Sanlihe Road, 100046. Four stars. Tel. 68313388. Fax 68314577. $110 to $130.*

The Xiyuan boasts 707 spacious rooms. This recently resurrected old hotel now has in-room safes, in-house videos, USTV, a boutique brewery, an appetizing-looking Moslem restaurant, and Shandong and Sichuan restaurants. It also has a revolving restaurant, a fast Chinese food restaurant, and a health-food restaurant. 24-hour business center. Small heated pool. Health club due soon. Cathay International Hotel Management. Breakfast buffet $10.

YANXIANG HOTEL *(Fandian), A2 Jiang Tai Rd., Dong Zhi Men Wai, 100016. Three stars, Tel. 64376666, Fax 64376231. Y580 to Y680. Dist.A.P. 17 kilometers. Dist. Tiananmen 15 kilometers.*

Attractive garden and Shandong restaurant with live fish. Pool of questionable hygiene. USTV but no CNN. Clean, polished but very dark, depressing and cheaper than other hotels, but the newly renovated rooms are all right. Spotted carpets. Soviet-style hotel with poor English.

ZHAOLONG HOTEL, *2 Congti Bei (Workers Stadium) Rd., Chaoyang Dist., 100027. Four stars, Tel. 65002299, 65003625. Fax 65003319. $148 to $170. Dist.A.P. 28 kilometers. Dist.R.W. six kilometers. Dist. new railway station seven kilometers.*

Built 1985. Renovated 1996. 19 stories. 259 rooms. Small bathrooms. Indoor pool. Gym.

WHERE TO EAT

Beijing is a gourmet's delight, with excellent food from all over the country and the world, and some of the local variety is incredably cheap. The top restaurants now fly seafood in from the Gulf of Thailand and import Chinese produce from Hong Kong because the best is sent there. Prices listed are subject to change and a there's a 10 to 15%surcharge.

Beijing food is much like Shandong's, but was influenced by the imperial kitchens. It is usually salty (as opposed to sweet) and is not highly spiced. Sauces are used less frequently than in Cantonese cooking.

Unique are the previously mentioned **TINGLIGUAN** *(Pavilion for Listening to Orioles) in the Summer Palace, Tel. 62581608, 62581955. Open daily 10:30 am to 2:30 pm; 5:30 to 8:30 pm* and the **FANG SHAN RESTAURANT** *in Beihai Park, along the lake by the White Dagoba at 1 Wenjin Jie, Xichengqu, Tel. 64011879.* Their cooks were taught by the Empress Dowager's own cooks.

Everyone must try Peking duck at least once! The best part is the crispy skin, which is dipped in sweet, dark brown hoisin sauce, seasoned with a green onion, and then wrapped in a thick pancake and eaten by hand. Mongolian food is local too, especially hot pot which you cook yourself at your table. For the barbecue, you select the raw ingredients and sauces, and then someone else cooks it for you.

The best **Peking Duck** is at the **QUANJUDE KAOYA DIAN RESTAURANTS**. Try the Wangfujing branch (known as "Sick Duck" because of the nearby hospital), *13 Shuaifuyuan, east of Wangfujing, Tel. 65253310, 65228384. Open 10:30 am to 1:30 pm and 5 pm to 8:30 pm.* For eight people, it suggests salted beef for Y20, mushrooms and pine nuts for Y20, two Peking ducks at Y88 each; stir-fried mustard greens Y18, chicken with cashews Y30; shelled prawns with chili oil Y130, duck soup Y4 and fruit Y80. This restaurant has clean white table cloths, charming Chinese decor and bright chandeliers. The Quanjude has branches at *32 Qianmen Dajie, Tel. 65112418* (known as the "Big Duck") and *Hepingmen, Tel. 63018833,* (known as the "Wall Street Duck" to local foreigners because a wall was once beside this old six-story restaurant).

TWO UNIQUE DINING EXPERIENCES!

LOUISIANA RESTAURANT, Beijing Hilton Hotel, 4 Dong Sanhuan Bei Road, 1 Dongfang Road. Tel. 64662288, 64674754. It's open 11 am to 2 pm; 6 pm to 10:30 pm.

A mix of Pacific Northwest, Creole, and Asia-Pacific. The menu in this popular restaurant changes frequently so there is always some variety introduced by guest chefs like Keith Edgar, Claus Mayr, and Charles Saunders. It also matches local and foreign wines to each dish. This makes the Louisiana a very exciting restaurant. Popular are the winter squash bisque Y40, and gumbo Y45 soups. Highly recommended is the rack of lamb smoked with coffee beans, after marinating in sugar cane juice for Y135. Also great is the butterfly Norwegan salmon for Y150. Or try the tender supremo of free range chicken with mango sauce. The most popular dessert is the Mud Bug.

LI JIA CHAI (LI FAMILY RESTAURANT), 11 Yangfang Hutong, De Nei Dajie. Have your driver or hotel telephone 66011915 for directions.

Located across the lake from Soong Ching-ling's residence, this restaurant is a one-table, ten-seat restaurant in a private home in a lane full of tiny traditional old houses. But it has great imperial cooking and classy table settings, a special and exotic experience. A reservation could require weeks in advance but give it a last-minute try anyway. A party of ten gets priority. You can consult about the set menu. Please do not cancel without several days notice; the restaurant will have bought food only for you. The Li Jia Chai is very difficult to find, unless a sign has now been posted outside the gate.

Mongolian food is best at the Donglaishun restaurants. See below in the Qianmen area. For Mongolian food in a relatively authentic setting, you can eat in a **yurt** at the **Movenpick Hotel** below and at the **Swissôtel**, *Hong Kong Macau Center, Dong Si Shi Tiao Li Jiao Qiao, Tel. 65012288. 5:30 to 10 pm. Reservations required.*

For some popular restaurants, particularly the Louisiana, Justine's, the Fang Shan and the Wangfujing Beijing Duck Restaurant, you should make reservations in advance. Some foreigners have celebrated their weddings with dinner on a boat in Kunming Lake at the Summer Palace, or enjoyed picnic suppers on the night with a full moon at the Ming Tombs. Catering can be done by any of the good restaurants.

On the opposite end of the scale, you can also buy onion and sesame buns hot off the grill at a street stall for next to nothing, Y1 or Y2 each.

Great international **buffet brunches** are at the **Swissôtel** with Chinese, French, sushi and a big salad bar on Sundays *(Dong Si Shi Tiao Jiao Qiao. Tel. 65012288)*. This hotel also has a children's menu and excellent desserts. A very good Sunday brunch is at the **Kempinski**, 11:30 am to 3 pm for Y185, and with unlimited champagne it's Y225. Good brunches are also at the **SAS**, **Hilton**, and the **China World** hotels. The best continental food is at Justine's in the Jianguo Hotel. Please consult individual hotels below for addresses.

Holiday Inn Lido-Grace-Yanxiang Hotels area

BOROM PUNAN, *Holiday Inn Lido, Jichang Road, Jiang Tai Road, Tel. 64376688. Thai. Open 11:30 am to 2 pm; 6 to 10 pm.*

This is especially good and is worth the trip out. Prices are moderate to expensive. Soups cost Y31 to Y45; salads Y45 to Y61; vegetarian entrees Y37 to Y53; noodles and rice Y44 to Y75; fish and seafood Y120 to Y175; curries Y69 to Y77; and meat sautees Y61 to Y66. You sit on the floor or on chairs in a romantic Thai atmosphere.

BEIJING LIDO KOREAN RESTAURANT, *Jiang Tai Road, Tel. 64371517.*

This restaurant gives good value, an all-you-can-eat barbecue for Y58 from a choice of 60 dishes including dog. You can also order grilled sliced prime rib for Y50, kimchi for Y10, and beef short rib soup for Y30. No table cloths. It is behind, but has no other relation to the Holiday Inn Lido.

SHI CHUAN YAO DIAN ZI FANG ZHUAN, *#311 Lido Dong Men, Tel. 64373561 X 6028.*

Across from the front gate of the Holiday Inn Lido through the heavy plastic strips, this local restaurant has no sign in English but it does have a menu in English and good, simple food. You know you've found it from its wooden floor, the straw raincoat and wooden plough on the wall, and the large bottles with strange contents. It also has clean white tablecloths. A basic seafood hot pot is Y18 plus Y5 for noodles, Y5 for broccoli, etc.

JIANG TAI RESTAURANT, *Holiday Inn Lido, 7 to 9 am, 11 am to 2 pm, and 5:30 to 8 pm. Closed Sundays.*

Beijing food is featured here. This is a clean place and has standard local prices and modest decor. We did see a couple of chipped dishes. It is behind the Lido Club, back of hotel. It charges Y60 for hot pot, Y4 for jiao tze, and Y13 for bean curd soup.

City Hotel-Zhaolong Hotel-San Li Tun area
METRO CAFE, *6 Gong Ti Xi Lu (by Workers Gymnasium). Italian. Credit cards.*

Good pasta and reasonable prices. This pasta restaurant is known for its lasagne bolognese for Y50, fetuccini with chicken and pepper cheese sauce for Y48, and ceasar salad. Manager Marvin Lau is from Hawaii. See also bars with food in this area in *Nightlife & Entertainment* section below.

Sheraton-Kunlun-Kempinski hotels area
GENJI RESTAURANT, *Beijing Hilton Hotel, 1 Dong Fang Road, North Dong San Huan Road. Tel. 64662288 X 7402. Closed Sundays and public holidays.*

You can get great sushi here. Its set menus start from Y86. Three pieces of sashimi cost Y175, sushi Y180, tempura Y116, and sukiyaki Y360.

YUEN TAI RESTAURANT, *31st floor of the Sheraton Great Wall Hotel, Donghuan Bei Road, Chaoyang District. Tel. 65005566 X 2295. Open 11:30 am to 2 pm; 6 to 10 pm.*

Sichuan food.The Sichuan beef here costs Y50, Chengdu smoked duck Y70, hot and sour soup Y20 and stir-fried seasonal vegetables Y31. It also has Chinese decor and a great view.

SORABOL KOREAN RESTAURANT, *basement, You Yi Shopping Center beside the Kempinski Hotel. 50 Liangmaqiao Road. Tel. 64651845, 64653388 X 5720. Open 11 am to 2:30 pm, and 5 to 9:30 pm daily.*

You can get good Boolgahlbi or marinated short ribs for Y75, or Boolgogi (marinated beef) for Y60. Haemool Pahjuhn (spring onion and seafood pancake) goes for Y60. This restaurant is part of a good chain of Korean restaurants. While you're in the basement, there's a bake shop and edible snacks in the supermarket next door for the budget minded.

SHE SHI YUAN RESTAURANT, *across the street from the Kunlun Hotel, maybe with a sign in English outside. Telephone 64671155 X 3058. Open 11 am to 2:30 pm, and 5 pm to 9:30 pm.*

This is a simple, local, cheap Beijing food restaurant. Its mandarin fish in tomato sauce is Y80, and steamed pork with ground glutinous rice Y9.

Avoid the Hong Kong City in this area. But the **ZHI WEI ZHAI CHINESE RESTAURANT** just north of the Kempinski is good with reasonable prices. Do consider the restaurants in the hotels, especially the Sheraton, the Kempinski, and the Hilton.

Closer to the Canadian and Australian Embassies, the **CITY SATAY** across the street is cheap and modest. While the meat is not top quality, a meal of satay here with rice and soup is filling. At the **YU YUAN HOTEL** in the same general vicinity, you can get a good all-you-can-eat barbecue with drinks, salad and dessert for Y55. The address is *Xin Yuan Xi Li 18 Middle Street, Chao Yang District, Tel. 64669988.*

Jianguo-Friendship Store-China World Hotel area

JUSTINE'S, *Continental. Jianguo Hotel, 5 Jianguomenwai Dajie. Tel. 65002233. Open 6:30 to 9:30 am, 12 noon to 2:30 pm, and 6 to 10 pm.*

With its draperied ceiling, and maroon-and-gold striped chairs, this restaurants offers the best continental food in the city. The goose liver terrine appetizer costs Y148 and escargot Y90. Grilled steak is listed at Y100 to Y320, prawns and mushrooms flamed with Black Label Whiskey and parsley potatoes is Y240.

TRADERS HOTEL COFFEE SHOP, *1 Jianguomenwai Dajie. Tel. 65052277.*

Behind the China World Hotel. This coffee shop has a great lunch time buffet and Starbuck's coffee.

RITAN PARK RESTAURANT, *southwest corner of Ritan Park, within sight of the sign on top of the CITIC Building, Tel. 65004984.*

Good jiao tze. In a Chinese palace, it has Sichuan, Huiyang, and Imperial food with moderate prices but the service and quality are not consistently good. Open daily 11:30 am to 2:30 pm; 5 to 8 pm.

Much cheaper is the **Yong An Li vegetable market** opposite the Friendship Store. This has many small restaurants, some stalls, but is not necessarily clean. Of these, especially good is the "hot and prickly" **SICHUAN HOMETOWN RESTAURANT**. Forget about Uncle Sam's. Avoid Maxim's. Avoid the Broadway Cafe in front of the Friendship Store. Do line up early for the **PIZZA HUT** there if you miss your pizza; it's cheap and crowded. And don't ignore the **BASKIN-ROBBINS** because you can get very good snacks there as well as ice cream.

Shangri-La-Xiyuan Hotels area

PEPPINOS, *Shangri-La Hotel, 29 Zizhuyuan Lu, Tel. 68412211 x 2732, 2733. Monday to Saturday, 11:30 am to 2:30 pm, 6 to 10:30 pm.*

Charming decor with checkered table cloths and guitar player. Spaghetti Marinara Y68, or Tortelloni all-Aragosta con salsa dizafferano Y86.

SHANG PALACE, *Shangri-La Hotel. 11:30 am to 2 pm; 5:30 to 10 pm.*

Try the sweet corn soup with crab at Y35 per person, sweet and sour pork with fresh fruits Y48, wok-fried beef with spring onion Y50 and traditional Beijing duck for Y138.

XIYUAN HOTEL, *1 Sanlihe Road. Tel. 68313388.*

For cleaner, better-quality Moslem food, try the ground floor of the

Xiyuan Hotel. On the grounds of this hotel is a cheaper snack food street open 11:30 am to 2:30 pm, and 6 to 10 pm.

Look for "**Uygurville**," a street marketwith cheap Moslem food and great shishkebobs and breads (also known as **Xinjiang Village** – Xinjiang Cun). There's a good Korean restaurant between the Xiyuan and the Shangri-La Hotel. A **McDONALD'S** is across the street from the zoo.

Wangfujing area
   PALACE HOTEL, *8 Goldfish Lane (Jinyu Hutung), off Wangfujing Avenue. Tel. 65128899.*
   Among its many good restaurants, its Sichuan restaurant offers shredded chicken in chili sauce for Y50 or spicy smoked fish for Y50; Hot and sour shark's fin soup is Y260 per person; diced chicken and cashews in hot sauce is Y50; Sichuan smoked duck is Y100; Shrimps in hot garlic sauce is Y160 and Mapo Bean Curd is Y45.
   SAWASDEE, *ground floor, Novotel Hotel. No reservations. Open 11 am to 2 pm; 5:30 pm to 10 pm.*
   Thai, with a genuine Thai cook. Not as fancy as the Lido's Thai restaurant but good. Try the Tom Yam Goong (hot and spicy lemon flavored prawn soup) for Y45, the Kratong Toung (crispy rice lotus flour stuffed with minced chicken and shrimp) for Y38. Then there's the green curry paste with fish, beef or chicken with sweet basil Y55; or fried noodles with bean curd, shrimp, beansprouts and egg Y60.
   GONIN BYAKUSHO, *second floor, east block of Beijing Hotel, 33 Chang'an Dong Avenue, Tel. 65137766 X 666.* 11:30 am to 2 pm, and 5:30 to 9 pm.
   Reasonable prices for Japanese food. Set Tempura meal Y100 to Y170. Sushi Y8 to Y60.
   HANWOORI KOREAN RESTAURANT, *Peace Hotel. 11 am to 2:30 pm; 5 to 10 pm. Takes credit cards.*
   Good Korean restaurant, with the same menu as Sorobal in Kempinski area (listed above).
   HONG KONG FOOD CITY, *18 Donganmen Dajie, just west of Wangfujing. Lunch 11 am to 2:30 pm, and dinner 5 pm to 10:30 pm.*
   This place has had mixed reviews, but if you're eager for Cantonese food, there's sweet and sour pork for Y42, and your pick of live fish from a tank for Y250. Good dim sum 7 am to 11 am.
   OMAR KHAYYAM, *Asia Pacific Building, 8 Ya Bao Lu, Chaoyang District, Tel. 65139988 X 20188. Open daily 11:30 am to 2:30 pm, and 6 to 10:30 pm.*
   This has the best Indian food in the city. See also Donglaishun Restaurant below.

Near Tiananmen Square

In the **Qianmen area** on the south side of Tiananmen Square are a few good restaurants, especially if you're looking for Western fare: **QUAN JUDE PEKING DUCK** restaurant, a **KFC**, **VIE DE FRANCE** (delicious French bakery cafe) and a **MCDONALD'S**.

On the east side of Tiananmen Square is a branch of the very good **DONGLAISHUN**, the good Mongolian hot pot restaurant with no signs nor menu in English. In spite of the poor staff English, you can get a good hot pot dinner for Y60 each without speaking a word of Chinese. There should be a branch now or soon at *198 Wangfujing Dajie, Tel. 65253562. Open 10:30am to 2 pm., 4:30 to 8 pm.*

About a block east is the **CAPITOL HOTEL**, where in its Yu Quan Hall on the ground floor, you can get a relatively good Cantonese meal that includes pan-fried lettuce with oyster sauce Y30, pork fillet in sweet and sour sauce Y38, fried Chinese cabbage for Y22, and sour and spicy soup for Y18.

Elsewhere in Beijing

DOU HUA RESTAURANT, *27 Guangqumenwai, Tel. 67712662. Open daily 11 am to 1:30 pm, 5 to 8:30 pm.*

Sichuan cuisine. About two kilometers south of the Friendship Store. For Y100 each, you can get the menu for foreigners: four cold dishes, deep fried prawns, egg rolls, sesame dumplings, abalone, fish, jiao tze, spinach, smoked duck, mapo do fu, and dan-dan noodles in this famous, traditional Sichuan restaurant. (The waiter pours tea high up from a copper pot and the decor is bamboo.) It's good and authentic but I've tasted better for cheaper in Sichuan.

One group I spoke with ate at the **XIAO BAIHE RESTAURANT** *(2, Zhishan Men, Jingshan West Street, West District. Tel. 64055005)*, on the first day of an 18-day trip and kept comparing all other restaurants with it. None surpassed it for sweet and sour pork, sizzling beef, crispy fish, and peanuts and chicken Sichuan style.

Also good but not quite up to Xiao Baihe standards is the **BEIHAI IMPERIAL RESTAURANT**, *in front of the Nine Dragons Well, North Bank, Beihai Park. Tel. 64015855, 64041088.* Good for chicken cashews, Peking duck, baby corn and cucumbers, and dumplings. If you want vegetarian food, try **GONGDELIN RESTAURANT**, *158 Qianmen Nan Dajie, Tel. 65112542. 10:30 am to 9:30 pm.*

Budget Dining

For budget travelers, there are the **food stalls** at night near the East Gate of the Forbidden City and also along many other streets. In the mornings, there are street vendors selling traditional rolls, or the Chinese equivalent of doughnuts, the long, deep-fried oil sticks dipped in sweet-ened hot soy milk (cheap), or baked sweet potatoes. In tiny canteens, you can find baozi meat dumplings, either steamed or boiled in soup. You should make sure the hygiene is good before you eat.

A popular bakery on the south side of the Xinqiao Hotel is the **ROSENBEC,** *open 7 am to 9 pm.* The **bake shop** in the China World Trade Center is fantastic. If you want what the Chinese consider a "snack" but something that can fill you up, fast-food Chinese restaurants are in the basements of the **Jing Guang New World Hotel** (shrimp dumplings and noodle soup for Y22) and the **Tianlun Dynasty Hotel** (**GOURMET BAZAAR,** *open 11:30 am to 2 pm; 5:30 pm to 9:30 pm*). Y58 buffet for all-you-can eat hot pot). A food street is beside the Xiyuan Hotel. See also Korean Barbecues and the Yuyuan Hotel for a cheap lunch buffet, above.

A **McDONALD'S** should still be at Changan Avenue and Wangfujing Street. It is said to be the largest in the world. And you'll find lots of cheaper local restaurants in the reviews above.

A PROPOSED ITINERARY

To help you plan your time so you can cover the most important sights, these groupings are suggested. The days can be interchangeable, depending on weather, train schedules, upset stomachs, traffic jams, and the hours a particular attraction is open. Your own interests and needs, of course will vary your time here.

For example, if you are traveling with children, you might want to head to the **Beijing Zoo** and see the pandas. The zoo is located on *Xizhimenwai Street in the western district near the Xiyuan Hotel, Tel. 68314411,* and is open 7:30 am to 6 pm daily.

Day One

You must see **Tiananmen Square**, the **Imperial Palace**, and **Jing Hill**. You can have lunch can be in one of the many restaurants on **Qianmen Xi Avenue** (cheaper) at the south end of the square, the Donglaishun Restaurant on the east side of the square toward the south, or at the Grand Hotel, McDonald's, or the Capital Hotel. There is also a snack stand in the **Forbidden City**.

Day Two

Do spend at least an hour at the **Museum of Chinese History**. This is China's best. The neighboring **Museum of Chinese Revolution** now has in front a clock counting down to July 1, 1997, the taking back of Hong Kong, but the museum itself has changing exhibits. For a pleasant park experience, there's **Beihai Park** and the more important **Temple of**

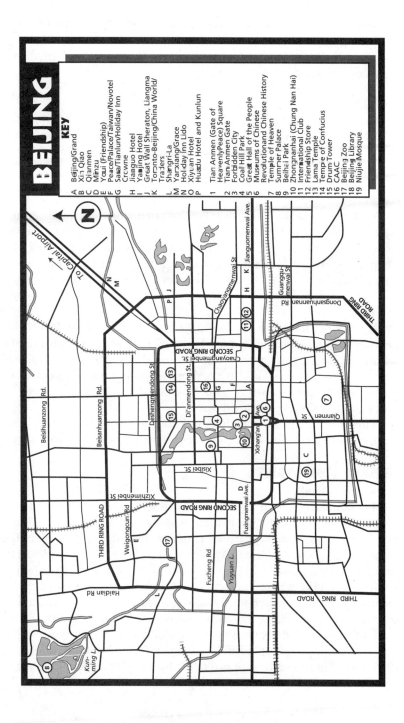

BEIJING

KEY

A Beijing/Grand
B Xin Qiao
C Qianmen
D Minzu
E Youi (Friendship)
F Peace/Palace/Taiwan/Novotel
 Saga/Tianlun/Holiday Inn
G Crowne
 Toronto-Beijing/China World/
H Jianguo Hotel
 Traders
J Yanjing Hotel
 Great Wall Sheraton, Liangma
K Huadu Hotel and Kunlun
L Shangri-La
M Yanxiang/Grace
N Holiday Inn Lido
O Xiyuan Hotel
P Huadu Hotel and Kunlun

1 Tian Anmen (Gate of
 Heavenly Peace) Square
2 Tian Anmen Gate
3 Forbidden City
4 Coal Hill Park
5 Great Hall of the People
 Museums of Chinese
6 Revolution and Chinese History
 Temple of Heaven
7 Summer Palace
8 Beihai Park
9 Zhongnanhai (Chung Nan Hai)
10 International Club
11 Friendship Store
12 Lama Temple
13 Temple of Confucius
14 Drum Tower
15 CAAC
16 Beijing Zoo
17 Beijing Library
18 Niujie Mosque
19

Heaven. You could also do some antique and window shopping at **Liulichang** or the **Hongqiao market**. Eat lunch if you make a reservation on time at the **Fang Shan (Imperial Kitchen) Restaurant** in Beihai Park or any of the other Day One restaurants.

Day Three
Go out to the northwest of the city to the **Summer Palace**, temples of the **Western Hills, Fragrant Hill**, ruins of the **Yuanmingyuan**, and **Great Bell Temple**. Avoid all but the temple if the weather is bad. Lunch at the Summer Palace (reservation needed at the **Tingliguan** there).

Day Four
Visit the **Great Wall** and **Ming Tombs**, but not on a weekend because of heavy traffic. Avoid these also in bad weather. Most tourists visit the Great Wall at **Badaling**. If you want a more remote part of the Wall with less people, ask for **Mutianyu** or drive a little further to an even more remote section. See *The Great Wall* section later in this chapter.

Day Five
My favorite temple is the **Lama Temple**. Nearby is the **Confucius Temple/Capital Museum**. These, along with the China Art Gallery, take half a day. For the remainder of the day and Day Six, there's a choice of arts and crafts factories, rural areas, shopping, cultural performances, or repeat visits to places already seen. You could also take the **hutong** or back-lanes tour in bicycle rickshaws.
This is a very heavy schedule and you may have to squeeze your shopping and strolling into the evenings. One really needs more time.

SEEING THE SIGHTS
Day One in Detail
Tiananmen (Tien An Men) **Square** is 98 acres and great for kite-flying in the spring. Try to imagine 1966 at the beginning of the Cultural Revolution when a million school children filled this square, chanting slogans and waving Chairman Mao's little red book of quotations. The father of Communist China stood at the front of the north gate and acknowledged the screams and cheers of the youngsters. Besides giving them a vacation from school, he also gave them a mandate to travel around the country on the trains with room and board in each city, all free.
Unfortunately, the Cultural Revolution had a serious downside as well, with many people killed and persecuted throughout the country. In 1976, after Mao's death, supporters of the Gang of Four and those of Premier Chou Enlai clashed in the square.

It will be hard for most foreigners to forget the much televised, idealistic young students demonstrating nonviolently for democracy in 1989. An estimated 300 to 3,000 people were killed in or around the square in what the Chinese government calls the quelling of the counter-revolutionary rebellion. No one is allowed to place memorial flowers without government permission, but sympathizers might accidentally drop a flower or two. Chinese government accounts of the turmoil and Western sources do not agree, as you might expect.

The square is bounded on the north by the **Tiananmen Gate** and on the west by the **Great Hall of the People**. On the east is the **Museum of the Chinese Revolution** and the **Museum of Chinese History**, and on the south you can't miss the imposing **Qianmen Gate**. In the center, from the north to south, are the **Monument to the People's Heroes** and the **Chairman Mao Memorial Hall**. Every first of May and October, the big portraits are displayed; from left to right, Marx, Engels, Lenin, and Stalin. Also prominent is Dr. Sun Yat-sen.

Let's start with **The Great Hall of the People**, also known as **People's Congress Hall**, *Tel. 63096156*, open 8:30 am to 3 pm if not used for meetings. Built in 1959, the Great Hall measures 171,800 square meters. Three main sections include a 5000-seat banquet hall, a three-story, 10,000-seat auditorium, and lounges in the style of each of the provinces. This is China's equivalent of a parliament. To some observers, it is merely a rubber-stamp group of representatives. To others, the People's Congress is a forum for the opinions of the masses.

Magnificent, beautiful **Qianmen Gate** has a folk museum. To the south is **Dazhalan**, a Chinese shopping area.

Beijing's gates are marvelous. Each had a very specific purpose; for example, night soil could only go through **Andingmen** in the north and prisoners to be executed plodded through the west gate, **Xuanwumen**. Departing soldiers marched through another of the north gates even if they had to fight in the south. The impressive **Deshengmen** (Victory Gate) can be climbed and may still have good contemporary art for sale.

In the **Monument to the People's Heroes**, the sculptures represent the burning of opium and the Opium War, 1840-42; the Taiping Heavenly Kingdom, 1851-64; the Revolution of 1911; the May 4, 1919 demonstration against the Versailles Treaty and for the New Cultural Movement (calling for plain literature rather than the generally incomprehensible classical language); the May 30, 1925 Incident in Shanghai, a protest against foreign powers in China after a Chinese worker was killed by a Japanese foreman. Look also for the August 1, 1927 uprising in Nanchang and the Anti-Japanese War, 1937-45.

In April 1976, during the Qingming (Ching Ming) festival, when the dead are honored, attempts by the Gang of Four to remove wreaths brought by private citizens in memory of Premier Chou En-lai were resisted by pro-Chou supporters at this monument. Hundreds were wounded and thousands arrested. This protest is now referred to as the **April Fifth Movement against the Gang of Four**, and encouraged pro-Chou politicians like Deng Xiaoping to attempt to overthrow them. In 1989, this statue was central to the student demonstrators.

The **Chairman Mao Memorial Hall** *(Tel. 65131130, 65249831)* was built in 1977. Whether it remains open depends on the political climate. In this mausoleum rest the remains of China's great leader. The simple white building, with 44 granite columns and glazed yellow trim, is 33.6 meters high and 105 meters square (open 8:30 to 11:30 am daily).

All visitors now enter together, and the visit takes less than 30 minutes. As a token of respect, visitors are advised not to wear bright colors, especially red, but no one was stopped when I was there. No cameras or purses are allowed. You first enter the North Hall where there is a seated, three-meter-high marble statue of the leader. Then, quietly, two by two, you enter the Central Hall where Chairman Mao (1893-1976) lies in state.

Tiananmen (Tien An Men; Gate of Heavenly Peace) is the second most famous structure in China. From its high balcony the imperial edicts were read, and this is where, on October 1, 1949, Chairman Mao Zedong (Mao Tse-tung) proclaimed the People's Republic of China. It is a symbol of old and new China. The country's leaders frequently appear here on national days to review the parades and festivities. It was built in 1651 and stands 33.7 meters high. The rostrum where Chairman Mao stood is open to tourists for Y30.

Through the gate under Chairman Mao's portrait and to the left is **Zhongshan Park**, the memorial park to Dr. Sun Yat-sen. To the right is **Working People's Cultural Park**. These two parks are great for a 6 am walk because of the magnificent walls, towers, gates, moats, and pavilions, and also because of the people limbering up for the day. You might hear some very beautiful voices resound off the walls from very shy singers hiding behind bushes and screens.

In the square between the two parks is a tiny white marble pavilion looking much like a Japanese lantern. In imperial times, if an official made a serious error, his black gauze cap was placed inside and he was taken out to be executed at the **Wumen** in front of the palace. Commoners were dispatched (i.e., killed) at the marketplace seven kilometers southwest of here near the Qianmen Hotel.

Gu Gong or **Imperial Palace** (also known as Palace Museum or Forbidden City), *Tel. 65132255*, is open 8:30 am to 4:30 pm (summer). No admittance after 3:30 pm. Visitors usually enter by the **Wumen** (Meridian Gate) inside the Tiananmen between the two above-mentioned parks, and head north. An acoustiguide, recorded by British actor Roger Moore, giving details about a limited area, is recommended.

The Gu Gong was the home and audience hall of the Ming and Qing emperors. Many buildings here are as the Qing left them, minus relics now in the National Palace Museum in Taiwan. Many of the buildings are exhibition halls for historic treasures from all over China. Thousands of imperial robes are stored there. Relics of the Last Emperor Pu Yi can still be seen, including his queue (which he cut off himself), his bicycle, and his cricket box. To walk at a leisurely pace from one end to the other takes about 30 minutes, but to explore it thoroughly takes at least a full day and some would say a week. And not all parts are open to the public!

The **Forbidden City** was originally built from 1406 to 1420 as the palace of the Ming emperors. It lies on more than 720,000 square meters (178 acres) of land. Over 8600 rooms cover a total floor space of about 150,000 square meters. The surrounding imperial red wall is over 10 meters high. Only imperial palaces were allowed to have yellow ceramic roofs. (Commoners could only use gray.) This massive city was built by 100,000 artisans and a million laborers.

Toward the end of the Qing, 280,000 taels of silver were needed annually to maintain the palace, the money collected in taxes and rents from 658,000 acres of royal estates. During the Ming, 9000 ladies-in-waiting and 100,000 eunuchs (castrated males) served here. Some eunuchs became more powerful than the self-indulgent emperors. Sacked by foreign powers in 1900, the Forbidden City was restored and now maintains a permanent staff of painters and carpenters so that every 20 years all the buildings are renewed.

The Forbidden City is divided into two major sections: the **outer palace** (for business) and the **inner residential courts**. Directly beyond the Meridian Gate are the five marble bridges like arrows reporting on the emperor to Heaven. The **River of Gold** below is shaped like a bow. Note the gates; red was used only for important places. Each has 81 studs – nine times nine, an imperial number. Seven layers of brick line the courtyards so no one could tunnel in from below. Note the white squares, on each of which a royal guard stood whenever the emperor ventured past.

Throughout the palace, huge cauldrons of water stand ready for possible fires. On the north side, beneath the cauldrons, are air vents that fan fires set in winter to keep the water inside from freezing. Note the lack of hiding places for possible assassins.

The first building is the **Taihedian** (Tai Ho Tien; Hall of Supreme Harmony), the most stately of all the buildings. It is surrounded by incense burners, 18 bronze ones representing the then 18 provinces, and others in the form of a stork (longevity) and a dragon-headed tortoise (strength and endurance). Note the copy of an ancient sundial and the small openings on the side of the pavilion to allow air to circulate inside. The building was used for major ceremonies like the emperors birthday, for imperial edicts, and for state affairs.

Imagine the area in front of the Hall covered with silk-gowned ministers and officials kneeling in rows, their heads to the ground while smoke poured from the incense burners and musicians played on the balcony. Can you see the child emperor being carried by a palanquin above them to the highly carved throne? If you can't, try to see the Chinese historical movie *Power Behind the Throne* and the American movie *The Last Emperor*. Good books to read are *Inside Stories of the Forbidden City*, published in China, and E. Behr's *The Last Emperor*.

Each of the 18-meter-high cedar pillars was made from one piece of wood. Each of the floor tiles took 136 days to bake, after which it was immersed in oil for a permanent polish. The bricks are solid, about five inches thick and 18 inches square. The base and throne are carved sandalwood.

The **Zhonghedian** (Hall of Complete Harmony) was used by the emperor to receive his ministers, to rest, and to dress before he entered the Taihedian. The two Qing sedan chairs here were for traveling within the palace. The braziers were for heat, the four cylindrical burners for sandalwood incense. Note the imperial dragon symbols on the ceiling.

The **Baohedian** (Hall of Preserving Harmony) the most decorative of these halls, was for imperial banquets and, during the Qing, the retesting of the top scorers in the national examinations. Note the ceilings and beams. Behind this hall, between the stairways, is a giant carving of dragons in one piece of marble from Fanshan county, 16.5 meters by three meters and weighing about 250 tons. Anyone caught touching this imperial symbol was executed. The carving and the timbers were brought here in winter by sliding them over ice made from water of wells especially sunk for the occasion. Nothing was too extravagant for the representative of Heaven!

Several buildings on both sides of these main halls were used for study, lectures, a library, and even a printing shop. Beyond this third hall are the **Inner Courts**, the three main buildings, similar to the three in the outer palace; the **Qianqingong** (Hall of Heavenly Purity) where the emperors used to live and where deceased emperors lay in state.

Cixi (Tzu Hsi), the infamous Empress Dowager, received foreign envoys in the **Jiaotaidian** (Hall of Union) where ceremonies involving empresses took place since women were not allowed in the outer palace! The **Kunninggong** (Palace of Earthly Tranquility) was a residence in the Ming and a shrine in the Qing. One of the Qing emperors used its eastern room as a bridal chamber.

East of the Kunninggong is a hall where clocks from all over the world are exhibited, gifts from foreign missions. In the back of the inner court is the **Imperial Garden**, where a snack bar might save thirsty tourists. The Imperial family sipped tea, played chess, and meditated in this beautifully designed but tiny garden. Can you imagine living here?

Then, continuing northward, you arrive at the back gate where tour groups usually meet their buses. But you're not finished yet! Retracing your steps to the entrance of the inner court, turn left (east) at the Qianqinggong, past the washrooms and the **Nine Dragon Screen**, and then turn left again.

Here are several pavilions with exhibitions well worth seeing, including a stunning collection of gold artifacts, bells, incense burners, table service (with jade handles), and scepters. There are also precious Buddhist relics and the biggest jade sculpture in China, a five-ton Ming statue depicting one of the earliest attempts in the Xia Dynasty to control the Yellow River. Look for paintings and antique jewelry, pottery and bronzes. Also notable, north of this area, is the 12-inch diameter well in which the obviously-thin Pearl Concubine was drowned by a eunuch after she incurred the wrath of the Empress Dowager in 1900. A clean toilet is in this area near the jewelry exhibit.

In each building, look at the ceilings and the palace lanterns, the distinctive blue Manchu cloisonne, and the western clocks. Where were the Imperial toilets? the kitchens? Think of the children who grew up within these walls and never set foot outside! Think of the eunuchs who gave up their manhood for a job that would benefit their families!

American Express has placed wooden signboards in the palace with historical information in English.

Jingshan (Coal) **Hill**, outside the north gate of the palace, was originally the site of a Ming coal pile. It was built with earth excavated from the moats and is 43 meters high. It is now a park with a good view of the Forbidden City and the lakes to the west and north. As the Manchus were breaking into the city, the last of the Ming emperors hung himself on a locust tree at the foot of the hill on the east side. There is a free market outside the **East Gate** every morning.

Day Two in Detail

The **Museum of Chinese History** *(Tel. 65128901, 65128986)* is China's best. It is divided into four sections: primitive society, slave society, feudal society, and semicolonial, semifeudal society. You can walk through without absorbing much in an hour, it is so large. You need at least a half day to do it justice. Please take it in short doses, especially if your feet tire easily. The entrance to the museum is opposite the Great Hall of the People. The history museum is to the right.

Relics here date from 1.7-million-year-old pre-human teeth to 1911. They include a model of the cave where the Peking Man was found. Also on display are a 14th-century B.C. ivory cup inlaid with jade, a Shang bronze wine vessel with four protruding ram's heads, and a Western Zhou sewer pipe with the head of a tiger. Intriguing, too, are a model of a Warring States irrigation system, tomb figures galore, and a model of a first-century B.C. wheel used to operate a bellows to melt iron. Here, too, is the **Flying Horse of Gansu**, which people around the world waited many hours to see when it was exhibited abroad. No queues here!

There is also a model of a 1700-year-old drum chariot with a figure of a child on top, always pointing south, and another miniature drum chariot with a figure that beats a drum every 500 meters, a Yuan water clock, and some Yuan rockets attached to spears. I can only whet your appetite. It is best to take a Chinese-reading friend since there are few signs in English.

The *Tiantan or **Temple of Heaven** (8:30 am to 5:30 pm, but parts are open earlier and closed later) is about five kilometers south of the Forbidden City. Think of the processions of incense-swinging priests, spear-bearing palace guards, and the palaquin bearers carrying the emperor, all marching from the palace unseen by anyone else. Setting eyes on the emperor was a crime punishable by death.

The temple is set in the middle of a 667-acre park with many pine and cypress trees, some over 500 years old. Give yourself at least 20 minutes for a quick look, an hour for a more thorough tour. The Temple of Heaven was built in the same period as the Forbidden City (1420), and ranks among the most famous structures in China. It was used a couple of times a year when the emperor, bearing all the sins of the Chinese people, humbled himself before Heaven and performed the rituals calculated to bring good harvests. The temple has two concentric walls, both round at the north and straight at the south, heaven being round and earth square, or didnt you know!

The raised, 360-meter passage between the main buildings is the **Red Stairway Bridge**. To the north is the **Qiniandian** (Hall of Prayer for Good Harvests) with triple eaves, 38 meters high and 30 meters in diameter. The four central columns represent the four seasons. Around these four are two rings of 12 columns each, the inner symbolizing the 12 months and the outer the 12 divisions of day and night. Here, the emperor performed the rites on the 15th day of the first moon of the lunar calendar. All the columns are wood from Yunnan province.

South of this is the **Imperial Vault of Heaven**, originally built in 1530 and rebuilt in 1752. In this building without horizontal beams were stored the tablets of the God of Heaven, the Wind God, the Rain God, etc. Sacrifices were made on the circular Sacrificial Altar on the winter solstice. The surrounding wall has a strange echo effect. You can hear people talking softly beside it from an unusual distance. Also count the number of stone slabs on the floor, staircases, and balustrades. They are in multiples of nine.

Next head over to **Beihai Park** (North Sea Park), open 7:30 am to 4 pm, only a few blocks west of Coal Hill. (Take bus number 103 along Wangfujing Street from the Beijing Hotel if you wish.) If you are short of time, just head for **Baita Shan** (White Dagoba Hill) and then the **Nine Dragon Screen** (1756) on the opposite side of the lake. While the whole area is a historic site protected by the State Council, these are the highlights of this big, 168-acre park full of intriguing old buildings, the recently renovated **Jingxinzhai** (Serenity Study), winding paths, and interesting rocks that could take a half day to explore. Rowboats are for hire and, in the winter, ice skating on the lake is an exotic experience (but bring your own skates).

The **Fang Shan Restaurant** near the White Dagoba serves the same fancy, delicate dishes (well, almost!) once presented to the Empress Dowager. But you do have to make a reservation or risk going hungry.

In the 10th century (Liao), an imperial residence was built on the site and called **Precious Islet Imperial Lodging**. In the 12th century (Jin), auxiliary palaces were constructed here and a lake excavated, the earth used to build the artificial hills and the *Round City at the southern edge. Rocks from Kaifeng were also used. During the Yuan, the **Qionghua Islet** was expanded and the palace of Kublai Khan was made the center of the city. This palace is no longer standing.

Also on the islet, the 35.9 meter-high, bell-shaped **White Dagoba** was first constructed in 1271 in the Tibetan style. The current stupa was built in 1731.

Also noteworthy is Kublai Khan's 3000 liter jade liquor container (1265) and the **Jade Buddha** in Chengguang Hall in the Round City on the mainland, by the White Dagoba causeway.

The Nine Dragon Screen on the north side of the lake is of glazed brick and is five by 27 by 1.2 meters. Successive dynasties added buildings to Beihai, and this park was also looted by the foreign powers in 1900. In the summer, a giant lantern festival is held in the park.

Zhongnanhai, south of Beihai, has not been generally open to the public because it contains the residences and offices of China's leaders. Very special tour groups have successfully requested a visit. The Qing Guangxu (Kuang Hsu) emperor, who attempted to make modern re-forms, much to the displeasure of the Empress Dowager Cixi, was imprisoned here during the winters when he was not at the Summer Palace. The historically important **Pavilion of Purple Light** and **Fairy Tower** were recently repaired. The **South Gate**, brilliant red and fancy, is on Chang'an Avenue west of the Tiananmen, too prominent to miss.

Now, if you have more time, the antiques, arts, and crafts shopping center of **Liulichang** is nearby, a pleasant place to poke around. Built during the reign of Qing emperor Qianlong, it has been renovated in the old Qing style. For some, looking in antiques and curios can be just as interesting as looking at museums.

Day Three in Detail

The **Summer Palace, Temple of the Azure Clouds, Temple of the Sleeping Buddha**, and **Fragrant Hill** are all within 10 kilometers of each other, 20 to 30 kilometers northwest of Tiananmen. Because of traffic jams, avoid this area on the weekends. If time permits, you can visit the **Yuanmingyuan** and **Great Bell Temple** too.

The **Summer Palace** or **Yiheyuan** (Garden of Cultivating Peace), *Tel. 62581077*, is open 8:30 am to 5:30 pm, but parts are open earlier. A visit to this 717-acre garden usually takes half a day. It is three-quarters water. Originally built in the 12th century, it was expanded in 1750 for the 60th birthday of the mother of the Qianlong emperor and burned in 1860 by the British-French army. It was rebuilt by the Empress Dowager Cixi (Tzu Hsi) on the occasion of her 60th birthday (1895) and financed with funds meant for building the Chinese navy. It was badly damaged by the foreign powers in 1900; the existing buildings were restored in 1903.

The imperial court lived here every year, when possible, from April 15 to October 15, receiving diplomats and conducting business in the Renshoudian (Hall of Longevity and Benevolence). Empress Dowager Cixi, who was the power behind the throne from 1861 to 1908, lived in this hall near the Deheyuan (Grand Stage) where she could indulge in her passion for theatricals. The stage floor is hollow so that ghosts could emerge from it. The Grand Stage is now a separate museum requiring an additional fee. It contains Cixi's jewelry and dinnerware, and wax figures of Cixi and two imperial concubines. Attendants are in Qing palace costumes and you can have your photo taken with a live eunuch or the wax figures. In the exhibition hall behind the stage is the 1898 automobile given to the emperor by General Yuan Shikai.

Twenty-eight ladies in waiting, twenty eunuchs, and eight female officials waited on the Empress Dowager. For lunch, she was offered 128 courses daily.

In the Hall of Jade Ripples, to the south of the main entrance, she kept the Guangxu (Kuang Hsu) emperor imprisoned every summer from 1898 to 1908 after he tried unsuccessfully to institute reforms to modernize China and to take his rightful power back. Note the walls around the compound. The rooms here and elsewhere are furnished as they were then.

The **Long Corridor** extends 728 meters along the lake to the famous **Qingyan** (Marble) **Boat**. The 1,400 paintings here (count them if you don't believe it!) are a most spectacular display. To the north up the hill are the **Hall of Dispelling Clouds**, the **Tower of Buddhist Incense**, and the **Temple of the Sea of Wisdom** where the empress used to hold her birthday celebrations and religious services. The **Xiequyuan** (Garden of Harmonious Interests) was designed like the Jichangyuan (Garden) in Wuxi. Also on the hill is a Tibetan-style Lama temple. Crossing **Kunming Lake** is a 17-arch bridge and, on an island, the **Dragon King Temple**.

A good restaurant is in the **Tingliguan** (Pavilion for Listening to Orioles) and reservations are essential *(Tel. 62581955, 62581608)*. Open daily 10:30 am to 2:30 pm and 5:30 to 8:30 pm.

The **Summer Palace Hotel** is in the garden, near the Hall of Scalloped Clouds, an exotic experience if you don't mind being isolated. It is a long way from downtown. Accessible from the palace is **Suzhou Street**, reconstructed on its original site. Built in the 18th century, and destroyed in 1860 by foreign soldiers, it was the shopping area used by palace residents. Attendants in Manchu dress give demonstrations of crafts and music. Photos are best late morning and early afternoon.

Northwest of the Summer Palace are the **Beijing Botanical Garden** and the **Temple of the Sleeping Buddha** (also known as Wofusi, or Temple of Universal Spiritual Awakening). This was first built in the Tang and reconstructed and renamed in the Yuan, Ming, and Qing. The lacquered bronze **Sakyamuni**, which was cast in 1331 (Yuan), is 5.33 meters long and weighs 54 tons. It is the largest bronze statue in China. The Buddha here is giving his last words to his disciples before his earthly passing. Because he is barefooted here, successions of emperors have presented the statue with 11 pairs of huge hand-made cloth shoes, which are on display in the same room. You can also stay in the temple overnight.

The **Biyunsi** (Temple of Azure Clouds), is more important than the Sleeping Buddha because of its stunning collection of religious statues and the Diamond Throne Pagoda. The Biyun was first built in the Yuan as a nunnery. During the Ming, it was the burial place for powerful eunuchs. In 1748, Emperor Qian Long (Chien Lung) ordered to be built the **Hall of Five Hundred Arhats** and the **Diamond Throne** (or Vajra Throne) **Pagoda**. The 508 gilded, wooden Buddhist saints are life-size and strikingly beautiful, each different, and protected behind dirty glass. How many are not sitting? Which have two heads?

In 1925, the body of Dr. Sun Yat-sen lay in state at this temple until the completion of his mausoleum in Nanjing. A tiny museum is at the spot. The unique 34.7-meter Diamond Throne Pagoda consists of five small pagodas in the Indian style and has some excellent carvings and towers, showing a great deal of Indian influence.

Xiang Shan (Fragrant Hill) **Park** is open 7:30 am to 5:30 pm, and was a 150 hectare (384 acre) hunting ground for many emperors. A 20-minute chairlift to the top of the mountain now gives a spectacular view of the area, especially in autumn, when the air is less dusty and some leaves are red. The highest peak here is 557 meters above sea level. The lift goes by a small **Glazed Pagoda**, a Western-style mansion that was presumably the hunting lodge, and a Tibetan-style temple, which you can inspect later.

Avoid the pathetically run-down Xiang Shan (Fragrant Hill) Hotel until it is renovated. But there are several camels to ride at the village before you get to this hotel.

If time permits on the way back to town, glimpse the **Yuanmingyuan ruins**, open 7 am to 7 pm *(Tel. 62551488)*. This Garden of Clear Ripples was built in an area full of bubbling springs and was used as an imperial resort beginning in the 11th century. It became the site of a major palace in 1690 and later was rebuilt into a favorite 160-hectare palace garden by Qing Emperor Qianlong, with buildings copied from Suzhou, Hangzhou, and Yangzhou. Sacked by Anglo-French forces in 1860 (after the Qing defeated the foreigners at Taku and tortured their envoys), it was partially repaired only to be destroyed again in 1900. Foreigners wanted to punish the emperor who loved it in revenge for the siege of the legations.

The few remains of this Garden of Gardens and Palace of Palaces can be glimpsed at in 45 minutes if you are in a hurry to get to the Great Bell Temple. Enough remains of the marble archways of the Evergreen Palace to show the influence of the European missionaries who helped design it early in the 1750s. Since the imperial families favored the Yuanmingyuan over the Imperial Palace, they kept their most precious treasures and books here. The 1860 burning took two days and is documented in a good Chinese-made movie, *The Burning of the Summer Palace*. One of the best accounts in English is Garnet J. Wolseley's *Narrative of the War with China in 1860*. A small exhibition near the entrance tells the story. The maze and some other buildings have been reconstructed.

You are rushing now to get to the **Da Zhong Si**, the **Temple of the Great Bell** *(31A Beisanhuan Xilu, Haidian District, Tel. 62541971, 62550843)*. Open 9 am to 4:30 pm. This temple houses over 40 different ancient bells. The most spectacular bell was cast during the reign of Emperor Yongle of the Ming (1403-25) in a clay mold and weighs 46.5 tons. How would you have brought the bell here without a crane and truck? In 1733, the Chinese slid it on ice in winter or on wheat shells in summer and put it on a mound. After attaching the bell onto the beams, they dug out the mound and built the hall around it. The 220,000 amazingly-handsome Chinese characters decorating it are Buddhist scriptures and prayers.

The other bells in the exhibit were for various purposes. In religious ceremonies they drove away worldly worries and attracted the attention of the gods. Some bells here announced the time of day and the closing of the city gates. Some were used in music rituals. (See also *Wuhan*.) A small hall contains an exhibit on how the bells were made.

Day Four in Detail

Some people prefer to take their own box lunch to the *Great Wall even though restaurants are available. For an excursion to the Great Wall *(Tel.63011864)*, see *The Great Wall* section later in this chapter. Remember, there are some less crowded places to see the Great Wall.

The **Ming Tombs**, *Shisan Ling**, are among the most famous sights in China. Open daily 8 or 8:30 am to 4 or 4:30 pm, the tombs are usually combined with a trip to the Great Wall at Badaling. They are a 50-kilometer (100-minute) drive northwest of the Tiananmen Gate.

These 13 imperial tombs were built from 1409 to 1644 and spread over 40 square kilometers. Each tomb consists of a Soul Tower, a Sacrificial Hall, and an Underground Palace where the bodies were placed, surrounded by a wall. Approaching from the south, you can see a big, carved white marble archway, erected in 1590, beyond which are the **Great Red Gate**, ornamental pillars, and the **Tablet Pavilion**. The **Sacred Way** has 24 stone animals (lions, unicorns, camels and elephants), 12 larger-than-life-size humans (military officers and government officials), and an army of enterprising hawkers (also an old China tradition) selling everything from furs, porcelain, and fruit to junk.

At least two of the tombs are open to visitors: **Chang Ling**, the biggest and earliest. There's also **Ding Ling**, which has been excavated and can be entered. Ding Ling is the tomb of the 13th Ming Emperor Wanli, who ruled for 48 years, starting at age 10. The tomb was begun when he was 22 years old. It took six years and cost eight million taels of silver to build.

The underground palace consists of three halls, the central one with passages to annex chambers, totaling 1195 square meters. The marble doors each weigh four tons and were closed from the inside by propping two large stone poles against them. Note the two triangular depressions in the ground inside the door where the poles rested. Note also the blue and white porcelain jars with the dragons, which were half filled with oil when the tomb was opened. The oil was burned to create an oxygen-free vacuum inside.

In the central hall are three marble thrones, two for the empresses, one for the emperor, all real. Note the Five Altar Pieces and the porcelain lamp. The rear hall has the three coffins and plaster replicas of 26 chests. There is a separate museum, which has on display some of the objects found in the tomb, such as the gold crown, headdresses, a jade belt, and a gold bowl. A 20 minute movie about the opening of Ding Ling is shown. The **Ding Ling Restaurant** nearby is better for lunch than the exotic **Ming**

Yuan Hotel a few kilometers away. Better still is the restaurant at the golf course but it's more expensive.

Enjoy the rural beauty, the vast, open spaces between the tombs, and the peace when you escape the 10,000-a-day tourists and peddlers. If you have time, you should also wander around the other tombs, which are not repaired and are usually free of tourists. These other tombs are not opened because of the high cost of careful archaeological excavation. Besides, no one knows where the entrances are because their builders were executed and no records have survived. The exterior of the tombs and the Great Wall are best seen at dusk, when one feels the presence of ghosts. Seeing weeds growing on imperial terraces and birds making nests on once glorious beams is a good time to reflect on life and death.

The Beijing Municipal Government and a Japanese firm have opened a **recreation complex** with roller coasters, ferris wheels, hotels and camel-racing tracks. There is also a nearby 18-hole golf course.

Day Five in Detail

Another much-visited site is *Yonghegong (**Lama Temple**, or **The Temple of Harmony and Peace**), open 9 am to 4:30 or 5:30 pm, closed Mondays. Count on at least 40 minutes. First built in 1694, this Mongolian-Tibetan yellow-sect temple is at the subway exit and is within walking distance of the Overseas Chinese Hotel. It should not be missed. Beautifully renovated, it reveals pavilion after pavilion of increasingly startling figures, the largest in the back hall 18 meters high. This Buddha was carved from one piece of sandalwood from Tibet and the temple was built around it.

The steles are incised with Han, Manchurian, Mongolian, and Tibetan script. The statues in the main halls resemble those in most Buddhist temples, but some statues wear the pointed Himalayan caps and white Tibetan scarves, a traditional gift. On either side of the symmetrical structure, however, the more typically Tibetan demons, human skulls, and *tankas* (religious paintings) are displayed. Another admission ticket is required for the exhibition hall that shows many Tibetan silver utensils of very intricate craftsmanship.

The Yonghegong was built in 1694 as an imperial residence for Emperor Yongzheng, then still a prince. It was transformed into a Buddhist or Lama temple in 1744 during Qianlongs reign. Prayer wheels are for sale.

This temple was an attempt by Emperor Qianlong to unite the Han, Manchu, Mongol, and Tibetan peoples into one country. He also took a Uygur princess from what is now Xinjiang into his court as one of his favorite empresses. For more on Lamaism, see also Lhasa and Chengde.

If You Have More Time

The **Arthur M. Sackler Museum of Art and Archaeology**, *at Beijing University, Tel. 62751667*. Don't expect to get in the gate at the university. You should make arrangements beforehand, a couple of weeks in fact. CITS can arrange it or you can telephone the university directly at the number above. The Sackler contains fourteen galleries from Paleolithic to Ming from the university's own collection.

The **Shudian** (**Capital Museum**), *in the old Yuan dynasty Confucius Temple, almost across Yonghegong Avenue from the Lama Temple. 13 Guozijian Jie, Dongcheng District. Tel. 64012118*. Open daily except Mondays from 9 am to 4 pm. It is the second largest Confucian temple in China. The exhibits on Beijing history, Qing armor, and the stone drums are worth seeing. Look for maps and relics of the old Yuan city too.

The **China Art Gallery**, *Tel. 64017076, near the Guangdong Regency Hotel*. Open daily except Mondays, 9 am to 4 pm. The gallery has changing exhibitions. See also Victory Gate (Deshengmen). For art exhibitions, consult the free tourist literature listed in *Getting Around Beijing*, above.

Paleozoological Museum of China, *#142. Xizhimen Waidaijie, across from the main gate of the Xiyuan Hotel. Tel. 68355511 X 227*. A sign outside says it's open 9 am to 4:30 pm but it was closed then when I visited. It has two mechanical dinosaurs and nine complete skeletons.

CCTV Tower, *at Xisanhuan Zhong Lu in west Beijing*. You'll be treated to a great view from 238 meters up in the air. There's a coffee shop and restaurant.

Chinese Ethnic Culture Park, *in the north part of Beijing at Yayuncun, Asian Games Village just west of Beichen Road, Tel.62063626 or 62063678*. This is an introduction to the ethnic diversity of China's people. The reproduction of the architecture is good and signs are in English. You get a sanitized feeling of Tibet,however. It is smaller and less organized than a similiar park in Shenzhen. During high tourist season, you can see ethnic dances and costumes. It is open 8:30 am to 5:30 pm daily for Y120. About 25 minutes from city center.

Daguanyuan (**Grand View Garden**), *Tel.63262306*, 8:30 am to 5:00 pm, is a 100,000 square-meter theme park in southwest Beijing inspired by one of China's greatest novels, the Dream of the Red Mansions. The buildings are sometimes staffed by actors dressed in Qing fashions as characters from the beloved novel.

*White Dagoba Monastery *at Miaoyingsi (Temple of Excellent Confirmation) in Xicheng* is from the Yuan (1271). During repairs made in 1978 after the Tangshan earthquake, archaeologists found more than ten relics inside dated 1753, from the Qianlong emperor.

Residence of Mme. Soong Ching-ling, *46 Houhai Beiyan, Xichengqu, Tel. 64031633 or 64016306*, is interesting not only because she was an illustrious humanitarian, the respected widow of Dr. Sun Yat-sen, but the father of Emperor Pu-yi (the last Emperor) was born here. Canadians might be intrigued by a copy of Margaret Trudeau's book in the library. (Read *Soong Dynasty*.) It is open 9 am to 4 pm.

Niujie Mosque, *in the southwest of the city*, where about 10,000 Muslims live on Niujie Street. This mosque is primarily for visitors with an interest in Islam and religious buildings. The mosque was founded in the Liao dynasty (A.D. 996) by the Arabian Scholar Nasullindin and rebuilt and enlarged in subsequent dynasties. Although it is in classical Chinese architecture, the interior does have west Asian arches and Arabic writing. Note the curtained-off section for women. It is open 5 am to 7 pm.

*Beijing Gu Guanxiangtain *(Ancient astronomical observatory, Tel. 65242202 at Jianguomenwei Avenue, near the Friendship Store*. Built in 1442 (Ming), this building has some instruments dating from 1437 to 1442. Telephone ahead for times.

Baiyunguan (Temple of White Clouds), *outside Fuxingmenwai, southwest of Beijing Television*, this is the largest Taoist Temple in China. Built originally in the Tang, it burned down in the Jin and was rebuilt in the Ming. During the Qing, it was enlarged. It has some striking incense burners and gilded statues, including that of Taishang Laojun, the initiator of Taoism.

Prince Gong's Mansion, *23 Lu Yin Jie*, is open 8:30 am to 4 pm daily and is included in the Hutong Tour. It was built from 1776 to 1785 and owned at one time by the great-uncle of the Last Emperor. Go for the pretty garden, the theatre, and the traditional style buildings.

Lugouqiao (Reed Valley Bridge), *also known as Marco Polo Bridge, is 20 kilometers southwest of the city, Tel. 63813163*. Built in the 12th century, it is 250 meters long with 11 stone arches and 485 stone lions spaced along its railing, each one different. The bridge is named for Marco Polo because the Venetian explorer described it at length to his biographer. It is the site of the incident that touched off the Japanese war on July 7, 1937. The bridge was renovated in the late 1980s with the addition of a museum of Chinese resistance to the Japanese invaders. The museum is inside the neighboring, quaint walled village.

*Zhoukoudian, *48 kilometers south of Beijing*, is where the Peking Man, who lived 400,000-500,000 years ago, was found in a cave in 1927. At least 44 skulls have been discovered there. A small museum has some relics, but many of the bones were lost during the Japanese war.

Aviation buffs should be interested in the **Aviation Museum**, *(Tel.62912457)* with its 151 planes.

For other overnight excursions, see the following destinations later in this book: Chengde (three days), Tianjin, Shijiazhuang, Beidaihe, Shanhaiguan, and Datong. See also Zunhua for the Qing imperial tombs.

Walks

You might begin with the area north of the Xinqiao Hotel and south of the Beijing Hotel for the old European architecture. This **foreign legation area** was under siege during the Boxer uprising from June 13, 1900. On June 20, most foreign diplomats and missionaries and 2,000 Chinese Christian refugees took shelter in the British Legation until the International Relief Force arrived on August 13. That British Legation building has been torn down to make way for a housing project. Some of the old buildings are now used by the Beijing Municipality and the Communist Party.

THE HUTONG TOUR

This tour was started by a photographer obsessed with preserving the old architecture and can now be booked through the travel agencies. It takes you through the old alleys near the Drum Tower, visits one of the courtyard homes (remember the one-story house in the movie M. Butterfly) and then ends up at the palatial and beautifully-renovated Prince Kong's Mansion and garden.

Before the 1970s, the whole city of Beijing consisted of these charming tiny houses. The privately-operated Hutong Tourist Agency has 50 bicycle rickshaws and drivers. While blankets are provided in cold weather, we do recommend it only in warm, dry weather.

The three-hour tour starts twice a day from 100 meters west of the north entrance to Beihai Park (you can't miss the maroon- canopied tricycles). It goes past Xi Sha lake to the Drum Tower (69 high stairs) where there is an exhibit of hutong photographs and one 13th century Yuan dynasty drum. From there you go to the old Silver Ingot Bridge. You also visit one of the houses. We had tea with a 78-year old Communist cadre, then went to the other extreme to Prince Gong's digs where you can chuckle about the reproduced piece of the Great Wall there to remind him of his Manchu past. Then you too can relax over tea in his fancy theatre. The mansion was originally built by a Ming eunuch in the southern style.

*Contact: **Beijing Hutong Tourist Agency**, West BLD, 10 Gan Mian Hu Tong, Dongcheng District, 100010. Tel.65254263, 65248482. Fax 65249357. Ask for Miss Liang Li, who speaks English.*

The areas around the Minzu Hotel, Drum Tower, and between the Xi Dan Market and the Forbidden City are full of old houses with antique doors, carvings, grinding stones used as steps, and fancy, carved stone door hinges. These **back alleys** with tiny houses and crowded courtyards with paper windows, are fascinating and are an endangered species.

The names of the alleys immediately around the Forbidden City are appealing. Nai Zi Huton (Wet Nurse Lane) was the street where the new mothers who nursed the imperial babies lived. Flower Lane was for those who hand made all the silk flowers for the imperial ladies. There were also Goldsmith Lane, Laundry Lane, and Bowstrings Lane.

You can consider your visit to the **Temple of Heaven** grounds a good place to walk. Or try circling outside of the Forbidden City. A good time is early in the morning, about 6:30-7:00 am when there is a street market with vegetables and outdoor barber shops by the East Gate of the old palace. This market helps bring to life what it must have looked like back in the Ming dynasty.

NIGHTLIFE & ENTERTAINMENT

There's a lot of good stuff here: opera, ballet, symphony orchestras, movies, art exhibitions, martial arts. Check *China Daily* or tourist hand-outs for events and times.

For traditional Chinese arts, see the **Beijing Opera** in the pleasant Liyuan Theater *in the Qianmen Hotel, 175 Yungan Road, just south of Liulichang antique street, Tel. 63016688*. Performances are held every evening at 7:30, usually with English titles to help you understand the plot.

For a traditional Chinese variety show, there's the delightful **Lao She Teahouse** *in the Da Wan Cha Building, third floor, 3 Qianmen Xi Avenue, 50 meters west of Kentucky Fried Chicken at the south end of Tiananmen Square. Tel. 63036830*. Look for the neon tea cup. From 7:30 to 9:30 pm every evening, it offers some of Beijing's top talent, including Beijing opera, magicians, cross-talk, and comedy acts. Theres a 1920's atmosphere with dirty floors and watermelon seeds. The talent transcends language. There's also the **Tianqiaole Tea House**, *113 Tianqiao Market. Tel. 63040617*. Performances at 7 pm, with folk arts performances and Beijing snacks. Closed Mondays.

The **Hotel Beijing-Toronto**, *Tel. 65002266,* has a Chinese puppet show every Saturday evening at 8 pm on the fourth floor. The **Beijing Wuyi Diyuan Theater**, *at the East Gate of the Olympic Sports Center at Xiao Guan. Tel. 64912157 or 64912233 X 450* performs martial arts demonstrations from time to time. The **Huaxia Cultural and Martial Arts Center**, *Tel. 63095819 or 66167831 X 180*, has performances daily at 7:30 to 8:40 pm. They also give courses.

Every second Friday, **Sophia's Choice** *at the Sino-Japanese Youth Exchange Centre, 40 Liangmaqiao Lu, Tel. 65004466 X 103*, shows good Chinese movies and frequently the film maker gives a talk. Call the **Art Salon** *at the Holiday Inn Crowne Plaza (65133388)* about Chinese movies with English subtitles every other Friday evening. It also has concerts on Thursdays and Saturdays *(Tel.65122288 X 1209)*.

The **Peking Acrobatic show** is not as good as Shanghai's, so it can be missed if you're going to that city. But it is still good. Book through your hotel, about Y30. The address is: *Chaoyang Theatre, 36 Dongsanhuan Bei Lu, Chaoyang. Tel. 65072421, 65004473.*

The Swissôtel and China World hotels have western and Chinese classical music with orchestras in their lobbies on Sundays, not the quietest place for it. And there's an interesting open-air night food market near the East Gate of the Forbidden City where you can see local food being prepared, and even sample some if you dare.

If you're tired of things Chinese, Beijing also has other fare: The **Gloria Plaza Hotel** (Tel. 65158855) has a daily **dinner show** with prices ranging from $28 to $36 depending on the menu. The show is professional quality, the food quite good but not exceptional, the music canned.

BEIJING'S JAZZ & CLASSICAL HOT SPOT!

*The **Sanwei Book Store** has live, smoke-free jazz on Fridays evenings (with not-so-good food) and live classical music on Saturday evenings. This tiny "book store" is on a side street across the street south from the Cultural Palace of the Nationalities which is on Fuxingmennei Ave. Tel. 66013204.*

For complete relaxation, there're massages at the hotels. Among the best hairdresser is Gary at Roger Craig at China World. The larger hotels offer cocktail lounges with live music. One of the more popular hotel bars with foreigners is **CHARLIE'S** *at the Jianguo Hotel.* Pleasant, small, privately-run Chinese bars have opened, but have also been periodically closed for prostitution or drugs.

Among the watering holes frequented by foreigners is **MEXICAN WAVE RESTAURANT** (poor food) *behind the Gui You Department Store on Dong Da Qiao Road, Tel. 65063961.* It's usually packed after 11 pm. It has sidewalk tables in the summer, and moderate prices.

There's the American-owned **FRANK'S PLACE**, *East Sports Stadium Road, Tel. 65072617, near City Hotel.* Hamburgers are Y35 and considered by some the best in town. Try also the fried cheese for Y35. Beer costs Y20 to Y35 a bottle which you can enjoy al fresco in warmer weather. A good bake shop, **BELLA'S**, is next door, and close by is **BERENA'S**, a moderately-priced Cantonese restaurant favored by foreigners.

The **HARD ROCK CAFE**, *in the Landmark Arcade, 8 North Dongsanhuan Road, Chaoyang District, 100004. Tel. 65016688 X 2571,* has good fries and is open Sunday through Thursday 11:30 to 2 am; Friday and Saturday 11:30 to 3 am. Yankee burgers cost Y62 to Y72; apple pie is Y45 and thick fountain shakes, Y28. Tee-shirts are on sale. This is one of the best discos but it's very noisy especially after 10 pm.

FRIDAY'S (*19 Dong San Huan Bei Lu, Tel. 65951380, one block south of the Zhaolong Hotel on the west side*) has good food but atrocious service and hardly any English. Some guests have waited two hours. It has fajitas, fried mozzarella, and buffalo wings, each for Y45. Nachos cost Y98 to Y125, hamburgers Y40, soup and salad Y40, and loaded potato skins Y68. The waiters dress in cute costumes. It's on Second Ring Road.

POACHERS, *at 7 San Li Tun, is above a Friendship Store, Tel. 65323063.* Cheap draft beer, live entertainment, informal and somewhat disorganized, this place is cheap and funky. It has guest disk jockeys and bands on weekends, hopefully Cobra, an all-women band. The crowd is young.

MINDER CAFE, *Dong Da Qiao Xie Jie (behind the City Hotel), Tel. 65006066,* has a pub atmosphere, and good steaks, sandwiches, burgers, and spaghetti. It has a good band Wednesday through Saturday evenings and serious darts on Thursday evenings. Open 11 am to whenever, its happy hour is 2 pm to 8 pm or 9 pm.

PAULANER BRAUHAUS, *in the Kempinski Hotel, Lufthansa Centre, 50 Liangmaqiao Road, Tel. 64653388,* is a boutique brewery with huge shining beer vats, long tables, and benches. It has good food, too, like half-grilled pork knuckles with sauerkraut and roast potatoes for Y125 and Nuernberger Sausage with sauerkraut and mashed potatoes for Y85. Half a liter of beer will set you back Y35 during the day, Y45 after 6 pm.

SCHILLER'S, across the road north of the Lufthansa Centre, is a popular expatriate hangout with club sandwiches, spaghetti, fries and burgers. They have a dart board. In summer there's sidewalk service.

The **brewery** *in the Kempinski Hotel*, open 11:30 to 1 am, is also popular.

Festivals

The week before and after the **lunar new year**, a temple fair takes place at the **Temple of the Earth**, the **Ditan**. Ice sculpture shows are at Long Qing Xia, Bohai Park, and Olympic Village. The **Golden Autumn Festival** is at the Yuanmingyuan. Look for dragon boat races in June and kite-flying contests in the spring.

SHOPPING

You can buy top quality goods from all over the country and the world (at higher prices, of course). Locally made goods include cloisonne, lacquerware, jade carving, filigree jewelry, carpets, and woodblock prints. Also made locally are felt hats and track suits. Chinese antiques can be cheaper than outside of China, and the quality and variety is very good.

Beijing has the best shopping after Shanghai. The Beijing Tourism Administration has a list of shops approved for foreign visitors.

The **Palace Hotel** has top-of-the line international name brands, but when Wangfujing Avenue gets rebuilt, you'll find some of these there too. At the moment, the Palace has the likes of Louis Vuitton, Celine, Bally, Gianni Versace, Hugo Boss, MCM, and Givenchy.

The main traditional shopping street is the very crowded **Wangfujing Avenue** along the east side of the Beijing Hotel and extending to the Regency Hotel, only seven short blocks, which are parallel to the Forbidden City. This area is in the process of being transformed from an interesting old traditional shopping street to a mix of traditional Chinese shops with bargains, and expensive, giant modern shopping malls like anywhere else in the world.

The stores that were torn down will be given space in new malls when completed. Still up are the **Arts and Crafts Centre**, *200 Wangfujing (Tel. 66124165)* with its good prices, some of the big book stores, the **Bi Chun Tea Store** *(Tel. 65254722)*, a couple of pharmacies, and stores specializing in musical instruments, hats, and furs. There's also the **Beijing Department Store** *(on the west side, Tel. 65126677)*. The **Huaxia antique store** is at *293 Wangfujing*.

Outside of Wangfujing is the **White Peacock**, *East Bin He Lu, Deshengmen, Tel. 62011199, which is on Second Ring Road almost north of the Forbidden City*. It has arts and crafts and silk.

The silk store with the biggest selection is the **Yuan Long Embroidery and Silk Store**, *55 Tian Tan Lu, Chongwen District, Tel. 67020682, near the Temple of Heaven*. It's open 9 am to 6:30 pm and has silk textiles as well as jewelry, carpets, embroidery, furs, and silk clothes.

The **Jianguo-Friendship Store** area is less crowded than Wangfujing. It also has the good **Gui You Department Store** (open 9:30 am to 8:00 pm) with prices cheaper than the Friendship Store. Almost across the street from the Friendship Store is the **CVIK department store**, a little more expensive.

The big department store in the **You Yi Shopping City** *(52 Liang Ma Qiao Road, Tel. 64651188)* is beside the Kempinski Hotel north of the Great Wall Sheraton and is also good. Check out the **Lan Dao Shopping Area** (cheaper than Gui You) between Jianguomenwai and Frank's Place, and take a look at the huge **Parkson shopping mall** at *101 Fuxing Men Street, Tel. 66013377 or 66017374*. The fifth floor has an exhibition of arts and crafts.

At the **Friendship Store**, *on Jianguomenwai Avenue near the Jianguo Hotel*, you can buy any locally-made crafts and much else besides. There are furs, down coats, groceries, books in English, and even fresh flowers. The Friendship Store can reset jewelry and develop photos, and a tailor here does a reasonable job in three weeks. Merchandise bought here can be easily customs-cleared (twice a week) and packed for shipping. Prices are reasonable and can be used as a yard-stick for other stores.

A very good market for export-quality overruns and seconds in clothing and linens is the **Xiushui Free Market** or Silk Street, *between the Jianguo Hotel and Friendship Store*. Avoid the Yabaolu Market near Ritan

Park which sells in large quantities to rude Russians — unless you want bargains in large sizes. The small **San Li Tun market**, *near the City Hotel,* also has name brand seconds and good styles.

For antiques, the best bargains are at the Sunday or Ghost Market or **Pan Jia Yuan**, *two blocks west of Second Ring Road, behind the Le You Hotel, west and north of the imposing Henan Building (seen from the sight).* Goods are laid out on concrete slabs in an open construction site. Go early (about 8 am) for the best selection. They start to pack up about 2:30 pm. This street market is full of reproductions and fakes, but people with a good eye will find real treasures if they haggle well. This market is very muddy in wet weather. The similiar Sunday antique market in neighboring Tianjin is better for prices and variety, though both are fun.

Try the tiny antique stores on the third floor of the **Hongqiao Market**, in the building with the traditional Chinese roof across the street and east of the Temple of Heaven on *Tiantan Dong Lu.* Here you can buy souvenirs like cloisonne wholesale if you haggle hard.

A total of 238 antique stores are at the **Jin Song Antiques Market**, *Dong Sanhuan Nan Lu/Third Ring Road South, in the southeast of the city.* They take credit cards, have a restaurant, and occasionally have auctions. There's also the **Chai Wai market** mostly for antique furniture beyond the northwest corner of Ritan Park (open 10 am to 5 pm). Antique carpets are at **Huaxia**, *12 Chongwenmennei Dajie and 44 Xingfu Dajie, Tel. 65015079.* Many hotels and crafts stores sell carpets, and remember, factories are not necessarily cheaper.

A minor street market with curios is across the road from the Kunlun Hotel. And the Ping'anli flower and bird market, north of Beihai Park, and south of Houhai Lake, also sells a few curios.

The largest collection of stores selling antiques, arts and crafts is **Liulichang** *(on both sides of Naxinhua Street),* the main street where the buses stop. In 1277, artisans made glazed tiles here. In the Qing, it was a market with 140 shops selling the same sort of arts it does today, including reproductions of paintings, the Dunhuang murals, bronzes, and porcelains. Some of the merchandise then was stolen from the Forbidden City and other wealthy homes. Small shops are also next to and behind the Rong Bao Zhai art store on the west side at 64. There's also antique furniture.

Prices here could be better than the Friendship Store if you haggle. It is less crowded too. Try the east side for tiny shops and more adventurous shopping. The **Beijing Cultural Relics Store** at *64 Liulichang Dong Street, Tel. 63033848,* is allowed to sell pre-Qing relics.

The Landmark Towers Hotel's second and third floors also have good souvenir shopping. A shoppers hotline, *Tel .61601234,* should be able to tell you where to buy things.

If your antiques are expensive and do not have a red wax seal, take them to the **Beijing Arts Objects Clearance Office** *in the Friendship Store* for permission to export. Unfortunately this service is only open Tuesdays and Friday afternoons.

PRACTICAL INFORMATION

- **American Express**, *West Wing L115D, China World Trade Center, 1 Jianguomenwai Da Jie, Tel.65052888, Fax 65054972*
- **American Chamber of Commerce**, *Sheraton Great Wall Hotel*
- **Beijing Tourism Administration**, *Beijing Tourism Tower, 28 Jianguomenwai Avenue, 100022, Tel. 65158255, Fax 65158215*. For complaints, problems, and information.
- **Business Hours**: for offices 8:30 am to 4:30 or 5:30 pm with lunch 12 to 1:30 or 2 pm. Beijing Tourism Tower 8:30 am to 11:30 am; 1:30 to 4:40 pm. Store hours on Wangfujing about 9 am to 8:30 or 9 pm. The stores in the Beijing Hotel are open at 8:15 am. At Liulichang, stores are open 8:30 or 9 am to 5:30 pm (winter) or to 6 pm or even 9 pm (summer).
- **Customs Office for clearing of relics for export**, *Ground floor, Friendship Store, Jianguomenwai.* Mondays and Fridays 1:30-4:30 pm. Wool carpets department. For authenticating relics, contact the **Beijing Municipal Quality Inspection Bureau**, *Tel. 65014455, 64213478 or 67022173*. You should get a refund if it's a fake and you have a detailed receipt.

Embassies *(Da She Guan)*
- **Australia**, *21 Dongzhimenwai Street, Sanlitun, 100600, Tel. 65322331*
- **Britain**, *11 Guanghua Road, Jianguomenwai 100600, Tel. 65321961; Fax 65011977. Cultural Sections, Tel. 65011903*
- **Canada**, *19 Dongzhimenwai Dajie, Chao Yang District, 100600, Tel. 65323536; Fax 653284311.* Monday through Friday. 8 am to 5 pm. (Has Catholic mass in English Sunday evenings).
- **CIS** (most of the former USSR), *Dongzhimen Bei Zhong Jie Number 4, 100600 (Not open daily), Tel .65321267, 65322051*
- **France**, *3 Sanlitun Dong Road, Chao Yang District, Tel. 65321331, 65321332*
- **Germany**, *5 Dongzhimenwai Dajie, Chaoyang District, Tel. 65322161.* Moving across from Canadian embassy.
- **Japan**, *7 Ritan Road, Jianguomenwai, Tel. 65322361*
- **Mongolia**, *2 Xiushui Bei Jie, Tel. 65321203, 65321810. Fax 5325045.* Not open daily. Phone for hours. Accepts only US$ for visas.
- **Myanmar** (Burma), *Tel. 65321425, 65321488*
- **Nepal**, *Tel. 65321795, Fax 6532325*

- **Netherlands**, *1-15-2 Ta Yuan Building for Diplomatic Missions, 14 Liang Ma He Nan Road, 100600, Tel. 65321131. Fax 5324689*
- **New Zealand**, *1 Ritan Dong Er Street, Chaoyang District, 100600, Tel. 65322731. Fax 65324317*
- **Pakistan**, *Dongzhimenwai, Tel. 65322504, 65322695*
- **Philippines**, *23 Xiu Shui Bei Street, Jianguomenwai, 100600; Tel. 65322451, 65324678 (Consular).*
- **Poland**, *1 Jianguomenwai Baitan Road, and 1 Ritan Road, 100600, Tel. 65321235.* Not open daily, mornings only.
- **Thailand**, Tel. *65321903, 65323955*
- **U.S.**, *Xiushui Beijie 3 (Chancery), 100600, Tel. 65323831. Fax 65054574. Bruce Bldg., Xiushui Dongjie 2, 100600. (American Citizen Services), Tel. 65323831, 65323431, 17 Guanghua Road, (Press and Culture), Tel. 65321161. Fax 65323297, 65323178, 65322483*
- **Vietnam**, *Tel. 65321155, 65321125*

- **Fire**, *Tel. 119*
- **Medical Concerns**: for minor ailments, consult your hotel. For an ambulance: *Tel. 120.* For **Asia Emergency Assistance** (AEA): *Tel. 63018060, 64629112.* Has a pharmacy and can arrange medical evacuation which is very expensive unless you have insurance. For **Beijing Union Hospital Emergency**: *Tel. 65127733 X 251.* For **International First Aid Center** (Gi Jou Chong Xin): near Qianmen Kentucky Fried Chicken on Qianmen. They have ambulances. *Tel. 65003419, 6555678, 66014336.* The **International Medical Center**, *(24 hour service: Tel. 64651561-63),* has a pharmacy in the Lufthansa Centre. Very expensive.
  Try also the **Sino-Japanese Hospital**, *Tel. 64221122 extension for Foreigners, 3412*, and the **Sino-German Policlinic**: *Landmark Tower, B-1, 8 North Dongsan Huan Road, Tel. 5011983. Fax 5011944.* Open 24 hours. Western-trained doctors.
- **Monkey Business Infocenter**: *Beijing Commercial Business Complex, Number One Building, Yu Lin Li, Room 406, 4th floor, Youanmenwai, 100054. Tel. 63292244 X 4406. E-mail CompuServe 100267.2567.* Specializes in the Trans-Siberian Railway.
- **Police**, *Tel. 110*; Foreigners Section of the Beijing Public Security Bureau, *Tel. 65255486.*
- **Telephone Operators**: *information Tel. 114; long-distance information, 116; overseas operator, 115; time 117; weather 121*
- **Tourist Complaints: Supervisory Bureau of Tourism Quality of Beijing Municipality**, *Room 1001, Beijing Luyou Building, 28 Jianguomenwai Street, 100022, Tel. 5130828 (24 hours). Fax 5158251, 5158255*

• **Tourism Hotline**, *24 hours, Tel. 65130828*. Questions, complaints, compliments. Free information from Beijing Tourism Tower, between the Chang Fu Gong and Gloria Plaza Hotels.

Travel Agents
• **Beijing Huayuan International Travel Service**, *Huitongci, West Deshengmen Street, Xicheng District, 100035, Tel. 66057496, Fax 6014154*
• **CTS**, *Beijing Tourism Tower, Tel. 65158264, 65158844, 65158565. Fax 65158557*
• See also **Monkey Business Infocenter** above for train travel to Russia.

THE GREAT WALL
(Wanlichangcheng; 10,000 li-long wall)
   The length of ***The Great Wall** has been officially given as 12,700 Chinese li, or 6,350 kilometers (3,946.55 miles) long from Jiayuguan to Shanhaiguan. Some scholars, however, add another 1,040 kilometers all the way to the Yalu River on the Korean border. The length depends on what you measure, as there are many offshoots and parallel walls. The Wall is in various states of repair.
   The best time to visit is after 2 pm, when most of the tourists have left. Stay to see the sunset if you can. The autumn is also good when the air is clearer and red leaves add interest to photos.

ORIENTATION
   The Great Wall was first built in shorter pieces, starting in the fifth century B.C., as a defensive and boundary wall around the smaller states of Yen, Chao, and Wei. The first Qin emperor (221-206 B.C.), who unified China for the first time, linked up and extended the walls from Liaoning in the east to Gansu in the northwest as protection from the Huns and other nomadic tribes to the north. The wall was subsequently repaired and extended by succeeding dynasties, especially the Ming.
   Originally built by slave labor, it has been called the world's longest graveyard because many of its builders were buried where they fell. It was designed in places to allow five horsemen or ten soldiers to march abreast along the top. It was almost a superhighway, considering the rough mountain terrain. A system of bonfires communicated military information to the emperor at a speed considered rapid for that period.

VISITING THE WALL
   The Great Wall is most frequently visited at ***Badaling** (Padaling), about 75 kilometers (two hours) by road northwest of Beijing. It is extremely crowded. You still need to avoid the weekend traffic jams.

Usually the trip can be done by taxi in four hours if you don't linger. Most tourists now go from Beijing by tourist buses, which leave Beijing daily at 8 am and stop at both the Great Wall and Ming Tombs. They are open 8 am to 5:30 pm.

Badaling is about 1000 meters above sea level. Here the wall averages 7.8 meters in height, is 6.5 meters wide at the base, and 5.8 meters wide at the top. Watchtowers are located every few hundred meters. Note the giant rocks and bricks of uniform size, the gutters, and the waterspouts. You can walk, and in some places climb, for several hundred feet in either direction or you can take a cable car. Skateboarding on the wall has been allowed, but is not recommended when it is thick with people, which is most of the time.

A **restaurant** and usually a shaggy Bactrian camel or pony for photographing are available. Taking a box lunch is recommended, especially in pleasant weather, so you can spend more time at the wall rather than waiting for service in a crowded restaurant. You can also see a 15-minute **movie** with English subtitles.

Also of note is the **gate** in the center of **Juyongguan** (Chuyungkuan Pass), about 10 kilometers south of Badaling. It is built of finely-carved marble and called ***Guofie** (Cloud Terrace). Originally the base of a tower built in 1345 (Yuan), the walls are decorated with carvings of buddhas, four celestial guardians, and the text of a Buddhist sutra in Sanskrit, Tibetan, and four other languages. Currently, tours do not usually stop here except by request.

A three-kilometers-long section of the Great Wall is at **Mutianyu**, 70 kilometers northeast of Beijing in Miyun County. It is less crowded and more beautiful, less commercial, with more rugged hills than Badaling. But you do have to ask for it. A 720-meter-long Swiss-built cable car can take you from the parking lot uphill to the base of the Wall. You still have to climb or take the cable car down. All buildings including a restaurant are tastefully built in matching Ming style. Open 8:30 am to 4:30 pm. You can also go by road from Mutianyu to the Ming tombs.

You'll find a very steep section about 90 kilometers from Beijing at **Huang Ya Pass**. Also open is the Wall in **Huairou County** (two-kilometer-long reconstruction), 60 kilometers northeast of Beijing. You can go by road from Beijing to Chengde following the Wall and stop at Simatai and Jinshan Ling.

Simatai, 140 kilometers from Beijing also in Miyun County, is spectacular but you have to walk about one kilometer from the parking lot to the base. At **Jinshan Ling** (150 kilometers from Beijing and 110 kilometers from Chengde), there is camping (bring your own tent) and a dirty, modest hotel with edible food. Officials here say you can see the lights of Beijing from the top. About two kilometers of the wall has been repaired here.

An 850-meter section is open in **Jixian County**, 60 kilometers northeast of Tianjin, and two sections are available near **Datong**. The Great Wall has also been restored and opened to visitors at 3,000-year-old **Shanhaiguan** (with cable car), over 40 kilometers north from Beidaihe, and about 30 kilometers from Qinhuangdao in the east. The tower was built in 1381. Nearby, at **Old Dragon Head**, the Great Wall meets the sea. In west China, it can be seen in Ningxia close to **Yinchuan**, and in Gansu at ***Jiayuguan**, its western terminus (Ming) where it is much narrower but still fascinating.

Museums are at Jiayuguan and Shanhaiguan. See separate listings under these destinations for more details.

THE GREAT WALL

15. SHANGHAI

Shanghai straddles the Huangpu River 28 kilometers from the Yangtze River on China's east coast, bordering on Jiangsu and Zhejiang provinces. It is due west of the southern tip of Japan. The urban population is 7.3 million plus three million "floaters;" the greater Shanghai area has at least 13 million people. The hottest temperature is 35 degrees centigrade in July and August; the coldest is minus five degrees centigrade in January and February. Most rain falls in June.

This municipality, directly under the control of the central government, started out 6,000 years ago as a tiny fishing village. It celebrated its 700th birthday in 1991. It became a port in the 16th century. In 1840 its population was 500,000. In 1842, the British seized it, and although the Chinese paid a $300,000 ransom to keep it from being sacked, British soldiers and Chinese thieves severely looted it. The **Treaty of Nanking** of that year opened Shanghai to foreign trade and settlement. This led to its partition into British, French, and, later Japanese concessions, which is still reflected in its downtown architecture. These concessions continued until the 1940s. Each of the concessions had its own tax system, police, courts, buses, and electrical wattage. A criminal could escape justice simply by going from one concession to another.

Shanghai thrived as a port, trading principally in silk, tea, and opium. Most of the foreign trade was British, and one fifth of the opium reached China in fast American ships. From 1853 to 1855, the **Small Sword Society** seized the walled section of Shanghai. This was a Cantonese-Fukinese secret society that wanted to restore the Ming dynasty and prohibit opium. It was helped in its struggle by some foreign seamen, but many other foreigners helped the Manchus regain the city. In 1860, the **Taiping Heavenly Kingdom** tried unsuccessfully to take Shanghai. In 1915 students and workers demonstrated here against the **Twenty-One Demands** of Japan. And in July 1921, the first Congress of the Communist Party of China met secretly here.

In 1925, a worker striking for higher wages was killed at a Japanese factory. This led to a demonstration by workers and students in the

International Settlement, during which the British police killed several demonstrators. A rash of nationwide anti-imperialist protests followed. In April 1927, Chiang Kai-shek ordered a massacre of the Communists here, and Chou En-lai barely escaped with his life. The 1920s and 1930s was the golden age of Shanghai.

In 1932, Shanghai resisted a Japanese attack for two months and made a truce. China appealed to the League of Nations and the United States, neither of whom did anything to help. Japan attacked again in August 1937. The Nationalists fought back for three months before retreating to Nanjing and later to Chongqing. The movie and book *Empire of the Sun* is set in this period and parts were shot in Shanghai. The Japanese stayed until 1945. In May 1949, the Communists took the city. During the Cultural Revolution, it was the scene of many intense political struggles, especially in January 1966.

ARRIVALS & DEPARTURES

From Shanghai you can get air, land, and water services to other parts of China. The train to Hangzhou is three hours, to Suzhou one. Shanghai is at about the same latitude as Jacksonville, Florida.

By Air

Shanghai is about a two-hour flight northeast of Hong Kong and less than two hours southeast of Beijing. It is also linked by air with 74 other cities including Los Angeles, Macau, New York, Osaka, Paris, San Francisco, Seattle, Seoul, Tokyo and Vancouver, and by sea with Hong Kong and Japan.

Major airlines include:
- **Aeroflot**, *Tel. 64711665*
- **Air China**, *Tel. 63272676, 63277888*
- **Air France**, *Tel. 62558899 X 5325. Airport 62688899 X 5325*
- **All-Nippon Airways**, *Tel. 62797000*
- **CAAC/China Eastern Airlines**, *200 Yan'an Xi Road, Tel. 62475953 for domestic, 62472255 for international. Fax 6276761.* Ticketing offices in many hotels. Airport information, *Tel. 62537664*
- **Canadian Airlines International Limited**, *6th floor, Jin Jiang Tower, Tel. 64153091, 62687720*
- **Dragonair**, *Tel. 62798099. Fax 62797189. Airport 62558899 X 5307*
- **Japan Airlines**, *Ruijin Building, Tel. 64723000*
- **Korean Airlines**, *Equatorial Hotel, Tel. 62588747*
- **Northwest Airlines**, *Shanghai Center, Tel. 62798088; airport Tel. 62558899 X 5319*
- **SAS**, *Tel. 64712455*
- **Shanghai Airlines**, *555 Yan'an Road, Tel. 62551551, 62688558*

• **Singapore Airlines (SIA)**, *Tel. 62798090*
• **Thai Airways**, *Tel. 62798000*
• **United Airlines**, *Hilton Hotel, Tel. 62798009. At airport, Tel. 62558899 X 5304*

By Train

If you're departing Shanghai by train and are booking tickets yourself, go to the **Foreigner's Ticket Office** in the Shanghai Railway Station or the ticket office in the Longmen Hotel, beside the railway station. This hotel booking office could be easier for same day tickets and next day tickets if you get there before 2 pm. You can, however, also book six days in advance through any travel agent or hotel.

SOME GOOD BOOKS TO GET YOU IN THE MOOD FOR SHANGHAI

Try Noel Barber's **The Fall of Shanghai***; Pan Lin's* **In Search of Old Shanghai***; and especially Sterling Seagrave's* **The Soong Dynasty** *– very readable and revealing book about the Soongs, sons-in-law Gen. Chiang Kai-shek and Dr. Sun Yat-sen, son T.V. Soong (reluctant premier and finance minister) and their Soviet, gangster, and wealthy Christian, American and Chinese friends.*

ORIENTATION

Shanghai is China's largest city and one of the biggest ports in the country. It is still an important trading city and one of the biggest industrial cities. As an agricultural area, it is highly developed. Its natives speak a dialect unlike that of Beijing and more akin to that of Hangzhou and Suzhou, only faster.

Shanghai is also pleasant because the people are outgoing and lively. They are less reserved than Beijing people; making friends is easier here. Every Sunday morning in People's Park there is an English-speaking corner. Someone is sure to approach you to practice English. In about five parks, you can exchange postage stamps with other collectors, another good way to meet people. Shanghainese have been known for centuries for their quick wit, business talents, and efficiency.

Today, Shanghai is China's foremost international class city. Parts are reminiscent of Manhattan or Paris. It is striving hard to clean up the air and has had campaigns to forbid spitting, littering, foul language, jay walking and the burning of coal — although not always enforced. The air is still dirty but not as bad as before.

Shanghai is one of the 14 **Open Coastal Cities** especially chosen for intensive economic development. It has been experiencing four years of double digit economic growth and its average per capita income of about Y11,000 is one of China's highest. It has a stock market. It is the "dragon's head" of the burgeoning **Yangtze River basin**. Its population density is about 50,000 people per square kilometer, a world high.

Shanghai's cosmopolitan heritage is reflected in its architecture and in the relative sophistication of many of its citizens. Its fashions and standards for products and services are more international than other Chinese cities, a result of its longer, more concentrated period of dealing with fussy foreigners. Its shopping is the best in the country.

It is a big, very crowded city that is more redolent of trade, commerce, and industry than it is of ancient Chinese culture. Its relics are mainly outside the city. Many visitors think Shanghai can be missed, especially if you're not interested in shopping. But I think you should at least look at this city with six million bicycles and 300,000 motor vehicles, that is expecting to surpass Hong Kong in the next century. Get a feel for its vibrancy. Will it catch up even with New York? It is the most liveable city now for foreigners in China.

PUDONG

*Pudong means "east of the Huangpu River." The older part of Shanghai is **Puxi**, "west of the Huangpu River." Ten years ago, this community south and east of Shanghai proper was nothing but rice fields and villages. The government has given it first priority for economic development and you can see the results today. It is booming; its annual growth rate in some areas has reached 30% to 50%.*

*You can get there by a tunnel and two bridges, a second tunnel currently being built. The metro should reach it in 1997, and the **new airport**, the largest airport in China, should be finished in 1999. The Shanghai Stock Exchange will move there. It already has Asia's biggest department store and its highest television tower. It expects to have a population of two million people by the year 2000.*

GETTING AROUND TOWN

Streets running east-west downtown are named after cities and those running north-south after provinces. Shanghai floods when it rains, so you need extra time to get around then, an extra hour to get to the airport from downtown.

By Public Bus

Good buses to know are the **Number 20** from the Jingan Temple, past the Shanghai Centre and down Nanjing Road almost to the Bund. The Number 505 goes from People's Square, past the Hilton, Westin, Zoo, Nikko Longbai Hotel to the airport. The double-decker **Number 911** goes past the Isetan Department Store, the Holiday Inn and then to the airport. Buses are incredibly crowded and subject to frequent breakdowns. Minibuses ply fixed routes.

By Subway (Di Tie)

The first 14-kilometer stage of Shanghai's subway system is now operating. Eventually there'll be seven lines totalling 176 kilometers. The line now starts from the Shanghai Railway Station (Longmen Hotel) with stops at Han Zhong Road, Xin Zha Road, People's Park (Nanjing Road, Shanghai Museum, Flower and Bird Market), Huang Pi Nan Road (Huai Hai Road and Isetan shopping center), Shan Xi Nan Road (Garden Hotel, Jin Jiang Tower, Huai Hai Road), Chang Shu Road (Hilton and Shanghai Hotels, U.S., French and Japanese consulates), Heng Shan Road (Heng Shan Hotel), Xu Jia Hui (Jianguo Hotel, Orient Shopping Centre), Shanghai Stadium (Sheraton, Olympic and Hua Ting Hotels), Cao Bao Road (near carpet and jadeware factories, and Mongolian barbecue), Xin Long Hua, and Jin Jiang Amusement Park. Look for the logo, a circle with two mountain peaks or "M" inside. Signs in the Metro are in English and Chinese.

By Taxi & Rental Car

These range from Y10.80 to Y14.40 per kilometer. You should address any complaints to the Shanghai Tourism Corporation and to the address of the taxi company in each taxi.

The quickest way to get around by car is by elevated expressway, one of which, the six-lane Inner Ring Road, is 48 kilometers long and takes 36 minutes to circle the city. This is connected by the east-west expressway and the new north-south expressway, like a pizza roughly cut into four pieces. A new expressway from the airport to Pudong should be completed soon.

WHERE TO STAY

The best five-star hotels are the **Garden** and **Portman**, then the **Westin** and **Hilton**. The best four-star is the **Holiday Inn**.

All the hotels listed here are very good unless specified otherwise. Some still have problems with English, more so with the lower stars. You might not have much of a choice because Shanghai is booming. Hotels are packed full especially in May, and September through the middle of November. The low season when prices go soft goes from late November or December to early March. July-August is the not-quite-so-busy 'shoulder season.' Because of the five-day work week, you should also haggle on weekends in top hotels when Hong Kong business people return home. The four-star hotels seem to be doing better business than the fives.

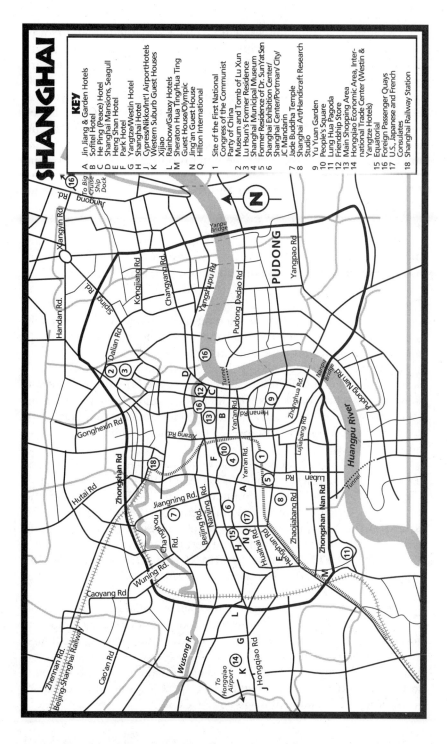

SHANGHAI

KEY

A Jin Jiang & Garden Hotels
B Sofitel Hotel
C He Ping (Peace) Hotel
D Shanghai Mansions, Seagull
E Heng Shan Hotel
F Park Hotel
G Yangtze/Westin Hotel
H Shanghai Hotel
J Cypress/Nikko/Int'l Airport Hotels
K Western Suburb Guest Houses
   Xijiao
L Rainbow/Galaxy Hotels
M Sheraton Hua Ting/Hua Ting
   Guest House/Olympic
N Jing'an Guest House
Q Hilton International

1 Site of the First National
   Congress of the Communist
   Party of China
2 Museum and Tomb of Lu Xun
3 Lu Hsun's Former Residence
4 Shanghai Municipal Museum
5 Former Residence of Dr. Sun Yat Sen
6 Shanghai Exhibition Center/
   Shanghai Center/Portman/City/
   JC Mandarin
7 Jade Buddha Temple
8 Shanghai Art/Handicraft Research
   Studio
9 Yu Yuan Garden
10 People's Square
11 Lung Hua Pagoda
12 Friendship Store
13 Main Shopping Area
14 Hongqiao Economic Area, International Trade Center (Westin &
   Yangtze Hotels)
15 Equatorial
16 Foreign Passenger Quays
17 U.S., Japanese and French
   Consulates
18 Shanghai Railway Station

Because of the tight hotel situation, I have also listed hotels of lesser but acceptable quality (depending on needs), and hotels in the suburbs in case you find yourself without a bed. In the lowest price range, there are no acceptable dormitories for backpackers. Of the cheapest hotels downtown, our first choice is the Seagull with its fantastic location on the Bund even though it is a seaman's hotel! Then there's the YMCA Hotel.

If you want a feeling of old Shanghai, do consider the Peace, Park, Jin Jiang or Garden - all of which have some 1920s ambiance. If you want something different, ask about the hotel rooms 230 meters up on the television tower in Pudong. See *Seeing the Sights* below.

Shanghai is building at least 10 new hotels. As they come on the market, you can expect prices to get softer and the quality to improve even more.

Prices listed here are subject to change, negotiation, a 10 or 15% surcharge, and a Y5 government tax. Prices are given either in US dollars or Chinese yuan (the price is preceded by a "Y" sign).

The Bund area

The best location for visitors and business people is near and along the **Bund**. The flavor of old Shanghai is still here, the western-style waterfront buildings, and the ships in the harbor. The Nanjing shopping area is visited by 200,000 people daily. Still if you're willing, the Peace, Seagull, and Shanghai Mansions are closest to the Friendship Store and some good department stores. The Sofitel on Nanjing Road is also within walking distance of the Bund and is the best location for shoppers. Both areas are within walking distance of the Bank of China and Chinese business offices.

The YMCA Hotel is about 1.5 kilometers from Nanjing Road towards the Yuyuan Garden, a very modest hotel. All but the Ocean are about five kilometers from the railway station and about 20 kilometers from the airport. The Ocean is about nine kilometers from the railway station and is nearest the Yangpu Bridge. The hotels closest to the two Pudong bridges are those near the Bund. The best hotel here is the Sofitel.

HOTEL SOFITEL HYLAND SHANGHAI *(Hailun Binguan)*, *505 Nanjing Dong Rd., 200001. Four stars. Tel. 63515888. Fax 63514088. In US, Tel. 1-800-221-4542. $200 and up.*

Ten-minute walk to People's Square subway station. Built 1993. 30 stories. 389 rooms. Compact hotel with poor bedside reading lamps but good service. USTV. In-room safes. Executive and non-smoking floors. French, Italian and Cantonese food. You can watch the activity on Nanjing Road from its restaurants. Mini-brewery/Fun Pub, 24-hour room service. Health club with weight-losing space capsule and Alpha 33 relaxation pad. No pool. Managed by ACCOR.

OCEAN HOTEL *(Yuan Yang Binguan), 1171 Dong Da Ming Rd., 200082. Four stars, Tel. 65458888. Fax 65458993. $110 to $160.*
Next to department store and old Jewish ghetto. Built 1988. 28-story building. 370 rooms. Executive floor. 24-hour business center. Gym. USTV. Sauna. English could be a problem.

PARK HOTEL *(Guoji Fandian) 170 Nanjing Xi Rd., 200003. Three stars. Tel. 63275225. Fax 63276958. Y870 and Y958.*
Near People's Park subway station, Nanjing Road shopping, winter theater of the Shanghai Acrobats, and bird market. Built 1934. Deteriorating but ren. 1996. 24 stories, 208 rooms. Poor bedside reading lights. USTV but no CNN. In-room safes. Cantonese, Beijing, continental food.

PEACE HOTEL *(Heping Fandian), 20 Nanjing Dong Rd., 200002. Four stars. Tel. 63216888. Fax 63290300. At least $110 to $150.*
Built 1929, ren. 85 rooms in 1996. 11-story North Building (with famous 1920's jazz band, daily 8 pm to 11 pm.) I can only recommend one section of this hotel; avoid the no-star South Building. 279 large rooms. USTV. Small TV sets. A bit rundown and dirty with dark hallways. Ask about the charming Indian suite. Good Sichuan-Cantonese-Shanghai restaurants on eighth floor. This hotel is for romantic travelers only, who don't mind socialist-style hotels.

YMCA HOTEL *(Qian Nian Hui Binguan), 123 Xizang Nan Rd., 200021. Three stars. Tel. 63261040. Fax 63201957. Dist.A.P. 15 km. Dist.R.W. four km. Y550.*
Built 1929. 11 stories, 165 small rooms. 24-hour coffee shop. Budget travelers only. Jin Jiang group.

SHANGHAI MANSIONS *(Da Sha), 20 Suzhou Bei Rd., 200080. Three stars, Tel. 63246260. Fax 63999778. $100 to $110.*
Built 1934, renovated 1992 above 9th floor. 19 stories, 254 large rooms. Sound-proof windows. Somewhat grubby, not polished and deteriorating. Dark halls. Soft beds. Yangzhou, Cantonese and Sichuan food. USTV. Desperate budget travelers only.

SEAGULL HOTEL *(Hai Ou Fandian), 60 Huangpu Rd., 200080. Two stars, Tel. 63251500. Fax 63241263. Y530.*
Built 1985. Ren. 1990. 12 stories, 104 rooms. Modest. Business center has IDD. Great view of Bund from south side. Grubby carpets, poor food and sluggish staff. For desperate budget travelers and seamen.

LONGMAN HOTEL *(Binguan), 777 Heng Feng Road, 200070. Three stars, Tel. 63170000. Fax 63172004. Dist.A.P. 13 km. Dist. Bund three km. Y476.*
Located beside the railway and subway stations. You might hear trains all night. 25 stories, 365 small rooms. 17th-21st floor for foreigners. 24-hour room service. Good place to buy train tickets. Sauna. Stained carpets. USTV. For easy-going budget travelers only.

The Old French Concession area

The most popular hotel area is the **old French Concession**. It is about 13 kilometers from the airport and six kilometers from the Bund in a pleasant residential area increasingly becoming commercial with tourist stores, restaurants and bars.

The Jin Jiang Hotel, Jin Jiang Tower and Garden Hotels are close together and within walking distance of shopping in the Jin Jiang Hotel, Huaihai Street and Shanxi Nan Road metro station. The Hilton, Jingan, Shanghai and Equatorial Hotels are clustered together near the Children's Palace, and closer to the U.S. Consulate. The Portman (in the Shanghai Centre), City (cheapest) and JC Mandarin surround the Shanghai Exhibition Center with its two overpriced crafts stores and innumerable restaurants. They are near the Ruijin Center.

The Shanghai Center is the main international business center and downtown exhibition center. It houses airlines, American Express, DHL, travel agents, supermarket and a "drug store" and a 1,000-seat theatre. These three groups are within about three kilometers of each other and are served by the Shanxi Road subway.

CITY HOTEL *(Chen Shi Jiu Dian), 5-7 Shan Xi Nan Rd., 200020. Three stars, Tel. 62551133. Fax 62550211. In US, Tel. 1-800-942-5050 or 1-800-44UTELL. $110 to $140.*

Good location within walking distance of good Korean (Sam Sung) and new seafood restaurants. Built 1988-89. 304 small rooms. Soft beds. Good elevators and executive floors. Sichuan and Cantonese food. USTV but no CNN. Some worn carpets are to be replaced soon. Generally good standards. Managed by Chains International (Singapore).

HOTEL EQUATORIAL SHANGHAI *(Gui Du Da Fandian), 65 Yan'an Xi Rd., 200040. Four stars. Tel. 62481688. Fax 62481773. In US, Tel. 1-800-44UTELL. Y1600 to Y1800.*

Near park. Vuilt 1991-92. 26 stories. 526 rooms. Small bathrooms. Hairdryers. USTV. Executive floor. International Club. Thai, Japanese, Chaozhou, Sichuan and Cantonese food. Indoor pool, bowling, gym, tennis and squash. 1000-seat theater. UPS office. Managed by Equatorial International Singapore. Breakfast buffet Y88.

JIN JIANG HOTEL *(Jin Jiang Fandian), 59 Mao Ming Nan Rd., 200020. Tel. 62582582. Fax 64725588. North Building $155 to $165. Centre Building $400 to $3000 (presidential). South Building $80.*

Built 1929, reconstructed 1986. About 18 stories. 628 rooms. North Building okay with big rooms and four stars. Middle building is now five stars, with classy art deco lobby, and all suites. USTV. Sichuan restaurant. Book and crafts stores and supermarket. China Eastern airlines. Expects to upgrade North Building to five-star standard in 1997.

JIN JIANG TOWER *(Xin Jin Jiang), 161 Changle Road, 200020. Five stars, Tel. 64151188. Fax 64150045 to 48. $190 to $230. Presidential suite $1500 and $2000.*
Built 1988-1990. 43 stories. 728 rooms. In-room safes. Choice of Chinese or western decor. Executive floors. Gym, outdoor pool and jacuzzi. Revolving restaurant, Korean barbecue, and French restaurant. USTV. Year- round outdoor pool. Dim bed lamps in Chinese rooms. Good hardware but tiny twin beds and maintenance needs work. Canadian and China Eastern Airlines.Breakfast buffet $13.

PORTMAN SHANGRI-LA *(Po Ter Man Jiu Dian), Shanghai Center, 1376 Nanjing Xi Rd., 200040. Five stars with excellent standards. Tel. 62798888. Fax 62798999. Sales office in North America, Tel. (703) 715-3000; Fax (703) 648-1523; Reservations 1-800-942-5050. $195 to $305. Presidential suite $1,220 and $1,500.*
Managed by Shangri-La Hotels and Resorts (H.K.). Built 1990. 50 stories, 620 large rooms (three telephones in each). In-room safes. Japanese restaurant, grill room. 24-hour coffee shop and room service. Executive and non-smoking floors. Good telecommunications including voice mail. USTV with HBO. Tennis, squash, aerobics, gym, and tai chi classes. Indoor-outdoor lap pool. Clinic. Good hotel for children.

GARDEN HOTEL SHANGHAI *(Huayuan Fandian), 58 Maoming Nan Rd., 200020. Five stars. Tel. 64151111. Fax 64158866. In US, Tel. 1-800-223-5652. $210 to $275. Presidential suite $2,800.*
1989-90. Major renovations 1997 and 1998. Incorporates 1926 Cercle Sportif into building. 34 stories, 500 spacious rooms each with three telephone jacks and scales. Gleaming white bathtubs. Non-smoking floor. Classiest-looking business center in China. Large garden. Pool with retractable roof, gym, and tennis. USTV. Japanese and continental food. Parking for 240 cars. Hotel Okura management. Member of Leading Hotels of the World. Steigenberger Reservation Service. Breakfast buffet $19.

SHANGHAI HILTON INTERNATIONAL *(Jinan Dajiudian), 250 Hua Shan Rd., 200040. Five stars, Tel. 62480000. Fax 62483848. $250 to $315. Presidential suite $1,800.*
Built 1988. 43 stories. 800 rooms each with three telephones. Good standards. European, Cantonese and Sichuan cuisine. Teppanyaki. Its basement fast Asian food is budget-priced and good. Clark Hatch gym. Indoor pool. Tennis. Squash. USTV with HBO. Non-smoking floors. Two Japanese-speaking floors. Business studios. Executive floors. Lufthansa Airlines. This hotel can book a whole train car for groups to Suzhou, clean out coach and cater it with food and open bar.

SHANGHAI HOTEL *(Binguan), 505 Wulumuqi Rd., 200040. Three stars, Tel. 62480088. Fax 62481310, 62481056. Y850 to Y950.*

Built 1983, ren. 1996. 23 stories, 562 rooms. China Eastern airlines. Chaozhou and Japanese food. Gym. Jacuzzi. USTV. Small televisions. Huating group. Breakfast Y55.

SHANGHAI JC MANDARIN *(Jing Chang Wen Hua), 1225 Nanjing Xi Rd., 200040. Five stars, Tel. 62791888. Fax 62792314, 62791822. Member Leading Hotels of the World: in North America, Tel. 1-800-44UTELL.*

Built 1990-91. 30 stories. 600 large rooms each with three telephone jacks. CITS counter. Cantonese and continental cuisine. Patisserie. Clinic. Tennis, squash. and gym. All-weather pool, sauna, jacuzzi and steamroom. Playroom for children. USTV with HBO. Clinic. Managed by Singapore Mandarin International.

Shanghai Stadium Metro area

This is the third best location. The **Sheraton Hua Ting**, **Hua Ting Guest House**, and **Olympic** hotels are in this area (in order of quality, with Sheraton the best) and are conveniently located at the Shanghai Stadium metro and beside the elevated highway. There are two relatively good shopping areas nearby, new restaurants, the Shanghai Stadium, the 80,000-seat soccer stadium (due 1997), and a little further away, the Cao He Jing High Tech park. This area is about 12 km from the airport and about 15 km from the train station. The Hong Qiao Development Zone is six km away.

HUA TING GUEST HOUSE *(Hua Ting Binguan #2), 2525 Zhong Shan Xi Rd., 200030. Three stars. Tel. 64391818, 64391380. Fax 6390322. Y680.*

This is not to be confused with its neighbor, the Sheraton Hua Ting. Built 1987. 17 stories, 187 rooms. Non-smoking floor. USTV. Slow elevators. Food and service tolerable but standards and prices not as high as the Sheraton. Guests here can use facilities next door but must pay cash. For budget travelers.

SHANGHAI OLYMPIC HOTEL, *1800 Zhongshan Rd., Nan Er Lu, 200030. Three stars.Tel. 64391391, Fax 64396295. Y650.*

Beside new stadium and across the road from the Sheraton. Three stars. 200 rooms. USTV. Squash, gym, sauna and use of outdoor pool. While it has a good continental restaurant, the hotel itself is for budget travelers who aren't fussy, for sports fans and for athletes. Breakfast buffet Y30.

SHERATON HUA TING HOTEL AND TOWERS *(Hua Ting Binguan #1), 1200 Cao Xi Bei Road, 200030. Five stars, Tel. 64391000. Fax 62550830. $190 to $280.*

Built 1986, renovated 1995-96. 26 stories. 885 rooms. Japanese, executive and non-smoking floors. Wide twins. Voice mail. Offices. 24-hour laundry (regardless of time collected). 24-hour business center and room service. Indoor pool, gym, bowling and tennis. USTV. Shuttle bus. Cantonese, Sichuan, Continental, Asian and Italian food. Popular 24-hour American sit-down deli. Good shopping center.

JIANGUO HOTEL *(Binguan), 439 Caoxi Bei Road, 200030. Xujiahui metro station. Four stars, Tel. 64399299. Fax 64399433, 64399714. Y1100 to Y1500. Dist.A.P. 11 km. Dist.R.W. eight km.*

This hotel is within one km of the Sheraton towards downtown and closer to the Orient Shopping Centre. Built 1993. Renovations 1996. 18 stories, 473 rooms. Gym. USTV. Cantonese and Chaozhou food. 24-hour coffee shop. Shanghai New Asia Group.

Near the Hongqiao area

The fourth best location and relatively close to the Hongqiao area is:

HOLIDAY INN CROWNE PLAZA YINXING *(Yin Xing Jia Re Jiu Dian), 388 Panyu Road, 200052. Four stars aiming for five. Tel. 62808888. Fax 62802353, 62802078. $200 and $220. Dist.A.P. 15 km. Dist.R.W. nine km.*

Best hotel for Shanghai Film Festival next door. Built 1991-92. Continuous renovations and high standards. 26 stories, 534 rooms. Wide twin beds. Executive and non-smoking floors. USTV. Gym. Indoor pool. Steam bath, sauna, squash, and tennis. Cantonese, Sichuan, and international food. 24-hour room service and coffee shop. Claims longest happy hour in town 11 am to 7 pm. Children have playground with free nanny service at lunch and for some kids free food. Teens and seniors' rates. In-house movies. Friendly, helpful staff.

Near the Exhibition Centre

The **Hongqiao Development Zone (HQDZ)**, is less than 10 km from the airport, and about 12 kilometers from the train station. This area features a 37-story International Trade and Exhibition Centre with an exhibition hall for big trade shows. Also some major government offices, apartments, a recreation center, and several hotels are located here: Westin Tai Ping Yang (top), the Yangtze New World, then the Galaxy (larger rooms) and the Rainbow (more recently renovated) in that order of quality. An entertainment center, upscale department store, shopping center, and restaurants are also here. Towards the airport is the International School, government guest houses, the zoo, and a growing number of expensive single family houses for foreigners.

GALAXY *(Ying He Binguan), 888 Zhongshan Xi Road, 200051. Four stars, Tel. 62755888. Fax 62750201. $140.*

Built 1990. Renovations in 1995 and 1996. 35 stories, 760 rooms. Soft beds. Has FIT and group lobbies. Helipad. Cantonese food. Gym and bowling. Huating Group. USTV.

RAINBOW HOTEL *(Hongqiao Binguan), 2000 Yan'an Xi Road, 200051. Four stars. Tel. 62753388. Fax 62757244 (reservations), 62753736 (guests). In North America, Tel. 1-800-44UTELL. $110 to $150.*
Built 1988, renovations 1995. 31 stories, 630 rooms, narrow halls and beds. Clean and adequate. CITS airline ticket desk and Asiana airlines. Korean restaurant. 24-hour room service. Pool and gym. Huating Group.

THE WESTIN TAI PING YANG SHANGHAI *(Tai Ping Yang Da Fandian), 5 Zunyi Nan Road, 200335. Five stars, Tel. 62758888. Fax 62755420. In US, Tel. 1-800-223-6800. $198 and $325. Royal suite $2,888.*
Built 1990-92. Excellent standards. 27 stories. 578 spacious rooms. In-room safes. Voice mail. Non-smoking and executive floors. USTV. Good Japanese and Italian food. 24-hour room service. Japanese-style bath. Gym, tennis and outdoor pool. Classy-looking lobby with bowing staff. Excellent antiques. Shuttle bus. AT&T. Managed by Caesar Park Hotels and Resorts and franchised by Westin Hotels and Resorts.

YANGTZE NEW WORLD HOTEL *(Yangtze Jiang Da Jiudian), 2099 Yan'an Xi Road, 200335. Four stars, Tel. 62750000. Fax 62750750. $160 to $250.*
Built 1990-91. 34 stories, 570 rooms. Non-smoking and executive floors. Outdoor pool. Gym. Asian, Sichuan, Chaozhou and Cantonese food. Karaoke. USTV. Disco. Bar has "hungry hour" with substantial snacks free with drink. China Eastern Airlines. Managed by New World International.

Slightly outside the Hongqiao Development Zone (HQDZ) are:
SHANGHAI WORLDFIELD CONVENTION HOTEL *(Guoji Hui Yi Da Jiudian), 2106 Hong Qiao Road, 200335. Aiming for four stars. Tel. 62703388. Fax 62704546. In US, Tel. 1-800-44UTELL. H.K.J.V. $160 to $250. Presidential suite $1,000.Dist.A.P. five km. Dist.R.W. 15 km.*
Nothing much of interest in neighborhood. 1994. 360 spacious rooms and small baths. In-room safes. Executive floors. USTV. 24- hour coffee shop and business center. 600-seat auditorium. Gym. 25-meter outdoor pool. Only the dim sum is exceptionally good here. Buffet breakfast available.

XI JIAO GUEST HOUSE *(Xi Jiao Binguan), 1921 Hong Qiao Road, 200335. Tel. 62198800 Fax 64336641. $120 in Building #7. Dist.A.P.six km. Dist.R.W.11 km. Dist.HQDZ two km.*
Built 1984. #2 and #3 buildings renovated 1992 and 1996. Seven buildings of one to three stories. 150 big rooms. Bit grubby and worn. Queen Elizabeth had suite in #7 building ($1,000). Tennis, squash and bowling. For the desperate, the curious and garden lovers. The service is not very good.

The Nikko-Airport-Cypress Hotels area

The Nikko-Airport-Cypress Hotels area (in order of quality with the Nikko best and the Airport a close second) are within two kilometers of the airport and 19 kilometers of the railway station. The closest to the airport is the International Airport Hotel, which has frequent downtown shuttle buses and no crowds.

CYPRESS HOTEL *(Long Bai Fandian), 2419 Hongqiao Road, 200335. Three stars, Tel. 62688868. Fax 62423739. Set in a vast garden.*

Built 1982, ren. 1993. Six stories, 161 rooms. Villas total 71 rooms. China Eastern bookings (domestic). Book store. Villas and apartments. USTV. Scruffy and rundown. Recreation Center with indoor pool, bowling, tennis, and squash. Lots of smokers. Recommended for budget travelers and garden lovers only.

NIKKO LONGBAI HOTEL *(Re Hong Longbai), 2451 Hongqiao Rd., 200355. Four stars, Tel. 62689111. Fax 62423739.*

Built 1987, renovations 1995-96. 11 stories, 419 rooms. Attractive garden. USTV but no CNN. Karaoke bar. Tennis, gym and outdoor pool. Should have golf practice range by now. Cantonese and Japanese restaurants. 24-hour room service. Plastic bathroom. Disco. Karaoke.

SHANGHAI INTERNATIONAL AIRPORT HOTEL *(Guoji Ji Chang Binguan), 2550 Hongqiao Rd., 200335. Three stars, Tel. 62558866. 62688888. Fax 62558393. $75 to $120 but ask about their cheaper rate.*

Built 1988. 8 stories, 308 small rooms. Teppanyaki. Japanese joint venture transit hotel. USTV. Massage. China Eastern (domestic and international) ticketing office.

Less Touristy Neighborhoods

If you want to get into wholly Chinese neighborhoods, look for isolated hotels like the Novotel, the Regal, or the Holiday Inn. The Novotel however is very far out for tourists. It is also frequently full of long-staying guests. The Regal is isolated in the northern part of the city and is quite good. It is usually the last to fill up, so try there for a discount. It's about 20 minutes by taxi to Pudong via the Yangpu Bridge.

The only hotel in Pudong open before 1997 is the Tomson. Shangri-La and Hyatt hope to open theirs in 1998.

NOVOTEL SHANGHAI YUAN LIN, *201 Bai Se Road, 200232. Three stars. Tel. 64701688. Fax 64700008. In US, Tel. 1-800-221-4542. $80 to $90. Dist.A.P. 15 km. Dist.R.W. 17 km. Dist.Bund 16 km.*

Next to Botanical Garden. Built 1990. Renovations 1995 and 1996. Six stories, 183 rooms. Shuttle bus. One non-smoking floor. USTV. Indoor pool, gym and tennis. 40 Canadian-style villas.

NEW ASIA TOMSON HOTEL, *777 Zhangyang Road, Pudong, 200120, Tel. 58318888, 58772237. Fax 58317777.*

In Lujiazui trade and financial zone. Walk to Asia's largest department store. Thirty-five minutes by expressway from the Sheraton Hua Ting. Five-star standard. Partially open 1996. 24 stories, 400 large rooms. In-room safes. Voice mail. USTV. Executive floors. Cantonese, Chaozhou and Italian restaurants. 24-hour fast food and business centre. Delicatessen. Italian restaurant, grill room and Cantonese restaurant. Gym, golf and indoor-outdoor pool. 21-story atrium. Will be managed by a multinational team.

New Asia will also open a 24-story, three-star hotel, 10 minutes drive away in Pudong nearer the Huangpu River also due in 1996. It should have about 300 rooms and a 24-hour supermarket.

WHERE TO EAT

Shanghai food is sweeter, lighter and prettier than other Chinese foods. It has a delicate consistency. See Chapter 11, *Food & Drink*. Every top hotel should be able to lay on a great Chinese banquet. But if you want to impress anybody, take them to the JC Mandarin, Westin, Garden, Hilton or Portman Hotels.

For Shanghai food, there's also the old-tried-and-true **MEILONGZHEN**, *Nanjing Xi Road, Lane 1081, Tel. 62535353*, about 100 meters east of the JC Mandarin Hotel. It is especially good in November with Shanghai's famous crabs. It also has pleasant traditional Chinese decor.

Good too for Shanghai food is the **OLD SHANGHAI RESTAU-RANT**, *Yu Yuan Garden, 242 Fuyou Road, Tel. 63282782*, particularly for big eels, and fish-head soup.

The **DRAGON-PHOENIX RESTAURANT**, *eighth floor, Peace Hotel*, open 11:30 am to 2 pm, and 5:30 to 8 pm) is another old favorite with a view of the sunset about 6 pm. Its popular Chinese dishes are seafood noodles in soup Y39; steamed perch with sour vegetables Y175 for a half kilogram of fish; sweet and sour pork for Y49; braised fillet of beef for Y56; barbecued whole duck for Y160; braised seafood hotpot Y108; mixed vegetables for Y57 and combination sour and pungent soup Y35.

The **FRIENDSHIP RESTAURANT**, *Shanghai Exhibition Centre, 1000 Yan'an Zhong Road, Tel. 62474078*, is good but nothing exciting, with one exception: the stir-fried duck with vegetables was amazing. Good also is the **MONGOLIAN BARBECUE RESTAURANT**, *33 Chao-Bao Road south of the Sheraton*, but how can you go wrong with Mongolian barbecue when you pick your own ingredients and sauces? But you may not like its factory-like atmosphere, noise, and line-ups. There is some good shopping around here (see *Shopping* below).

Cheap street food markets operate from 7 to 9:30 pm near Yunnan and Nanjing Road, and at Huanghe Road. Take your own bowl and chopsticks!

THE GRAPE (Pu Tao Yuan), *Xin Le Road* diagonally opposite the Dong Hu Hotel (Binguan) near Changle Street, is the current 'in' restaurant among knowledgeable expatriates. It serves Cantonese and Sichuan specialties on only six tables, and no reservations. It's usually hot, crowded, noisy, but great. The service is surly. Get there early for lunch. The **NEW GRAPE** (Xin Pu Tao Yuan) *also near the Dong Hu Hotel and the back door of the Garden Hotel at 142 Xin Le Road, Tel. 64720499,* is even better. Ask for pork ribs fried in salt and pepper. The **HYLAND SOFITEL HOTEL'S CANTONESE RESTAURANT** is introducing some new Chinese dishes like soft-shelled turtle from a secret imperial Qing recipe. And we all know about the energy turtle gives you! Ask also about its neo-Cantonese cuisine and its dim sum. It has some great Japanese sashimi (Seafood Boat). The dim sum is good also at the **YANGTZE NEW WORLD** and the **JC MANDARIN** Hotels.

Good for Cantonese seafood is the **FORUM SEAFOOD RESTAU-RANT** across from the Yangtze New World Hotel in Hongqiao. It has a branch on Huai Hai Zhong Road and has good dim sum too. For good Chinese food, there's the **HOLIDAY INN CROWNE PLAZA** for roast duck Cantonese style, sharks' fins dumplings, and fried Mandarin fish. The Sichuan food in the **BEIJING HILTON** hotel is special, but expensive.

The top hotels have excellent western food, especially at the Hilton, Garden, Holiday Inn, Portman and Westin. Sofitel's and Worldfield's Sunday hotel brunch is good. For Italian food, there's **TONY ROMA'S**, *Shanghai Centre, 1376 Nanjing Xi Road, Tel. 62797129, 62798888,* particularly for ribs.

GIOVANNI'S *at the Westin Hotel* has an Italian executive chef. Try the home-made lasagne with mixed vegetables, and the grilled fresh Norwegian salmon with Sabayon sauce, and finish with dark and white chocolate mousse with orange peel. Also Italian but less expensive is **PASTA FRESCA DA SALVATORE**, *6 Zunyi Nan Road, Tel. 62700000, 62704693,* near the Westin Hotel. It has good pizza.

New restaurants of all varieties are opening — and closing — all the time. Some like the popular **THE GAP RESTAURANT AND BAR**, *ground floor, Jing Ming Building, 8 Zun Yi Road. Tel. 62782900, 62704693,* across from the Yangtze New World Hotel in an alley to the left of the Friendship department store, has a mixed menu of Chinese and western food. Ask for the German braised pork knuckles and the Dai Yu, the deep fried fish Chinese style. The Gap even offers a choice of Italian, French, Australian and South African wines. Decorated with Charlie Chaplin and

James Dean posters, it has a cute atmosphere and sometimes a live American band. The Gap has smaller branches, one of which, **MINI ONE**, is behind Giordano's to the left as you go out the Sheraton Hotel. They take credit cards.

SHANGHAI JAX RESTAURANT, *at the Shangri-La Portman Hotel, Shanghai Centre,* has big, juicy beef burgers for Y72, charbroiled sirloin steak for Y145 and a dinner buffet for Y178. Open 24 hours.

JIA JIA LE RESTAURANT, next door to the domestic airport terminal, *Tel. 65371688 X 81881, or 62684018,* is a modest cafe with good, authentic Singapore and Malaysian food and affable manager Peter Yap. The pork spare rib soup (bak kut teh for Y20) tasted just like my Cantonese father's. Popular are the chicken rice for Y25, the laksa (fiery, spiced noodles with coconut milk soup) Y24, choi tau kueh (carrot cake) Y20, nasi lemak (coconut milk rice) Y28, and Mee Siam (spiced vermicelli soup) for Y24.

For Mexican, **EL POPO**, *12, Lane 19, Rong Hua Xi Dao, Gubei New Area, Tel. 62199279,* near the airport, has a laid-back and cheerful atmosphere, a mariachi band, delicious burritos, fajitas, and excellent Margueritas.

For Indian, **TANDOOR** *at the Jin Jiang Hotel, New South Building, 59 Mao Ming Road, Tel. 62582582 X 9301,* is expensive but has a good set lunch and Indian ambience. For vegetarians, there's the **JADE BUDDHA VEGETARIAN RESTAURANT**, *172 Anyan Road, Tel. 62585596,* near the temple.

A **KFC** is on the Bund beside the Dongfeng Hotel, across from the Park Hotel and other locations. Revolving restaurants are in the Jin Jiang Tower and the Ocean Hotel where the food is overpriced but the top floor view is great. Forget about the Seagull Hotel restaurant. The view might be spectacular but the food and service are terrible.

A PROPOSED ITINERARY

Four days in Shanghai is sufficient to cover the important sights, but you have to make choices as there is plenty to see. The following is a suggested itinerary.

Day One: In the morning, visit the **Yuyuan Garden**, **Huangpu Park**, and a walk along the **Bund** (preferably between 6 and 7 am), with lunch at the Peace or Hyland Sofitel hotels; there's also the **Shanghai Museum**, Friendship Store, Nanjing Road shops, or CITS for any bookings.

Day Two: The **Jade Buddha Temple** with vegetarian lunch, **Children's Palace**, any of the modern history sites, and/or a workers' residential district, (call CAAC/China Eastern or CTS for bookings), a look at the monumental **Shanghai Centre**, or the lovely **Garden Hotel**. (Ask Public Relations for a tour.)

On either of these days, you could substitute or try to squeeze in shopping, the zoo, a boat trip, an arts and crafts factory, the **Shanghai Industrial Exhibition Hall**, an antique or clothes market for shopping, or **People's Square** and the nearby **Huangpu Bird Market**.

Day Three: The **Botanical Gardens**, **Longhua Pagoda**, **Square Pagoda**, carpet factory, **Zuibai Ci Pond** and **She Shan Roman Catholic Church**. Take a picnic lunch with you if you want.

Day Four: **Jiading County**, the **Confucian Temple** museum, and **Qiuxiapu**.

On these last two days, you could also try to squeeze in a village. In the evening, try to see the **Shanghai Acrobats** or **Shanghai Kunqu Opera** (more melodic, quieter, and graceful than Beijing Opera). For tickets, ask your hotel or contact Kunqu Opera Troupe, *9 Shaoxing Road, 200020. Tel. 64331935.*

On another day, plan a day trip to **Suzhou** or an overnight in **Hangzhou** or three days in **Putuoshan**. A travel agent should be able to arrange train tickets or a tour.

SEEING THE SIGHTS

Huangpu Park is the oldest and smallest park in the city, *Zhongshan Dong-1 Road*, across the bridge from Shanghai Mansions. Open daily from 5 am to 10 pm, even for foreign tourists). Started in 1868 by the British, next to the Suzhou and Huangpu Rivers, this once displayed the infamous sign 'No Dogs and Chinese Allowed.'

The **Bund** (Embankment) starts at Huangpu Park on the east. It was even more active between the mid-19th and mid-20th centuries when 240 foreign banks flourished here: look at the grandeur of the **Bank of China** lobby and the Greek columns of the **Customs House**. Look into the lobbies: smile at the guard innocently and say 'Just looking.' Historical plaques are posted outside important buildings.

The Bund is now an elevated walkway beside the harbor. There are plans to extend it south beyond Yan'an Road. If you make it from the Peace Hotel to Yan'an Road, you can walk about the same distance onward to Yuyuan Garden.

The ***Yu Yuan Garden***, *Yu Yuan Road, Tel. 63260830, 63289850*, is a major tourist attraction. Open daily, 8:30 am to 5 pm. Should you see it if you are also going to the gardens of Suzhou? It depends on how much time you have and how much you like gardens. This one is pretty good, but it is crowded. It was originally laid out between 1559 and 1577 by a financial official from Sichuan and now covers 20,000 square meters.

From 1853 to 1854, the Yu Garden itself was used as the headquarters of the **Small Sword Society**, which staged an armed uprising and held part of Shanghai for 18 months. The pavilion opposite the exquisite stage is now a mini-museum. The top of **Rockery Hill** is an artificial mountain made with rocks carried from Jiangxi province. Until it was dwarfed by Shanghai's skyscrapers, this was the highest point in the city from which you could see and hear the Huangpu River nearby. The five dragon walls wind concentrically around the garden. Look for their heads. Note the unusually-shaped doors, some like vases, and, of course, the lovely moon gate. Look for the **Pavilion to See the Reflection of the Water on the Opposite Side** (these names are really something!) and don't trip over the step-over doorways. The south side of the garden was for the aristocratic women, kept out of sight of all but family members. There's a snack bar and souvenir store. A Sunday morning antique market is on a nearby street.

About 100 years ago, a part of the Garden was sold to merchants, and that is now the 98-shop **Yu Yuan Market**, once the busiest in the city and still bustling. Its old architecture helps make it a fun place to visit. Here you can buy dressmaking patterns (six sizes on one pattern) and novelties, and watch *jiao zi* and other Chinese dumplings being made. It is a good place for souvenirs and antiques. The large **Old Town Restaurant** is famous.

The excellent **Shanghai Museum**, *People's Square; 201 Renmin Da Dao, 200003. Tel. 63723500, 63270271*, is open Monday through Friday, 9 am to 5 pm, no admissions after 4 pm; and Saturdays 9 am to 4 pm, with no admissions after 3 pm. Admission is Y35. From the outside, this four-story building in the middle of the square looks like a giant Chinese bronze with four huge handles, its shape symbolizing that heaven is round and earth is square. The exhibits are well lit and signs are in English and Chinese.

If you like temples, see the **Jade Buddha Temple**, *170 Anyuan Road, Puto District; Tel. 62550477, 62538805*. Open daily, 8 am to 5 pm, but closed for lunch at noon. This is a good introduction to Buddhist temples, but nearby Suzhou has better and older ones. The Jade Buddha Temple was built in 1882 in the southern outskirts of Shanghai. It was bodily moved to Shanghai in 1918 and now occupies about two acres in the western part of the city. Many monks live in this temple, and you might hear them singing or reading the scriptures. At your request and donation, monks will chant prayers for the well-being of your soul.

In the first hall, a 2.6-meter-high, gold-faced **Wei Tuo**, the military protector of the Buddhist scriptures, menacingly greets visitors. On each side are two temple guardians: the Eastern King, with a mandolin-like instrument, using music to defend and praise Buddha; the Southern King, with his dark, angry face, and sword; the Northern King, with a Chinese parasol; and the Western King, who 'looks after the whole world with penetrating eyes and carries a snake which is actually a net to catch converts.'

The three largest figures inside the next parallel building are Sakyamuni (center), to his right the Amitaba Buddha (with lotus), and the Yuese Buddha, carrying the Buddhist wheel of law. Along the sides are the 20 guardians of heaven. Guanyin is centered behind the three main Buddhas. Note the very thin Sakyamuni, above, paying homage, and the 18 arhats.

On the second floor the seated 1.9-meter-high Jade Buddha, carved from one piece of white jade in Burma, and brought to China in 1882. The shelves on both sides of the room contain 7240 volumes of Buddhist scriptures, printed in the Qing 200 years ago. They are similar to the book under the glass. In another building is a Reclining Buddha, also of white jade. A good vegetarian restaurant, small antique store, a small museum, and a Buddhist Academy with at least 100 students are also in this temple.

The **Jingan Temple**, *1686 Nanjing Xi Road, Tel. 62583335*, is tiny, eclectic, but conveniently located downtown. It's relatively new, having been relocated several times. There is also the **Xiaotaoyuan Mosque** at *52 Xiaotaoyuan Street, Tel. 63775442*, and the **Baiyunguan Taoist Temple** on *Xi Lin Hou Road*, for those interested in religion.

Many group tours include a visit to a **Children's Palace**. These are after-school programs for seven to 16 year-olds, much like community centers. Specially-chosen children get extra opportunities to learn and practice art, sciences, music, and sports, Some of the 23 palaces in the city are in old mansions built by wealthy capitalists. A visit to one will not only give you a chance to learn something of the education of children but also to explore the buildings themselves.

Best set up for tourists is the **Children's Municipal Palace**, *64 Yan'an Road, Tel. 62481850*, for exact visiting hours. It has been open Wednesday and Saturday mornings for visitors but not all summer. Children's Palaces were a project of Soong Ching-Ling, the widow of Dr. Sun Yat-sen. Money is being solicited internationally for the Soong Ching-ling Foundation to continue and expand this work.

The former **residence of Dr. Sun Yat-sen**, *Shangshan Road, Tel. 64372954*, is in the old French Concession, but not open daily. Once inside, you are back in the 1920s. The house was bought by Chinese-Canadians for the father of republican China for 16,000 pieces of silver. Dr. Sun lived here with his wife intermittently from 1920 to 1924, just before his death of cancer in 1925. His widow, Soong Ching-ling, lived in the house until 1937, when the war forced her to move to Chongqing.

Here, in 1924, Dr. Sun met Communist leader Li Dazhao (Li Tachao) publicly for the first time to work out Nationalist-Communist cooperation. Dr. Sun was much influenced by Marx and Lenin. Besides the antiques, there are some old photographs, a 1920 China train map, Sun's medical instruments, clothes, and glasses. The railway map is significant because Dr. Sun was in charge of railways for a short time after he resigned as president. The house contains his library: a 1911 Encyclopedia Britannica, biographies of Bismarck, Cicero, Lincoln, and Napoleon in English, books in Japanese, and ancient works in Chinese. No photos are allowed. See also *Nanjing* for more about Dr. Sun.

An interesting place is the **Museum and Tomb of Lu Xun** (Lu Hsun), *Hongkou Park; Tel. 66661181,* museum open daily, except Sundays, 8:30 am to 4 pm but closed for lunch at 11:30. These are in the northern part of the city. Lu Xun (1181-1936) was an author of short stories who wrote in the colloquial language about poor people, impoverished literati, and oppressed women. Chinese literature until then had primarily been about the wealthy elite, written in a snobbish literary style, too difficult for the masses to grasp. Although he was not a Communist, Lu Xun is considered a national hero. He died in Shanghai.

The site of the **First National Congress of the Communist Party of China**, *76 Xingye Road, Tel. 63260664,* is open daily from 8:30 am to 4 pm except for lunch at 11 am; closed Monday and Thursday mornings. This was the living room of a small rented house in the former French Concession. There, 12 representatives of the Party from all over China including Mao Zedong, met secretly for four days starting on July 1, 1921.

Another relic from a previous era and still in use is the **Shanghai Industrial Exhibition Hall**, *1000 Yan'an Zhong Road, Tel. 2563037.* Completed in 1955 with Soviet help in the massive Soviet style, it is used for trade exhibitions. There are two large arts and crafts handicraft stores here, not recommended for careful shoppers.

The **Shanghai Zoo**, *2381 Hongqiao Road, Tel. 62687775, 62557775,* usually open daily, 6:30 am to 5:30 pm, but check before you go. One of the better zoos in China, it's on 70 hectares, and has 280 species, including giant pandas, rare Chinese birds, and Yangtze crocodiles.

If you wish to pay your respects to a very distinguished humanitarian and revolutionary, visit the beautiful white statue and tomb of **Song Qingling** (Soong Ching-ling) in *Wang Guo (International) Cemetery, 21 Lingyuan Road, Changning District near Hongqiao Road.* The widow of the founder of republican China died in May 1981. Her parents, and the maid who served her for 52 years are buried nearby. Do read *The Soong Dynasty.*

Soong Ching-ling was the sister of Mme. Chiang Kai-shek. She eloped with the already-married Sun Yat-sen and was virtually disowned by her wealthy Christian father, up to that point a strong supporter of Dr. Sun. She was tolerated by her family and her powerful in-laws, although she was outspoken in her opposition to their exploitation of China. She was, after all, the widow of the widely respected father of the country. She chose to remain in China after Liberation, and worked to promote the welfare of the Chinese people.

You have a choice of two **Huangpu River** boat trips. The cheaper one is booked from the wharf near Huangpu Park at the foot of Beijing Dong Road across from the Peace Hotel, *229-239 Zhongshan Dong Road, Tel. 63744461, 63745854.* This 3 1/2-hour, 60-kilometer trip sails to the Changjiang (Yangtze) River at Wusong Kou at 9:30 am and 2 pm daily, with a 1 1/2-hour night cruise at 7 pm during the summer. You should go if you want to relax and see sailing junks and rusty ships from all over the world on a muddy river with industries along its shores. On the return trip, however, you might find a magician and acrobatic show.

The longer, more expensive cruise is operated by **Regal Cruises**, *Third floor, 110 Yangtze Road, 200080, Tel. 63069801 or fax 63069902.* It has higher standards, good food, and overnight accommodations.

Also fun is **Renmin** (People's) **Square**, measuring 467 by 100 meters and used for parades, ceremonial occasions, people-watching, and ball-playing. It also has a daily free market with flowers, *penjing* (miniature landscapes), and goldfish of many varieties. The **Huangpu Market** (open 7 am to 5 pm) is a block west. The **Botanical Garden**, *1100 Longhua Road, Tel. 64365523*, is also worth a visit. Open 8 am to 4 pm (it might be closed on Sundays) is in the southwestern suburbs. On 70 hectares, there are rock gardens and potted miniature trees, some several hundred years old.

Longhua Pagoda and Temple, *2853 Longhua Road, Tel. 64397797, 64385963*, open 7 am to 4 pm, is in the southwestern suburbs and can be combined with the Botanical Gardens and Songjiang county for a one day trip. It is a noted scenic spot, the park formerly was an execution ground. It was originally built by Sun Quan of the Three Kingdoms (222-280 A.D.) for his mother and rebuilt several times since, the latest in the early 1980s. It is considered the oldest temple in Shanghai district. Note the fine brick carvings on its walls. The seven-story brick and wood Song dynasty pagoda stands about 40 meters high. It tolls good luck bells on New Year's eve.

The **Oriental Pearl Television Tower** (Dongfang Ming Zu), *2 Lane 504 Jujiazui Road, Pudong, 200120. Tel. 58827333, 58824999 or 58828888 X 116 or fax 58796660*, open 9 am to 9:15 pm, has been the tallest such structure in Asia and the third highest in the world. You can see it as you look east on Nanjing Road. It has an observatory.

Shanghai also has private museums, with collections of folk art, theatrical costumes, calculation instruments, paper fans, boat models, coins and root sculptures. There is a traditional Chinese medicine museum and a navy museum. The Shanghai Tourism Administration has the addresses.

Shanghai's Jewish History

Jews in Shanghai? Yes, there have been three migrations. A handful of Sephardic Jews arrived from west Asia in the mid-1800s. These were the

Kadoories, Hardoons, and Sassoons, who invested in much of Shanghai's real estate and whose mansions today are across from the City and Equatorial Hotels. The music conservatory used to be the Russian Club.

Then came White Russian Jews, refugees from the Communist revolution who arrived in the early 1920s. The third and latest group came to escape Hitler's Europe in the late 1930s. The 19,000 or so who reached Shanghai were mainly from Poland,Germany, and Austria. They were encouraged to stay by the then Japanese rulers even though Japan was an ally of Germany, because the Japanese incorrectly thought they could borrow large sums of money from these Jewish refugees.

This last wave of refugees arrived with only their clothing, choosing Shanghai because they needed no visas and passports here. They just walked off their ships or trains, and were helped by earlier migrants and Jews from other parts of the world. There were also Jews from Russia who arrived via Harbin. In 1943, the Japanese forced all Jews into Hongkou district. They endured U.S. bombs and very few married Chinese people.

After the war, most discovered they had no family in Europe. With the communization of China, they left for other parts of the world. The last of the resident Shanghai Jews died in the 1980s.

Part of the **Ohel Moshe Synagogue**, built in 1927, is now a museum organized by the district government. A good sign in English points to two rooms with a few relics and photos. *Located on the second floor of 62 Chang Yang Road in Hongkou District, Tel. 65120229, and 65416312.* Open 9 am to 4:30 pm Monday to Friday.

Ask for guide Wang Fah Liang, a neighborhood resident who can tell you about the area. It is behind the Ocean Hotel where a memorial plaque (in English and Hebrew) also sits in a nearby park. If you want to do more research, contact the Israeli Consulate in Shanghai or the **China-Judaic Institute**, *232 Lexington Drive, Menlo Park, CA 94025.*

Walks

Downtown Shanghai is too crowded and the air too polluted for much walking, but there are parks near the Jin Jiang Hotel. People's Park doesn't have much greenery, so head for the suburbs, unless you like walking around air conditioned urban malls. Or follow the circular route of the old city wall and moat that winds in a big loop around the Yuyuan Garden. Start at Ren Min and Zhong Hua Roads, then head north on Ren Min Road.

In the suburbs are the Botanical Gardens, the airport hotels, the zoo and further out, Suzhou. There's interesting hiking on the hill around the She Shan Basilica.

NIGHTLIFE & ENTERTAINMENT

Shanghai has high standards for music, art, and drama. It is a good place to sample China's rich cultural life and to look for the contributions of its various migrant groups. For current offerings, look through the monthly tourist handouts free at many of the hotels. I suggest looking at what's playing at the Shanghai Art Theater and Shanghai Concert Hall. Shanghai is generally safe after dark.

The **Shanghai Acrobatic and Magic Troupe** is a fun show with magicians, sword-swallowing, juggling and sometimes performing pandas. Its theater is near the Park Hotel *at 400 Nanjing Xi Road*. When rebuilt about 1999, it will have other entertainment venues as well. Its current temporary home for its regular performances is in the Shanghai Centre.

Among the free concerts at the hotels, the Portman has a 14-member orchestra playing Beethoven and Mozart on Sunday afternoons in **Zhou's Bar**. Be careful about scams: in some bars you'll pay unreasonably high prices for hostesses to drink with you. Among those that are okay:

New York, New York, *146 Huqiu Road, Tel. 63216097*, a good disco with reasonable prices. It appeals to the younger crowd. There's also a good disco in the **Galaxy Hotel**, *888 Zhong Shan Xi Road, Tel. 62755888*.

The **Long Bar**, *Shanghai Center, Tel. 62798888*, is a hangout of usually boisterous Americans – but avoid the hamburgers. There might be a T.G.I.F. happy hour organized by diplomats, so ask at the Australian, U.S., or Canadian consulates about Friday evening. **Charlie's Bar**, *Holiday Inn*, has a Filipino band.

Other drinking holes favored by foreigners are: **Churchill's**, *Dong Hu Hotel, 167 Xin Le Road, Tel. 64158158 X 12130*, a real British pub with good value for the money. There's **Hyland 505**, *second floor, Hyland Sofitel Hotel, 505 Nanjing Dong Road, Tel. 63515888*, which has happy hour 6 pm to 8 pm daily, a mini-brewery and pub with darts, pool and live entertainment. A small beer costs Y30. **Shanghai Sally's**, *4 Xiang Shan Road, Tel. 63271859*, open 5 pm to 2 am daily, is another English pub with pool and darts.

Malone's American Cafe, *257 Tong Ren Road, Tel. 62472400*, is a sports bar on the street immediately south of the Shanghai Center. It has good hamburgers (Y75) and salads (Y40 to Y75), and American movies on Sunday nights. It's good even for kids before 6 pm and it takes major credit cards.

L.A. Cafe, *188 Huai Hai Road, Tel. 63587097*, has draft beer, sandwiches, and a good salad bar. A Hard Rock Cafe should open soon on the west side of the Shanghai Center and after that there'll probably be a Planet Hollywood close to the Garden Hotel.

For sheer relaxation, try a massage in your hotel.

SHOPPING

Shanghai is the best place in China for selection and quality, and time should be set aside here to shop if interested. Produced in the city are jade, ivory and whitewood carvings, lacquerware, needlepoint tapestries, silks, carpets, embroideries, gold and silver jewelry (especially filigree), artificial flowers, painted eggs, reproductions of antique bronzes, and such proletarian articles as cheap jogging suits, bedroom slippers, winter jackets, heavy tee-shirts, and gloves. Please note: crafts factories do not necessarily have the lowest prices.

Serious souvenir shoppers should check out the prices first at the Arts and Crafts Sales Service Centre store on Nanjing Road below, or the Friendship Store, or the stores in and the one across the street from the Old Town Gods' Temple Arts and Crafts in Yuyuan Garden. These are the cheapest. However, there are also a few good buys at the Sheraton Hotel shopping center too. You'll find most places cheaper than Hong Kong for crafts and antiques with a much bigger selection.

The **Old Town Gods' Temple Market**, *Hua Bao Building, 265 Fong Bang Zhong Road, Yu Yuan Garden. Tel. 63559999*, is open 9:30 am to 6:30 pm. It's basement has many interesting little antique shops with a good variety for hagglers. Other floors have souvenirs at reasonable prices. The **Shanghai Friendship Store**, *40 Beijing Dong Road, Tel. 63234600*, two blocks north of the Peace Hotel, is one of the largest in China. It can also crate and ship purchases. Prices are reasonable with a good variety of lacquerware, cinnabar, eggs, peasant paintings, cloisonne, teapots, old porcelain shard boxes, pearls, musical instruments, ordinary stone carvings, painted silk screens, calligraphy, cross-stitch, antique embroidery, and dough figures.

The best general shopping is along **Nanjing Road** between the Peace and Park Hotels, but of course this means oppressive crowds and the possibility of pickpockets. You have to be a dedicated shopper to face this. The Shanghainese themselves shop along **Huaihai Road**, a very long street with fewer people than Nanjing Dong Road. Among the many stores there is **Isetan's**, the Japanese department store, *527 Huaihai Zhong Lu at Yang Dang Road, Tel. 63751111*.

For sportswear, the **Huating Market** *off Huaihai Road near the Hilton* is good for better quality factory overruns than other street markets. Look for great buys on silk shirts but lots of junk too. Tailors everywhere might take two weeks to three months to make anything. Make sure they know the latest western styles.

A western-style 'drug store' with no pharmacist is in the Shanghai Center. Supermarkets with imported goods are at the Jin Jiang Hotel,

Shanghai Center and Friendship Store. Good Chinese supermarkets are everywhere.

Shanghai Arts and Crafts Trading Corp., *1000 Yan'an Zhong Road, Shanghai Exhibition Center, open 8:30 am to 6 pm, Tel. 68790279, X 2130*, is to be avoided. The two stores have good quality but are overly expensive, badly maintained, and served by don't-care clerks. The **Shanghai Carpet Factory** is at *256 Cao Bao Road, Tel. 64361713, 64360126* (across from the Huaxia Hotel beyond the Sheraton). **Number One Silk Printing and Dyeing Factory**, *1133 Chang Ning Road, 200051, Tel. 62519900, 62578766*, is expensive compared to factories in Suzhou and Hangzhou, and shops in downtown Shanghai, but selections and styles are good for ready-made garments. Avoid tourist traps like CTS's Xing Hua Tourist Souvenir Store on Huaihai Xi Lu near the Holiday Inn Crowne Plaza, and the Qing Xiang tourist store next to the Mongolian barbecue restaurant at 33 Chao-Bao Road where our test item was about nine times the price elsewhere.

Shopping on Nanjing Dong Road is crowded, but you don't have to walk far to find what you want.

Nanjing Road Stores & Services in Detail

The following are located east to west from the Peace Hotel on the north side. CITS has a small office in the Peace Hotel but is moving back to 66 Nanjing Dong Road soon.

Number 30 Telegram and Telephone office (open 24 hours) has videophone and card phones. After Sichuan Zhong Road, there isHui Luo Company, a good Hong Kong joint-venture department store which might save you a trip to the Friendship Store. It's open 9:30 am to 9:30 pm. Nearby is Jeans West. At Number 114 is a music store, and then Giordano for sportswear. At Jiangxi Zhong Lu, there's the Guan Long Photo Store where cameras can be fixed (open 9 am to 9:30 pm). You will probably be able to get unusual-sized camera batteries here.

Number 51 is the Lao De Ji Dispensary; at Henan Zhong Road, there's Bausch and Lomb for frames and a resident eye doctor. At 200 is the Donghai Leather Co. (purses and suitcases, open 10 am to 10 pm); 204 is the Hong Feng Stationery; 212 is the Marboro City Jewellery. Nearby at 222 is Shanghai Computers. Number 238 has wedding dresses; 244 has Chinese postage stamps for collectors; 262 is the Hengdali Watch Co. (the Citizen dealer). Across Henan Zhong Street is Number 270, the Li Hua Department Store.

A bakeshop, decent grocery store and the fast food Rong Hua Chicken place is at 300. Number 320 is a traditional medicine store; 328 to 334 sells electronics; 340 is the Zhong Lian Department Store (open 9 am to 10 pm); 386 is a leather store; 388 is the Weng Long Sheng Tea Shop; 392 has traditional Chinese medicines; 402 has jewellery.

After crossing Shanxi Nan Road, there's the Ningpo Food Store at 414; the Duo Yun Art Gallery with painting supplies where you can have scrolls mounted and buy top paintings and calligraphy is at 422. The Shanghai Jewelry Store and Arts and Crafts Jewelry and Jadeware is at 432 and 438. 448 is a department store; 460 the Shanghai Gold Shop; 490 is Zhang Xiao Quan knives and scissors.

The Sincere Co. (H.K.) and the Manhattan Plaza with many boutiques are next to the Sofitel across the street. Number 505 Sofitel Hotel is where you can leave your purchases and lunch at the Hyland 505 brewery (pizza and beer for less than Y50) with free use of darts.

Continuing west along the north side of Nanjing Road, across Fujian Zhong Road, there's a porcelain shop at 550, and a deparment store at 580. Number 588 has a McDonald's in the basement. 616 is a dispensary with some western medicines; 630 has groceries; 636 has fast shishkebobs; then after crossing Zhejiang Zhong Road, there is a big clothes store at 690. Cross Guanxi Bei Road, and at 720 is a department store. Cross Guizhou Road to 740, a bedroom store; 748 a pharmacy; and 764 an optical store. 766 has food, 772 is another optical store and after the construction site and Liuhe Road Number One Department Store (good for linens, *Tel. 63223344*) is at the circle overpass over Xizang Road. The four department stores here are handy to each other. The fanciest seems to be New World City. Here also is the metro stop on the southwest side.

The Pacific Hotel at 104 Nanjing Xi Road (same road) is next. It was formerly the Overseas Chinese hotel and has a CTS office. (It's relatively cheap, grubby, but adequate.) The Park Hotel is next at 170. The recommended **Arts and Crafts Sales Service Centre** is at *190-208, Tel. 63275299.* Jewelry is on the ground floor and crafts on upper floors. Here you can buy silver chop sticks, silk tee shirts, quilts, clothes, shoes, gloves, ties, children's dresses, carpets, cloisonne, yard goods and furniture. Across the road is a KFC.

Starting on the way back east at the east end of People's Park, at Xizang Road, there a watch and jewellery store, and the Quan Long Photo Store. After Yunnan Zhong Road, a jewellery store is at 751, a store for hats and shoes at 747, and a electronics store at 739. After Guizhou Road is the good **Sunya Cantonese Restaurant** *at 719, Tel. 63224393.* Then comes a wool yarn shop and Guangxi Road, and the **Baodaxiang Department store**. Cross Jinhua Road to the **Hualian Department Store**, *Tel. 63224466*, open 9 am to 10 pm, and past a huge construction site which might be built-up by the time you get there. 549 is a pharmacy, and 541 an electronic company. Cross Fujian Road to the Sofitel Hotel which also houses an optical store. After the large Hong Kong department stores, one of which is similar to the top-of-the-market Landmark in Hong Kong, there's a Singapore fast food place at 463.

At Shanxi Nan Road going east on the south side, 397 Nanjing is a textile store, 391 a cheap restaurant, 373 another textile store, then the Xin Hua Book Store. After you cross Shandong Zhong Road is 311, a camera store. Numbers 297 and 259 are optical stores, 285 for ham, and 257 is yet another department store. Then cross Jiangxi Zhong Road for the computer store at 171, Adidas at 157, and a pharmacy at 151. Cross Shashi Yi Road and then there are alleys for buying cheap sportswear. 123 is Benetton.

Also within walking distance of the Sofitel Hotel is the **Foreign Language Book Store** at *390 Fuzhou Road, 200001, Tel. 63224109, 63223200.* Open 9 am to 5:30 pm. It will mail books. Another good store with books in English is in the Jin Jiang Hotel. Other hotels also have book stores. For musical instruments, try the department stores or the Shanghai Piano Co., 369 Yunnan Road at Nanjing Road.

A clean, modern shopping mall that looks more like Hong Kong than China is under People's Square. In the eastern-most corner is a booth marked "Shanghai Information" which gives out a free tourist map. Nearby is a Park 'N Shop supermarket.

Antiques

The best bargains in antiques is at the Sunday morning street market at **Fu You Road** about five short blocks north of Yu Yuan Garden. This opens at about 6 am until about 3 pm. It has great buys if you know what you're buying and start at a quarter of their first asking price. The market stretches along eight blocks of Fu You Road. Wares are spread out on the ground or on tables. And an interpreter just might volunteer to help you.

The next best market, especially in inclement weather, is the **Old Town Gods' Temple Market** *in the Hua Bao Building, Yu Yuan Garden above.* Then there's the semi-outdoor **Dongtai Antique Market**, *around 54 Dong Tai Road. If you have problems finding it, Tel. 63288282.* It's near the site of the First National Congress of the Communist Party. Guides are reluctant to take you to any of these markets partly because they don't get any commissions. But the markets are fun; you can find tiny shoes for bound feet, old silver jewellery with real kingfisher feathers, and the cricket boxes — things you can see in museums and couldn't handle before.

Try **Chine Antiques**, *1660 Hong Qiao Road west of Xi Jiao Guest House, Tel. Julie Yu, 62701023.* Open 9 am to 4 pm weekdays for refinished antique furniture. It also has a warehouse and can ship. Several antique stores are between the Hilton and the Shanghai Hotels on Hua Shan Road. Especially good is the **Kuo Yue Cha Artware** shop in the Hilton itself on the second floor with good quality stone carvings, porcelain and jade — with negotiable prices, but avoid the other shop at the Hilton because of high prices. Avoid also the shop at the Equatorial, except for the miniature paintings found nowhere else. Go to the **Xuzhong Antique Shop**, *445 Wulumuqi, Tel. 62481856*, for knowledgeable private dealers, good embroidery, jewellery, jade, and porcelain.

For more expensive antiques and government guarantees, there's the **Shanghai Antique and Curio Store**, *218-226 Guangdong Road, Tel. 63212864, 63212864*, Open 9 am to 5 pm; **#Antiques and Curio Branch, Friendship Store**, *694 Nanjing Xi Road, Tel. 62539549*; and **#Shanghai Antique Store**, *218-226 Guangdong Road, Tel. 63214697, 63212864*. The latter is especially good for antique scrolls.

EXCURSIONS FROM SHANGHAI

Songjiang County, about 40 kilometers southwest of the city, has a history of 2,500 years. Plan on a full day. The rare **Square Pagoda** *in the Xingsheng Monastery, Sangong Street, Songjiang, Tel. 57833310*, open daily 5:30 am to 5 pm, is 48.5 meters high. It was first erected in 949 and rebuilt in 1086-94 in the basic Song dynasty style with the tetragonal shape of the Tang. It still has some original brick and wooden brackets. Renovations in the late 1970s uncovered two Song murals of Buddha, Song and Tang coins, bronze buddhas, and animal skeleton-offerings. Its nine stories lean slightly seaward to compensate for prevailing winds.

The screen in front is the oldest brick carving in the area, erected in 1370 to keep evil spirits out of the Temple of the City Gods, which no longer exists. Very well preserved, the mythical animal is a tuan, greedily eating everything in sight. Note the money in its mouth. Other ancient relics have been assembled here from different parts of the county.

Also in Songjiang County is the **Zuibai Ci** (Pond for Enjoying Bai's Drunkenness) **Garden**, outside the West Gate of Songjiang town. First built in 1652 and expanded in 1958. The lotus flowers in the pond are said to date from the 17th century. Look for a stone engraving of 91 leading Songjiang citizens from the Ming and early Qing. Skip this garden if your time is short.

The **Roman Catholic Basilica** (Xu Jia Hui, She Shan), *Zao Xi Bai Road, Tel. 57813349*, is high on a hill beside the Academy of Science's Observatory. It is northwest of Songjiang. It looks most impressive but intriguingly and incongruously European. The Jesuits built both, the observatory in the 1860s and the basilica in the 1920s. A Jesuit seminary is still at the base of the hill. Stations of the cross line the driveway up and pilgrimages take place in May.

I highly recommend **Qiuxiapu**, a 450-year-old classical garden, once belonging to a Ming officer. It gives yin-yang contrasts of stillness and liveliness, reality and dream, with 20 scenic spots in a small space.

The **Confucius Temple**, *183 Nan Da Street, Chexiangzhen, Tel. 69530379*, open 8 am to 5 pm, except for lunch from 11 am to 1:30 pm, is one of the largest such temples in South China. A major part of it is a museum of local history, with maps showing how people migrated, an old fishing boat, and famous stone tablets relating to important events from the Ming. The temple itself was founded in 1219 and enlarged in the Yuan and Ming.

The **Daguanyuan** (Grand View) Garden, 65 kilometers north of Shanghai *on Dianshan Lake west of Qingpu town, Tel. 69266629, 69266831*, open 8 am to 4:30 pm, is not international class but people who know the 1886 book *Dream of the Red Chamber-Mansions* might want to see this theme park which is better than the one in Beijing. It can be combined in a one-day tour with Zhou Zhuang village, a beautiful little town with canals like Suzhou's.

Other excursions can be easily arranged from Shanghai to Hangzhou, Ningbo and Putuo Shan, Suzhou, and Wuxi. See separate listings.

PRACTICAL INFORMATION

• **Business Hours**: Most offices are open five days a week; some offices 8:30 am to 5 pm, or 9 am to 5:30 pm. Lunch time goes from 11:30 or 12 noon to 1 or 1:30 pm. Friendship Store 9 am to 10 pm. Many stores open 9:30 or 10 am to 9:30 to 10 pm. Store hours vary.

• **Arts Clearance Office**: for permission to export major antiques contact the **Shanghai Antique and Curio Administration**, *7, Lane 567, Huai Hai Zhong Road, Tel. 63586965*. Every Thursday afternoon 1:30 to 3:30 pm.

• **ATM** in Citibank, outside the Peace Hotel, and on the sixth floor of the Union Building near the Bund and Yan'an Dong Road.

Consulates

Hours are usually Monday to Friday, about 8:30 am to 5:00 pm.

• **Australia**, *17 Fuxing Xi Road, Tel. 64334604. Fax 64376669*
• **Britain**, *244 Yongfu Road, 200031, Tel. 64330508. Fax 64330498, 64711849*
• **Canada**, *West Tower, Suite 604, Shanghai Centre, 1376 Nanjing Xi Road, 200040, Tel. 62798400. Fax 62798401*
• **France**, *1375 and 1431 Huaihai Zhong Road, 200031, Tel. 64332639, 64377414. Fax 64377073, 64339437*
• **Germany**, *151 and 181 Yongfu Road, 200002, Tel. 64336953. Fax 64714488, 64714448*
• **Israel**, *Tel. 62098008. Fax 62098010*
• **Italy**, *121 Wuyi Road, Tel. 62524373. Fax 62511728*
• **Japan**, *1517 Huaihai Zhong Road, 200031, Tel. 64336639. Fax 64331008*

- **Korea**, *2200 Yan'an Xi Road, 200335, Tel. 62196417. Fax 62196918*
- **New Zealand**, *Room B, 15th floor, 1375 Huaihai Zhong Road, 200031. Tel. 64332230, 64711127. Fax 64333533*
- **Poland**, *618 Jianguo Xi Road, 200013. Tel. 64334735, 64339288*
- **Russian Federation**, *20 Huang Pu Road, 200002, Tel. 63242682 Fax 63069982*
- **Singapore**, *400 Wulumuqi Zhong Road, 200031. Tel. 64331362, 64370776. Fax 64334150*
- **Switzerland**, *Tel. 62480599. Fax 62480688*
- **U.S.**, *1469 Huaihai Zhong Road, Tel. 64379880, 63242682, 64336880. Fax 4334122. Press and Cultural Affairs, 4th Floor, Qi Hua Tower, 1375 Huaihai Zhong Road, 200031, Tel. 64718689. Fax 64317630.* Email, *demr@usia.gov*

- **Emergencies**, *Ambulance: Tel. 120; Fire Tel. 119; Police Tel. 110*
- **Medical**, *Hua Shan Hospital, 12 Wulumuqi Zhong Road, Foreigners' Clinic, 19th floor. Dr. May Yuan, Tel. 62483986. Sino-Canadian Dental Clinic, Ninth People's Hospital, 7th floor, main building, 639 Zhi-Zhao Ju Road, Tel. 63774831. Dr. William Xi extension 5279. Or 63763174. Fax 63776856.* Some western medicines are available. Try Watson's at the Shanghai Centre. Call your consulate for help.
- **International ship passengers enquiry**, *1 Taiping Street, Dongdaming Road, Tel. 65419529*
- **Information telephone line for shopping, hospitals**, *Tel. 63200200. Or 115.*
- **Shanghai Municipal Tourism Administration**, *2525 Zhong Shan Xi Road (in Hua Ting Guest House), 200030. Tel. 64391818 extensions 2414, 2309, 2311 or Miss Cheng Mei Hong, Tel. 64810905. Fax 64391519. (Administration, complaints, brochures.)*
- **Taxi Complaints**, *Tel. 63216611*
- **Tourist Complaints**, contact **Supervisory Bureau of Tourism Quality of Shanghai Municipality**, *Tel. 64390630*
- **Tourism Hotline**, for help with translations, logistical questions, telephone numbers, etc.: *Tel. 62520000 extension 100, 195, 210, 211. Or 64390630.*

Travel Agents
- **CITS**, *Booking office, 66 Nanjing Dong Road or the Peace Hotel. Tel. 63214565, 63210032. Fax 3291788. Head office, 2 Jinling Dong Road, 200002 (near Yan'an Road and the Bund.) Tel. 63238748 for tickets. Tel. 63217200, 63234202. Fax 63291788*
- **China Shanghai Spring International Travel Service**, *1558 Xing Xi Road, 200050. Tel. 62520000. Fax 62523734.* Ask for Sally Shao,

Manager, F.I.T. Department. Contact **Shanghai Spring** in the United States for cheaper Shanghai hotels, etc.: *300 N. Continental Blvd. #450, El Segundo, CA 90245. Tel. (310)7260183. Fax (310)7260185*
- **CTS**, *881 Yan'an Zhong Road, 200040. Tel. 6475521, 62478888. Fax 62475521. Booking office, 104 Nanjing Xi Road, Tel. 63226606, 62470246, 63279112, 64338338*
- **CYTS Tours**, *2 Heng Shan Road, 200031. Tel. 64331826. Fax 64330507, 64335521*
- **Shanghai Express Company**, *Suite 312, Dadi Business Center, 50 Pu Hai Tang, 200030. Tel. 61690177. Ask for travel agent Emily Pang.*

16. EAST CHINA

FUZHOU

(Foochow)

The capital of **Fujian** province on the east coast across from Taiwan, **Fuzhou** is over 2000 years old. The hottest temperature is 39 degrees centigrade in July and August; the coldest, minus 0.8 degrees centigrade in February. The urban population is 1.3 million.

ARRIVALS & DEPARTURES

There are flights from Hong Kong and 37 other Chinese cities, bus connections, and a 37-hour train ride from Guangzhou. A new international airport should open in 1997.

ORIENTATION

Opened to foreign trade in 1842, Fuzhou had British and American dockyards, and factories for making tea bricks. Once home to about 10 foreign consulates, its foreign cemetery was dug up and replaced by a school. The old British Community Church is still a church. Across the street is the Hua Nan Women's College which is looking for native English-speakers willing to teach English in return for room and board. The city is noted for its **hot springs**, with over a dozen in Fuzhou itself.

WHERE TO STAY

The most important hotels here are centered around the **Foreign Trade Center** (FTC), except the Lakeside. The best is the classy **Lakeside** (if you like modern, glass-walled high-rises). It is also best for walks. The **Hot Springs** is next best, then the **Foreign Trade Center Hotel**.

The **Ming Jiang** is the best three star. All the downtown hotels have hot spring water and all are convenient to shopping. Prices here are subject to change and negotiation.

FUJIAN FOREIGN TRADE CENTER HOTEL *(Wai Mao Zhong Xing Jiudian)*, *Wusi Rd., 350001. Four stars, Tel. 7523388. Fax 7536552. $90. Dist.A.P. 25 km.. Dist.R.W. three km. Credit Cards.*

Built 1985, ren. 1991. Next door to FTC. Seven stories, 163 rooms. IDD, B.C., attractive rooms, pool, tennis, and conference hall. Preferred by business people because of location, though second best. USTV.

HOT SPRING HOTEL *(Wen Quan Daxia), Wusi Zhong Rd., 350003. Four stars, Tel. 7851818. Fax 7835150. Reservations in North America 1-800-44UTELL. $100 to $110. Dist.A.P. 13 km.. Dist.R.W. four km. Credit Cards.*

Built 1986, ren. 1989. 15 stories, 311 rooms. IDD. Outdoor pool, gym, tennis, bowling. B.C. Qigong. 'Bubble' elevator. Large rooms with balconies, small closets, no drawers. Japanese cuisine.

LAKESIDE HOTEL *(Xihu Dajiudian), 158 Hubin Rd., 350003. Four stars, Tel. 7839888. Fax 7839752, 7831097. Y800 to Y1230. Dist.A.P. 15 km.. Dist.R.W. three km.. Credit Cards.*

Built 1988. Ren. 1994. 22 stories, 436 rooms. Gym, disco, outdoor pool, B.C. Japanese and Cantonese restaurants. IDD. CITS. Even-numbered rooms have lakeview. Non-smoking rooms and executive floors. USTV.

MIN JIANG HOTEL, *Wusi Road, 350001. Three stars. Tel. 7557895. Fax 7551489. $75. Dist.A.P. 13 km.. Dist.R.W. 3.5 km.. Credit Cards.*

This hotel has 412 rooms, IDD, Cantonese and Huaiyang cuisines. B.C. A CTS hotel.

WHERE TO EAT

In addition to the hotel restaurants, try the famous **JU CHUN YUAN RESTAURANT** *(Tel. 7553038).*

SEEING THE SIGHTS

Visit **Gushan** (Drum Hill), topped by a huge drum-shaped boulder in the eastern suburbs, at least 969 meters high. It is 10 kilometers outside the city, open 8 am to 4:30 pm. The **Yongquan Si** (Surging Spring Temple) was founded in 908 A.D. and has a white jade buddha. Monks chant twice a day for one hour. The **Qianfo Taota** (Thousand-Buddha Pottery Pagoda) and the **Shuiyun Ting** (Water and Cloud Pavilion), east of the Yongquan Si are both from the Song dynasty. Views from the 18 caves west of the temple are famous. Several hundred inscriptions on the cliff are near the **Lingyuan Dong** (Spirit Source Cave). Over 100 of these writings are from the Song.

The most famous temples are the plain-looking **Baita** (White Pagoda) on the west side of Yushan Hill, and the **Wuta** (Black Pagoda), at the base of Wushi Hill, both in the center of town. The main hall of the *Hualin

Temple, from the Song, is worth seeing. The **Jinshan** (Gold Mountain) **Temple** is snugly perched on an island west of the city.

The **Memorial Hall of Lin Zexu**, the official who burned the 20,000 chests of opium near Canton in 1839, is a small shrine with a statue of the national hero. Ask your hotel to write directions in Chinese. Known also as a calligrapher and a poet, Lin was one of the first Qing officials to take an interest in things foreign. Because the British fired on China as a result of Lin's actions, the emperor exiled Lin to Yili in Xinjiang. The **Xi Chen Si Buddhist Temple** is at *Yang Ziao Road*, open 8 am to 4:30 pm.

NIGHTLIFE & ENTERTAINMENT

There's a disco at the Hot Springs Hotel and a night market near May Square. The **Festival of Goddess Mazu** is held in April and May on Meizhou Island in Putian City, 108 kilometers south.

SHOPPING

Good bodiless lacquerware, cork carving, and Shoushan stone carvings are made and sold here. Stores are open 8 am to 9 pm.

EXCURSIONS

Xiamen seems to be the most developed for tourists in the province, with good hotels. **Quanzhou** is next, for some interesting things to see. Fuzhou itself has less to offer.

Wuyi Mountain, in the northwestern part of the province, is a summer resort (snow in winter) with 86 hotels, rafting through beautiful Guilin-type scenery with peaks up to 717 meters, and a Song Dynasty replica shopping street. They're aiming for three million visitors a year by 2000. There's hiking, climbing and a nearby UN Biosphere Reserve. From Fuzhou, take train T91/92 or a 40-minute flight MFFJ8815 (three times a week). There are also flights from Shanghai and Xiamen. To arrange travel, contact **CITS**,*Tel. (0599) 32258* or **CTS**, *Tel. 32981.*

The three-star **JADE MAID HOTEL**, *Tel. (0599) 5252988 or fax 5252776* is the best for $80. Two-hour bamboo-raft-trips leave from nearby Xingcun Village.

Aside from Wuyi, Fujian is mainly for those interested in maritime history, in Koxinga (museums in Xiamen and Quanzhou), and in the relics of Arab traders, Manichaeanism, and Nestorian Christianity. Some of its native sons have returned from Southeast Asia with wealth. They have built monuments, schools, hospitals, and temples. The religious buildings are uniquely flamboyant with cosmopolitan touches.

The Fujian dialect is distinct, neither Cantonese nor Mandarin. This language is spoken also by the majority on Taiwan, just across the straits. The weather is subtropical, and most of the province is mountainous.

PRACTICAL INFORMATION

- **Business Hours**: Offices, 8 am to 5 pm. (some until 6 pm); stores, 8 am to 9 pm.
- **CITS** and **Fujian Overseas Tourist Enterprise Corporation**: *73 Dong Da Road, 350001. Tel. 7555496. Fax 7537447, 7555497. FOTEC Tel. 7557755 x 85204, 7527549. Fax 7523456.*
- **CTS**, *Fujian Branch, Wusi Road, 350001; Tel. 7556304, 7557603. Fax 7553983*
- **CYTS**, *20th Floor, International Plaza, Wusi Road, 350003. Tel. 7810001. Fax 7810021*
- **Fujian Provincial Tourism Bureau**, 24 Dong Da Road, 350001, Tel. 7553794, 7555148. Fax 7538758.
- **Telephone code**, *0591*
- **Tourist complaints**, contact **Supervisory Bureau of Tourism Quality of Fujian Province**, *1 Daying Street, Dongda Road, 350001, Tel. 7554153. Fax 7538758*
- **Tourist Hotline**, *Tel. 7554153*. For complaints and questions.

GRAND CANAL

The oldest and longest in the world, the **Grand Canal** was built in the Sui dynasty (581-618 A.D.) and originally extended 1,794 kilometers from Hangzhou to Beijing, an inland shipping route safe from seafaring pirates.

Today, visitors can still take tour boats on parts of the canal for an intimate look at life on the water. You can sleep on ferries between cities to save paying for a hotel room. But the water is dirty and the trip can be noisy as traffic moves on the canal all night. However, that was the way it was 1000 years ago too!

At individual cities along the route, you can visit parts of the canal. **Wuxi** has a 36.5-meter-long, two-storied 'dragon boat' with flashing eyes. Tours cruise mainly between Yangzhou and Suzhou.

HANGZHOU

(Hangchow)

Hangzhou, the capital of Zhejiang province, is on the Qiantang River at the southern end of the Grand Canal on the east coast of China. The coldest weather is in January, a little below minus ten degrees centigrade; the hottest is in July, with highs of 37 degrees centigrade. The annual precipitation is about 1452 millimeters, mainly May-June. The population is 1.3 million.

ARRIVALS & DEPARTURES

Located 140 kilometers southwest of Shanghai, it is best reached from there by a three-hour train. It is also linked by expressway. It has air connections with Hong Kong, Singapore, and 28 Chinese cities. A new international airport is due in 1999.

ORIENTATION

Hangzhou is one of the most famous beauty spots of China because of **Xihu** (West Lake). It is also of historical importance. Founded over 2,200 years ago in the Qin, it began to prosper as a trading center after the completion of the Grand Canal in 610. It was the capital of the tiny state of Wuyueh (893-978), at which time the first dikes forming the lake were built. It was also capital of the Southern Song after 1127.

The best book giving a detailed picture of the city from 1250 to 1276 is Jacques Gernet's *Daily Life in China on the Eve of the Mongol Invasion*, essential for visitors who want to know a lot of history, to compare life then with today, and to look for old ruins. The city was seized by the Mongols under Kublai Khan in 1279 and visited by Marco Polo the next year when it was known as Kinsai. The Venetian explorer raved about the city, then the largest and richest in the world, its silks and handicrafts much in demand in China and abroad.

Hangzhou has been a famous resort for centuries, attracting famous painters, poets, and retired officials as well as tourists. It is also an industrial city now, with machine-making, chemicals, an oil refinery, and electronics. Of tourist interest are its crafts factories, temples, and museums. Villages here grow the famous *long jing* (Dragon Well) tea and silk worms. Today Zhejiang province produces one-third of China's silk. These make a rural excursion especially worthy.

WHERE TO STAY

The best hotel is a toss-up between the **Dragon** and the **Shangri-La**, depending on your tastes and needs. The Shangri-La is more for romantics and closer to the lake. The Dragon hums with activity and will be even busier with a new International Exhibition Centre due to open nearby in 1997. The Dragon has smaller rooms, television sets, and twin beds. The Friendship is a downtown hotel more for shoppers. The Wanghu isn't bad, but I could find no one who spoke English.

The high tourist season here is April, May, September, October. The shoulder season is March, June through August, and November. All prices listed below are subject to change, negotiation and 15% city tax. All these hotels are within a few kilometers of each other. A new five star and a new four-star hotel should open soon.

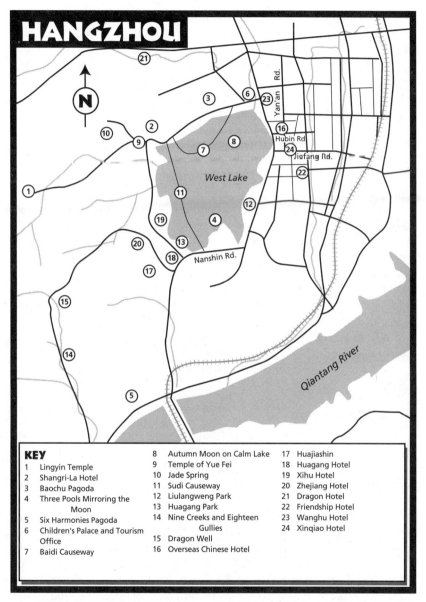

HANGZHOU

West Lake

Yan'an Rd.

Hubin Rd

Jiofang Rd.

Nanshin Rd.

Qiantang River

KEY

1	Lingyin Temple
2	Shangri-La Hotel
3	Baochu Pagoda
4	Three Pools Mirroring the Moon
5	Six Harmonies Pagoda
6	Children's Palace and Tourism Office
7	Baidi Causeway
8	Autumn Moon on Calm Lake
9	Temple of Yue Fei
10	Jade Spring
11	Sudi Causeway
12	Liulangweng Park
13	Huagang Park
14	Nine Creeks and Eighteen Gullies
15	Dragon Well
16	Overseas Chinese Hotel
17	Huajiashin
18	Huagang Hotel
19	Xihu Hotel
20	Zhejiang Hotel
21	Dragon Hotel
22	Friendship Hotel
23	Wanghu Hotel
24	Xinqiao Hotel

DRAGON HOTEL *(Huang Long Fandian), 11 Shuguang Road, 310007. Four stars, Tel. 7998833. Fax 7998090. In US, Tel. 1-800-637-7200. $130 to $140. Dist.A.P. 14 km.. Dist.R.W. seven km. Near Bao Chu Hill and Yellow Dragon Cave. Credit Cards.*

Built 1987-88. Looks a little worn but should renovate some guest rooms in 1996. Six, seven and nine stories, 536 rooms. IDD. USTV. B.C.

SIA and Dragonair offices. Gym, outdoor tennis courts and pool. Bicycles. Managed by New World Hotels International. Buffet breakfast $12.

FRIENDSHIP HOTEL *(You Hao Fandian), 53 Pinghai Road, 310006. Three stars, Tel. 7077888. Fax 883942. $72 to $85. Dist.A.P. 15 km. Dist.R.W. 3.5 km.. Credit Cards.*

Built 1986, ren. 1991. 23 stories, 220 rooms. Small bathrooms. B.C. Discos. In-room safes. USTV. Japanese J.V.

SHANGRI-LA HOTEL HANGZHOU *(Shang Gorilla Fandian), 78 Beishan Road, 310007. Five stars, Tel. 7977951. Fax 7073545, 7996637. $100 to $140. In US, Tel. 1-800-942-5050, booked through Hangzhou Overseas Tourist Company. Dist.A.P. 20 km.. Dist.R.W. 5 km.. Credit Cards.*

On north end of lake. East building, seven stories, 156 rooms. Chinese decor. West main building dates from 1956, six stories, 199 rooms. Smallish bathrooms. More western decor and more convenient to store and restaurants. These two buildings are joined by a covered walkway. Three villas. Total 387 rooms. 24-hour B.C. CITS. IDD. USTV. Italian and Cantonese restaurants. Fast-food restaurant on grounds. Gym. Boating, bicycles and games. Shangri-La International management since 1985.

WANGHU HOTEL *(Binguan), 2 West Huancheng Road, 310006. Three stars aiming for four. Tel. 7071024. Fax 70711350. $75 to $120.*

Close to lake. 364 rooms, big and clean. In-room safe. Executive floor. USTV.

WHERE TO EAT

Hangzhou claims "beggar's chicken," the first made with lotus leaves and mud from West Lake, as its very own. The lake fish is very bony.

The food and ambiance in the hotels, especially the **Dragon** and **Shangri-La** (**SHANG PALACE** for Chinese and **PEPPINOS** for Italian) are generally the best. For good local food, the **LOU WAI LOU RESTAURANT** is at *30 Gushan Road, Tel. 7969023, 7029023 near the Shangri-La.* Near the Dragon Hotel is the **DA FU HAO RESTAURANT** *at 9 Shuguang Road, Tel. 5117646, 5118384.*

Vegetarian food is featured at the **LINGYIN TEMPLE**. The **HU QING YU TANG RESTAURANT** serving "healthy food" is across from the Traditional Medicine Museum *(Da Jin Lane, Wu Shan, Tel. 7025896).*

SEEING THE SIGHTS

Xihu (West Lake), is a 5.6-square kilometer lake, originally part of the Qiantang River until its outlet silted up. It was first dredged under the leadership of the famous Song poet, Su Dong Po, then mayor. It is now 15 kilometers in circumference, with an average depth of 1.8 meters. The lake is now linked with the **Qiantang River** and is usually renewed with fresh water once a month. Just strolling around the edge of the lake is worthwhile. Many of the tourist attractions are close to its shore.

Visitors with only one day to spend in the city should take a **boat ride** with stops at various famous sites. Then take in the **Pagoda of Six Harmonies, Lingyin Temple, Jade Spring**, and a **silk factory**. You can hire boats at different places around the lake.

You can also rent a bicycle from a hotel or hire a pedicab. That way in one day you can ride along the 1.8 kilometer, 1,000 year old **Baidi Causeway** with stops at the Autumn Moon on Calm Lake Pavilion, Wenlan Ge (next to Zhejiang Provincial Museum), Xiling Seal Engraver's Society, Tomb and Temple of Yue Fei, and Jade Spring.

Explore Lingyin Temple and then visit the **Feilaifeng Grottoes** across the stream from the temple. Turn back to the **Yue Fei Tomb** and then south onto Sudi Causeway. Follow Nan Shan and then Hubin roads. Stop to enjoy Liulanwenying Park if only for its name, which means Park to See the Waving Willow and Hear the Singing of the Birds.

The best times to see the lake itself is in the mist, in the moonlight, or just at sunrise before the sun makes strong shadows, and when the birds are singing in the willows. One of the favorite spots for viewing the lake, especially during the harvest moon, is at **Pinghuqiuyue** (Autumn Moon on Calm Lake Pavilion) at the southeastern end of **Gu Shan** (Solitary Hill). But don't expect to be alone.

On the islet also is the **Wenlan Ge** (Pavilion for Storing Imperial Books), built in 1699 (Qing), and one of the seven imperial libraries. This one was especially built to store the *Sikuzhunsu*, a 33,304 volume Chinese encyclopedia ordered by Emperor Qianlong. It took 10 years to copy it by hand. The stone Chamber to the Three Venerables Han San Lao Hui Zi here was carved in 52 A.D. The island has a provincial museum and a good restaurant, the Lou Wai Lou.

You can look for lively giant golden carp at **Huagang Park** at the southwest end of the lake, beyond the Sudi Causeway. A Song official once had a vacation home here.

The 2.8-kilometer **Sudi Causeway** is the more beautiful of the two causeways here, lined with grass, willows, and peach trees. No motor vehicles are allowed because of its hump-backed bridges. It's a pleasant bicycle or pedicab ride, but please give the driver a break. Get off and walk up those bridges.

The famous **Zig-Zag Bridge** is on the islet **Xiaoyingzhou** (Three Pools Mirroring the Moon) and can be reached only by boat. It is east of Sudi Causeway. Did you know that bad spirits have to move in a straight line?

Stand on the bridge here and nothing can harm you. This islet was first constructed in 1607 (Ming) with mud cleared from the lake. Look for the 'island in a lake and the lake in an island.'

During the **Moon Festival**, candles light up the small pagodas, thus creating 'Three Pools Mirroring the Moon.' In June, this is a good place to enjoy water lilies and lotus flowers. Everywhere around West Lake are exquisite gardens, some with artistically cobbled foot paths.

You can also go by boat to **Ruangongdun Island** on the northwest side of West Lake just south of Gu Shan Hill. Here you'll find **Huanbi Zhuang**, an attempt to reproduce a Song Dynasty village with period costumes, sedan chair rides, wine shop, and music. Some tourists have found it fun, but others might find it too commercial and poorly done.

The *Liuhe Ta (Pagoda of Six Harmonies), *91 Zhijiang Road, Tel. 7038911, 6082980,* is on the north bank of the Qiantang River. Built in 970 A.D., it is 59.89 meters or 13 stories tall, octagonal, and made of brick and wood. It can be climbed for a good view. West of this temple is the shallow and clear Nine Creeks and Eighteen Gullies, which cut through the rugged but tranquil **Yangmei Hill**. Great for hikers, the paths wind for about seven kilometers.

The **Lingyin** (Soul's Retreat) **Temple**, *1 Fa Yun Si Nong, Tel. 7996657, 7968665,* is nine kilometers from the city, west of West Lake. Founded in 326 A.D., its Celestial King's Hall and 33.6-meter-high Buddha Hall are all that is left of the original 18 pavilions and 72 halls. Lingyin at one time housed 3000 monks. The statues have been replaced now. The seated Sakyamuni inside is 19.6 meters high. The temple guardian behind the Four Celestial Kings was carved from camphor wood during the Song. Lingyin is still one of the largest and most magnificent temples in China. Two restaurants serve vegetarian food, the one inside is better than the one next to the temple.

Across from Lingyin temple is *Feilaifeng (Peak that Flew from Afar), named by an Indian monk after a similar-looking Indian peak that must have flown here! The 380 carvings along the narrow, hilly trails are from the Five Dynasties to the Yuan.

It could take three or four days to cover all the important spots in Hangzhou. The 45-meter-high **Baochu** (Precious Stone Hill) **Pagoda** is on a 200-meter-high hill north of the lake, two kilometers from the city. It was first built in 968 to pray for the safe return of the unjustly arrested Qian Hongchu, a successful effort. The pagoda, last reconstructed in 1933, is now filled with dirt and no one can enter.

The *Tomb and Temple of Yue Fei, *Tel. 7969670,* is at the northwest corner of the lake, next to the Shangri-La Hotel. He was a famous Song general who was unjustly executed in 1142. Public reaction forced a retrial 20 years later that reversed the verdict. A temple was built with statues of his four accusers kneeling for forgiveness before his grave. These four are spat on even today.

Yue Fei was also a calligrapher and poet who came from a family that valued patriotism. His mother tattooed his back with four characters to remind him of his duty to his country. His son was murdered on the day of Yue Fei's death. Their tombs are next to each other, but only contain their clothing. An exhibition hall illustrates Yue Fei's battles and shows his handwritten proposals to the Song emperor.

At the **Hupao** (Tiger) **Spring Park**, *Tel. 7967213*, you will find water that will not overflow from a full cup even though you add coins to it. The high surface tension will also support a carefully placed Chinese coin, a trick that also works in Toronto, so don't be gullible. The spring is near the **Hangzhou Zoo**, about six kilometers from the city southwest of the lake on Hupao Road. A handy tea house is here. The well is named after a tiger who revealed the location of the water in a dream to a monk.

The **Longjing** (Dragon Well), *Tel. 7986060*, to the northwest of Hupao, is another spring. The water here has a curious ripple effect when you stir it, especially on rainy days. This phenomenon is explained by the differences in the specific gravity of the rain water and the spring water, and is a good ploy to encourage business in wet weather.

Two kilometers southwest is **Longjingcun** (Dragon Well Village) where you can see the famous tea growing on hillsides. It is usually picked in late March or early April. Connoisseurs of good tea pay fabulously high prices for the best of the harvest, the most tender leaves are hand-picked before the spring rain. The quantity is also limited because only a few villages have the proper soil and water. The best Longjing tea, when brewed, has a fresh, crystal-green color, a mild and pure fragrance, and a slight sweetness.

The third of Hangzhou's famous springs is **Jade Spring** *on Yugu Road*, off the northwest corner of the lake within walking distance of the Shangri-La Hotel. It is for gold fish and flower lovers, as multicolored ornamental fish are bred here. It is inside the 200-hectare **Hangzhou Botanical Garden**, *Tel. 7961908*, which has 3700 species of plants, including 120 varieties of bamboo.

A cable car runs from 8 am to 5 pm between Beigao Feng (North Peak) and near the Lingyin Temple, giving a good view of the lake. You can also drive up **Wushan Hill**, east of the lake, the highest spot in the city. This has an 800-year-old camphor tree and the ruins of the former Song palaces, trashed by the Mongols. At 6 am it is full of taiji and disco people.

The **Tea Museum** has good exhibits and is open daily 8:30 am to 4:30 pm all year, *Tel. 7964778*. It's four kilometers from the Shangri-La past the Xihu Guest House west of the lake.

The **Silk Museum**, just south of the lake, has the oldest weaving machines in China, ancient silks and Ming and Qing court robes. It also has a silk fragment from 2715 B.C.

The **Hu Qing Yu Tang Museum of Traditional Chinese Medicine**, *Tel. 7027507*, should be seen for its beautiful old wood panelled store as well as its exhibits, one of the two most famous herbal medicine stores in the Qing. Open 8 am or 8:30 am to 5 pm Monday to Friday, it closes for lunch from 11 am to 12 noon. It is in an old area full of interesting old buildings east of the lake. All these museums have signs in English.

You should be able to visit a silk factory. Try the **Dujinsheng Silk Weaving Factory** downtown, *Tel. 7061103* or the **Hangzhou Silk Printing and Dyeing Complex**, *Tel. 8017824*.

Ask about the special events: the **marathon race** and **international boat festival** (September), **traditional medicine festival** (May), and **New Year's Eve**.

NIGHTLIFE & ENTERTAINMENT

Try **Casablanca Bar**, *23 Hubin Road, Tel. 7025934*, five minutes by taxi from the Shangri-La. There is the **West Town Bar** on the other side of the lake. And, of course, the hotel bars.

SHOPPING

This province is known for silk textiles, woven silk pictures, satin, brocades, silk parasols, lace, mahogany and boxwood crafts, fresh water pearls, Longquan celadon, sandalwood fans, woven bambooware, distinctive Tianzhu chopsticks, and stone and wood carvings. Look for the incredible multicolored stone carvings from Qingtian. Hangzhou produces some fancy scissors that are useful souvenirs as well as longjing tea.

The main shopping areas are **Jiefang Road** and **Yan'an Road**. You can find lots of crafts even in local department stores; try the **Hangzhou Department Store** *at 739 Jiefang Road*. The **Friendship Store** here has good quality and unusual things, like finely carved stones shaped like insects, sandalwood, and Buddhas.

For silk fabric and garments, look in the department stores and then the **Hangzhou Sichou Shichang** (wholesale silk market), *Tel. 5159166*; open daily about 9 am to 4 or 5 pm. It is about a 20-minute taxi ride from downtown. This market has stalls from all the different silk factories in the area and prices should be good. Avoid the store at the Silk Museum. While the tourist quality silk is cheaper than some, the fine art quality is twice the price of other stores.

Lots of tea pots are for sale in the Tea Museum. The cheapest prices for curios are at the **Bird and Flower Market** two blocks east of the

Friendship Hotel on Ping Hai Road. (Open 9 am to 5 pm.) Three tiny charming real jade carvings have cost Y50 each after haggling first thing in the morning.

Wushan Road in the same neighborhood is a good place for serious antiques. It has about five stores. Especially good is **Zheng Li Zin** *at Number 118, Tel.* 7060926, for ancestral portraits (at one-third Hong Kong prices), jade, and porcelain. The government **Antique and Curio Store**, *90 Dongpo Road just east of the lake, Tel.* 7069821, has good quality goods but prices a little high except for shard pendants for Y20. A branch is at *2 Hubin Road nearby, Tel.* 6029585. The Friendship Hotel has a good quality store with prices to match.

EXCURSIONS FROM HANGZHOU

For Ningbo (about 150 kilometers southwest), Shaoxing (about 50 kilometers southeast), and Huangshan (200 kilometers), see separate listings.

Mogan Mountain, 700 meters high (about 75 kilometers northwest), is a well-known summer resort with over 300 hectares of waterfalls, bamboo forests, stone trails, ponds, and caves. It's good for hiking and relaxing in beautiful surroundings. You can stay at the **MT.MOGAN HOTEL** *in Deqing, Tel. 8033184.*

The large limestone **Yaoling Cave** is 120 kilometers southwest of the city, close to Tonglu County, and is 25 meters high and more than one kilometer long with many stairs. This is usually a one-day trip, combined with lunch 25 kilometers away at the **JINGXIU HOTEL** *in Tonglu town.* The specialty is live drunken shrimp but you can get other food as well. You can also visit **Angling Terrace** and **Monk's Island** (40-minute boatride from Fuyang) where the farmers can organize a lion dance, noisy firecrackers, buffalo-cart ride and goat fight. You can also try papermaking, peddling a waterwheel and grinding wheat the hard way. There is an exhibition of old farm tools. This is not the most exciting excursion, but these destinations are an opportunity to see the countryside with its unique whitewashed, geometric architecture, and lifestyle.

These places are on the way between Hangzhou and Huangshan via the 30 year-old **1,000 Island Lake**, a two-day trip with an overnight at the **1,000 ISLAND LAKE HOTEL** *(Qian Dao Hu), Tel. 4872181. Fax 4872788.* This 105-room, three-star hotel is on the southeast side of the lake near a small village, about a five-hour drive from Hangzhou. It is related to the Wanghu Hotel in Hangzhou. This 1988 Hong Kong joint venture is quite acceptable and takes credit cards. But it has five stories and no elevators. Good food if you like fish.

The undeveloped lake is 580 square kilometers, very pretty and pristine. Mountains rise up to 200 meters. On its 1078 islands are a couple of temples. One island has 200 wild, free-roaming monkeys (15-minute stop but no disembarking). Another has a thousand snakes in pits (a worthwhile 30-minute stop). From the hotel, you can take a ferry to Anhui province on the other side of the lake and then go by road to Huangshan.

In **Tiantai**, about 100 kilometers from Hangzhou, the **Guoqing Temple** is the home of the Tiantai Buddhist sect. The **Tidal Bore of the Qiantang River** is most spectacular on the 18th day of the eighth month (lunar calendar). In 1974 it reached a height of nine meters, but it is not usually that dramatic. You can best see it in Yanguantown at Zhan'ao Pagoda, 45 kilometers from Hangzhou, or at Haining. Check with a travel agent for dates and bus tours if you are in Hangzhou in late September or early October.

Huzhou, which is about two hours drive or train north of Hangzhou, is a silkworm breeding centre. Here you can also watch the silk-making process on a large scale.

PRACTICAL INFORMATION
- **Business & Sightseeing Hours**: offices, 8:30 am to 5:00 or 5:30 pm with lunch about 11:30 am to 1:30 pm, Monday to Friday; stores daily 9 am to 9 pm; banks 9 am to 4 pm; most temples open daily from 8:30 am to 5:30 pm., museums from 9 am until 4 or 4:30 pm daily. Some parks close at 6 pm.
- **Ambulance**, *Tel. 7024078; Police, Tel. 110*
- **CITS**, *Zhejiang, 1 Shihan Road, Hangzhou 310007. Tel. 5152888. Fax 5156667, 5156576*
- **China Comfort Travel**, *78 Beishan Road, 310007. Tel. 7075005, 7077951. Fax 7075008.*
- **China Hangzhou Overseas Tourist Company**, *45 Shuguang Road, 310013. Tel. 7993888. Fax 7994366, 7994365*
- **CTS**, *Tel. 7080988. Fax 7089220*
- **CYTS**, *Tel. 7012333, Fax 7070025*
- **Dragonair**, *Dragon Hotel, Tel. 7998833 X 6061; Fax 7987902*
- **Zhejiang Provincial Travel and Tourism Bureau**, *1 Shihan Road, Hangzhou, 310007. Tel. 5152377. Fax 5156429.* Brochures available. For tourist complaints, contact **Supervisory Bureau of Tourism Quality of Zhejiang Province**, *Tel. 5156631, 5158831. Fax 5156429*

HEFEI
(Hofei)

Hefei is the capital of **Anhui** (Anhwei), a province north of the Yangtze River. The urban population is 1.1 million.

The coldest weather in January is minus five degrees centigrade; the hottest in July and August is 39 degrees centigrade.

ARRIVALS & DEPARTURES

Flights from 21 cities and Hong Kong are available now, and are planned to Japan and Southeast Asia. There's also train service from Beijing (14 1/2 hours); Nanjing (six hours); and Shanghai (11 hours). Hefei is connected by expressway to Nanjing, a 185 kilometer trip in two to three hours.

ORIENTATION

Anhui is famous for its dramatic mountains that have inspired poets, mystics, and painters for centuries. In the province live Han, Hui, She, and other nationalities. Because of its strategic location, numerous battles were fought here in the ancient past. Hefei's tourist attractions can be squeezed into one day.

WHERE TO STAY

The best should be the Novotel Hefei when open. The next best is the Anhui Hotel.

ANHUI HOTEL *(Fandian), 18 Meishan Rd., 230022. Three stars, Tel. 2811100, 2812998. Fax 2817583. Dist.A.P.20 km. Dist.R.W.10 km. Credit Cards.*

Ren. 1996. 320 rooms. IDD.

NOVOTEL HEFEI, *25 Wu Hu Rd., 230001, Tel. 2647777. Fax 2644584. Three to four-star standard.*

WHERE TO EAT

Anhui specialties are freshwater crabs from Lake Chao and locally-produced *Gujing Gongjiu* wine, once sent as tribute to the Ming emperors. Try cured Mandarin fish, stewed turtle, Fulizi braised chicken, Wenzhenshan bamboo shoots and sesame cakes. Dishes are somewhat salty and slightly spicy hot, with thick soups.

Try the restaurant in the **ANHUI HOTEL**, *Tel. 2811818.* There's also the **HUISHANG RESTAURANT** *on Yangtze Road, Tel. 2653088.*

SEEING THE SIGHTS

In **Xiaoyaojin**, near the center of the city, during the Three Kingdoms period 1700 years ago, General Zhang Liao of the State of Wei fought against General Sun Quan (Sun Chuan) of the State of Wu. The site is now a **park** with three islets, on one of which is the tomb of General Zhang. Near the park is a **zoo**.

Two kilometers south of Ximaoyaojin, the **Lecturing Rostrum/ Archery Training Terrace** is where Emperor Caocao trained Wei troops in using crossbows. These sites are marked with pavilions in traditional architecture. The **Mingjiao Temple** (from the Tang dynasty) is on the terrace. Destroyed in the 19th century during the Taiping War, it was rebuilt by General Yuan Hongmo of the Taiping Heavenly Kingdom.

The **Temple to Lord Baozheng**, situated in a park in the center of the city, was built in honor of this honest and outstanding magistrate and vice minister of the Northern Song. The **Provincial Museum** has a pleasant dinosaur garden.

SHOPPING

Grown in the province are pears, pomegranates, grapes, kiwi fruit, and herbal medicines. Made are candied dates, tea, bamboo mats, and iron pictures. Hefei is also noted for its four scholarly treasures: Xuan writing brush, Hu ink stick, She ink slab and Xuan paper. Try the **Hefei Department Store**, *124 Yangtze Road, Tel. 2647133* or the **Hui Tong Department Store**, *277 Yangtze Road, Tel. 2672835*. The **Chenghuangmiao shopping center** was built in the Ming style and surrounds the 900-year-old Town God's Temple.

EXCURSIONS FROM HEFEI

Near **Bengbu**, on the railway line between Beijing and Shanghai, 169 kilometers from Hefei, is the ancestral home of the first Ming emperor, who proclaimed it a royal city. Among the tombs here are Tang He, who was one of the Ming Dynasty founders. The *ruins of the Imperial City of the Middle Capital**, and stone inscriptions at the Imperial Mausoleum, are now under State Council protection. Bengbu also has the **Temple of King Yu**. One of the first attempts at the 'Responsibility System' was started here in 1978. You can stay at the three-star **ZHANGGONGSHAN HOTEL**, *128 Zhanggongshan Road, Bengbu, 233010. Tel. (0552)4091888. Fax 4091588*. Takes credit cards and has IDD.

Huangshan (Mount Huangshan) **Scenic Area** is reached from Hefei. The bus takes about 10 hours; the plane 35 to 50 minutes. See separate listing immediately below for more details.

Jiuhuashan (Mt. Jiuhua), one of the **Four Buddhist Mountains** (altitude 1,341 meters), is at least a three-day trip by road taking 5 1/2 hours each way. It is 301 kilometers south. It is 116 kilometers from the closest airport and railway station. It has 78 Ming and Qing temples, 6,800 buddhas which were untouched by the Red Guards, and 99 peaks. Motor vehicles can drive up to 600 meters. There is cable car service. **Roushen Hall** and **Qiyuan Temple** are both important sites. In **Baisui Gong**

(Buddhist Mummy Hall), there is a 400-year-old cadaver of a monk. There's a **Temple Fair** on the 30th of the seventh lunar month for 10 days. The coldest mean temperature in January is minus three degrees centigrade. The hottest mean temperature is 18 degrees centigrade in July. The best hotel is the two-star **JULONG HOTEL**, Jiuhua Street, *Qingyang County, 242811. Tel. (0566)5011368, 5011227. Fax 5011022.* The hotel does not offer IDD, and no credit cards are accepted. **CITS** is on *Jiuhua Street, Jiuhua Mountain, Qinyang County, 242811. Tel. 5011318. Fax 5011202.*

Ma'anshan (Horse Saddle Mountain), south of the Yangtze near the eastern provincial border, is 175 kilometers from Hefei. It has impressive stone outcrops into the Yangtze. This large industrial city is on the railway line between Nanjing and Wuhu. The **Taibai Pavilion** at Caishiji has relics related to Li Bai, the world-famous Tang poet whose grave is at the foot of Qingshan. An international poetry festival is on the ninth of the ninth lunar month. You can stay at the two-star **CHANGCHENG HOTEL**, *14 Hubei Road, Ma'anshan, 243000, Tel. (0555)2479888. Fax 2479790*, which takes credit cards and has IDD. **CITS** is at *22 Hu Song Road, Tel. 2475251. Fax 2476024.*

Tunxi is the administrative part of Huangshan City and is 60 kilometers from the Huangshan Mountain Scenic Area. Here you can see **Tunxi Old Street** (with antique and curio market), the **Tangyue Memorial Arches** (with China's only hall for women) in Shexian (five kilometers from Tunxi), and take the **Xinan River Cruise**. The best hotel is the three-star **HUANGSHAN INTERNATIONAL HOTEL**, *Xiaohuashan, 245000. Tel. 2526999. Fax 2512087.* It is four kilometers from the airport, and two from the railway station. It has international direct dialing but no credit card service.

The following agencies and offices can help you with information and travel arrangements: **Anhui Overseas Tourist Corporation**, *60 Qianyuan Nan Road, Tunxi District, Huangshan, 245000. Tel. 2514266, 2518262. Fax 2514689;* **Huangshan CITS**, *6 Xishan Street, 245011. Tel. 2515231. Fax 2514014;* **Huangshan Municipal Tourism Administration**, *63 Yan'an Road, Fax 2514019, 2511850* for brochures. Tunxi's telephone code is 0599.

Wuhu, in the southeastern part of the province, is where the Qing-yi River joins the Yangtze. On the railway line from Nanjing and Hefei, it is the main foreign trading river port for the province and the fourth largest port on the Yangtze. It also produces silk and those lovely pictures made of forged iron, usually painted black. Its **Alligator Breeding Center** (4,000 alligators) is in Diadulin District in the southern suburb of Xuancheng County.

PRACTICAL INFORMATION

- **Anhui Overseas Travel Corp.**, **Anhui Tourism Administration**, and **CITS Hefei Branch**, are together at *8 Meishan Road, 230022. Tel. 2821418, 2812930. Fax 2812855*. They can arrange home stays with local families. For tourist complaints, *Tel. 2821821*. For information, *Tel. 2812930, 2812931*.
- **Anhui Provincial Tourist Bureau**, *6 Meishan Road, 230022. Tel. 2821701* for tourist information.
- **Business Hours**: offices 8 or 8:30 am to 5 or 6 pm, lunch 12 to 2 pm. Bank of China, 8 am to 5 pm.
- **CTS Anhui**, *Tel. 2651522. Fax 2654308*
- **Huangshan Comfort Travel Service**, *12 Qian Yuan Bei Road, Tunxi. Tel. 2511203. Fax 2514040*
- **Telephone Code**, *0551*
- **Tourist Hotline**, *Tel. 2821821*
- **Tourist Complaints**, contact **Supervisory Bureau of Tourism Quality of Anhui Province**, *4 Meishan Road, 230061, Tel. 2821825. Fax 2824001*

HUANGSHAN SCENIC AREA

Located in southern Anhui province, **Huangshan Mountain** is one of China's top ten tourist attractions, and has been designated a UNESCO World Heritage site. Climbing the mountain has been described by one writer as 'walking into an unending Chinese landscape painting.' It is part of Huangshan City.

The coldest month is January, with a low of minus six degrees centigrade; the warmest is July, with a high of 20 degrees centigrade. The annual precipitation is 1600 millimeters, mainly from June to September. The urban population of the scenic area is 360,000.

ARRIVALS & DEPARTURES

A proposed airport is expected to be located at the Huangshan Scenic Area; there is talk of direct U.S. and Hong Kong flights. Huangshan can now be reached by road from Hangzhou via 1,000 Island Lake, from Tunxi by road (60 kilometers), or by train from Nanjing (eight hours) or bus (10 hours).

ORIENTATION

Huangshan Scenic Area is 154 square kilometers with 45 kilometers of paved paths. Unfortunately there are no signs in English. One of the best views is the **Peak for Dispelling Clouds** where lovers can put a padlock on a fence and throw away the key into the clouds below. As with most mountains in China, paths are crowded with hikers during the summer. The end of April is the most beautiful time, and hiking is good to the end of October.

WHERE TO STAY & EAT

No hotel has USTV. The best hotels for foreign tourists are the **West Sea** and then the **North Sea** on the mountain, and the Peach Blossom and then the Cloud Valley at the base. The summit hotels lends coats to unprepared guests. Travelers should leave heavy bags at the base and take only what they are able to carry in case they can't find help.

These hotels are currently about 65 kilometers from the closest airport and railway station, and they're also where you'll be eating too.

CLOUD VALLEY VILLA HOTEL *(Yungu Binguan), Yungu Si, 242709. Three stars, Tel. 5562466, 5562477. Fax 5562346. $45. Credit Cards.*

Altitude 800 meters. Renovated 1995. 102 rooms. Set in a beautiful valley surrounded by bamboo and pines. This hotel rarely gets sun and smells musty. Charming Ming architecture, built like a maze on the side of a mountain. Connecting three-story buildings. Narrow beds. Stores. Bar. Air-conditioning. Whitewashed walls. USTV.

NORTH SEA HOTEL *(Beihai Binguan), 242709. Two stars, Tel. (0559)5562555. Fax 5562708. $60.*

Altitude 1600 meters. Half kilometer walk and 340-meter climb from upper cable car terminal. Built 1958, ren. 1984. 130 rooms. Hot tap water evenings only. Bar.

PEACH BLOSSOM HOTEL *(Tao Yuan Binguan), 3 Yanan Rd. Three stars. Tel. 5562666. Fax 5562888. $80. Credit Cards.*

Near stores and swimming pool, 7 1/2 km. to cable car. 137 rooms. Traditional Chinese architecture. Small televisions. Tiny tubs. Narrow beds. Good food. Great view. IDD. B.C. Built 1992, 40-room Yi Yuan building looks like a motel with fish pond and free-ranging rabbits. Small televisions, bigger baths.

WEST SEA HOTEL *(Xi Hai Fandian), Xi Hai Scenic Area, 242700. Three stars. Tel. 5562818 and fax 5562988. $150. Only hotel on summit taking Credit Cards.*

The West Sea has 108 rooms. On summit, half hour (one kilometer) walk and climb from cable car. Should be 300 m from new cable car. Altitude 1600 meters. Built 1988. IDD. H.K. management. High season Mar 1 to Nov. 15. Small televisions.

SEEING THE SIGHTS

Huangshan is worth making an effort to visit. But one has to take a chance with the weather for the best effect: for serious photographers, the weather should be cloudy, which it is 208 days a year (mainly in the spring). For perfect photos, you must patiently wait for clouds to float to the right place between the mountains, silhouetting twisted, horizontal 400-year old pines that add depth. One full day on top is enough for covering all the designated photo spots but not for taking the perfect photo.

The highest of the 72 peaks, **Lian Hua** (Lotus Flower) rises 1,873 meters above sea level. To reach the valley before the final ascent to the top means climbing 800 stone steps cut into an 80 degree angle cliff, nose almost to rock.

One section of the second highest peak, **Tian Du** (Heavenly Capital Peak, 1,864 meters), has a ridge less than a meter wide called **Carp's Backbone**. Although iron chain railings are there to assure the unsure, some people resort to crawling to get across. This is just to say that Huangshan is for the strong and adventurous, who will be rewarded by giant vertical peaks, pines (at least one over 1,000 years old), hot springs (42 degrees centigrade), lots of streams, mist, magnificent views, and a great feeling of achievement if you make it.

You can spend the night on the summit to see the sunrise. But you have to walk and climb to the hotels on top even after the cable car ride. The summit is not for people prone to heart attacks nor for the fussy. And one must consider cable car rest days.

The 1986-built, 2,800-meter-long **cable car** on the east slope leaves from near the Cloud Valley Hotel and makes the ascent in eight minutes to near the North Sea Hotel. Otherwise it takes three hours by foot up 40,000 stone steps. The cable car operates daily 8 am to 4 pm, with one car leaving every 15 minutes with a maximum of 40 people. Expect up to an hour's wait during high season. The cable car runs all year except for a half day between the 22nd and 26th of each month. It is closed once a year from December 20 to 31. It does not operate during windstorms, nor during maintenance.

There are plans for a second 3,000-meter-plus cable car on the north side of the mountain. This would go from Taiping County, the lower terminal closest to Jiuhua, Taiping Lake, and the Huangshan Hotel. There is also talk of a third cableway from the Peach Blossom Hotel to Jade Screen Peak. You can also ride human-powered sedan chairs up and on the mountain. One way up the mountain costs at least Y600. You can negotiate for a porter to carry bags.

SHOPPING

Paintings of Huangshan, Huangshan tea, bamboo, and straw curtains are made here. It is traditional to buy a special stone and find someone to carve your name on it. And don't forget the padlock.

PRACTICAL INFORMATION

See *Excursions from Hefei*, section on Tunxi above for travel agencies.
- **Business Hours**: Offices 8 am to 6 pm. Bank of China 8 am to 5:30 pm.
- **China Overseas Travel Service**, *Hot Spring Area, Huangshan. Tel. 215555*
- **Telephone Code**, *551*

NANJING

(Nanking: Southern Capital)

Located in the southwest part of Jiangsu Province (of which it is the capital), **Nanjing** lies on the Yangtze River. Nanjing's hottest temperature is a rare 40 degrees centigrade in August; its coldest is seven degrees centigrade in January. The annual precipitation is more than 1,000 millimeters, with rain mostly in summer. The urban population is 2.2 million. A good time to visit is late October to mid-November when the streets are lined with chrysanthemums.

Nanjing is important because of its historical relics and its beauty. It was settled 6,000 years ago and became a walled city 2,400 years ago. From 229 to 1421 A.D., it was intermittently the capital of the Eastern Wu (229-280 A.D.), Eastern Jin (317-420), Song (420-479), Qi (479-502), Liang (502-557), Chen (557-589), Southern Tang (937-975), Ming (1368-1421) and Taiping Heavenly Kingdom (1853-64).

Many of the ancient relics in the present city are Ming, built by Zhu Yuanzhang (Chu Yuan-chang), first emperor of the dynasty (1368 to 1399) whose reign name was Hongwu. After his reign, the capital was moved to Beijing, where his successors built the Forbidden City and were buried in elaborate tombs north of it.

In 1842, England and China signed the **Treaty of Nanking**, ending the First Opium War, and the city became an open port. On January 1, 1912, it became the capital of the Sun Yat-sen government and remained the Nationalist capital until April 5, 1912, when the capital was moved to Beijing. After a period of much confusion, Chiang Kai-shek unilaterally declared Nanjing the capital on April 18, 1927.

The Japanese captured Nanjing on December 12, 1937, and massacred 300,000 civilians in what is referred to as the **Rape of Nanking**. A museum was recently opened to commemorate this tragic event. The Nationalists moved their capital to Chongqing but returned to Nanjing after the Japanese surrender in 1945. Most buildings survived the war. The Communists took the city in 1949, and moved the capital to Beijing. Nanjing is still the provincial capital.

For background on Nanjing, read Barry Till's *In Search of Old Nanking*.

ARRIVALS & DEPARTURES

Nanjing is four hours by train or one hour by air (300 kilometers) northwest of Shanghai, and 16 hours by train or 1 3/4 hours by air southeast of Beijing. There are also flights from Hong Kong and 31 other Chinese cities. The 12 meter-wide 274 kilometer Nanjing-Shanghai highway should be completely finished now. You can also arrive by ship from Shanghai. A new international airport should be completed after 1997, 35 kilometers from the city, hopefully with connections to Japan, South Korea, and Malaysia.

ORIENTATION

Nanjing today is a beautiful city of broad avenues thickly lined with 240,000 sycamore trees. Centrally located is the **Drum Tower**, with **Zhongshan Road**, the main shopping street, running south, northwest, and east, intersecting in the center of town. The earlier dynasties were centered in this section of town. **Xuanwu Lake** dominates the northeastern sector. Above it to the east looms 450-meter **Zijin (Purple Gold) Mountain**. The magnificent Ming **city wall** snakes around most of the urban area.

Two thousand factories make metallurgical and chemical equipment, ships, telecommunication instruments, and synthetic fibers. The **Zhong Xin Yuan Silk Factory** manufactures brocade, and the **Arts and Crafts Carving Factory** works in ivory and wood. The city is building a 16.4 kilometer subway line.

WHERE TO STAY

The best hotel is the five-star **Jinling**, then the four-star **Central**. The five-star, 570-room Dingshan Garden Hotel should open soon. Of the cheaper hotels, there's the three-star Nanjing and the Mandarin Chamber. For getting close to things China, there's the Mandarin Chamber which is smack in the middle of the Confucian Temple area.

CENTRAL HOTEL, *75 Zhong Shan Rd., 210005. Tel. 4400888, 4400666. Fax 4414194. Four stars. Dist.A.P.nine km. Dist. R.W.eight km. Credit Cards.*

Built 1991. Managed by the Jinling Institute of Hotel Management. 10 stories. 354 rooms. USTV. IDD. Tennis, bowling, gym, sauna, and outdoor pool.

DINGSHAN HOTEL *(Binguan), 90 Chahaer Rd., 210003. Four stars, Tel. 8801868. Fax 6636929. Isolated on a hill apart from the city. Dist A.P.16 km. Dist.R.W. seven km. Credit Cards.*

Note: The telephone number of the new **Dingshan Garden Hotel** at the same address *is 8802888, Fax 6636929.*

Built 1975, ren. 1993. Main building eight stories, 256 rooms. IDD. B.C. USTV.

JINLING HOTEL *(Fandian), 2 Han Zhong Rd., 210005. Five stars, Tel. 4455888. Fax 4703396. Dist.A.P. 10 km. Dist.R.W. 10 km. Credit Cards.*
Built 1983, ren. 1990-91. 37 stories, 818 rooms. USTV. IDD. Gym and sauna. Tanning machine. Pool. B.C. Dragonair. Reserve through Omni Hotels.

MANDARIN CHAMBER HOTEL *(Zhuang Yuan Lou), 9 Zhuang Yuanjing, Fuzi Temple, 210001. Three stars, Tel. 2202555, 2202988. Fax 2201876. Dist.A.P. 12 km. Dist.R.W. 20 km. Credit Cards.*
On a narrow street north of the Confucius Temple. You can sit in its fancy lobby and watch 'old China' outside. Near street food market. Built 1991. Five stories, 120 rooms. Gym. IDD. B.C. Singapore J.V.

NANJING HOTEL, *259 North Zhongshan Rd., Tel. 3302302. Fax 3306998. Dist.A.P. 13 km. Dist.R.W. five km. Credit Cards.*
Gym. B.C., IDD.

NANJING GRAND HOTEL, *208 Guangzhou Rd., 2100214. Tel. 3311999. Fax 3315385. Four stars. Credit Cards.*
USTV. Japanese restaurant. Japanese J.V.

WHERE TO EAT

Nanjing people say the recipe for Beijing roast duck originally was from Nanjing, so you might want to try the Nanjing version. Among the other local specialties are: salted duck, especially August Sweet Osmanthus duck, salted duck gizzard, roast chicken with coriander, salted shrimps, casserole cabbage heart, Big Flat Pork Croquette (outside crisp, inside soft), chrysanthemum-shaped herring, long-tailed shrimp and squirrel-like mandarin fish. Restaurants in the top hotels are very good.

Recommended restaurants include: the **DASANYUAN RESTAU-RANT**, *38 Zhongshan Road, Tel. 6641027* and the **NANJING PALACE RESTAURANT**, *31 Beijing Dong Road, Tel. 3364600*. For good Western food, try the **Jinling** and **Central hotels**, especially the Jinling.

SEEING THE SIGHTS

Nanjing takes two days to see, but if you only have one day in the city itself, most important are the **Sun Yat-sen Mausoleum**, **Linggu Temple**, and **Ming Tomb** in the eastern part of the city, usually combined in a half-day tour.

In the afternoon, you can choose from the Observatory (for the view), the museum, the Drum Tower, the Yangtze River Bridge or whatever you want from the following menu. The Zhonghua Gate and city wall, the Confucian Temple, Qinhuai River, and the Taiping Museum are close together.

The **Dr. Sun Yixian** (Sun Yat-sen) **Mausoleum**, *Tel. 4446458*, open daily, is on an 80,000-square-meter site. The building was designed to be more impressive than those of the emperors whom the father of the Chinese republic overthrew. Eight kilometers from the Jinling Hotel, it is on the south side of Purple Gold Mountain, its feng-shui ideal. Dr. Sun (1866-1925) was buried here in 1929 in the rear of the hall. The mausoleum, 158 meters above sea level, has 392 steps and a five-meter-high statue, and is well worth visiting. But you must leave bags and purses behind.

Sun Yat-sen was born of peasant stock in Guangdong province, near Macau, in what is now called Zhongshan County, renamed after its most distinguished son. Zhongshan was Dr. Sun's honorific name. Dr. Sun actually spent most of his life outside China, leaving home at the age of 12 to study at an Anglican school in Hawaii, where his older brother had settled. He studied medicine in Hong Kong and for a short time set up practice in Macau. He spent much of his life traveling in Europe and America, living in Japan, writing and plotting against the Manchus, and planning a government for China. His teachings have been slavishly followed in Taiwan, where he is almost worshipped. He is highly respected on the mainland, too.

An intriguing, complex man, Dr. Sun became a Christian early in life and, although he attacked missionaries as being imperialists, he admitted on his death bed that he remained a Christian. He fought the Manchus because they could not rid the country of the foreign imperialists. After becoming president, he did make it a point to inform the first Ming emperor of what had happened! Dr. Sun did not remain president for long. Because of problems in uniting the country, he abdicated in 1912. The north was not willing to accept a Southerner as head of state, he reasoned. He later accepted a post as director of railways for the country. At the same time, he flirted with socialism, coming under the influence of Russian advisers.

He was married first to a peasant woman and later to Soong Chingling, much against her father's wishes. The second marriage shocked the Christians but not most Chinese, who were used to the idea of several wives. Mme. Sun was the sister of Mme. Chiang Kai-shek of Taiwan. See also *Shanghai and Zhongshan.*

Linggu (Valley of the Soul) **Temple**, open daily, is just an empty building, the only survivor of a whole complex of Buddhist structures, its statues destroyed during the Taiping war, when the Qing army slept here. Eight kilometers from the Jinling Hotel, a Liang princess built it originally in 513 A.D. in memory of the famous monk Xuan Zhuang. The first Ming emperor moved it to its current location at the eastern foot of Zijin Mountain because he wanted the original site for his own tomb. Built

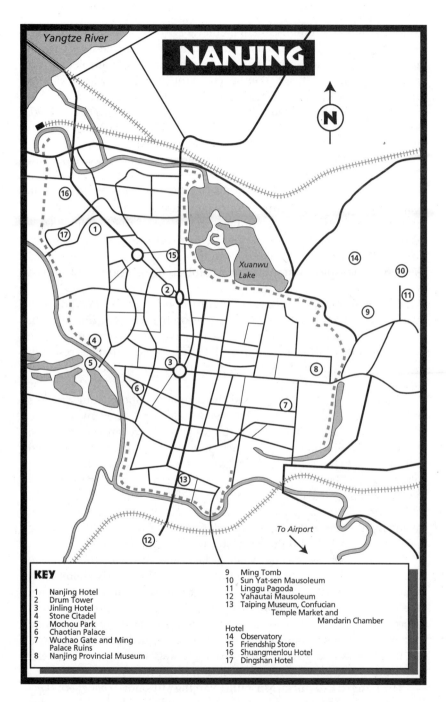

NANJING

Yangtze River

N

Xuanwu Lake

To Airport

KEY

9 Ming Tomb
10 Sun Yat-sen Mausoleum
11 Linggu Pagoda
12 Yahautai Mausoleum
13 Taiping Museum, Confucian
    Temple Market and
                Mandarin Chamber

1 Nanjing Hotel
2 Drum Tower
3 Jinling Hotel
4 Stone Citadel
5 Mochou Park
6 Chaotian Palace
7 Wuchao Gate and Ming
    Palace Ruins
8 Nanjing Provincial Museum

Hotel
14 Observatory
15 Friendship Store
16 Shuangmenlou Hotel
17 Dingshan Hotel

without beams, it is reminiscent of medieval Europe because of its arches. Its eastern and western walls curve outward. Nearby is a nine-story pagoda built in the 1920s to complement the area around the mausoleum, two kilometers to the northeast. You can climb the pagoda for a good view of this beautiful, wooded area. The Sun Yat-sen Museum is nearby.

The **Xiaoling Mausoleum** (Ming Tomb) is open daily, *Tel. 6642990*. This mausoleum, for the first Ming emperor, Zhu Yuanzhang, and his empress (1398 and 1382 respectively), is not as impressive as those north of Beijing, but is worth a visit. Zhu Yuanzhang was an unemployed peasant and former Buddhist monk and beggar who fought his way to the throne and was a brilliant emperor. The **Sacred Way** has over a dozen well-proportioned, larger-than-life mythical animals, four generals, and four ministers. The stone statues are beautiful. Most of the buildings were destroyed in the early days of the Qing, who overthrew the Ming dynasty. The mausoleum is six kilometers from the Jinling Hotel. The **Botanical Garden**, with tropical and subtropical plants, is on one side of the Sacred Way.

Zijinshan (Purple or Bell Mountain) dominates the northeastern skyline. The **Observatory**, *Tel. 6642270*, is on the west side and you can combine it with a visit to Xuanwu Lake. This major research center of the Chinese Academy of Science, built in 1934, is involved with space research such as man-made satellites. You can go there for the view and to see copies of ancient instruments.

Chinese astronomers invented the armillary sphere (four dragons and spheres) 2000 years ago to locate constellations. They invented the abridged armillary sphere (three dragons) in the Yuan for the same purpose. The Germans and French stole both of these 500-year-old replicas in 1900 but returned them later. Astronomers used the gnomon column next to the abridged sphere (a 3,000-year old invention), to survey the seasons and calculate the days of the year. It faces due south and north. In the large column is a small hole through which the sun shines at noon, casting light on the gauge below. Because of this instrument, the Chinese decided very early that there were 365 1/4 days a year.

Xuanwu Lake is outside Xuanwu Gate, northeast of the city, *Tel. 6633154*, five kilometers from the Jinling Hotel. Twenty-five kilometers in circumference, this lake is now used for recreation and fish farming. One to two meters deep, it was originally built in the fifth century, and several emperors used it to train or review their navies and for private recreation. A black dragon was spotted here in the fifth century, so if you visit it on a dark and stormy night, you might want to look for it. You can walk from the railway station and take a ferry.

The **Jiangsu Provincial Museum** (Nanjing Museum), *Zhongshan Dong Road, Tel. 6641554*, is a traditional Chinese-style building and contains exhibits ranging from the era of Peking Man to revolutionary times. Three thousand items are on display, among them a 3,000-year-old genuine duck egg; the jade burial suit that was exhibited in America in 1973 (Eastern Han, from Xuzhou City, Jiangsu); a sixth-century Soul Pot covered with many birds, placed in a tomb so the birds could fly the soul of the deceased to paradise; maps of the early capitals in Nanjing from 229 to 589, so you can try to locate ancient landmarks in the modern city; a 20-meter scroll showing the inspection tour by Qing Emperor Kangzi (Kang-shi) from Nanjing to Zhenjiang; the anchor from a British merchant ship lost in Zhenjiang; a photo of a British-built electric company in 1882; and a list of institutions set up by the United States in China, with numbers of Chinese students and teachers and of foreign teachers. The museum is four kilometers from Jinling Hotel.

The **Gulou** (Drum Tower) is at the intersection of Zhongshan Bei Road, and Zhongyang and Beijing Roads, in the center of the city. Built in 1382, it holds a six-foot diameter drum and an ancient giant stone tortoise carrying a stele added in the Qing, a report on the inspection tour of Qing Emperor Kangxi. Nearby is the Big Bell Pavilion.

The **Nanjing City Wall** is 12 meters high, 33.4 kilometers in circumference, and from 7.62 to 12 meters thick. Built from 1368 to 1387, it once had 13,616 cannons on top. Roughly 10 kilometers north-south by 5.62 kilometers east-west, it is believed to be the longest city wall in the world. The bricks were made in five provinces, and each is inscribed with the name of the superintendent and the brickmaster, plus the date made. The mortar was lime, tung oil, and glutinous rice paste. Originally built with 13 gates, 11 more were added later. You cannot miss this magnificent wall.

The **Zhonghua Gate**, *Tel. 6625752*, on the south side, is the best gate to see. It has four two-story gates in succession (in case the enemy breaks through one), 12 tunnels, and room to garrison 3,000 soldiers. You can walk along the top of the wall here.

They built the **Jiu Hua Hill** (Monk Tang Pagoda) originally in the Song, about 1,000 years ago, to house a fragment of the skull of Xuan Zhang (Hsuan Tsang). This was the monk who traveled to India in search of the Buddhist sutras and was immortalized in the novel *Pilgrimage to the Western World*.

If You Have More Time or Special Interests

Inside the city wall, **Qingliang Shan Park** was a lovely gathering place for painters and writers of old, on a hill overlooking the northern part of Nanjing near the university. It is on the main road to the Yangtze River Bridge. Among the writers was the author of the Nanjing-based classic novel *The Scholars*. A crematorium used to be in the area, and as a result few Chinese come here. It is a good place to get away from crowds.

The **Confucius Temple** (Fuzimiao), adjacent shopping center, hotel, and free market, are major tourist attractions, featuring Ming and Qing architecture and worth a visit. The Temple was originally built in 1034 A.D. as a place of sacrifice. Wars destroyed it many times and the current building is a post-Liberation reproduction. Moving wax statues of scholars in period dress demonstrate how examinations were written. Birds, fish, and clothes are on sale. Nearby on the Qinhuai River is the former residence of famous Ming sing-song (courtesan) girl Li Xiang; you can rent boats (but the ride is short and the water dirty).

Originally built in the Ming dynasty, 600 years ago, the palace that now houses the **Taiping Museum**, *Tel. 6623024*, was rebuilt for Yang Xiuqing (Yang Hsiu-ching), eastern prince of the Taiping Heavenly Kingdom in the mid-19th century. It now contains exhibits reflecting the background of the revolution; uprising at Jintian village; Nanjing as capital; regulations and policies; insistence on armed struggle; resisting aggression; safeguarding the capital; and continuing the revolution.

Prominently displayed inside the museum is a plaque 'in memory of the organizer and leader of the Ever Victorious Army, erected by the Frederick Ward Post, American Legion, May 27, 1923.' Frederick Ward was an American mercenary who fought against the Taipings and died in 1862.

Another relic of the Taipings well worth seeing is the **Tianwang Mansion** (The Heavenly King's Mansion), *292 Changjiang Road in the eastern part of the city, Tel. 6641131*. The palace was made for Hong Xiuquan (Hung Hsiu-chuan), the head of the Taipings, with materials from the Ming palace. After the 1911 Revolution, the Tianwang Mansion became the Presidential Residence.

You can study the **Ming Palace** ruins in the eastern part of Nanjing in about five minutes. It was built between 1368 to 1386 for the first Ming emperor. The Forbidden City is about the same size. Qing troops partially destroyed it in 1645 and the Taipings pulled down the remainder. In 1911 only a gate was left standing, but in 1958 the government restored some of the relics.

Also in the city is a memorial hall to Zheng He, the Muslim eunuch who became one of China's most famous maritime commanders, making seven voyages to 30 countries of Asia and Africa from 1405 to 1433. His tomb is 10 kilometers south of Nanjing. The **English Corner** is at the foot of Drum Tower Park, every Saturday 1 to 10 pm, where locals go to practice their English.

Walks

Great walks include Purple Mountain and along the top of the city wall.

Outside the City Wall

The **Meiling Palace** is about three kilometers outside the Zhongshan Gate. This 1930s building was the weekend home of Generalissimo Chiang Kai-shek and his wife from 1945 to 1949. They held church services here, sometimes with the American ambassador.

Yuhuatai (Rain-Flower) **People's Revolutionary Martyr's Memorial Park**, *Tel. 6624003*, is just south of the Zhonghua Gate, five kilometers from the Jinling Hotel. This ancient battleground was later an execution ground used by the Japanese and warlords. Here the Nationalists killed 100,000 Communists and sympathizers from 1927 to 1949. Now a memorial park with exhibit hall and flower garden, it is known also for its multicolored agate pebbles which are sold everywhere.

Mochou (Sorrow-Free) **Lake Park**, *Tel. 6623243*, southwest of the city, contains several buildings from the Qing and a small 47-hectare lake. The white marble statue of Mochou is a local landmark. She was the good-hearted wife but submissive daughter-in-law who ended up killing herself, alas, because of her oppressive father-in-law. Open daily.

The **Stone Engravings of the Southern Dynasties** can be seen any time. Scattered around the suburbs of Nanjing are relics of the Six Dynasties (222-589). Some of the 31 tomb sites (11 emperors and 20 nobles) are in the middle of a field off the main road. Many of the tombs are protected by distinctive pairs of stone mythical animals, pillars, or tablets, symbols of authority and dignity.

The **Southern Tang Tombs** are more than 30 kilometers south of the city. You can enter two tombs and see old murals, reliefs, and coffins of the first two emperors of the Tang dynasty, Li Bian and Li Jing, who ruled over 1300 years ago. The tomb of the founder of that glorious dynasty is 21 meters long by 10 meters wide and at least five meters high. The highly decorated coffins of the imperial couple are in the rear under a chart of the stars and planets.

NIGHTLIFE & ENTERTAINMENT

The best **disco** is in the Jinling. The **Nanjing Acrobatic Troupe** has won international prizes.

SHOPPING

Made in Nanjing are 'Yunjin (Figured) Satin' brocade, velvet flowers, tapestry and carpets, imitations of ancient wood and ivory carvings, silver jewelry, and paper cuts. Made in the province are inlaid lacquer (Yangzhou), purple sand pottery (Yixing), Huishan clay figures, fresh water pearls, silk underwear, batik (Nantong), and Suzhou embroidery. Around the Confucian temple is a lively free market (jeans, fish, birds, back scratchers, etc.) with a good dumpling restaurant. On the nearby river, the flower girls used to solicit customers.

You can visit the **Brocade Research Institute**, *240 ChatingDong Road, Tel. 6611377*; **The Arts & Crafts Company**, *31 Beijing Dong Road, Tel. 7711193*; and **The Nanjing Jade Workshop**, *233 Zhongshan Dong Road, Tel. 4412910.*

There's lots of shopping in the **Golden Shopping Centre** next to the Jinling Hotel, *2 Hanzhong Road, Tel. 4455888.* An antique store is at the Zhongshan Gate and the Cultural Relics Shop is at the **Nanjing Museum**, *321 Zhongshan Dong Road, Tel. 4450324.* The **Shizhuzhai**, Nanjing Cultural Relics Shop, is at *72 Taiping Nan Road, Tel. 6643313.* The **Nanjing Central Department Store** is at *79 Zhongshan Nan Road, Tel. 4408288.*

EXCURSIONS FROM NANJING

You can make day trips from Nanjing to Zhenjiang and Yangzhou. Also in the province are Suzhou, and Wuxi. See separate listings. Further away are the following:

Changzhou is the home of a still productive, 1,500 year old imperial comb factory and the *****Tianningsi** (Heavenly Tranquility) **Temple** with its 500 Tang arhats. It is a stop on some Grand Canal cruises and 20 kilometers southeast are the ruins of Yancheng, the capital of Yan State (11th century B.C.), with a small museum, ongoing excavations, and pearl farming in its moats. It is halfway between Shanghai and Nanjing on the Grand Canal, three hours by boat from Wuxi. The urban population is 600,000.

You can stay at the **CHANGZHOU GRAND HOTEL** *(Dajiudian) is at 65 Yanling Xi Rd., 213003. Three and four stars. Tel. 6609998. Fax 6607701. Credit Cards.* Downtown location. Dist.A.P. 30 km. Dist.R.W. five km. 360 rooms. Diet therapy restaurant with food to 'prolong life and beautify women. B.C. Clinic. IDD. USTV.

You can contact **CITS** at *Tel. 6600481 or fax 6689455*, or **CYTS** at *7 Luo Han Road, 213003, Tel. 6601925.* The Telephone code is 0519.

Lianyungang is on the Yellow Sea, the eastern end of the train line from Rotterdam in the Netherlands. About 300 kilometers by road north of Nanjing, this sprawling, open port city has an airport connecting with six Chinese cities and soon hopefully Hong Kong, Japan, and Korea. There's not much else to recommend it except for a 625.5-meter-high mountain which was the fictional setting for the Monkey King, mischievous hero of the popular Qing novel *Pilgrimage to the West.* Guides can show you his "birthplace." There is also a clinic for treating illnesses with bee stings. The best hotel is the three-star **TIAN RAN JU HOTEL**, at *32 Hailian Zhong Road, 222004. Tel. 5411688. Fax 5411851.* Another good choice is the three-star **SHENZHOU BINGUAN** at *1 Yingzui Bei, Xugou,*

222042. *Tel. 2310088. Fax 2311535. Credit Cards.* Dist.A.P.60 km. Dist.R.W. five km. It has five Swedish modules and is close to a swimming beach and near the port. IDD. B.C., H.K.J.V. For **CITS**, *Tel. 5415079. Fax 5413374.* Telephone Code is 0518.

Nantong is for textile lovers: the Textile Museum (8 Wenfeng Road) is a reproduction of a 1900s factory and is worth seeing. It also has three pagodas, and a March festival for whistling kites (also made here). Nantong is an open port city (population 450,000) west of Shanghai on the north bank of the Yangtze, and reached by road and bridge from Wuxi and Suzhou. Twice-a-day high-speed ferries from Shanghai's north suburbs take two to three hours. It is also connected to six other cities by air.

One of the two three-star hotels is the **NANTONG DAJIUDIAN**, *43 Qingnian Dong Road, 226007, Tel. 518989. Fax 518996. Credit Cards.* It is in the suburbs near the Foreign Economic Business Building and textile museum. Dist.port eight km. Dist.A.P. 40 km. 300 rooms. IDD. USTV, B.C. Tennis. For **CITS**, *Tel. 518023. Fax 518019.* Telephone code is 0518.

Xuzhou in northwest Jiangsu is on two train lines. Its Han Dynasty Museum is on the site of Prince Chu's tomb (201 to 154 B.C.). Here archeologists found the jade burial suit that once toured North America. They also found 3,000 terracotta horses and warriors 27-54 cm high. You can stay at the two-star **SOUTH SUBURB GUESTHOUSE** *(Nanjiao Binguan), 55 Heping Road, 221009. Two stars. Tel. 841980, 847980. Fax 844995.* Dist.A.P. 10 km. Dist.R.W. five km. **CITS** is at *Tel. 5415079. Fax 5413374.* Telephone Code is 0516.

Yixing, due west of Shanghai and Suzhou and on the west side of Lake Taihu, is the home of the famous purple clay pottery in Dingsu. You can visit factories and the huge exhibition hall. It's also known for its limestone caves.

Shanjuan Cave, 25 kilometers southwest of the city, was discovered about 2,000 years ago. The 700-meter walk takes about an hour. It has a 120-meter-long underground river. The **Zhonggong Cave**, 22 kilometers southwest of Yixing was the home of Zhang Daoling (one of the founders of Taoism) and Zhang Guolao (one of the Eight Taoist Immortals). With 72 small, interconnected caves, it's one kilometer walk includes 1,500 stone steps. **CITS** and **CTS** is at the **YIXING GUEST HOUSE**, *214200. Tel. (0518)702172. Fax 705491.*

PRACTICAL INFORMATION

• **Business Hours**: offices 8 am to 5,30 pm; stores 9 am to 7 pm.
• **CITS** and **Overseas Tourist Co.**, *255 Zhongshan Bei Road, Tel. 3342328. Fax 3306002; 202-1 Zhongshan Xi Road, 210003. Tel. 3422328. Fax 3438954*

• **CTS**, *313 Zhong Shan Bei Road, 210003. Tel. 8801502. Fax 8801533; Also 289 Zhujiang Road, 210018. Tel. 3366227. Fax 3366228*
• **CYTS**, *160 Hanzhong Road, Tel. 6523344. Fax 6523355*
• **Jiangsu Travel and Tourism Bureau**, *259 North Zhongshan Road, 210003. Tel. 3327144. Fax 3343960. For complaints Tel. 3423221*
• **Jinling Business International Travel**, *2 Hanzhong Road, Tel. 4455745. Fax 4702788*
• **Nanjing Municipal Tourism Bureau**, *4 Donggushi Nan Road, Tel. 3362686. Fax 7711959. Complaints, Tel. 7711005*
• **Telephone Code**, *025*
• **Tourist Complaints**, contact **Supervisory Bureau of Tourism Quality of Jiangsu Province**, *255 Zhongshan Bei Road, 210003. Tel. 3301221. Fax 3328795*
• **Tourist Hotline**, *202-1 Zhongshan Bei Road, Tel. 3301221, 7711005*

NINGBO
(Ningpo)

Ningbo is on the Zhejiang coast south of Shanghai. A community of 1.13 million people, Ningbo is known for its great ship builders and prominent business people and booming commerce. It is also noteworthy for the oldest extant library in China, two major temples, and the nearby home of the Goddess of Mercy in Putuo Shan.

ARRIVALS & DEPARTURES

Ningbo can be reached by train (in about four hours) or by road (over two hours) from Hangzhou, and by expressway from Shanghai. It is linked by plane with about 22 Chinese cities and Hong Kong, and from Shanghai it's a 30-minute flight or a four-hour ferry and bus ride – a convenient weekend trip.

ORIENTATION

The Ningbo area has been settled with an advanced culture at least since 4800 B.C. and some scholars now claim the cradle of Chinese civilization was here, and not confined to the Yellow River.

Ningbo has been recorded since the Spring and Autumn Period (700-476 B.C.). It has been a major port since the Tang, trading with Korea, Japan, and Southeast Asia. Ice-free, it was made a treaty port, open to foreign trade and residence in 1842. After 1860, a French military detachment was stationed here. Ningbo was reopened as a port for foreign trade in 1979 for the first time in 30 years.

If you have only one day, see **Hemudu**, the library and the two temples to the east. If you have one more day, there's Chiang Kai-shek's home town and the temple home of the Laughing Buddha in Xikou Town, Fenhua city. From Ningbo, Putuoshan is a two-day visit. Forget about crafts shopping. There isn't much.

WHERE TO STAY & EAT

The East Port Hotel is best, then the Asia Garden. Add 15% tax to prices.

EAST PORT HOTEL, *52 Caihong Bei Road, 315040. Four stars. Tel. 7373188, Fax 7333646. $90 to $130. Credit Cards.*

In commercial district near big department stores. 14 stories, 248 rooms, IDD, B.C., 24-hour room service, pool, gym, clinic. Dragonair.

ASIA GARDEN HOTEL *(Yazhou Huayuan Binguan), 72 Mayuan Road, 315010. Three stars, Tel. 7296888. Fax 7292138, 7296554. Y550 to Y930. Dist. A.P.15 km. Dist.R.W. 0.5 km. Credit Cards.*

Close to Friendship and antique stores. Built 1987. 10 stories, 170 rooms, IDD, B.C., USTV. Clean, adequate, but badly managed. Buffet breakfast Y80.

SEEING THE SIGHTS

The *Tianyige Library, completed in 1561 (Ming to Qing) is half a kilometer from the Asia Garden Hotel. It still has more than 300,000 books. It started as a private library and now has in its more modern extension next door over 80,000 rare books, mostly from the Ming, plus numerous stone tablets. Scholars can see these books upon request. The library is worth visiting for its simple elegance and its peaceful, tastefully-designed gardens. It was the blueprint for the other seven imperial Qing libraries.

At the entrance to the library is a sign that says something like 'This is not an amusement park. No fun inside. Keep out.' Don't be intimidated by the blunt Ningbo manner. Note also the conversations of the man-in-the-street, which might sound like intense, bitter arguing.

Both the **Tiantong Temple,** (35 kilometers) and the **Ayuwang** (King Asoka) **Temple** (30 kilometers) are east of the city in rural hill country, and are bigger and more impressive than city temples, with bigger-than-life-size statues. The Ayuwang, *Tel. 4880624* (open daily 8 am to 5 pm) was founded in the third century. The Ayuwang Temple has about 70 monks, and relics of Sakyamuni (Buddha) in its highest hall. The famous Buddhist monk Jianzhen (see *Yangzhou*) once lived here after he failed in his third attempt to reach Japan in the Tang dynasty. The **Tiantong Temple** is one of the largest temples south of the Yangtze, with over 700 halls and over 100 monks. The Tiantong has sent many teachers to Japan and consequently attracts many Japanese visitors. It is the second holiest shrine of the Zen or Chan sect. Zen Buddhist statues are supposed to have deepset eyes looking at their noses as the nose safekeeps one's heart to avoid temptation. See if you can find any. Better still, try crossing your eyes when you feel tempted to sin.

On the way back to Ningbo from these temples, you might be interested in a huge wholesale market for sweaters made in the area.

The **Hemudu** site is west of the city in Yuyao County about 90 minutes by road in the flourishing countryside. It has a small but good **museum**, *Tel. 2670158*, with English signs. The display includes a still-playable 6,000 to 7,000 year-old bone flute, rice, plough shares, weaving, inlaid-bone and wood carvings, and jade ornaments. (Open daily 8:30 am to 4:30 pm all year round)

The ***Bao Guo Temple**, built in 1013 (Northern Song), is the oldest extant wooden structure south of the Yangtze, and is in Yuyao, 20 kilometers north of the Asia Garden Hotel. Unlike other temples, which have large beams for support, this one uses many small ones. The **Tainfeng Pagoda**, built in 695, was traditionally a place for scholars to gather to compose poems and enjoy the scenery. It is hexagonal, seven stories high, but not as beautiful as younger pagodas. This needs another half day to see.

EXCURSIONS FROM NINGBO

Putuo Shan is the home of **Guanyin** (Kuan Yin), the Goddess of Mercy, and is one of the **Four Sacred Buddhist Mountains**. This 12.5-square-kilometer island is reached by ship from Ningbo, a two-hour trip offered four times a day; a ferry is also available from Shanghai. An airport is at Zhu Jia Jian with flights from Shanghai. This is a 30-minute ferry trip away from Putuo Shan.

On the way you pass the famous **Zhaoshan-Qundao fishing ground** with triangular fish nets, a picturesque view, especially at sunset.

Putuo Shan has been a religious site since 847 A.D. It once had over 200 temples and nunneries, but the years and the Red Guards have done their worst, and about 80 are now open. Those who remember hiking from innumerable nunneries to innumerable temples may be disappointed. No more tiny Buddhist statues inscribed with religious poems to help keep one single-mindedly devout line the narrow mountain paths. But you can still climb thousands of steps and hike through bamboo groves, and along the rocky shore and beaches. Along with the hospitable and warm- hearted villagers, enough of the religious atmosphere remains for first-time visitors to enjoy the island.

The best hotel is the three-star **PUTUO SHAN ZHUANG**, *Tel. (0580) 6091666 or Fax 6091667*, but the **XILAI XIAO ZHUANG**, *Tel.*

(0580)6091522 or fax 2031378, is more convenient. It's beside a temple and the chanting might awaken you early in the morning. It's a three star hotel.

Visitors can also see the kowtowing pilgrims, forehead to ground every three steps, as they pay homage or ask special favors of this favorite deity. Especially touching are the sick and handicapped, carried on the backs of friends or family, who come to pray for healing. Devout Buddhists try to make a trip to Putuo at least once in a lifetime.

It is customary to purchase a yellow sack from one of the temples and, for a fee, have each temple rubber-stamp its seal on the sack to prove you've been there.

Putuo Shan is especially famous because repeated storms kept some Japanese worshippers from carrying away a statue of Guanyin from China. Near a cliff is the **Won't Go Temple**, to commemorate the goddess's desire to remain in China.

PRACTICAL INFORMATION
• **Ambulance,** *Tel. 120*
• **CITS,** *75 Yanyue Street, 315010, Tel. 7312850. Fax 7298690, 7312831*
• **Ningbo Overseas Travel Co.,** *8th floor, Wanghu Building, 2 Nanzhandong Road, 315010, Tel. 7303017, 7364451. Fax 7294481, 7364481*
• **Ningbo Travel and Tourism Bureau,** *59 Yanyue Street, 315010, Tel. 7303716, Fax 7291266*
• **Police,** *Tel. 110*
• **Tourist Complaints,** *Tel. 7291299*
• **Telephone Code,** *0574*

QUANZHOU
(Chuangchou)

Located 103 kilometers north of Xiamen in Fujian, the ancient city of **Quanzhou** was considered one of the two largest ports in the world by Marco Polo, who knew it as Zaiton or Citong. At that time it exported silks and porcelain as far away as Africa. In the Song it had a population of 500,000. It declined because maritime trade was forbidden and the harbor silted up.

The hottest day has been in July at 32°C. Winters are mild (no snow). Precipitation is 1,400 millimeters, from July to September.

ARRIVALS & DEPARTURES

It is 100 kilometers from an airport, but should have its own soon linking it with Hong Kong, Guangzhou, Shenzhen, Beijing and Shanghai. For now, you'll have to get here by train or bus.

ORIENTATION

Today, Quanzhou is one of the 24 cities protected by the State Council as a historical monument. Its downtown area still has a great deal of slow-paced old China flavor plus charming touches of Muslim architecture. It also has bicycle rickshaws with sideseats and China's largest collection of Nestorian Christian and Manichaean relics.

If you only have one day, in the morning visit the Kaiyuan Temple, East and West Pagoda, Overseas Communication Museum, and Old God Rock. In the afternoon, see the Grand Mosque, Wind-Shaken Rock, Holy Islamic Tombs, and Luoyang Bridge. If you have more time, visit the Mazu Temple especially on a feast day if you don't mind crowds.

WHERE TO STAY & EAT

The best hotel is the Quanzhou or the Zai Tong. The Golden Fountain Hotel and the Overseas Chinese Building are downtown beside the park and walking distance to the mosque.

GOLDEN FOUNTAIN HOTEL *(Jinquan Jiu Dian), Baiyuan Qingchipan 362000. Three stars, Tel. 2825078. Fax 2824388.*

Built 1965, ren. 1985. The lobby is dark and overall the place is a bit scruffy.

OVERSEAS CHINESE HOTEL *(Huaqiao Da Sha), Baiyuan Qingchipan 362000. Tel. 2282192. Fax 2284612. Credit Cards.*

Built 1951, ren. 1993. 12 stories, 221 rooms. USTV. IDD.

QUANZHOU HOTEL *(Fandian), Zhuang Fu Lane, 362000, Three stars, Tel. 2235395, 2285395, 2182108. Fax 2289958, 2132108.*

A nice hotel, this is closer to Kaiyuan Temple than the others.

ZAI TONG HOTEL *(Fandian), Yingbin Rd., 362000. Three stars, Tel. 2182108. Fax 2183028.*

SEEING THE SIGHTS

The **Kaiyuan Temple** is one kilometer northwest of the Overseas Chinese Hotel and dates from the Tang. The main hall has 100 heavy stone Greek-type columns. On top of 24 of these columns are gaudy part women/part bird creatures, whose crowns appear to support the beams. These flying musicians are gilded clay and most unusual. Indian figures and Chinese dragons and tigers also decorate the temple. Look also for the 1000-armed, 1000-eyed Guanyin. Note the corners of the roof, the curled swallow tails, and the lively dragons that are distinctive aspects of southern Fujian temple architecture.

Two large pagodas, the trademarks of the city, are on the temple grounds. These are the **East** and **West Pagodas**. The 48-meter-high Zhenguo Pagoda is east. Originally built of wood in 865, it was rebuilt of

EAST CHINA 313

stone in 1238. The west **Renshou Pagoda**, 44 meters high, was originally built in 916 and rebuilt in 1228. In the Song dynasty, this temple was home to over 1000 monks.

There is also the nine-story **Museum of Martime Navigational History**, which houses relics from many religions, including Nestorian Christian, Manichean, Hindu, and Islamic. Look for the Franciscan tombstone with a cross. It also has the remains of a 13th-century ship, 24-meters long, found in Quanzhou Bay.

Old God Rock is four kilometers from the city. This stone statue of Laotze, the founder of Taoism, is beautiful, 600 years old, standing about five meters tall and grandfatherly, with a long beard.

At one time, 10,000 foreigners from Persia, Syria, and Southeast Asia lived in the southern part of the city. Most of them were Moslem. The *****Qingjing** (Grand Mosque) on Tushan Street, half a kilometer from the Overseas Chinese Building and open daily, was built by local Moslems in 1009. One of the earliest mosques in China, it was copied from a mosque in Damascus and renovated in 1310. It is one of the few mosques in eastern China with west Asian architecture.

While much of it has been in ruins, it is lovingly maintained. Arabic writing and central Asian arches point to its former glory. Inside is a small museum with text in English pointing out such events as Moslems fighting beside Zheng Chenggong (Koxinga) and the continuing observance of customs like Ramadan, weddings officiated by an imam, and abstinence from eating pork. Three thousand Moslems still live on Tushan Street.

The **Islamic Tombs** are on Ling Shan Hill, outside the East Gate, four kilometers from the city. They are protected by a Chinese-style pavilion. They could belong to two trader- missionaries who arrived in the city during the Tang. Koxinga prayed here before his fifth voyage to Southeast Asia. Inscriptions are in Arabic. A few steps away is the 50-ton **Wind-Shaking Rock**, an elephant-sized boulder that anybody can wobble. Honest!

In the neighborhood of the **Luoyang Bridge** is a stone-carving factory that makes Japanese lanterns, balustrades, temple pagodas, and photo-graph-like pictures. It provided the stone columns of Chairman Mao's mausoleum in Beijing.

If you have more time, **Wanshan Peak** has some rare Manichaean relics. This religion, brought to China in the seventh century from Persia, was a combination of Zoroastrianism, Christianity, and paganism. At one time, St. Augustine was an adherent. On a stone tablet near the site of the monastery are inscribed the activities of the cult during the Song, when it was associated with Taoism. Behind the ruins is a circular Manichaean statue of a man.

About 13 kilometers outside the south gate of Quanzhou is the **Caoan Temple**, the only Manicaean temple left in China and the best preserved such temple in the world. There used to be temples in Xi'an and Luoyang as well, but the religion was persecuted in 843 A.D. and its leaders fled to Quanzhou. From here it spread along the east coast but died out in the Qing. This temple was first built in the Song and renovated in the Yuan. It has a 1.5-meter-high carving of Mani Buddha inside dating from 1339.

The **Heavenly Princess Palace** and **Confucian Temple** are half a kilometer from the Overseas Chinese Hotel. Further afield – one hour by car from the city, at the shore – is the five-story octagonal stone **Tower of the Two Sisters-in-law**, built in 1162. The 21-meter high structure was originally built as a navigational aid, but its name symbolizes the loneliness of the women left behind by the sailors and emigrants. The 161-acre **Overseas Chinese University** is in the mountains east of the city. Its students are drawn from Southeast Asia, Hong Kong, and Macau.

The **Tomb of Zheng Chenggong** (Koxinga) is at Nan'an, about 25 kilometers northwest of Quanzhou. He was a pirate who allied himself with the defeated Ming forces in the mid-1600s, fighting the Manchus. With his fleet of 800 warships, this national hero successfully rid Taiwan of the Dutch.

A nice day trip from Quanzhou is the hometown of the sea goddest **Mazu**, who is worshipped by fisherfolk in 1,500 temples around the world, including Hong Kong, Macau, and Taiwan. She was originally a woman named Lin Mo or Lin Mazu who lived from 960 to 987 A.D. and is credited with saving members of her own family and later other fishermen from shipwreck. Her birthday is the 23rd day of the third lunar month at which time the temple is full of worshippers and smoking incense. The original 1000-year-old temple is on **Meizhou Island**, 88 kilometers from Quanzhou, and is on the list of important national historic sites.

The nearby **TIANFEI HOT SPRING HOTEL** is at the foot of Phoenix Hill near the Fuzhou-Xiamen Highway (*at the entrance to Xue Yuan Road, 351100. Tel. 265588, Fax 265068*).

SHOPPING

Local products are embroidered blouses, life-like artificial flowers, stone carvings, woven bamboo, Dehua porcelain, and Anxi Guanyin tea.

PRACTICAL INFORMATION

- **CTS**, *Overseas Chinese Building, Baiyuan Road, 362000; Tel. 2282192. Fax 2284388.*
- **Quanzhou International Travel Service**, *4th Floor, Food & Oil Building, Dongda Road, 362000. Tel. 2282039, 2287295. Fax 2182056*
- **Telephone Code**, *0595*

SHAOXING

(Shaohsing)

Shaoxing is in Zhejiang province. The urban population is 240,000. You go to Shaoxing to get a feel of old traditional China. It is a 2000 to 3000 year-old town, best known for its wine. Its charm will not last forever so go soon. It was the birthplace of China's most famous pre-Liberation writer, **Luxun** (Lu Hsun). Some of his stories, notably *The Story of Ah Q*, were set in this town, and a highly recommended but very sad 1982 movie was made of the *Ah Q* novella here. Literary types should pay a visit to his former residence and the **Luxun Memorial Hall**.

Shaoxing was the capital of the State of Ye during the Spring and Autumn period. The 'tomb' of Emperor Yu, the Xia dynasty founder, is in the south suburbs at the base of Mt. Kuaiji. No one knows if the remains of this third century B.C. pioneer in irrigation are actually here in Yuwang Miao Temple. In any case, he died in Shaoxing during a visit. The name Shaoxing means 'gathering place,' for example, of the people celebrating the miraculous engineering feats of Emperor Yu.

Shaoxing is famous throughout China for its distinctive **opera**. It is less formal, full of emotion, action, and audience-pleasing lyrics, gorgeous costumes, and flashy sets. All parts are played by women.

ARRIVALS & DEPARTURES

Shaoxing is 60 kilometers from Hangzhou by train or road, three hours from Ningbo. An airport should open soon. It is 65 kilometers from the closest airport in Hangzhou.

ORIENTATION

Shaoxing is attractive because it still has many houses, streets, canals, and boats hardly changed from centuries ago. Much time can be spent walking around in this time warp.

Changes have been made, however: the addition of a local television station and the lovely sycamore and plane trees lining the streets. The Second Hospital was the former mission hospital.

Shaoxing today is the capital of one of the ten most prosperous small counties in China, its wealth based on textiles. Don't miss the Wine Festival if you're here in September.

WHERE TO STAY & EAT

Until the new four star hotels open, the best is the **Shaoxing Hotel**.
SHAOXING HOTEL *(Binguan), 9 Huanshan Rd., 312000. Three stars. Tel. 5155888. Fax 5155565. Dist.A.P. 67 km. Dist.R.W. three km. Credit Cards.*

At the foot of Fu Hill, convenient to stores and government offices.
Built in the 1950s. Two and three stories. 115 rooms. Ren. 1988; 85
additional rooms and pool. Traditional late Ming garden-style architecture, beautiful, adequate but smelling mildly of mold. The dining hall is
an old family temple. IDD, B.C.

As for food, the restaurant at the Shaoxing Hotel is good. There
should also be a Pizza Hut by now.

SEEING THE SIGHTS

If you want to visit East Lake, Yuwang Miao, Lang Ding (Orchid
Pavilion), Luxun's home and museum, Qiu Jin's home, and stroll about
the town, you need at least two full days. You could also ask about the story
of the scholar writing with a brush made of mouse whiskers. Tours can
visit a home for the aged.

Shaoxing is known for its lovely canals and **East Lake**, alive with boats
of all descriptions. Especially striking are its distinctive foot boats, the oars
worked by feet. I highly recommend a trip onto the lake, through its
canals, and into caves cut out of the lake's quarried cliffs to see the hanging
gardens. You can also glide under some of its 3,000 stone-arched bridges
to old temples and the market, a good way to see the city.

You can take another boat trip near ancient **Keqiao**, 12 kilometers
from Shaoxing, pulled by two men along part of a five-kilometer stone
towpath to a 800-year old stone bridge. Tour groups can also arrange a
demonstration of Shaoxing opera on board.

Also of interest are the **Orchid Pavilion**, dating back to the fourth
century, and the **Shen family garden**, which commemorates the meeting
between Song dynasty lovers. **Jianhu Lake**, first dredged in the second
century, covers more than 200 square kilometers. The home of the early
20th century female revolutionary Qiu Jin is open as a museum. Premier
Chou En-lai, though born in Jiangsu province, was brought up in this city
and you can visit his home.

SHOPPING

Shaoxing wine, brewed with two thousand years of experience, is a
"must purchase" item. You can stop in at the **Xian Heng Wine Shop**, *44
Luxun Road*, named after a Luxun short story. Other locally made items
include lace, felt hats, paper fans, silk, porcelain, bambooware, and ink
stones. The Shaoxing Antique Store is on Jiefang Nan Road.

PRACTICAL INFORMATION
• **CITS Shaoxing Branch**, *360 Fu Shan Xi Road, 312000, Tel. 5167672. Fax
5165766*

• **CTS**, *Huanshanxi Road, Tel. 5133252*
• **Telephone Code**, *0575*
• **Zhejiang Shaoxing Tourism Bureau**, *9 Huan Shan Road, 312000. Tel. 5155888 X 763. Fax 5155565*

SUZHOU

(Soochow)

In the Yangtze basin, in Jiangsu province, **Suzhou** is famous for its gardens, silk, canals, and old architecture. Choosing between Suzhou and its rival Hangzhou is not easy, for both are interesting and beautiful. Suzhou is closer to Shanghai, but you can fly direct to Hangzhou from Hong Kong and Singapore.

The hottest temperature is 36 degrees centigrade (usually one to two days in late July, early August); the coldest is the end of January, averaging zero degrees to seven degrees centigrade. It snows once or twice a year. Rain falls mainly from May to July. The population is almost 860,000 in the old city; the metropolitcan area has over 5.3 million people.

He Lu, King of Wu, founded the city as his capital in 514 B.C. Suzhou is one of China's oldest cities. Iron was smelted here more than 2,500 years ago and silk weaving was well developed in the Tang and Song. Marco Polo visited in the latter half of the 13th century. Textile manufacturing flourished during the Ming. From 1860 to 1863, 40,000 troops of the Taiping Heavenly Kingdom controlled the area. During the Japanese occupation, the Jiangsu provincial puppet government was headquartered in the Humble Administrator's Garden.

People here speak the Wu dialect, which is similar to that of Shanghai, only with softer tones and more adjectives. Industries include the manufacturing of television sets, wristwatches, chemicals, and electronics.

You can see the factories where artisans weave and print silk, make sandalwood and silk fans, and create one of the four most famous embroideries in China. They also make musical instruments. The villages raise silkworms, jasmine flowers for tea, shrimp, and tangerines, and are therefore particularly good places to visit. The old city proper is under state protection as a historic and cultural treasure. No one can build any new factories, and existing factories that pollute have to move out to the suburbs.

ARRIVALS & DEPARTURES

The fastest way to Suzhou is by train from Shanghai and is about one hour (86 kilometers) west. This can be booked two days before departure through hotels or travel agencies in Shanghai. The 6 am train is easiest, the double-decker trains the most comfortable.

Until the new Suzhou airport opens in Guang Fu District 15 kilometers from Suzhou (the airport will be linked by expressway), the closest major airport is at Shanghai, where you can pick up an express bus to Suzhou. The new airport will have service by China United Airlines with flights from Guangzhou and Beijing.

There's a 3 1/2 hour direct bus from Hangzhou March to November only. From Shanghai, on the 100 kilometer expressway, the bus takes about 1 1/2 hours if you're lucky.

ORIENTATION

The former walled city is about three by five kilometers and is criss-crossed by many canals (most in need of cleaning). The western and southern **moats** are actually part of the famous Grand Canal (610 A.D). The **city wall** was built in 514 B.C. and remnants, including three gates, remain. Also remaining is one of the eight **water gates**, now topped by a watch tower and museum.

Suzhou is one of the prettiest towns in China, its streets thickly lined with plane trees and its tiny whitewashed houses of uniform design. Unlike many other Chinese cities, the Japanese war inflicted little damage here. It is known primarily as a cultural and scenic city, similar in this respect to Japan's Kyoto. Its classical gardens are among the best in China.

The main street, **Renmin** (People's) Road, runs north-south; **Guanqian Street** runs east-west, meeting with Renmin almost in the center of the city. Taxis are double the price of Shanghai's. The city is small, and you can get around more cheaply by bicycle rickshaw or public bus.

WHERE TO STAY

With its growing economy, hotels here will be increasingly difficult to obtain. Book early. The best hotel for tourists is currently the beautiful **Bamboo Grove** with its restful garden, good service, and convenient location in the old city. A close second is the **Suzhou**. Third are the Nan Lin Hotel, also in the old city, and the new 150-room Dongshan Hotel. The Dongshan is villa-style, set against a hill. Dongshan town is in a national holiday resort 40-minutes drive in the southwest part of the city. The five-star Panmen Hotel near the water gate is a Singapore joint venture to be finished soon. The best for business people is the **Aster**, west of the city wall in the business district close to Suzhou Customs and the trade center.

The new 400-room Sheraton Suzhou International Hotel at Dong Da Road and Xin Shi Road should be five-star standard when it opens.

Prices mentioned below are subject to change, negotiation and a 15% surcharge.

BAMBOO GROVE HOTEL (*Zhu Hui Fandian*), *Zhu Hui Rd., 215006. Four stars, Tel. 5205601. Fax 5208778. $120. Dist.R.W. six km. and south of the Master of Nets Garden. Credit Cards.*

Built 1990-91. Ren. 1994. Five stories. Three connecting buildings. 405 rooms. IDD, B.C. Executive floor. Cantonese food. Gym. Tennis. Sauna. Bicycles. USTV. Clinic. Lee Garden International management.

NAN LIN HOTEL (*Fandian*), *20 Gun Xiu Fang, Shiquan St., 215006. Four stars, Tel. 5194642. Fax 5191608. $88 net. Dist.R.W. 10 km. Credit Cards.*

Walk to Master of Nets Garden. Built 1986. Ren. 1991. San Shiu Lou (main building), seven stories, 212 rooms. IDD, B.C. Great garden. Generally run-down. Dark. Needs better management. Cantonese and Sichuan food.

ASTER HOTEL (*Yadu Dajiudian*), *156 Sanxiang Rd., 215004. Four stars, Tel. 8091888. Fax 8291838. Dist.R.W. six km. Credit Cards.*

Built 1991. 29 stories, 410 rooms. IDD, B.C., USTV. Food Street with Cantonese, Chaozhou and Suzhou snacks. Revolving restaurant, 24-hour room service. Outdoor pool. Clinic.

SUZHOU HOTEL (*Fandian*), *115 Shi Quan St., 215006. Four stars, Tel. 5204646. Fax 5204015, 5209191. $70 to $100. Dist.R.W. seven km. Credit Cards.*

Quiet setting in garden. Built 1958. Ren.1992, 1996. Total 321 rooms. Newer 1992 section better with 174 rooms. B.C. IDD. USTV. A few chipped dishes. Sauna. Stuffy. Poor maintenance. Large garden.

WHERE TO EAT

The **BAMBOO GROVE HOTEL** has the best western food. The Bamboo Grove and Aster Hotel have good Cantonese food.

The **SONGHELOU (PINE AND CRANE RESTAURANT)**, *141 Guanqian Street, Tel. 7277006*, is famous from Qing emperor Qianlong's time. The **WANGSI RESTAURANT** specializes in local food like beggar's chicken. A movie was made about the **DE YUE LOU RESTAURANT**. All three are on the same street downtown near the Taoist Temple off Guanqian Street.

The **EAST VENICE RESTAURANT**, *8 Renmin Road, Tel. 5295969*, is good. A night food street market is on Guanqian Street.

SEEING THE SIGHTS

If you only have one day, you might consider visiting two of the gardens, Tiger Hill, one handicraft factory, and definitely a boat trip. However, there is enough to do here for three hurried days, more if you just want to poke around in museums, meditate in temples, and indulge in shopping for silk.

Shizilin Yuan (Lion Forest) **Garden**, *23 Yulin Road, Tel. 7272428*, four kilometers from the Nan Lin Hotel, was built in 1350 during the Yuan and is so named because the teacher of the monk who built it lived on Lion Rock Mountain. Some of the rockeries are shaped like lions. It was once owned by the granduncle of American architect I.M. Pei.

At the entrance, the maze inside the rockeries is notable, and some of the rocks have clearly been carved and then weathered in **Lake Tai** for scores or hundreds of years. The rock structure above the stone boat was a waterfall, which in the early days was hand-poured. The **Standing-in-Snow Study** is exquisite, so named because a student once went to visit his teacher there and, too polite to awaken him, stood patiently in the snow.

Changlang Ting Yuan (Gentle Wave or Surging Wave) **Pavilion**, *3 Canglang Street, Tel. 5306148*, is one kilometer from the Nan Lin Hotel. About two acres, it is the only garden that is not surrounded completely by a view-blocking wall. A pond lies outside to be enjoyed from a View-Borrowing Pavilion. A hall houses 125 steles with the images of 500 sages, dating from the kingdom of Wu to the Qing. Carved in relief in 1840, the deeds of each one are confined to 16 poetic characters. The poet Su Tzu-mei founded the garden, one of the oldest in the city, in 1044 (Song). In the Yuan and early Ming, it was a Buddhist nunnery.

Look for the set of dark brown furniture made from mahogany tree roots that look like chocolate-covered peanuts. This garden is not as spectacular as the others, so if you're short on time, skip it.

Yi Yuan (Joyous) **Garden**, *340 Renmin Road, Tel. 5249317*, was built by a Qing official and, at 100 years old, it is the newest. It has taken the best of all the gardens, concentrating them into about an acre. The rockeries are from other older gardens. The dry boat is an imitation of the one in the Humble Administrator's.

*Liu Yuan (Lingering) **Garden**, *79-80 Liuyuan Road, Tel. 5337940*, six kilometers from the Nan Lin Hotel, was originally built in 1525 (Ming). The eight-acre garden consists of halls and studios in the east sector, ponds and hills in the central, and woods and hills in the western section. In late autumn, these woods are red. Look through some of the 200 different flower windows at the scene beyond. You are in a living picture gallery. A huge five-ton, six-meter-high rock from Lake Tai stands in the eastern section.

Wangshi Yuan (Master of Nets) **Garden**, *11 Kuotao Xiang, Tel. 5203514*, 0.5 kilometers from the Nan Lin Hotel, originally built in 1140 (Southern Song), is one of the best. The Metropolitan Museum of Art in New York City has reproduced the Peony courtyard as the Astor Chinese Garden Court.

This garden is very pretty, especially when decorated with colorful palace lanterns for the Classical Night Garden in summer when tourists rotate among the pavilions to hear musicians and storytellers and to see folk dancers. Don't miss this charming experience.

*Zhuozheng Yuan** (Humble Administrator's) **Garden**, *178 Dong Bei Street, Tel. 7203378*, five kilometers from the Nan Lin Hotel, is the largest in Suzhou. A humble administrator, a dismissed official, laid it out in 1522 (Ming). Later it was divided into three gardens after the owner lost it gambling. The largest and most open of the gardens, three-fifths water, is typical of the water country south of the Yangtze. Almost all buildings are close to water. If you only have a short time, visit the central part. At **Fragrant Island**, there is a two-story stone 'dry boat' complete with gangplank, 'deck,' and 'cabin.' The **Mandarin Duck Hall** has blue windows and classical furniture, with live ducks in a cage at the side of the hall. A garden blooms within a garden. A covered walkway in the western section follows the natural contours of the land. Look also for the Little Flying Rainbow Bridge, the Pavilion of Expecting Frost, and the Pavilion of Fragrant Snow and Azure Clouds.

Note also the **Lingering and Listening Hall** for listening (of course) to the raindrops on the lotus leaves. Who else but aristocratic Chinese constructed buildings just for something like that! Ramps instead of stairs make one wonder about wheelchairs back then. Look for the wood carving and the cloud designs on the glass. A 200-year-old miniature pomegranate tree is included in the excellent collection of penjing-bonsai. A museum of gardens with titles in English is near the exit.

Important but not spectacular is the *Hu Qiu** (Tiger) **Hill**, *8 Huqiu Shan, Tel. 5314921*, nine kilometers from the Nan Lin Hotel. The 45-acre site is northwest of the city outside the moat. The grounds were an island many years ago, but are now about 100 kilometers from the East China Sea. It was originally called Hill of Emergence from the Sea. Named Tiger Hill because a white tiger appeared here at one time, the entrance is the head, the pagoda is the tail, and in-between is the back of the tiger.

On the right after entering is the Sword Testing Rock which **He Lu**, King of Wu, was supposed to have broken in the sixth century B.C. On the left is a large magic rock. If the stone you throw stays on top, you will give birth to sons, so beware! On the right is a pavilion with red characters, the Tomb of the Good Wife, a widow sold by the wicked brothers of her deceased husband to another man. Forced to be a courtesan, she committed suicide.

Here is also where Fu Chai, King of Wu, is said to have built a tomb for his father, He Lu, in the early fifth century B.C., after which the tomb builders were slaughtered to keep the location a secret. Hence, no one is sure if this is indeed the right place. If you look carefully, legend has it that you can still see the red of the blood on the large flat rock!

The **tomb of He Lu** is believed to be beyond the moon gate. In 1956, unsuccessful attempts were made to enter it. The foundation of the pagoda started to protest. Inside are supposed to be 3000 iron and steel swords. You can see the cave, blocked by large, cut stones, from the bridge to the pagoda. Is it or isn't it the 2500-year-old tomb? The two holes on the bridge were for hauling up buckets of water.

The **Tiger Hill Pagoda**, known also as Leaning Tower of Suzhou, was built originally in the 10th century A.D. (Northern Song) but was burned down thrice. The latest repairs were made in 1981, when its foundation was strengthened. At 47.5 meters high, it tends to tilt to the northwest. Pilgrims used to climb the 53 steps here on their knees. Note the Indian arches.

GRAND CANAL BOAT TOURS

The Grand Canal Boat Tours go from:
• *the Panmen Water Gate, 2 Dongda Street, Tel. 5230827 and passes the Wumen Arch Bridge, and Ruiguang Pagoda eastward along the city wall. Some boats go to the Precious Belt Bridge with its 53 arches and return along the same route.*
• *Suzhou to Wuxi, 45 kilometers in three hours.*
• *Suzhou to Jiaxing near Hangzhou, 3 1/2 to 4 hours.*
Dragon boats can meet tour groups at the train station on request to take you to your hotel.

If You Have More Time

The **Beisi Ta** (North Temple) **Pagoda**, *Tel. 7531197*, at the north end of Renmin Road at 652, is nine stories and 76 meters high, the tallest pagoda south of the Yangtze River, first built in the 10th century. You can climb it. On the grounds are exhibition halls and across the street to the northwest is the excellent Silk Museum (see below).

The Theatrical, Embroidery, Silk, and Folk Arts museums are relatively near this pagoda and are worth visits:

The **Silk Museum**, *661 Renmin Road, Tel. 7276538*, should fascinate lovers of textiles. You can see reproductions of ancient brocades, giant looms (with weavers balanced on top), and 'stone washing' which is actually stone grinding. The **Theatrical Museum** is in the fancy old Shaanxi Provincial Guild Hall in the east of the old city. The **Folk Arts Museum**, *Tel. 7272349*, is charming.

The **Suzhou Museum**, *204 Dongbei Street, Tel. 7274203*, near the Humble Administrator's Garden was the official residence of a royal Taiping prince, first built in 1860.

Han Shan (Cold Mountain) **Temple**, *8 Hanshansi Long, Tel. 5336317*, 10 kilometers west of the Nan Lin Hotel, was the home of two Tang monks, Han Shan and Shide. To the right of the central, gold Sakyamuni Buddha is Wu Nan, the young disciple who wrote the sutras; the older man is disciple Ja Yeh. Japanese pirates stole the original bell but Japan replaced it with a bell cast about 100 years ago. Originally built in the Liang dynasty (sixth century), the current buildings are Qing and the pagoda was built in 1993.

Travel agents organize special excursions to hear the bronze bells here on midnight December 31, New Year's Eve. If you hear the bells chime 108 times on this night, you should have few troubles in life! Monks chant and pray for guests. Lions and dragons dance. Open 7 pm to 1 am on this occasion.

Xiyuan (West Garden) **Temple**, *18 Liuyuan Road, Tel. 5334359,* is also very beautiful. Near the Han Shan Temple, it is the largest group of Buddhist buildings in Suzhou. It was originally built in the 16th century but was destroyed by fire, and rebuilt in 1892.

The ceiling in the main building is ornamented with magnificent bats (happiness) and cranes (long life), as in Beijing's Forbidden City. The central Buddhas are seven meters tall, including base and mandala. Behind the Buddhas to the right is the Bodhisattva of Wisdom, with a crown on his head. To the left is the Bodhisattva of Universal Benevolence.

The 500 arhats here are worth studying, each face so real, expressive, profound, individual. Outstanding is the crazy monk, who can look sad, happy, or wry, depending on the angle from which you look at him. Gilded on modeled clay, each statue is larger than life. But can you find any women? Enjoy those incense burners. During the Great Leap Forward (1958-60) they were supposed to be smelted. But the CITS director said no! Look also for the five-colored carp and giant soft-shelled turtles in the pond in the back garden.

A visit to the pearl farm in the eastern suburbs is fun for groups. After a 15-minute boat ride, you can choose a living, breathing oyster and keep the pearls found within. (Pick a big one.) Contact **Suzhou Fishery Industry**, *Marine Tourism Service, Huangshiqiao, Fengmen, Suzhou 215006. Tel. 7261987.*

The 16 colored arhats in the **Zijin** (Purple Gold) **Nunnery** are older (Song) and said to be better than those in the West Garden Temple. See them for yourself in **Luhua Cun**, *Dokongshan, Tel. 6201126.* The **Twin Pagodas**, almost in the middle of Suzhou, are known as the big and small 'brushes' (used by Confucius for writing). They were built in the Song in honor of the sage.

The **Xuan Miao Guan** (Mysterious Wonder Taoist Temple), *Guanqian Street, Tel. 7274348,* in the middle of the city, has been described as the tallest, most magnificent temple in the area and probably in China. Three giant, gilded sculptures of the founders of Taoism dominate. Originating in the Jin (265-420 A.D.), the temple's current central Sanqing Hall was built in the Southern Song.

In **Guang Fu,** 25 kilometers east of the city, is a tiny village amid fields of stunted mulberry trees. Here all the women embroider in their homes. I watched a 73-year old work on a Japanese obi. A visit can also give you an opportunity to experience rural life.

The Singapore Labour Federation and Suzhou Municipality are building a huge industrial, commercial, and tourism project in the eastern suburbs. Its 'integrated resort facilities' will include a 36-hole golf course and amusement park. All should be completed before the year 2003.

Walks

The gardens are good but can be crowded at times, a little difficult if you want fast-moving exercise. They are lovely, however. Try the large Humble Administrator's and Tiger Hill.

Explore the alleys and follow the canals near the Nan Lin, Suzhou, and Bamboo Grove Hotels. Some gardens are open 7:30 am to 5:30 pm or 8 am to 5:00 pm in summer, until 4:30 pm in winter.

NIGHTLIFE & ENTERTAINMENT

On summer evenings, Chinese musicians perform classical Chinese music in the Master of Nets Garden. Popular bars are in the Aster and Bamboo Grove Hotels. A night market is in front of the Taoist temple on Guanqian Street.

A **Silk Festival** takes place in early September.

SHOPPING

Inkstones, brushes, jewelry, embroideries, silks, traditional musical instruments, antiques, iron reproductions of ancient relics, excellent woodblock prints of Suzhou, and reproductions of some of the arhats are available. This is one of the best cities to buy sandalwood fans (always smell them to be sure but it might just be perfume) and rubbings.

For general shopping, head for **Ca Yuan Chang Industrial Products Market** which is linked under Renmin Road by a tunnel to the **Number One Department Store**, *Tel. 5223328.* The Ca Yuan Chang is better. Behind the Number One is Guanqian Street, closed to vehicles and full of stalls, tailors, shops and the Taoist Temple. Except for hawkers with loudspeakers, shopping here is even pleasant. You can rest in any of the nearby restaurants and even Kentucky Fried Chicken.

For silk, the **Suzhou Silk Garments Factory**, *46 Lu Jia Xiang, 215001, Tel. 7271278, 7271453,* has a 20-minute show of ancient and modern clothes and a wide selection of garments and cloth for sale. They have the most variety and best quality, but higher prices. Groups should be able to get a 15% discount. The store takes credit cards. Other silk factories also have demonstrations of how silk is made.

Prices at the **Silk Museum** are about the same as the Silk Factory but it has more interesting colors. Compare prices at the **Huanghuo Chodu** (Princess Silk Capital), *537 Renmin Road, Tel. 7292245*, open 8:30 am to 7:30 pm. You might also find small quantities of silk in stalls around tourist attractions where you can haggle. But silk in most places frequented by tourists and offering credit card service is expensive. Prices are high but the quality is good at the **Bamboo Grove Hotel**; compare prices down the street at the **CYTS Store**, *15-2 Minzhi Road, Tel. 5201461*. Look into stores at the Nan Lin and Nan Yuan Hotels (across from each other).

Local Chinese buy their silk in department stores, or at the **Dong Hu Silk Factory Store**, *540 Renmin Road*. They talked also about the **Quan Kai Xiang store** for goods by the yard. The cheapest silk would be from one of the many non-tourist silk factories in the suburbs. Pretend you're in the business and are looking for samples. Unfortunately, there's not much variety as each factory specializes in one or two designs.

There are lots of tiny curio shops on **Shiquan Road** near the Nan Lin Hotel and some outside the Bamboo Grove Hotel. Look also in the hotels. For antiques and crafts, there's the **Suzhou Cultural Relics Shop**, *238 Renmin Road, Tel. 5202439*, with pottery, porcelain, ivory, wood and bamboo carving, old jewelry, snuff bottles, paintings, rice paper and bronze. There's also hardwood furniture, jadeware, old textiles, ink-slabs and seals.

The **Suzhou Shopping Centre** is at *9 Renmin Road, Tel. 5206307*.

PRACTICAL INFORMATION
- **Business Hours**, 9 am to 9 pm daily for stores; 8 to 11 am and 1 to 5 pm for offices, five days a week.
- **CITS** and **CTS**, *115 Shiquan Street, 215006. CITS, Tel. 5303952, 5222401. Fax 5225931, 5223793. CTS, Tel. 5221276, 5239278. Fax 5225931*
- **CYTS Tours**, *102 Zhu Hui Road, 215007. Tel. 5291746. Fax 5291929*
- **Telephone Code**, *0512*
- **Tourist Bureau**, *115 Shiquan Street, 215006. Tel. 5226280. Fax 5235535*
- **Tourism Hotline**, *Tel. 5223327. For complaints.*

WUXI

(Wushi)

Wuxi sits on the northern shore of Lake Taihu and south of the Yangtze River in southern Jiangsu province. This industrial and resort city also straddles the ancient Grand Canal. Wuxi is one of the oldest cities in China, founded over 3000 years ago during the Zhou dynasty. After deposits of tin became depleted, its name was changed to Wuxi, meaning 'no tin.'

The urban population is one million. The hottest weather is in July at 38 degrees centigrade; the coldest in January, minus four degrees centigrade. The annual precipitation is 1056 millimeters mainly in June.

ARRIVALS & DEPARTURES

Wuxi is less than an hour by train from Suzhou, and 100 kilometers west of Shanghai on the Beijing-Shanghai railway. By car, take State Highway Number 312 and the Shanghai-Nanjing Expressway.

It is a two-hour flight south of Beijing and also has air connections with four other cities and maybe eventually Hong Kong.

ORIENTATION

Contrary to its image of a placid, sail-filled lake, Wuxi has the fifth highest industrial output in China. But it's known as a beauty spot, with classical Chinese gardens and a famous lake from which many of the best gardens get their rockery. Notable are the Liyuan (Li Garden) and Meiyuan (Plum Garden).

WHERE TO STAY

The best hotel is the **Wuxi Grand**, the second best the **Holiday Inn Milido** and then the **Lakeside**. The Grand and the Holiday Inn are downtown, and convenient for business people and tourists who want to shop. But the best choice for tourists is the Lakeside right beside Lake Taihu next to Li Garden, and close to the big buddha. The Taihu Sunshine has a good view of the lake.

HOLIDAY INN MILIDO *(Milido Dajiudian), 2 Liangxi Rd. 214062. Three stars, Tel. 6765665, Fax 6701668, 6707348. In US, Tel. 1-800-HOLIDAY. Dist.A.P. 20 km. Dist.R.W. five km. Dist. Lake Taihu four km. Credit Cards.*

Built 1987-1988. Ren. 1995. Nine stories, 251 rooms including apartments with kitchenettes. Pub. Pool. B.C., IDD. Clinic. Gym and USTV.

LAKESIDE HOTEL *(Hubin Fandian), Hubin Rd., Li Yuan, 214075. Three stars. Tel. 607888, 603824. Fax 602637. Dist.A.P. 23 km. Dist.R.W. 12 km. Dist.city center four km.*

Built 1976-78. Ren. 1995. 10 stories. 186 modest, comfortable rooms. B.C., pool. IDD. USTV. Clinic. B.C. Choice Hotels International Management. Has floating restaurant on Taihu.

TAIHU (SUNSHINE) HOTEL *(Fandian), Mei Yuan, 214064. Tel. 6707888. Fax 6702771. Dist.A.P.26 km. Dist.R.W.14 km. Credit Cards.*

Thirty minute walk to lake. Built 1991, Jing Ming Lou. Three stars. 90 rooms. B.C. IDD. H.K.J.V. The Taihu itself has never practiced good maintenance. The Taihu became the Sunshine Hotel in 1995.

WUXI GRAND HOTEL *(Dajiudian), 1 Liangqing Rd., 214061, Four stars, Tel. 6706789, 606789, 666789. Fax 200991, 362055. Dist.A.P. 22 km. Dist.R.W. four km. Credit Cards.*

Built 1989. 22 stories. 342 rooms. Non-smoking floor. B.C., IDD. CITS and CTS. Japanese, Cantonese and Sichuan food. Should have indoor pool by now. Has gym. Massage. Clinic. Cheaper west wing. Pan Pacific management.

WHERE TO EAT

Local specialties include ice fish, spareribs, deep-fried eel, crabs, and shrimp. The hotels listed above will be your best bet here.

SEEING THE SIGHTS

The **Liyuan** has a 'thousand-steps veranda,' with 89 windows on the inside wall. At the **Meiyuan**, the plum blossoms are best appreciated in the early spring. The **Yuantouzhu** (Turtle Head) Islet is in Lake Tai, (the lake is 2,235 square kilometers), 17 kilometers southwest of the city. Here some of the sets of the **Tang Cheng Television Studio** are open to tourists. The Tang dynasty palace where the famous concubine Yang Guo Fei dazzled the emperor is there with guards dressed in period uniforms and armed with swords and spears. The studio also produced the Chinese television series *Romance of the Three Kingdoms* and it has 20 reconstructed warships on the lake from 1,800 years ago. Don't waste time at the adjacent Journey to the West exhibition. It is not that well done.

On this peninsula also and opening soon if not already is a 88 meter-high standing **Buddha**, 400 tons of bronze, the biggest in the world. Five kilometers north of the Buddha is the three-star holiday resort **BEER GARDEN HOTEL** (aimed at domestic and Asian tourists) and a New Zealand joint-venture brewery, at *Mei Liang Road, Mashan, Wuxi 214092. Tel. 6795891, 6795736 or fax 6796704.*

Historical sites include **Xihui Park**, west of the city, with its **Tianxia Di'Er Quan** (Heavenly Second Spring, dating from the Tang), **Jichang**

(Garden to Entrust One's Happiness) and the **Longguang** (Dragon Light) **Pagoda** (great view), the latter two from the Ming. Jichang is one of the best-known South China gardens. A copy of this garden is in the Summer Palace in Beijing. Bells ring at midnight 'for luck' on December 31 at the **Kaiyuan Temple**.

Wuxi is also a silk-producing center, the hills around the city filled with mulberry trees. Tourists can learn about silk, from silkworm rearing through the printing and dyeing process at a silk factory. There are the **Hui Shan Clay Figures factory boat trips** with lunch on Lake Tai and trips on the Grand Canal. You can take a 15 kilometer cruise in Wuxi itself. A trip across Lake Tai can also involve a tour of Huzhou (ancient writing brush factory) before you go to Hangzhou.

You can also visit **Huaxi Village**, 1 1/2 hours away for demonstrations of ancient farming and village life. A good time to visit is the **Mid-Autumn Festival**, with lots of colored lanterns, moon cakes, and an evening cruise on the lake and, one hopes, a full moon.

Festivals

The week-long **Lake Tai Arts Festival** features folk dancing and singing; and the **Cherry** and **Pottery festivals** are held in April.

SHOPPING

Good locally-made products include clay figurines, embroidery, fresh-water pearls, pearl face cream, and silk. Also made in the province are porcelain and Yixing pottery (especially tea pots in all kinds of shapes and sizes). **Number One Silk Spinning Mill** has a display of silkworms and reasonable prices for garments. The clothes at the **Number Three Silk Spinning Factory** seemed too expensive.

The **Friendship Store** here is at *28 Liangxi Road, 214062. Tel. 668915* and is good with an antique store beside it. The **Wuxi Antique Store** is at *466 Zhongshan Road, Tel. 226520*.

EXCURSIONS FROM WUXI

You can take excursions to nearby (69 kilometers) Yixing purple sandware **ceramic factory** and the **Yixing caves**, and to **Jiangyin** (home of Ming dynasty scientist and traveler Xu Xiake). Jiangyin and **Huaxi village** can be combined in one day's sightseeing. See also *Changzhou, Zhenjiang, Yangzhou, Suzhou, Nanjing,* and *Shanghai*.

PRACTICAL INFORMATION

• **Business Hours**, offices 8 am to 5 pm five days a week. Stores 9 am to 7 pm daily.

• **CITS**, *Tel. 2706702, 2303420. Fax 2701489.*
• **CTS**, *59 Chexhang Road, 214002, Tel. 2304906. Fax 2302743*
• **CYTS**, *6th Floor, the Youth Culture Center, Jin Yan Dong Bridge, 214023. Tel. 5748904. Fax 5757653*
• **Telephone Code**, *0510*
• **Wuxi Municipal Travel and Tourism Bureau**, *7 Xingsheng Road, 214002. Tel. 2704314. Fax 2729644 or 2703851, or 26 Meiliang Road, Mashan, Wuxi. 214092. Tel. 6795177. Fax 6795003*
• **Wuxi Overseas Tourists Corp.**, *7 Xing Sheng Road, 214002; Tel. 2712303. Fax 2716780. Complaints to Xu Jirong or Wang Bosheng*

XIAMEN

(Hsiamen, Amoy)

Xiamen is on the southeast coast of Fujian (Fukien) province, over 200 kilometers across the straits from Taiwan, but just 2 1/2 kilometers from Quemoy (Jinmen/Kinmen), one of Taiwan's offshore islands.

Xiamen was the home base of General Zheng Chenggong (Cheng Cheng-kung, or Koxinga), who repelled the Manchu invaders for a while and then rid Taiwan of the Dutch in 1662. Xiamen was a minor trading port when the British seized it in 1839. In 1842, the Treaty of Nanking allowed foreigners to build residences and warehouses here. For many years, especially in the late 1950s, both explosives and propaganda shells were lobbed to China from Quemoy, off the southeast coast of Xiamen.

Xiamen is part of a 131 square-kilometer Special Economic Zone. While the national language is also spoken, local people speak the Xiamen dialect, Fukienese, which is different from both Cantonese and Mandarin. Fukienese is also spoken by the majority of people on Taiwan.

The hottest weather is July and August when the temperature soars to 38 degrees centigrade; the coldest is in February, when it dips to minus four degrees centigrade. The annual precipitation is 1206 millimeters, mainly from May to July. The urban population is 370,000.

ARRIVALS & DEPARTURES

You can reach Xiamen by air, sea, or air-conditioned bus from Guangzhou and Hong Kong. The passenger ships *Gulangyu* and *Jimei* sail every Tuesday and Friday between Hong Kong and Xiamen, a journey of 17 hours. Direct trains are available from Nanjing and Shanghai. Ships and direct flights should soon be available from Taiwan.

It is a 1 1/2-hour flight southwest of Shanghai and one hour flight northeast of Guangzhou. It is linked by air with 38 other Chinese cities and Hong Kong, Jakarta, Kuala Lumpur, Macau, Manila, Penang, and Singapore.

ORIENTATION
If you only have one day for sightseeing, take in Gulangyu, South Putuo Temple, and hurry through Jimei.

WHERE TO STAY
Fujian is particularly busy with Taiwanese visitors and business people. Reservations are recommended. The top hotel is the **Holiday Inn Crowne Plaza Harbourview** downtown. The **Mandarin** has a quiet, isolated setting on a hill surrounded by factories. The **Lujiang** has a historical location on the waterfront, close to shopping and the Gulangyu ferry pier. We like its old architecture but it was rundown the last time we saw it. An Omni Hotel joint venture should open soon.

HOLIDAY INN CROWNE PLAZA HARBOURVIEW *(Haijin Jiari Dajiudian), 12-8 Zhen Hai Rd., 361001. Aiming for five stars. Tel. 2023333. Fax 2036666. Dist.A.P. 15 km. Dist.R.W. six km. Dist.ferry 0.6 km. Credit Cards.*

Built 1992. 22 stories, 367 rooms. IDD. B.C., USTV. In-room safes. Non-smoking rooms and executive floors. American Express, Philippine Airlines, and Silkair offices. Sichuan and Cantonese food. 24-hr. room service. Pool. Gym. Clinic. Planning tennis court and golf packages.

LUJIANG HOTEL *(Binguan), 54 Lujiang Rd., 361001. Three stars, Tel. 2022922. Fax 2024644. Credit Cards.*

Built 1989. Six stories. Large rooms. IDD. B.C. Sichuan, Cantonese, Chaozhou and continental food.

OMNI MARCO POLO HOTEL, *Hubin Road in the Yuandang New Urban District of the Special Economic Zone.*

Seven stories, 265 rooms including one executive floor. In-room safes, IDD, and USTV. Shuttle bus to city centre, clinic, gym, B.C., in-room movies, non-smoking rooms, sauna, swimming pool and 24-hour room service.

XIAMEN MANDARIN HOTEL *(Yue Hua Jiudian), Huli Dist., 361006. Four stars. Dist.A.P.six km. Dist.R.W.10 km. Tel. 6023333. Fax 6021431. Credit Cards.*

Built 1984; three stories, 74 rooms. Ren. 1988; now seven stories, 133 rooms, 22 two-story villas. Conference hall, sauna, jacuzzi, health club, French, Japanese, Sichuan, and Cantonese food, pool, bowling, tennis, shuttle bus to city. IDD, USTV. Adding another 300 rooms. H.K.J.V.

XIAMEN MIRAMAR *(Meilihua Dajiudian), Xinglong Rd., Huli Dist., 361006. Three stars, Tel. 6031666. Fax 6021814. Credit Cards.*

Built 1988, ren. 1996-97. Dist.A.P. five km. Dist.R.W. six km. Near government trade offices. Ren. 1992. 12 stories, 128 large rooms. IDD, B.C., USTV. Gym, pool. Ask about direct computer hookup to business satellite. Singapore J.V. (Eastwind International Hotels).

WHERE TO EAT

Fujian food is much like Cantonese, and heavy on seafoods, of course, with some distinctive dishes. See Chapter 11, *Food & Drink*, for recommended local dishes.

Try the **HAO QING XIANG RESTAURANT** and the vegetarian food at the **Nan Putuo Temple**. Hotels have the best food, however.

SEEING THE SIGHTS

The southeastern part of the city contains the downtown shopping area, the botanical gardens (where among the tropical and subtropical plants is a redwood tree brought by then-U.S. President Richard Nixon). Also in this area are the South Putuo Temple, Xiamen University (built by Tan Kah Kee in 1921), and the ferry pier to Gulangyu.

The 1,000-year-old **Nan Putuo** (South Putuo) **Temple** is named after the home of the Goddess of Mercy. Most of the current buildings are from the 1920s and 1930s, but the tablets, scrolls, sculptures, bells, etc., were made in the Song and Ming. On the lotus base of the statue of Buddha is carved the biography of Sakyamuni, and the story of the monk Xuanzang who went to India. The eight three-meter-high 'imperial tablets' in Mahavira Hall tell about the Qing suppression of an uprising and are written in Manchu and Chinese. Most famous is the stunning, three-faced, multi-armed statue of Guanyin. A festival is held here New Year's Eve.

Behind the temple is **Five Old Men Peaks**, which you can climb for a good view of the Taiwan Straits. The famous Chinese writer Lu Xun taught at **Xiamen University** in 1926-1927 and a five-room memorial hall on his life is here. He helped to found the **Museum of Anthropology**, with exhibits from prehistoric man to the Qing, and relics from the national minorities. Look also for the Australian boomerang and the 700 year-old Japanese sword.

At the foot of Five Old Men Peaks is the **Overseas Chinese Museum**, outlining the contributions of natives who emigrated overseas.

See the Islands

You can charter a tour boat around the islands. **Gulangyu** (Drum Wave) **Island** is 1.7 hilly square kilometers, seven minutes across the 'Egret River' by ferry. Ferries are every five to 15 minutes. The Gulangyu population is 25,000. Formerly the foreign ghetto, it is good for another half day unless you want to hike or go swimming too. It has the best beach (**Gangzi Hou**), frangipani, flame trees, magnolias, and other heavily scented trees, and tiny shops. A very charming collection of old mansions built for foreigners have now been converted into guest houses.

Gulangyu is a car- and bicycle-free resort area, great for children and relaxing. It is cleaner and more prosperous-looking than the fishing villages of Hong Kong's outlying islands, to which it bears some resemblance. Staying here, however, makes it difficult for hectic sightseeing and shopping unless a special ferry to the guest houses is laid on. The dominating statue is of Koxinga. Gulangyu has two small museums, two churches (one from 1882), and a temple. It formerly had 14 foreign consulates. A high percentage of music lovers live here and you will probably hear strains of Bach and Verdi floating on the breeze. The island has a concert hall, which is especially good for chamber music groups.

Everyone must climb 90-meter-high **Riguang Yan** (Sunlight Rock), the highest peak here, for the view and the story of the two devoted egrets, the male killed by a greedy, unromantic goshawk. Also here is the **Lotus Flower Nunnery** (also known as Sunshine Temple), the camp where Koxinga stationed his men, and Zheng Chenggong Memorial Hall, with souvenirs of his life, and a history written by a Dutchman about the fall of Taiwan/Formosa. The **city museum** is nearby.

The **Shuzhuang Garden** was built by a Taiwan resident who moved here after the Japanese took over that island in the late 1890s. Unlike most gardens of China, it incorporates the sea into its design. 'The garden is in the sea and the sea is in the garden.' You can rent sailboards near the ferry pier.

Jimei, 2.83 square kilometers, is worth an hour and is 15 kilometers north of downtown. You can reach it by 2.8-kilometer granite causeway from Xiamen Island on the road to Quanzhou. Eighty percent of the 23,000 people here have relatives abroad. On Jimei is a most interesting monument built by an Overseas Chinese philanthropist, Tan Kah Kee, who made his money from rubber, rice, and pineapples in Singapore. **Turtle Garden**, built in 1950, is an encyclopedia in stone, full of pictures of the things Mr. Tan wanted to teach people: factories, machinery, exotic animals, Chinese literature, history, and culture. How many scenes can you identify? His elaborate tomb is typically horseshoe-shaped. His biography is in pictures around the tomb.

Nearby is the huge Jimei Middle School, one of many which he financed. Here, mainly Overseas Chinese students from all over the world come to study. For those curious about the man, a tiny museum nearby also shows pictures of his life.

EXCURSIONS FROM XIAMEN

In the vicinity of Xiamen, closer to Fuzhou, is the **tomb of Koxinga**. Reached by road is the historical city of **Quanzhou** and the capital of Fujian, **Fuzhou**. See separate listings.

SHOPPING

Locally made are Caiza silk figures, lacquer thread-decorated vases, colored clay figures, and bead embroidery. You may want to try the Yupi peanuts, the gongtang crisp peanut cakes, dried longan fruit, and preserved olives. Locally grown are longan, litchis, peanuts, sugarcane, and, of course, rice. The main shopping street is **Zhongshan Road**.

Highlights include: **Xiamen Antiques and Curios Store**, *211 Zhongshan Road*, *Tel. 2023363*; **Friendship Store**, *Tel. 2023817, 2024385*; **Tourist Shopping Center**, *103 Si Ming Bei Road, Tel. 2020133*; **Lacquer Thread Sculpture Factory**, *Tel. 2020529*; **Arts and Crafts Factory**, *Tel. 2024784*; **Arts and Crafts Factory**, *Tel. 2024784*.

Also open is the **Donghai Shopping Center**, *Zhongshan Bei Road, Tel. 2021094*.

PRACTICAL INFORMATION

- **Business Hours**, 8 am to 5 pm for offices, five to 5 1/2 days a week. 8 am to 9 pm for stores.
- **CITS**, *Second floor, 2 Zhongshan Road, 361001. Tel. 2031781, 2078831. Fax 2025077. Tel. also 5051825. Fax 5051819*
- **CTS**, *Overseas Chinese Building, 70-74 Xin Hua Road, 361003; Tel. 2022053, 2025602. Fax 2031862*
- **CYTS**, *65 Bai Road, 361003. Tel. 2053188. Fax 2020024*
- **Telephone Code**, *0592*
- **Xiamen Tourism Bureau**, *2/F, 7 Haihou Road, Tel. 2054021, 2054022*

YANGZHOU

(Yangchow)

Yangzhou is 20 kilometers north of the Yangtze on the Grand Canal in Jiangsu province. Its population is 400,000.

Yangzhou is almost 2,500 years old and famous for its gardens and pavilions. It is a nice change from the hectic pace of other Chinese cities. Because of its location, it was a very prosperous port after the Sui emperors had the canal built. In the Tang dynasty, it was the residence of over 5,000 foreigners. One of the Prophet Mohammed's descendants is buried here, and starting in 1282 Marco Polo is said to have spent three years as inspector here. Yangzhou's wealth declined with that of the canal, and by the Qing it was famous only as an imperial resort city.

The hottest temperature is 34 degrees centigrade in July-August; the coldest is minus two degrees centigrade in January-February. The annual precipitation is about 1000 millimeters, mainly from June to September.

ARRIVALS & DEPARTURES

Yangzhou can now be reached by ferry and bus from Zhenjiang on the south shore, two hours by expressway from Nanjing, or by boat along the Yangtze or the Grand Canal. An international airport is planned between Yangzhou and Nanjing. Until it opens, you have to use the Nanjing Airport 120 kilometers away. The closest railway is in Zhenjiang.

ORIENTATION

Yangzhou is one of the 36 historical and cultural cities protected by the State Council, and is one of the nicest cities, with lots of old Chinese architecture and a relaxed atmosphere. All new buildings must be in traditional Chinese styles and industries built in the suburbs.

If you only have one day in Yangzhou, take the 2 1/2-hour Emperor Qian Long's boat tour.

WHERE TO STAY

The best located hotels for tourists are the **Xi Yuan** and **Yangzhou**, with good gardens and within walking distance of the museum and tourist stores. The Yangzhou has more services and liveliness. Both had dirty carpets. The **Qiong Hua** seems to be the best equipped and better located for business people. Whether it can maintain its initial high quality is a question. The Yangzhou is best all around.

QIONG HUA HOTEL *(Dasha), 3 Pi Fang Street, 225001. Three stars, Tel. 231321. Fax 231079. Dist.city hall and trade offices two km. Dist.He Garden 200 meters. Credit Cards.*

Built 991. Four adjoining buildings, 22 stories. 120 rooms. IDD. B.C. Dorm. Gym and tennis, USTV.

XI YUAN HOTEL *(Fandian), 1 Fengle Shang Street, 225002. Two stars, Tel. 344888. Fax 233870. Credit Cards.*

Built 1976. 210 beds for foreigners. No western breakfast. IDD from lobby only. No elevator in five-story building. B.C.

YANGZHOU HOTEL *(Binguan), 5 Fengle Shang Street, 225002. Three stars, Tel. 342611. Fax 343599. Credit Cards.*

Built 1985. Nine stories. 150 rooms. B.C. gym, pool, IDD. Elevator.

WHERE TO EAT

Thousand-layer oily cake may sound awful, but it is delicious. People also go to Yangzhou from Nanjing just for the dumplings. Both the **Yangzhou** and **Xiyuan hotels** can reproduce a banquet from the novel *Dream of the Red Mansion* (the author's father lived here).

SEEING THE SIGHTS

Along Emperor Qian Long's boat tour you'll see:

Shouxi (Slender West) **Lake**, in the northwestern suburbs, 4.3 kilometers long and surrounded by lovely, peaceful scenes: curled-roof pavilions, the Five Pavilion Bridge, and the imposing **White Dagoba** (Qing), all packaged in the north and south Chinese garden styles. At the **Diaoyutai** (Fishing Terrace), Qing Emperor Qianlong is supposed to have fished there once. (He must have been a good politician.) The **Five Pavilion Bridge** was built on the occasion of his visit. It is best seen on the night of a full moon, when 15 moons are supposed to reflect from the water under the arches, a Chinese puzzle that must be seen to be understood.

The **Daming Temple** was founded in the fifth century. An impressive arch commemorates a famous nine-story pagoda that used to be here but was destroyed by fire in 843. The Daming has 18 three-meter-high carved Buddhist statues.

The **Jian Zhen Memorial Hall**, near Daming Temple, was built in 1973 to commemorate the 1,200th anniversary of the death of Monk Jian Zhen. It, too, is lovely in spite of its youth; it is a copy of the Toshodai Temple in Nara, Japan. This abbot of Daming Temple persisted in going to Japan to teach Buddhism in spite of five unsuccessful efforts and his blindness. He succeeded at age 66. Because he and his disciples also introduced Tang literature, medicine, architecture, sculpture, and other arts to Japan, he is highly honored in that country, where he died and is buried. A 1,000 year-old-plus statue of Jian Zhen, now a national Japanese treasure, was brought back for a visit 'because it looked homesick.'

Along the way, you can also see a delightful potted landscape garden, and the **24-Maid Bridge**. You can visit all these places on foot or by bus, but a boat is more fun. In the afternoon, there's a lacquerware, jade-carving and paper-cutting factory, and shopping.

The **Yangzhou Museum**, small, informal, and pleasant, has a Marco Polo Hall. The Italians sent a bronze lion, the symbol of Venice. Curiously, there are two Italian tombstones on display, dated 1342 and 1344.

The **Geyuan Garden**, started as a private garden, later became the home of the Ye Chun Poet's Society in the Qing. It is full of gnarled rockeries, moon gates, bamboo, latticed doorways, wavy walls, and real picture windows. The rockeries are built around a spring-summer-autumn-winter theme. Do these inspire you, too, to poetry?

The **Heyuan Garden**, in the southeastern part of the city close to the Geyuan, is typical of Yangzhou's gardens. The Islamic-styled **Tomb of Puhaddin** is on the east bank of the Grand Canal, near the Heyuan. Built in the 13th century, it contains the remains of this 16th generation descendant of Mohammed, the founder of Islam. Puhaddin (Burhdn Al-Dan) came to China as a missionary in the Southern Song. The 700-year-old **Xianhe** (Crane) **Mosque** is one of the four most famous in China, and was built between 1265 and 1275. It is worth a visit. Open daily except Fridays. A 2,000 year old Han tomb has recently opened four kilometers away.

If you have more time, Yangzhou has five kilometers of canals, a seven-story pagoda, and Guang Ling, a classic book publishing house, the only place in China where you can see the Song Dynasty printing process.

Further afield, you can visit Zhenjiang and Nanjing from here on day trips; there are longer excursions along the canal.

Festivals

The **Food Festival** is in autumn. An unusual boat festival in Qintong 60 kilometers away was held in the Qing and Ming. The Daming Temple bells bring luck to those who hear them at midnight on December 31.

SHOPPING

Locally made are lacquerware, red lacquer carving, jade carving, velvet flowers, paper cuts, and silk lanterns. At the paper-cutting factory, a master craftsman can cut lacy paper chrysanthemums for you. Yangzhou also exports potted landscapes, miniature trees and mountains.

Check out the **Friendship Store**, *454 Guoqing Bei Road*, with adjacent antique stores, and the **Yangzhou Antique and Curio Store**, *1 Yanfu Road*, selling antiques, arts, and crafts.

PRACTICAL INFORMATION

- **CITS**, *1 Upper Fengle Street, 225002, Tel. 348925. Fax 344278*
- **CYTS Tours**, *8 Xi Men Road, 225002. Tel. 344844. Fax 345070*
- **Telephone Code**, *0514*
- **Tourism Administration**, *1 Fengle Shangjie, 225002*
- **Tourist Bureau**, *1 Fengle Street, 225002. Tel. 342001*

ZHENJIANG

(Chinkiang, Chenchiang, Chenkiang)

Zhenjiang, 'to pacify the river,' is in central Jiangsu Province, where the Grand Canal meets the south bank of the Yangtze. It is bounded on three sides by hills and on the north by the Yangtze River.

Zhenjiang is an historic old city, the streets lined with plane trees, some of its houses small and whitewashed like Suzhou's, others black brick with courtyards. The city was founded in the Zhou. It boasts 2,500 years of history, including seven years as the capital of the Eastern Wu (third century), when it was called Jingko (entrance to Nanjing). In the Qin dynasty (221-206 B.C.), 3,000 prisoners were sent here to build canals and roads. Many battles were fought in the area and the city is mentioned in the *Romance of the Three Kingdoms*.

During the Yuan, Zhenjiang was visited by Marco Polo. The first British missionaries arrived in the 17th century. Toward the end of the First Opium War, it was the only city that strongly resisted the imperialists. After that failed, however, about 1,000 foreigners, mainly merchants and missionaries from Britain, Germany, and the United States lived here. The foreigners left their mark on some of the architecture.

In 1938, Marshall Chen Yi's New Fourth Army was stationed about 50 kilometers away, and some skirmishes with the Japanese took place in the area. In April 1949, the British warship *H.M.S. Amethyst*, while rescuing British citizens upriver, was caught in the crossing of the Yangtze by the People's Liberation Army and held for over three months here. The captain refused to cooperate or admit his ship fired first. Under cover of a passing passenger boat, the *Amethyst* finally escaped.

Its hottest temperature, in July and August, is 35°C, with breezes from the Yangtze; its coldest is minus three degrees centigrade from the middle to the end of January. The annual precipitation is 1000 millimeters mainly in July. The urban population is 500,000.

ARRIVALS & DEPARTURES

Zhenjiang is about one hour by train (63 kilometers) east of Nanjing, and about four hours (220 kilometers) northwest of Shanghai. The closest airport is about 60 kilometers away at Nanjing, but it should have its own airport in 1998.

ORIENTATION

Today, Zhenjiang has 500 factories and mines, and makes industrial chemicals, textiles, silk, and paper (from rice stocks) for export.

WHERE TO STAY

The Jinshan Hotel in the suburbs is adequate but smells musty. The **Zhenjiang Hotel** is better for business people and Pearl Buck fans. It is downtown near her home. The **Zhenjiang Yiquan Hotel** is four stars and new, and should be best of all. The Jinshan is in the western suburbs close to the Jinshan Temple.

JINSHAN HOTEL *(Jiudian), 1 Jinshan Xi Road, 212002. Two stars, Tel. 5623888. Fax 5624530. Dist.R.W. four km. Credit Cards.*

Built 1979. At least 143 rooms. IDD, B.C. China Eastern booking office. Number Four had dim reading lamps, but was fine. Pool and tennis. Building Number Four is undergoing renovation and will merits three stars when finished.

ZHENJIANG HOTEL, *92 Zhong Shan Xi Road, 212004. Three stars. Tel. 5233888. Fax 5231055. Dist.R.W.300 meters. Credit Cards.*

Built 1963. Six stories, 128 rooms. IDD. B.C. 188 rooms and 10 suites. USTV.

ZHENJIANG YIQUAN HOTEL, *1 Yiquan Road, 212002, Tel. 5624061. Fax 5623341. 500 meters to railway station. Credit Cards.*

Brand new, this hotel is supposed to have IDD and many other amenties.

PEARL S. BUCK, FRIEND OF CHINA

The American Nobel and Pulitzer Price-winning author **Pearl S. Buck** *(1892-1973) grew up here, studied in what is now the Zhenjiang Second Middle School (founded 1884) and taught here (1914-17), a total of 18 years. In the past, China criticized her for being 'imperialist' and ignored her writings. In the 1950s, U.S. Senator Joseph McCarthy accused her of being a Communist. Zhenjiang and sister city Tempe, Arizona, have renovated one of her homes as the Zhenjiang Friendship House or Sino-U.S. Cultural Exchange Center for the 100th anniversary of her birth.*

The home is also for the study of foreign missions and her books. They would appreciate copies of her books: **Good Earth, Imperial Women, Dragon Seed, My Several Worlds**, *etc. You can see the tomb of Buck's mother and talk with some of her old students. Pearl S. Buck has a foundation based outside Philadelphia supporting American-Asian children.*

WHERE TO EAT

A local specialty is crab cream bun, a steamed meat pastry. Make a hole first and slurp out the soup inside. Food here is concerned with fragrance, shape, and color, and is neither too sweet nor too salty. You might find your hors d'oeuvres looking like butterflies, peacocks, or fans. Everything can be dipped in vinegar.

In addition to the hotel restaurants above, try the **YANCHUN RESTAURANT**, *Renmin Street, Tel. 5271615.*

SEEING THE SIGHTS

If you only have one day, consider seeing Jinshan Hill, Jiao Shan Island, the museum, Pearl Buck's house, and the Thousand-Year-Old Street.

Tiny **Xiao Matai Jie Street**, which is four kilometers from the Jinshan Hotel, has an unusual Song or Yuan stupa built above the sidewalk. **Jiao**

Hill (150 meters high) on Jiao Shan Island is less than half a kilometer from the city (13 kilometers from the Jinshan Hotel). Up 250 steps is a magnificent view of the Yangtze. All three of Zhenjiang's hills have magnificent views of the Yangtze, and you can see the place where the Chinese held the *Amethyst*. What would you have done if you were captain?

Back at the base of Jiao Hill, you can look at the **Battery**, which was used against the British in 1842. Also below is a garden with steles of many calligraphers, including that of the father of modern calligraphy, Wang Hsi-chih, who lived 1,500 years ago. At the loquat orchard and the **Din Hui Buddhist Temple**, the Red Guards destroyed most of the Ming statues. The existing statues were made in 1979. For the ferry to Jiao Shan Island, *telephone 8815502*. It operates 8 am to 5 pm.

Jinshan (Golden Hill), *at 62 Jinshan Road, 212002, Tel. 5281631,* one kilometer from the Jinshan Hotel, looks better from afar than close up. The temple here was first built 1500 years ago (Jin) and rebuilt several times since, a victim of lightning, fire, and weather. The current pagoda was finished in 1900 with animal carvings, in time for the Empress Dowager Cixi's birthday. It reflects her crude tastes. Seven stories tall, 30 meters high, it is easier climbing up the 119 steps than down because the steps are shallow.

There are some fun **caves**, all the more interesting because of the presence in one cave of the white, ghastly-looking, life-size figure of the monk Fa Hai, and in another the two beautiful women said to be the White Snake and the Blue (sometimes Green) Snake, both fairies. The cave is said to reach Hangzhou!

Other Sights & Tours

The **museum** is housed in the former British consulate building, *85 Boxian Road and Daxi Road, 212002, Tel. 5277317, 5277143,* open 8 am to 5 pm daily) It includes the former Southern Baptist mission residences. It is four kilometers from the Jinshan Hotel. Its permanent collection includes an anchor from the British ship *Amethyst*, a land lease dated 1933 referring to the 'former British Concession lot and the tomb stone of the famous missionary Hudson Taylor.' A tiny silver coffin found under the nearby Iron Pagoda contains two gold coffins and the ashes of a Buddhist saint. Charming is the Song porcelain pillow in the shape of a sleeping child. No titles in English.

If you have more time, the **Bei Gu** (North Consolidated) **Hill**, nine kilometers from the Jinshan Hotel, is the site of the temple where Liu Pei, of *The Romance of the Three Kingdoms*, was married to the sister of Sun Chuan. After he died, his wife mourned for him at the pavilion on top of the hill now called Mourning over the River Pavilion. On this hill also is an 11th-century **Iron Pagoda** (from the Northern Song period), *Dongwu Road, Tel. 8823043*, originally nine stories high. Struck by lightning several times, it was repaired in 1960 and now has only its first, second, fifth, and sixth stories. Open 8 am to 5 pm.

Zhenjiang has the **Sericulture Research Centre** at the China Agricultural Science Academy (six kilometers away at Sibaidu, *Tel. 5626721*), and a **Silk Garment and Prop Factory** for fancy old-style garments for theatres and films, *11 Huangshan Road, 212004. Tel. 5231678 or 410 Daxi Road, Tel. 5285011.*

Zhenjiang also offers **boat tours** on the Yangtze and the Grand Canal, and a Children's Palace. Annual events include the December 31 bell tolling for luck at the Jinshan Temple.

Yangzhou is 25 kilometers away by road and ferry across the Yangtze. **Yixing** is 150 kilometers away. See separate listings.

THE SNAKE STORY & CHINESE OPERA

The story of the Snakes is also the plot of a famous Beijing opera. Briefly, the several thousand-year-old **White Snake** *from Mount Emei (the* **Blue Snake** *is the maid) becomes a beautiful woman and goes to Hangzhou. There, at the Tuanqiao (the Bridge of Breaking Up), she falls in love with a scholar, and eventually the two marry.*

The White Snake, using her magic powers, takes money from a government official to build a house, but because the official's seal is still on the money, the young man is arrested and ordered beaten for theft. The White Snake again uses her magic so that whenever her husband is beaten, the official's wife feels the pain. Consequently, the young man is expelled to Zhenjiang. After his arrival, the monk master Fa Hai, jealous of their happiness, tries to separate the couple, but the White Snake floods the area, including Jin Shan temple. They are reunited at the Tuanqiao. The unrelenting monk master retaliates by imprisoning the White Snake under the Leifeng pagoda in Hangzhou. There she is rescued by the Blue Snake. The White Snake, her husband, and her son are reunited and live happily ever after.

This is a popular Chinese tale and a study of its symbolism and the psychology of its popularity could keep a folklorist busy for years.

SHOPPING

Dashikou is Zhenjiang's main shopping area. Zhenjiang's factories make elaborate palace lanterns and are famous for their 'crystal' meat and vinegar. Also made in the city are silk, jade carvings, paper cuttings, and silk birds.

Try the **Friendship Store** at *87 Jiefang Road, Tel. 5010019.* Open 8 am to 5 pm.

PRACTICAL INFORMATION

- **Business Hours**, 8 am to 5,30 pm for offices, six days a week.
- **CITS**, *25 Jianking Road, 212001; Tel. 5236361. Fax 5244818*
- **CTS**, *6 Jiankang Road, 212001. Tel. 5016926, 5207663. Fax 5017911, 4417288*
- **Telephone Code**, *0511*
- **Tourist complaints**, *Tel. 5236996*
- **Tourist hotline**, *Tel. 5231806*
- **Zhenjiang Culture Travel Service**, *25 Jiankang Road, 212001. Tel. 5231806. Fax 5012245*. Ask for Pearl S. Buck specialist Hsu Heping.
- **Zhenjiang Friendship House**, the home of American author Pearl S. Buck, organizes tours, one of which follows Buck's life in Shanghai, Zhenjiang, Nanjing, Suxian, Taishan and Beijing. Contact Sun Weier, President, Zhenjiang Friendship House, *6 Runzhoushan Road, 212004. Tel. 5234174 or Fax 5236425.*
- **Zhenjiang Travel and Tourism Bureau**, *92 Zhongshan Xi Road, 212004. Tel. 5232959. Fax 5236425*

17. NORTH CHINA

CHENGDE

(Chengteh, Chengte, Jehol, Jehe)

This historic mountain resort of **Chengde** is in Hebei province, 250 kilometers northeast of Beijing, at an altitude of 340 meters, has an urban population of over 130,000.

Chengde oozes with history. The Qing court lived here from May to October each year. It was in a yurt here in 1793 that Lord Macartney of Britain refused to kowtow to Qing Emperor Qianlong. The emperor dismissed the Englishman as a bearer of tribute from King George III, and refused his requests for trade.

In 1860, the Manchu court fled to Chengde as Anglo–French forces approached Beijing. The death of Emperor Xianfeng in 1862 led to the rise of Cixi, the Empress Dowager, as regent. Think of the plotting that went on as he lay on his deathbed. Cixi visited here again, by train, in 1900.

In the 1930s, warlord Tang Yu Liu looted and destroyed many of the buildings. The most important have been repaired.

Its coldest temperature is minus 19 degrees centigrade; hottest is 35 degrees for a very short time. Most rain falls in June and July.

ARRIVALS & DEPARTURES

An express train leaves Beijing daily at 7:15 am, arriving at noon. You can leave Chengde daily about 2:30 pm arriving in Beijing at 7:14 pm. (Times subject to change.) It should take 2 1/2 hours by highway. The drive follows the Great Wall and you can see Simatai and Jinshan Ling. See *Great Wall*. (In the last century a one–way trip took the Manchus three to 20 days by horseback, palanquin, or bumpy chariot).

ORIENTATION

The Qing **Imperial Summer Resort** was built for Emperors Kangxi and Qianlong, not just to relax in, but to curry favor with the Mongolian nobles in the area. To help win them over, Emperor Kangxi (1703–1790) built 11 Buddhist temples also. Chengde is well worth seeing, especially if you don't go to Tibet. It is one of the 24 historical cities protected by the State Council. The Imperial Summer Resort covers an area of 5.6 million square meters, which is larger than the Summer Palace in Beijing. Most of it is surrounded by a 10 kilometer–long wall.

WHERE TO STAY

The only near–international–standard hotels for foreigners is the **Yunshan** and the **Guest House for Diplomatic Missions**. The Mongolian Yurt Holiday Village beside the Summer Palace is primarily a novelty with a good location. Think of it as camping. Also exotic is the Qiwanglou which should be better after its renovations.

GUEST HOUSE FOR DIPLOMATIC MISSIONS, *Wutie Road, Fax 2022269. Three stars.*

MONGOLIAN YURT HOLIDAY VILLAGE *(Meng Gu Bao Fandian), Wanshu Yuan, Summer Palace. Two stars. Tel. 2023094, 222269. Credit Cards.*

Direct access to the summer palace grounds next door. Built 1987. Ren. 1993. 51 felt, tent–like structures, sleeping two or three to a yurt, a total of 91 beds. IDD. On my last visit here, this place was very dirty with musty smells, peeling paint, plywood walls, no shower curtains and bad management. It does have televisions, desks, carpets and 24–hour room service. It has arranged Mongolian barbecue with singers and dancers, campfires and fireworks. Bicycles can be rented. Open April to November 30 only.

QIWANGLOU *(Binguan), Be Feng Men Gate, 1 Dong Road, 067000. Two stars, Tel. 2024385.*

Next to Summer Palace with attractive Qing architecture. Built 1985, ren. 1993. 34 small rooms.

YUNSHAN HOTEL, *6 Nanyuan Dong Rd., 067000. Three stars, Tel. 2026171. Fax 2024551. Beside river. Dist.R.W. 0.5 km Dist.Summer Palace one km.*

Near CITS, CTS, and crafts store. Built 1988, renovated 1994. 12 stories, 219 rooms. Generally good but a bit sloppy. IDD. Massage. B.C.

WHERE TO EAT

At almost every meal you'll find the locally–grown apricot kernels, sweetened and delicious. Try the sweet hawthorn juice, and almond milk.

Food is better at the hotels, but if you want to try a restaurant not part of a hotel, there's the **FANGYUANJU RESTAURANT**, *inside the mountain resort, Tel. 2023429,* for braised prawns and camel's foot in brown sauce; and the **TIANHELOU RESTAURANT**, *Zhonggutou Hutong, Tel. 2029901,* for lamb.

SEEING THE SIGHTS

You can explore the main palace and garden in one day and five of the outer temples on a second day. If you rush and avoid the climb to the Club Stone, you can cover all the open temples and the summer resort in one full, hurried day.

The Imperial Summer Resort

The **Imperial Summer Resort** has nine courtyards. It is not as palatial as Beijing's Summer Palace, but it is worth seeing. The building to the right inside the second gate has a painting of the Macartney visit and a hunting scenes (with officials sporting animal head masks and imitating mating calls to attract the animals.

To the left is the **Hall of No Worldly Lust but True Faith**, also called the Nanmu Hall because of the scented wood from which it is made. You might get a whiff of it. The emperor received subjects and envoys in this ceremonial hall. On either side are waiting rooms, one for foreign visitors and one for relatives and tribal leaders. Among the exhibits in these and other halls are Manchu coats with sleeves shaped like horses hooves, sedan chairs, an elephant dotted with pearls and brilliant blue kingfisher feather ornaments. In a hall displaying fine porcelain are Qing imitations of Ming vases.

The **Refreshing-at-Mist-Veiled-Waters Pavilion** was the imperial bedroom. On either side are the pavilions of the two empresses. The imperial bedroom has a hollow wall (seen from the back) where Cixi listened carefully as the emperor lay dying inside. As a result of her eavesdropping, she was able to seize power. Cixi lived in the Pine Crane Pavilion, which was originally built for the mother of Emperor Qianlong. The emperor used the two–story pavilion beyond to enjoy the moon with his concubines. It has no interior stairs. The Qian Long Emperor studied in the pavilion.

The **garden** is beautiful and great for walks. Visitors should be able to rent ice skates and bicycles. The trees planted by the Qing are tagged with identifications numbers. The two most influential emperors chose 72 scenic spots and wrote poems about each. Kangxis poems have four characters; Qianlongs have three. Thirty of these places are still marked by pavilions from which you can enjoy the view, including one on the top of the hill to view the snow. There is even one to view the Club Stone.

Among the buildings counterclockwise around the lake is the **Jinshan Pavilion**, copied from one of the same name in Zhenjiang, and the **Yanyulou** (Misty–Rain Tower), the latter built by Qianlong, a copy of one now destroyed in Zhejiang. It was used to watch the misty rain, of course, and to read.

On the flatland area here, Emperor Qianlong stooped to receive the equally arrogant Lord Macartney, the envoy from Britain. One of the scenes from the television movie *Marco Polo* was filmed in this garden, the scene where Polo meets the Yuan emperor.

The walled garden on the Changlang Islet is a copy of the Changlang Garden in Suzhou. Some people collect postcards when they travel; the Qianlong emperor collected buildings! Nearby, on a side road, is a herd of about 40 spotted deer, started here during the Qing because some of the emperors drank deer's blood as a tonic.

The two-story **Imperial Library** has a pond in front and a few trees as a precaution against fire. The library is a copy of one in Shaoxing. It is approached through the rockeries. If you notice tourists in front of the library staring into the water, its because they are looking for the reflection of a crescent moon. Look for it yourself.

As a Chinese garden, this imperial summer resort is one of the best, a microcosm of the whole country with lake, grasslands, and mountains. For information on the **Mountain Resort** and **Eight Outer Temples**, *call 2023502.* The Outer Temples, outside the walls, are a mixture of Manchu, Mongolian, Tibetan, and Han Chinese architecture with a similar mix of artifacts inside. Once housing 1,000 lamas or monks, they are now primarily museums. The steles usually have Manchu writing in front, Chinese behind, and Mongolian and Tibetan on the sides. If you are short of time, the Putuozongsheng and Puning are the most important to include. Otherwise, start with the ***Pule**, which is also known as the Round Pavilion, as it was built in 1766 to resemble the Temple of Heaven. Inside is a statue of two hard-to-see copulating gods from the tantric sect of Tibetan Buddhism. From this temple you can climb or take a cable car to the Club Stone, the giant, malle-shaped stone, for a marvelous view.

The small **Anyuan Temple** is patterned after a temple in Xinjiang that no longer exists. Inside is a statue of Lu Du Mo, a female goddess. The Puren should be open for your visit.

Inside the gate of the Puning Temple is a stele about Qianlongs suppression of a rebellion of the minorities. The ***Puning Temple** contains a copy of the spectacular 1,000-headed and 1,000-armed Guan Yin, Goddess of Mercy, which should not be missed. Actually he/she has only 42 hands and arms, each representing 25. On each palm is an eye. The statue in Mahayana Hall is 22.28 meters high. A warlord stole the original.

The Puning Temple is patterned after the Sumeru temple in Tibet and is known also as the Temple of Universal Peace or Big Buddha Temple. Inside are a drum and a bell tower, a laughing Buddha, and four guardian kings. About 100 larger-than-life-size arhats remain of the original 508; the others were destroyed by fire. Only eight of the arhats are Chinese. The mural of 18 arhats is 230 years old and original, remarkable for its preservation. Look for the big bronze cooking pot that fed 1000 lamas. The number of buildings and stupas are symbolic. The center of the world was Sumeru Mountain, with four great continents around it.

In the Puning are live, chanting red-robed monks, probably from Inner Mongolia and Qinghai on a three-year contract. They chant every morning. If you can't go to Tibet, this is the place to come.

The **Xumifushou** (Longevity and Happiness) Temple was inspired by the Xiashelumpo (Zhaxilhunbu) Temple in Shigatse, Tibet, and used as a residence for the sixth Panchen Lama. Dragons seem to scamper along the edges of the roof, most unusual for a Han temple. Built in 1780, it is the newest of the temples and commemorates Qianlong's 70th birthday, at which point he started to learn Tibetan. In the main building is a statue of the founder of Lamaism and behind him Sakyamuni. The tent-like pagoda in the back is similar to the one in Fragrant Hill Park in Beijing.

The ***Putuozongcheng Temple** is patterned after the Potala Palace, home of the Dalai Lama, in Lhasa. It was built from 1767 to 1771 for the 60th birthday of Qianlong and for the 80th birthday of his mother. The elephant symbolizes the Mahayana sect. (One elephant equals 500 horses.) The five pagodas on several of the buildings symbolize the five schools of Buddhism. Dancers perform here every morning.

Not to be missed is the **Donggang Zi Dian** (East Hall) where embarrassed guides try to explain what is happening under the yellow aprons. These are statues of the Red Hat sect of Tibetan Buddhism, where sex with a person other than one's spouse was part of the religious ritual. In the opposite hall on the same level are other metal Buddhist statues. Another 164 steps lead up to the main building, which is decorated by Buddhas in niches – the 80 at the top representing Qianlong's life. Some birthday cake! The temple was built to commemorate the birthdays, as well as a visit by tribal leaders. This temple is the largest.

Finally, the Yongning Temple, built in 1751, is worth a quick look.

SHOPPING

The **Friendship Store** is at *Lizhengmen Street, Tel. 2024279*. Gardeners of miniature plants might be interested in the cheap water stones, which absorb water and plants can grow on top of them. But they are heavy! The area also produces silk, walnut walking sticks, and wood carvings.

PRACTICAL INFORMATION

• **CITS** and **CTS**, *6 Nanyuan Dong Road, 067000; Tel. 2026827, 2026418. Fax 2027484, 2028930*

• **Chengde Tourism Bureau**, *11 Zhong Hua Road. 067000. Tel. 2023454, 2026706. Fax, 2027484*
• **Tourist Complaints**, *Tel. 2024548*
• **CYTS**, *2nd Floor, Box Office of Theatre, Nan Ying Zi Road, 067000 Tel. 2030466, Fax 2024049*
• **Telephone Code**, *0314*

DATONG

(Tatung)

Datong is most famous for the **Yungang** (Yunkang) **Grottoes**, said to be the best-preserved, the largest, and the oldest sandstone carvings in China. Founded during the Warring States, about 2,200 years ago, this was a garrison town built between two sections of the Great Wall. The Northern Wei (386–534) declared it their capital and instructed Monk Tanyao to supervise the carving of the Yungang Caves.

The population is over 300,000. The highest temperature in summer (July–August) is 37.7 degrees centigrade, the lowest (December–February) minus 29.9 degrees centigrade. Rainfall is a scant 400 millimeters a year, mainly May–October. The best time to visit is May–October. The altitude is 1000 meters.

ARRIVALS & DEPARTURES

Located in northern Shanxi province, Datong is eight hours by train from Beijing. You can continue from here by once-a-week train to Ulan Bator and thence onward to Moscow.

ORIENTATION

Datong is basically a coal-mining town, one of the largest open pit coal-producing areas in the world, with a 600-year supply at the current rate of production. The city is industrial and heavily polluted. Outside Datong coal deposits are visible, with all kinds of coal transport equipment on the roads. Some of the equipment is the most advanced in the world.

The mining may be ugly but it is worth your time. Because the mines have unearthed some old burial grounds, Shanxi has an extremely large number of excavated tombs and neolithic sites.

WHERE TO STAY

YUNGANG HOTEL *(Fandian), 21 Yingbin Dong Road, 037008. Two stars. Tel. 521601. Fax 290006.*

WHERE TO EAT

Look for people preparing Knife-cut Noodles on the street. Ask about the chefs who put noodle dough on their heads and slice the dough with a knife into a cooking pot.

SEEING THE SIGHTS

If you only have one day to spend in the city, good choices are the Yungang caves, Huayan Monastery, Shanhua Monastery, and the Nine-Dragon Screen.

You can reach the *Yungang (Yunkang) Grottoes by public bus or taxi about 20 kilometers west from Datong. Fifty-three caves here contain over 51,000 stone carvings of buddha, bodhisattvas, apsaras (angels), birds, and animals. These statues range from 17 meters to a few centimeters high and some of them still retain their original color. They were restored in 1976. The grottoes are at the southern foot of Wuzhou Hills. They were built between 460 and 494 A.D. after a period of persecution against the Buddhists supposedly led to the illness of Emperor Taiwu. The grottoes extend east-west for a kilometer. The Wei dynasty later moved its capital to Luoyang and built another set of grottoes there.

Although the exposed caves have suffered natural erosion as well as damage by man, they are nicely preserved and well worth visiting. The walking is easy, with no lighting problems. The best are at the Five Caves of Tanyao (Nos. 5, 6, 16-20), which include the largest statues. The large ears mean deliberate poverty (no earrings). Although Datong was not on the Silk Road, the carvings carry strong Indian, Persian, and even Greek influences. You can expect to spend at least half a day here, strolling from cave to cave. During tourist season, English-speaking guides are available for hire. There are several restaurants. Open 8:30 am to 4:30 or 5 pm.

The *Huayan Si (Huayan Monastery) is one of the largest temples in China. You can easily spend from two hours to a half day there, there is so much to absorb. It is in the southwest of the city, three kilometers north of the main tourist hotel. A good antique store is at the temple, *Tel. 233629.*

The monastery is well preserved and is separated into the Upper Huayan and the Lower Huayan. You pay two entrance fees. In Upper Huayan is the magnificent main hall, Daxiong Bao Dian, built in 1062 and rebuilt in 1140. It is 53.75 meters wide and 29 meters long. The beam structure, murals, five large Ming buddhas, and 26 guardians are most impressive. In Lower Huayan is the main hall, the Bhagavan Stack Hall, built in 1038. Along its walls are 38 two-story wooden cabinets, housing the Buddhist sutras. The temple's exquisite 31 clay statues were made in the Liao. The Datong Municipal Museum has prehistoric fossils and cultural relics and is in the Municipal Exhibition Hall.

The *Shanhua Monastery, in the south part of the city, was founded in 713 A.D. Surviving are relics of the Liao and Jin. The Nine Dragon Screen, in the southeast of the old city, is almost 600 years old, and at 45.5 meters, larger than the two in Beijing. The morning is better for photographs. A nearby Christian church is worth a 10-minute visit.

SHOPPING

Locally made products include porcelain, brassware, knitting wool, furs, leather, silk dolls, and carpets. The **Brassware Factory** is at *9 Nan Cung Street, Tel. 232786.* The **Friendship Store** is at *17 Nanguan Nan Street, Tel. 232333.*

EXCURSIONS FROM DATONG

If you have more time, the 67.3-meter-high *Sakyamuni Wooden Pagoda** at Foguang Temple may be worth the 1 1/2 hour drive if you are interested in unusual pagodas. It is the tallest ancient wood-frame structure in China. It was constructed in 1056 (Liao), with eight corners and nine stories. From the outside it looks like five stories. Local folklore says that the pagoda only sits on five of its six vertical beams. One of the beams is always resting, and you can pass a piece of paper underneath it. Each beam takes its turn at being weightless. Bring a piece of paper and test it for yourself. This pagoda is usually locked, but ask for permission to view the interior. It is 75 kilometers south of Datong in Yingxian county.

The **Great Wall** is 40 kilometers and 150 kilometers away. You can also visit **Hengshan Mountain**, 80 kilometers south, for the **Xuankongsi** or Temple in Mid-Air (or Hanging Monastery). This is a two hour drive southeast of Datong, a marvel of cliff-side architecture. The temple literally clings to an almost vertical mountainside. It was first built over 1400 years ago (Northern Wei) and rebuilt in the Tang, Jin, Ming and Qing dynasties. Its clay statues are poor. The bronze and iron castings and stone and wood carvings are better and probably older. Take lunch in Hongyun County town nearby. From here its another three hours to Wutai Mountain, 240 kilometers south of Datong. You pass some 11th century Liao dynasty tombs.

On **Wutai Shan**, one of the Four Great Buddhist Mountains of China, there are about 50 temples from the fifth century. Important are the *Main Hall of the Nanchan Temple (Tang to Qing), *Foguang Temple (Tang to Qing) and the *Xiantong Temple (Eastern Han). The main halls of the Nanchan and Foguang temples are the oldest extant wood-frame buildings in the world. Both have histories of over 1200 years and are worth the white-knuckle trip through the mountains.

Visitors can hike on a paved path to the summit. The liveliest time to visit is during its festival here in July and August. Dr. Norman Bethune's model hospital is also in the area. You can stay at the **FRIENDSHIP GUEST HOUSE** (three stars).

PRACTICAL INFORMATION

• **CITS, CTS**, and **Datong Tourist Bureau**, *21 Yingbin Dong Road, 037008, Tel. 522265, 524176. Fax 522046. Tourist Bureau, Tel. 521601 X 915*
• **CYTS Tours**, *1-1, Building 2, Nanguan Xi Road, 037008, Tel. 269205. Fax 263303*
• **Telephone Code**, *0352*

HOHHOT

(Huhehot, Huhehaote)

Hohhot, the capital of **Inner Mongolia** (Nei Monggol Autonomous Region), is northwest of Beijing in the south central part of this 1800-kilometer-long region. The urban population is over 700,000.

Genghis Khan united the tribes living here in 1206, and his descendants went on to conquer the rest of China and then parts of Europe. The traditional religion, as reflected now in its monasteries and temples, is a distinctive branch of Buddhism and is related to that practiced in Tibet.

Hohhot dates from the Ming, at least 400 years ago. It was called Guisui under the Nationalists. After Liberation it was renamed Hohhot (Green City), the name preferred by the natives. In the past, Inner Mongolia has been a home for nomads.

The best time to visit is June through August. The highest temperature in Hohhot is 30 degrees centigrade, but the nights are cool. The winters are very cold and windy, with a minus 32 degrees low in January, and you need long johns even in early May. The spring has sandstorms; the annual precipitation is between a scant 50 and 450 millimeters, mostly late summer and early autumn. The altitude is 1500 meters above sea level and it has from 90 to 160 frost-free days.

ARRIVALS & DEPARTURES

Hohhot can be reached by train or plane from Beijing, or plane from Hong Kong, Tokyo and Ulan Bator, and eleven other Chinese cities. A train also connects it with Ulan Bator.

ORIENTATION

Today Hohhot's population includes Han, Daur, Ewenki, Oroqen, Hui, Manchu, Korean, and, of course, Mongolian nationalities. The

Mongolians are now actually a minority. Hohhot looks like any other Chinese city, except for the horse statues.

WHERE TO STAY

The **Zhao Jun** is better than the Inner Mongolia; the cheapest is Xin Cheng.

INNER MONGOLIA HOTEL *(Nei Mongol Fandian), Wulanchabu Xi Road, 010020. Three stars, Tel. 6964233. Fax 6961479. Dist.A.P. 10 km. Dist.R.W. 1.5 km.*

Built 1982-86. 20 stories, 250 rooms. Shopping. IDD. Disco. Mongolian consulate. $55.

ZHAO JUN HOTEL *(Zhaojun Dajiudian), 53 Xinhua Road, 010050. Three stars, Tel. 6962211. Fax 6968825, 6967645. Dist.A.P. 15 km Dist.R.W. 0.5 km Dist.city hall 200 meters. Credit Cards. $62 to $68.*

Built 1987. Ren. 1995, 1996. 262 units. USTV. IDD.

XIN CHENG, *Hu Lun Nan, 010010, Tel. 6963322. Fax 6968561. Rooms start at Y200 and they take major credit cards.*

WHERE TO EAT

Meat, mainly mutton but also beef, is the big thing here. Notable dishes are barbecued lamb, mutton hot pot, sesame pancakes, braised oxtail, beef kebab, ox tendon in egg white, camel hoof, and facai (the edible black hair-like algai that is a favorite in China.)

Mongolian food is better in Hohhot at the hotels than in the grasslands. Try also the **FRIENDSHIP RESTAURANT** for good Mongolian hotpot.

SEEING THE SIGHTS

In summer, visitors can travel out from here, if they wish, and sleep in a yurt in the beautiful sparsely settled grasslands. You can drink tea laced with milk, butter, and grain, said to be very filling and great for cold winter days – it's too greasy for hot weather. Visitors can go to one of several rural communities located 90 to 180 kilometers away, on roads cut through the rolling prairie lands.

Mongolian **yurts** or tents are made of compressed sheep's wool with no windows unless you count the roof. They are shaped somewhat like igloos, and can be folded up and carried by camel. Eight people can put up a large one in 40 minutes. Visitors staying in yurts sleep on padded earthen mattresses. Everything smells of sheep. (Put a bag between you and the wall if the smell keeps you awake.)

Up to three people to a yurt is very comfortable, and over six very crowded. Sometimes you can hear bugs eating the felt. A mosquito net might be useful. Most Mongolians now live in houses but keep yurts around because they are cooler in summer.

In some yurt hotels, there is a separate bathhouse with running water and flush toilets (when the pump is working). The people are charming and wear their traditional costumes. The food might be barely edible, with tough fresh-killed mutton, fried millet, boiled millet, rice, boiled eggs, and cake. Do not expect traditional Mongolian hot pot or barbecue except in winter or in the cities. Take some snacks to fill up. Also soap. Each travel agency has a different hostel on the grasslands, some better than others.

You can visit Mongolian homes and an **aobo**, the rock mounds at high points where people worship, gather, and leave messages for each other. Mongolians now ride motorcycles much more than horses. Hohhot used to have many temples but the Cultural Revolution destroyed them. Among the survivors is the oldest, **Dazhao Temple** (Ming), with a rare silver Buddha and many musical instruments, and the **Xiaozhao Temple**. At the **Wutasi Temple**, the tallest of its five pagodas is 6.26 meters and all are made of glazed bricks carved with Buddhist symbols and inscribed in three languages: Mongolian, Sanskrit, and Tibetan. Behind the pagodas is a Mongolian astrological chart.

The **White Pagoda** on the eastern outskirts of the city at the **Xilitu Lamasery** (monastery) is from the 10th century and is 40 meters or seven stories high. Inside are native tapestries. For more on Tibetan Buddhism, see *Tibet*.

The **Tomb of Wang Zhaojun** is about 10 kilometers south of the city. In 33 B.C., she was an imperial Han concubine, married off to a Xiongnu tribal chief to form an important political alliance. The story goes that the Han emperor picked his bed partner from paintings of his many concubines. Consequently, the women bribed the painter to make them look beautiful. Wang Zhaojun refused and he made her look awful. She was continually ignored. In choosing a gift for the tribal leader, the emperor decided on the ugliest of his wives. He never saw Wang Zhaojun until the day of the presentation. She was beautiful, but it was too late. The Xiongnu liked her too. And the peace was kept for 40 years!

The **Great Mosque**, built in Chinese style, is worth seeing, as is the Provincial Museum, *2 Xin Hua Avenue, Tel. 6964924,* with a highly recommended exhibition about the Mongolians. For those serious about Mongolians, there is a Mongolia Society in the U.S.

You might also be interested in the **Mongolia Art Performing School** and the **Horse Rodeo School** with displays of singing, dancing, and horsemanship. Ask about them at the local tourist office for more details on events.

Walks

Out in the rolling grasslands, you can see for miles, and hiking is a pure joy.

Festivals

The dates of the **Nadamu Festival** are now set by the province and depend on the harvest. Some areas celebrate in July, others in August. This annual fair in Hohhot is held August 15-20th. Tourists then go on to celebrations outside Hohhot.

At **Siziwang**, about 160 kilometers outside of Hohhot, there is a demonstration of Mongolian culture with a parade, wrestling, archery, horsemanship, and traditional songs and dances. You eat Mongolian food, sleep in yurts, use flush toilets, and visit Mongolian homes. You can ride horses and camels. Tourists sometimes outnumber Mongolians.

At **Xilinhot**, 700 kilometers from Hohhot, foreigners might sleep in yurts or in town and commute about 40 minutes to the fair grounds carrying their own food. The 10,000 Mongolians attending Nadamu sleep in yurts, put up booths to sell kitchenware, boots, carpets, and motorcycles, but no native clothes or jewelry. They wear traditional dress, and used muddy open pit toilets with canvas covers. There could be circus acts, wrestling, archery, and horse– riding competitions with lots of chaos and no explanations, no dancers, and no horseback rides. Only a few foreigners attend.

You have to choose. Because of the crowds, I urge you to book a place through a travel agency and expect no star accommodations. These will probably improve as organizers get more experience.

SHOPPING

Today, in addition to less exotic goods, Inner Mongolia produces woolen textiles, cashmere sweaters, carpets, and tapestries. It also manufactures Mongolian-style boots, daggers with chopsticks, silver bowls, brass hot pots, cheap but fancy tweezers, wrestlers jackets, saddles, stirrups, and felt stockings. Also available are antique bottles of jade or agate.

Try the **Inner Mongolian Minorities Handicraft Factory** and **Minzu Shang Chang** (Nationalities Market, *Tel. 6968822*), the **Hohhot Antique Shop**, *10 Xilin Nan Lu, Tel. 6968430, 6966748* and the **Hohhot Carpet Factory**. Shopping is better in Hohhot than in the grasslands.

EXCURSIONS FROM HOHHOT

Baotou in western Inner Mongolia, twenty kilometers north of the Yellow River, is a 14 hour train trip, or a 1 1/2 hour flight from Beijing.

It can be reached from Hohhot also by train. It is connected to four other cities by air. The average altitude is 1000 meters, its annual rainfall a sparse 312 millimeters. The city was founded in the 17th century (Qing) on a neolithic site. The urban population is about 1,800,000, of whom the Han are 90%, the Mongolians 2.5%, and the rest 21 other national minorities.

Locally produced goods in this region include carpets, cashmere knitwear, leather and furs, porcelain, and arts and crafts.

If you only have one day, you might want to visit the **Wudangzhao Lamasery** and take a quick city tour. The Wudangzhao Lamasery is 70 kilometers east of town in **Huluntu Mountain**, Guyang county. It is a massive 2,500 room complex established in 1794 (Qing), once home to 1,200 monks and covering about 50 acres. The largest monastery in western Inner Mongolia, it contains statues, murals, and tangkas typical of the yellow sect of Tibetan Buddhism. (More about Tibetan Buddhism under *Lhasa* and *Chengde*.)

If you have more time, visit the **Meidaizhao Lamasery**, originally built in the Ming, which is at Tumd You Banner, 80 kilometers east of Baotou. It is also known as the Sanniangzi Temple after the concubine of its Mongolian founder who is buried here. A Han Chinese, she helped to bridge the two groups. The ***Tomb of Genghis Khan** was moved about 200 kilometers south of Baotou to **Ejinhoroq** (Elinhoro) in 1954. It contains ashes, said to be his. Pilgrims gather here to pay homage for one day in the third, fifth, ninth, and tenth lunar months.

You can also visit the **Great Wall**, 40 kilometers and 70 kilometers north of Baotou. And all places of interest are open 8 am to 6 pm daily.

The best hotel here is the **TIAN WAI TIAN HOTEL**, *50 Hu De Mu Lin Avenue, Qingshan District, 014030. Three stars. Tel. 3137766. Fax 3131771. No Credit Cards, but you can use the Bank of China nearby. Dist.A.P. 20 km Dist.R.W. 20 km. IDD.*

CITS and **CTS** are at the *Baotou Hotel, Kundulun District, 014010, Tel. 5156655. Fax 5154615.* Address tourist complaints to the **Baotou Tourism Bureau**, *City Hall, Kundulun District, 014010, Tel. 5152255.*

PRACTICAL INFORMATION

- **Business Hours**, offices 8,30 am to 5,30 pm. Stores 9 am to 7 pm.
- **China Comfort Travel Service**, *32 Xin Hua Aveenie, Tel. 6920995, 6951394. Fax 6967336*
- **CITS**, *Tel. 6924494*
- **CTS**, *Tel. 6927924. Fax 6862774*
- **CYTS Tours**, *9 Zhong Shan Dong Road, 010020. Tel. 6964968*
- **Inner Mongolia Tourism Bureau**, *95 Yishuting Nan Street, 010010. Tel. 6964233 X 8567. Fax 6968561*

• **Inner Mongolia International Travel Service,** *Tel. 6968822*
• **Police,** *Tel. 110*
• **Telephone Code,** *0471*
• **Tourism Administration of Inner Mongolia,** *Inner Mongolia Hotel, 010020. Tel. 6964233. For complaints, Tel. 6914196*
• **Tourist Complaints,** contact **Supervisory Bureau of Tourism Quality,** *1 Xinhua Street, 010055. Tel. 665978. Fax 668561*
• **Tourist Hotline,** *Tel. 6914197, 6914199*

JINAN

Jinan, the capital of Shandong province, is due south of Beijing, 15 kilometers from the south shore of the Huanghe (Yellow River), at the junction of the Beijing–Shanghai and the Qingdao-Jinan Railways.

Jinan dates as a city with a wall from the sixth century B.C., when it was made capital of the State of Qi. However, it was settled here more than 5000 years ago by neolithic cultures, the Dawenkou and the Longshan. It was named Jinan, meaning south of the Ji River, a name it has kept even though that river dried up centuries ago.

Jinan was a busy commercial center during the Tang, and Marco Polo wrote favorably of its garden atmosphere and its thriving silk industry. It has been the capital since the Ming. It is now an industrial center producing trucks, textiles, and paper, and as a tourist destination, famous primarily for its springs, its Buddhist temples, and its proximity to Taishan Mountain and Qufu.

The climate is temperate. The hottest in late July to early August is 33 degrees centigrade; the coldest in January, minus 10 degrees. The annual precipitation is about 700 millimeters, mainly in July and August. The urban population is 1.5 million.

ARRIVALS & DEPARTURES

Jinan is on the main Beijing–Guangzhou train line, six hours from Beijing. Jinan can also be reached by plane from Hong Kong, Singapore and 24 cities. The airport is 40 kilometers from town.

ORIENTATION

A geographer first recorded the excellent quality of the water in this **City of Springs** 2,500 years ago. The Chinese kept records of pretty much everything! During the Jin (1115–1234), someone else listed 72 springs on a tablet. He missed a few: a 1964 survey mentions 108 natural springs.

The springs are not just holes in the ground spouting water. They have been embellished with gardens, rockery, pavilions, and tea houses. A subterranean wall of volcanic rock forces the water to the earth's surface. But unless you have a water fixation, a trip to one or two springs will suffice. The performance of the water is seasonal because of the lowering water table. The best time seems to be after the rains in August and through the autumn.

If you only have one day, take in the Baotu Spring, Daming Lake, Yellow River, Qianfo Hill, museum and a crafts factory.

WHERE TO STAY

The best hotel for tourists and business people is the **Qilu**. The glitzy **Pearl** is better located for business people. The Guidu is new, as yet untried. The Novotel is due in 1997. The following prices are subject to change, negociation and 10% service charge.

GUI DU HOTEL, *1 Sheng Ping Road, 250001, Tel. 6900888. Fax 6900999. Three stars. Dist.A.P. 30 km Dist R.W. 0.2 km. $40 to $60. Credit Cards. IDD.*

NOVOTEL JINAN, *399 Jinshi Road, 250022. Tel. and Fax 7952895.1997.*

QILU HOTEL *(Binguan), 8 Qianfoshan Road, 250014. Four stars. Tel. 2966888. Fax 2967676. Dist.A.P. 40 km Dist.R.W.six km. $80 to $120. Credit Cards.*

Good view of 1000 Buddha Hill in the suburbs. Walk to CITS. Built 1985– 86, 11 stories, 255 rooms. Tennis. B.C., IDD. Pool, gym, USTV. A new five-star section of the Qilu Hotel is due soon.

SHANDONG PEARL HOTEL *(Zhen Zhu Dajiudian), 164 Jingsan Road, 250001. Three stars, Tel. 7932888. Fax 7932688. Y398 and Y488. Dist.A.P. 38 km Dist.R.W. 1.5 km. Credit Cards.*

Next to park and within walking distance to city hall. Built 1991–92. 24 stories, 153 rooms. USTV, B.C., IDD. Revolving restaurant. Cantonese cuisine. Very small driveway.

WHERE TO EAT

Exotic local fare are cattails, lotus roots and lotus seeds from Daming Lake, roast duck, winding–thread cakes, and monkey–head mushroom.

Try the **ORIENTAL PEARL RESTAURANT**, *150 Lishan Road, Tel. 2964280* and the **GOLDEN WORLD RESTAURANT**, *48-1 Heping Road, Tel. 6943718.*

SEEING THE SIGHTS

The **Baotu Quan** (Jet Spring) in the southwest corner of the old city, is the best, with 16 fountains and the greatest amount of water. It is in the center of a square pond. In 1995, it gushed up one meter high. Tel. 6920439, open 8 am to 5 pm.

The **Heihu Quan** (Black Tiger Spring Park), *Tel. 6925603*, is another of the four most famous springs. It is a 10–minute walk from the east side of Jet Spring. In this park the water flows from the mouths of three stone tigers. Does it sound like the roar of tigers? Open 24 hours.

The third famous spring is the **Zhenshu Quan** (Pearl Spring), *Tel. 2655522*, in the courtyard of the Pearl Spring Auditorium. The Five–Dragon Pool completes the four most famous. It is outside the West Gate.

The **Shandong Provincial Museum**, *Wenhua Xi Road at the foot of Qianfo Hill; Tel. 2960284, 6923012*, (open 8:30 to 11:30 am; 1:30 to 5 pm; closed Mondays) contains both historical and natural history relics. The history dates from neolithic times and includes Sun Bin's famous treatise on the art on war, written on bamboo about 2000 years ago. Also note the frescoes from Sui dynasty tombs, musical instruments, paintings from the tomb of the Prince of Lu (Ming), and musical instruments from the Confucian Family Mansion in Qufu.

If you like mosques, you might be interested in **The Grand Mosque**, *13 Libai Si Xiang, Tel. 6925281*. Open daily.

The **Qianfo** (Thousand-Buddha) **Hill**, *Tel. 2951792*, open 24 hours, 2 1/2 kilometers south of the city. You'll find the entrance beside the Qilu Hotel. Here are Buddhist images carved into the side of a cliff. Much climbing is involved for the **Xingguo Si** (Revive the Nation Temple), with 60-70 buddhas from 20 centimeters to over three meters tall, ranging from the Sui to the Tang. Look for three caves at the foot of the cliff and in the rooms of the west courtyard of the temple. There you find, yes, more buddhas.

In the **Yilan Ting** (Pavilion of Panoramic View), the tallest building around, you can get a good view of Jinan. On Jueshan you can see the 10-meter-high cave with the head of a buddha, seven meters tall.

West of Xingguo Temple about three kilometers is the **Yellowstone Cliff**, a 40-meter-high rock around which were carved more buddhas, and heavens! – flying devas – some of them nude! These were made during the Northern Wei, about 1,600 years ago. A stimulating time to visit this temple is on the ninth day of the ninth lunar month, when the hill is full of chrysanthemums and market stalls are set up.

If you want to get out into the countryside, the ***Lingyan Si Temple**, *Tel. 7463198*, 55 kilometers from Jinan, is one of the four finest temples in China. It was founded by a famous monk in 354 A.D. who was much moved by the beauty of the surroundings and whose sermons caused birds to listen, animals to stop, and even a rock nearby to nod in agreement. Hence the name. The current temple is from the Tang. Open 8 am to 5 pm.

The temple expanded in the Song when over 1000 monks studied and worshipped here. Surviving the centuries are the rock grotto from the

Northern Wei, the Tang halls and pavilions, the Song clayimages, and various rock carvings. Important is its Thousand Buddha Hall, built in the Tang, and repaired in the Song, Yuan, and Ming. Here are three large statues of Buddha, one of wood and two of bronze. The 40 painted clay arhats are very lively and about 102 centimeters tall. Northwest of this hall is the nine-story, 52.4 meter-high **Pizhi Pagoda** from the Tang, restored in the Song. The iron spire on the top is unusual, with its eight or nine Buddhist wheels chained together.

To the West is another cemetery with tiny dagobas marking the graves of monks, no two dagobas the same. This is the second best graveyard of this type in the country. (See Shaolin Temple in *Zhengzhou*).

Walks

Lots of parks around the springs. The **1,000 Buddha Hill** above the Qilu Hotel is a good easy climb.

SHOPPING

Made in the province are human hair and silk embroidery, lace, wool carpets, straw articles, kites, feather pictures (lovely), and dough modeling (yes, they do last!). The **carpet factory** is at *108 Beixiao Xin Zhang Dong Street, Tel. 7963608*. Open 8 am to 5 pm. The province also produces **Qingdao** (Tsingtao) **Beer**, the most popular Chinese beer. The main shopping area is **Quanchen** and also along Jin 2-Road. The **People's Department Store** is on *Jingsi, Tel. 6919888*. Open 9 am to 8 pm.

The **Shandong Antique Store** is west of the Department Store, *401 Quancheng*; Also **One Gong Qing Tuan**, *3rd floor*. The **Shandong Arts & Crafts** is at *Jing Qi Wei Yi*. The **Jinan Embroidery Factory**, *11 Baotu Quan Bei, Tel. 6913132,* open 8 am to 5 pm.

EXCURSIONS FROM JINAN

You really need a couple of days to take in **Taishan**, over 50 kilometers away, and **Qufu**, the hometown of Confucius, 140 kilometers south. Taishan is listed under Taian in this book. Both are very worthwhile. *Linzi, the former capital of Qi, is from the Zhou dynasty. In the province also are Qingdao, Yantai, Weihai, and Weifang. See separate listings.

PRACTICAL INFORMATION

• **Ambulance and Fire**, *Tel. 119; Ambulance, 5959955, 6920900*
• **CITS**, *88 Jing Shi Road, 250014. Tel. 2965858. Fax 2965651*
• **CYTS Tours**, *2-1 Road, Ying Xiong Shan Road, 250002. Tel. 6925488. Fax 6916806*

- **Police,** *Tel. 110*
- **Shandong International Tourism Corporation,** *88 Jinshi Road, 250014. Tel. 2961080. Fax 2961085*
- **Tourist Complaints,** contact **Supervisory Bureau of Tourism Quality of Shandong Province,** *Tel. 2963423, 2965858. Fax 2964284*
- **Shandong Travel Service,** *240 Jing San Road, 250021. Tel. 7923623, 7923624. Fax 7937799. Attention Miss Wei Wei, Manager, North America Department.*
- **Telephone Code,** *0531*
- **Tourist Hotline,** *Tel. 2963423*

QINGDAO

(Tsingtao)

Qingdao lies on a peninsula on the southern coast of Shandong province, 393 kilometers east of the provincial capital Jinan.

Starting as a fishing village, Qingdao (pronounced Ching Dow) has been an important trading port since the seventh century. During the Ming, it was fortified against pirates. The Germans seized the area in 1897 in retaliation for the assassination of two German missionaries. Here they built a naval base and trading port, and protected them with at least 2000 men. The large number of Germans accounted for its German architecture and its beer recipe.

In 1919, the Versailles Peace Conference confirmed Japans 1915 capture of the German territories in Shandong, including Qingdao. The Japanese stayed long enough to build huge cotton mills before they were forced to withdraw in 1937. (During this period, the British built cigarette factories.) The Japanese navy regained the city early in 1938, but not before a Chinese mob smashed the breweries, sending rivers of beer into the streets!

Qingdao's breweries were rebuilt, of course, and still produce the most popular **Tsingtao Beer.** Qingdao also bottles **Laoshan mineral water** from the mountains behind the city, and wines.

The climate is temperate: the highest in August an average, 25 degrees centigrade; the coldest in January an average -1.2 degrees centigrade. The annual precipitation is 715 millimeters. The population is two million.

ARRIVALS & DEPARTURES

Qingdao can be reached by rail, or by a two hour flight south from Beijing or north from Shanghai. There are direct air connections with 28 other Chinese cities and air links with Hong Kong, Macau, Osaka, and Seoul, and in the future probably Singapore and Bangkok.

Qingdao is on the Huanghai (Yellow Sea) and you can also reach it by ship from Shanghai (26 hours), Yantai, Guangzhou, and Dalian. There's also an expressway from Yantai.

ORIENTATION

Qingdao is an ice-free port and summer resort, famous for its beer and mineral water. It should be put at the end of a hectic, tight schedule in summer. Full of hills and trees and red-tiled roofs, it is very pretty with its 19 very different Asian and European architectural styles, most from its imperialist past. How many can you identify? It is now concerned about preserving the best of them.

Qingdao is the largest city and industrial center in Shandong. Its factories make diesel locomotives, automobiles, television sets, textiles, and cameras. Its oceanic research institute is internationally famous. Huangdao District, on the west coast of Jiazhou Bay, is its economic and technical development zone. Qingdao is one of the 14 Open Coastal Cities.

WHERE TO STAY

Many hotels have opened recently. The top hotel with luxury standards is the **Huiquan Dynasty**, but up and coming is the new **Grand Regency Hotel** which is aiming at five stars. Third is the four-star Haitian Hotel. A four-star Shangri-La is due in 1997.

Among the new cheaper hotels is the 410 room Huanhai Gloria Inn, one of the more modest hotels of this Hong Kong joint-venture chain. There's also the three star Huatian.

BADAGUAN HOTEL *(Binguan), 19 Shanhaiguan, 266071. Tel. 3864822, 3864888. Fax 371383. Dist.A.P. 30 km Dist.R.W. four km. Credit Cards.*

Twenty buildings between 10 and 200 meters from a swimming beach. Built 1903, started by the Germans. In the 1920s, the Japanese and Spanish added villas. In 1953, the Badaguan became a hotel and in 1988 expanded with its current main building. Total 420 beds. Nos. 1, 5, 13, 17, and 18 for foreigners. Pool, tennis, gym and bicycles. This is an old but interesting hotel for people who don't care about modern standards.

GRAND REGENCY HOTEL, *1 Taiwan Road, 266071. Tel. 5881818. Fax 5881888.*

HAITIAN HOTEL *(Dajiudian), 39 Zhanshan Da Road, 266071. Four stars. Tel. 3871888. Fax 3871777. Dist.A.P.25 km Dist.R.W. five km. Credit Cards.*

Dist. swimming beach 200 meters. Built 1988–1989, ren. 1994. Extension completed 1993. 15 stories. 641 rooms. IDD. Tennis, pool, gym and bowling. B.C. USTV. In-room safe.

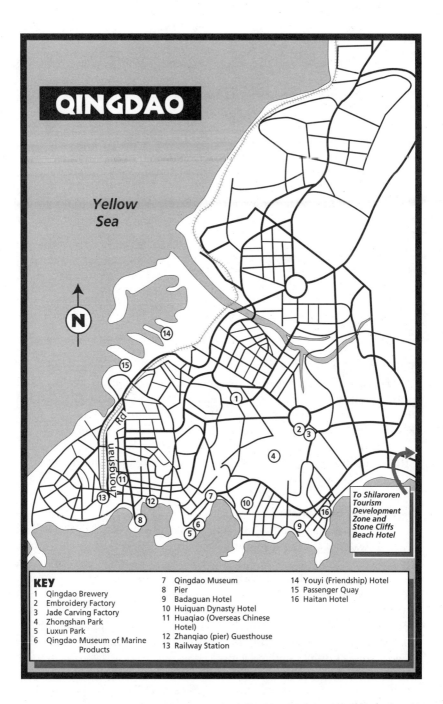

QINGDAO

Yellow
Sea

N

To Shilaroren
Tourism
Development
Zone and
Stone Cliffs
Beach Hotel

KEY

1 Qingdao Brewery
2 Embroidery Factory
3 Jade Carving Factory
4 Zhongshan Park
5 Luxun Park
6 Qingdao Museum of Marine
    Products

7 Qingdao Museum
8 Pier
9 Badaguan Hotel
10 Huiquan Dynasty Hotel
11 Huaqiao (Overseas Chinese
    Hotel)
12 Zhanqiao (pier) Guesthouse
13 Railway Station

14 Youyi (Friendship) Hotel
15 Passenger Quay
16 Haitan Hotel

HUATIAN HOTEL, *20 Taiping Road, 266002. Three stars. Tel. 2871900, 2873918. Fax 2867128. Overlooks The Pier. Dist.A.P. 35 km Dist.R.W. less than one km. Credit Cards.*

Close to shopping. Built 1995. 17 stories, 198 rooms. USTV, IDD and B.C.

HUANHAI GLORIA INN, *21 Donghai Road, 266071. Tel. 3878855. Fax 3864640.*

HUIQUAN DYNASTY HOTEL *(Huiquan Wang Chao Dajiudian), 9 Nanhai Road, 266003. Four stars aiming for five. Tel. 2873366. Fax 2871122. Dist.A.P. 35 km Dist.R.W. five km. Credit Cards.*

Across the street from Number One swimming beach. Built 1969. 12 stories; ren. 1994, 23 stories. Total 420 rooms. IDD. B.C. USTV. Korean Restaurant and revolving restaurant. Gym, bowling, pool and tennis. Its three–story penthouse suite is due soon. Bicycles. Managed by Dynasty International H.K.

RAMADA HOTEL, *Shandong Zhong Road, 266071. Tel. 5814688. Fax 5827294. In US, Tel. 1-800-8547854. Dist.A.P. 26 km. Dist.R.W. and ferry terminal nine km. Credit Cards.*

Built 1995. 239 rooms. B.C. and IDD. USTV. Cantonese and Asian cuisine. Ten–minute drive to swimming beach. Single rooms have only showers, no tubs.

WHERE TO EAT

You'll want to try seafood here, of course, especially abalone and prawns. Lots of sea cucumbers and scallops are available too. The food in the top hotels is very good. With the arrival of business people from Korea, joint-venture Korean restaurants have become popular.

Good choices are the **GAO LI RESTAURANT** near the Dynasty Hotel, and the **JING FU GONG RESTAURANT** opposite the Haitian Hotel. A **KFC** is on Zhongshan Road.

SEEING THE SIGHTS

You can cover all of Qingdao's urban attractions in a day, unless you want to walk leisurely through this museum of European architecture. You need a second day or two for Laoshan Mountain if you enjoy hiking in exotic settings and want to savor it all. Qingdao's four kilometers of city beaches slope gently into the sea and are protected by four large bays east from **The Pier** (1891). This 440-meter pier is a good place to absorb the sunrise, and its Huilan Pavilion is Qingdao's famous landmark. Southeast of the Pier and linked with the shore by a 700-meter-long dyke is **Xiaqingdao** (Little Qingdao Island).

Zhongshan Park is best seen when its 700 cherry trees bloom in April. It also has osmanthus, roses, and peonies. Luxun Park with its many hilly paths, rocky hills, and old pine trees, has an excellent view of Number One Beach, Xiaoqingdao, and the European buildings. The castle-like **Museum of Marine Products** is in this park. A good view is also from **Xiaoyu Shan** (Little Fish Hill), a tastefully-designed park with a recent three-story pavilion, and three large ceramic screens showing the likes of the eight Taoist ferries crossing the sea. Qingdao's nine other major peaks are similarly developed.

If you can borrow a bicycle, ride through the **Badaguan** area, where the streets are named after the eight passes of the Great Wall and each street is lined with a different kind of blossoming tree: cherry, peach, or crape myrtle. Behind the streets are individually-designed houses with spacious gardens, each one-of-a-kind with interesting features, a bit of old Europe. You can rent some of these houses by the month with cooks and housekeepers.

One of the most famous is at 18 Huanghai Road. Built in 1903 in the shape of a castle, with large blocks of granite, it was originally a hunting lodge for the German governor. Protected by Qingdao as a historical monument, the Stone House is now part of the Badashan Hotel.

Qingdao's 18-hole **golf course** is a Japanese joint venture. The city is also building a subway, starting from Xizhen in the south and running to the Number Nine Textile Mill in the north, a 16.68 kilometer line with 13 stations.

The largest and best of the six city beaches is the **Number One Huquan** (Pearl Spring) **Beach**, with lifeguards, medical station, and changing facilities. Be prepared to share any city beach with 100,000 other people in summer. They are open from early July to the end of September. If you are worried about pollution, **Yangkou Beach** in Laoshan is being developed as the pollution-free bathing beach. **Shilaoren** is 17 kilometers east of Qingdao and should be less crowded. However, this is where the new **Shi Lao Ren National Tourist and Resort Area** is located, *Tel. 3861667 and fax 3875344.* This is also where the hi-tech zone is being built. It is too early to assess what is happening to the beach in this area.

However, at Shi Lao Ren, there's the new 35-hectare, **Qingdao International Beer City** at the *Xujiamaidao Armed Police Base, Zhanliugam Road, 266071.* Currently finished is the two-hectare **Beer Plaza**. Soon to be finished is the three-hectare Beer Street with several bars. If you get there before I do, please let me know if it's worth a visit.

The same goes for the **Ocean Theatre** at Qingdao Ocean Park, also at Shi Lao Ren, *63 Zhanliugan, 266071. Tel. 5815718 X 3301 or fax 5814541.* Its whales have been trained in Japan. When entirely opened, this park should have an Aquatic Museum, aquarium, water rides, children's playground, wave pool, restaurants, gym and hotel.

Festivals

The annual **International Beer Festival** begins the second Sunday in August and runs for 15 days. The **Candied Haw** (Crab Apple) **Festival** has attracted 500,000 people at the Haiyun Temple on the 16th day of the lunar new year.

SHOPPING

Shops are along **Zhongshan** and **Jiaozhou Roads**. Local products include beautiful shell pictures, feather pictures, carpets, weaving, embroidery, and knitting. The shell products and embroidery are especially good buys. A large **market** is on Jimo Street with clothes, handicrafts and bicycles for sale.

You can buy these and other items at the **Friendship Store**, *12 Xingjiang, Tel. 2827570*; **Arts and Crafts Products Store**, *212 Zhongshan, Tel. 2828627.* and at the big **Guo Huo Department Store**, *Zhongshan Road.*

EXCURSIONS FROM QINGDAO

The **Laoshan Mountains** are roughly 40 kilometers east of the city, reached by land or sea. The range is said to be the home of the Eight Taoist Immortals (genii, fairies). The **boat trip**, *Tel. 7895185*, gives an excellent view of the city.

You may have to choose one of three routes to tour Laoshan. On the South Route you cover the upper and lower Taiqing temples, Longtan Water Fall, and Dragon Well Falls. The North Route takes you to Shuilienbi (Water Fall Screen), Camel Head Rock, Fishscale Gorge, and Tsaoying Water Fall. The East Route goes to Lion Peak (to soak in the sunrise), Fairy Bridge, Yuelong Cave, and Sheep Rock. A leisurely three-day trip would be ideal for hikers. There's a 400-meter-long chairlift.

Do not expect large temples. Many of the temples here are Taoist, with small buildings, small doorways, and small courtyards. The mystical Taoists didnt want to be distracted in their meditative search for eternal peace, their communion with nature.

Laoshan is famous for the masculine shape of its mountains and its rushing waterfalls. It is full of legends. The highest peak, **Mt. Laoding**, is 1,333 meters above sea level. The mountains extend over 386 square kilometers and are full of granite canyons, grotesque crags, old temples, rivers, streams, and the Laoshan reservoir. The **Taiping** (Great Peace) **Taoist Temple** was founded in the Song. The home of Qing writer Pu Songling (1640-1715) is open to the public. He lived in a very modest corner of the Taiping Temple. Pu wrote his famous *Strange Tales* from a Lonely Studio here. The trees he described are still standing.The biggest temple, **Taiqing Taoist Temple**, has over 150 buildings.

An inscription about the visit of the first Qin emperor in 219 B.C. is also on the mountain. The builder of the Xian ceramic army searched for pills of immortality in this area.

PRACTICAL INFORMATION

- **CITS**, *9 Nanhai Road, 266003. Tel. 2879215, or Service Center, Huiquan Hotel, Tel. 2870876. Fax 2870983*
- **CTS**, *Tel. 5822095. Fax 5844234*
- **Qingdao Overseas Tourist Corporation**, *Tel. 3861259. Fax 3862954*
- **Qingdao Tourism Administration**, *16 Guanhai 1st Road, 266001. Tel. 2882314, Fax 2882427*. Information and complaints.
- **Telephone Code**, *0532*
- **Tourist Hotline Center**, *16 Guanhai 1st Road, 266001. Tel. 2882349. Fax 2882427*

QINHUANGDAO

(Chinwangtao)

Qinhuangdao, at the northeastern tip of Hebei province on the Bohai Sea, is more of a commercial than a tourist city. It is however the capital of the prefecture that includes Beidaihe, 15 kilometers away, the better seaside resort. It is also 20 kilometers from Old Dragon Head, where the Great Wall meets the sea.

The city is one of China's busiest harbors. Ice-free, it is the port for a nearby oil field to which it is joined by a pipeline. With an urban population of 448,000, it is one of the 14 Open Coastal Cities.

ARRIVALS & DEPARTURES

Qinhuangdao is a 280 kilometer road trip from Beijing, or a five hour train trip. The closest airport is 15 kilometers away, in Shanhaiguan.

ORIENTATION

Originally a small village, Qinhuangdao was opened as a seaport in 1898 and became a base for foreign (especially British) shipping. In 1902 the British army also built a small pier. The railway was finished in 1916.

The city is named after a legend. The Qin emperor passed through here about 2,200 years ago looking for pills of longevity. Suddenly, he recognized a special tree described by his teacher. Surprised and afraid, he bowed to the tree and a branch bowed back.

WHERE TO STAY & EAT

QINHUANGDAO CINDIC HOTEL, *Yinbin Road, 066000. Three stars, Tel. 3032243, 3032443. Fax 3032253. Dist.R.W. 0.5 km Dist.A.P.12 km. Dist.beach five km.*

Built 1984. Ren. 1992. Over 100 rooms. USTV. IDD. Cantonese, Sichuan, and French-style food. H.K.J.V.

SEEING THE SIGHTS

Dong Shan (East Mountain) is where the Qin emperor searched for the pills of longevity and boarded his ships. There's a good view of the sea and the sunrise. A cruise boat goes to a fishing village at the mouth of the Xin Kai River and sometimes visitors can come across teams of fishing boats going out together, dragging their big nets between them. In the old days, the fishermen used to sing to each other.

You can visit a **shell-carving factory** and the **Sea God Temple**, where the Qin Emperor searched for those longevity pills. You can also go swimming at **Dong Shan beach**. A natural **wildlife park** is now open.

EXCURSIONS

A good nearby excursion is **Beidaihe**, primarily a seaside resort 10–15 kilometers south of Qinhuangdao. For more information, see the selection on *Beidaihe* immediately below.

Shanhaiguan in northeastern Hebei province 20 kilometers north of Beidaihe, is an important pass in the Great Wall. Its Qinhuangdao airport can be reached by air from seven Chinese cities. It's a five-hour train ride from Beijing.

Six kilometers north is the **Meng Jiang-nu Temple**, built in memory of another of China's chaste, almost supernatural heroines. Lady Meng traveled on foot during several winter months in search of her husband, one of the hundreds of thousands of workers building the Great Wall. Her deep sorrow and tears moved Heaven so much that the Great Wall collapsed to reveal her husbands bones. The temple was originally built in the Song dynasty, but the Red Guards destroyed the statues. The government restored them in the late 1970s in gaudy, crudely painted clay. But the view of the hills to the north is interesting.

Laolongtou (Old Dragon Head), the place where the Great Wall meets the sea, is four kilometers south of Shanhaiguan. **Chenghai Tower**, on the seashore, was originally built in 1579. It has been rebuilt and decorated with soldiers in Ming costume. The **Great Wall Festival** in June has races, 18 to 40 kilometers up and down the Wall. It also has costumed Ming and Qing performances, lantern shows and large scale fireworks at Old Dragon Head. A small temple to the Sea Goddess is nearby.

At **Jiao Shan**, where the Great Wall is very steep, there is an 1,833 meter-long chair lift almost to the top. The town itself is surrounded by a well-maintained wall of its own.

Hotels are better in nearby Qinhuangdao and Beidaihe.

SHOPPING

Grown locally are peaches, pears, sea cucumbers, and crabs (biggest in September-October). Made locally are pictures, lamps and ashtrays of shell. Also manufactured are mirrors, magnifying glasses, painted eggs, painted stones, butterfly and insect specimens, bird-feather crafts, and necklaces of red beans (symbol of longing between lovers).

PRACTICAL INFORMATION

- **CITS**, *Tel. 4041748. Fax 4042478; also 46 Minzu Road, Tel. 3066988. Fax 3065974*
- **CYTS Tours**, *45 Wen Hua Road, 066000. Tel. 3036402. Fax 3032633*
- **Telephone Code**, *335*

BEIDAIHE

Beidaihe is primarily a seaside resort, built after the completion of the Beijing-Shanhaiguan railway in 1893. By 1949, 706 villas and hotel buildings had been completed, many of them for foreign diplomats and missionaries as well as wealthy Chinese. After Liberation, the Chinese government rebuilt some of the old buildings and added new ones as rest and recreation centers for its employees.

The population is around 20,000.

ARRIVALS & DEPARTURES

Beidaihe is about 40 kilometers from Shanhaiguan, 10 to 15 kilometers south of Qinhuangdao, and about a five hour train trip or a six hour drive (with lunch) due east (290 kilometers) of Beijing. The railway station is about 18 kilometers away. Cars are generally not permitted into the downtown area, but you can get permission to access the hotels there.

The closest airport is near Shanhaiguan. There is also air service with Shijiazhuang.

ORIENTATION

The resort stretches along 12 kilometers of hard, golden sand sloping gently out into the **Bohai Sea**, a good place to walk. Swimming is good too though there may be a few jellyfish. Rock promontories divide the beaches. At the Pigeons Nest in the east, you can look at Qinhuangdao across the bay and the best sunrise. At the Tiger Stone in the center, crab fishermen sell their catch in the summer.

Several **swimming areas** are attached to each of the hotels, manned by life guards and protected by nets. Each hotel has changing rooms on the beach with hot and cold fresh-water showers, open 8 am to 10 pm. The swimming season is from May to September, depending on how cold you like your water. The hottest days are in August (maximum 36 degrees centigrade for a few days), but the high is usually 31 degrees, sometimes dropping to 24 or 25 degrees at night.

SEEING THE SIGHTS

A **Guanyin Temple**, built in 1911, is on the grounds of the West Hill Hotel. The buildings were beautifully restored in 1979, the two statues and frescoes inside replaced after being destroyed by the Red Guards. The temple is about 1.5 kilometers behind the hotels service bureau, a nice mornings walk. The **Xiaobaohezhai Village** is also a good place to visit. It was one of the first in China to have pensions for its older citizens and one of the first with a birth-control program. It grows apples, peaches and pears for export, so an ideal time to visit is late August-September.

An incredible seaside playground built by Changli County is located less than 60 kilometers south of Beidaihe. It has fake castles, sand slides, water slides, cabanas, hotels, amusement parks – none of which appears to be up to North American standards. Only foreigners wanting a do-nothing seaside vacation with something to amuse the children would probably be interested.

WHERE TO STAY

The top hotel is the **Jinshan**, but don't expect anything fancy. The Diplomatic Missions is quite good too. Both are close to the beach. The airport is 30 kilometers east; the railway station 12 kilometers north.

BEIDAIHE GUESTHOUSE FOR DIPLOMATIC MISSIONS, *1 Bao San Road, 066100. Tel. 4041287, 4041587. Fax 4041807. Credit Cards. Three stars.*

Note:This hotel is not restricted to diplomats. It's closer to shops than the other hotels and a few feet from the beach. Next to the Tiger Stone. Built 1988. Renovations in 1994 and due again soon. Garden with ten three-story villas, one of which is rented by an embassy. Some not air-conditioned. 185 rooms. IDD. USTV. Ticketing service. Tennis court.

JINSHAN HOTEL *(Binguan), 4, the Third Road of East Beach, 066100. Tel. 4041678, 4041748. Fax 4042478. Three stars, Credit Cards.*

Built 1986. Ren. 1991. 500 beds. Several buildings joined together by covered walkways and beautiful private gardens. Half a block from beach. Better ambiance than North Star Hotel in Qinhuangdao. 100 rooms.

Dirty carpets. USTV. B.C. Outdoor pool. Good food. Bowling. They expect their own fleet of Mercedes soon. High season July 1 to September 15. Open all year.

PRACTICAL INFORMATION

- **CITS**, *Tel. 2026828, 4041748. Fax 2027484, 4042478*
- **CYTS**, *Tel. 2030466. Fax 2024049*
- **Tourist Bureau**, *9 Pingan Road, Tel. 4042195*
- **Telephone Code**, *0335*

QUFU

(Chufu)

Qufu is in southwestern Shandong province. The population is 60,000.

The hometown and grave of **Kong Fuzi** (Master Kong), known to the west as **Confucius**, is a good place to be immersed in old China. Take your time. Meditate in these beautiful, exotic surroundings. Read the *Analects of Confucius*. The discipline he advocates might be just what your hectic life lacks. Go back in time.

Confucius was born in Nishan, 35 kilometers southeast from his temple. He moved with his mother to Qufu after the death of his father, when he was three. His father was a general of the State of Lu. Qufu was the capital of a minor kingdom during the Shang (14th-11 century B.C.). The city is named Winding City Wall after the old wall built 3,000 years ago. The current wall is Ming.

One-fifth of the people in Qufu are surnamed Kong, and those in a direct line of descendance received state pensions for centuries (with no need to earn their living otherwise). Currently living are the 73rd to 77th generations. The sage's birthday, September 28, is now celebrated with a reenactment for tourists of the sacrificial ritual and homage by an emperor in the hypnotic, slow movements and music of the times. It is part of the annual **Confucian Cultural Festival** in late September and early October. A telephoto lens is necessary for photographers.

The hottest temperature in summer is 39 degrees centigrade; the coldest temperature in winter is a chilly minus seven.

ARRIVALS & DEPARTURES

Qufu is about 150 kilometers south of Jinan, and 80 kilometers from Jiaxiang Airport. You can get there by road from Jinan and from Tai'an (70 kilometers). You can go by train from only Jinan and Rizhao to Yanzou on the Beijing-Shanghai line. Then you have to go by road for 18 kilometers.

At one time, it was believed that a railway would disturb Confucius' grave and its *feng shui*, so a new railway station was opened closer to Qufu.

ORIENTATION

Spend at least two days for this small, charming city, one day for the three Kongs (mansion, temple and forest), and one day for the tomb of Mencius, the birthplace cave of Confucius, and the Temple of Shao Hao.

This is a good place for bicycling or hiking. It is relatively flat and has many interesting things to explore. At least a week is necessary for adventurous bicyclists. You can rent bicycles near the Qufu bus station or in the Forest of Confucius.

The old city is centered around the Confucian monuments.

WHERE TO STAY

The best hotel is the charming **Queli**, which has western food, but needs work. It is the best location within walking distance of the Mansion, Temple, and shops, and just a ten minute ride from the forest.

QUELI HOTEL *(Binguan), 15 Zhong Lou St., 273100. Three stars, Tel. 411300. Fax 412022. Almost adjacent to the Temple of Confucius. Credit Cards.*

Built 1986. Ren. 1993. Exquisite Chinese architecture with court-yards and ponds. Two stories. 164 rooms. Striking murals and sculptures. Good furniture. Concerts of classical Chinese music if enough interested guests. Video of Confucian ceremonies on request. B.C. Good food. USTV. IDD. U.S. management company.

WHERE TO EAT

Confucian food is not as salty as Shandong and each dish has a meaning, for example, turtle for longevity. A genuine banquet used to have 400 courses! The food at the **QUELI HOTEL** is edible. You might want to try the **GRAND INN**, *Tel. 4412647*, 100 meters southeast of the Queli Hotel, for a change.

SEEING THE SIGHTS

The Confucian monuments are in and near the old city, and can be seen in a day. The *Confucian Temple, occupying more than 20 hectares (about 50 acres), is the most important one in China and the largest in the world. First built in 478 A.D., it was rebuilt and enlarged to its present size during the Ming and Qing. Its gold-tiled roofs, its arches, red doors, and carved tile dragons are Ming. The two stone soldiers/generals, over two meters tall and near the gate, are from the Han Dynasty (917-971). They once guarded a nobles tomb in another part of the city. Live egrets and cranes nest in the gardens here.

THE PHILOSPHY OF CONFUCIUS

Confucius lived from 551 to 479 B.C. during the Spring and Autumn Period, a time of small warring kingdoms and political chaos. He was an itinerant teacher who preached that stability could be achieved by a return to the classics and the old Zhou dynasty rituals. He defined and promoted an already existing system of interpersonal relationships with its emphasis on responsibility and obedience.

The virtuous or benevolent man does not lose his temper; the virtuous man thinks ill of people who criticize others in their absence, who talk badly of other people to make themselves look better, or who persist in promoting deceptions they know are false. He did not concern himself with insignificant things, material gain, fame, or ambition. He was moderate in all things.

He was no democrat. People who do not hold office in a state should not discuss its policies, he said. He advocated that subjects be unquestionably subordinated to rulers, sons to fathers, younger brothers to older brothers, wives to husbands, younger friend to older friend.

His philosophy was the official ideology in China for over 2,000 years, promoted because it supported the oligarchic power structure. Filial piety was essential to the system, and the state enforced this policy. If a child failed to care for his aged parents or was rude to them, the authorities would punish the child. Children owed their lives to their ancestors. They were obligated to respect and worship these people.

The philosophy deteriorated into a religion where descendants performed rituals to keep ancestral spirits happy, so the dead would influence the fortunes of the living.

One finds elements of his theories still stifling Chinese people everywhere. Confucius was behind the famous civil service system, based on the memorization of the classics and his analects. The imperial examinations and the arrogant, insular thinking did, however, outlive their usefulness. The civil service examination system was abolished in the early 1900s, and Confucius is now being studied dispassionately again.

In some family temples, food is still shared with ancestors, heads bowed and incense burned in worship especially during the Qing Ming Festival in spring, and the autumn equinox. And vestiges of the traditions surrounding the cult remain to this day, in spite of governmental discouragement: things like arranged marriages, marriages between two deceased people, or between one living and one deceased person, etc. This is not, however, as common as it was before 1949. Rote memory is still the basis of much education, but hopefully this is changing today.

The **Dacheng Hall** is the main hall for paying homage. Only an emperor could be carried over the carved dragons up to its door. The hall is over 31 meters tall and 54 meters wide, with the same appearance of some of the buildings in Beijing's Forbidden City (which was copied from this temple). Important are the ten carved stone columns, two dragons with a pearl on each, slithering between clouds and a pearl. Note the set of ritual bronze bells, which are played on ceremonial occasions. (See also Provincial Museum, *Wuhan*.)

The *****Kong Family Mansion** has nine courtyards, over 400 rooms, and a garden, on 14 hectares.The gate in front is Ming. The Main Hall, Second Hall, and Third Hall were offices of the Duke of Yansheng, the 46th generation grandson, who was made a noble by Emperor Renzong of the Song. These offices, with his desk under a yellow canopy and painted beamed ceiling, give authenticity to opera stage sets of the period. Ancient weapons, banners, and drums line the walls. The mansion was started in 1038.

Gifts to the family from emperors and high-ranking visitors include Zhou and Shang dynasty bronzes. Visitors would do well to read *In the Mansion of Confucius' Descendants* by Kong Demao and Ke Lan before arriving. From it you can get a feel for the human drama that took place here. Kong Demao, who is still living, was the daughter of the second wife of the Duke of Yansheng, her mother was believed to be poisoned by the first wife. Her tale of being confined behind these walls is pathetic, but she was also party to great events as well as family misfortunes. Some photographs of the family are on display. The current Duke of Yansheng is said to be living in Taiwan. The **Kong Family Mansion Hotel** (first built in 1038 A.D.), *Tel. 4412421*, and next to the family mansion has an exhibition of antiques.

The Confucian Forest contains 200,000 family tombs and is reputedly the oldest and largest cemetery in the world. The trees were collected by disciples from all over the country. It is about three by four kilometers and has over 30,000 trees. Elaborately crafted gates, stone lions, and a stone-arched bridge punctuate the lovely greenness. Tall stone nobles and animals guard the gate to the *****Tomb of Confucius**, a tumulus marked with stone tablets and fancy incense burners.

A small brick house, Zi Gong's Hut, stands nearby. One of the master's disciples built it and lived there for six years after Confucius death, to show respect. Lady Yus Arch was named after a daughter of Qing Emperor Qianlong, who was married to the then Duke of Yansheng. The title was hereditary until the Nationalists officially stopped the practice.

Also in Qufu is a Sacred Way with stone animals and steles, the Temple of Yan Hui, the Temple of the Duke of Zhou, and the remains of the former capital of the State of Lu.

The Tomb of Shao Hao, one of the five legendary rulers, is about eight kilometers away. The **Temple of Mencius**, the later disciple who spread the teachings of Confucius to the rest of China, is 27 kilometers south of the city. Here is also a small museum, a temple to the mother of Mencius, and a hall for the wife of Mencius.

The Birthplace of Confucius in Nisan is also open as a museum. A theme park based on the Six Confucian Arts is between the Forest and the Temple on Chun Qou Road in Qufu.

SHOPPING

Locally produced are wood carvings, stone rubbings, carpets, and Nishan inkstones. The **Antique Store** *in the Mansion, Tel. 4412757,* sells beautiful carved and gilded wooden beds and can ship them. A souvenir market is between the Queli Hotel and the Confucius Temple, and a market in Ming architecture is one block to the left as you leave the Queli Hotel. A small **Friendship Store** is on the same street as the Mansion. The **Qi Lu Department Store** is on *Wu Ma Ci Street, Tel. 4414403.* Chun Qou Ge is at *5 Bei Men Street, Tel. 4411014.*

PRACTICAL INFORMATION

• **CITS**, *1, Kongmiao Shendao, 273100. Tel. 4412491, Fax 4412492*
• **Tourist Complaints**, *88, Jing Shi Road, Jinan, 250014. Tel. (0531) 2965858 or 2963423*
• **Telephone Code**, *0537*

SHIJIAZHUANG

(Shihchiachuang, Shihkiachwang)

Shijiazhuang is the capital of Hebei province.With a population of over 900,000, Shijiazhuang is primarily an industrial city.

It is of importance to Chinese revolutionary history as the burial place of the Canadian who became a Chinese hero. **Dr. Norman Bethune** arrived in China in 1938 to help the Communist Eighth Route Army in its fight against the Japanese. Working almost in the front lines, he died of blood poisoning on November 12, 1939, in Huangshikou village, Tangxian county, in Hebei. That year, Chairman Mao wrote a much publicized article, pointing him out as an example of utter devotion to others without any thought of self. He became known to every school-child, and statues were made of him all over the country. I highly recommend the Canadian feature film, *Bethune, the Making of a Hero.*

ARRIVALS & DEPARTURES

Shijiazhuang is a few hours by train south of Beijing, on the main line to Guangzhou, east of the Taihang Mountains on the Hebei Plain. It is also connected by the 224-kilometer-long Jingshi Expressway with Beijing and now linked by air with 15 Chinese cities and, hopefully in the near future, with Hong Kong, South Korea, and Japan.

The airport is 33 kilometers from city centre and is one of Beijing's alternatives, should Beijing's airport be unexpectedly closed.

ORIENTATION

The **Bethune International Peace Hospital**, first set up in 1937 in the Shanxi-Chahar-Hebei Military Area, was moved here in 1948. Dr. Bethune is buried in the western part of the North China Revolutionary Martyrs Cemetery, where there is also the Bethune Exhibition Hall and the Memorial Hall for Revolutionary Martyrs. The city also has the **Hebei Provincial Exhibition Hall and Museum**.

WHERE TO STAY & EAT

The **Tatai Grand** has the most services, the International Building the second most.

HEBEI GRAND HOTEL *(Binguan), 23 Yucai Road, 050011. Three stars, Tel. 5815961, Fax 5814092.*

INTERNATIONAL BUILDING, *23 Changan Xi Road, 050011. Three stars. Tel. 6047888. Fax 6034787. Credit Cards.*

IDD. B.C.

TATAI GRAND HOTEL, *48 Qingyuan Street, 050021. Three stars. Tel. 6012901. Fax 6011071. Credit Cards.*

IDD. Sichuan, Shandong, Cantonese, Chaozhou, Japanese and Beijing food. Tennis. Gym.

SHOPPING

Locally made are painted-on-the-inside snuff bottles, paper cuts, and ceramics. There are also white marble carvings from Quyang County, and Liuling wine. Elsewhere in the province golden-thread tapestry (Zhuoxian), shell crafts (Qinhuangdao), horse saddles (Zhangjiakou), ink slabs (Yishui), woven straw (Chengde), Handan ceramics, and Tangshan porcelain are made.

Good shopping is at the **Cultural Relics Store**, *24 Yucai Street, Tel. 5814487*, and the **Hualian Commercial Building**, *Zhanqian Street, Tel. 7025991.*

PRACTICAL INFORMATION

- **CITS**, Shijiazhuang Branch, and **Hebei Overseas Tourist Corporation** *are both at 22 Yucai Street, Shijiazhuang, China, 050021. Tel. 5814766. Fax 5815368*
- **Hebei Oriental Travel Service**, *22 Haizhong Zhong Road, Tel. 6019083. Fax 6019074*
- **Hebei Tourism Bureau**, *22 Yucai Street, 050021. Tel. 6014319. Fax 6015368*
- **Telephone Code**, *0311*
- **Tourist Complaints**, contact Supervisory **Bureau of Tourism Quality of Hebei Province**, *22 Yuzhong Street, 050021, Tel 6014239. Fax 6015368*
- **Tourist Hotline**, *Tel. 5814319, 5814239*

TAI'AN

Tai'an is about 80 kilometers south of Jinan, which has the closest airportto Tai'an. The hottest time (36 to 37 degrees centigrade) is in July and August; the coldest is December and January, minus 10 degrees. The annual precipitation is 700 millimeters, mainly from July to September.

It is about 10 degrees colder at the top of Mt. Tai. The best time to climb is from April to October, but one can climb all year round except in inclement weather. The urban population at the base is over 250,000.

ARRIVALS & DEPARTURES

Taian is accessible by road and rail, and is usually combined with a visit to Qufu, 80 kilometers away.

ORIENTATION

Taian is where you go to ascend **Mt. Tai** (Taishan), one of China's **Five Sacred Mountains**. It is a 2.5 billion year old mountain, one of the oldest in the world.

In ancient times, emperors came here to offer sacrifices to Earth and to Heaven; if they went up the mountain, they were probably carried up, and visitors today have the same choice, but by bus or taxi.

WHERE TO STAY

At the foot of the mountain, the best hotel is the **Overseas Chinese Hotel**. On the summit, the best is the **Shenqi**. If your schedule is tight and there is a strong wind threatening to cancel the cable car, you better stay down below. Prices listed, as always, are subject to change.

TAISHAN OVERSEAS CHINESE HOTEL *(Huaqiao Dasha)*, *Dongyue Avenue, 271000. Four stars, Tel. 8228112. Fax 8228171. $30 to $50. Dist.R.W. three kilometers. Credit Cards.*
Built 1990. 14 stories, 204 rooms. IDD. Cantonese food.

SHENQI HOTEL *(Binguan)*, *10 Tian St., Taishan, 271000. Three stars, Tel. 8223866, 8223821. Fax 8333150. $40 to $60.Credit Cards.*
About two kilometers upward from the top of the cable car, 20 kilometers from the railway station. Built 1991. Two stories, 102 rooms. IDD. Sauna. Great view. Seven restaurants, traditional medicine banquet. Clinic. Cantonese and Sichuan food. Sauna.

WHERE TO EAT

The hotel restaurants are good here. There's also the **TAI YUAN RESTAURANT**, *199 Yingxuan Da Jie, Tel. 8213737*, and the **INTERNATIONAL RESTAURANT**, *Longtan Road, Tel. 8214593*.

SEEING THE SIGHTS

If you have only one day, you can be driven halfway up to the **Zhongtian** (Middle Celestial) **Gate**. Then you can take the 2078-meter-long suspended cable car almost to the top at **Nantian** (Southern Celestial) **Gate** between 7 am and 7 or 8 pm (no service during high winds.) From the top of the cable car to the peak at an altitude of 1,545 meters are 500 more steps.

You can lunch at the **Shenqi Binguan** near the summit and then return to see the **Daimiao Temple** and a free market.

Ascending on Foot

The longer, more satisfying way is to climb (at least one way) because the mountain has 30 old temples and 66 well-documented scenic spots, including beautifully carved memorial arches, Han dynasty cypress trees, white water, breathtaking views of forests and crags, and a stone pillar that looks suspiciously like a lingam. If you do it the hard way, you are following in the footsteps of Confucius!

The top can be reached in five or six hours on foot through the **Path of Eighteen Bends**. Note the 7,000-plus stonestairs, each carefully placed by human labor! Like an almost vertical Great Wall! And they are not narrow! It is difficult to get lost. The stairs are very steep and in some places difficult to climb.

The **Temple of Azure Clouds** is over 970 years old (Song). Note the bronze or iron roof ornaments, rafters, bells, and tiles of the main hall, made of metal to endure the severe mountain storms. Inside are nine huge gilt statues. Can you imagine having to carry these and the bronze

Ming tablets up here! The top is at **Tianzhu Feng** (Heavenly Pillar Peak), which is also known as Yuhuang Ding (Jade Emperor Peak).

The **Tomb of Feng Yuxiang** (Feng Yu-hsiang) may be of interest to students of modern Chinese history. This was the famous Christian General who fought with the Nationalists against the Japanese and baptized his men with water hoses. His tomb is at the east end of the Dazhong Bridge, downhill from the Dragon Pool Reservoir. He is known more for his eccentricity than his military successes.

The 72 visiting emperors used to offer their sacrifices at the **Daimiao** (Temple to the God of Taishan), *Hong Men Road,* close to the Taishan Guest House at the base. Open 8:30 am to 5 pm. On special occasions like the Climbing Festival, actors perform a reenactment of the rituals by Song Emperor Zhengzong at the impressive Daimaio. Though slow-moving, this should not be missed. The **Tain Kuang Hall**, which is the main hall, has a mural 3.3 by 62 meters, painted in the Song, showing the pilgrimage of this emperor here. It includes 570 to 657 figures. (Count them!) This hall was built in 1009 A.D. and is considered one of the three eminent halls of China. It's on Travel agencies can arrange sightseeing by helicopter and the re-enactment of the rituals at the Daimiao.

Festivals
During the third or fourth lunar month or early in September, there is the **mountain climbing festival**.

SHOPPING
Carpets and baskets are made locally. Peaches, walnuts, chestnuts, and dates are grown.

PRACTICAL INFORMATION
· **CITS** and **Tai'an Tourism Bureau**, *46 Hongmen Road, 271000, above the Dai Temple and the Taishan Arch; Tel. 8223259, 8227020, 8221183. Fax 8332240*
· **Telephone Code**, *0538*

TAIYUAN
Taiyuan is in the center of Shanxi province, of which it is the capital. Taiyuan was founded in the Western Zhou (1066-771 B.C.). Because of its strategic location, it was the site of many wars, changing hands five times between 396 and 618 A.D. It was a silk center under the Sui and has been growing grapes for a thousand years.

The hottest temperature is 35 degrees centigrade for a few days in August, the coldest is minus 14 degrees in January. The annual precipitation is 400 millimeters from July to September. The altitude is 800 meters. The population is 2.05 million.

ARRIVALS & DEPARTURES

Taiyuan is over an hour's flight southwest of Beijing, and 2 1/2 hours north of Guangzhou. Taiyuan can be reached by air from Hong Kong and 22 other cities, and by train from Beijing, Xian, Zhengzhou, Hohhot, and Datong, and others.

ORIENTATION

Although it used to be a highly cultured city with many architectural wonders, the wars and modern industry have changed its complexion.

WHERE TO STAY

SHANXI GRAND HOTEL *(Shanxi Dajiudian), 5 Xin Jian Nan Road, 030001. Three stars, Tel. 4043901. Fax 4043525. Credit Cards.*

This is the best hotel in town. Built 1989. 14 stories, 168 rooms. B.C., IDD. USTV. B.C. Cantonese and Russian restaurants. Indoor pool. Bowling. Gym. Qigong.

WHERE TO EAT

Shanxi people love noodles and vinegar-flavored dishes. Five hundred-meter-long Food Street, in the southern part of the city, has 46 food shops and restaurants.

SEEING THE SIGHTS

Taiyuan is most famous for the **Jinci Temple**, 25 kilometers southwest of the city at the foot of Xuanweng Mountain. One source says it was initially built in the Northern Wei (386-534) in memory of the second son of King Wu of the Western Zhou. The Jin Temple was renovated, with additions, in 1102 (Northern Song). The temple has female statues, which, aside from goddesses, is very rare in China. Was this second son a lush? A son much pampered by women? Are the women here to continue indulging him in the after-life?

Alas, no! Centuries ago, Shanxi was very short of water. Sea and water deities have usually been female. In Shanxi a spring was found near Jinci, so people started worshipping Shuimu (Mother of Water). The maids-in-waiting and the mermaids were her retinue.

The temple is the oldest wooden structure in the area and is charming. In the Shengmu (Sacred Lay Hall) are 43 dusty, lifesize clay figures, 30 of these court maids-in-waiting, all lithesome, each different in expression, and still retaining much color. They were made in the Song.

Uphill from the Jinci about 40 minutes by road, the **Tianlong Shan** (Mountain of Celestial Dragon) has a little temple with four lohan and 24 small caves with many old, damaged statues. The **Chongshan Monastery** in the city itself is believed to have been a Sui palace once. Only part of the original (Tang) monastery is standing, and part of that is the **Shanxi Provincial Museum**. The monastery is famous for its ancient 1000-handed, 1000-eyed Goddess of Mercy. It, along with the two other bodhisattvas are eight meters tall. The beams and ceiling are quite remarkable. During the Sino-Japanese War, a bomb went through the ceiling without exploding, and the repair work is still visible. It is three kilometers from the Yingze Hotel.

Next door is the Shanxi Provincial Museum. **Museum Number One** has a vast collection of neolithic artifacts. So far, 200 paleolithic and 500 neolithic sites have been unearthed in the province, plus over 500 tombs and other ancient ruins. **Provincial Museum Number Two** is considered more important than Museum Number One. Located at the site of the Chunyang Palace on the west side of May 1 Square, the palace itself was built between 1573 and 1619, and renovated in the Qing. It contains 20 exhibition halls with ceramics, bronzes, carvings, lacquer, calligraphy, embroidery, books, and other documents unearthed around the province. There is also a huge coal museum.

The **Shuangta Temple**, also known as the Yongzuo Monastery, has twin pagodas, symbols of Taiyuan, eight kilometers from the Yingze Hotel. The pagodas were built in the Ming and are over 50 meters high. They are octagonal and of carved bricks. Inside the monastery are exhibitions of old coins, pottery, etc., and a corridor with 207 stone tablets of Ming calligraphy.

There are also a great number of important historical monuments in Shanxi province: 70 kilometers southwest is the **Qiao Family Compound** and folk museum, originally the home of a wealthy Qing merchant. This is highly decorated with carvings and should be of interest to those who saw the internationally-acclaimed Chinese movie *Raise the Red Lantern*. Built in 1755 in Qixian County, it was used as the main set for this Oscar-nominated movie. The mansion has 313 rooms.

SHOPPING

Locally made are fur coats, including rabbit and wild rat(!) skin, gold and lacquer inlaid crafts, reproductions of ancient ironware, black-glazed porcelain, Junco brand carpets, Fen Chiew wines, vinegars, fine glass-ware, lacquerware, jade carving, and brass and copperware (especially fancy charcoal-burning hot pots). Grown locally are dates, pears, persimmons, walnuts, and wild jujubes.

EXCURSIONS FROM TAIYUAN

In the southern tip of Shanxi province is ***Yong Le Palace** in Ruicheng County, with beautiful 400-meter-long Yuan dynasty murals. From it, you can also study social and architectural history.

Nearby in Yuncheng County is the **Guan Di Temple**, founded in the Sui and completely renovated in the Qing. **Pingyao**, about 100 kilometers southwest of Taiyuan, is a well-preserved ancient city with 6.7 kilometers of city walls, and shops and homes untouched since the Ming and Qing.

At Hongdong, about 200 kilometers southwest of Taiyuan, is the ***Guangsheng Temple**, listed as Yuan and Ming. It has excellent colored ceramic figures and frescoes. An intricate, stunning collection of about 1,000 lively Buddhist and animal figures over 300 years old is at the **Xiaoxitian** (Miniature Western Paradise), northwest of Guangsheng Temple and north of Xixian county town. These are also worth a visit. Be prepared to climb and crane your neck. Take a flashlight and binoculars. And recently opened for tourists is a Ming dynasty jail in Hong Dong County. There a woman, wrongly accused of poisoning her husband, was incarcerated.

*Dingcun paleolithic ruins are in Xianfen county, roughly 25 kilometers southwest of Hongdong. Also in this area is a Han (nationality) folk museum, with 19 Ming and Qing courtyards, the oldest built in 1593. **Houma**, another 50 kilometers southwest of Linfen, is a Jin site from the Eastern Zhou. A low but spectacular (depending on the season) waterfall is at Hukou on the Yellow River, northeast of Dingcun. Guesthouses are at Yuncheng City. You could spend a fruitful month exploring this province alone! Much of the Chinese collection in Toronto's Royal Ontario Museum is from southern Shanxi.

See *Datong* for the Yungang Grottoes, the Great Wall, Wutai Mountain, Sakyamuni Pagoda, the Huayan and Shanhua Monasteries and the Mid-Air Temple.

PRACTICAL INFORMATION

- **CTS Shanxi**, *Fax 4035024*
- **CYTS Tours**, *34 Qing Nian Road, 030001. Tel. 4048017, Fax 4046475*
- **Shanxi CITS**, *38 Ping Yang Road, 030012. Tel. 7042109, 7042109*
- **Shanxi Provincial Tourism Administration**, *282 Ying Ze Avenue, 030001. Tel. 4080073, 2027161. Fax 4048289. (Information); for Tourist Complaints, Tel. 4047544. Fax 4048289*
- **Telephone Code**, *0351*
- **Tourism Hotline**, *Tel. 7042126, 7042109*

TIANJIN

(Tientsin: Ferry to the Imperial Capital)
Tianjin is China's third largest city. The urban population is four million.

Tianjin was a trading post in the 12th century during the Jin. It developed as a port in the Yuan. During the Ming (1404), city walls were built and the city was called Tianjinwei by the Duke of Yen, who crossed the Haihe River here on a military expedition. After the Grand Canal opened in 1412, inland commerce and Tianjins fortunes improved. A city wall was built about this time, and an imposing old fort once stood at the confluence of the three rivers.

The British and French invaded Tianjin in 1858. In June of that year they and the Chinese signed the **Treaty of Tientsin** giving Christian missionaries freedom of movement and protection because the Christian religion as professed by Protestants and Roman Catholics inculcates the practices of virtue, and teaches man to do as he would be done by. In 1860, British and French troops from Tianjin marched on Beijing and forced the Qing rulers to ratify the Treaty of Tientsin; they then burned down the Summer Palace. The resulting Treaty of Peking opened Tianjin and nine other ports to foreign trade.

Nine countries eventually controlled over 3,500 acres of this city: Britain (with over 1,000 acres), France, Germany, Japan, Russia, Italy, Belgium, Austria, and the United States. The concessions lasted from 20 to 80 years and, as in Shanghai, left the Chinese some very interesting old European architecture as well as bitter memories. The Treaty of Peking also forced the Chinese to permit French missionaries to own or rent property anywhere, and further helped to inflame smoldering anti-Christian and anti-foreign resentment.

Many of these feelings resulted from what the Chinese saw as Christian arrogance, which insisted that the Christian god was the only true god. Added to this were cultural misunderstandings. Quite a few Chinese actually believed that the children in Catholic orphanages were either eaten by nuns or ground up for medicine. The French Catholics did pay money for female babies – to keep them from being killed. By 1870, the atmosphere grew so tense that after the French consul fired at a minor Chinese official, the consul was immediately hacked to death. Ten nuns, two priests, and another French official were also brutally killed in what is now known as the Tientsin Massacre, or what the Chinese prefer to call the Tientsin Revolt. In 1976, an earthquake centered in nearby Tangshan severely damaged the city.

The weather is hottest in July, 40 degrees centigrade, and coldest in January, minus six degrees. Annual precipitation averages 600 millimeters, mostly between June and August.

ARRIVALS & DEPARTURES

Tianjin, 70 kilometers from the Bohai Sea, is two hours (120 kilometers) southeast of Beijing by train on the Beijing-Shanghai and Beijing-Harbin railway lines. It is also joined by expressway to Beijing and by Number 17 Express Bus every 30 minutes from the Beijing's Zhaogongkou Long-distance Bus Station between 7 am and 6:30 pm.

There are air connections with Hong Kong, Irkutsk, Kiev, Macau, Seoul, Tashkent, and 20 Chinese cities, and by ship from Inchon (Korea), Kobe (Japan), Dalian, Yantai, Qingdao, and Shanghai (708 nautical miles).

ORIENTATION

Tianjin is more of a gateway to elsewhere than a tourist destination in itself, though interest in the Last Emperor (who lived here from 1925 to 1931) has brought tourists here. Tianjin is a port city, the largest commercial seaport in North China. One of the treaty ports open to foreign trade by the Opium Wars, it is now one of China's biggest industrial centers and one of the 14 Open Coastal Cities. It has China's first free trade zone.

Tianjin is mainly for business travelers but in between appointments, there are things to do in addition to **golf**. Resident foreigners say it is a good place to live because the people are friendlier and more polite than in Shanghai and Beijing, and the sightseeing is less crowded. Many of Beijing's foreign residents drive the two hours to Tianjin on weekends for a change for peace and the antique market.

Tianjin, like Beijing and Shanghai, is a municipality directly under the central government. It has eight urban and four rural districts and five suburban counties. Its factories make Flying Pigeon bicycles, Seagull watches, petrochemicals, textiles, and diesel engines. The city is rather smoggy. The Dagang Oil Field is 60 kilometers away. You would probably be interested in seeing its arts and crafts factories. Its counties grow walnuts, chestnuts, dates, Xiaozhan rice, and prawns. Cultural presentations here sometimes include traditional opera, Beijing opera, Tianjin ballet, acrobats, and puppets.

The city proper sprawls on both sides of the **Hai River**. The area immediately southwest of the Jiefang (Liberation) Bridge was formerly French. The section south of that, around the Astor Hotel, was formerly British. Liberation Road was Victoria Road. The city is of interest primarily to fans of old European architecture, modern history, and handicrafts.

WHERE TO STAY

The **Sheraton** and the **Hyatt** are the best hotels here. Both are good and luxurious with executive floors. You should choose between the two based on location. The Hyatt borders the Heihe River and is more central, closer to government offices and the antique market. The Sheraton is in the quieter suburbs within walking distance of the 400 meter-high telecommunications tower, CITS, Crystal Palace Hotel, and the Friendship/antique store. It is also near the World Economy Trade and Exhibition Centre which has its own hotel, the Geneva, a cheaper alternative. The area around the Sheraton is also a little closer to the economic zone and harbor. The Astor Hotel is almost next door to the Hyatt and the Friendship Hotel is nearby.

ASTOR HOTEL, *(Lixun De Fandian), 33 Taier Zhuang Road, 300040. Four stars. Tel. 3311688, 3311112. Fax 3316282. Dist.A.P.eight km. Dist.R.W.two km. Credit Cards.*

H.K.J.V. originally built by the British in 1863, and expanded in 1924 and 1987. U.S. President Herbert Hoover slept here. The charming old wing has 94 big rooms. The new wing has 129 rooms. Four and seven stories. IDD. 24-hour B.C. USTV.

FRIENDSHIP HOTEL *(Youyi Binguan), 94 Nanjing Road, 300040. Three stars, Tel. 3310372. Fax 3310616. Dist.A.P. 22 km. Dist.R.W. four km. Credit Cards.*

Built 1977. Ren. 1990. Nine stories, 272 rooms. USTV. IDD. B.C. Korean and Japanese joint venture bars. Gym. For budget travelers.

GENEVA HOTEL *(Jin Li Hua Dajiudian), 30 Youyi Road, Hexi District, 300061. Three stars, Tel. 8352222. Fax 8359855. Credit Cards.*

105 rooms. 165 apartments. Soft beds. IDD. B.C. Cantonese food. Gym.

HYATT TIANJIN *(Kai Yue Fandian), 98 Jiefang Bei Road, 300042. Four stars, Tel. 3318888. Fax 3310021. Dist.A.P. 20 km. Dist.R.W. two km. Credit Cards.*

Built 1986. 19 stories, 450 rooms. IDD. USTV. B.C. Cantonese and Japanese restaurants. Dumplings. 24-hour room service and bars. Bicycles, gym. Steam bath and sauna. Shuttlebus.

SHERATON TIANJIN HOTEL *(Sher Er Don), Zi Jin Shan Road, Hexi Dist., 300074. Five stars. Tel. 3343388. Fax 3358740. Dist.A.P. 15 km. Dist.R.W. nine km. Credit Cards.*

Built 1987. Ren. 50 rooms each year. Six stories, 282 rooms. Non-smoking rooms. USTV. B.C. Italian restaurant. Bicycles, gym, indoor pool, tennis, putting green and steam bath. Small hotel with comfortable, unpretentious atmosphere. Six-story atrium lobby with water fountains.

WHERE TO EAT

The top hotels have the best food. The **Nanshi Food Street**, *Tel. 7351784 or 2350900*, has three stories of shops, restaurants, wine shops, and tea houses. The food here is from all over China and abroad, and includes typical Tianjin snacks such as goubuli (steamed meat dumpling), erduoyan (fried cake), and shibajie (deep-fried dough twist).

SEEING THE SIGHTS

The standard city tour includes the Water Park, Ancient Culture Street, a carpet factory, television tower, Food Street and New Years Picture factory.

The **Dabei** (Grand Mercy) **Temple**, *Tianwei Road, near the Grand Canal, Tel. 6352320*, is the city's biggest Buddhist temple, founded in 1656 (Qing). The Grand Mosque (Dafeng Road, near the Grand Canal) was built in 1644 (Qing). The **Tianjin History Museum**, *4 Guanghua Road; Tel. 4314660*, contains exhibits on the ancient and revolutionary histories of Tianjin, and has some bronzes, jade, paintings, and calligraphy.

The **Tianjin Arts Museum**, *77 Jiefang Bei Road, Tel. 3392484*, has sculptures and other traditional works of art from ancient times. The **Tianjin Museum of Natural History**, *206 Machangdao, Hexi District, Tel. 3352504*, has fossils of mammoths and dinosaurs.

The **Friendship Club**, *268 Machang Dao*, was built in 1925 and is open to both Chinese and foreigners. Formerly the Tientsin Club, it reeks of Britain in the early 1900s, with beautiful, high mahogany paneling and a drab, dismal interior. There are billiards, badminton, tennis, four bowling lanes, a 1300-seat theater, a 600-seat banquet hall, and a ballroom with an elastic wooden floor. (Real springs are beneath it.) Swimming is in a 33 degree centigrade mineral-water pool.

The **Zhou Enlai** (Chou En-lai) **Museum**, *Tel. 7371961*, is in the western part of the city, south of the Grand Mosque at 20 Sima Street, Nankai. The former premier studied at Nankai Middle School here from 1913 to 1917, and briefly at Nankai University (1919), where he led student uprisings.

The 100-room, **Grand Mansion of the Shi Family** is in *Yangliuqing Township, Xiqing District, Tel. 2355062*. It is worth seeing for architecture and its folk arts.

Near Food Street is **Ancient Culture Street** in Qing dynasty style, and the 1326 A.D. **Temple of the Sea Goddess**. But it is nothing like Beijing's Liulichang or Nanjings' Confucian Temple area. I found nothing much to buy except traditional musical instruments. It does have a well-stocked antique shop. Do let me know if this changes.

The **Theater Museum**, *31 Nanmennei Street, Nankai District, Tel. 2355017*, is a must for theater lovers. The building itself is a gem in the gaudy south China style, a guild hall for Guangdong merchants built in 1907. The **Catholic Cathedral**, *Tel. 7301929*, is next to the International Market.

The Last Emperor Pu Yi lived in the Zhang Yuan Garden and the Jing Yuan Garden, neither of which has been renovated nor are open to the public. He was an honorary member of the Tientsin Club (now the Friendship Club). No other Chinese were allowed to be members then.

Festivals

Festivals are held on Ancient Culture Street with stilts and dragon dances and special exhibits. On the first Sunday of April is the International Marathon; the Rose Festival is in May; the Great Wall Mountain Produce Festival is in the autumn; and the New Year Picture Festival is during the Spring Festival.

VISIT A FACTORY

Tianjin is a good place to visit factories. The **Number Two Carpet Factory**, *(Heincheng Road, Hexi District, Tel. 2382113) is one of the biggest carpet factories here, and has been making Junco-brand carpets for more than 100 years in Tianjin. These include thick carpets of pure wool, with no synthetics. Knots are made by hand, either 70 rows per square foot (ordinary) or 120 rows (refined). Embossing is also done by hand. Washing in a chemical solution adds gloss.*

Other factories you might want to visit: **Tianjin Painted Sculpture Workshop** *(202 Machangdao, Hexi District, Tel. 3359866);* **Tianjin Special Handicrafts Factory** *(16 Liuwei Road, Hedong District, Tel. 2344105). The* **Yangliuqing New Year Picture Society** *(111 Sanheli, Tonglou, Hexi District, Tel. 7351531) has New Year's pictures of deities, like the Kitchen God, who informed Heaven of what happened during the year in the family. These pictures are much brighter and more cheerful than traditional Chinese art.*

You can also visit and buy from factories making Pierre Cardin clothes, Italian bicycles and Oneida cutlery. The sales managers at the Sheraton and Hyatt should know about these factory outlets and about factory overruns at the **Arts and Crafts Centre** *on Heping Road.*

Note: visitors allergic to dust or wool should avoid carpet factories.

SHOPPING

The main shopping streets are **Binjiang Dao** and **Heping Road**. Wool carpets, painted clay figurines by Master Zhang, New Year pictures, porcelain vases, tablecloths, accordions, cloisonne pens, soccer balls, basketballs, kites, jade, wine and inlaid lacquered furniture are all made in Tianjin. Cloisonne is better in Shanghai and Beijing. If you're looking for carpets, hotel sales managers should know where to buy old Beijing carpets.

Tianjin Friendship Corporation, *21 Youyi Road, Hexi District, 300201, Tel. 8352477*, has all of the above plus antiques, jewelry, jade, ivory, fur coats, and hats, suede coats, padded silk jackets, men's suits shell work, cloisonne, carved lacquer, screens, inlaid chests, cork and boxwood carvings. They also ship purchases, tailor clothes, and arrange certificates of origin and orders.

You may also want to shop at: **Quanyechang Emporium**, *290 Heping Road, Tel. 7303771*; **Wenyuange Antique Store**, *191-263 Heping Road, Tel. 7303450*; **Yangliuching New Year's Picture Studio**, *Gu Wenhua Street, Nankai District, Tel. 2355191*. Good prices for scrolls, reproductions, and prints; **#Tianjin Cultural Relics Company**, *161 Liaoning Road, Tel. 7300308*. Branches in the Friendship Hotel, and Astor Hotel.

The **Sunday Antique Market** (Shen Yang Dao) starts about 9:15 am with goods spread out on the ground for about seven blocks alongside three regular blocks of full-time more expensive antique stalls. Individual peddlers, eyes alert for the antiquities police, let you peek inside their bags at what they hope you think is a genuine Ming vase. There must be over 100 merchants here with Victrolas, old handsewn clothes, jewelry, old silver and clocks. You can see plenty of the cricket boxes shown in the movie *The Last Emperor* and if you look hard enough, there might be embroidered shoes for bound feet. Be prepared for some hard haggling and crowds. Dealers from antique stores elsewhere do their buying here too. It is one of the best markets in China. If you know your antiques, you can probably get great buys.

EXCURSIONS FROM TIANJIN

Beidaihe seaside resort and **Qinhuangdao** are 3 1/2 hours northeast by train; see these two selections above. Other nearby excursions include Beijing, Chengde, and the Qing Tombs (about three hours drive northeast).

*Dule (Temple of Solitary Joy), 120 kilometers north, about two hours drive, is in the western part of Jixian city and can be combined with a trip to **Panshan Mountain** and the **Great Wall** in one day. It was founded in the Tang. Its Guanyin (Goddess of Mercy) Hall and the Gate to the Temple were rebuilt in 984 A.D. (Liao). The magnificent **Guanyin Hall,** 23 meters high, is the oldest existing multi-storied wooden structure in China. The 16-meter-high, 11-headed goddess is one of the largest clay sculptures in China. The mythical animals at the gate are the oldest extant chiweis in China! The Great Wall at Huangyaguan in Jixian County has a museum. See also *Great Wall*.

The **Panshan** (Screen of Green) **Mountain** (about 100 kilometers north of Jixian City) has been a mountain resort since the Tang. The highest peak is 1000 meters above sea level, on top of which is a pagoda said to contain a tooth of Buddha. Its 70 Buddhist temples were burned by the Japanese during World War II. Some of the buildings have been replaced or renovated.

PRACTICAL INFORMATION
• **CITS** and **Tianjin Overseas Tourist Corporation**, *22 Youyi Road, 300074. Tel. 8358309, 8350104. Fax 8358479. Also O.T.C. Tel. 8358479, 8350821. Fax 8352619. CITS Tel. 8358501, Fax 8352619*
• **CTS**, *10 Youyi Road, 300074. Tel. 8353925. Fax 8353924*
• **CYTS Tours**, *11 Mu Nan Road, He Ping District, 300050. Tel. 8309818, 3115017. Fax 3318017*
• **Telephone Code**, *022*
• **Tianjin Tourism Bureau**, *18 Youyi Road, 300074. Tel. 8354860, Fax 8352324. (Information)*
• **Tourism Complaints**, contact **Supervisory Bureau of Tourism Quality of Tianjin**, *Tel. 8358814, 8358812. Fax 8352324*
• **Tourism Hotline**, *Tel. 8358814 (day); 8358812 (night). 24-hourTel. 3318814*

WEIFANG
Almost in the center of Shandong province, **Weifang** is noted for its international kite festival (the first five days in April) every year, its unique kite museum, and home stays. The urban population is 400,000.

ARRIVALS & DEPARTURES
There's a twice-weekly air connection with Beijing, with more flights during the kite festival.

KITE HEAVEN!
Kites are the main draw and they are fun. You can visit the kite and woodblock print-making village of Yangjiabu to watch the process and professional adult kite fliers testing their goods. You can buy a kite and learn flying techniques from the champions, or explore the kite museum with room after room of the worlds best kites from 350 meter-long centipedes to tiny matchboxes that fly.

The **festival** *itself draws 300,000 spectators. You should book early or go on a tour to ensure transportation and hotel. Contestants have come from all over the world.*

SEEING THE SIGHTS

There are Buddhist relics from the Sui and Tang dynasties here, and a 7.5 meter high stone Longevity character, the biggest such character in China, carved over 500 years ago. In **Shanwang**, southwest of the city, 18-million-year-old prehistoric fossils have been found. The **Shanwang Paleontological Museum** here has 10,000 specimens. Tourists can live with farming families in **Shijiazhuang** village.

Students of modern history might be interested in the **Second Middle School**, a little over a kilometer from the Weifang Hotel. This was once the **Weihsien Concentration Camp**. British, Canadian, and American prisoners were held here by the Japanese in the 1940s, including Eric Liddell, the hero of the movie *Chariots of Fire*. A gold medalist in the 1924 Olympics for winning the 400 meters, this Scottish athlete refused to race on Sundays. He later became a Congregational missionary in China and died of a brain tumor in 1945. He was buried near the prison camp six months before the end of the war. Look for the seven-foot-high memorial stone in Chinese and English. Some of the original prison-missionary buildings are still standing.

WHERE TO STAY

Hotels here have higher prices during the kite festival.

RENAISSANCE FUWAH HOTEL, *Bei Hai Road, 261031. Should be close to five star standard. Tel. 8881988. Fax 8880766. Credit Cards.*

Located in the hi-tech development zone 15 kilometers northeast of the airport, and seven kilometers from the railway station. Combined with an international convention centre and close to Fuwah Amusement Park with waterworld. Built 1995-1996. Nine stories, 246 rooms. USTV. IDD. Cantonese and Korean restaurants. 12-lane bowling, gym, heated indoor pool, sauna, steam bath and tennis. There is no surcharge for 1-800 number calls, credit card calls, or collect calls.

YUAN FEI HOTEL *(Dajiudian), 46 Shengli Street, 261041. Three stars, Tel. 8226901. Fax 8237749, 8223840. Dist.A.P. eight km .Dist.R.W. 2.5 km. Credit Cards.*

Near parks, a reconstructed Qing wall, fascinating decibel counter, and kite museum. 21 stories. 225 rooms. USTV. B.C. Qigong. Has charming Chinese room with kong at no extra charge. A second building of four-star quality should be finished now.

WHERE TO EAT

One of the food treats here is fried scorpions or cicadas, actually quite tasty. I've eaten several of them and survived. Honest!

Your best bet for good food is in the top hotels.

SHOPPING

Made locally are woodblock prints, kites, lacquer furniture inlaid with silver, cotton toys and bronze imitations.

PRACTICAL INFORMATION

- **Business Hours**, 8:30 am to 6 pm (summer) or 5:30 pm (winter) five days a week; 9 am to 6:30 pm for stores.
- **CITS**, *381, Dong Feng Street, 261041, Tel. 8238119. Fax 8233854*
- **CTS**, *Tel. 8223447*
- **Telephone Code**, *0536*
- **Weifang Tourism Bureau**, *127 Shengli Road, 261041, Tel. 8236901. Fax 8238688* Information and complaints.

WEIHAI

(Wei-hai-wei)

Weihei is in northern Shandong province on the Bohai Sea, 95 kilometers east of Yantai and northeast of Qingdao. The urban population is 230,000.

Weihai was developed in the Ming because of its excellent harbor. Some of the funds to strengthen the navy base here were squandered by Empress Dowager Cixi on her Summer Palace in Beijing.

In 1894, the Japanese won a naval base on a 25-year lease, which was used to keep an eye on the Russians at Port Arthur (now Dalian), 100 kilometers north. The British tutor of the Last Emperor, Reginald Johnson – remember Peter O'Toole in the *Last Emperor* movie? – was the British administrator here.

The hottest temperature is 28 degrees centigrade in August; the coldest is minus 12 degrees in January. Rain is mainly in August.

ARRIVALS & DEPARTURES

This off-the-beaten track family vacation city can be reached by road or rail (soon), flights from Beijing and Jinan, and a ferry from Dalian and Inchon, Korea.

ORIENTATION

For the American navy and other foreigners, it was a summer resort. Today it is still a beautiful little open-port city off the tourist track, with small but good beaches and hot springs. Natives are proud of its appearance and cleanliness. There has been a rule that no two buildings downtown should look alike.

WHERE TO STAY

There are no fancy resorts. The **Dongshan Hotel** overlooks a beach and fishing village, has no air-conditioning and few other services, but is adequate for families. It is surrounded by interesting old European houses. The **Weihaiwei Mansion** is better located for business people.

DONGSHAN HOTEL *(Binguan), 27 Dong Shan Road, 264200. Two stars, Tel. 5231184. Fax 5234764.. Dist.A.P.42 km. Dist.city center 12 km. No Credit Cards.*

Built 1980, ren. 1989. Three buildings, two and three stories, 84 rooms. Number Two building best and closest (50 meters) to beach. High ceilings, thin drapes, and big bathrooms.

WEIHAIWEI MANSION *(Dasha). 82 Haigang Road, 264200. Three stars, Tel. 5232542, 5247888. Fax 5232281. Dist.port 100 meters. Dist.A.P.30 km. Credit Cards.*

H.K.J.V. Built 1990-91. 17 stories. 153 rooms IDD. Tennis (across street). B.C. Clinic. Long, narrow rooms. Hot spring water and USTV. French, German, Korean, Sichuan, and Cantonese food.

SEEING THE SIGHTS

Liugong Island (three square kilometers) has a **navy museum** with incredible Qing navy dress uniforms and models of ships. Wax figures of the men who fought the Japanese in 1895 are in the former headquarters. In Weihai you can also find factories that produce carpets, leather goods, embroidery, artificial fur, etc. You can also drive to the easternmost tip of China at **Chengshan Gap**, where the Yellow Sea meets the Bohai Sea. There's not much here except a marker and a fishing village, **Yuanya**, five kilometers from Weihai, which is open for overnight home stays.

PRACTICAL INFORMATION

• **CITS** and **CTS**, *27 Heping Road, 264200, Tel. 5223616, 5225296. Fax 5231152*
• **CYTS TOURS**, *75-2 Tong Yi Road, 264200. Tel. 5233124*
• **Telephone Code**, *0896 or 05451*

YANTAI

(Chefoo, Cheefoo)

Yantai, also known as **Zhifu**, is on the northern coast of Shandong province, about 250 kilometers northeast of Qingdao. Inhabited almost 2,200 years ago, this fishing village was visited by the first Qin emperor early in its existence. (That guy really got around!) In 1398, during the Ming, a military post was set up, and beacon towers built for transmitting messages. Yantai means smoke tower.

Yantai was opened to foreign trade in 1862. It was a summer resort for the U.S. Navy's Yangtze Patrol (with White Russian bar girls). The China Inland Mission operated a school here for missionary children; the buildings now are used by the Chinese Navy. Yantais harborside area and Chaoyang Street still reflect the old architecture. Yantai Hill once housed 10 foreign consulates.

The weather is hottest (28.3 degrees centigrade) in July and August; coldest minus 10 degrees in January. Annual precipitation is about 700 millimeters mostly in June. The urban population is now over 780,000.

ARRIVALS & DEPARTURES

Yantai can be reached by train from Qingdao or by a five-hour superhighway, and can be reached by plane from Macau and 10 Chinese cities. It can also be reached by ship, and by a direct 16 hour train from Beijing and Shanghai. The airport is 25 kilometers from town.

ORIENTATION

Yantai is one of the prettiest little cities in China, nestled between the sea and, on three sides, gentle hills. Many of its buildings are topped with orange tiles, and some are of rose- colored stone. It does not have the depressing look of neglected structures that many Chinese cities unfortunately have. It has a cheerful atmosphere of vitality and prosperity. Off the main tourist track, it is more for relaxed family sightseeing and swimming than hectic tourism.

Yantai is one of the original Coastal Cities recently opened to trading and accelerated industrial development.

Today, Yantai is an important ice-free port that has received international cruise ships. It farms prawns, abalone, scallops, and jelly fish. It grows peanuts (one fifth of China's crop), cherries, grapes, and apples, and grows and cans white asparagus. It mines one quarter of China's gold. The closest mine is about 80 kilometers from the city.

WHERE TO STAY

Hotels here are mainly rundown and have water shortages in the summer. The top is the **Yantai**. The **Zhifu**, the favorite of resident foreigners, is closest to swimming and has a cozier atmosphere. The **Asia Hotel** is downtown and newer. All are three stars.

The **Cheefoo Club** has the most historical setting at one end of the bund and next to Yantai Hill where the foreign consulates were. In its beautiful suites (with the cigarette burns in the stained carpets), its magnificent dining room with its 15-meter ceiling (once used as a church), and its 1870 bowling alley, one does get a feeling of faded imperialist grandeur.

ASIA HOTEL, *116 South Street, 264000. Tel. 6247888. Fax 6242625. Credit Cards.*

IDD. Gym. B.C. Cantonese and Japanese food.

YANTAI HILL GUESTHOUSE *(Yantai Shan Binguan), 34 Haian Road, 246001, Tel. 6224491, 6224493. Fax 6216313. Dist.A.P. 25 km. Dist.R.W. two km. Some Credit Cards.*

Two buildings for foreigners. The **Cheefoo Club** was the former British Consulate built in the late 1800s. In 1913 it became a hotel and was renovated last in 1994. Three stories, 19 rooms. No elevators. Suites 1201 and 1203 face the bund. 1201 has its own wide balcony. Its double rooms are adequate. The Seaview Restaurant, 1988. Three stories, 38 rooms. IDD.

YANTAI HOTEL *(Dajiudian), 1 Huanshan Road, Eastern Suburbs, 264001. Three stars, Tel. 6248468. Fax 6248169. Dist.A.P. 25 km. Dist.R.W. eight km. Dist #2 beach 1.5 km. Credit Cards.*

Hong Kong J.V. Built 1989. Eight stories, 183 rooms, IDD. Low hallway ceilings. Dim sum. Sichuan, Cantonese and French food.

ZHIFU HOTEL *(Zhifu Binguan), 1 Ying Bin Road, 264001. Three stars, Tel. 6248422. Fax 6248289. Dist.A.P. 23 km. Dist.R.W. eight km. Dist.#2 beach 500 meters. Credit Cards.*

Built 1981. Six stories. 115 rooms. IDD. B.C. Sichuan, Cantonese and Continental food.

Home Stays

Yantai is a pioneer in home stay programs for tourists bored by temples. By Chinese standards, some of the rural villages here are incredibly wealthy, and a visit will explain why. **Xiguan Village**, 23 kilometers away, is one of the places where you can spend the night with a family (usually part of a package, and not cheap). Contact CITS or the Yantai Tourism Bureau (see *Practical Information* below) for more information.

WHERE TO EAT

Seafood, of course, is the food of choice here! Shandong food is not peppery hot or overly sweet. Lots of garlic, onions, and salt. Yantai people say that Beijing duck originated when two indigent Yantai peasants went to Beijing and found a dead duck on the road. Improvising an earthen oven, they cooked the duck. An official happened by, liked the smell, and asked for a taste. Pleased, he presented the dish to the emperor, who rewarded the official and the poor peasants.

The best restaurants are in the hotels.

SEEING THE SIGHTS

Penglai Pavilion is the most important tourist attraction here and is 83 kilometers northwest of the city, past the Yantai Economic and Technology Development Zone. A visit to Penglai can take a day.

Penglai Pavilion was a favorite place for centuries of scholars and poets, for it was from here, legend says, that the Eight Taoists Immortals flew across the seas. After getting drunk, each tried to compete with the other using his or her own treasure. (See Attributes of the Eight Taoist Genii in Chapter 5, Land & People). Some people say they flew to Japan, fighting on the way with the dragon king of the sea. A Japanese legend speaks of seven fairies. But some people say these fairies achieved immortality or arrived in paradise. Myths vary. The pavilion was first built in the Northern Song (1056-63) and extended in 1589. The buildings themselves cover 19,000 square meters.

From the Penglai Pavilion, mirages have been seen on the calm summer surface of the sea by many people. A recent sghiting was in 1988. CITS says a video was made and can only be shown in Penglai. Natives have conflicting opinions about the ideal conditions for mirages, but they seem to be in summer and autumn, with the east wind blowing shortly after a gentle rain, between 2 and 3 pm. The mirage is of a high mountain, an island or old city, which some people believe to be Dalian or Korea across the straits.

The pavilion with the tables and chairs has a chair of longevity. If people sit on it, they will live a long time. It was in this room that the Immortals had their party!

Movies about the Taoist Immortals have been shown regularly on television. Ask about them, at your hotel. A good Hong Kong movie is the *Eight Immortals Cross the Sea*. These mythical people were each from different periods of history but legend says they did get together during the Song! Fairies can do anything!

Among the other buildings nearby are the **Temple of the Sea Goddess Tian Hou**, a Taoist temple, and the **Wind Protection Hall**, where lit matches will not blow out even if the wind is from the north. Important is the room full of calligraphy by a famous Ming calligraphist who lived here for three years waiting unsuccessfully to see a mirage. Let that be a lesson to you!

The *****Penglai Water Town** or Beiwocheng, immediately to the south of the pavilion, was built as a fortress, particularly against Japanese pirates. The Song and Ming navies trained here, and the Ming expanded the defenses. Intriguing is the water gate. In the old days, pirates were lured inside and the gate closed behind them. Then, after the water level rose, the gate was opened and the dead pirates flushed out. Originally built in 1376, the gate was rebuilt in 1596.

A replica of the Ming town **Dengzhou**, including an old style bazaar, is on the way from the bus stop to the pavilion. Two recently built Ming warships take visitors for rides. Nearby is the **Dengzhou Ancient Ship Museum**. On special occasions, spear-carrying guards in Ming dress, waving dynastic flags, stilt and boat dancers, and firecrackers enliven the gateway and market.

The **Eight Immortals Palace** is a nearby exhibition with moving figures of these famous mythological people. It can give you some background, but its not Disneyland.

Also important in Yantai is the **Museum**, *2 Yulan Street, Tel. 6222520*, in the middle of town. Open daily, except Mondays. It is in a gaudy Fujian-style guild hall with a temple dedicated to the sea goddess. The beautifully restored building was constructed from 1884 to 1906 in Fujian, and brought in three sections here. Note the jawbone of a whale and the remains of a giant sea turtle. A statue of the goddess, destroyed during the Cultural Revolution, has been replaced in wax. The museum has a few relics from 8000 B.C. to more recent times, with labels in English. It can be seen in 40 minutes. There's an antique store there.

Pleasant to visit is the 600-year old white **Yuhuang** (Jade Emperor) **Temple**, at 70 meters above sea level, with a good view of the city. The temple building is original, the tower built in 1984, and the memorial arch in 1876. A 600-year old white pomegranate tree here still bears fruit. Nearby is another garden, **Little Penglai**, inspired by the real one to the north.

A visit to the Zhang Yu Wine Company and the Woolen Embroidery Factory are also recommended if you are interested. The wine-making and the embroidery styles date from imperialist days, the needlepoint probably taught by missionaries. Some of the patterns are European. The woolen embroidery of China's mountains in Chairman Mao's Mausoleum in Beijing was made here.

If you have more time, a **lighthouse** was built on top of a Ming dynasty beacon tower on Yantai Hill,. It has a good view of the harbor.

Yangma Dao (Horse Racing Island or Elephant Island, because of its shape) is one hour by road away. Here the first Qin emperor raised horses and visited three times. A one-kilometer horse-racing track with bleachers opened in 1985.

Yantai has two bathing beaches in the city proper: **Number One Bathing Beach**, in central Yantai, and **Number Two Bathing Beach** farther east. Both have all facilities. CITS here claims that Yantai has no sharks, but rival summer resort Qingdao does! The swimming season goes from June to early September.

Kongtong Isle is 4 1/2 nautical miles off Yantai, and you can visit a fishing village here; there are lots of wild rabbits.

Walks

There are good walks on **Yantai Hill**, and along the Bund and the beaches.

SHOPPING

Riesling wines, vermouth, Gold Medal Brandy, lace, tablecloths, straw weaving, wooden-framed clocks, and partially completed woolen needlepoint pieces (very cheap). The best selection is at the **Arts and Handicrafts Service Counter** at *Nan Da Avenue*, but selection is limited. Try the factories and department store.

PRACTICAL INFORMATION

· **CITS**, *17-2 Yuhuang Ding Xi Road, 264000; Tel. 6234145, 6234144. Fax 6234147. Contact Yantai Tourism Bureau here for brochures or complaints.*
· **CTS**, *Overseas Chinese Hotel, 30 Huanshan, 264001; Tel. 6224431. Fax 6246124*
· **Telephone Code**, *0535*
· **Yantai Municipal Tourism Bureau**, *17-2 Yueding Xi Road, 264000. Tel. 6243148. Fax 6247387*

ZUNHUA

(Tsunhua)

Located in Hubei province, **Zunhua** is about 125 kilometers northeast of Tianjin and 135 kilometers east of Beijing. There are no decent hotels to recommend here, so make this a day trip from Tianjin or Beijing.

SEEING THE SIGHTS

Among the imperial **Qing tombs** (built 1743-1799) at nearby Dongling (Eastern Tombs) are those of **Emperor Qianlong** (Chien Lung) at **Yuling**. Qianlong snubbed Britain's envoy. He is buried with his five wives. A devout Buddhist, his tomb is covered with religious statues and sutras in Indian, Tibetan, Chinese, Manchurian, and Mongolian.

The tombs of **Empress Dowager Cixi** (Tzu Hsi) and **Empress Cian** are together at **Dingdongling**. The Empress Dowager was the fascinating, outrageous, scheming, brilliant, scandalous but short-sighted woman who built the Summer Palace in Beijing. Her tomb, covered with phoenixes deliberately and arrogantly placed above the dragons (symbolizing the emperor), was completed in 1873 and renovated in 1895, with an additional 4590 taels of gold as decoration. She died in 1908.

Both mausoleums can be entered. The carving is more elaborate than that in the Ming tombs, with Buddhist sutras (in Tibetan and Sanskrit) and figures inside. You can study an exhibition of her clothes, utensils, a coat for her dog, and photos. Her tomb was robbed in 1928 by a Nationalist warlord who used explosives to open it. He stripped over 500 pearls off her clothes.

Like the Ming tombs, there is also an animal-lined Sacred Way, the figures here smaller but more elaborately carved. It seems each dynasty tried to outdo its predecessors, the Ming being more elaborate than the Song (see Zhengzhou). The tombs of the emperors and empresses have glazed yellow roofs. Tombs of lesser importance have green roofs.

These tombs are a leisurely overnight excursion from Beijing, a slight detour on the way to Beidaihe or Chengde. They are several kilometers from the poor hotels in Zunhua City. A better three-star 70-room hotel should open soon, six kilometers from Qianlongs tomb. Cixi's is one kilometer from Qianlongs.

The Qing Tombs here are less spread out from each other than the Ming Tombs. Six of the 15 are open to the public. The atmosphere is quieter, less commercial. In the vicinity live 10,000 Manchu farmers.

A word of warning: No decent bathrooms nor running water exists except in the guest house in the courtyard to the right of Qianlong's Tomb.

The **Xiling** (Western Tombs), 120 kilometers southwest of Beijing at Yixian are not as illustrious. The 14 mausoleums hold the remains of Emperors Yongzhen (Tailing), Jiaqing (Changling), Daoguang (Muling), and Guangxu (Chongling), plus the usual retinue of wives and children. Visitors can enter Chongling, the last royal tomb in China, but it has no funeral objects as it was robbed.

WHERE TO EAT

The **restaurant** in the spartan **management office** at the Qing tombs serves good Hebei meals, including donkey meat, a provincial tradition. Hebei food is very salty. The attendants here are dressed in Qing imperial costumes with eye-catching Manchu hats, and high heels attached to the center of their shoes. Some heels are in the shape of vases or bells.

PRACTICAL INFORMATION

• **CITS**, *Zunhua Hotel, Tel. 3083*
• **Management Office**, *Western Qing Tombs Cultural Relics, Zunhua 064206. Tel. 7524 or 7396. English-speaking guides.*
• **Telephone Code**, *03421*
• **Tourism Administration of Zunhua City**, *2 Haidu Road, Zunhua 064200. Tel. Zunhua 2920, 2083. Or in Beijing, Room 3037, Qianmen Hotel, 100059. Tel. (01)3016688. Fax (01)3013883*

18. NORTHEAST CHINA

CHANGCHUN

Capital of Jilin province (formerly Manchuria), **Changchun** is noted mostly as an industrial city manufacturing automobiles (China's first plant), trucks, railway carriages, tractors, and textiles. The urban population is 1.6 million.

Changchun is very cold in winter (lowest minus 30 centigrade). Average annual rainfall is 600-700 millimeters, mainly in the east, in July and August. There are about 150 frost-free days!

ARRIVALS & DEPARTURES

Changchun is a 1 1/2 hour flight northeast of Beijing. It can also be reached by plane from 22 other Chinese cities; or by train, via Shenyang and Harbin.

ORIENTATION

Changchun was founded in 1800. Invaded by Tsarist Russia in the 1890s, it became a Japanese concession in 1905 and the capital of Japanese-controlled Manchukuo from 1931 until 1945. It can be very attractive with its lovely broad avenues flanked by beautiful hospital and university buildings.

The province of Jilin borders on Korea and Russia. Its 24 million people include Koreans, Manchus, Hui, Mongols and Xibos. Settlements have been recorded since the Qin dynasty. It has developed a regional opera based on song-and-dance duets.

WHERE TO STAY

When the **Shangri-La Hotel** opens – hopefully by the time you read this – it should be the best.

CHANGBAISHAN GUEST HOUSE *(Binguan), 12 Xinmin Street, 130021. Three stars, Tel. 5643551. Fax 5642003. Dist.A.P. 13.5 km. Dist.R.W. eight km.*

In attractive setting near park, hospitals, and university. Built 1982. 12 stories, 268 rooms. CITS. IDD. USTV.

CHANGCHUN OVERSEAS CHINESE HOTEL, *1 Hubin Road, 130022. Tel. 5688728. Fax 5686099.*
Near South Lake. B.C., IDD. Ticketing service. Cantonese cuisine. Karaoke, Disco. H.K.J.V.

SHANGRI-LA HOTEL, *Corner Xian Avenue and Chongqing Road. Four stars. In US, Tel. 1-800-942-5050.*
In the diplomatic, financial, business and entertainment district. Due to open in 1996. 458 rooms plus 63 serviced apartments and 84 offices. Cantonese restaurant. Karaoke lounge. B.C. Gym, jacuzzi, sauna, steambath, indoor pool, children's playground, and outdoor tennis court. In-room safes, IDD, in-house movies. Three executive floors.

WHERE TO EAT

Exotic specialties: houtou (golden orchid monkey head) mushrooms, ginseng chicken, thick deer antler soup (with sea cucumber, prawns, egg white, ham, and chicken), and frog oil soup. Frog oil is said to be very nutritious and tastes better than it sounds. Please, no endangered species! And yes, you can get other dishes too!

The best restaurants are in the hotels.

SEEING THE SIGHTS

If you have only one day in Changchun, you must take in the **Museum of the Former Palaces of the Last Emperor Pu Yi**, 10 kilometers from the Changbaishan Hotel. From 1932 to 1945, Pu Yi lived and worked in this complex. He was head and then Emperor of Manchukuo. The Ton De Palace was actually used as one of the sets in the movie *The Last Emperor*. (The movie company put in the chandelier). Only one of Pu Yi's wives lived in this palace which was built for Pu Yi by the Japanese and now holds provincial relics. A good guide can tell you which rooms she lived in. Pu Yi himself lived in a neighboring building; he believed the Ton De Palace was bugged and used it only for receptions.

You can see the emperor's throne in the white trim building, the Qian Ming and his living quarters. Wax figures, photographs of the emperor, his wedding, wives, parents, and English teacher are on display. The palace was looted after the Japanese surrender and Pu Yi was taken off to the Soviet Union. After 1949, an automobile factory used it as an office. A hall was built in 1963 to teach young people about the cruelty of the Japanese invasion, but this museum was neglected again during the Cultural Revolution. (Mao badges were produced here.) A tunnel goes from here to the railway station.

In Changchun, you might want to include: the **Changchun Film Studio**, one of China's largest. The Changchun Movie City has movie sets, musical fountain, exhibition hall of movie props and trick photography, sedan chairs, and the like. At the **Changchun Number One Motor Vehicle Plant**, you can watch a more labor-intensive manufacturing process than in America or Europe. You won't believe the wages! You can skate in the winter and swim in the summer in Nanhu Park, the largest park in the city.

If you have more time, **Xinlicheng Reservoir** in the suburbs has some sika deer, ginseng root, and is stocked with fish. The 480-square-kilometer Songhua Lake is about 20 kilometers southeast of the city. The **Changbaishan Nature Reserve**, with tigers, deer, and sable is in Antu County about 300 kilometers southeast, with its own mythical monster and at least two hotels.

Jilin has a Korean area and an ancient Korean capital, dating back 1,400 years, with Korean festivals. It also offers a white river expedition.

For fans of steam locomotives, tourism officials boast that Jilin has no diesel engines stationed here (which says a lot about the air quality). In one of its forest areas is a **narrow-gauge train** that tourists can ride. Because it is hilly and engines have to work harder (and thus produce more photogenic steam, especially in wintertime), photos are good at the East Junction (Tong Har Tao Kao), 15 minutes by taxi from the Changbaishan Hotel. Another good site for photos is the South Bridge (Quan Ping Tao Quo tram 53 or 54).

One of my most moving experiences in China has come at 6 am, in front of the palatial **Geological College** here, watching over a thousand people enjoying themselves dancing in unison.

Festivals

Every year, from September 3 to 6, **Liberation Day** festivities are held, celebrating the Japanese surrender.

A fun time can be had at the **Mongolian Festival** in Baicheng, 400 kilometers from Changchun, for five to six days with horse racing, archery, wrestling, and dances. A **Ginseng Festival** is held for three days, usually in August, in Fusong county at the foot of Changbai Mountain. In August-September is the **Port Wine Festival**.

SHOPPING

Locally produced are: wine, ginseng, sable furs, deer antlers (aphrodisiacs), and frog oil (tonic). Tonghua and Changbaishan wines are made from wild grapes. Changchun produces carpets, embroidery, feather patchwork, mushrooms, azalea, wood carving, and bark pictures. The deer farm also has a retail shop. Please avoid furs from endangered species. I found a leopard skin coat in this city.

EXCURSIONS FROM CHANGCHUN

Jilin is in the center of Jilin province, 90 kilometers east of Changchun. The population is nearly one million. It can be reached by rail from Beijing, Changchum, Shenyang, Harbin, and Tianjin. The airport is 25 kilometers away and flights connect with three Chinese cities. Like the rest of the area formerly known as Manchuria, this also is extremely cold, with snow in winter and an average minimum temperature in December-February of minus 24 degrees centigrade to minus 15 degrees.

Tourist attractions include the **Deer Farm** at Longtan Hill, which produces antlers (for aphrodisiacs), ginseng, and sable. Also of interest are the ginseng gardens, the Jilin Exhibition Hall (with a 1770-kilogram meteorite, believed to be the largest in the world), and Jiangnan Park. **Songhua Lake** is a 480-square-kilometer man-made lake, and is 20 kilometers from the city center. The **Songhua River** runs through the city and beautiful hoarfrost forms on the trees lining its banks in minus 20 degree centigrade weather, and is celebrated with the **Rime Festival**. Ice lanterns are sculpted in the winter.

Jilin and the **Changbai Mountains** have alpine skiing with lifts from December to February. These mountains are 380 kilometers southeast of the city, their highest peak 2,691 meters. Its crater is beautiful **Heaven Lake** with its own mythical monster. Changbai Mountain can be reached by road from Jilin and Yanji, by rail from Tonghua and tourist helicopter from Yangji. The other side is Korea. You can also see **Arladi Village**, 70 kilometers from Jilin, where Korean customs are still practiced.

Local specialties include venison, frog oil soup, steamed whitefish, raw salmon and carp, and chicken and ginseng in earthenware pots.

Visitors can stay at the three-star **JIANG CHENG HOTEL**, *4 Songjiang Road, 132001, Tel. 457721* or the three-star **YINHE HOTEL**, *175 Songjiang Road, 132011. Tel. 841780. Fax 841621.* **CITS** and **CTS** are at *4 Jiangwan Road, 132001. CITS, Tel. 443451. Fax 453773.* The telephone code is *0432.*

PRACTICAL INFORMATION

• **CITS**, *10 Xinmin Street, 130021, Tel. 5647052. Fax 5645069*
• **CYTS**, *Building Number 114, Xi Chang Residential Area, 130061. Tel. 8940520. Fax 829702*
• **Jilin Provincial Tourism Bureau**, *14 Xinmin Street, 130021; Information and suggestions. Fax 5642419*
• **Tourist Complaints**, contact **Supervisory Bureau of Tourism Quality**, *Tel. 5609246. Fax 5642053*
• **Telephone Code**, *0431*

HARBIN

(Haerhpin)

Harbin is the capital of China's northernmost province of Heilongjiang, formerly part of Japan's Manchuria, and is 159 kilometers from the Daqing oil fields, China's biggest. The city has a population of over two million and is an industrial city.

Its highest summer temperature is 36 degrees centigrade; its lowest in winter is minus 38 degrees. The winter is six months long, so take your longjohns. Wintertime, however, is brightened by the **Ice Sculpture Festival**. You can also bring skates and skis. The annual precipitation is 250-700 millimeters, mostly June through August.

Harbin is building a mass transit railway.

ARRIVALS & DEPARTURES

Harbin is a 1 1/2-hour flight northeast of Beijing or a five-hour train ride from Jilin. Flights are with Khabarovsk (Siberia), Chita, Vladivostok, and 31 Chinese cities.

ORIENTATION

The area was first settled by people of the Nuzhen nationality in 1097. In the Yuan, the city was renamed Harbin. In 1898 it was opened as a port and became a Russian concession. Tsarist troops and police patrolled the Russian ghetto. After the Russian revolution it became home for thousands of White Russians and had several synagogues. From 1932, the Japanese occupied the area until the end of the war. You can observe a lot of neglected tsarist and Japanese architecture, and cobblestone streets (in Dao Li District).

Today, Heilongjiang numbers among its population Han, Manchu, Korean, Hui, Mongolian, Daur, Orogen, Ewenki, Kirgiz, Hezhen, and other nationalities.

WHERE TO STAY

The best are the newer Flamingo, Gloria Inn, Holiday Inn and New World Hotels. Cheaper is the older Swan. Prices here are subject to 15% surcharge.

GLORIA INN, *257 Zhongyang Ave., Daoli District, 150010. Tel. 4638855. Fax 4638533. $130 to $150.*

There are 304 rooms (including duplex apartments). B.C.

HARBIN FLAMINGO HOTEL, *119 Minsheng Road, Dongli, 1994-96. Tel. 2603677, 2636698. Fax 2657028. $105 to $115.*

Near Trade Centre. 225 rooms. Offices. B.C. 24-hour room service. IDD. Cantonese food. Gym. A Zenith Hotel, under KYZ management.

HOLIDAY INN CITY CENTRE HARBIN, *90 Jingwei St., Daoli District, 150010. Four-star standard. Tel. 4226666. Fax 4221661. Tel. 1-800-HOLIDAY. $110 to $160. Dist.A.P 36 to 60 km. Dist.R.W. four km. Credit Cards.*

153 rooms. Gym with sauna, steam bath. USTV. B.C.

NEW WORLD BEI FANG HOTEL HARBIN, *403 Huayuan Jie, Nangang Qu, 150001. Four-star standard. Tel. 3628888. Fax 3622828. Reservations in North America 1-800-6377200. $145-$195. Dist.A.P. 45 km. Dist.R.W. five km.*

In business and commercial district next to the Provincial Economic Trade Exhibition Centre. 15 km from ice festival. Built 1995. 329 rooms. Executive floors. B.C., IDD. USTV, inhouse movies. Clinic.

SWAN HOTEL *(Tian E Fandian), 73 Zhongshan Road, 150036. Three star, Tel. 2620201. Fax 2623727. Quiet location. Dist A.P. 45 km. Dist.R.W..five km. Credit Cards.*

Built 1983. 15 stories, 258 rooms. Soft beds. B.C., CAAC, IDD. 24-hour bar.

WHERE TO EAT

The most exotic dishes are moose nose and hazel grouse. Please, don't eat any endangered species! For those who want something less questionable, try monkey-head-shaped mushrooms. Russian food is available in hotels, as is other cuisine.

SEEING THE SIGHTS

The most important attraction is the magical **Ice Sculpture Festival**, from January 5 to February 25 at Zhaolin Garden. You can easily spend three hours there if you can stand the cold. This international competition has attracted teams from all over the world. Full of giant ice pagodas, bridges, giant lanterns, human figures, mazes, palaces, and childrens slides, it is best seen at night with its twinkling colored lights.

Although it has what is probably China's best ski area and wooded forests north of here, and a good red-crested crane sanctuary, there's not much else to come here for except business and to get away from the summer heat. If you only have one day in Harbin, you might want to tour the harbor and the **Song Hua River**, with its 10 kilometers dike; in summer you can rent sailboats and sampans; in winter you can sail-sled on ice. There's a Confucian Temple and a Temple of Happiness. Among the animals at the zoo you can find a Manchurian tiger, a red-crested crane, and a moose. The **Heilongjiang Provincial Museum** has one of the best skeletons of a mammoth found in China.

Travel agents have bird-watching, gold panning, horse riding (Mongolian), and skiing tours. Bicycle tours go from Wuying, Dafen Nanchan, and Dailing to Langxiang. You can take steam locomotive tours on narrow-gauge mining and logging trains and wait for the trains from the railway bridge near the International Hotel.

For skiing, see Chapter 10, *Sports & Recreation.*

IF YOU'RE A BIRD WATCHER ...

China's biggest bird sanctuary, the 210,000-hectare **Zhalong Nature Preserve** *is near Qiqihar, 280 kilometers away. Its cranes, storks, swans, geese, and herons are best seen from April to September. The famous red-crested cranes are considered a symbol of luck. For more information, CITS in Qiqihar is at Tel. (0452) 2472056, Fax 2475836.*

Heilongjiang also has China's largest **ski resort** at Yabuli, 195 kilometers by expressway from Harbin. On 2,255 hectares, with an elevation of 1,374.8 meters and two ski lifts, it is used also for training China's national ski team. A three-star ski lodge with IDD, and fax service was open for the 1996 Asian Games.

Also in the province is the **Taiyang Island** summer resort, another ice festival in Qiqihar, and Jingpo Lake in Mudanjiang. You can make a day trip from Heihe on the northern border of Heilongjiang province adjacent to Siberia. Daqing is a six hour train ride northwest of Harbin. **CITS** is at *Tel. (04610) 6662546. Fax 6324959.*

NIGHTLIFE & ENTERTAINMENT

Ask about the leather-silhouette show, and the annual **Harbin Summer Music Festival**.

SHOPPING

Sable, mink and muskratat hats, jackets, and collars can be purchased. Handicrafts include straw patchwork, horn carving, knitting, and ivory, jade, stone, and wood carving. Good to eat are its pine nuts and good for you, is ginseng.

There's good shopping at **Harbin Number One Department Store**, *146 Diduan Street, Tel. 6649291;* **Harbin Embroidery Factory**, *Arts and Crafts Building, Tel. 6225055* (for tablecloths); and **Tourist Fur Store**, *88 Zhongyang Street, Tel. 6649683.*

PRACTICAL INFORMATION

• **Ambulance**, *Tel. 120*
• **Business Hours**, 9 am to 7 pm.
• **CITS**, *Heilongjiang, 73 Zhongshan Road, 150036. Tel. 2327758, 2622655. Fax 2622476*

- **Heilongjiang International Travel Service**, *95/1 Harbin Zhong Shan Road, 150036. Tel. 2302579. Fax 2302476*
- **Heilongjiang CTS**, *72 Hong Jun Street, 150001. Tel. and Fax 3644679*
- **Heilongjiang Overseas Tourist Corporation**, *4 Dazhi Street, Harbin, 150001. Tel. 3641441. Fax 3621088*
- **Heilongjiang Tourism Administration**, *4 Xi Dazhi Street, Nangang, 150001, Tel. 3637410, 3631441 X 826. Fax 6330860, 3630860*
- **Police**, *Tel. 110*
- **Tourist Complaints**, contact **Supervisory Bureau of Tourism Quality**, *Tel. 3625269. Fax 3630860*
- **Telephone Code**, *0451*

SHENYANG

(Formerly Mukden)

Shenyang, the capital of Liaoning province, borders on Korea. With a recorded history of over 2,000 years, Shenyang was the Manchu capital from 1625 until 1644. After that, the Qing capital moved to Beijing. Shenyang is the biggest industrial city in this region, which was formerly Japanese-held Manchuria. The **Mukden Incident** on September 18, 1931, a surprise attack on the Chinese army stationed here, marked the beginning of Japanese aggression in China.

The weather is hottest in August, averaging 23.8 degrees centigrade; the coldest in January is minus 30 degrees. Rain is mainly from June to August. The urban population is about 4.7 million, with Manchus the largest group.

ARRIVALS & DEPARTURES

Shenyang is 1 1/4 hours by air northeast of Beijing. Flights with Hong Kong, Irkutsk, Macau, Seoul, and 42 Chinese cities are available. You can also reach it by train (in about five hours) and expressway from Dalian, about 400 kilometers away (four hours or so).

ORIENTATION

Shenyang today is a cultural center also, with institutions of higher learning and research. It is the home base of the **Shenyang Acrobats**, among China's best.

WHERE TO STAY

The top hotel is the **New World**. Then comes the Zhongshan and the Phoenix, until Traders is open.

NEW WORLD HOTEL SHENYANG, *2 Nanjing Nan St., Heping District, 110001. Four stars. Tel. 3869888. Fax 3860018. US Reservations, Tel. 1-800-637-7200. Four stars. Dist.A.P. 30 km. Dist.R.W. 15 km. Credit Cards.*
Built 1994. 22 stories. 252 rooms. IDD. Executive and non-smoking floors. Cantonese restaurant. Shuttle service. Clinic. B.C. Indoor pool. Gym. Sauna. Video golf room.
PHOENIX HOTEL *(Fenghuang Fandian), 109 Huanghe Nan St., 110031. Three stars. Tel. 6805858, 6846501. Fax 6087207, 6862507. Credit Cards. Dist.A.P. 35 km. Dist.R.W. 10 km.*
Built 1984, ren. 1991. 15 stories, 360 rooms. B.C. IDD. Sauna.
TRADERS HOTEL, *Zhong Hua Road, Heping District. Three stars. In US, Tel. 1-800-942-5050.*
Due soon. 595 rooms. Korean restaurant. Gym, jacuzzi, sauna, and steambath. In-room safes, IDD, in-house movies and 24-hour room service. Executive floors. B.C. Traders is the Shangri-La's International Hotel Management Group's mid-price business class hotel chain.
ZHONGSHAN HOTEL *(Dajiudian), 65 Zhong Shan Road, 110011. Three stars. Tel. 3833888. Fax 3832732, 3839189. Dist.A.P. 30 km. Dist.R.W. 15 km. Credit Cards.*
Built 1991, 27 stories, 208 rooms. B.C., IDD. Barbecue. Gym, bowling. H.K.J.V.

WHERE TO EAT

Local delicacies include monkey head mushrooms. The best food is in the top hotels. Also good are the restaurants of the **LIAONING MANSION**, *105 Huanghe Nan Street, 6809502* and the **SHENYANG DONG SHEN MANSION**, *9 Beijing Street, Tel. 2736363.*
Consider also **MONGOLIAN BARBEQUE AND HOT POT RESTAURANT**, *89 Bawai Road, Shenhe District, Tel. 2851011.*

SEEING THE SIGHTS

If you only have one day, do consider the **Imperial Palace** and **Beiling Tombs**.
The 19-year reigns of Nurhachi/Nulhachi and Huangtaiji (Huang Tai Chi) were enough to build the very impressive ***Imperial Palace**, 171 Shenyang Road, 10 kilometers from the city, Tel. 4843227*. The palace dates from 1625 to 1636, and is now restored to its original gaudy splendor. In an area of almost 60,000 square meters, it is also one of the best museums in China. Although this palace has a lot of Han influence, look for Mongolian and Manchu-style touches.
The most impressive section is the eastern one, with its octagonal **Dazhen Dian** (Hall of Great Affairs) and **Shiwang Ting** (Pavilions of Ten

Princes). Does the Beijing Palace have such dragons on its pillars, and the yurt-like design? The hall was used for important ceremonies and meetings with top officials.

Huangtaiji commanded his military forces and political business from the **Chongzhen Dian** (Hall of Supreme Administration). At the back of this hall is a road to the **Fenghuang Lou** (Phoenix Tower) and the **Qingning Gong** (Palace of Pure Tranquility). The Manchu leaders lived in the Qingning Gong, which is the most distinctively Manchu.

In the western section is the **Wenshuo Ge** (Hall of Literary Source), especially constructed for the Complete Library of the Four Treasures of Qing Emperor Qianlong. Unfortunately, no signs are in English.

The **Beiling* (or North) **Tombs**, also called the Zhaoling Tombs, are on *Beiling Street, Tel. 6896337*, in the north of the city. They are of Huangtaiji and his wife Borjigid (Poerchichiteh). Huangtaiji was the son of Nurhachi. Begun in 1643, the tombs were completed in 1651. If you still want to study more Manchu tombs, the **Dongling** (East) **Tombs** (or Fuling Tombs), of Nurhachi and his wife Yihnaran, are 20 kilometers from the city, *Tel. 8842494*. During the Ming, Nurhachi unified the tribes, became Khan in 1616, and made Shenyang his capital in 1625.

Other Sights

Also of interest is the **Shenyang Steam Locomotives Museum**, *Sujiatun Jiwuduan, Sujiatun District*, and an overnight in Tieling Village with a peasant family. The 40-square-kilometer **Qianshan Mountain Park** is 130 kilometers south.

At Yixiang, about 250 kilometers west of the city, is **Fengguo* **Temple**, dating from the Liao and said to be the second largest temple in China. Does anyone dispute that? Ask also about the **Xin Le Neolithic Museum** on the site, *Tel. 6809440*. It is near the entrance to the Friendship Hotel in Shenyang on 7 Longshan Lane.

SHOPPING

Produced in the province are diamonds, ginseng, sable and carvings of jade, agate, jet, and amber. Also produced are ceramics, feather patchwork, the musical instrument zheng, shell carvings and pictures.

Try the **Liaoning Department Store**, *63 Zhonghua Road, Tel. 3863312*. There's also the **Zhongxing-Shenyang Department Store**, *86 Taiyuan Bei Street, Tel. 3838888*.

EXCURSIONS FROM SHENYANG

Also in the province and worth side trips if you have the time are Anshan, Dalian, Dandong, and Fushun.

Anshan

Anshan is the home of China's biggest iron and steel works where fans of steam locomotives can ride a train for 38 kilometers. It is 1 1/2 hours by regular train, about 375 kilometers southwest of Shenyang. The urban population is two million. Its mines and smelting date back to the second century B.C. The other main tourist attraction is **Tanggangzi Hot Spring Sanatorium**, 15 kilometers south of Anshan where you can get treatment for arthritis, sciatica, and psoriasis. A room was built for the Last Emperor here, but he seldom used it.

Haicheng silk, ginseng, and Nanguo pears are specialties of the city.

The best place to stay is the five-star **INTERNATIONAL HOTEL**, *219 Yuan Lin Road, Teidong District, 114001. Tel. 5555888. Fax 5555988. Credit Cards., IDD. Dist.A.P. 30 km. Dist.R.W. five km.*

CITS is at *29 Shengli Road, Teidong District, 114002. Tel. 5553685. Fax 5530465. The Telephone Code is 0412.*

Dalian

Dalian (Talien, or Luda), a one hour to 80 minute flight south of Shenyang, is an ice-free port near the southern tip of Liaoning province, and an important industrial center. You can reach it by train from Beijing or Shenyang, and also by plane from Tokyo, Fukuoka, Hong Kong, Macau, Osaka, Seoul, and 34 Chinese cities. A 375 kilometer toll highway also joins it with Shenyang. It can also be reached by ship from Shanghai, Tianjin, Qingdao, and Yantai. Ocean cruise ships sometimes stop here.

With an urban population of about 2.2 million, its hottest temperature (August) is 34 degrees centigrade, and its lowest is minus 21 degrees. The annual precipitation is 600 to 800 millimeters. The best time to visit is May 1 to October 1.

Known during imperialist times as **Port Arthur**, Dalian was seized briefly by the Japanese in 1894, but was leased as a naval base for 25 years to Russia in 1898 in return for a loan to pay China's indemnity to Japan following the first Sino-Japanese War. Russia was also given the right to build a railroad connecting the base with the Trans-Siberian railroad. As the result of the Russian defeat by Japan in 1905, Japan took over the base until 1945.

Dalian is a very attractive city, with a lot of old tsarist and Japanese architecture and a high percentage of first-rate hotels. It also has 1,800 kilometers of coastline. Tourists might be interested in its ornamental glass factory, the centrally-located zoo, the harbor and its beautiful beaches. The best swimming beach is at the Bangchuidao Hotel. If the guard at the gate tries to stop you, telephone CITS. The second best swimming beach seems to be at the Tiger Park Beach. This beach is rocky and usually very crowded. You might try hiring a sampan to go to an outer island.

You can visit **old Port Arthur** and **Snake Island**, 25 nautical miles away, northwest of Lushun. With an estimated 15,000 pit vipers, this is a snake sanctuary, partly open to visitors. It supplies a research center studying the medical benefits of the venom. Look for the **Snake Museum** in Lushun. You can also hike and raft in **Bingyu Valley** with its Guilin-like scenery, 400 kilometers from the city. Take tents.

The Economic and Technical Development Zone is about 30 kilometers from Dalian and has its own three-star hotel. The Trade Fair building is in downtown Dalian with a 248-room hotel of its own.

Travel agents can arrange for scuba diving (water temperature is 16 degrees centigrade to 22 degrees in summer), fishing, and mountain climbing. You can best photograph steam locomotives from Victory Bridge.

If you'd like to stay in Dalien, the top hotels are now the **Furama**, **Holiday Inn**, and the **Dalian International**. In 1997 a Shangri-La International Hotel should open at the junction of Ren Min Lu and Zhi Gong Street with 520 rooms, B.C. and gym with indoor pool, tennis courts, and sauna. A four-star New World Hotel International should also open in 1997 with 500 rooms.

The best hotels are:

DALIAN INTERNATIONAL HOTEL *(Guoji Jiudian), 9 Stalin. 116001. Four stars, Tel. 2638238. Fax 2630008. Dist.A.P. 15 km. Dist.R.W. two km. Credit Cards.*

Built 1987; ren. 1991. 27 stories, 380 rooms, 24-hour room service. IDD. B.C. Chinese herbal medicine and acupuncture clinic to stop smoking. Gym and sauna, All-Nippon and Dragonair offices. USTV. Handy central location.

FURAMA HOTEL *(Fulihua), 74 Stalin Road, 116001. Five stars, Tel. 2630888. Fax 2804455, 2803100. In North America, Tel. 1-800-44UTELL.Dist.harbor one km. Dist A.P. 14 km. Dist R.W. two km. Credit Cards.*

Close to shopping. Built 1988. Ren. 1992. 22 stories, 500 rooms. No relation to the Furama Hotel in Hong Kong. IDD, B.C., office suites, free shuttle. Indoor pool, gym, whirlpool, and tennis. USTV.

GLORIA PLAZA HOTEL, *5 Yide Avenue, Zhongshan District, 116001. Tel. 2808855. Fax 2808533.*

The Gloria Plaza has 240 rooms. IDD, USTV, and in-house movies. B.C., Cantonese food.

HOLIDAY INN DALIAN *(Jiu Zhou Jia Ri Fandian), 18 Sheng Li Square, Zhong Shan District, 116001. Four stars, Tel. 2808888. Fax 2809704. In North America, Tel. 1-800-HOLIDAY. Dist.A.P. 11 km. Dist.harbor one km. Credit Cards.*

Next door to railway station. Built 1988. Ren.1995. 23 stories. 405 rooms. IDD, B.C. executive club. Non-smoking floor. Pub. Cantonese and Sichuan food. Gym, indoor pool, USTV, and tennis. Clinic.

CITS and **CTS** are at *One Changtong Street, Xigang District, 116011, Tel. 3687660, 3640273. Fax 3687733. CTS: Tel. 3635385. Fax 3638523.* **CYTS Tours** are at *94 Shen Yang Road, Xi Gang District, 116011, Tel. 3686139. Fax 3686070.*

Contact the **Dalian Tourism Bureau** at *One Renmin Square, 116012. Tel. 3631258* for brochures. The Dalian telephone code is *0411.*

And when you get hungry, try the hotels (seafood is the main specialty here). Two other good restaurants are the **QUN-YING LIU Restaurant** and the **DALIAN BO HAI RESTAURANT** (near the Holiday Inn).

Dandong

Dandong is at the border with North Korea and can be reached by air from six Chinese cities. You can boat on the **Yalu River** (famous for those who know about the Korean War), and visit the **King of Medicine Temple** on Feng Huang (Phoenix) Hill, a visit to which should cure you of all ills.

The best hotel here is the **DANDONG INTERNATIONAL HOTEL**, *88 Xinan Street, 118000. Three stars. Tel. 2137788 X 3004. Fax 2146644. Credit Cards. Dist.A.P. 30 km. Dist.R.W. five km.* **CITS** is on *Shanshang Street, 118000. Tel. 227721, 220187. Fax 231853.* The telephone code is *0415.*

Fushun

Fushun, 50 kilometers northeast of Shenyang, is known now for the prison where the Last Emperor spent the years 1950 to 1959. You can see the greenhouse where Pu Yi learned gardening, and the room where his concubine stayed with him for 48 hours (and afterwards filed for divorce). You can see the bed platform where he slept. His captors moved him in 1952 from this room along with 11 other Manchu companions because he didn't know how to tie his shoelaces.

Fushun is also important as the first Manchu capital (1616) with the oldest imperial Manchu tombs, containing the ancestors of the Machu emperors. At **Soldier Lei Feng's Museum**, you can muse about how today's heroes are made and visit the **Fushun Open Coal Mine**. The best hotel is the **FUSHUN FRIENDSHIP HOTEL**, *4 Yongning Street, Xi Fu District. Three stars, Tel. (0413) 2622181. Fax 2626773.*

PRACTICAL INFORMATION

- **Business Hours**, most tourist attractions 9 am to 4:30 pm in summer, shorter hours possible in winter; the large department stores above are open 8:30 am to 6 pm.

• **CITS**, *113 Huanghe Nan Street, Shenyang, 110031. Liaoning CITS, Tel. 6807005. Fax 6808772.* They can book trains to Russia and Korea.
• **CYTS Tours**, *21 Wu Jing Bei Road, Heping District, 110003. Tel. 2714356. Fax 2712917*
• **Liaoning Overseas Tourist Corporation**, *26 Kun Shan Zhong Road, 110031, Tel. 6225075. Fax 6228632.* They can arrange tours to North Korea but not for U.S. citizens.
• **Liaoning Tourism Administration**, *113 Huanghe Nan Road, 110031, Tel. 6807316, Fax 6809415.* For information and brochures.
• **Telephone Code**, *024*
• **Tourist Complaints**, contact **Supervisory Bureau of Tourism Quality of Liaoning**, *113 Huanghenan Street, Huanggu District, 110031, Tel. 6116668. Fax 6809415*
• **Tourist Hotline**, *Tel. 2722999.* For complaints, comments and information.
• **U.S. Consulate**, *52, 14th Wei Road, Heping District, Tel. 2820068. Fax 2820074.* There are also Japanese, Russian, and North Korean consulates.

19. NORTHWEST & CENTRAL CHINA

NORTHWEST CHINA

DUNHUANG

(Tunhuang, Tunhwang)

Here in isolated western Gansu is one of the world's greatest art treasures, now protected by UNESCO, the **Thousand Buddha Caves**.

Summers are hot; winters are very cold. The warmest is about 41 degrees centigrade in July, the coldest minus 21 degrees centigrade in December, but it can be minus 15 degrees centigrade in April. The annual rainfall is only 36.8 millimeters. The best time to visit is May, September or October. The altitude is 1,000 to 1,200 meters.

ARRIVALS & DEPARTURES

You can reach Dunhuang by train from Lanzhou (24 hours and 1,148 kilometers) but the train station is 130 kilometers away. Flights with Jiayuguan and Lanzhou are regular but infrequent. You can take a charter flight in the summer only from Beijing and Xi'an.

A bus from Jiayuguan takes five to six hours to cover the 383 kilometers.

ORIENTATION

Dunhuang was an important cultural exchange center and oasis on the **Silk Road**. It was founded in 111 B.C. during the Western Han. From here, the Silk Road west splits into northern and southern routes and ends 7,000 kilometers away at the Mediterranean Sea. Dunhuang was a military outpost under the Tang. In 400 A.D., it became the capital of the Xiliang kingdom. An enemy army of 20,000 attacked the city and flooded it 21 years later. It changed hands several times. In 1227, Genghis Khan seized it, and in the Ming, it was a military headquarters. You can see the ruins of the walls and a 16-meter-high tower in the old part of town, 250 meters west of the current one. The population now is 150,800 urban and rural.

Between the fourth and 14th centuries, more than 1,000 caves were cut out of the cliffs 25 kilometers southeast of the city and filled with Buddhist carvings, gilt and colored frescoes, and murals. These are the famous Thousand Buddha Caves.

WHERE TO STAY & EAT

Apricots, jujubes, pears, melons, peaches, and wine grapes are grown locally. For restaurants, the hotels below are your best bet.

DUNHUANG GRAND HOTEL, *32 Mingshan Road,* is four-star quality.

DUNHUANG HOTEL *(Fandian), Dong Dajie, 736200. Three stars. Dist.A.P. 13 km. Dist.R.W. 130 km. 1980. 130 rooms. No air conditioning in rooms. Only credit card accepted is American Express.*

SEEING THE SIGHTS

Known as the *Mogao Grottoes or the **Thousand Buddha Caves**, 492 of these fascinating caves remain today in three or four rows on a 1.5 kilometer-long wall. The State Council has renovated murals like the Feitian (Flying Apsaras) fresco (Tang) and repainted over 2,000 statues. Some of the statues, in about 20 caves, were repainted in the Qing. Note the intricately painted ceilings.

The most important cave is the **Cangjing** (Preserving Buddhist Scriptures) **Cave**, now **Number 17**. Dating from the Jin to Song (or late Tang to Western Xia, depending on sources), a span of 600 years, this is where 40,000 important old documents were found, including the **Diamond Sutra** (868 A.D.), said to be the oldest existing printed book. It is now in the British Museum in London.

Other important caves include **Number 45** (clay figures); **Number 158** (the 15.6 meter-long Sleeping Buddha) and **Number 96** both have 26- and 33-meter-high Maitreya Buddhas respectively. Entrance to some of these might require additional payment.

The caves have stories. One of the most famous is outlined in a series of pictures about a woman who was badly treated by her husband. While returning to her mother, she encountered a wolf that killed her two children. After becoming a nun, she learned that her miseries were punishment for mistreating her stepsister in a previous incarnation.

Some of the statues are damaged, many by Moslems in the distant past and a few by the Red Guards. Signs indicate which museums abroad have stolen the pieces originally here. Some of the colors are still original and vivid. The red might be from pig's blood or cinnabar. One could get a real feeling of history and mysticism here. Caves were used as temples because they were conducive to meditation and were secure, like a mother's womb, perhaps symbolizing reincarnation.

The caves are a half-day trip at least and there is a decent restaurant and lots of souvenir shops. You could take your own lunch. Buses from Dunhuang city leave every half hour arriving 30 minutes later. Make sure you find out what time the last bus leaves. Ask your hotel if it has a shuttle. The caves are open from 8:30 to 11:30 am and 2:00 to 5 pm with the last admissions about 3:30. They could be closed in February and in bad weather. Knowledgeable guides are available for hire on the site to show you around, and about twenty speak English. As with all cave temples, it is best to take a flashlight to zero in what you want to see. (You can also rent them.) And do not expect to observe an entire mural as you would in a spacious museum. You have to piece each section together in your own mind. This fragmentation has disappointed some tourists. A heavy metal door protects each cave.

Cameras and bags are not generally allowed. Photography needs special permission in advance. Tourists cannot wander around the site without a guide. About 30 or so caves are available at any onetime, of which you will visit a fraction. If you are anxious for more, ask for special permission in advance.

Other Sites

Visitors also can see the **White Horse Pagoda** (only a 12-meter-high pagoda in the desert and a five-minute stop). It commemorates the horse of the Indian monk Fumoluoshi, which died here. The **Yangguan Pass** (70 kilometers south of Dunhuang) is just a beacon tower now, of interest to people who like deserts or have a feeling for history. It was a military command post from the Han to the Yang, but the sands of the desert have inundated it.

The **Yumen** (Jade Gate) **Pass**, 80 kilometers northwest of the city, has remains of the old wall. Jade used to be carried here. These three sites are in themselves really not worth the hardship of getting here, but if you think of what went through here, the caravans of camels and merchants supplying the wealthy homes of Europe, and the envoys bringing tribute to the emperor, they can be emotional experiences. A recent Chinese movie, *Dunhuang,* makes an attempt to recapture the spirit of the era and could help you appreciate the relics here.

Dunhuang also has a **carpet factory**, *Danghe Bei Road, 736200,* and the **Mingsha** (Singing Sand) **Hill**, five kilometers south, where a whole army was buried during a sandstorm. Their ghosts are still heard from time to time playing military drums and horns! You can get a short camel ride to **Crescent Moon Spring**, climb sand dunes, and visit a folk custom museum. Twenty kilometers south of the city you can visit a movie set of old Dunhuang.

PRACTICAL INFORMATION
- **CITS**, *1 Dong Dajie, 736200. Tel. 22494*
- **Dunhuang International Travel Service**, *32 Mingshan Road. 736200. Tel. 23312, 22598. Fax 22173*
- **Dunhuang Solar Energy International Travel Service**, *Tel. 22306. Fax 22121*
- **Dunhuang Tourist Bureau**, *1 Dong Dajie, 736200. Tel. 22529; Fax 22334. Tourist complaints, Tel. 22403*
- **Guansu Silk Road International Tours**, *1 Dong Dajie, 736200. Tel. 24726. Fax 24727*
- **Fire**, *Tel. 119*
- **Police**, *Tel. 110*
- **Telephone Code**, *09473*

JIAYUGUAN

Jiayuguan is at the western end of the Great Wall, in the Hexi Corridor of the western part of Gansu province in the eastern Gobi desert. The altitude is 1600 meters, the population 190,000. The hottest weather in August is 34 degrees centigrade. The coldest, in January, is minus 21 degrees centigrade. The best time to visit is May-October. Sandstorms occur March to May, especially around Anxi, and strong winds in November and December could make for an unpleasant trip.

ARRIVALS & DEPARTURES
Jiayuguan can be reached by infrequent regular flights from Dunhuang and Lanzhou, and from Dunhuang by thrice-a-day public bus. During the high tourist season, there are more frequent chartered flights.

A tour bus on the 383-kilometer paved road takes five or six hours from Dunhuang, more if you lunch at the Yumen Guest House in Anxi, and stop in Qiao Wuan town to see the 300-year-old earthen ruins of an imperial scam, 100 kilometers east of Anxi.

WHERE TO STAY
The best is the **Great Wall Hotel**. The airport is 13 kilometers away. **CHANGCHENG BINGUAN** or **GREAT WALL HOTEL**, *6 Jianshe Xi Rd., 735100. Tel. 226306. Fax 225255. $48 to $58. Dist.A.P. 14 km. Dist.R.W. four km. Credit Cards.*

Three stars. Built like a fort, on the edge of town with a great view of the snowcapped Qilian Mountains, this hotel is close to the Great Wall Museum. Built 1990-91. Five stories. 160 rooms. IDD.

JIAYUGUAN HOTEL *(Binguan), 1 Xinhua Bei Rd., 735100. Two stars, Tel. 226185, 226285. Fax 227174. $30 to $60. Dist.A.P. 14 km. Dist.R.W. five km. Credit Cards.*

Five stories. 65 rooms. IDD.

WHERE TO EAT

The **CHANGCHENG HOTEL** is best, but you can also try the **YUAN SHONG XUAN**, *1 Shengli Bei Road, Tel. 281829* and the **CITS RESTAURANT**, *Changcheng Xi Road, Tel. 226470.*

SEEING THE SIGHTS

The western end of the **Great Wall** is marked by a fort, seven kilometers from town, and first built in 1372 when the first Ming emperor had the wall repaired to keep out the defeated Mongols. He sent government and military officers to develop the region and to protect commerce on the Silk Road. It covers over 33,500 square meters and has three imposing gates with fancy 17-meter-high towers. In addition to military structures, it has a theater built in 1502, a reading room for officials, and a temple to the God of War. The god must have worked. No army ever captured the fort. *Tel. 225518.* 8:30 am to 6 pm.

The end of the Great Wall here is a mere trickle of its eastern magnificence, but it still fascinates. It continues from here west for 7.3 kilometers to the first beacon tower.

The **Wei** and **Jin Tombs** (220 to 420 A.D.) are 20 kilometers east of the city and open 8 am to 10 pm. You can enter them to study the famous bricks with delightful paintings of old lifestyles and mythology. The modest museum is well worth seeing. Jiayuguan also has a **Great Wall Museum**, *Tel. 225881*, open 8:30 am to 6 pm and a glacier (136 kilometers away and a one-day trip). You can also go gliding at the Gliding base of the civil airport 10 kilometers northeast of the city which claims one of the three best airflows in the world.

Jiuguan is 25 kilometers away, with a **Bell and Drum Tower** originally built in 343 and renovated in the Qing, a Han pagoda, and a carpet factory. The 'wine spring,' the Western Han relic after which the city is named, has now dried up. The other city attraction is the **Luminous Jade Cup Factory** (open 9 am to 6 pm) which makes almost eggshell-thin goblets of 'jade'. There is also the Jiuquan City Museum, open 9 am to 5:30 pm.

For shopping, there's the **Damofeng Art Factory**, *Tel. 225598*, and the **Friendship Store**, *Tel. 225266 X 1128.*

PRACTICAL INFORMATION

- **Jiayuguan International Travel Service**, *2 Sheng Li Bei Road, 735100. Tel. 226280, 226598. Fax 226931, 222586*
- **Police**, *110*
- **Telephone Code**, *09477*
- **Tourist complaints**, *Tel. 226068*

KASHI

(Kashgar)

At the far western tip of Xinjiang province, 164 kilometers from the former Soviet republic of Kirghizstan, **Kashi** is one of the highlights of a **Silk Road** trip because of its Central Asian ambience, architecture, and extraordinary Sunday market.

Kashi has about 300,000 people, urban and rural, of whom 74% are Uygur. The altitude is 1,289 meters. The annual rainfall is below 100 millimeters so take precautions against dust. The highest temperature in summer is 40° centigrade. The lowest in winter is minus 24° C. Early May to early September is fine to visit. The end of September can be cold.

The **Sunday market** is a medieval crush of 100,000 Uygurs, Afghanis, Pakistanis, Kirghiz, Tadjik, and Mongols, blacksmiths, barbers, 'dentists,' and donkey carts. Peppercorns, mutton shish kebabs, pomegranates, grapes, cloth, bright felt carpets, jeweled knives, and boots, camels, and goats are traded here. Tinkerers repair kettles and repair bicycles. This market is more interesting for photographing than for buying, and needs at least three hours. Most residents don°t mind cameras. Go early to avoid the heat.

Government officials, hotels and tour guides operate on Beijing time, but some shops keep 'Kashgar time,' and others keep 'Pakistan time', which could be a three hour difference.

ARRIVALS & DEPARTURES

You can get there by air (1,085 kilometers in 1 1/2 hours at least once and sometimes twice a day), or by land (three-day jeep ride) from Urumqi. You can also get there by land from Lhasa but it's even harder.

Kashi is also accessible by road, but not without a long, tiring, and sometimes spectacular journey from Pakistan (520 kilometers), or from Kirghizstan (quite risky). Plans to fly between Urumqi and Islamabad via Kashi have been considered for years but have not materialised so far.

ORIENTATION

Kashi is over 2,000 years old and has been fought over by many contenders. In the mid-10th century, a Uygur-Turkish coalition, the

Karahanid (Qurakhanid) Dynasty took over the area. Its leaders later converted to Islam and made Kashi their capital. Today it grows rice, wheat, fruit, and cotton. It exports tomato sauce.

WHERE TO STAY & EAT

Prices listed here are subject to change and negotiations. Kashgar's accommodations are generally poor with limited services. Unless things have improved by the time you arrive, there's no IDD and not all hotels can change money, but the Bank of China will. The **Qiniwak** is the best hotel. The Seman's new section is second. Dine only in the top hotels.

KASHGAR HOTEL *(Binguan), Tazris/Tawuguzi Rd., 844000. Building Number Four is two stars, Tel. 222367. Fax 224679. $30. American Express credit card only.*

This hotel is nine kilometers from the airport and four kilometers to town center and set in a large garden, it is the closest hotel to the Sunday market, Moslem dining room. Good hot water but terrible plumbing. IDD. Okay for backpackers.

QINIWAK HOTEL *(Qinibah), 93 Seman Rd., 844000. Two stars, Tel. 222103, 225006, Fax 223842, 223087. Dist.A.P. 12 km. $38. Credit Cards.*

The old British Consulate building is still there. Its 1990 addition has five stories and 140 rooms. Bigger bathrooms than Kashgar Hotel. CITS nearby. IDD. Read *The Antique Land* by Diana Shipton, who lived here in 1946.

SEMAN HOTEL, *170 Seman Rd., 844000. Two stars, Tel. 222129, 222150. Dist.A.P. 13 km. $32.*

More central with notice board for travelers. Bicycles. Western coffee shop. Exchange desk. IDD.

SEEING THE SIGHTS

You can get around locally by taxi, but if you want to try something different, go for the bumpy donkey cart experience!

Like other cities of Xinjiang, Kashi gives you a feeling more of Central Asia than of China. It is the only place in China where women veil their faces, by choice. The city centre is near the **Idkah Mosque**, Tel. 223235, (1442 A.D.) which holds 7,000 people. Nearby is a giant pomegranate, symbol of the city (and fertility). Just sitting in this square is like watching a movie of life and death in the Middle Ages. I saw a funeral pass by, the deceased on a stretcher, not a coffin. Behind the mosque are streets with old buildings, wrought-iron balconies, and alleyways with mud townhouses more typical of north Africa than China. The local people are friendly. Carpet and musical instrument factories are close by, the best instruments made of snake skin. The area has 9,500 mosques.

You should go to the huge **Abakhojia Tomb**, *Tel. 222638* (Ming and Qing), the final resting place of 70 descendents of Muhatum Ajam, an Islamic missionary. It is five kilometers from the Kashgar Hotel and has a jewelery shop. A museum is being built close to this hotel. The **San Xian** (Three Immortals) **Buddhist Caves** are 16 kilometers north of the city with a decent road. Three rectangular holes high in the side of a cliff beckon the fit and curious. Unless they have been recently repaired, the frescoes inside are not in good condition.

Recent visitors have seen the snow-covered **Pamir Mountains** from Scholar Mohamed Kashgari's Tomb 45 kilometers southwest of Kashgar on the road to Pakistan. You can visit **Karakuli Lake**, 196 kilometers west of the city, on a one-day excursion.

Thirty kilometers east of Kashi is the town of Hanoi, abandoned after the 11th century and now just a ruin. In the area, you can also cruise South Lake, but it is only a respite from all the dryness. South of the city and east of the **Sino-Pakistan Highway** toward Afghanistan are the 7,719-meter-high **Mt. Kongur** and 7,546- meter-high **Mt. Muztagta**, part of the Pamirs. If you keep in mind that Hunza in Pakistan and Kashmir in India are also to the south, you will get an idea of the magnificence and isolation of the area here. Think Himalayas!

There's a good walk behind Idkah Mosque. Actually, this whole city is good for walking and bicycling. You can rent bicycles from the hotels.

SHOPPING

Kashi produces gold and silver ornaments, leather boots, bronzeware, jewelry, rugs, jade carving, embroidered caps, daggers, and musical instruments made of apricot wood. The jewelry bazaar is on **Zhiren Street**. The **Odali Bazaar** on *Jiefang Bei Road* sells daggers and caps. The **Handicraft Centre** is on the same road.

If you buy the fancy 'jewelled' daggers, put them in your checked luggage during your flight, or leave them with the cabin crew (for a fee).

PRACTICAL INFORMATION
• **CITS**, *Qiriwak Hotel, 93 Semar Road, Tel. 223156, 228473. Fax 223087*
• **Telephone Code**, *0998*
• **Tourism Hotline/Complaints**, *Tel. 228473*

LANZHOU
(Lanchow)

In western Gansu province, of which it is the capital, **Lanzhou** is almost in the center of China. Founded about 220 years ago, Lanzhou was called the 'Gold City' after gold was found here. Gansu province today has a population of 24 million, including Han, Hui, Tibetan, Dongxiang, Yugur, Bonan, Mongolian, Kazak, Tu, Salar and Manchu nationalities.

The area was settled 200,000 years ago. Three thousand years ago, the inhabitants started farming the eastern part of Gansu. The province is the setting for Yuan-Tsung Chen's excellent autobiographical novel *The Dragon's Village*, a book based on her own experiences with land reform shortly after Liberation in 1949.

Situated on the Yellow River and at an altitude of 1,524 meters, the coldest winter temperature is minus 10 degrees centigrade in January; the hottest is 35 degrees centigrade in summer. The annual precipitation in the province is between 30 and 800 millimeters, the rain mainly in the southeast. Sandstorms occur in April and May.

With an urban population of 1.4 million, the city is industrial, with petrochemicals, machine building and smelting.

ARRIVALS & DEPARTURES

Lanzhou can be reached by air from Hong Kong and 25 Chinese cities including Beijing, Dunhuang, and Xi'an (800 kilometers away). Lanzhou is also serviced by train from Baotou, Urumqi, and Yinchuan.

From Xining in Qinghai it takes 4 1/2 hours by express tourist train. The airport is about 64 kilometers from the city by expressway.

ORIENTATION

Lanzhou is important as a stop on the **Silk Road** and as a gateway to two cave temples, the ***Bingling Si Grottoes** and the ***Maijishan Grottoes**. Stop here if you're interested in cave temples and have at least three days and the strength to climb. In any case, the infamous pollution here has been reduced by the growing use of electricity instead of coal.

WHERE TO STAY

The best hotel is the **Lanzhou Legend**, then the Jincheng.

LANZHOU LEGEND HOTEL, *599 Tian Shui Rd., 730000. Four stars. Tel. 8882876. Fax 8887876. Dist.A.P. 76 km. Dist.R.W. two km. Credit Cards.* The hotel has 389 rooms, B.C., gym, Korean restaurant. Singapore management.

JINCHENG HOTEL *(Binguan), 363 Tianshui Rd., 730000. Three stars, Tel. 8416638, 8827759, Fax 8418438. Dist.A.P. 76 km. Dist.R.W. three km.* In the center of town, this hotel offers 300 rooms. IDD., B.C. and gym. Built 1982.

WHERE TO EAT

Local specialties include roast piglet (delicious), sweet and sour

Yellow River carp, facai (black moss), steamed chicken, fried camel hoof (ugh) and fried sheep's tail. For snacks, try toffee potatoes and toffee melon. The hotels are best, but try the **FLYING HORSE RESTAURANT**, *361 Tianshui Road, Tel. 8416638.*

SEEING THE SIGHTS

In Lanzhou itself, of mild interest is the **Baita** (White Pagoda Park) on a hill on the north bank of the Yellow River. First built in the Yuan, then rebuilt and expanded in the Ming and Qing, it has seven stories and eight sides and is about 17 meters high. Open 8:30 am to 4 pm.

Five kilometers from the Jincheng Hotel, you should visit the **Wuquan** (Five-Spring) **Hill** for its genuine temples, the oldest, the spooky Ming Dynasty Chung Wen. Legend credits General Ho Qubing (Huo Chu-ping), in 120 B.C., with stabbing the ground with his sword after finding no water for his horses. Five streams of water appeared and have been flowing ever since. Other important relics to see are the **Taihe Iron Bell**, three meters high, weighing five tons, and cast in 1202; and the **Tongjieyinfo Buddha**, cast in bronze in 1370 and weighing nearly five tons. Open 8:30 am to 5 pm. Good walks here.

The Yellow River cruise is not special, but the **Provincial Museum**, *Xijin Dong Road*, five kilometers from the Jincheng Hotel (open 9 to 11 am; 2 to 5 pm; closed Saturdays and Sundays), is well worth the trip for the famous 1,800-year-old **Galloping Horse of Gansu** that toured the U.S. and Canada. It was found in Wuwei in the middle of the province. A replica of its original presentation is in the Jincheng Hotel. Also important are the 2000-year-old-wooden 'slips' (documents of history and medicine) from north Gansu and 7,800-year-old painted pottery. Another good museum is in Guyuan near Pingliang.

If you have a chance, see the authentic Chinese dances, inspired by the paintings in the caves, performed by the **Gansu School of Dance** in Lanzhou.

EXCURSIONS FROM LANZHOU

The elaborate fifth-century *Bingling Si Grottoes are 129 kilometers southwest of the city, near Linxia, open April to November, depending on the water level. From Lanzhou, you go 75 kilometers by road and then 54 kilometers by boat (an 11-hour excursion in all). You can also take an eight-hour train to Tian Shui from Lanzhou and then a one-hour bus. It's not easy.

Here you'll find 183 caves and shrines with 694 stone Buddhist statues and 82 clay ones, the biggest Buddha 27 meters high, the smallest only 25 centimeters. Like other cave temples, this has a lot of stairs. The statues range from Northern Wei to Ming, the youngest, at least 350 years old. The most spectacular is the Xiasi (Lower Temples).

The *Maiji Grottoes, also Northern Wei to Ming, are 45 kilometers southeast of Tian Shui, itself 350 kilometers southeast of Lanzhou. Tianshui was a trade distributing center on the Silk Road and has two temples, the Fuxi and the Nanguo, and is accessible by train and bus.

At Maiji, there are 194 caves full with over 7,000 stone and clay Buddhist statues, and 1300 square meters of murals dating from the end of the fourth century to the 19th, a period of 1500 years. These caves are on a mountain, which rises almost vertically, and are reached by wooden staircases and protected by doors and windows. Some of the statues are completely unsheltered. One statue 15.28 meters high is from the Sui. The work on the mountain was done by craftsmen who piled blocks of wood up to the top and started carving while standing on them. As the artisans worked their way down, they gradually removed the blocks. The Maiji is better than Bingling.

Also near Tianshui, at Dadiwan in Qin'an County, is an on-the-site museum similar to Banpo in Xi'an. Its 1,154-square-meter hall covers a 7,800-year-old primitive village with painted pottery tripods, stone and bone artifacts, and ground paintings. Of the 200 houses so far discovered, one covers 600 square meters, the largest such building found so far in China.

From Xiahe, 280 kilometers southwest, it is a two-day trip by road to the **Labrang/Labuleng Monastery**, the largest outside of Tibet, built in 1709. It's best seen in July, but yearly festivals (March 2 to 6, and August 14 to 21 in 1996), during which the Buddha *thangka* is put out in the sun, are interesting times to visit. Belonging to the 'Yellow sect,' the monastery has a 10 meter-high statue of Maitreya. The **LABULENG SI HOTEL** here is three stars *(Laizhoucun Ciahe, 747100)*. It is two kilometers from the monastery, has 74 beds, and is built in Tibetan court tent architecture.

Ask about **Qingyang**, a village devoted to the making of those flat, stuffed, whimsical animals sold in stores here. In the evening, you can watch Tang Dynasty dances. Also in the province are Dunhuang and Jiayuguan. See separate listings and ask about the 6,000 Roman troops (Han dynasty) who 'lost' their way and ended up in Wuwei.

SHOPPING

Lanzhou produces many kinds of melons, red dates, the best tobacco for water pipes, carved ink slabs, luminous 'jade' cups, and bottle gourds. It also manufactures carpets, lanterns, and reproductions of ancient paintings based on the Silk Road murals. Some of its replicas of the famous Flying Horse of Gansu are made from molds directly from the original in the local museum. Museum reproductions and cloth animals at the **Tianma** (Heavenly Horse) **Store**, *361 Tianshui Road*. See also the **Gansu Cultural Relics Shop**, *3 Xinjinxi Road, Tel. 2336461.*

Try the **Provincial Arts and Crafts Shop**, *West Donggang Road*, and the **Nanguan Department Store** with its Friendship Store branch. The **Foreign Language book store** is at *Jiu Quan Road.*

PRACTICAL INFORMATION

- **Ambulance**, *Tel. 120*
- **Bank of China hours**, 8:30 to 11:30 am; 2:30 to 5:30 pm, Monday to Friday.
- **CITS**, *Gansu Overseas Tourism Corporation (sales) and Gansu Tourism Administration (brochures and complaints) are all at 361 Tianshui Road, 730000.*
- **CITS**, *Tel. 8416164, 8416638. Fax 8418556; GOTC, Tel. 8826188. Fax 8824670*
- **Gansu Silk Road International Tours**, *Euro-American Department, 361 Tianshui Road, 730000. Tel. 8830138, 8827098. Fax 8418457*
- **Gansu Tourism Administration**, *Tel. 8418443. Fax 8418443*
- **Lanzhou Tourism Bureau**, *14 Xijin Xi Road, 730050, Tel. 2333051*
- **Police**, *Tel. 110*
- **Telephone Code**, *0931*
- **Tourism Hotline**, *Tel. 8830138, 8826860*
- **Tourist Complaints**, *Tel. 8826860. Fax 8418443*

SILK ROAD

The term **Silk Road** was first used by a German author in the 19th century and is still used because it is so apt. Silk was the main commodity carried along the caravan routes between Cathay and Europe. It dazzled the eyes of Marco Polo who traveled here in 1275. Bales of silk were buried in ancient tombs along the way, it was that highly valued.

Informal trade between China and West Asia goes back over 2,000 years. In 138 B.C. (Han), Emperor Wudi sent his emissary Zhang Qian (Chang Ch'ien) on missions westward to get help fighting the Huns. Zhang returned 13 years later, having been imprisoned most of that time by hostile tribes, but he fired the emperor's interest in trade. The Han emperors encouraged trading caravans with imperial protection and the building of beacon signal towers.

From then on, the routes flourished periodically until the 14th century, especially in the Tang. It declined because sea-going ships were able to trade more efficiently and because of hostilities along the land routes.

Trade was mainly in high-value or easily transported goods. The Chinese exchanged silk, tea, and seeds for peach and pear trees. They also exchanged skills, such as iron-, steel-, and paper-making; they received grapes, pomegranate and walnut trees, sesame, coriander, spinach, the Fergana horse, alfalfa, Buddhism, Nestorianism, and Islam. Goods were exchanged along the route especially with India and West Asia. A few items even reached Rome. The road went west from Xi'an along the Weihe River valley, Hexi Corridor, Tarim Basin, Parmirs (in Central Asia), Afghanistan, Iran, Iraq, and Syria. It was about 7000 kilometers long. (2,700 kilometers within China).Northern and southern routes divided at Dunhuang on either side of the Taklamakan/Takelamagan Desert.

Many Arab and Persian merchants settled in Xi'an and even as far east as Yangzhou. Some of the cities on the Silk Road are open to foreigners, and tourists find themselves in a world of onion-domed mosques, bazaars, oasis, grapes, central Asian and Turkish faces, embroidered caps, and languages their national guides cannot understand. Spontaneous dancing and singing, uncontrolled by Han reserve, make people here delightful. Visitors are frequently asked to join in and contribute to the festivities.

You can find giant rock carvings and murals, some of the best in the world, and can explore earthen-walled ghost cities, the western end of the Great Wall, old tombs, and Buddhist temples. You can look for mummies. Try to figure out how and what the beacon towers communicated and learn how water is channeled to make this desert flourish. Carpets, jade goblets, jeweled daggers, and musical instruments are good buys here.

But the Silk Road is not Turkey, Pakistan, or Afghanistan. It is China, an ingredient that makes this region of mixed cultures special and worth the hardships.

Arranging Travel

Conference Travel of Canada and China Rail Express Travel Service have deluxe train tours through this area. Several agencies have less elegant land tours. China Nature Tours of Urumqi can arrange week-long camel tours along this road.

Regular charter flights during the April to July tourist season have served Dunhuang, Jiayuguan, Lanzhou, and Xi'an. Kashi and Dunhuang should not be missed.

Travel Realities

Tourists in this area should be fit and adventurous. It is not for the finicky and inflexible. While good hotels exist, there are few luxury hotels here. Do not expect international direct dial, convenient hotel money changing, good plumbing, air conditioning, or a constant flow of electricity. Some visitors get sore throats and upset stomachs. Careful backpackers and the adventurous traveler who want to jeep through the desert and eat in canteens and street markets where no foreign tour groups go, should take their own chopsticks and bowl. You are okay on the tourist track in hotels three stars and up, and even in the two-star Turfan hotel, but not in all two-star hotels. The area is extremely dry and cold even on summer nights. Long train and bus rides through the desert are not comfortable. Tourist buses, but not trains, are air-conditioned. Buses have broken down in the desert and the coolest retreat has been the shade of a rock or a sand dune, if you're lucky.

Be prepared for delays and be pleasantly surprised if they don't happen. While waiting, think about the peasants and herdsmen who struggled to raise crops and animals here while the spring or autumn sandstorms howled mercilessly. Think of the sand smothering the crops. Think of the caravans passing through. What did the camels and traders do when they couldn't see a foot ahead of them?

Carry your own liquid refreshments and something to protect your nose and eyes from dust. Also imperative for travel here is an inflatable pillow to cushion bumpy roads, a strong flashlight for caves, a flask for water, and if you want to buy a carpet, a folding bag with lock, perhaps. Try to plan your trip for the Sunday bazaar in Kashi.

The government is in the process of upgrading services in this area. By the time you go, planes may be flying into most of the cities on the route. Paved roads already reach the most important cave temples.

EATING & DRINKING ON THE SILK ROAD

If you don't want to risk spoiling your trip with diarrhea, read about how to avoid upset stomachs in Chapter 10, Food & Drink. Do not eat anything from the local markets. The meat beyond Xi'an is mainly mutton. Wise is the traveler who says something like 'I would love to try it, but it doesn't agree with me. Thank you anyway,' when handed a glass of mare's milk buzzing with flies. The well-meaning tribesman in his yurt is not going to appreciate the pain you will go through later. Don't drink it because you don't want to hurt his feelings. You are the one who will suffer!

Ethnic Groups

As you travel around, try to pick out the characteristics of the different nationalities. Attempt to identify people from their facial features and their distinctive dress. Among the groups along the Silk Road are the Han, Huns, Huis (Moslems), Kazaks, Kirghiz, Manchus, Mongols, Russians, Tarjiks (Tajiks), Tartars, Turfans, Uzbeks, Uygurs (Uighurs), and Xibos.

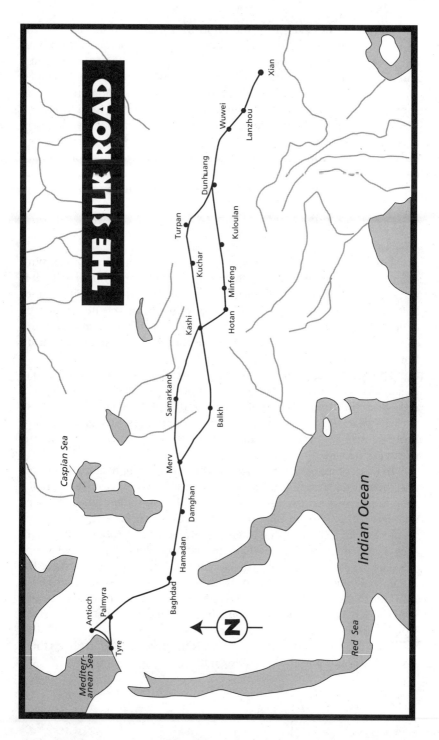

You might be taken to some minority villages and left to fend for yourself. Do some reading beforehand. Prepare some questions about lifestyles, schooling for nomads, number of children allowed, handicrafts and courtship customs. Many guides know nothing about these people. On the other hand, one of our highlights was stopping spontaneously on spotting a nomad yurt by the road, and being invited in for a look.

Read William Dalyrimple's *In Xanadu, A Quest*, about his 1986 trip here and Peter Hopkirk's *Foreign Devils on the Silk Road* about archaeological raids here in the early 1900s. There are many books on China's national minorities.

See *Xian, Dunhuang, Kashi, Lanzhou, Turpan,* and *Urumqi*.

TURPAN

(Turfan)

Turpan is located in the desert of northeast Xinjiang province. With so many Chinese cities clogged with traffic and frentic with activity, it is refreshing to find this sleepy, charming, exotic little town. It still seems to have more donkey carts than cars and traveling by bicycle here is not the ordeal it is in Chengdu, for example. In fact, it is downright pleasant, especially under the grape arbors that line the downtown streets which are bordered by canals of rushing water.

The weather here is the hottest in China! Turpan is in the Turpan Basin, which is known as 'the oven.' Temperatures reach over 40 degrees centigrade in summer. Rainfall averages 16.6 millimeters a year, and in very dry years, it has been as little as four millimeters. Strong winds blow more than 30 days a year. The hot air from the basin and cold air from the north create violent storms.

In winter, people wear fur coats in the morning, light clothes at noon, and dine in the evenings around hot stoves. The temperature has fallen to minus 17 degrees centigrade in January. For summer nights, you need a sweater. It is an area of extremes. Weather people and geographers would love it. The best time to visit is late May to October. Sandstorms blow in April and early May. The population is 200,000, mostly Uygurs.

The lowest point of the basin is Aydingkol Lake, its water surface 154 meters below sea level. It is second only to the Dead Sea as the lowest body of water in the world but you need special permission in advance to visit it. It is not usually included on tours because of the poor road. Nearby is Bogda Mountain with an altitude of 5,445 meters.

But wait! Don't stop reading! Some of the people who have been there say the dust and plumbing are worth it!

ARRIVALS & DEPARTURES

Roughly 200 kilometers, or a four hour drive southeast of the capital, Urumqi, the Silk Road city of Turpan can be a three-day tour by road or train from Urumqi. Your tour should include visits to Gaochang, Jiaohe, the Baziklic Caves, Astana Tombs, Imin Minaret and Karez wells. You can also reach it from Lanzhou by road or rail, a long, long journey. An airport, 90 kilometers away, is planned. The train station is 45 kilometers from town at Daheyan.

ORIENTATION

Turpan was once an oasis on the Silk Road. It existed then and now because of subterranean water from the Karez wells some 2,400 years old. During the Western Han (206 B.C. to 24 A.D.), soldiers were sent to develop agriculture here. Some sources say the technology for the wells came from Shaanxi province. Other historians say from farther west, since Karez is a Persian word. In any case, the wells are most common in Turpan and nearby Hami, to the east.

In spring, snow from the **Tianshan Mountains** melts, and this water flows into the Turpan Basin, soaking into the ground and stored in vast natural underground reservoirs reached by sloping channels tapped in turn by the wells. You can see the desert dotted with lines of wells.

Modern irrigation methods based on these wells have transformed Turpan into an agricultural area. Californians, and anyone else who has made deserts produce food, should be fascinated. Grain, grapes, cotton, and the famous Hami melons are grown here. Grapes have grown here for 2,000 years. The wooden huts with the holes are for drying the September-harvested seedless raisins in the hot, dry air. Ask to see the drying process. Hami melons are much in demand. They have a sweet perfume, somewhat like face powder, with the texture of cantaloupe and the taste of honeydew.

Visit the Karez well museum, which explains with diagrams just how those 40 kilometer-long irrigation tunnels were dug. There are 5,000 kilometers of tunnels, the oldest dates from 400 B.C.

Turpan's grapes are very sweet with a 15-20% sugar content. Grapes grow almost everywhere, along streets and beside private homes. Turpan is also a good place to experience the different cultural minorities. Uygur (Uighur) and Hui nationalities live here with the Han.

WHERE TO STAY & EAT

The **Turfan** is a much better hotel than the Oasis. Both have air-conditioning (turned off for the winter in September and October) but both need work. They are within walking distance of each other and the markets. The Turfan has a good Uygur dance show in the evenings. Both hotels are capable of very good Moslem banquets.

The cheaper **John's Cafe**, *Tel. 524237 across from the Turfan Hotel*, is a hangout for foreign backpackers. Some hotels might be closed in winter.

OASIS HOTEL *(Liuzhou Binguan), 41 Qinian, 838000. Two stars, Tel. 522478, 522491. Fax 523348. No Credit Cards.*

Ren. lobby 1995. Best rooms in FIT section. Soft beds. B.C. Post office. Karaoke. Rooms for backpackers. IDD.

TURFAN HOTEL *(Tulufan Binguan), 838000. Two stars, Tel. 522301, 522642. Fax 523262. Should be able to take major credit cards in high season.*

Renovations 1994. Five stories. IDD. Money exchange. B.C. Good service considering the isolated location. Attractive dining room. Wide twin beds. No second set of stairs in case of fire. Dorms for backpackers.

SEEING THE SIGHTS

The 37-meter-high **Imam Minaret**, (1778) stands two kilometers east of Turpan, its geometric patterns in the Uygur style. However, its smooth inverted-cone shape with rounded top is reminiscent of those towers south of New Delhi on the road to Agra.

There'a a small **museum** near the Turpan Hotel with five well-preserved 1,300-year old human mummies on display. It is open 9:00 am to 8 pm daily in high tourist season (May 1 until the winter).

Walking around town is good if it's not too hot, as some streets are topped with shady grape arbors. The **Grape Festival** is on August 20.

EXCURSIONS FROM TURPAN

The dry climate has preserved historical monuments. The area has many ancient tombs, Buddhist grottoes, and the ruins of ancient cities.

The ghost city of *****Gaochang**, 40 kilometers southeast of Turpan, was capital of the State of Gaochang (500-640) and reached its peak in the ninth century, with a population of 50,000. Try to imagine it as it was then. It was on the Silk Road and flourished from the first century B.C. until the Mongols ravaged it in the 14th A.D. Here were once 30 to 40 monasteries! The buildings were made of mud bricks and are now without roofs. Take a donkey cart if it's too hot to walk.

The equally ancient city of **Jiaohe** (see below) on the other hand shows the effect of its UNESCO and Japanese help: a scale model, signs in English saying the likes of "five minutes to the temple," or "Do not enter." UNESCO has opened new areas like the small northeastern temple. The paths are now paved and it is hard to get lost.

Eight kilometers from Gaochang and 40 kilometers southeast of Turfan are the **Astana Tombs** dating from the third century to about the eighth A.D. This is where 500 mummies, plus their belongings, were found, along with 2100 documents and books. Take a flashlight. Visitors routinely see only a couple of Tang mummies in a dark room. The dry weather has preserved the bodies with still discernible eye lashes and eyeballs. Was Astana the Uygur capital? Astana means capital in Uygur.

  ***Jiaohe** (also known as Yarkhoto, and possibly Yaerhu), 10 kilometers west of Turpan, existed from the second century B.C. to the 14th A.D. Its mud brick buildings are better preserved than Gaochang's and are in an area 1.65 x 0.3 kilometers. It also had a population of 50,000. In the northwestern part are temple ruins with the remains of Buddhist images. There is also a rare brick Buddhist temple. Take a donkey cart if you tire easily. Jiaohe is different in structure from Gaochang; the city was carved out rather than built. One source says it was abandoned in the Ming for lack of water; another source says it was destroyed by fire during fighting in the Yuan dynasty.

  The ***Pazikelik** (or Baziklic, Bazeklik) **Thousand-Buddha Caves** are 16 kilometers northeast of Turpan by dusty road, on a cliff on the Flaming Mountains. About 80 of the grottoes are still intact but in poor condition, destroyed by looters, earthquakes, and archaeologists. Many of the murals were taken to the Berlin Museum in Germany and destroyed by bombs during World War Two. (Read *Foreign Devils on the Silk Road* by Peter Hopkirk.) Faces were mutilated by Moslems. They were built over a period of 1,400 years, starting in the Southern and Northern Dynasties (420-550 A.D.). Dunhuang's are more interesting and younger, but it is good to compare the two.

  The **Flaming Mountains** themselves are historical, so named because the incessant sun is supposed to make the red rocks seem on fire from a distance. Perhaps this happens at sunset only in the classic fairy tale *Pilgrimage to the West*. In that story, the monkey king helps put out the fire so that Monk Xuan Zhang can go to India. The mountains are 100 kilometers long and 10 kilometers wide, their highest peak 800 meters above sea level. Unless you know the story, this is just another set of hills and may not be worth a special stop. They are between the Caves and Turpan, in the hottest part of the depression.

PRACTICAL INFORMATION
• **CITS** and **CTS**, *Oasis Hotel, Tel. 522907. Fax 522768*
• **Telephone Code**, *0995*

URUMQI
(Urumchi; pronounced Oo-roo-moo-chi)
  Urumqi, the capital of the Xinjiang (Sinkiang) Uygur Autonomous Region, has an area one-sixth of China's total, and borders on Mongolia,

Russia, Kazakhstan, Kirghizstan, Tajikistan, Afghanistan, Pakistan and India. The province has 16 million people.

Urumqi is at an altitude of 650 to 910 meters and is surrounded on three sides by mountains. Its hottest weather is in August, 40.9 degrees centigrade. Its coldest weather is in December, minus 41.5 degrees centigrade. Pack also for cold summer nights. In May and June, the coldest has been minus 8.9 degrees centigrade and minus 4.2 degrees centigrade! Consider yourself warned. Maybe you can use the weather as an excuse to buy a fur jacket! The annual precipitation is 200 to 800 millimeters. There is snow between November and March. The best time to visit is May to September.

The urban population is 1.5 million, mainly Uygurs (Uighurs), but also Hans, Kazaks, Mongolians, and Huis. The city has 13 nationalities, the region 47. The region produces oil.

ARRIVALS & DEPARTURES

You can reach Urumqi by plane from Beijing (2,631 kilometers in 3 1/2 hours), Lanzhou (three hours) and Shanghai (4 1/2 hours). Flights connect with Almaty, Islamabad, Karachi, Moscow, Novosibirsk, Tashkent and 29 Chinese cities. Flights with Hong Kong are only from July to September. The Beijing-Urumqi express train covers almost 4,000 kilometers in 64 hours, the longest train ride in China. Passenger and freight train service arrive from Almaty in Kazakhstan and beyond that from Moscow and Rotterdam. See Chapter 6, *Planning Your Trip*.

ORIENTATION

Urumqi dates from the Tang, 618 to 907 A.D., but its attractions are its people and nearby scenery. It is a bustling city, at least 25 years behind eastern China but starting to develop commercially. Tourists usually go there on the way to somewhere else.

WHERE TO STAY

The best and better-located hotel is the attractive **Holiday Inn Urumqi**. The Hotel World Plaza is next. Except for the joint-venture hotels, don't expect much. Taxis might be cheaper from the airport than some hotel buses. The high tourist season is June through October. Prices listed below are subject to change and negotiation.

HOLIDAY INN URUMQI *(Xinjiang Jia Ri Da Jiudian), 168 Xinhua Bei Road, 830002. Four stars. Tel. 2818788. Fax 2817422. $96 to $125. Dist.A.P. 20 km. Dist.R.W. six km. Credit Cards.*

Central location. Built 1992. 24 stories, 383 rooms. Money exchange only on weekdays. IDD, B.C., USTV. Executive floor. Moslem, Sichuan and Cantonese food. Deli. Pub. Beer garden. Gym, sauna, jacuzzi, tennis, solarium and steam bath. Video projection room. Shuttle service. Clinic. This hotel boasts the only western restaurant in Xinjiang, a region four times the size of France.

HOTEL WORLD PLAZA *(Huan Qiu Dajiudian), 2 Beijing Nan Road, 830011. Four stars, Tel. 3836360, 3836409. Fax 3836399 or 3839007. $90 to $100. Dist.A.P. 17 km. Dist.R.W. 12 km. Credit Cards.*

In the South Road Technological Development area. Built 1992, ren. 1995-1996. 24 stories, 400 rooms. Non-smoking floor. B.C. IDD, USTV, gym, sauna and indoor pool. 24 hour room service. Lee Garden (H.K.) management.

ISLAM GRAND HOTEL, *22 Zhong Shan Road, Tel. 2811017, Fax 2811513, Three stars, cheaper than the other two hotels.*

The Islam Grand is better located for business people, but I haven't had a chance to see it.

WHERE TO EAT

Local specialties include roast whole goat or sheep, kebabs, thin-skinned steamed buns with stuffing, fried rice (eaten with bare hands), deep-fried nan, mare's milk, and dried sour cheese. The food can be chili hot. Local fruits include seedless white grapes, pears, Hami melons, apples, and raisins. The meat in Xinjiang is mainly mutton, because Moslems do not eat pork.

Eat only in the **Holiday Inn**, the **World Plaza**, and the **Overseas Chinese Hotel**, though the latter is dirty and falling apart. So far, I haven't gotten sick there. Try the crispy chicken, and fake crab soup in the Cantonese style. It's at *51 Xia Hua Street, Tel. 2860793.* There is also a night food market with Uygur and Moslem food there of questionable hygiene.

SEEING THE SIGHTS

A one-day trip is possible to **Tianshan** (Heaven Mountain) and **Lake Tianzi** (Heavenly Lake), 115 kilometers south of the city. These are about 1,980 meters above sea level and colder than Urumqi. They've had snow in early May. Take something extra for warmth, especially if you want to climb. Tianzi has beautiful scenery but the boat trip on the lake can be missed as you can experience the same things walking. The lake is five square kilometers and 100 meters deep. An ancient glacier, about 100 meters thic and two by five kilometers wide, sprawls near ice caves and valleys. But visitors are frequently too cold to stay to explore. Your visit to a minority yurt is usually not well planned as guides explain very little.

This area might look like the Rockies or Switzerland. But did you ever find yurts and herds of cashmere goats near Lake Louise?

On a second day you can drive about 75 kilometers south of Urumqi to the **Nanshan Pasture** for more mountains, valleys, fountains, waterfalls, and cypress and pine trees. The pasture is in Kazak country. Horseback riding, mountaineering, and digging for valuable ginseng roots are among the attractions.

Here, if you are lucky, or unlucky, you might find a game of polo played with an initially live goat instead of a ball! Shades of Afghanistan! Or you might cheer on women chasing and beating men on horseback, a courtship ritual. You might also be able to dine and/or sleep in a yurt. Barbecued mutton drowned by tea with mare's milk has been offered to some groups. The Kazaks are traditionally nomadic herdsmen, whose ancestors rode and plundered with Genghis Khan.

In the city itself, you can visit the nine-story **Hong Ding Shan Ta** (Red Pagoda Hill), *Tel. 2828416,* founded in the Tang, the current building finished in 1788. There is a good view of the city from the pagoda. The excellent **Xinjiang Museum**, *132 Northwest Road, Tel. 4816436,* closed on Sundays) has gold Roman coins, silver Persian coins, and other artifacts from the Silk Road. One hall contains murals; another displays 3,200-year-old mummies. A special exhibition hall shows traditional relics and the customs of 12 minorities in Xinjiang. The museum is good for two hours.

The **Moslem Market** near the Grand Mosque, *11 Jiefang Road,* is dirty and not well organized, but you can see local Moslem snacks, halal meats, and local vegetables there. The Russian market is interesting because it has goods from Central Asia and Russia like cameras, shoes, and appliances. But the trade is more from China to Kazakhstan. The Qiao Livestock Market has camels and horses.

THE UYGURS

The different minority groups make this an interesting region. The **Uygurs** *controlled northwest China during the Tang. In 788 A.D., a Tang princess married a Uygur khan, by no means a love match. In subsequent years, Chinese silk and sugar were exchanged for Uygur horses and furs. Uygur cavalry often helped the Tang emperors. Strangely enough, the Uygurs were the main supporters of the Manichaean religion (see Quanzhou).*

The power of the Uygurs declined after their capital was sacked by the Kirghiz of western Siberia. In 842, a food shortage turned the Uygurs into very aggressive raiders and China retaliated with force and the execution of Uygurs in Xi'an. The Uygurs also fought with Genghis Khan but because they had a written language, they were the bookkeepers and administrators, not the warriors.

SHOPPING

Urumqi is just about the best place on the Silk Road to shop for minority handicrafts. These include carpets, decorated daggers, jewelry, embroidered caps, jade carving, embroidery, musical instruments, and fur and leather articles. Hand-knotted wool carpets in Persian designs are especially good buys but are probably cheaper in Pakistan. The **Overseas Chinese Hotel** has a shop with reasonable prices for cashmere sweaters. The **Holiday Inn** has books in English and some unusual crafts, at high prices.

Other stores of interest are the **Urumqi General Carpet Rug Factory**, *40-64 Jinger Road, Tel. 5813297*; **Musical Instrument Factory,** *245 Jiefang Nan Road, Tel. 5813293, 2823284;* **Xinjiang Antique Store**, *325 Jiefang Nan Road, Tel. 2825161;* **Jade Sculpture Factory** (jasper, topaz, crystal, Hotan jade), *7 Pearl River Road, Tel. 5812395;* **Urumqi Foreign Trade Carpets Factory**, *14 Li Yu Shan Road, 830000, Tel. 5812395.* There is also a **Cashmere Sweater Factory** at *7 Juan Jue Road, Tel. 2863678.* The biggest **department store** is at *51 Xin Hua Nan Street, Tel. 2860793.*

The **Friendship Hotel** *(Youyi Binguan), Yan'an Road, Tel. 2868088* has had very nice, but small, mounted prints of camels, autographed by the artist.

EXCURSIONS IN XINJIANG

This is a huge region, the largest in China. It is much less populated than other parts of China as most of it is desert and mountain. Two cave temples are at **Baicheng** and **Kuqa**, almost halfway in between Kashi and Urumqi, and 285 kilometers from Urumqi. (Turpan's caves are better). Kuqa has an airport, so you can fly there if you want to see the ***Kezil/Kerzil Thousand Buddha Grottoes**; these caves are from the Han and have 236 grottoes. Xinjiang has at least eight important groups of grottoes.

Another interesting place is **Yili via Yining**, near the Kazakhstan border where you should be able to see hundreds of yurts. This can also be done from Almaty on a long weekend. See Chapter 6, section on *Getting To China Via Central Asia.*

Travel agents can arrange jeep, camel, motorcycle, bicycle or bus tours on the Silk Road, a tour of the southern, less traveled route to Tibet and Pakistan, treks in the mountains or the Taklamakan Desert, and a land tour from Urumqi to Almaty in Kazakhstan and back through Kashgar.

For other caves and tourist attractions in the region, see *Silk Road, Turpan,* and *Kashi.* Ask about the Corban Festival, the Moslem New Year, with its songs, dances, horse races, courtship rituals on horseback, wrestling, and lamb snatching.

PRACTICAL INFORMATION

- **Business Hours**, 10 am to 7 pm (winter) and 9,30 am to 6,30 pm (summer) for offices five days a week. 10 am to 7 pm (summer) and 11 am to 8 pm (winter) for stores.
- **China Xinjiang Nature Travel Service**, *9 Dong Hou Street, 830002, Tel. 2616843, 2632596, 2626343. Fax 2617174. Attention Xia We Hui, Manager, European and American Department.* Specialists in bird watching, trekking, jeep, horse and camel tours, in off-the- beaten-track areas around the Silk Road.
- **CITS** and **Overseas Tourist Corporation**, *Xinjiang Branches, 51 Xinhua Bei Road, 830002, Tel. 2825794 or 2821529 or 2825913. Fax 2810689, 2818691*
- **CTS**, *47-51 Xinhua Nan Road, 830001, Tel. 2861970, 2861806, 2860238. Fax 2867131, 2862131. Attention Yang Yi, Sales Manager.*
- **CYTS**, *9 Jianshe Road, 830002. Tel. 2818447. Fax 2817078*
- **Telephone Code**, *0891*
- **Tourism Hotline**, *Tel. 2831902 for information and complaints.*
- **Xinjiang Tourism Bureau**, *16 Hetan Nan Road, 830002, Tel. 2831907. Ask Lincoln Cui for information.*
- **Tourist Complaints**, contact **Supervisory Bureau of Tourism Quality of Xinjiang**, *Tel. 2831902. Fax 2824449*

XI'AN

(SIAN: Western Peace)

Xi'an, the capital of Shaanxi province on the Guanzhong Plain, borders on the Loess Plateau to the north and the Qinling Mountains to the south.

Xi'an was the capital intermittently for 1,183 years and 11 imperial dynasties, including the Western Zhou (of the ritual bronzes), the Qin (of the Great Wall and **terracotta army**), the Western Han (of the jade burial suits), the Sui (of the Grand Canal), and the Tang - ah, the Tang! This city was the center of China's world from the 11th century B.C. to the early 10th A.D. Commerce on the Silk Road thrived west of here to the Mediterranean and beyond. (See *Silk Road.*) Thousands of foreigners lived in the Western Market then.

In spite of the occasional invasions and sackings by rebels and tribesmen, Xi'an, then named Chang'an (Everlasting Peace), reached its peak in the Tang, when the population was nearly two million. It was one of the world's largest cities, with walls measuring 36 kilometers in circumference. It declined because of late Tang debauchery and corruption, the eunuchs ruling the court and increasingly powerful governors-general controlling the provinces. In 906, one of the last Tang emperors allowed one of his generals to take complete charge while he enjoyed his lady love. Xi'an rolled downhill from there on, following the fortunes, also, of the Silk Road. Read Cooney and Alteri's novel about this period, *The Court of the Lion*.

A short-lived peasant regime made Xi'an a capital again in the 17th century, but it never regained its past glory. Xi'an did, however, continue to be a tourist resort and destination for religious pilgrimages because of its Buddhist roots. In 1900, when the Empress Dowager fled Beijing, she went to Xi'an.

During the **Xi'an Incident** in 1936, one of his top officers, known as the Young Marshall, devised a plan to kidnap Generalissimo Chiang Kai-shek. They forced him to cooperate with the Communists against the Japanese, and the Communists set up a liaison office here which is now the *Museum of the Eighth Route Army**. On May 20, 1949, the Communists eventually took over the city.

The altitude is 400 meters. The hottest weather is 40 degrees centigrade in July; the coldest is minus 14 degrees centigrade in January. Rain falls all year round, but especially July through early September with an annual precipitation of 550 to 770 millimeters. The best weather is May, and September-October. The urban population is six million, inside and outside the wall.

ARRIVALS & DEPARTURES

Xi'an is a 1 3/4 hour flight or about a 22-hour train ride southwest (1,165 kilometers) of Beijing. It is about a seven hour train ride west of Luoyang. Air routes with 42 cities now include Hong Kong and Hiroshima and soon if not already, Bangkok, Macau, Nagoya, Osaka, and Singapore. Check with travel agents about summer plane charters with Tianshui and Dunhuang.

Upon arrival at the airport, be prepared to walk from your plane to the terminal. The bridges are too high for small planes, even 737s. The airport at Xianyang is between 38 to 53 kilometers from the city's hotels, depending on where you're staying. The one-hour CAAC airport bus to Xi'an is 1/10th the price of most hotel airport transfers. On the way, look for the 2,200-year old Qin imperial burial *tumuli* (pointed tops) and almost as old Han imperial *burial* mounds (rounded top).

ORIENTATION

Next to Beijing, Xi'an is the best city to visit in China, especially if you are interested in ancient Chinese history, traditional culture, and archaeology. It is one of the 24 historical cities protected by the State Council and, unfortunately, it has been sinking due to lack of water.

Just to glimpse all it has to offer takes a full week. To savor Xi'an slowly, to study it deeply, read about Empress Wu and her lover-protector-henchman while sitting in the shadow of a Tang pagoda - or reading about that crafty fictional Tang detective Judge Dee, two giant silk-flower petals sticking sideways out of the back of his magisterial cap – that kind of depth could take months.

Ancient Xi'an is the setting for many Chinese operas, their sweet young heroines waving flowing ribbon sleeves and their flag-pierced generals galloping away to battle amid the clash of cymbals. Here the real camels, caravans, and traders exchanged silver, furs, horses, and sesame for Chinese silk and porcelain. It is here that the egomaniac emperor ordered the burning of all books except those he liked, and demanded that his subjects create an army of life-size soldiers so he could maintain his empire after his earthly death.

TOURIST SIGHTS IN XI'AN BY LOCATION

• *In Xi'an and immediate vicinity:* Wild Goose Pagodas, Bell Tower, Drum Tower, City Wall, Great Mosque, Xi'an Stele Museum, Shaanxi Provincial History Museum, Xingqing Palace Park, Banpo Museum, Memorial Museum of the Eighth Route Army, Xi'an Film Studio.

• *West and South of Xi'an:* Chariot and Horse Pits, Xingjiao Temple, Xiangji Temple, Qinglong Temple, Temple of Du Fu, Cao Tang Temple, Peasant Painting of Hu County.

• *East of Xi'an:* Huaqing Hot Springs, Qinshihuang's Tomb and Terracotta Army, and Bronze Chariots.

North and Northwest of Xi'an: Xianyang Museum, Maoling, Zhaoling, and Qianling tombs, and Famen Temple and the international airport.

Xi'an today is a textile and manufacturing center. It also produces Chinese and western medicines and airplanes. It is an educational center, with about 40 colleges, universities, and research institutes. **Xi'an Jiaotung** (Communications) **University** is the best known, and one of the 11 'super-key' universities in the country. The municipal government has embarked on a program to bring Xi'an up to international standards between now and 2010. It plans to make the city more green and develop its high-tech industries.

Xi'an's agricultural areas grow cotton, maize, wheat, vegetables, pomegranates, and persimmons. Many houses and walls have been made of loess soil mixed with straw. If cared for properly and protected with bricks on top, mud walls can last 100 years. Cheap too! Today many farmers are rebuilding entirely in brick.

The walled city is laid out in the classic Chinese style in a rectangle, most streets parallel, the bell tower almost in the center. If you only have one day, try to see the Qin Army Vault Museum (Terracotta Warriors), Bronze Chariots, Banpo Village, the Big Wild Goose Pagoda, the Provincial Museum, the Bell Tower, and the City Wall and gates. If you've never experienced a Chinese-style mosque, try to fit in the Great Mosque, too.

This is a very rushed itinerary, better done in two days. Be aware that many taxi drivers do not use their meters. Settle on a price before you get in. Judge distances by the size of the city wall.

WHERE TO STAY

Hotels here add a 10-15% surcharge. Some hotels charge for local as well as long distance telephone calls. The best hotels are the **Hyatt** (especially for business guests), **Sheraton Xi'an**, and the **Shangri-La Golden Flower**, all modern-day international class palaces. The Hyatt has the smallest twin rooms, but the best furniture.

Also of international luxury quality are the Grand Castle, the Xi'an Garden and the Grand New World. Of the three-star hotels, we prefer the modest Bell Tower for location and service. A new three-star hotel, the Min Sheng Grand opened recently near the South Gate on South Street with 120 rooms, and should be good.

The best location for business people and individual tourists is inside the city wall but traffic jams are common and the air is not as fresh as outside the wall. The Bell Tower and the City Hotels have the best spots, convenient to stores, KFC, the telecommunications office and Bell Tower. They are walking distance to the Drum Tower, the Mosque, the South Gate, a good antique market and general shopping.

The Xian Grand Castle just outside the South Gate and the Hotel Royal Xi'an, tie for the second best locations. The Royal Xi'an is west of the Hyatt, both inside the wall, but the Royal is closer to an interesting vegetable market, the East Gate, the Friendship Store, department stores, the south Heping (Peace) Gate and the Small World Restaurant. The Xi'an Castle is closest to the stairs up the South Gate, the Stele Museum and the attractions in the south of the city.

The Hyatt and People's Hotel (Renmin Binguan) have the third best location inside the wall. The People's is closest to the City Hall. Budget travelers should use the Jianguo Inn, the Jiefang Hotel (at the railway station), and the People's Hotel. Romantic travelers should consider the lovely garden architecture of the Xi'an Garden Hotel and forget its price for one night. The sampling of prices here are subject to change, negotiation and 15% surcharge.

BELL TOWER HOTEL *(Zhong Lou Fandian)*, *Southwest corner of Bell Tower, 710001. Three stars. Tel. 7279200. Fax: 7271217, 7218767. In US, Tel. 1-800-HOLIDAY. Dist.A.P. about 46 km. Dist.R.W. three km. Credit Cards.* Located 200 meters to Great Mosque. Built 1985, ren. 1994, and 1995. Seven stories, 321 rooms. Best view from odd-numbered rooms. Executive floor. B.C., IDD. USTV. Cantonese restaurant, Fun Pub (with karaoke and disco). Mongolian food in yurts in winter. Friday and Saturday barbecue in April to October. Gym. Bicycles. Managed by Holiday Inns Asia-Pacific.

CITY HOTEL XIAN *(Xin Shi Jie Jiudian)*, *5 Nan Da St., 710002. Three stars, Tel. 7219988. Fax 7216688. Credit Cards.*
Excellent location near Bell Tower. Built 1988. Six stories, 138 small rooms. IDD. B.C. Chains International Hotels (H.K.) management. Budget travelers only.

GRAND CASTLE HOTEL XIAN, *12 Xi Duan Huan Cheng Nan Lu, 710068. Four stars. Tel. 7231800. Fax 7231500, 7231244. Credit Cards.*
Just outside South Gate. Built 1993. 10 stories. 359 spacious rooms. Kettles. IDD. Huge atrium lobby. Looks like a castle. B.C. IDD. Japanese, Cantonese, Mediterranean cuisines and health foods. 24-hour room service. Gym. Managed by ANA Hotels.

GRAND NEW WORLD HOTEL *(Gu Du Dajiudian)*, *48 Lian Hu Rd., 710002. Four stars, Tel. 7216868. Fax 7219754, 7210708. Dist.A.P. 45 km. Dist.R.W. four km. Credit Cards.*
Near West Gate and park. Built 1989-90. Ren.1994. 14 stories, 480 rooms, tending to be small with attractive but unusual color schemes. B.C., IDD. Planning executive floor. Cantonese restaurant. Food Street. Indoor pool. Gym, sauna, steam bath and tennis. 1200-seat theatre on odd-numbered days during high season has a Terracotta Warriors historical dance drama. USTV. Managed by New World Hotels International.

HOTEL ROYAL XI'AN *(Huang Cheng Binguan)*, *334 Dong Da Jie, 710001. Four stars. Tel. 7235311. Fax 7235887. Credit Cards.*
Built 1992. 12 stories, 439 rooms. (Kitchenette in all suites). USTV. B.C. Cantonese food. 24- hour room service. Un-inspired architecture. Nikko Hotels International (JAL).

HYATT REGENCY XIAN *(Kaiyue Fandian)*, *158 Dong Da Jie, 710001. Five stars. Tel. 7231234. Fax 7216799, 7277650. In US, Tel. 1-800-233-1234. Internet: http://www.travelweb.com/hyatt.html Dist.A.P. 45 km. Dist.R.W. two km. Credit Cards.*
Built 1990. 8, 10 and 12 stories. 404 classy but small rooms, some of which have attractive Japanese paper windows. Executive club. IDD, B.C. 24-hour room service. Cantonese and Italian cuisine. Gym, aerobics. Steam room. USTV. Jacuzzi. Bicycles.

JIANGUO HOTEL *(Fandian), 20 Jin Hua Nan Rd., 710048. Three stars, Tel. 3238888. Fax 3235145. Dist.A.P. 50 km. Dist.R.W. five km. Next to tourist shopping in residential area. Credit Cards.*
Built 1989-90. Six and 14 stories, 888 large rooms. Wide twins. Televisions in beautiful cabinets. Wicker furniture. B.C., IDD. CITS and CTS. Popcorn machine. USTV. 24-hr. room service and coffee shop. Chaozhou, Sichuan, Cantonese, and hot pot food. Gym. Jianguo Inn in the same complex has 160 smaller, cheaper rooms (showers only) and a cafeteria. Indoor pool.
JIEFANG HOTEL, *across from railway station, 710004. Two stars, Tel. 7213417, 7213419. Fax 7212617.*
B.C. Musty. No dorms. No IDD but DDD. Bicycles (cheap). For budget travelers only.
PEOPLE'S HOTEL *(Renmin Dasha), 319 Dongxin St., 710004. About two-star quality. Tel. 7215111. Fax 7218152.*
There's a garden here, but the rest of the place is seedy. Dirty carpets. Thin curtains. Big baths. Backpackers only.
SHANGRI-LA GOLDEN FLOWER HOTEL *(Shang Gorilla or Jinhua Fandian), 8 Chang Le Xi Road, 710032. Four stars, Tel. 3232982. Fax 3235477. In US, Tel. 1-800-942-5050. Dist.A.P. 49 km. Dist.R.W. three km.*
Night market outside with food and clothes. Credit Cards. 1985 wing, seven stories. 1989 wing, 11 stories. 510 rooms (including apartments with kitchenettes). Old wing has bigger rooms and larger beds. B.C. Executive floor. Non-smoking floor. IDD. USTV. 24-hour room service. Gym, indoor pool, jacuzzi, and sauna. In 1995 it was in the process of renovations.
SHERATON XIAN *(Xilaidun Jiudian), 12 Feng Hao Rd., 710077. Five stars, Tel. 4261888. Fax 4262188, 4262983. In US, Tel. 1-800-3253535. Dist.A.P.45 km. Dist.R.W. 4.5 km. Credit Cards.*
In a quiet location, two kilometers west of West Gate. Built 1991. 16 stories, 450 rooms. Some apartments with kitchenettes. Executive floor. IDD, 24-hour B.C., CITS. Non-smoking floors. Cantonese and international food. USTV. Indoor pool. Gym, sauna, steambath and jacuzzi.
WANNIAN HOTEL XI'AN, *B11 Changle Zhong Rd., 710032. Three stars. Tel. 3231932. Fax 3235460.*
XI'AN GARDEN HOTEL *(Tang Hua Binguan), 4 Dong Yan Yin Rd., Da Yan Ta, 710061. Four stars, Tel. 5261111, 5255840. Fax 5261778, 5261998. In US, Tel. 1-800-223-6800. Dist.A.P. 53 km. Dist.R.W. eight km. Credit Cards.*
Garden-style hotel on southern edge of city outside wall. Walk to Xi'an Film Studio and Big Wild Goose Pagoda. Small but good. Tang dynasty museum on premises with titles in English. Theatre restaurant open for groups. Built 1988, Four stories, 301 rooms. Small twin rooms.

Small televisions and bathrooms. Could be a long walk from lobby to your room. IDD. B.C. USTV. Japanese restaurant. Fast food. Gym. Member Leading Hotels of the World. Managed by Mitsui (Japan).

XI'AN HOTEL (*Binguan*), *36 North Section, Chang'an Rd., 710061. Four stars. Tel. 5261351. Fax 5261796. Dist.A.P. 55 km. Dist.R.W. 10 km. Credit Cards.*

Near CITS and Small Wild Goose Pagoda. Built 1982; North Building ren. 1994, 14 stories, 286 rooms. 1986 South Building, ren. 1991, 1993. 14 stories, 264 rooms. B.C., USTV. IDD. Post office. Japanese and Cantonese restaurants. Bicycles. Gym. Indoor pool. English poor.

XI'AN LEE GARDENS (*Li Yuan Jiudian*), *8 Laodong Nan Rd., 710068 Four stars, Tel. 4263388. Fax 4263288. Dist.A.P. 38 km. Dist.R.W. eight km. Credit Cards.*

Southwest of walled city near Northwest Technical University and Gao Xing Gi Shu Kai Fa (Gi Shu Hi-Tech Development Area). Built 1992-93. Eight stories, 296 rooms. IDD. B.C. USTV. Executive floor. Chaozhou and Cantonese food. 24-hour room service. Outdoor pool and gym due soon.

WHERE TO EAT

Xi'an food is similar to that of Beijing: somewhat bland. Its famous local dishes are crisp fried chicken or duck, and dried fish shaped like grapes. A typical Moslem dish is Yang Rou Pao Mutton Soup. Much of its food has been inspired by imperial tastes.

Two celebrated wines are made here: one is thick and sweet with the appearance of milk. Served hot, **Chou Jiu wine** inspired Tang poet Li Po, who drank 1000 cups and wrote more than 100 poems. The other wine is **Xifeng Jiu** (55% alcohol), one of the eight Most Famous Wines in China. Most hotels have good Chinese food, but only joint ventures have good western food.

The popular jiaotze dumpling restaurant **DE FACHANG**, near the Bell Tower serves over a hundred different kinds of dumplings, which all seem to taste the same. The hygiene needs work here and in the popular **QINGYA ZHAI MUSLIM RESTAURANT**, *Dong Da Jie* near the Bell Tower. The food at the **MOSLEM MARKET** is cheap, quite good, but also of questionable hygiene.

There are street food markets in the evenings: near the Jianguo Hotel, the Xi'an Hotel, and New World Xi'an. Take your own bowl and chopsticks. You can get good Cantonese snacks and dim sum are at the **GRAND NEW WORLD HOTEL'S FOOD STREET**.

Except for the hotels, Xi'an still hasn't got any good restaurants suitable for foreigners. The **SMALL WORLD RESTAURANT** for back-packers is at *6 Heping Lufu, Tel. 7432448*, on the west side of Heping Road between the Hyatt and Victory Hotels. The floors are cement, the menu limited and the ambiance modest, but it claims "the best French fries this side of the International Dateline" and is popular with foreign backpackers. The **SINGAPORE FAST FOOD RESTAURANT** is on the south side of Dong Da Jie between the Nikko Hotel Royal Xi'an and the Hyatt, across from the covered market. So-so food, but at least it looks clean. **KFC** is south of the Bell Tower.

The **WANNIAN HOTEL** has good jiaozi dumplings, and a well-served hot pot banquet. The **TANG DYNASTY THEATER RESTAU-RANT**, *39 Changan Road, Tel. 7211633, 7211655,* across from the Xi'an Hotel, has Cantonese food, but no one recommends it.

SEEING THE SIGHTS

*The Museum of Emperor Qin's Terracotta Army**, 38 kilometers northeast of the city (Qin Yung Bo Wu Guan. 8 am to 5:30 pm) is the most spectacular and important place to visit because of its 2,180-year-old painted-ceramic army of more than 8000 soldiers buried to 'protect' the tomb of the first Qin emperor. You can purchase slides and photos of reasonable quality in souvenir shops. It costs quite a bit to take a photo here so do ask before you raise your camera. In Vault or Pit Number One, staff can take a photo of your group in front of the soldiers for Y150. If you are caught taking photos without permission, there is a fine of Y300 to Y800, payable to the museum. Get a receipt. Guides have been known to pocket this themselves.

Local peasants digging a well discovered the relics in 1974. The terracotta army is a puzzle because the emperor left no record of its existence. Excavation started in 1976. A permanent building protects the army and tourists from most of the elements, and you are able to walk around the periphery of the once-buried relics. If you look carefully, you should see bits of the original colors, lost because of exposure to air.

There are three vaults. **Vault Number One**, opened to the public in 1979, is 62 by 230 by five meters deep. Most of the army was found facing east, toward the tomb, 1 1/2 kilometers away. The soldiers were in lines of roughly 70 across and 150 deep, separated by 10 partition walls and 11 corridors.

The men are hollow from the thigh up and made in two parts; they are 1.78 to 1.87 meters tall. The soldiers in front hold crossbows; also in front were bells and drums. Charioteers hold their hands out before them as if clutching reins. The horses originally wore harnesses with brass ornaments and are a breed native to Hechu in Gansu. You can distinguish the officers from the soldiers by their clothing and armor. Is every one of the 2,000 faces here different? Judge for yourself.

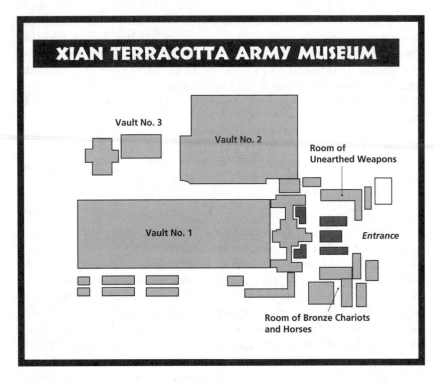

Researchers believe that kilns were built around the molded figures (probably two horses at a time) and destroyed after firing. There are remains of 30 wooden chariots.

In separate buildings are **Vault Number Two**, holding 1,400 cavalrymen, archers, charioteers and infantrymen, some kneeling and shooting and **Vault Number Three**, which has 68 officers and was probably the 'command post.' You pay extra to visit these two other museums. Near the main museum is a smaller building with two of the 20 tiny bronze chariots found. These are also outstanding and you can see them at close range.

Seven human skeletons believed to be the murdered children of the first Qin emperor are also on display at the Terracotta Warriors museum. Their brother killed them in a palace coup 2,200 years ago.

You pass the **Tomb of Emperor Qinshihuang** (Chin Shih Huang-ti) on the way to and from the Terracotta Warriors. The first emperor of the Qin Dynasty, the builder of the Great Wall, and first unifier of China, lived from 259 to 210 B.C., and became king of Qin State at age 13. What he achieved in so short a reign is incredible, and it is no wonder that he searched his empire for pills of longevity. Over 700,000 people worked on his magnificent underground palace tomb, begun in 246 B.C. when he was 14 years old.

Archaeologists have made preliminary excavations at this site and so far believe that the tomb has not been robbed, and that the ancient records are correct. 'Rivers of mercury' probably flow through it. Lack of money and technology has postponed the excavation of this extremely important tomb. At press time, all you can see is a **tumulus** (an ancient grave mound) six kilometers in circumference and 40 meters high, covered with pomegranate trees and a small pavilion.

A reconstruction of the first Qin emperor's tomb based on the 2,000-year old description by Szuma Chien, China's first historian, is now 200 metres from the real tomb.

You can book tours for the Terracotta Warriors from most major hotels. Cheaper bus tours go from the Jiefang Hotel and Xi'an Railway Station but make sure you have an English-speaking guide and know what you're paying for. You pay entrance fees yourself at the sites.

The **Huaqing Hot Springs*, the site of the Xi'an Incident, have been so overshadowed by modern events that their ancient history is frequently overlooked. They are at the base of **Lishan Hill**, 30 kilometers northeast of Xi'an, and a visit here is usually combined with the Terracotta Warriors and lunch. Huaqing has been an imperial resort since the mid-Tang, about 1,200 years ago, its most famous tenants were Emperor Xuanzong (Hsuan-tsung) of the Tang, and the woman blamed for his downfall, and his favorite concubine Yang Guifei (Kuei-fei). The influence of Yang Guifei and her relatives caused much dissatisfaction at court. In 755, an adopted son of hers rebelled, and the emperor's troops refused to move as long as she remained alive. The Japanese say she escaped to Japan. The Chinese say she was strangled. The emperor lived on even though they had vowed to die together. Promises! Promises! His son returned eight years later and proclaimed himself emperor.

The imperial couple used to winter here because it was warmer than Xi'an. They bathed in the **Jiulong** (Nine Dragons) **Hot Spring** and the **Lotus Bath**. You can find a reconstruction of Yang Guifei's personal bath. The current buildings are post-Liberation in the old Tang style.

You can also trace the flight of Chiang Kai-shek, the Chinese Nationalist leader, from his bedroom as he panicked at the sound of gunfire at 5 am on a cold December morning in 1936. He left behind his false teeth and wore only one shoe. A pavilion today marks the spot up the hill where the "Young Marshall" captured him.

The ***Dayan Ta Pagoda**, or the **Big Wild Goose Pagoda** of the Da Ci'en Temple, along with the **Little Wild Goose Pagoda** in Jianfu Temple, are the most famous pagodas in China because of their age and their important historical connections. They are not, however, the most beautiful or spectacular. The bigger pagoda was built to house the sutras brought back from India in 652 A.D. (Tang) by the famous monk Xuan

Zhang (Hsuan-Tsang). It was probably named in memory of the temple in India where the monk lived, on a goose-shaped hill. Or it could have acquired its name because some monks were starving and Buddha, in the form of a wild goose, dropped down close to them. The monks, being vegetarians, refused to eat it.

The pagoda has seven stories, 248 steps, and a great view from the top. In the adjoining Da Ci'en Temple (647 A.D.) are painted-clay statues of 18 lohan (Ming), most with strong Indian rather than Chinese features.

The *Little Wild Goose Pagoda (Xiao Yan Ta), outside the south wall, is 45 meters high and was constructed of brick in 684 A.D. Thirteen stories high, it is missing two of its original stories, which were destroyed during earthquakes in 1444. This is all that remains of the great Da Jianfu Temple, so important in the Tang.

While both pagodas are historical monuments protected by the State Council, only a stop at one is really necessary.

The **Shaanxi Provincial History Museum**, *Shaanxi Li Shi Bo Wu Guan, 91 Yanta Zhong Road, 710061*, is south of the walled city. It is well laid out with some explanations in English. Separate entrance and higher fees for foreigners pay for a shopping area, toilets, lockers (purses are not allowed in the museums), and the use of a snack bar. This is one of China's best museums and is worth visiting. It requires a minimum of one hour, more if you want to savor it. It covers prehistory to the end of the Qing and has original Tang frescoes never exhibited before. The entrance fee is high for a Chinese museum.

The 36-meter-high *Bell Tower (Zhong Lou) was first built in 1384 (Ming) in another location, and moved to its current central site here 200 years later. Three sets of eaves weaken 'the force of the rainfall,' and actually only two stories are here. The furniture is gorgeous (Qing) and the very fancy traditional ceiling is Ming. From the second story you can look at all four gates of Xi'an. Parking is impossible. It is on Dong Da Jie near the Bell Tower Hotel, west of the main shopping area, and north of the South Gate.

The nearby **Drum Tower** (Gu Lou) within walking distance to the west is also impressive and contains a large antique store. The tower was built in 1384 and is original. Drums used to be beaten about 800 times in 10 minutes before the city gates closed for the night.

The *Great Mosque, *Qing Zhen Si, Tel. 7271504, 7272541*, the largest in Xi'an, is on a back street north past the Drum Tower. It was founded as a mosque in 742 (Tang), but the present buildings are mainly Ming, with some subsequent construction. The buildings are a good example of the sinofication of foreign religious buildings right down to the bats, dragons, unicorns, marbletop tables, and mother-of-pearl-inlaid furniture. The Great Hall (Ming) is, however, more west Asian, the writing Arabic, the arches and flowers more like Istanbul or Baghdad. You remove your shoes before entering. Prayers are said five times a day. Moslems first came here from Xinjiang and Guangzhou, and they founded this mosque with help and encouragement from the Tang emperors. A gilded wooden Koran, said to be the largest in the world, has been carved here. Today in Xi'an, 14 other mosques and this one serve 60,000 or so Moslems.

Banpo (Panpo) **Museum,** *Banpo Wu Guan, Tel. 3279240, 3279248,* in the eastern suburbs of the city, is the actual archaeological site of a 6,000-year-old neolithic village. The site covers 50,000 square meters, of which the museum encloses 3,000. There you see living quarters, one of the oldest pottery kilns in the country, and a graveyard.

The museum encompasses a communal storage area, moat, grave-yard (skeletons under glass), and fireplaces. In the museum are a bow drill, barbed fish hook, clay pots, and pottery whistle believed to be the earliest musical instrument in China. Among its other artifacts are hairpins, stone axes, and a pot with holes in the bottom, probably used as a steamer. Its narrow-necked, narrow-based water jugs, with two handles, look surprisingly like amphoras also used by the ancient Greeks and Romans! Is there a connection? The exhibits are labeled in English.

This culture is believed to be matrilineal: (1) because of the burial customs. Most of the 174 graves had one skeleton each; the few graves that contained more than one skeleton had no male-female couples; (2) the women gathered wild food at first while the men hunted. After the women discovered how to plant seeds, land became valuable and it was passed on from mother to daughter; (3) because of the burial system (with no couples), scientists concluded that there were no fixed marriages. Besides, did neolithic people know where babies came from! (4) the village consisted of one big house in the center for old and young, and smaller houses for visiting males. The men kept their belongings in their native villages, where the men were later buried.

As agriculture developed, men started pursuing it too. As surpluses grew (and probably the basic principles of physiology were discovered), fixed families started. In later neolithic gravesites in Gansu, male skeletons were found lying straight, females leaning toward them. Since the women were bound, they were probably buried alive. So much for early women's lib! Now, what is your theory?

The new theme park **Banpo Village** on the same grounds as the Banpo Neolithic Museum is a waste of time and money. The dances are poorly choreographed and executed. The costumes are not authentic. Did they really wear sneakers 6,000 years ago? The buildings are badly made, so forget it.

The *****City Wall** was built from 1374 to 1378 (Ming), probably with material from the old Tang wall: 3.4 kilometers (north-south) by 2.6

kilometers (east-west); 12 meters high. The walls follow the boundaries of the Tang imperial city. The gates open to the public are on each of the four sides from which you can climb the wall. Six new gates have been added to the original four to facilitate the flow of traffic. You can see a small section of the south wall in its original Tang dynasty state. You can walk on top of most of the wall.

If You Have More Time or Interest

The **Xi'an Stele Museum**, *Bai Shu Lin Street, Tel. 7210250*, is at the first gate east of the South Gate and can be combined with a day in the city. It is in an old (Qing and Ming) Confucian temple, and is primarily of interest to calligraphers. The museum has the most important collection of steles in China, with over 3,000 from the Han through the Qing, including 114 Tang engravings of the 13 Confucian classics. These have been used by centuries of scholars to copy and study for content as well as calligraphy.

Important for Christians here is the seventh-century Nestorian stele, written in Syriac with a cross at the top. You really have to search for it in this forest, but it is a rare piece of church history, the commemoration of the establishment of the church in Xi'an. This stele is in the second pavilion of steles at the back of the museum, the first stele on the left. You can buy rubbings of this and other steles in the souvenir shop. The Nestorian sect started in the fifth century but was declared heretical by Rome in 431 A.D. The sect flourished in west Asia, but relics have also been found in Quanzhou, China.

This museum also has giant stone carvings, the largest from the eastern Han, including a life-size rhinoceros and ostrich (inspired by live animals given as tribute). Four of the bas-reliefs of horses from the Zhaoling tombs are here. (One is in Philadelphia.)

On a third day, you may want to go to *Qianling, Tomb of Tang Emperor Gaozong (Kao-tsung) and the Empress Wu, 79 kilometers from Xi'an. She was as ruthless and outrageous as Qing Empress Dowager Cixi, but a more successful ruler. He died in 683 A.D. and she in 705 A.D. This unexcavated tomb is 75 kilometers northwest of the city, a worthwhile full day's excursion that can include other tombs as well. While earlier tombs were built to create their own artificial hills on the plains, the Tang tombs were built into existing hills. This one is 400 meters high, 1049 meters above sea level.

Approaching the hill, you pass statues of horses and ostriches, and 10 to 12-foot high guardian figures holding swords. Then on the left are the life-size statues of guards, tribal heads, and foreign diplomats who paid their respects at the funeral. The 61 statues are now without heads, alas; look for names on their backs. One is labeled "Afghanistan." The wall around the tomb is 4470 meters long. There are plans to open the actual tomb to the public. Although many of the structures at Qianling were destroyed in the war at the end of the Tang, the museum here contains about 4000 pieces.

Some of the minor tombs in the neighborhood are excavated, and you can also go underground to find the coffin and fine murals of court scenes in the tombs of Princess Yong-tai and Prince Yide.

Famen Temple, 120 kilometers from Xi'an, can be included in a one-day trip along with the Qianling Tomb, and a small but extremely valuable museum of ancient Zhou bronzes in **Shaocheng Village** where they were excavated (nine kilometers from Famen). These are near Baoji on the old Silk Road.

Famen Temple is extremely important because it houses a finger bone of Prince Gautama, the founder of Buddhism whose statue is in every Buddhist temple in China and who lived in the fifth century B.C. Unfortunately a tourist town has been built around this shrine. This and loud rock music has destroyed the mystical atmosphere but the museum is worth the trip. While tourists will not normally be shown the rare relic, you can see some of the treasures that were buried with it.

Among the over 900 pieces are well-preserved gold-inlaid ceremonial vessels, ancient glass and jade, gilt buddhas, jewelry, gold walking stick, gold chain basket, fake 'bones' of jade - the largest group of Tang artifacts found since 1950. They were gifts from Tang Emperors Yi Zong and Xi Zong. Empress Wu donated gilded embroidery with threads finer than those made today. Titles are in English in the air-conditioned museum.

The temple was founded in the Han Dynasty, 2000 years ago. The bone and the treasures found with them were re-discovered in the 1980s during repairs to one of the pagodas here. Additional payment to visit the vault under the reconstructed pagoda is overpriced.

More Tombs?

*****Maoling** on a plateau north of the Wei River, 40 kilometers northwest of Xi'an, has more than ten tombs, small grassy pyramids, about 46.5 meters high. The main tomb is that of the fifth Han emperor, built 139 to 87 B.C. According to records, it contains a jade suit with gold threads (seems to be a Han fad), and, in a gold box, more than 190 different birds and animals, jade, gold, silver, pearls, and rubies.

The other identified tombs are of the emperor's favorite concubine, Madame Li; General Huo Qubing, who fought the Xiognus/Huns, and strengthened the dynasty from the age of 18 until he died of disease at 24!; General Wei Qing; his horse breeder Jing Min Ji, who remained faithful even after the emperor defeated Jing's tribe; and General Huo Guang.

You can also study some of the earliest and, therefore, most primitive massive stone carvings, originally placed in front of the tombs. Look for the horse stomping a Hun aristocrat. Each stone has a few lines added to the natural shape of the rock. Also in the museum are Han artifacts found by local peasants, including an irrigation pipe and ceramic animal figures. Near Maoling is the **Xianyang Museum**, containing 3,000 painted terracotta warriors and horse figures from the Western Han (206 B.C. to 24 A.D.). They are each between 55 and 68 cm high, and artistically better than the Qin Army.

Also near Maoling is the **Tomb of Yang Guifei**, the beautiful, tragic imperial concubine. Women have taken earth from here to put on their faces, hoping it will make them equally alluring.

*Zhaoling, 70 kilometers northwest of Xi'an near Liquan, is the tomb of the second Tang Emperor Taizong. The 20,000-hectare cemetery contains 167 minor tombs (children, wives, generals) and took 13 years to build. You can visit its small museum with Tang pottery, stone tablets, and murals. This tomb is not worth visiting unless you can read classical Chinese. The six famous bas-reliefs of the emperor's favorite horses in the Stele Museum are from here.

The **Horse and Chariot Pit,** Zhangjiapo, Chang'an county, can be combined with Huxian county for a half-day tour. It is the burial site of two chariots, six horses, and one slave (11th century B.C. to Western Zhou) and is the best of seven such pits found. It is of special interest to archaeologists.

Tired of Tombs?

In town, the **Xian Film Studio** is worth a visit if only for the magnificent reproduced Qin palace used for the strongly recommended Sino-Canadian movie (and book), *The First Emperor*. There are other exhibits as well. It is near the Garden Hotel.

The **Kaiyuan Men Gate**, in the western part of the city, was the starting point of the Silk Road and is now marked with a huge recent photogenic statue of a caravan. The ruins of ***Daming Palace**, built in 634 A.D. (Tang) are about two kilometers north of the railway station. Now reconstructed, it should be furnished in the Tang style.

Head southwest of Xi'an to Huxian County Town. Here you can visit the **Huxian Peasant Painting Exhibition Hall**. Some of the 2,000 painters in the county have also exhibited abroad these recordings in gay colors of their everyday lives and achievements. While you can buy these paintings everywhere in Xi'an, you might want an opportunity to meet the artists.

About 25 kilometers away from the city is the thatched-cottage **Caotang Temple** (Tang), where Indian monk Kumarajiva Jiumoluosi translated the Buddhist sutras into Chinese. He died in 413 A.D. The current buildings are recent, with a fine rose garden. Japanese Buddhists have presented a modern wooden statue of the monk. The two-meter-high stupa has some elaborate carvings and, from a well in the ground, a cloud used to come out at dawn, travel to Xi'an, and return at evening, said one guide. But this hasn't happened since the Cultural Revolution!

*Xingjiao Temple**, about 25 kilometers east of the city wall, is on a sylvan hillside, which, with a little mist, could look like the lonely setting of the famous Japanese movie *Rashomon*. The place oozes with atmosphere, although the buildings are recent. It was founded by Tang Emperor Gaozong in 669 A.D., but destroyed and rebuilt several times. The remains (at least some of them) of monk Xuan Zhang, who first walked to India 'day and night' and brought back the sutras, are buried in the small, five-story pagoda here. About 20 monks are in residence. It is peaceful with few tourists.

Other sights include the **Qinglong Temple**, in the Tang-dynasty Chang'an city in the southern suburbs at Tian Lumiao. Six famous Japanese monks were initiated into Buddhism here between 794 and 1192 A.D., and links with Japan still exist.

The **Louguan Taoist Temple** has now been restored. It is beyond Huxian, about 70 kilometers west of Xi'an. It is said to be the place where Lao Tzu, founder of Taoism, taught. The temple has resident monks and makes traditional medicines. The setting and especially the entrance gate are very fine. A big yearly fair is held here. A porcelain museum where porcelain is thrown by hand the way it was in the Tang and Song dynasties is two hours by road north of the city at Yaozhou.

Xi'an also has an **English Corner** Sunday mornings at the Foreign Language Institute at the Xingqing Palace Park, and at the south wall near the Victory Hotel. Many schools have their own corners. The annual **Cultural Arts Festival** in September is highly recommended.

NIGHTLIFE & ENTERTAINMENT

There's not much aside from the theater restaurants. The **Tang Dynasty Theater Restaurant** is best, an international-quality show of Tang-inspired dances and disco afterwards, maybe to 2 am, which has been free to dinner guests. The show is cheaper if you don't eat there. The Grand New World, Royal Xi'an, and Garden Hotels also have shows but not on a regular basis. Hotels have the usual discos and karaoke, the best at the Hyatt and Sheraton. The **Bell Tower Pub** and the bar in the Xi'an Hotel are popular. Unfortunately there are lots of prostitutes frequenting locally-run bars, but not bars in good hotels. And as usual, be aware of over-priced drinks and bar hostesses.

The **City Wall** has some drink stands on summer evenings. You can probably see some local outdoor dance halls from the top of the South

Gate. The Wall is lighted and decorated with huge lanterns during festivals and it is very pleasant up on top. Groups can arrange a fireworks display. Ask about the powerful Shaanxi waist drum dances.

The **Red, Blue and Green Bar** (karaoke and dancing) is said to be hostess-free, *Tel. 7211135.*

SHOPPING

The main shopping area is east of the Bell Tower on **Dong Da Jie**. Made locally or in the province are: rubbings, reproductions of three-color Tang camels, and horses, and murals. Also made are inlaid lacquer, cloisonne, stone and jade carvings, gold and silver jewelry, peasant paintings, silk embroidery (south Shaanxi province), and celadon. Cloisonne seems cheaper in Shanghai and Beijing than here. You can start haggling at half the first asking price with all private merchants.

You will also find cheap reproductions of the Terracotta Warriors. Some of these are not kiln-dried and are extremely delicate. The better quality is usually found in government- approved stores. A 200-meter-long Tang Dynasty-style street, with food and souvenirs, is near the Big Wild Goose Pagoda.

At stalls outside many tourist attractions, you will find cheap tiger slippers for children and red cotton vests with appliqued snakes, scorpions, lizards, and pandas. These are very popular with tourists and are the cheapest in China. The yucky bugs are to frighten away the evil spirits. The **Xi'an Friendship Store**, *Nanxin Street, near Dong Da Jie, Tel. 7210551, 7213898*, has batik, linens, silk jackets, cloisonne, cashmere sweaters, carpets, clothes, jewelry, stone carvings, decorated tiles, opera shoes, ceramics, a few antiques, lacquer, and folk crafts. Across the street is the **Xi'an Arts and Crafts Store**, *Tel. 7212085*, with less variety, where you might be able to haggle lower prices than the Friendship Store.

The **Xi'an Cloisonne Factory** is at *33 Dong Road, 710005*. The **Arts & Crafts Studio** is next door at *19 Yanta Road, Tel. 7251607*. Consider the **Phoenix Embroidery Factory**, *33 Dong Road, 710005, Tel. 7271437*, the **Xi'an Antique Store**, *Stele Museum, Tel. 7213672*, and the **Xi'an Jade Carving Workshop**, *173 Xi-1 Road, Tel. 7218232*. An **Arts and Crafts Factory**, 90 kilometers outside Xi'an near Qianling, makes Tang and Buddhist art reproductions. There's the **Xi'an Luxury Friendship Store**, *5 Nan Street*, the **#Shaanxi Cultural Relics Store**, *Shaanxi Provincial Museum, Tel. 7213691* and the **#Xi'an Cultural Relics Shop**, *375 Dong Da Jie. Tel. 7215874.*

The **Tang Cheng Department Store** is on *Dong Da Jie at An Ban Street*, west of the Friendship Store. Walk south from the Friendship Store, cross Dong Da Jie, turn right and then left at Lo Ma Shi for a street of stalls selling cheap clothing.

The best shopping for antique embroidery has been near the restaurant by the Hot Spring, and especially on the street between the Drum Tower and Mosque, open 9 am to 6 pm. (There might not be much left now.) The small shops around the Banpo museum are good for peasant paintings, cloisonne, and ceramics.

At the South Gate behind the head of the gold dragon is a street in ancient architecture where some traditional arts like writing brushes are made. There's also a fur store (with endangered species), and closer to the Stele Museum, an antique store. Art reproductions of the Terracotta Warriors can be bought at the **Art Ceramics Factory**, *East Electricity Road, Buzi Village, Tel. 3279063*. Ask about colored reproductions. There's a souvenir market outside the Shangri-La Hotel.

EXCURSIONS FROM XI'AN

Binxian County is about 130 kilometers northwest of the city, and is a two-day trip. It is famous for its caves of Tang Buddhist statues, the largest about 25 meters tall. These were recently renovated with German help.

*Huangling County is almost halfway between Xi'an and Yan'an, about four hours by road. Important there is the ***Tomb of the Yellow Emperor Xuan Yuan**. This is 3.6 meters high and 50 meters in circumference, originally built in the Han but moved here to its present site in the Song. The Yellow Emperor is the legendary ancestor of the Chinese people believed to have lived about 2,000 B.C. The tomb is at the top of Qiaoshan Hill, one kilometer north of Huangling town. At the base is **Xuan Yuan Temple** built in the Han. The throne stands in the middle with information about Xuan's life on both sides. In ancient times, travelers had to dismount from their horses and pay their respect to their First Ancestor as they passed by. His memorial day is the 5th day of the fourth lunar month.

Of its 63,000 cypress trees, the Yellow Emperor himself is supposed to have planted one. It is the largest known ancient cypress in China. In front of the tomb is the Platform of Immortality built by Emperor Han Wu (156-87 B.C.) to announce his victory over his enemy and to pray for longevity. The **Cave Temple of a Thousand Buddhas** (Tang) is halfway up Ziwu Hill in the western part of Huangling county.

Huashan Mountain, 150 kilometer east of Xi'an, peaks to 2,100 meters. Cable cars are due soon. Until then, it is mainly for serious climbers because of its 80-degree cliffs (there are iron chains to hang on to) and a '1000-foot-long Flight of Stone Steps.' You can also squeeze through the '100-foot-long Gorge.' Famous as one of the Five Sacred Mountains, it is dotted with old temples.

The best hotel is the **HUASHAN BINGUAN** at the foot of the mountain. Hostels are on the slopes. The cable car is a Sino- Singapore joint venture using Austrian hardware. It is otherwise a nine-hour climb. A hotel is on the north peak, but it is best to stay overnight below.

In Tongchuan City, Yao Xian county, 200 kilometer north of Xi'an, are the ruins of ancient celadon kilns and workshops. A museum should be open there now. Yao Xian county also has a grotto with 40 Ming statues, the largest 11 meters tall.

Yan'an, in northern Shaanxi, was the headquarters of the Communist revolution at the end of the famous Long March. In 1936 it had a population of 3000 and grew to 100,000 in 1945. Today it has about 50,000 people. It is of interest to revolutionaries and students of modern history. For others it has only a 44-meter Tang pagoda famous primarily because of the revolution, and a tiny cave of 10,000 Buddhas (used as the Communist print shop). The city is now largely industrial. Nearby are oil wells and coal mines.

Yan'an has flight connections once a week with Xi'an and Beijing. You can also get there by road or rail north from Xi'an in about eight hours. Its altitude is 800 to 1000 meters. During the rainy season, planes may be postponed or canceled.

Important to see are the **Yan'an Revolutionary Memorial Hall** and the four Residences of Chairman Mao (now museums and 'caves'). Ask about performances of the Waist Drummers and the Ankle and Wrist Drummers. Ask also about China's second largest waterfall, 210 kilometers from Huangling County on the Yellow River, and the Mausoleum of Hua Mulan, the warrior woman who inspired Maxine Hong Kingston's famous book.

The main hotel is the 168-room **YAN'AN GUEST HOUSE** *(Binguan), 56 Yan'an Street, 716000. Tel. 213122, 10 kilometers from the airport. 168 rooms.*

PRACTICAL INFORMATION

- **Business Hours**, 8,30 am to 5,30 pm, five days a week for offices; 9 am to 8 or 8,30 pm for stores. About 5 pm to about 11 pm depending on weather for night food and clothing markets.
- **CITS**, *Xi'an Branch, 32 Chang'an Bei Road, 710061. Tel. 5262066. 5261453. Fax 5263959, 5261454, 5261558. Branches in many hotels.*
- **CTS**, *Xi'an Branch, Tel. 3232999, 3241060. Fax 3241060, 3241070*
- **CYTS Tours**, *155 Zhu Que Da Jie Road, 710068. Tel. 5256418. Fax 5256409*
- **Shaanxi Overseas Travel Corporation**, *(for sales from abroad) 15 Chang'an Bei Road, 710061. Tel. 5261425. Fax 5250761*

• **Shaanxi Provincial Tourism Administration**, *15 Changan Bei Road,*
  710061. Tel. 5261434, 5261179, 5261337. Fax 5261483, 7211660
• **Tourist Complaints**, contact **Supervisory Bureau of Tourism Quality**
  of Shaanxi Province, *Tel. 5261437. Fax 5250151, 5261437*
• **Telephone Code**, *029*
• **Tour East Holidays Company**, *2nd Floor, 334 Dong Da Jie, Tel. 7433459,*
  7420038. Fax 7270011
• **Xi'an Tourism Administration**, *159 Beiyuanmen, Xi'an 710003. Tel.*
  7295670, 3233131. Fax 7295607

YINCHUAN

Yinchuan is the capital of the Ningxia Hui Autonomous Region,
which lies between Inner Mongolia and Gansu on the north central
border of China. It has no international class tourist attractions and
whoever goes there has to be adventurous and intrigued by its mysteries.

In the northern part of the province, Yinchuan is a few kilometers
west of the **Huanghe** (Yellow) **River**, and in the middle of a mesh of
irrigation canals in the plains, but close to mountains and sandy deserts.
Its regional weather is coldest in January at minus 22 degrees centigrade;
its hottest is 33 degrees centigrade in May to September. It has very little
rain, but it has sandstorms, which blow hard in spring and autumn.

ARRIVALS & DEPARTURES

Yinchuan is linked by air with Beijing, Chengdu, Guangzhou, Shanghai and Xi'an and hopefully in the future with Singapore and India. It is
also reached by train from Beijing and is on the Lanzhou-Baotou-Hohhot
railway line.

ORIENTATION

Yinchuan has only recently been opened to tourists, It is not as far
from Beijing as the Silk Road, but the weather is more severe, and it is still
being developed. It was founded in the Tang. It was the capital of the
Western Xia dynasty during the early part of the Song (1038) when it was
known as Xingqing. The Xia kings reigned for about 190 years, until
Genghis Khan destroyed them. Very little is known about them. Today,
850,000 people live in the urban part of Yinchuan.

Ningxia was inhabited 30,000 years ago, and archaeologists have
collected 8000-year-old neolithic relics here. It was home to the Yong and
Di tribes in the Western Zhou dynasty. The first Qin emperor conquered
the tribes and connected parts of the Great Wall. He sent thousands of
men to settle and defend this area but the Xiongnu tribal federation took
it over in the fifth century.

Ningxia was close enough to the trade routes for Persian coins to be buried in its Northern Wei tombs. It exists because parts have been irrigated by the Yellow River for the last 2000 years. Its fight against the relentless sands is admirable, and visitors from places like California should be especially interested in how the Chinese manage here. A great deal of the region is covered by the Liupan Mountains, through which the Long March passed in 1935.

Ningxia Hui Autonomous Region was founded in 1958, and the Cultural Revolution sent many people here from urban China in the 1960s. Today, it has many national minorities, including the **Huis** (31.7%), Mongolians, Manchus, and Turfans. The provincial population is 4.65 million of whom a quarter are Hui (Moslem).

It produces an edible black hair-like moss called facai. The region exports coal and also produces petroleum, mica, asbestos, and lime.

WHERE TO STAY & EAT

The top hotel is the 159-room three-star **INTERNATIONAL HOTEL**, *25 Bei Huan Dong Road, 750004. Tel. 6028688. Fax 6091808*. It is 15 kilometers from the airport and 13 kilometers from the railway station, has USTV and accepts credit cards. A four-star hotel is being built.

The food is mainly Moslem (mutton, no pork). Corn on the cob and oil sticks (like long donuts) are delicious. The hotels are the best place to eat.

SEEING THE SIGHTS

Of importance to visitors is the **Chengtian Monastery Pagoda**, built in 1050 A.D.(Western Xia) and renovated in the Qing. Like many of the area's pagodas, it is unusually plain. The old Tanglai Canal and Hanyan Canal (Han) should be seen as examples of ancient irrigation efforts. Note the old waterwheels. The **South Gate Mosque**, *Tel. 4012704*, is recent, with an onion dome. The **Zhongda Mosque** is more in the Chinese style. Both these mosques are downtown.

The **Tongxin Mosque** is from the early Ming and was repaired in the Qing. It is one of the largest mosques in the region. The imposing Jade Emperor Pavilion (Ming) is good for photographs, with its delicate towers, as is the unusual Drum and Bell Tower. The *Haibo (Sea Treasure) or North Pagoda is also unusual, a naked structure without fancy eaves, and appearing more like a strange sort of Masonic temple, perhaps of Indian origin. Dating from the early fifth century, it was destroyed by an earthquake but rebuilt in the 18th century in its original style. It is one kilometer north of the city.

The **Twin Pagodas** at the Baizi Pass on Mt. Helan, and the **Western Xia Mausoleum** at the base of Mt. Helan, are 80 kilometers southwest of

Yinchuan. The mausoleum is rather crude and of interest primarily to people keen on history. In treeless surroundings, it has a stark kind of primitive beauty.

The founder of the Western Xia kingdom built over 70 tombs, most as decoys. The nine imperial tombs are being rebuilt. Archaeologists believe that octagonal glazed-tile pagodas once stood by each tomb. For atmosphere, tourists should visit at night when the tombs are illuminated and accompanied by ancient music. You can enter the tomb of Li Yuanhao, the dynasty's founder. The 23rd grandson of the last emperor of the Western Xia Dynasty is still living and doing research into his family history.

Adventurers can also take river rides on rafts buoyed by inflated sheep skins. Normal watercraft are also available. At **Qingtongxia** south of the city is a gorge and an impressive dam. Nearby on a barren hill, the mysterious 108 white dagobas have been arranged in the shape of a triangle in 12 rows from one to 19 across in odd numbers. The smallest one is about six feet and three arm-spans around. They are Buddhist structures from the 13th and14th centuries, apparently built to ward off the '108 human frustrations' and are unique in China.

The city also has a museum and a **Russian Orthodox Church** (another mystery to be solved). The Guyuan grottoes, the mosque in Tongxin county, the Kangji Buddhist Pagoda in Tongxin County, and the Wanshou Pagoda (the latter two dating from 1038 to 1227 A.D. respectively) were all renovated in 1988.

Also in the region are 2,000-year-old rock paintings on **Helan Mountain**, and the ruins of the **Great Wall** (Warring States: 475-221 B.C.), mainly earthen mounds, no stone. Especially important are the *Buddhist grottoes** on Mt. Xumi (also known as Sumeru) in Guyuan County. They are Northern Wei to the Ming and have a 19-meter-tall bust of Buddha rising from the floor of a cave. In the south of the province, these caves are impressive, although many of their 300 statues are damaged. Unless they have been recently built, few, if any sidewalks and stairs connect the 132 caves. This cave temple covers an area one by two kilometers and the trip is rugged.

The **Gao Temple**, in Zhongwei County in the western part of the province, is striking because of its sandy monotone. A temple for Confucianism, Buddhism, and Taoism, it also has statues of the Jade Emperor, the Holy Mother, and Guan Yu, the God of War. These point to the eclecticism of Chinese religion. Multi-purpose temples of this broad range, however, are rare.

The **Yellow River Festival** is celebrated in Yinchuan every September.

SHOPPING

The region produces sheepskin garments, licorice root, Helan inkstone carvings, rugs, and blankets. Try the **Shopping Center** on *Gulou Nan Street, Tel. 6023046.*

PRACTICAL INFORMATION

- **Business Hours**, 8 am to 6 pm for offices; 9 am to 9 pm for stores.
- **CITS** and **CTS**, *150, Jiefang Xi Street, 750001, Tel. 5043720. Fax 5043466. CTS, 4th floor, Tel. 5044485*
- **CYTS Tours**, *Xi Xia Hotel, 20 Min Le Xi Road, 750004. Tel. 6030578*
- **China Comfort Travel Service**, *19 Gongyuan Street, 750001. Tel. 5045678. Fax 5045600*
- **Ningxia Tourism Bureau**, *117 Jie Fang Xi Street, 750001 Tel. 6022397. Fax 6041783*
- **Tourist Complaints**, contact **Supervisory Bureau of Tourism Quality of Ningxia**, *Tel. 622265. Fax 641783*
- **Telephone Code**, *0951*

XINING

Xining is the capital of Qinghai (Tsinghai) province. The urban population is about 500,000.

Qinghai is the source of both the Yellow and Yangtze rivers and has a lot of hydro-electric power. It is rich in aluminum, coal, and oil. Its hottest weather is about 32 degrees centigrade in July and August, but could hit 50 or more out in the desert sun in its northwest; its coldest is minus 16 degrees centigrade in January and December. The annual precipitation is 450 millimeters in July and August.

Its eastern section is a grass-covered plateau ranging from 2,500 to 3,000 meters, up to 5,000 meters. You could be affected by altitude sickness. If you go in summer, you also might be kept awake by the open-air karaoke bars.

ARRIVALS & DEPARTURES

Xining is a two-hour flight from Beijing and is important to visit because of the Taer Monastery and a bird sanctuary. It also has direct flights with five other Chinese cities.

WHERE TO STAY

QINGHAI HOTEL *(Binguan), 20 Huang He Rd., 810001. Three stars, Tel. 6144018, Fax 6144545. Dist.A.P. 27 km. Dist.R.W. three km. Credit Cards.*

Near government trade offices and tourist shopping. Built 1989. 23 stories, 395 rooms. B.C. IDD. Gym. USTV. This is the best hotel.
XINING GUEST HOTEL (Binguan), *215 Qiyi Rd., 810000. Two stars, Tel. 38701. Fax 38798. Dist.A.P. 12 km. Dist.R.W. four km.* Built 1957. 400 rooms.

SEEING THE SIGHTS

A one-day visit to Xining can include the Taer Monastery, Dongguan Mosque, and North Mountain Temple.

The **Dongguan Mosque**, one of the biggest in Northwest China, was built in 1380 and is two kilometers from the Qinghai Hotel. The **North Mountain Temple** is also two kilometers from the hotel.

The *Taer Monastery (Ming), the center of the Yellow Hat sect of Tibetan Buddhism, is at Huangzhong, about 40 kilometers south of the city. Built in 1379, it is worth a visit if you are interested in Tibetan culture. Its kitchen has three bronze cauldrons that are said to cook 13 cattle at one time to serve 3,600 people. Ask why meat is served in this Buddhist monastery! In the winter, frozen butter, two meters high by 26 meters long, is sculptured into Buddhist scenes and displayed on the 15th day of the lunar new year. It also has 20,000 religious paintings and embroideries. CTS has a branch in the monastery and there is the two-star **TAERSI HOTEL**, *57 Yingbin Road, Lushaer Town, Huangzhong, 810000. Tel. (09822)32452.*

Qinghai Lake (China's largest saltwater lake) is 3,196 meters above sea level and 130 kilometers from the capital. A bird sanctuary, **Bird Island**, is about 350 kilometers away from Xining in the northwest section of the lake and is best seen April to June. The small island attracts 100,000 migrating geese, black-neck cranes, gulls, Griffon vultures, Mongolian larks, minivets and skylarks especially from April to July. The island has bird-watching pavilions and Tibetan-style hotels. This trip can be a two-day tour from Xining. Birders should ask also about the **Longbao Black-necked Crane Sanctuary**. The province has wild antelope, yak, donkeys, camels, lynx, deer, snow leopards, and pheasant, all protected.

About 60 kilometers east of Xining in Lu Du county is the *Qutan Monastery (Ming). Also in the vicinity is the 6282-meter **Ma Qing Gang Re Mountain**. Ask about the Regong Tibetan artists with their 300-year old tradition.

SHOPPING

Good buys are handicrafts made by the minorities like wooden bowls inlaid with silver. Also facai (edible moss), a favorite ingredient of new year's banquets.

EXCURSIONS FROM XINING

Golmud is a new industrial city in the **Gobi Desert** in the western part of the province. It has a population of 130,000, is 800 kilometers from Xining, and is a trans-shipment point for Tibet. The highway to Lhasa from here is now asphalt, (the highest highway in the world). A railway joins Xining with Golmud (and also with Lanzhou and Xi'an, eastward). Currently being built is a 1200-kilometer rail line from Golmud to Lhasa. When it is finished in the next century, it should be one of the most spectacular train rides in the world.

GOLMUD HOTEL is modest but adequate. For **CITS** and **CTS**, *Tel. (09822) 33126.*

The **Qinghai** region, which covers one-thirteenth of China, lies in the Qinghai-Tibet Plateau. It was settled 2,100 years ago in 121 B.C. It has less than four million people, mainly Han (60%), the rest Tibetan, Hui, Mongolian, Kazak, Salan, and Tu. Many of these are nomadic herders. Ninety-six percent of its land is pasture for 22 million horses, yak, and sheep. Livestock breeding has been practiced here for 4000 years, and cow dung is used for fuel. Half of China's yak and one third of all the world's yak are in Qinghai.

Times are changing however: recently, a 3,500-gram gold nugget was found, and a gold rush is on. The national government is focusing its economic development on the northwest region. Pasture land is now contracted to herdspeople for 30 years, thus encouraging the users to manage it more wisely. Counties give bonuses to families who send their children to school, not an easy task for nomads. The government is building railways and highways.

Qinghai has mountaineering with several peaks up to 6860 meters and trekking between April and November. There is also white water rafting. You can visit the birthplaces of both the current Dalai Lama and the 10th Panchen Lama.

The region is also known as the **Gulag** of China. Here criminals who have served their sentences continue to live because they cannot get residence permits elsewhere. Stores in Xining are stocked with products made from forced prison labor.

PRACTICAL INFORMATION

• **CITS**, 215 Qiyi Road, 810000. Tel. 6143950. Fax 8238721
• **CYTS Tours**, *2nd Floor, Qinghai Hotel, 20 Huanghe Road, Xining, 810001. Tel. 6144018. Fax 6144545*
• **Qinghai Provincial Tourism Administration**, *21 Huanghe Rd., 810001. Tel. 9006002. Fax 8238721.* Brochures and information.
• **Telephone Code**, *0971*

• **Tourist Complaints**, contact **Supervisory Bureau of Tourism Quality of Qinghai Province**, *57 Xida Street, 810000, Tel. 8239630. Fax 8239515*

CENTRAL CHINA

KAIFENG

The former imperial capital of **Kaifeng** is in northern Henan province. It is 10 kilometers from the southern bank of the **Huanghe** (Yellow River), and is highly recommended for its history and quiet, exotic charm.

With a history of 2,600 years, Kaifeng was the capital of several imperial dynasties, including the Wei, Liang, Later Jin, Han, Later Zhou, Northern Song, and Jin. During the Song it was an important commercial and communications center, producing textiles, porcelain, and printing. It was sacked by Jurched tribesmen in 1126 and never recovered.

With 120 recorded Yellow River floods due to dams breaking near Kaifeng between 1194 and 1948, you might wonder why Kaifeng exists at all. In 1642, during a peasant uprising, Ming forces destroyed the Yellow River dike and completely inundated the city killing 372,000 people. In 1938, the Nationalists destroyed the dam upriver near Zhengzhou to stop the Japanese and 840,000 people died. Today, the river bed, raised by centuries of silt deposits, is about 10 meters higher than ground level near Kaifeng. Since Liberation, the Chinese have given top priority to controlling the Yellow River.

The population is 620,000. The hottest weather in July to early August is 38 degrees centigrade, the coldest in January is minus nine degrees centigrade. Its annual rainfall is about 600 millimeters mainly in July and August. Spring is dry, dusty, and windy.

ARRIVALS & DEPARTURES

On the Shanghai-Urumqi railway line, Kaifeng is joined with Zhengzhou to the east. Its closest airport is reached by an 81 kilometer expressway. Kaifeng is on National Highway 106 (Beijing-Guangzhou) and Highway 310 (Tianshui- Lianyungang).

ORIENTATION

Kaifeng is one of the 24 cities of historical importance protected by the State Council. It is laid out in the classic Chinese plan, and has a well-preserved but decaying earthen Song city wall.

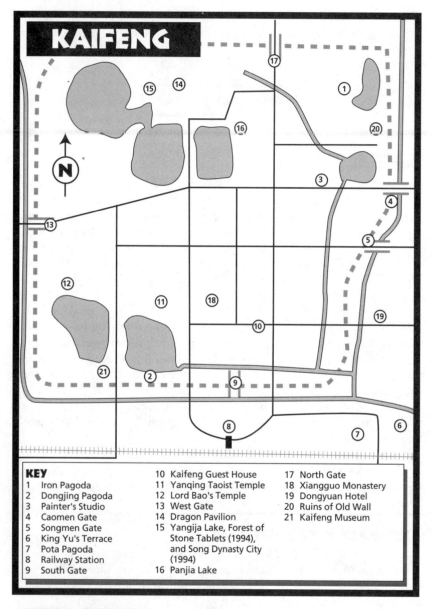

KEY
1 Iron Pagoda
2 Dongjing Pagoda
3 Painter's Studio
4 Caomen Gate
5 Songmen Gate
6 King Yu's Terrace
7 Pota Pagoda
8 Railway Station
9 South Gate
10 Kaifeng Guest House
11 Yanqing Taoist Temple
12 Lord Bao's Temple
13 West Gate
14 Dragon Pavilion
15 Yangija Lake, Forest of Stone Tablets (1994), and Song Dynasty City (1994)
16 Panjia Lake
17 North Gate
18 Xiangguo Monastery
19 Dongyuan Hotel
20 Ruins of Old Wall
21 Kaifeng Museum

WHERE TO STAY

Of the two main hotels, the **Dongyuan** especially was in very bad shape. Hopefully both have since improved. The **Dongjing** has bigger rooms, and is within walking distance of the museum, the old wall, and the lake. It is on the Number One bus route downtown to Song Dynasty street.

The standard of English is very low in both, but the Dongjing had an English-speaking general manager and is involved with the new economic zone.

DONGJING HOTEL *(Dongjing Dafandian), 14 Ying Bin Road, 475000. Two stars. Tel. 5958936, 5958938, Fax 5957705, 5956661. No credit cards.* In the southwest part of the walled city. Built 1988-89. Three stories, 200 rooms. IDD. Penjing garden. Sichuan and Shanghai food. Owned by tourism bureau. No elevators.

DONGYUAN HOTEL *(Dajiudian), 1 Xin Song Road at Gongyuan, 475002. Aiming for three stars, Tel. 5958888. Fax 5956816. Dist.R.W. 3.5 km. No credit cards.* Just outside the east city wall. Built 1992. 14 stories. 198 small rooms. IDD. Gym. H.K. management.

WHERE TO EAT

The Dongjing and Kaifeng Binguan have the best food. You can also get Song-style food and entertainment in the **FANLOU RESTAURANT**, *Song Dynasty Street, Tel. 5956480,* where the architecture, decor, music, costumes and food are in the Song court style.

SEEING THE SIGHTS

Kaifeng has 22 historic and cultural sites, a large number for such a small city. Except for the **Yellow River**, all important sites are inside or near the four by eight kilometer-long wall. You need a full day, preferably two, to see everything important: temples, museum, reproduced Song dynasty street, Jewish relics and iron pagoda. The annual Song Dynasty Culture Festival in Kaifeng is celebrated every April.

The 13-story *Tie Ta ('Iron Pagoda') in the northeast corner inside the wall was built over 900 years ago. It began to lean towards the wind but it is now standing straight. At a height of 55.6 meters, it is actually made of glazed brick. The **Xiangguo Temple** in its south-center, built in 555 A.D., was rebuilt in 1766 after a flood. It has a famous thousand-armed, thousand-eyed Buddha of gingko wood. The **Longting** (Dragon Pavilion) in the north center is at the site of the Northern Song palace. The existing buildings here are from the Qing, the stone lions in front from the Song.

Also worth seeing are the **Yanqing Taoist Temple**, **Lord Bao's Memorial Hall** (wax figures) on Baogong Lake, and the very fancy **Guild Hall of Three Provinces**, all within walking distance of the Dongjing Hotel. The **Yuwang Miao** (King Yu's Temple) was built in the Ming in honor of Emperor Yu, who tried to control the floods; it is outside and to the south of the east wall. Near the Yuwang Miao is the **Pota Pagoda**, its bottom built in 977, and its top section replaced in the Qing.

Kaifeng has plans for a new economic zone in its west suburbs. There is talk about tearing down the old city and rebuilding it in Song dynasty style. A theme park should be opening soon, bigger and better than the Song village in Hong Kong, which is based on the famous painting of the ancient city. **Qing Ming Festival** takes place at the Riverside. Ask about these after you get there.

Kaifeng is great for bicycling. Walks are interesting along the path on top of the old Song wall and in any of the monuments.

Canadians in particular might be interested in the grave of Canadian Dr. Tillson Lever Harrison, who died in Changqiu in 1947 after delivering three box cars of medical supplies, under horrendous conditions, through Nationalist areas to the Communists. It is in the Revolutionary Martyrs Cemetery with a stone almost two meters high. There is also a Tillson Lever Harrison Memorial School in the city, probably on the site of the old Anglican church where he was first buried.

THE JEWISH COMMUNITY OF KAIFENG

*The **Kaifeng Jewish community** is believed to have first arrived at least 2,000 years ago. About 200 descendants of Jews still live in Kaifeng today although they don't practice Jewish traditions. Many of these people still live in Nan Jiao Jing Hutong. The **Kaifeng Museum** (open 8:30 am to 12 noon, and 3 to 5:30 pm) has a top floor room with a stele explaining the history of the local Jews with a reproduction of a seventh century drawing of the synagogue. Most of these early Jews came as silk merchants and migrants from Persia, their descendants moving elsewhere in China later. In the Song dynasty, thousands of Jewish merchants arrived from India. Most left in the Ming because of the floods. Marco Polo also came across groups of Jews in Beijing, Hangzhou, Suzhou, Guangzhou, and Kunming.*

*In the late 13th century, there were about 4,000 Jews in Kaifeng. Three Jews who succeeded in the imperial examinations funded the synagogue. For more information, ask about a woman writer named Qu Yinan who studied Judaism in Los Angeles, and 60-year old Zhou Pingmao. The **Kaifeng Jewish History Research Society** is soliciting money to rebuild one of the synagogues as a Jewish museum.*

SHOPPING

Kaifeng is famous for its embroidery and fighting kites. Shopping is extensive at the **Xiangguo Temple Market's** 3,000 stalls. For antiques, try the *Kaifeng Cultural Relics Shop, 23 Madao Street.

PRACTICAL INFORMATION

• **CITS** and **CTS**, *14 Ying Bin Road, 475000. Tel. 3930070, 5958938. Fax 5955131, 5957705*

• **Kaifeng Tourism Administration**, *Dongjing Hotel, 475000, Tel. 5958936 X 6503 (complaints and information).*
• **Telephone Code**, *0378*

ZHENGZHOU

(Chengchow)

Zhengzhou is the capital of Henan province, the cradle of China's civilization. As such it has a lot to offer visitors.

Zhengzhou is historically important as one of the first cities to be built in China. This was during the Shang dynasty 3,500 years ago. It is also important because of its proximity to **Shaolin Monastery**, known to every kung fu fan. Zhengzhou is a good place to start a driving tour (avoiding airports). In one week you can cover Mangshan, Anyang and Kaifeng, and then the Song Tombs, Dengfeng, Luoyang, Sanxiamen and some of the countryside at your own pace.

For historians, Zhengzhou has one of the best museums. It was in nearby Anyang that the oracle bones with one of the first Chinese writings were found. The capitals of the Eastern Zhou, Han, Wei, Jin, Northern Song, Tang, and Liang were in this province. At least one of the capitals and possibly four of the five other capitals of the Xia dynasty were also in this province. The Xia was China's first dynasty, and until recently was clouded in legend, traditionally dating from the 16th century B.C. China's first Buddhist temple, the **Longmen Grottoes**, and the earliest astronomical observatory are also located in the province.

More recently, Zhengzhou was the site of the February 7th Beijing-Hankou Railway Workers' General Strike of 1923, part of a larger workers' movement for better wages and conditions. Over 100 railroad workers were killed. The strike is commemorated with a modern 14-story double pagoda-like clock tower in February 7th Square, built in 1971.

The coldest average temperature is minus 10 degrees centigrade in January; the hottest is 27 degrees centigrade in July. The annual rainfall is 500 to 900 millimeters, especially July through September. The urban population is 1.7 million.

ARRIVALS & DEPARTURES

On both the Beijing-Guangzhou and the Shanghai-Xi'an railway lines, Zhengzhou is about 20 kilometers south of the Yellow River on the main railway line between Luoyang and Kaifeng. It is a two hour flight south of Beijing, and can be reached by air from 26 other Chinese cities and Hong Kong.

ORIENTATION

Zhengzhou itself doesn't have much to offer. One day is enough for the provincial museum and sight-seeing along the Yellow River at Mangshan Mountain (40 kilometers from the Holiday Inn).

If you are interested in archaeology, there are the Shang ruins and the old city wall. And then there are the egrets: at least 2,000 of them have been in the city causing a big mess, unless by now, city officials have figured out a way to move them outside the city limits.

WHERE TO STAY

The top hotel is the **Holiday Inn**, the second best is the Novotel. Both are together in a restaurant and bar district near the Henan Chinese Medical University and provincial government offices.

NOVOTEL ZHENGZHOU *(formerly the International Hotel), 114 Jinshui Dong Rd., 450003. Three to four stars, Tel. 5956600. Fax 5951526. In US, Tel. 1-800-221-4542. Dist.A.P. three km. Dist.R.W .five km. Credit Cards.* Built 1981-82. Renovations and extension 1996. 610 rooms. B.C. IDD. Gym, sauna, and clinic. A pool, bowling and tennis are due soon.

HOLIDAY INN CROWNE PLAZA, *115 Jinshui Rd., Zhengzhou 450003, Aiming at five stars. Tel. 5950055. Fax 5953851, 5990770. In US, Tel. 1-800-HOLIDAY. Dist.A.P. three km. Dist.R.W four km.*

Five floors, 222 rooms (including 32 two-story suites and executive floor), in-room safes, IDD, USTV and some non-smoking rooms. B.C. Bank. Airport shuttle. Bicycles. Patisserie, Cantonese and western restaurants. English pub, night club and karaoke. Swimming pool and gym due soon.

WHERE TO EAT

The best food is in the top hotels but there are also some good restaurants nearby. The modest **YUE XIU** (Cantonese) is 100 meters west of the Holiday Inn. There is also the nearby **HAI XIAN CHEN RESTAURANT**.

The **LI ZHU RESTAURANT**, *2 Shunhe Road, 450004, Tel. 9558411,* owned by the Henan Tourism Bureau is good, clean, and not only serves scorpions, it keeps them live for patrons to cringe over before they eat them. The Li Zhu Restaurant says to rinse about 25 live scorpions three times in cold tap water. Toss them into boiling water for about 10 seconds and drain. Stir in 1/3 cup flour. In a wok, heat cooking oil to the point of fragrance and smoke. Toss in the scorpions at high heat for 28 seconds. Turn off the heat for another ten seconds. Drain and serve scorpions garnished with herbs. **The heat kills the poison.**

SEEING THE SIGHTS

Dahecun Village, a 5,000-year-old site of the Yangshao and Longshan neolithic cultures and the Shang ruins, are northeast about 12 kilometers. The 3,500-year old fragment of wall is in a small museum near the Holiday Inn.

The **Mangshan/Yellow River Scenic Area** is a diverting but tacky theme park on the south shore, about 40 kilometers north of the city. 150-meter-high statues of two Xia dynasty kings are being built there. There's fortune-telling by computer (in Chinese) and a Chinese "wedding" procession. Autographs on two-by-four foot stone tablets include that of the Lieutenant-Governor of Kansas and you – if you want to pay.

If you climb the mountain, you get a good view of the river. The 45-minute cruise of the Yellow River nearby not only gives a view of the impressive 5.5 kilometer-long bridge but you can actually bounce on a mud flat on the most heavily silted river in the world – as if it were a bowl of jelly.

The **Provincial Museum** in downtown Zhengzhou not far from the Holiday Inn is good, but it has no titles in English. It also has one of the few Mao statues left in China.

SHOPPING

Made here are reproductions of three-color Tang porcelain figures, jade and lacquerware, calligraphy and paintings. It's a good place to buy Chinese writing brushes, paper, inkstones, and inkbars. Made in the province are also Jun porcelain and embroidery from Kaifeng.

The **Friendship Store** is at *96 Erqi Bei Road*, north of People's Park. The **#Henan Cultural Relics Shop** is at *4 Jinshui Dadao, Tel. 5955347*.

EXCURSIONS FROM ZHENGZHOU

In the province, there's **Kaifeng** (above) which is 70 kilometers away and a two-day trip from Zhengzhou. **Anyang** is a one day trip from Zhengzhou. You can take in the other highlights of this varied and interesting province in another four day trip by road, visiting **Gongxian**, **Dengfeng** (overnight), **Luoyang** (overnight), and **Sanmenxia** (overnight). There are flights between Hong Kong and Zhengzhou, Hong Kong and Luoyang, and a train goes from Sanmenxia to Xi'an.

For destinations close to Zhengzhou in Shanxi province see *Taiyuan*. For Hebei province, see *Shijiazhuang*.

Anyang

In the northern part of Henan province, **Anyang** lies about 200 kilometers (two hours) north of the Yellow River and Zhengzhou by express highway or via the Beijing-Guangzhou railway line. A quick visit can be made by car in one day from Zhengzhou.

With 700,000 people, Anyang is one of the oldest cities in China. Inhabited at least 4,000 years ago, it was for 273 years in the 14th century B.C., a capital of the State of Yin during the Shang dynasty. It was here that the oracle bones, an ancient means of divination were found. The earliest writings, inscribed on tortoise shells and the shoulder blades of oxen and then cracked with heat, were found here. The direction of the crack foretold the future.

Visitors can see a reproduced Shang palace and tomb, a Shang museum, the mausoleum of the man who proclaimed himself emperor after the republican revolution, some temples, jade carving and carpet-weaving. This is also the birthplace of the I Ching.

Anyang is primarily of interest to people who like history, archaeology and air sports. It is the only place in China for hang gliding, parapente, sky diving, hot air ballooning and parachuting.

Important sights include the 24-square-kilometer *Yin Ruins on the edge of town, Tel. 331689. These include the palace foundations, 11 royal tombs, bronze and jade artifacts, and a small but good museum. There are reproductions of the palace, Shang chariots, guardian tomb figures and the largest bronze vessal found anywhere in the world, the 875-kilogram Simuwu Tripod. (The real relics are in museums in Beijing and Zhengzhou.) You can also see the tomb of Fu Hao, concubine of King Wuding, the first woman general in Chinese history. Many of the pits hold remains of human sacrifices. One pit has 16,000 oracle bones.

The Yue Fei Temple in Tangyin County, Tel. 23664, 20 kilometers from Anyang commemorates the birthplace of the exemplary but maligned marshall of the Song dynasty. See also Hangzhou where he is buried. It is also worth a visit for its very ornate front gate. Serious followers of the I Ching (Yi Jing), Book of Changes, might want to touch the platform where official Xi Bochang worked to develop 384 combinations of the eight trigrams. On these are based a whole school of divination and philosophy. Xi was jailed for seven years because he incurred the displeasure of his king in the 11th century B.C. Youli, 25 kilometers south of the city, is thus considered China's first recorded jail.

The five-story 40-meter high Wen Feng Pagoda is unusual. It is wider above than below and is crowned with a tiny white stupa. Built in 952 A.D., it can be climbed if you don't mind high stairs. The City Museum, 2.5 kilometers from the Anyang Hotel, is in the Mausoleum of Yuan Shi Kai, Tel. 425959. Yuan was the warlord and was an overly ambitious, brilliant official of the Qing court who took over the presidency of republican China from Dr. Sun Yat-sen in 1913. He declared himself emperor in 1915 and died of a heart attack in 1916. He reigned for 83 days.

If you have the Chinese surname Lin or Lim (as in 'forest'), you might be interested in the temple of the first Lin, a Shang dynasty prime minister. At Bigan Miao Temple, a short way off the expressway halfway between Zhengzhou and Anyang, you can learn about the maligned Bigan who had to take out his own heart to prove his honesty. His son changed the family name to Lin.

If sky sports are essential to your visit here, you can make arrangements with the **Anyang Aerial Sports School**, *Tel. 424686, 422675*; the **Aviation Sports Association**; or a travel agency before you go. The annual Shang dynasty festival takes place September 16 to 25.

In Anyang, your main choice is the **ANYANG GUEST HOUSE**, *One You Yi Rd., 455000. Two stars, Tel. 422244, 422219. Fax 422244. Dist.R.W. one km. Built 1959, ren. 1984. 157 rooms. IDD. USTV. Travel agency.* Unfortunately, the guest house is badly in need of more renovations. For more travel information: **CITS** is at *Zhongyuan Guest House, 62, Beimen Dong, 455000. Tel. 425650. Fax 427740.* The telephone code is *0372.*

Cave Temples & Tombs

If you can take a four day trip from Zhengzhou and are looking to get well off the beaten path, go to **Gongxian County** on the way to Songshan Mountain, where you can see the ***Gongxian County Cave Temple***. Its 7,743 small Buddhist figures date from 517 A.D. (Northern Wei) to the Song dynasty. Some of these are very well preserved. They are not as big or as impressive as Luoyang's, but they are certainly worth a look.

There are also several groups of imperial ***Song Tombs*** here, at least one with 60 impressive giant stone statues, among them foreign envoys wearing turbans. The tombs themselves are less spectacular than those of the later Ming and Qing emperors and are spread over an area 15 kilometers long. They were built in a much shorter time than those of their successors, and without the personal supervision of the emperors who were going to reside there. These are worth visiting if you are in the area, 65 kilometers west of Zhengzhou. They are from the Northern Song, when that illustrious dynasty had its capital in Kaifeng.

There are plans to open other scenic spots here in Song architecture. The **Tomb of Song Emperor Yong Ding** is due to be reconstructed. One of the imperial tombs is expected to be opened in the near future.

The cave home of Tang poet **Du Fu/Tu Fu** also in the neighborhood is not worth a visit unless you're into Tang poetry. There are also the Han Tombs at Dahuting (Tiger-hunting) Pavilion in Mixian County. They are worth a short stop for their paintings and stone carvings. Then you arrive in Dengfeng for a night or two.

Dengfeng County Area

Songshan Mountain in Dengfeng County is about 75 kilometers southwest of Zhengzhou, where you'll find the closest airport and railway station. The mountain stretches more than 60 kilometers east to west. The highest peak is 1,512 meters above sea level. It is one of China's Five Sacred Mountains, and emperors used to come here to worship. During the Southern and Northern Dynasties (420-589 A.D.), 72 temples and monasteries flourished here. It is well worth visiting also for the lovely Chinese countryside, and air so clean you might want to stay an extra day.

From your hotel in Dengfeng County town (population 50,000), you can bicycle or drive to China's largest Taoist temple, China's most famous temple, and a pagoda from 520 A.D. 13 kilometers northwest of Dengfeng County town is **Shaolin Temple**, *Tel. 2749116*, the home of gong fu/kung fu. Shaolin Temple was first built in 495-496 A.D. and became famous because 13 fighting monks from here supported the first Tang emperor. Here you can see the depressions in the floor worn by generations of monks practicing martial arts.

Among the murals and frescoes are some of 500 arhats (Ming), and some depicting fighting monks. At one time, 2,000 to 3,000 monks lived here. The *Ta Lin (Forest of Pagodas) is the largest group of memorial pagodas in China. A cemetery for abbots, it has over 240 miniature pagodas, dating from the Northern Wei.

Northwest of the temple is a cave where the sixth century Indian missionary Bodhidharma, was reputed to have spent nine years in meditation before achieving Nirvana. He was the founder of Chan Buddhism, more popularly known as Zen, and is frequently depicted in art in his robes, crossing the Yangtze River standing on a reed.

The **Shaolin Martial Arts Training Center** (Wu Shu Guan), *Tel. 2749120*, is close to the temple, and it gives exhibitions and classes. The kung fu here is somewhat different in style from western kung fu. There's a Wushu (martial arts) Festival in September. Foreigners can also study and live at the school, but foreigners cannot become monks. The 20-room hostel at the school is spartan and you can stay there too.

The 43-meter-high *Songyue Pagoda at Fawang Temple is the oldest proven extant pagoda in China, and is four kilometers from Dengfeng. Built of brick about 520 A.D. (Northern Wei), it is also unusual because it has 12 sides and is curved like an Indian sikhara tower. It is of importance to those studying pagoda architecture. The **Songyang Shuyuan** (Songyang Academy of Classical Learning) at the foot of the mountain has two cypress trees said to be over 3,000 years old, each measuring 12 meters in circumference. The school was one of the four imperial academies preparing students for the imperial examinations.

Zhongyue Miao (Central Mountain Temple) at the base of **Taishi Peak** and four kilometers east of Dengfeng town, was founded in the Qin and moved here in the Tang. It has four feisty 3.5-meter-high iron figures (Northern Song) guarding it. Children pat these 'to gain strength.' One of the earliest Taoist temples, it is huge, the largest extant monastery in the province. It was enlarged during the Qing, along the lines of the Forbidden City in Beijing. The *Taishi Tower is from the Eastern Han. You can climb to the top of Huanggai Peak for an overall view of the 400 or so buildings and the 300 2,000-year-old cypresses. 10-day temple fairs occur during the third and tenth lunar months.

SEARCHING FOR CHINA'S OLDEST DYNASTY

A search for the first Xia capital, China's oldest dynasty, has been centered in Dengfeng County, half a kilometer west of the town of Gaocheng at **Wangcheng Gang** *(Royal City Mound).*

This site is not usually included in a tour, but people interested in archaeology might ask about it. City walls, skeletons (probably of slaves buried alive in foundation pits), wine vessels, bronze fragments, and ceramic pots have been uncovered. However, Wangcheng Gang was found to be of a later date.

Across the river and half a kilometer northwest of Gaocheng is another site where the earliest bronze vessels in the province were found and carbon-dated to 2000 B.C.

The *Shaoshi Tower and the *Qimu Tower also on the mountain, are from the Eastern Han too. The *Astronomical Observatory, 14 kilometers from Dengfeng town, was built early in the Yuan, based on a Zhou dynasty concept. It is the oldest in China. Ancient astronomers here proved that the earth revolved around the sun once every 365.2425 days, 300 years before the Gregorian calendar. China's first astrological museum is nearby.

The best hotel is the three-star **Shaolin International Hotel**. If you want two-star standards, try the **Songshan Guest House**. Martial arts fans might want to stay at the **Shaolin Wushu Training Center**, also two-star standards.

SHAOLIN INTERNATIONAL HOTEL, *16 Shaolin Dong Rd., 452470. Three stars. Tel. 2870888. Fax 2871447, 2871440. No Credit Cards.*

Built 1993. 61 rooms. IDD. B.C. Cantonese restaurant. Sauna, and massage. Game room.

SHAOLIN WUSHU TRAINING CENTER *next to Shaolin Temple, 452470. Tel. 2749018. Fax 2749017. IDD. No Credit Cards.*

SONGSHAN GUEST HOUSE, *48 Zhongyue St., 452470. Tel. 2872755. IDD. No credit cards.*

For area travel information: **CITS** is at *48 Zhongyue Street, 452470. Tel. 2872137, 2877038. Fax 2873137*; **Dengfeng Tourism Bureau**, 177 Zhongyue Street, 452470. Tel. 2873043. Fax 2873137. For information ask for Guo Mengzhu. Home telephone number 2872198.

Tourist Hours: 8 am to 6 pm for tourist attractions and kung fu demonstations in summer, 8 am to 5 pm in winter. The telephone code for Dengfeng is *0371.*

PRACTICAL INFORMATION

· **CITS Henan**, *15 Jinshui Road, 450003. Tel. 5952072. Fax 5957705*
· **CTS Henan**, *Fax 5959624*
· **CYTS Tours**, *17 Jin Shui Da Road, 450003. Tel. 5952191. Fax 5952191*
· **Henan Province Tourist Corporation**, *288 Chengdong Bei Road, Tel. 5961133. Fax 5952273*
· **Henan Tourism Bureau**, *16 Jinshui Road, 450003. Tel. 5957880. Fax 5955656, for information.*
· **Tourist Complaints**, contact **Supervisory Bureau of Tourism Quality of Henan Province**, *Tel. 5955913. Fax 5955656*
· **Telephone Code**, *0371*

LUOYANG

(Luoyang: North Bank of Luo River)

Luoyang, about 25 kilometers south of the Yellow River, is important because of the Longmen Grottoes, the White Horse Temple, the Ancient Tomb Museum, and because it was an imperial capital for many centuries. It is one of the 24 cities of historical importance protected by the State Council.

Luoyang was first built in the 11th-century B.C. From 770 B.C. it was the capital at one time or another of the Eastern Zhou, Eastern Han, Wei, Western Jin, Northern Wei, Sui, Tang, Later Liang, and Later Tang dynasties. The imperial leaders moved here frequently because of drought in Xi'an, a city that they preferred.

Because there are hills on three sides, it was relatively easy to defend, and whoever wanted to control western Henan had to take Luoyang. Consequently, many battles were fought in this area and many treasures were buried to save them from the soldiers.

Luoyang was one of the earliest centers of Buddhism, dating from the first century A.D. During the Tang, it was the biggest city in China. It declined later because the capital moved away. Luoyang people will proudly tell you that the Silk Road actually started from Luoyang and not from Xi'an, as is commonly supposed. 'Knowledgeable merchants always came here for silks,' they say. 'It was cheaper.'

The hottest temperature is 39 degrees centigrade in July and August; the coldest in January and February minus 12 degrees centigrade. The weather is usually mild. The altitude is 145 meters above sea level. The urban population is about one million. The city has had a quiet, provincial atmosphere, but is starting to get lively.

ARRIVALS & DEPARTURES

Luoyang is two hours by train west of Zhengzhou. It's an eight-hour train ride east from Xi'an. There are frequent air connections with seven Chinese cities and Hong Kong.

ORIENTATION

The older, eastern part of Luoyang is more interesting than the newer sectors. Today, there are over 400 factories manufacturing everything from truck cranes to ball bearings. Tourists might be interested in its arts and crafts factory which makes palace lanterns and reproductions of three-color Tang porcelains and Shang bronzes.

Area farms grow cotton, corn, winter wheat, a little rice, sesame, sorghum, sweet potatoes, apples, pears, and grapes. They also raise yellow oxen, goats, and donkeys. The city is also noted for its peonies, first grown 1400 years ago in the Sui! Flower lovers should aim for the Royal City (Wangcheng Park) between April 15 and 25.

WHERE TO STAY & EAT

The best hotels are the **Peony**, and then the Friendship Guest House (with bigger rooms) and the New Friendship Hotel (with smaller rooms), both close together. A new five-star hotel and the four-star Small Swan (Xiao Tian E Binguan), a U.S.joint venture should open soon.

Your food options here are pretty much limited to the hotels.

FRIENDSHIP HOTEL *(Youyi Binguan), 6 Xiyuan Dong Road, 471003.Western part of Luoyang. Tel. 4912780. Fax 4913808. Dist.A.P. 15 km. Dist.R.W. seven km.*

Two four-story wings. Built 1956. 325 rooms. West Building, two stars, East Building, three stars. In residential district. Pool, gym. Bicycles. Dorms. IDD.

NEW FRIENDSHIP HOTEL, *6 Xiyuan Rd., 471003. Tel. 4913770. Fax 4912328. Three stars, Dist.A.P. 15 km. Dist.R.W. seven km. Credit Cards.* USTV. Ren.1995.

PEONY HOTEL *(Mudan Dajiudian), 15 Zhong Zhou Xi Rd., 471003. Three stars, Tel. 4013699. Fax 4013668. Dist.A.P. 15 km. Dist.R.W. four km.*

In city center. Built 1990. 17 stories, 196 rooms. IDD, B.C. Gym. Hong Kong joint venture.

SEEING THE SIGHTS

The following can be covered in one day if you don't dawdle.

The *Baima Si (White Horse) **Temple**, *Tel. 351285*, 25 kilometers from the Friendship Hotel, was founded in 68 A.D. after second Han Emperor Mingdi dreamed that a spirit with a halo entered his palace. His ministers convinced him that the spirit was the Buddha, so he sent scholars to India to bring back the sutras. After three years, the famous Indian monks Shemeteng and Zhufalan arrived here with the scriptures, having made the last part of the trip on a white horse. The emperor put the monks up in his resort, the Cold Terrace, at the back of White Horse Temple, the first Buddhist temple in China. There they translated the scriptures into Chinese. Both monks died in China and were buried in the east and west corners of the grounds beyond the moon gates.

None of the buildings here are original: the red brick foundation of the Cold Terrace is Han, and none of the others are earlier than Ming. The State Council lists them as Jin to Qing. The abbot here was one of Tang Empress Wu's favorites.

In the main hall to the right of Sakyamuni is Manjusri, the Bodhisattva of Wisdom carrying the sutras, and at Sakyamuni's left, Samantabhara, Bodhisattva of Universal Benevolence. In the next hall are 18 clay arhats, each with a magic weapon. These are the oldest statues here (Yuan). One is Ceylonese, one Chinese (the Tang monk Xuan Zhang went to India), and the rest Indian. Inside the back halls are statues of the two Indian monks, the Pilu Buddha (Sakyamuni), and the drawers where the sutras are kept.

The **Qiyun** (Cloud Touching) **Pagoda** nearby is in the Tang style, first built in 1175. Only the base with the darker brick is original. It was repaired in the Northern Song and Jin dynasties and has 13 stories. You get a strange echo effect if you stand either north or south of the pagoda and clap your hands.

The **Luoyang Municipal Museum**, *Tel. 337107*, has 2,000 pieces on display and roughly 50,000 pieces in its collection. Relics include historical maps of the city, and they show that the first imperial city is where **Royal City** (formerly Laboring People's Park) is now. The *Han and **Wei city** was east of the White Horse Temple; the Sui and Tang cities were on both sides of the Luo River.

Other items include two mammoth tusks found right in town in 1960; double boilers used 3,700 years before the British used double boilers; a crossbow with a trigger (476-221 B.C.); iron farming tools (Han); figures from the tomb of a Northern Wei prince, including a band with one musician falling asleep; and original three-color Tang horses and camels from which the copies are made. Study these carefully for comparison if you want to buy reproductions.

Longmen Grottoes

China has 19 important 'cave temples' and the *Longmen (Lungmen) Grottoes*, *Tel. 339498, 339499*, is among the top three. Although predating these caves and built also by the Wei, those at Datong are better preserved, more elaborately colored, and bigger. The stone at Longmen, however, is better. The grottoes are 20 kilometers south of the city from the Friendship Hotel and extends north along the Yi River for about 1000 meters. They were not touched by the Red Guards, but the heads and hands of some were damaged at the beginning of this century. The buses stop by a 303-meter copy of a famous Sui bridge built in 1962 of only stone and cement.

Work on the caves began about 494 A.D., when Emperor Hsaio Wen of the Northern Wei moved his capital from Datong to here. Work continued at a great pace from then until the Tang. A few statues were added during the Five Dynasties and Northern Song. There are 1352 grottoes, over 750 niches, and about 40 pagodas of various sizes. They contain more than 100,000 Buddhist images, ranging in size from two centimeters to 17.14 meters.

The **Wan Fo** (10,000 Buddhas) **Cave** actually has 15,000 buddhas on the north and south walls. It was completed in 680 A.D. (Tang). Note the musicians and dancers at the base. The back wall has 54 bodhisattvas, each sitting on a lotus flower. Outside the cave is a Guanyin with a water vessel in her left hand and a whisk in her right. There used to be two lions here, but they are now said to be in the Boston Museum of Fine Arts. The **Guyang Cave** was the earliest, built around 494 A.D.(Northern Wei). The corn-like design represents a string of pearls. The ceiling is covered with buddhas, lions, and tablets.

Fengxian Temple, the largest and most spectacular, was completed in 675 A.D. The main statue (17.14 meters) is the Vairocana Buddha (i.e. Sakyamuni). If you look carefully, on the left side of the face are traces of a five-centimeter crack extending from the hairline to the chin. This was repaired recently. The square holes around the statues were used to hold the roof structure that was taken down when it was found that sunlight was good for limestone. Behind the smaller disciple to Sakyamuni's right is an imperceptible cave large enough to hold 400 people and from which climbers used to negotiate the top of the head. This is now blocked. On Sakyamuni's far left is Dvarapala, whose ankles are worn black and smooth by individuals trying to embrace them in return for happiness.

Compare the dress of the statues. Some are clothed in the plain robes of Indian holy men; others wear female Chinese court dress, sometimes with jewelry, a later development. You can understand that wealthy, devout worshippers wanted to clothe their gods in the best fashions of the day. This practice is much like that of medieval European religious art, which also ignored the mystical preachings of its teachers. The narrow, regular pleats are characteristic of the Northern Wei. The Tang statues tend to have rounder faces. While it is said that gods could change their sex at will, the feminine faces are because, as one adherent said, 'We want people to look at the face of Buddha. Since women's faces are more attractive than men's, the statues are made to look more feminine.   .

During imperial times, common people had to look at the statues from afar, and in later periods, peasants broke pieces off the statues to make lime fertilizer.

Other Sites

The **Tomb of Guan Yu** (Kuan Yu), *Tel. 357339*, or at least that of his head is nearby. Guan Yu was one of the heroes of The Three Kingdoms period, and he is also known as the Chinese god of war. His tomb, between the grottoes and the city, was built in the Ming. He was beheaded about 219 A.D. One of the buildings has a moving statue of recent vintage.

Outside of the city is the **Tomb of Liu Xiu**, *Tel. 338678*. He was first emperor of the Eastern Han 1,900 years ago. A visit could be combined with a trip to see the bridge across the Yellow River. The **Luoyang Ancient Tombs Museum** is seven kilometers from the city near the airport and is worth a visit if tombs interest you. These 22 are from the Han, Tang, Ming and Qing dynasties, some genuine, some reproductions. Tourists keen on tombs can compare the dynastic differences. Mainly in one building and underground, this museum is cool in summer and dark. Take a flashlight. Children would love it. An imperial Wei tomb is next door.

The **Folk Customs Museum**, *Tel. 351064*, is charming if you have a good guide explaining the symbols on tiny women's shoes, embroidered headbands and children's clothes. It has a special display of birthday and wedding customs and religious influences. The tombs and folk customs museums are not on the regular tour and must be asked for if you are interested.

Walks

Pleasant places to walk include the Longmen Grottoes, around the Friendship Hotel and in the Royal City, site of the Zhou dynasty palace (but don't look for ruins; there aren't any.)

SHOPPING

The **Friendship Store**, *Tel. 4912603*, has reproductions, along with brushes, chopsticks, artificial flowers and inkstones, all made locally. The **Arts and Crafts Store** sells palace lanterns and reproductions of Shang bronzes, and artistic tiles. Tang horses and camels are made upstairs.

EXCURSIONS FROM LUOYANG

Sanmenxia is 122 kilometers west of Luoyang, about a four-hour drive. It is almost halfway by tourist train between Zhengzhou and Xi'an. You can visit 'cave' homes, cruise the Yellow River, and visit two very impressive 3,000-year old horse-and-chariot pits. You can spend a second day visiting Hangu Pass. A performance of the Sanmenxia "monks" with lamps on their head is very worthwhile but takes some organizing in advance. The monks are actually farmers, and they are very good.

Sanmenxia has a **Yellow River Festival** in April and an **Apple Festival** in September every year. The modest **SANMENXIA FRIENDSHIP HOTEL** (Youyi Binguan) is at *16 Heping Zhong Road, Tel. 222222. Fax 223404. Credit Cards. 1989. 12 stories. 350 beds. USTV.* There's also the two-star **TOBACCO MANSION**, *Xiaoshan Zhong Road, 472000. Tel. 223883. CITS's Tel. 221061. Fax 223404.* The telephone code is *03891.*

PRACTICAL INFORMATION

- **CTS** and **CITS**, *Friendship Hotel, 6 Xiyuan Road, 471003. Tel. 4913701. Fax 4912200*
- **CYTS**, *15th Floor, Zhong Fang Plaza, 26, Zhong Zhou Xi Road, 471003. Tel. 4912727. Fax 4911211*
- **Luoyang Municipal Tourism Bureau**, *Garden Hotel, Nanchang Road, 471003. Tel. 4913825, 2921681. Fax 4913825*
- **Telephone Code**, *0379*

20. TIBET

LHASA

Lhasa, the capital of **Tibet** – the Chinese call the region Xizang – is your main point of entry into the 'land of snows.' Lhasa is situated north of Bhutan and Bangladesh and almost due south of Urumqi.

Tibet is generally safe for visitors, except those who get involved in local politics or can't take the altitude. I also suggest you avoid getting close to the many stray dogs here.

Tibet is one of the more exotic places to visit, almost a country in itself, with an area about the size of France, Spain, and Greece combined. It is isolated by the highest mountains in the world. It is important to see because of its unique culture, its celebrated monasteries, and its stark, spectacular scenery.

Good books to read before your trip here include Heirich Harrer's *Seven Years in Tibet*, about his adventures there in the 1940s, a good picture to compare with today's Tibet. Harrer, a German, taught the Dalai Lama English and was his cameraman. A sequel tells of Harrer's recent return trip. Also recommended are the classics *Tibet and Its History* by Hugh E. Richardson, and Peter Fleming's *Bayonets to Lhasa*.

Lhasa's population is about 175,000.

ARRIVALS & DEPARTURES

Lhasa is reached by two daily two-hour flights from Chengdu, and two flights a week each from Kathmandu and Chongqing. The Kathmandu flights might or might not continue all winter. (See also Chapter 6, *Planning Your Trip*, about Getting to China Via Nepal.)

There are also twice-a-week flights from Beijing, and soon flights with Qamdo, Shanghai, Kunming and Xi'an. Lhasa's **Gonggar Airport**, the third highest in the world at 3,542 meters, can now accommodate 747s. There is talk of direct flights from Hong Kong. The airport is over 100 kilometers from Lhasa and the road follows a river which becomes the Brahmaputra in India.

THE MAGNIFICENT POTALA

You can also go to Lhasa by daily bus from Golmud (1,100 kilometers) with an overnight stop in Amdo or wherever the driver wants to sleep. It's about 30 hours driving time with the possibility of snow in the passes, even in June. Take warm clothing, motion sickness pills, and your own food. Buses have no toilets and heat.

Travelers have also been going overland from Kathmandu; you can travel from the Nepal border to Lhasa in one long day if you don't stop to sightsee. Three days is better. You can also go by land from Chengdu via Chamdo; from Kashi; and via Yunnan province. Most road conditions are very poor, however; you should expect delays due to landslides in summer and substandard roads and months to get permits.

ORIENTATION

This is colorful National Geographic land: you can see prostrating pilgrims, fierce-looking tribesmen, people spinning prayer wheels on the street, a great variety of tribal dress, maroon-robed monks, unusual handicrafts and architecture, great mountains, and smiling, friendly people most of whom don't mind having their photo taken when asked. It's best to take a long lens for the ones who have never seen foreigners or cameras before. You are lucky if you encounter groups of 50 to 100 monks challenging each other with questions catechism-style amid much laughter and the clapping of hands.

And there are yaks – oxen who live at high altitudes.

While visiting Tibet is no longer an experience just for the adventurous few, it is still not for the weak. The average altitude in Tibet is over 5000 meters (very hard on the skin, so take some good sunscreen). Usually it takes about two days to decide whether you'll be sick, and two weeks to feel at home. Just don't push yourself too hard. Taking it easy is difficult, as a lot of climbing is involved just to sightsee. Do not go if you have asthma or other pulmonary problems. In addition to the altitude and dust, the temples are full of incense smoke and are lit by butter lamps all of which might make breathing difficult. Qualified doctors may not be available.

Since most food, energy and building materials have to be imported by truck or plane, the cost of accommodations and sightseeing is higher than in other parts of China for the same quality. You should take your own flashlight, drinking flask, medicine for altitude sickness, and an alarm clock.

The Climate

The altitude in Lhasa is about 3,607 meters. Most of the year can be very dry with lots of dust blowing. A nose mask and goggles are helpful. Only light clothing is needed in summer for Lhasa, but warmer clothes are needed for higher altitudes. Winter days can be warm with highs of 20 degrees centigrade and you can get a sunburn. But the nights can be cold. The best weather is September to November. The hottest temperature in Lhasa is 27 degrees centigrade in July and August; the coldest, minus 15 degrees centigrade in December to February. The annual precipitation is about 500 millimeters, mainly in June and July.

When to Visit

The busiest tourist months are April, May, and July through October. At the height of the tourist season in August, you might have to queue up at the Holiday Inn's several restaurants or not get a room there at all. From November one to March 31, the valley is full of colorful nomads going on pilgrimages from monastery to monastery, and living in tents. A good time to go is October and November when there are fewer tourists. There's also mid-March when there are hardly any other tourists, and lots of sunny 15 degree centigrade days. At night the temperature dips to near freezing but there's nothing to do outside anyways. Be warned however

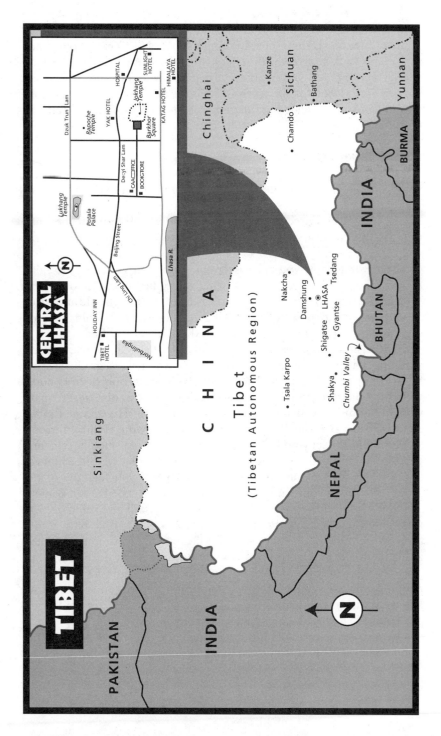

that there is no decent heat and hot water in hotels except in Lhasa's Holiday Inn, nor is there heat in minibuses. At New Years, houses and mountains look glorious with fresh prayer flags, and monasteries have special ceremonies, but markets are partially open and stores and factories are closed for two weeks. This is the best time for photography and tourist market haggling. Just take a hot-water bottle. You can visit Gyantse, Shigatse, and Zetang year round.

Altitude Sickness

If you only have two days, it may not be worth visiting Lhasa where you get about two-thirds the amount of oxygen at sea-level. In Shigatse, you get 50%!! Jogging or any physical exertion makes matters worse. About 60% of new arrivals get a headache. If you are one of the small minority afflicted with severe **altitude sickness**, you could spend much of your time in bed.

You won't know you are susceptible until you get to about 3,000 meters. You can travel successfully in high altitudes 20 times and get it on the 21st. It seems to hit the young and strong more than the old and weak. Young people have passed out checking into hotels. You should not jump onto a bicycle upon arrival or jog, even though you feel fine.

The symptoms are severe headache, dizziness, insomnia, nausea, vomiting, and difficulty in breathing. People who make a gradual ascent by road rarely get it, if at all. People who fly in are prone. So are people with colds, breathing difficulties, poor health, and heart disease. Pregnant women should stay below 3,600 meters, says the Himalayan Rescue Association in *Hints on High Altitude*, circulated by the Holiday Inn.

It is better to let your body adjust naturally. Avoid smoking, alcohol, and sleeping pills. Move about in slow motion. Drink over three liters of liquid a day. Get plenty of bed rest especially if you feel any of the symptoms. Open your windows. Breathe deeply. Relax. Do not panic.

Some hotels have oxygen in the rooms. This will give relief but will retard the time it takes the body to adjust. Some people have found aspirins helpful. Some have successfully taken the diuretic Diamox available in North America by prescription only. Most doctors will not prescribe it because they don't know its effect at high altitudes. With a few people Diamox has caused vomiting, confusion, and, of course, urination. Discuss it with a mountaineering club or travel agency doctor before you go. You have to start taking it a day before you arrive.

In very severe cases of altitude sickness, the only recourse is evacuation to a lower altitude – but you may not get a plane out for days.

HOW TO ARRANGE TRAVEL TO TIBET

Tibet has been officially open (except during times of civil unrest) only for prepaid tours with a guide, even for one person. Any Chinese travel agent can arrange these. You will need authorization sent from the **Tibet Tourism Bureau** *to the Chinese mission where you are applying for a visa. You can also arrange tours after you arrive in China. If you wait until you get to China, you should NOT mark 'Tibet' on your visa application form. If you mention Tibet, the Chinese consulate will need to see your permission from the Tibet Tourism Bureau first.*

Waiting until after your arrival could mean a cheaper trip depending on the number of people in your group. It can take three days to get permission, but better give yourself a week. For diplomats assigned to countries other than China and traveling as tourists, legal entry to Tibet is decided on a case-by-case basis which could take three weeks to a month once authorities receive your name and passport number.

As for journalists, what is a journalist? As long as you call yourself something else, and behave like any other tourist, journalists should have no problems. Just don't put "journalist" on any form, not even a hotel registration form.

From time to time, these official restrictions have not been enforced and a few people have entered without a permit. You do risk a fine and deportation if caught.

If you want an ethnic Tibetan rather than Chinese guide, make your request when you book your tour. A Tibetan guide might not speak English as well as a Chinese one, but a Tibetan guide will be able to communicate better with Tibetans. You can also request a guide with good English if available. Some Tibet-based travel agencies are listed in Chengdu. Tibetans can be hostile to Chinese guides.

Because tourists have complained of guides with little knowledge and poor English, please take this guide book with you or get something more detailed, like Elisabeth B. Booz's **Tibet**. *If you are worried about the political unrest, contact U.S. missions in China, especially the consulate in Chengdu, or the Sales Manager, Holiday Inn Lhasa, for current information. There could be demonstrations on important Tibetan anniversaries, but guides will steer you away from them. If something happens before your trip, your travel agent can always cancel for you.*

TIBETAN HISTORY

Tibetans were nomads or farmers who raised barley, yak, and sheep. Tho-tho-ri Nyantsen, 28th king of Tibet, introduced **Buddhism** into the country in 233 A.D. In 779, Buddhism became the state religion.

In the seventh century, the king of Tubo conquered the other tribes and made Lhasa his capital. He also invaded neighboring Sichuan, and although he was repulsed, his request for a Chinese wife was granted. His marriage with Tang princess Wen Cheng and his interest in Tang culture introduced much Chinese culture into Tibet. Among the innovations were silk, paper, and the architecture of the palace he built for her. His marriage to a Nepalese princess also meant Nepalese-Indian influences. Tibetan script is derived from Sanskrit, which was developed in India.

Both princesses promoted their own brand of Buddhism. The Tibetan kingdom subsequently expanded to include parts of Yunnan and northern India. The Mongols invaded Tibet in 1252 and adopted Tibetan Buddhism for themselves and propagated it to help control their subject tribes in other parts of China. Some Tibetan lamas, or high priests, became very powerful during the Yuan. **Kublai Khan** appointed a lama as king, to maintain overall power himself. This system has continued with varying degrees of Chinese enforcement ever since. Qing Emperor Qianlong (Chien Lung) especially asserted his authority in Tibet.

The Jesuits were the first western missionaries to arrive in 1624. During the lifetime of the **fifth Dalai Lama**, the office of Dalai Lama became political as well as religious. The first British mission arrived in 1774 and a British military expedition (Younghusband's mission) forced the Dalai Lama to flee to Mongolia from 1904 until 1909. In 1910, the Chinese again asserted their control and the Dalai Lama retreated for a time to India.

In 1911, the Tibetans repelled the Chinese. The British tried to maintain some control, but the Tibetans pretty much ruled themselves until the Chinese People's Liberation Army invaded in 1950-1951. The 1950's saw periods of turmoil as well as calm as the Chinese strengthened their hold.

An uprising by many Tibetans and a fierce Chinese crackdown in 1959 caused the current Dalai Lama (the 14th) to fear for his life; he and a large number of Tibetans fled to India. He has been living in Dharamsala, India, ever since, along with tens of thousands of Tibetans who live in exile throughout India, Nepal, and to a lesser extent Bhutan.

In 1964, China made Tibet an "autonomous region" within China. During the Cultural Revolution, the Red Guards destroyed most of the monasteries. Today, Tibet has at least 50 monasteries open, including seven for nuns, with at least 3,000 monks in residence and 138 nuns. More religious buildings are under repair, many of these by the Tibetan and Chinese governments which also maintain and regulate the monasteries. Before the Chinese army took over, Tibet had 2,770 monasteries. In 1980, the government agreed to rebuild a number of monasteries, which it is now doing.

The Chinese have started to train Tibetans to replace Han adminis-trators. The 2.1 million Tibetans here are over 95% of the population, not counting the Chinese military. Due to government incentives, many Han Chinese are moving into Tibet, especially Lhasa. Some estimates put the number of Chinese soldiers and security forces in Tibet at 300,000.

In 1987, again in 1989, and sporadically in the past few years, a number of Tibetans (led by monks) have demonstrated for indepen-dence. Several dozen people have been killed and hundreds imprisoned.

The current Dalai Lama was awarded the **Nobel Peace Prize** in 1989, for his nonviolent resistance in exile to Chinese occupation of his country, and for a peace plan offering the Chinese sovereignty of sorts in exchange for genuine autonomy in everyday life, with guarantees of political and religious freedom. China accused the United States and other countries then (and still does) of interfering in its internal affairs.

WANTED ~ DALAI LAMA PHOTOS

As you move around the region, be sensitive to the feelings of people. I have been appalled by the loud talking of my Chinese guide during Tibetan prayers. Walk clockwise around temples. If you hand a picture of the Dalai Lama to a Tibetan, make sure no Han Chinese is around because you and your Tibetan friend could get in trouble. Hold the photo (postcards are great) in both hands, put it to your forehead and then bow your head as you hand it over.

The Dalai Lama is considered by Tibetans to be an incarnation of God, and they might ask you for a 'Dalai Lama picture' in every monastery. You probably could give out 40 in the Potala alone. However, if you have pictures of the Dalai Lama in your possession, the police could conclude that you support Tibetan independence. They have arrested some foreigners for getting involved in this dispute. In the early 1990s, you could see photos of the Dalai Lama in monasteries, but in 1996, the authorities confiscated them.

TIBETAN BUDDHISM

Tibet's Buddhism is different from that of the rest of Asia, aside from Mongolia and northern China. It believes in reincarnation and there are both wrathful and peaceful aspects: the wrathful side includes a torturous hell for sinners, which is reflected in its art, full of demons and human skulls, witchcraft and magic, much influenced by the pre-Buddhist polytheism of the Tibetans.

The peaceful side of the religion is also reflected in Tibetan art. It has also many pre-Hindu influences and much recitation of spells. You might hear the chant *Om Mani Padme Hum*, which means 'Hail to the Jewel in the Lotus,' a mantra that helps the individual communicate with the eternal.

At the same time, Buddhism has many mystical elements, and a highly developed theology. The goal of Buddhism is the end of continuous reincarnations.

At one time, a quarter of the male population of Tibet were monks, and the theocracy was such that no matter how cold it was, on whatever day spring was proclaimed by the Dalai Lama, everybody had to change into summer clothes!

Like other religions, Buddhism is divided into sects: the two main ones in Tibet are often referred to as the Red Hats, where sex with a person other than one's spouse is part of the ritual, and the Yellow Hats (the **Gelukpa** sect), which is more strict about celibacy and other traditional Buddhist monastic practices. The Dalai Lama is head of the Gelukpa sect.

The title Dalai Lama comes from combining *Dalai,* which is a Mongolian word meaning '*ocean,*' and *Lama,* which means 'revered one,' 'teacher,' or, in this case, 'wisdom.' So Dalai Lama means Ocean of Wisdom.

Determining Reincarnated Lamas

How successive Dalai Lamas are chosen is a fascinating story. Toddlers recognizing objects used by themselves in their previous incarnations, answering questions correctly, and so on, is the usual way it's done. The current incumbent is from a peasant family from **Amdo** (northeastern Tibet, now in Qinghai province). The Dalai Lamas are earthly incarnations of the four-armed god **Chenrezi**, the God of Compassion, and when each incarnation dies, his spirit takes on the body of another Tibetan child at birth.

Disputes have arisen over who is the real reincarnated Dalai Lama or any other lama, and the issue is politically sensitive. To the chagrin of his followers, the current Dalai Lama has said there should be 'no more Dalai Lamas,' and 'there is no need to preserve this institution.'

Lamas are very learned monks or recognized reincarnations of previous lamas or monks, and their identities are determined in a similiar way. One American woman has recently borne the reincarnation of a high lama. In 1995, the Dalai Lama proclaimed one child as the reincarnation of the Panchen Lama while the Chinese government proclaimed another. The Chinese pointed to a Qing dynasty agreement that said it had to approve the appointment.

TIBETAN CUSTOMS

Tashi Delek is the Tibetan greeting. It means "good luck." Hello is *Wei.* Among traditional Tibetan customs is the giving of a *kata,* a long silk scarf, as a token of esteem and good luck. The sticking out of the tongue is a sign of respect. At one time, Tibetans practiced polyandry, brothers sharing one wife because of poverty. Every summer a festival celebrates the annual washing and cleaning.

Funeral workers cut up the remains of some Tibetans at dawn to feed vultures, a 1,000-year-old tradition. Tibetans believe these birds take the spirits to heaven. Those who cannot afford this expensive rite, like beggars or victims of serious illnesses, are fed to fish, which is why Tibetans don't eat fish. Burial in the ground is for the very poor and unfortunate, such as criminals or victims of murder. Some high lamas are covered in butter and cremated. The highest lamas are buried in monasteries; the previous Dalai Lamas in the **Potala Palace** (see below).

Tourists are forbidden from seeing the birds at work, because the families of the deceased fear strangers will scare the birds away.

Look for the *tangkas* hung on monastery walls. These are the scrolls used by itinerant preachers to illustrate the teachings of the Buddha and the best are valued by art collectors. You'll also see **prayer wheels**, with a written prayer inside, which adherents spin in the belief that each rotation sends a prayer to Buddha. Monasteries have giant prayer wheels. Prayer flags are blue symbolizing the sky, white for clouds, red for fire, green for water and yellow for earth. They are for protection.

Religious institutions usually decide the time and date of ceremonies and special events at the last moment. You have to telephone each morning for the time if you want to see these. No one really knows what is going on when, and you could find many changes to your itinerary.

WHERE TO STAY

The best hotel is the **Holiday Inn Lhasa** (with the best spoken English), then the **Tibet Hotel**. Third is the Sunlight. The Holiday Inn and Tibet are within walking distance of each other and the Norbulinka. The Kirey, Banok Shol and Yak are normally clean Tibetan inns, with no private baths. The Banok Shol has the better food of these. Aside from the Holiday Inn, few hotels honor reservations. You might have to send a scout a day ahead to secure rooms in high tourist season. Hotels outside of Lhasa's top two can be downright crude.

The cheaper Tibetan inns are within walking distance of each other and the central Jokhang Monastery in the old Tibetan city and have been off limits to foreigners from time to time. No Tibetan inn has western toilets. Few rooms have private baths and most have cheap dorms too. Most have concrete floors and lots of flies. Some offer free do-it-yourself laundry service and have only one telephone and one television for everyone.

HOLIDAY INN LHASA (*Lhasa Fandian*), *One Minzu Rd., 850001. Three stars but closer to four. Tel. 6332221, 6324509 (Sales office). Fax*

6335796, 6324509. Telex 68010 HILSA CN. Recent published rates subject to change: November to March 31, $57 to $104; April 1 to October 31 $69 to $140. Dist.A.P. 100 km. Credit Cards.

In the western suburbs. Built 1986. 468 rooms in five and six story buildings. Tibetan-style suites. Heat in winter. B.C., USTV, IDD (card phones), foreign exchange, Sichuan and Tibetan restaurants. Pub. Outdoor pool open April to the end of October. Western and Tibetan herbal clinics. Own bus to airport. Write for worthwhile newsletter. CITS, CYTS and Tibet Tourist Bureau on premises. Usually has at least one native English-speaking staff person on duty.

SUNLIGHT HOTEL LHASA, *27 Linju Road, 850000. One star, Tel. 6333768, 6322227.*

TIBET HOTEL *(Xizang Binguan), 221 Beijing Xi Rd., 850001. Two stars. Tel. 6326784. Fax 63236787.*

Behind the Holiday Inn. Built 1986, ren. 1993. Clinic on-site.

YAK HOTEL, *Beijing Rd., 850000. Tel. 6323496.*

Built 1985, ren. 1992. Bicycles. 10 rooms and private bathrooms

WHERE TO EAT

Tibetan tea is drunk with **yak butter** and salt, and tastes more like an overly rich beef broth. It does tend to give much needed energy for survival and is said to be good for colds. The proper way to drink it is to lightly blow the top cream away from you and allow it to settle on the sides of your cup. The thicker the cream, the more generous the host. Fresh, hot yak milk is sweet and 'heavenly' and has a higher fat content than cow's milk. Barley- like flour is often added to the milk or tea to form a dough. *Chang (tsang)*, a barley wine, is another favorite drink offered to guests. Most foreigners do not like yak butter and yak-butter flavored Tibetan food – it's very rich and high in fat.

Except for the main hotels, restaurants here are generally dirty and the food is not good. There are few vegetables. You can get Tibetan food (yak meat and cheese), Moslem (mutton or lamb), and Chinese food in Lhasa. At the **HARD YAK CAFE** *at the Holiday Inn*, you can get yak burgers and spaghetti. The **BHARKHOR CAFE**, *Tel. 6326892, in the main square in front of the Jokhang Temple*, is good and clean, and run by former Holiday Inn staff in the summers. Backpackers eat at **TASHI ONE** or **TASHI TWO**, which are good and are located around the corner from the Bharkhor.

The park at the front base of the Potala has food stalls, but take precautions when you eat there. If you are going outside of Lhasa, stock up on snacks before you leave for Tibet.

SEEING THE SIGHTS IN LHASA

The most important buildings are the **Jokhang Temple**, **Potala Palace**, **Sera Monastery**, and **Drepung Monastery**. You should also see the **Barkhor** or bazaar, and **Norbulingka Palace**. You might want to visit a carpet factory or traditional medicine hospital.

In your spare time you may want to go out on your own. Only the Yak Hotel has bicycles. You can flag down one of the frequent public mini-buses or take a bicycle rickshaw; jeep-type vehicles are expensive (almost three times the taxi rate in any other Chinese city). Monastery hours keep changing, so check at your hotel. The Potala has been open Mondays and Thursdays to the public, and daily except Sundays to tour groups, 9 am to 12:30 noon. Do check before you go. To travel to other parts of Tibet, ask your hotel, travel agents or other travelers. The Yak, Kirey, and Sunlight Hotels have notice boards with messages.

You can see the temples and palaces of Lhasa in two days if you are in good shape. You must not miss the *Potala Palace, *Tel. 6324587.* It is 3.5 kilometers from the Holiday Inn and one kilometer from the Jokhang. It dominates the city from its lofty cliff. Your group gets driven up to the entrance, but individual travelers could climb the 300 meters to the top. In spite of its 13 stories, there are no elevators. If you follow the crowds and go into every open doorway, you should be able to take in everything worthwhile in three hours. There are no signs in English or arrows. There are a lot of stairs, and the only toilet is near the east entrance.

Originally built in the seventh century by Songsten Gampo, the Potala was the official residence of the Dalai Lama, the religious and secular head of Tibet. The first Dalai Lama lived from 1391 to 1474. The Potala has 1,000 rooms, 10,000 chapels, and the tombs of eight Dalai Lamas, some gold-plated and studded with diamonds, turquoises, corals, and pearls. The largest tomb is 14.85 meters high. More than 200,000 pearls cover the Pearl Pagoda. The tombs are not always open so ask about them. Additional payment is worth it. Every room has a helpful monk-guide. To take photos you pay from Y10 to Y60 per room; he will tell you how much.

The building was destroyed and rebuilt several times, the latest structure dating from 1642. Among its 200,000 statues are those of King Songsten Gampo and his Chinese wife. Every wall is covered with murals. Noteworthy are those in the Sishiphuntsok Hall. In the West Grand Hall, the murals record the life of the Fifth Dalai Lama, including his meeting with Qing Emperor Shunzhi in Beijing in 1652.

The palace is 400 meters by 350 meters, and is made of stone and wood, its brightly colored walls between three and five meters thick, yellow for living quarters, and red for chapels. Black around doors is good luck. The White Palace was built during the time of the Fifth Dalai Lama (1617-1682) and the Red Palace afterward. From the 18th century, with the construction of the Norbulinka (Summer Palace), the Potala was used only in winter. Can you imagine a child growing up here? The current Dalai Lama was brought here at the age of four. Think of him flying his kite from the Potala's roof and exploring the city and its people with a telescope!

The *Jokhang Temple (Juglakang), *Tel. 6323129*, is the most important Buddhist temple in Tibet. It is here that most pilgrims prostrate themselves and you can take a great photo of them from its second floor. It is here that China's largest concentration of policemen seem to be, ready to show up whenever a crowd gathers. The Jokhang is 4.5 kilometers from the Holiday Inn and is the heart of the city. It was built in the mid-seventh century, also during King Songsten Gampo's time. It has been expanded several times since. Note the Nepalese and Chinese features. Princess Wen Cheng brought with her from China the seated statue of the child Sakyamuni. The Tibetans believe that the statue was made by the Buddha himself. The Great Prayer Festival is held annually here from the third to 25th of the first month of the Tibetan calendar.

The *Sera Monastery, *Tel. 6323139*, in the northern suburbs 10 kilometers from the Holiday Inn and four kilometers from downtown, was built in 1419. It was extended in the early 18th century, and is one of the four major monasteries in Tibet, at its height housing 10,000 lamas and monks. Today it has about 500. The 18 sandalwood arhats and four heavenly kings here were gifts from the Ming emperor. Look also for a gold statue of an 11-faced Guan Yin, the Goddess of Mercy.

The *Drepung Monastery, *Daipung, Tel. 6323149*, is in the western suburbs six kilometers from the Holiday Inn and 10 kilometers from the Jokhang. You can climb to the roof for a view of the valley. Financed by the same nobleman who built the Sera, the Drepung was founded in 1416 and extended several times. It is one of the four major monasteries. Among its treasures is a white conch and a gilded Buddha. Inside the abdomen of the statue in the main hall are the remains of a master translator named Dorjidak. At one time, this monastery also had a population of over 10,000 monks and lamas; today it has about 600.

If you have more time, **Norbulingka Park**, *Tel. 6322157*, was the summer residence of the Dalai Lamas. With 370 rooms, it is four kilometers from the Potala and set in a 100-acre garden. **Kalsang Podang**, the first building, was originally erected in 1755. The New Palace for the 14th Dalai Lama was built in 1954 and 1956. It is also full of statues and murals. The murals are of Princess Wen Cheng and her marriage to the king, the three worlds, and Buddha preaching under a banyan tree. The bedroom is as the current Dalai Lama left it when he fled to India. In the 1940s, the German mountain climber Heinrich Harrer set up a movie theater for the Dalai Lama in this park.

An exhibition of *tangkas* is usually in one of the temples in the back. If you don't like the toilets, go over to the Holiday Inn nearby. One of the temples in Lhasa has a bronze bell with Latin inscriptions. It should be from 17th-century Catholic missionaries. Ask about it if you're interested.

Also of interest is the **Sunday market**, down the hill and across the street in front of the Potala, a delightful innovation with rides for children, market stalls, and food to eat. At the Tibetan traditional medicine hospital, you can also learn about Tibetan medicine. If you want to ride a yak-skin raft, that should be possible too; inquire at your hotel.

Festivals

Dates are hard to pin down and some festivals have been canceled, even at the last minute.

• October-November: the **Gods Descending Festival**
• November-December: the **Fairy Maiden Festival** (Jokhang Temple)
• December: **Tsong Khapa's Festival**
• January-February-March: **Tibetan New Year**
• February-March: **Great Prayer Festival** (Jokhang)
• February-March: **Butter Lamp Festival**
• July: Giant **Tangka Festival** (Shigatse)
• August: **Shoton (Tibetan Opera) Festival**

SHOPPING

Tibetan boots, rugs, saddle blankets, jewelry, temple bells, prayer wheels, and woolen blankets are for sale. Look for the market around the Jokhang Temple, the **Barkhor**. There you can also buy Nepalese-made Tibetan *tangkas* which are finer than Tibetan ones, at several times the price of those in Nepal but cheaper than in North American, at **Syamukapu International**. Using the front gate of the Jokhang as 6 o'clock, this upmarket store is at about 10 o'clock.

There are other antique stores in the market. *Tangkas* and original art can also be bought at **Potala Arts & Crafts**, *Tel. 6326221*, at the foot of the Potala (bus stop). Not cheap. Unmounted prints of Tibetan *tangkas* are a great buy and have been found in the Holiday Inn and at the Potala. There's a Chinese-run **Friendship Store**, *Renmin Road, Tel. 6323954, 6323657*.

EXCURSIONS FROM LHASA
Shigatse & Gyantse

The most important town outside of Lhasa is **Shigatse** (Xigaze) for the *****Tashilhunpo** (Zhaxilhunbu) **Monastery**. On the new highway, this is about a five-hour, 260 kilometer journey west of Lhasa. It can be combined in a two-night, three-day trip with **Gyantse** (see below). You can return on the older, longer and more spectacular road that includes an hour in Gyantse, a climb up to a 5,000-meter pass full of stone cairns, and thousands of prayer flags, vibrating in gale-force winds. You can leave a cairn there yourself if you're not too cold. You also get spectacular views of snow-covered **Najun Gsancy** glacier and mountain (7,220 meters high). This is a journey of about 10 hours, including lunch and a drive around sacred **Lake Zambok**.

Shigatse is at an altitude of over 3,900 meters. The **Tashilhunpo** is usually open 9:30 am to 12:30 noon and sometimes 3:30 to 6:30 pm. It was founded in 1447 and was the home of the Panchen Lamas, the reincarnations of the Buddha of Eternal Light. The Chinese consider the Panchen Lama a political equal to the Dalai Lama, but this is also a very sensitive and controversial point.

At one time, the Tashilhunpo had a population of 3,800 monks. Today there are about 650. This monastery also has many halls and chapels, and statues of the 18 arhats. The **Hall of the Buddha Maitreya Champa/Qiangba** was built from 1914-18 with a 26.7-meter statue of the Buddha in gold and copper. The gold-plated reliquary of the fourth Panchen Lama is 11 meters high and is decorated with precious stones. The tenth Panchen Lama died here in 1989. Look for the photos of British Prime Minister Major and U.S. President George Bush on a stupa. There are also 15th century paintings. You can probably hear the lamas chanting in the **Grand Chanting Hall** three times a day. A good market for Tibetan handicrafts and unique boots is nearby.

Shigatse is a good place for walking around. It is flat and interesting especially around the market. Shigatse also has a traditional **Tibetan medicine hospital** to visit and the **Gang-Gyen Carpet Factory**, *9 Mount Everest Road, 857000, Tel. (9892) 22733*, with traditional Tibetan designs, which is owned by the Tashilhunbo monastery. It makes carpets, bags and jackets with sheep's wool and natural Tibetan-grown dyes. It's open 9:30 am to 12:30 noon then 3:30 to 6:30 am.

The **SHIGATSE HOTEL** *(Binguan) at 3 Beijing Zhong Road, 857000, Tel. (9892) 22525, 22527, 22550,* has only 123 rooms, no heat and no hot water. It's less than one kilometer to the Tashilhunpo. Almost next door is the Bank of China.

Gyantse is almost a two-hour drive from Shigatse, and 205 kilometers from the airport outside Lhasa. It is worth a stop, unless you're tired of monasteries by now. Gyantse's is the spookiest of the lot and has about 85 monks, but few visitors because of its isolation. The town itself looks positively medieval with the remains of an impressive old fort above it. Gyantse has a carpet factory and the two-star **GYANTSE HOTEL**.

Royal Tibetan Tombs

The *Royal Tibetan Tombs, from the seventh century, are at **Chonggye** (Qonggyai) in **Lhoka** (Shannan) prefecture, about 180 kilometers southeast of Lhasa. A hotel is in Zedang. The **Yumbulakang Palace**, built in 228 B.C. by the first Tibetan King, is on a hilltop. **Lake Yamdrok Yamsto** is a one-day excursion from Lhasa, a large undeveloped lake, but an opportunity to enjoy the stark countryside.

Ganden Monastery

The **Ganden Monastery**, 60 kilometers east of Lhasa, is listed as early Ming to Qing. At least 10 buildings have been restored. Less than 100 monks live there now. At one time, it had over 8,000 monks.

Elsewhere in Tibet

Nyingchi County, 400 kilometers from Lhasa, has the new **Parsong Co Lake Vacation Village** on a 12-kilometer long lake but we haven't had a chance to review it yet.

Tsedang is the first Tibetan capital, boasting the best hotel and food outside of Lhasa. **Samye** (reached by ferry and truck) is the oldest remaining monastery of the Red Hats.

Tsurpu is the new 'hot spot.' Two hours' drive from Lhasa, it has the newly rebuilt **Tsurpu Monastery**, the seat of the **Karmapa**, the head of the 'Black Hat' sect. He is the 17th reincarnation, discovered in 1992 at the age of eight years, but an old soul. The lineage is older than the Dalai Lama's. This remarkable child has given blessings (from a distance) to visiting tourists. Security is heavy and no cameras and purses are allowed. Audiences are not always possible and involve a one-day trip from Lhasa. Travel agents can make arrangement if the monastery is willing.

Zhangmu, on the Tibet side of the Nepal border, is now open to tourists, with a 100 bed guesthouse. The trip can take three days if you stop to sightsee or one day if you don't.

There are also tours to the **Quangtang grasslands**, a 200,000 square kilometer nature reserve with 60 kinds of rare wild animals like yak, argali, bear, and wild donkeys.

Treks

Several tour agencies now offer **treks** in Tibet, and prices for these are higher than similar treks in other countries. Mountaineering can be organized through the Chinese Mountaineering Association.

The best trekking months are June-July and September-October. August has the most rain, and landslides. There are treks to **Kailash** and **Rongbuk** (Everest Base camp) and various lakes, and soft treks from

Ganden to **Samye** (four to six days). (See also Chapter 6, *Planning Your Trip*, about Getting to China Via Nepal.)

PRACTICAL INFORMATION

• **CITS**, *Beijing Xi Road, 850001, Tel. 6322980, 6332980. Fax 6326315*
• **CTS**, *Tel. 6322980, 6336626. Fax 6335277*
• **CYTS**, *331 Zin Zhu Dong Road, 850000. Tel. 6323329. Fax 6335588*
• **Medical Emergencies** – The Holiday Inn has a local Chinese doctor who charges Y200 for a consultation, quite steep by Chinese standards. It can also give you the telephone number of a European doctor.
• **Nepalese Consulate**, *13 Norbulingka Road, Tel. 6322880*
• **Telephone Code**, *0891*
• **Tibet International Sports Travel**, *6 Linkhor Dong Road, 850000. Tel. 6323775, Fax 6326366*
• **Tibet Tourism Bureau**, *208-218 Beijing Xi Road, 850001, Tel. 6326793. Fax 6333241. For complaints, Tel. 6324584. Office in Tibet Hotel, Chengdu and 149 West Gulou Street, Beijing 100009. Tel. Beijing 4018822 X 1601. Fax 4015883 or 4019831*
• **Tourist Complaints**, contact **Supervisory Bureau of Tourism Quality of Tibet**, *208 Yuanlin Road, 850001, Tel. 6333476, 6334330. Fax 6334632*

21. SOUTH CHINA

CHANGSHA

Located south of the Yangtze River, **Changsha** is the capital of Hunan province, with a population of one million.

Changsha, in one of China's main rice-growing areas, was a small town 3,000 years ago. It was almost completely destroyed during the Japanese War. It is partly famous because Chairman Mao was born and lived nearby in **Shaoshan**. He studied for about five years at the Hunan Provincial First Normal School (1912-18). Yale University started a mission in about 1904 and eventually established a medical school, hospital, and middle school. The Americans left shortly after 1949.

Changsha is also known for its important Han excavation. Its embroidery is one of the four most famous in China.

The coldest temperature is about minus eight degrees centigrade in January; the hottest about 30 degrees in July. The rainfall is from 1250 to 1750 millimeters mostly April to June.

ARRIVALS & DEPARTURES

The city is a 95 minute flight southwest of Shanghai, one hour northeast of Guilin, and two hours south of Beijing. It has direct flights with Hong Kong, Macau and 35 other Chinese cities. Changsha is on the main Beijing-Guangzhou railway line, 726 kilometers north of Guangzhou.

ORIENTATION

The novel and movie *The Sand Pebbles* was set partly in Changsha during the Northern Expedition in the late 1920s. The hero was an engineer on an American gun boat, which sailed up the Yangtze through Lake Dongting and along the Xiang River. The movie is one of the few good Hollywood efforts on China. Changsha is also the setting of a more recent book, Liang Heng and Judith Shapiro's autobiographical *Son of the Revolution*, a refreshing look at growing up in Communist China and beating the system. The excellent novel *A Small Town Called Hibiscus* is set in the southern part of this province.

Hunan province's nationalities include Han, Tujia, Miao, Dong, Yao, Hui, Uygur, and Zhuang.

WHERE TO STAY & EAT

As in many other places in China outside the major cities, the better food is served in hotel restaurants.

HUATIAN HOTEL *(Dajiudian), 16 Jie Fang Dong Rd., 410001. Four stars, Tel. 4442888. Fax 4442270. Dist A.P. 23 km. Dist. R.W. 1.5 km. Credit Cards.*

Built 1990. 17 stories. 288 rooms. Eight-story recreation building. IDD., B.C. Executive floor. Chaozhou and Thai food. Pool, gym and disco.

HUNAN FURAMA, *Four stars, Tel. 2298888. Fax 2291979.*
Built 1995.

LOTUS HOTEL *(Furong Binguan), 8 Wuyi Dong Rd., 410001. Three stars, Tel. 4401888. Fax 4465175. Dist.A.P. 15 km. Dist.R.W. one km. Credit Cards.*

Built 1984, ren. 1995. 15 stories. 265 rooms. IDD. B.C.

SEEING THE SIGHTS

If you only have one day, the Hunan Provincial Museum, the embroidery factory, and the Yuelu Academy are good choices.

Hunan Provincial Museum is on *Dongfeng Road*. Because this is the main tourist attraction, skip everything else if you are short on time. The 1972 to 1974 excavations of three 2,100-year-old tombs overshadow the revolutionary and other ancient collections in this museum. You must see these Han relics, important because of their excellent state of preservation and vast number. You may want to return to savor the rest of the museum later.

The Han collection is in the white middle building on the right after you enter the gate. The three tombs were of Li Tsang, chancellor to the Prince of Changsha and Marquis of Dai, his wife, and his son. The son died in 168 B.C. The body of the woman, 1.52 meters long and weighing 34.3 kilograms, is incredibly well preserved, with flesh, 16 teeth, and internal organs. The lungs, intestines, and stomach were removed after disinterment and preserved in formaldehyde. They are all on display in the basement. An autopsy revealed arteriosclerosis, gallstones, tuberculosis, and parasites. Death came to her suddenly at age 50; there were undigested melon seeds in her stomach. The remarkable state of preservation is attributed to the body being wrapped in hemp and nine silk ribbons, and sealed from oxygen and water in three coffins surrounded by 5,000 kilograms of charcoal and sticky white clay. She died after her husband; maybe that is why her tomb is the largest and she is the best preserved of all. She probably planned it herself.

The 5,000 relics include 1,800 pieces of lacquerware, many of which needed only cleaning to appear new. Look for the ear cups for wine and soup, and a make-up box with comb, mirror, powder, and lipstick. She also had for her after-death use incense burners, clothes, silk fabrics, medicinal herbs, and nine musical instruments. Maybe she did use them! An inventory of the relics was written on bamboo strips, paper still being rare then. In the building to the left as you leave the marquise are the three coffins and a model of the tomb site. To the right is an arts, crafts and antiques store. Some reproductions are on sale.

The Han tomb site, only four kilometers away in Mawangdui, is now just a large hole in the ground under a roof. You can see the pyramid-shaped hill, the neat, earthen walls, and staircase inside. Geomancy students can figure out the feng shui. Was it practiced then? Did the tomb face south?

The **Hunan Provincial Embroidery Factory**, *285 Bayi Road*, is worthwhile, as you can study this ancient craft being performed and be amazed at the number of workers not wearing eyeglasses. Look for embroidery so fine it can be displayed from either side.

A tour of the city includes **Tianxin Park** with its small section of 600-plus-year-old city wall. Open daily, 6 am to 8 pm. **Juzi** (Orange) **Island**, five kilometers long in the middle of the Xiang River, is probably the 'long sand' after which Changsha is named.

The **Hunan Normal School**, *Shuyuan Road*, outside the south gate of the city, has a small museum. Mao studied and taught here in 1913-18 and 1920-21. The current structure, built in 1968, is a copy of the 1912 school and reflects its European connections. The **Lushan Temple** was built in 268 A.D. and reconstructed last in 1681. The **Yuelu Academy** was one of the four major institutes of higher learning from 976 A.D., rebuilt last in 1670. The **Aiwan Pavilion** was built in 1792. None of these is spectacular.

NIGHTLIFE & ENTERTAINMENT

Local Huagu opera originated from provincial folk songs and ditties. The **Hunan Provincial Puppet Show Troupe** is well known.

SHOPPING

Made in the province are the embroideries, brocade, batik, porcelain and pottery, chrysanthemum stone, peach stone, and bamboo carvings, fans, firecrackers, lacquer reproductions, smoky quartz and bloodstone carvings, handicrafts from minorities, and duck-down clothing.

EXCURSIONS FROM CHANGSHA

Wulingyuan is 400 kilometers west of Changsha (seven hours by bus; 22 by train). It is a 360-square-kilometer forest close to Dayong county in the western part of Hunan province, full of beautiful hills, stone pillars, flowers and wild boar, monkeys and leopards. Thirteen different ethnic groups live here including the Miao in Jishou City. There are karst caves in Longshan county and it's possible, by now, that you can go rafting on the Mongdong River in Yongshun County.

The best hotel is the Dragon International. A cheaper two-star hotel, the **PIPAXI GUEST HOUSE** is also in *Zhangjiajie, Tel. (07483)712393. Fax 713325.* There's the **WULINGYUAN HOTEL** in *Suoxiyu Town, Tel. 618288.* **DRAGON INTERNATIONAL HOTEL** *(Chelong Guoji Dajiudian), 46 Jiefang Road, Zhang Jia Jie, 416680. Four stars, Tel. (0744)8226888 or fax 8222935. Credit Cards. 223 rooms. Hong Kong joint-venture. $50. Hong Kong Tel. (852)2520-2266 or fax 2529-1868.* Built in 1994, this hotel is a 30-minute drive from the park and six kilometers from the airport. **CITS** is *Tel. (7483)222928. Fax 222938.*

Shaoshan is 104 kilometers southwest of Changsha, a worthwhile 2 1/2 hour trip by road, more by train. There is an airport. The countryside is lovely, with tea plantations, orange groves and rice fields. This is the *Birthplace of Chairman Mao, a simple mud-brick farmhouse where the founder of the People's Republic was born on December 26, 1893. He lived in this charming, and apparently tranquil, village until 1910, when he left for studies in Changsha. He returned briefly several times, holding meetings and conducting revolutionary activities. The Nationalists confiscated and destroyed the original house in 1929, but after 1949, the Communists rebuilt it along the original lines. Two families shared the house, the section on the left as you enter being the Mao's. It is very sparsely furnished. The dining room still has the original small table, typical even for large families. The master bedroom has portraits of the parents and the bed in which he was born. Another room holds original farm tools.

The **museum**, with ten large galleries, is a ten minute walk from the farmhouse. It is full of exhibits depicting his life although Mao's deposed widow, the late Jiang Qing and his unsuccessful assassin Lin Piao don't appear at all. Also open is the Water-Dropping 'cave' where Mao Zedong stayed hidden for 11 days in 1966 and planned the Cultural Revolution. It is 20 minutes by car from Shaoshan. You can also visit the family temple and stay at the modest **SHAOSHAN HOTEL**, a five minute walk from the museum or the villa formerly used by top leaders. **CTS** and **CITS**, *Tel. (0372)682197. Fax 682197.*

Yueyang, 2,000 years old, is on the north shore of **Lake Dongting**, just south of the Yangtze River, and is sometimes a stop on a Yangtze River cruise. It is 160 kilometers north of Changsha and is close to the mother of all dragon boat races. The 19 meter-high Yueyang Tower was first built in 716 A.D. to train the navy. It was rebuilt in 1867 in the original Tang style. One of the eight Taoist genii, Lu Tung-pin with the supernatural sword, is credited with saving the tower from collapsing.

You can also visit **Junshan Island** which grows Junshan Silver Needles tea and a tree with red leaves on one side and green on the other. It is a bird-watcher's paradise. Try to imagine the Song dynasty when 10,000 troops were stationed here.

As for the **dragon boats**, in 278 B.C. in the nearby Miluo River, Qu Yuan, the great patriotic poet, drowned himself in protest against the destruction of the State of Chu by the First Emperor of China. Ever since, this tragic event has been commemorated with races to feed the fish before the fish can eat Qu Yuan!

The three-star **YUEYANG HOTEL** is best, at *26 Dongting Bei Road, 414000, Tel. (730)8223011, 8225235. CITS is Tel. 8222482, 82222386.*

Hengshan Mountain is about 310 kilometers south of Changsha, one of the Five Great Mountains of China. It has 72 peaks and about 20 Taoist and Buddhist temples. The most noteworthy is at Nanyue, occupying 98,000 square meters. First erected in 725 (Tang), it has Song and Ming architecture. A hotel and botanical garden are also there. You can eat vegetarian food at the **Zhusheng Temple**. A 1,710 meter-long cableway should now be operating.

PRACTICAL INFORMATION

- **Business Hours**, 8 am to 5,30 pm for office; 8 am to 9 pm for stores.
- **CITS** and **CTS**, *Tel. 4410094. Fax 4446996*
- **CYTS**, *13 Ying Bin Road, 410011. Tel. 4423310. Fax 4441866*
- **Dragonair**, *Lotus Hotel*
- **Hunan Provincial Travel Bureau**, *Chunhua Road at Bayi Dong Road, 410001. Tel. 4446736. Fax 4446996.* Complaints and brochures.
- **Telephone Code**, *0731*
- **Tourist Complaints**, contact **Supervisory Bureau of Tourism Quality of Hunan Province**, *First Floor, Provincial Tourism Administration Building, Wulipai, Changsha, 410001. Tel. 4726736. Fax 4720348*

GUANGZHOU

(Kwangchow, Canton)

The capital of Guangdong province, **Guangzhou** is one of the fastest developing areas in the world. Travelers should avoid Guangzhou during the lunar new year holiday (late January or early February), trade fairs, and Qing Ming (early April), because of the crowds.

Guangzhou is known as the **Goat City** because five fairies came here supposedly in 1256 B.C, riding five goats from whose mouths the fairies drew the first rice seeds. The city was founded over 2,000 years ago. In 214 B.C., the first Qin emperor set up the Prefecture of Nanhai here. Guangzhou is best known as the largest and most prosperous trading city in south China, a role it has played since at least the Tang dynasty. Arab traders started arriving over 1,300 years ago. The Portuguese settled in Macau, 150 kilometers away in 1557, and foreign traders moved here seasonally here. More recently, it was the site of the Canton Trade Fair, for 23 years China's main foreign trade institution.

Being a long way from the political center of China, the people here developed a rebellious, independent spirit. Guangzhou was the starting point or site of many important historical events, including:
• the fight against the importation of opium. Chinese officials burned 20,000 chests of it near here in 1839;
• the struggle against foreign imperialism, at Shanyuanli, for example, during the Opium War in 1841;
• the movement against the Qing dynasty by the Taiping Heavenly Kingdom. Leader Hong Xiuquan (Hung Hsiu-ch'uan) was born about 66 kilometers north of the city and was given the Christian tract that changed his life and China's history in Guangzhou;
• the campaign against the Qing in the early 1900s led by Dr. Sun Yat-sen, who was born south of the city in Zhongshan county near the Macau border. The fight was fueled by the failure of the Qing emperors to repel the encroaching foreign powers;
• the general strike against the unequal foreign treaties, starting in June 1925. It lasted for 16 months and almost closed Hong Kong;
• the Communist Revolution. Mao taught peasant leaders here in 1926 at the National Peasant Movement Institute;
• the Northern Expedition, whose officers were trained at the nearby Huangpu (Whampoa) Military Academy. Chiang Kai-shek was director and Chou En-lai was in charge of political indoctrination. In June 1926, this expedition to unify China and to assert Chinese nationalism started off from Guangzhou.
• an uprising against the Nationalists led by the Communists in December 1927.

Many foreign missionaries established schools and churches here after the Treaty of Nanking in 1842 opened the city to foreign trade and residence. From 1938 to 1945, the Japanese occupied Guangzhou. The Communists took over on October 14, 1949.

The weather here is subtropical, the coldest about zero degrees centigrade in January and February; the hottest and most humid is about

38 degrees in July and August. The average rainfall is 1680 millimeters. The best time to visit is October to February. The urban population is about 3.85 million.

ARRIVALS & DEPARTURES

From Hong Kong, 165 kilometers northwest in Guangdong province on the Zhujiang (Pearl River), it is a non-stop two to two-and-a-half hour train ride, a three-hour hydrofoil ride, or a half-hour flight. You can also take buses direct from Hong Kong to your hotel.

There are overnight boats, fast catamarans and hovercraft leaving several times a day from Hong Kong China City at 35 Canton Road in Tsimshatsui, west of the Star Ferry. China Travel Service can make arrangements or you can buy tickets at the pier.

Guangzhou is also linked by air with Bangkok, Djakarta, Ho Chi Minh City, Kuala Lumpur, Manila, Melbourne, Osaka, Penang, Seoul, Singapore, Surabaya, Sydney, Vientiane and at least 64 cities in China. A second larger airport should be finished in 1997 in Huadu city about 35 kilometers from Guangzhou. It will replace the current Baiyun Airport.

Guangzhou is a 36-hour train ride south of Beijing. To get train information, call the **Railway Station**, *Tel. 87777112, 86661789, 87752409.* A superhighway connects it with Shenzhen on the Hong Kong border. Every time there is a long Hong Kong holiday, over 100,000 visitors try to get from Hong Kong to China and back.

Airlines
• **CAAC**, *next to main railway station, Tel. 86661803 or 86662749 (international),;86662969 (domestic)*; Airport Service Desk, Departure Lounge, *Tel. 86666123, 86678901.*
• **JAS**, *China Hotel A201. Tel. 86696688, 86666888 X 2871. Fax 8666-5603*
• **Malaysian Airlines**, *Garden Hotel, Tel. 83358828, 83338989*
• **Singapore Airlines**, *Garden Hotel, Tel. 83358999, 83338898 X 1056*
• **Thai Airways**, *Tel. 83823947, 83338989*
• **Vietnam Airlines**, *Tel. 83827187*

ORIENTATION

In recent years, Guangdong has been one of the main suppliers of food, water, and electricity for neighboring Hong Kong. It is rich in livestock, fruits, and vegetables. Guangdong has 11 institutions of higher learning, including Zhong Shan University, which is on the site of the missionary-founded Ling Nam University. Tourists would probably be interested in or disgusted by its ivory-carving factory, which makes about 50 concentric and free-moving balls within balls from one piece of ivory.

The city is divided by the **Zhu** (Pearl) **River**, which is crossed by at least five bridges, a tunnel and innumerable ferries to be avoided at rush hours (roughly 7:30 to 9 am and 4:30 to 6 pm). Most of the places of interest to tourists are located on the north side. An 18 kilometer-long subway is being built. There are two railway stations, the newer **Tianhe station** serving all Hong Kong and Shenzhen trains and others too, so ask about your arrival station before you depart.

The city is plagued with traffic jams. More elevated highways and bridges are being built to relieve the traffic congestion but parking problems and traffic jams are the price of prosperity. Cars from outside of town are now banned from the center of the city, and bicycles from some streets. But ring roads, wider roads, and express roads and multi-storied car parks are opening and making life a little easier.

While *pu tong hua* (Mandarin dialect) is understood by almost everyone, the language spoken in most homes is Cantonese.

GUANGDONG'S GIFT TO THE WORLD: HER PEOPLE

Guangdong province is the provincial 'home' of many Chinese immigrants to Australia, the United States, Canada, Hong Kong and Southeast Asia. These people have contributed to the economic development of their adopted lands and have also brought or sent back expertise as well as money to their ancestral home. Many are playing a leading role in China's modernization program, and are largely responsible for Guangdong's economic boom.

WHERE TO STAY

Guangzhou's hotels add 10% service, 5% tax and 5% subway tax. All hotels here give discounts depending on availability to walk-in guests. Rooms are cheapre when booked through travel agents. However, unless rooms are reserved in advance and for several nights, hotels certainly do not give discounts during the Canton Trade Fair when prices double or almost triple.

The top hotels are still the **White Swan** (for tourists), and the **Garden** and **China** (especially for business people). The Guangdong International has improved considerably and should be ranked close to the top three, above the Dong Fang. The Dong Fong would be rated higher except for the quality of English and the smaller rooms in its west wing.

Parkview Square is a good deal if you don't want a fancy lobby or lots of services. Its rooms are the largest in town for the price. The location across from the Han dynasty museum, near the Guangzhou Museum and Yuexiu Park, and around the corner behind the China Hotel is good for Trade Fair people as well as tourists.

The Equatorial Hotel looked deserted and uninviting during our inspection, but it does command one of the best locations across the street from the Canton Trade Fair, and it should be considered as a last resort for trade fair goers. The GITIC Riverside seems to be more for Southeast Asians. While it is good, it is not included here because of its lack of English speakers.

The China, Dong Fang, Equatorial, Liu Hua and then the China Merchants and Parkview are the best located for the Canton Trade Fair and tourists. It is within walking distance of two big parks, the Orchid Garden, the Han Museum, the Six Banyan Tree Temple and pagoda, Zhenhai Tower (museum), CAAC, CITS, and the main railway station.

The next best area for all visitors is about three kilometers east. Here are the Bai Yun, Garden and Guangdong International Hotels, the Holiday Inn City Center, Friendship Store and the World Trade Center. The zoo is nearby.

The White Swan Hotel is relatively isolated on a historic island, but an elevated highway means only a 15-minute drive to the Foreign Trade Center. It's near the U.S. Consulate, and you can walk to the Qingping Market. Also on the island are the cheaper Victory Hotel and a youth hostel. Within steps of the Pearl River Bridge downtown is the Landmark Hotel, close to CTS and shopping. The Ramada is in a less crowded area, far from anything but the river. It is the closest joint venture to the Tianhe railway station. The White Swan has the most beautiful lobby, its bar and coffee shop have the best view of the Pearl River, but the Ramada's river view includes a genuine pagoda. For the best gawdy Chinese atmosphere and garden, there's the Dong Fang.

All outdoor pools close in November for the winter. During trade fairs, many hotels demand that reservations be secured by a deposit. All hotels listed here of three stars and more have television reception from Hong Kong, sometimes in English. Most have a doctor or access to one.

BAI YUN HOTEL *(Binguan), 367 Huanshi Dong Rd., 510060. Three stars, Tel. 83333998. Fax 83336498, 83343032. Dist.A.P. six km. Dist.R.W. four km. Next to Friendship Store.*

Built 1975; ren. 1993 and 1994. 34 stories. Over 700 large rooms and suites. Worn carpets. Wide hallways. 28th floor best. USTV but no CNN. Not much English. Okay for budget travelers.

CHINA HOTEL *(Zhong Guo Da Jiu Dian), Liu Hua Rd., 510015. Five stars. Tel. 86666888. Fax 86677014, 86677288. In North America, Tel. 1-800-44UTELL. Dist.A.P. five km. Dist. R.W. one km.*

Built 1983; ren. 1995 to 1997. 18 stories, 1017 rooms including 128 suites. Executive floors. Separate check-in for commercial guests in the lobby. Bank of China. USTV and movies on demand. Deli. Asian, Chaozhou food. Hot pot restaurant. Expresso bar with latte and Starbucks coffee. Should soon have sports bar with billiards and darts. Gym, tennis, bowling and 25-meter outdoor pool. Benzes. 18-piece orchestra plays evenings. U.S. trade office, and consulates of Canada, France, and New Zealand. Managed by New World Hotels International.

CHINA MERCHANTS HOTEL, *111 - 8 Liu Hua Rd., 510010. Tel. 86681988. Fax 86662680. Dist.R.W. 500 meters.*

Three to four-star standard. Facing Liu Hua Lake. Built 1992. 240 rooms. Gym. Clinic. USTV. English poor.

DONG FANG HOTEL *(Dong Fang Binguan), 120 Liu Hua Rd., 510016. Five stars, Tel. 86669900, 86662946 (reservations). Fax 86662775. In North America, Tel. 1-800-44UTELL. Dist.A.P. five km. Dist.R.W. one km.*

Built 1961. Ren. lobby 1996. Eight and 11 stories. 1300 spacious rooms. Large twins. Smallish televisions. USTV. Generally charming. Executive floor. Old wing has larger rooms and high ceilings. Smoke hoods and umbrellas. Beautiful Chinese garden. Clinic. Thai, Japanese, and Indonesian food. Book store. Supermarket. Four-lane bowling, outdoor pool, tennis and mini-golf. Car park.

GARDEN HOTEL *(Huayuan Jiu Dian), 368 Huanshi Dong Rd., 510064. Five stars, Tel. 83338989. Fax 83324534. In North America, Tel. 1-800-44UTELL.Dist.A.P. nine km. Dist.R.W. five km.*

Built 1984-85. Good standards. 30 stories, 1,038 rooms. Narrow twin beds. Non-smoking floor. Executive floors with free use of meeting rooms. Office and residential tower. USTV. During trade fairs, has trade fair registration office. 24-hour room service. Red Flag limousines. Shuttle to railway station only. AT&T. Malaysian, Thai, Garuda, and SIA airlines. Pizzaria. Tennis and outdoor pool. Gym, sauna, jacuzzi and steam bath. China's largest bowling alley (AMF). Very fancy karaoke. U.S. cultural office. Clinic. A Summit International Hotel.

GUANGDONG INTERNATIONAL HOTEL *(Guangdong Guoji Liu Shi San Chen), 339 Huanshi Dong Rd., 510098. Five stars, Tel. 83311888. Fax 83313490, 83311565. Dist.A.P. 10 km. Dist.R.W. five km.*

Built 1992. In complex of four buildings with 63-story main building, Bank of China, DHL, Bud's ice cream, McDonald's, American Express and the Australian Consulate. Ren. 1994. 702 rooms. Executive floors. In-room safes. "Please wait" buttons. Wide twins. Non-smoking floor. USTV. Chaozhou, Japanese and European food. Outdoor pool, lighted tennis, gym, bowling, jogging track. Hi-tech karaoke. Helicopter pad.

HOLIDAY INN CITY CENTRE *(Jia Re Wen Hua Jiu Dian), Huan Shi Dong Rd., 28 Guangming Rd., Overseas Chinese Village, 510060. Four stars, Tel. 87766999. Fax 87753126. Dist.A.P. nine km. Dist.R.W. five km.*

Built 1989-90. 24 stories. 400 rooms. Exhibition center, gym,, outdoor pool, and 500-seat cinema. Bicycles. Executive floor. Free shuttle bus from railway station. Clinic. Children 19 and under free in parents' room.

HOTEL EQUATORIAL *(Guidu Jiu Dian), 931 Renmin Rd., Tel. 86672888. Fax 86672582.*

HOTEL LANDMARK CANTON *(Huaxia Dajiudian), 8 Qiao Guang Rd., Haizhu Square, 510115. Four stars. Tel. 83355988. Fax 83336197, 83331564. Dist.A.P. 10 km. Dist.R.W. four km.*
Built 1991-92. 39 stories. 730 rooms. Hairdryers. Business studios. Gym. Helipad. Pool. Tennis. Karaoke. Chaozhou, Sichuan, and Beijing food. Managed by CTS Macau.

LIU HUA HOTEL (Binguan), 194 Huanshi Xi Rd., 510017. Three stars, Tel. 86668800. Fax 86667828. Dist.A.P.four km. Dist.R.W. 300 meters.
Near post office, Trade Fair building, CAAC, and CITS. Built 1972. 7 stories. 718 small rooms. Small twins. North bldg., ren. 1989. Spacious rooms. Large in-room safes. Shanghai Airlines. Som restaurants very grubby. Service poor; no English. Chipped dishes – but great location. Has branch of Maxim's Fast Food. No USTV. Budget travelers only.

PARKVIEW SQUARE *(Tian An Da Sha), 960 Jie Fang Bei Rd., 510040. Three stars, Tel. 86665666. Fax 86671741. Dist.A.P. six km. Dist.R.W. two km.*
Built 1989-90. Ren. 1992. Lobby renovated 1995. 10 and 12 stories. 176 apartments mainly for long term. Executive club. USTV. Gym and saunas. Food Street, Chaozhou and Taiwan food. Room safes provided on check-in. H.K. management.

RAMADA PEARL HOTEL *(Hua Mai Da), 9 Ming Yue Yi Lu, Dong Shan Dist., 510600. Aiming at four stars. Tel. 87372988. Fax 87377481. Dist.R.W.Tianhe three km. Dist.A.P. 15 km.*
On 150 meters of waterfront. Near Guangzhou or Third Pearl River Bridge. Near some government offices but generally too far from any-where except for the 10- minute drive to International School. 1992, some renovations 1996. 25 stories. 330 rooms. Non-smoking rooms. Executive floor. USTV. Office tower and apartments. Asian buffet and California cafe. 24- hour room service. Gym, squash, tennis, indoor and outdoor pools. Good place for children. Lots of space. Malaysian consulate. Problem getting taxis but has shuttle bus.

WHITE SWAN HOTEL *(Baitian E Binguan), 1 Southern Street, Shamian Island, 510133. Five stars, Tel. 81886968. Fax 81861188, 81882288. Dist.A.P. 11 km. Dist.R.W. seven km.*
Member Leading Hotels of the World. H.K.J.V. Built 1983, continu-ous renovations. Good standards. 28 stories. 834 spacious rooms. Smoke hoods. 24-hour Business Center. Executive floor. AT&T. Grill room. Japanese food. Gym. Tennis. Squash. Beautiful outdoor pool and 20-meter lap pool. Golf-driving range. Rolls Royces. Convention center. U.S. and Thai consulates.

WHERE TO EAT

Guangzhou's garden restaurants are among the prettiest in China but unfortunately the food in the Beiyuan is no longer good and the Nanyuan is too far away. The best hamburgers are at the bar on the ground floor of the China Hotel, the one with the American manager – they have USDA prime beef.

The **BANXI (PAN HSI) RESTAURANT** is the only one of the garden restaurants left with good food and location. At 151, Long Jin Xi Road, Tel. 81815955 or 81817038, it is also extremely interesting for its hundreds of varieties of dim sum. A reservation here is mandatory for the fancy, private banquet rooms, especially the Reception Dining Hall with its traditional, redwood Chinese furniture and beautiful blue glass windows. This historic old restaurant is set around a large pond.

The restaurants in the top hotels – the **GARDEN, CHINA**, and **WHITE SWAN** – are excellent for both Chinese and western food. The **BAIYUN** and **DONG FANG HOTELS** are good for Chinese. Try the 'Drunken Prawns' and the crisp-skinned pigeon. At the **GITIC RIVER-SIDE HOTEL** try the steamed prawns, scallops, and deep-fried duck maws. Too adventurous? They have sweet and sour pork too.

The **GUANGZHOU RESTAURANT** *(four branches, the most convenient of which is at 112 Tiyudong Road; the telephone of the one near the Tianhe Railway Station is 87579138; the number for the branch at 1 Wen Chang Nam Road, close to a parking garage and closer to the White Swan Hotel is 81888388, 81862285 or 81862439).* is still one of the best Cantonese restaurants in town. The service is good, the food great and it has been inventing new dishes. Try the sauteed clams with Xo sauce and peppers, and sauteed shrimp with vegetables stuffed with Yunnan ham and mushrooms. There's also the vegetables with soup and sauteed preserved egg.

The dim sum restaurant at the **GARDEN HOTEL**, still considered one of the best such in town, has a new twist. It still has women rolling trolleys full of steaming pastries to your table, but you can also go to a buffet table where cooks will fry or steam on the spot anything you point at.

The **XIHU MARKET** also has food stalls (mostly dirty and not well developed) but some foreigners love it. It is open to about midnight, and is near the White Swan and the Cultural Park.

The two best Japanese restaurants are the **HIRATA**, *third floor, White Swan Hotel, Tel. 81886968 X 30009*; and the **SUISHAYA**, *third floor, 301-303 Huan Shi Zhong Road, Tel. 83382288 X 315.*

The best Korean Restaurants are the **JIANG NAN HAN GOU LIAO LI**, *first floor, 348 Jiu Nan Da Road, Tel. 84418888*; and the **JU GUI**, *World Trading and Exhibition Center, 117 Liu Hua Road, Tel. 86678000.*

> ## BEWARE THE KARAOKE CRAZE IN GUANGZHOU!
> *A word of warning. Guangzhou people have gone karaoke mad to the point of insisting on singing into a microphone at lunch and dinner. Many private restaurant dining rooms now have karaoke. If you can't stand amateur singing, let it be known, before you insult your host, that you'd like a nice quiet place in which to eat – without music.*

For lighter, cheaper food like noodles, congee, and dim sum, try China Hotel's **FOOD STREET**, Garden Hotel's **LAI WAN MARKET**, and the Holiday Inn"'s **DAI PAI DONG FOOD ALLEY**.

For western snacks like hamburgers, there's the Canadian joint-venture **TIMMY'S**, down river from the Nanfang Department Store. For fast food, **MEI XIN (MAXIM'S)** is in Liu Hua Park, **CAFE DE CORAL**, and two **PIZZA HUT's**. A **KFC** is between the railway station and the Garden Hotel on Huanshi Road, and **McDONALD'S** has opened at the Guangdong International Hotel.

SEEING THE SIGHTS

If you only have one day, visit the Chen (Zhen) Family Hall, the Han Dynasty Mausoleum Museum, the Temple of the Six Banyan Trees/ Flower Pagoda (for exotic Chinese architecture), and the Qing Ping Free Market (for genuine local color). You could also decide on a garden (if you like plants), or an arts and crafts factory.

Be sure to eat in one of the old garden restaurants, have dim sum at the Banxi Restaurant or China Hotel, and a drink in the riverside coffee shop or bar at the White Swan Hotel. If you have more time (at least a day), go to Foshan for the ancestral temple and ceramics. Guangzhou is not noted as a prime tourist destination, but it has enough to do for two or three days.

Taxis are plentiful. In 1998, the east-west metro line should go from the Guangzhou Steel Plant to the East Railway station with 16 stations (through Fangchun, Liwan, Yuexiu, Dongshan and Tianhe).

The **Chen Family Hall**, *7 Shongshan Road; Tel. 81841559, 81814559*, is well worth a visit. It was built in the 1890s with nine halls and six courtyards of different sizes and has been used as a school. Its windows, door frames, and pavilions are all lavishly decorated with intricate carvings and sculptures, almost too much for the mind to absorb at once. Take it in small doses. Because the army occupied these buildings during the Cultural Revolution, the artwork suffered very little damage.

The **Guangdong Folk Arts and Crafts Museum** is located here now, and it is a good place to shop for linens. Just don't let the bargains distract you from the ceramic opera scenes on the roofs and the charming carved mice eating the lichees on the pillars.

The **Liu Rong** (Six Banyan Trees) **Temple**, *Liu Rong Road, Tel. 83344926*, was founded 1,400 years ago. It was so named because the famous Tang poet Su Dong Po found six luxuriant banyan trees there in 1100. The present buildings were rebuilt in 1989. Its nine-story Flower Pagoda is 57.6 meters high and originally built in 537. It can be climbed for a good view and the exercise. Monks chant Tuesday and Friday mornings.

The **Qing Ping Free Market** (Qing Ping Ziyou Shi Chang), is the largest herb market in the city (about five blocks), where you can find dehydrated lizards, snakes, plants, and weird-looking roots. It has some live animals, too, for pets or food, including pangolins (an endangered species) and civet cat. This market is not for children nor the squeamish as it has skinned barbecued dog dangling in the stalls. It also has one block of antiques for sale.

This market is filthy, always crowded, but fascinating even if you don't want to buy anything. It is within a 20 minute walk of the White Swan Hotel, north and west about three blocks in each direction and open 6 am to 6 pm. As in all crowded places anywhere in the world, beware of pickpockets!

THE MUSEUM OF THE NANYUE KING

*Guangzhou has a 2,100-year-old "imperial" tomb now officially known as the **Museum of the Western Han Dynasty Mausoleum of the Nanyue King**, Tel. 86664920, 86678030. The Nanyue Kingdom was founded by one of the ruling generals of the first emperor Qin. After Qinshihuang's death in 210 B.C., his son and successor who lacked his father's fanatical drive, let loose the reins of empire. Chao T'o, the surviving general in charge of south China declared himself Emperor of Nanyue.*

*The Han dynasty took over China in 206 B.C. Five years later, the Nanyue Emperor was given the choice of uncrowning himself and renewing his allegiance to the Chinese empire, or bringing suffering on his people. Chao T'o chose the former, and died at the ripe old age of 93 in 137 B.C. (Read Herold J. Wiens' **China's March towards the Tropics**.) More than 1,000 burial objects were excavated. Included in the find were a chariot, ritual bronzes, gold and silver vessels, ivory and lacquerware, jades, musical instruments, weapons, and tools. They also buried human sacrifices, concubines, and servants with him. The relics are beautifully displayed, with English titles, at the actual site. Don't miss the video, in English, of the excavation. The museum is about half a block behind the China Hotel on Jiefang Road towards the river.*

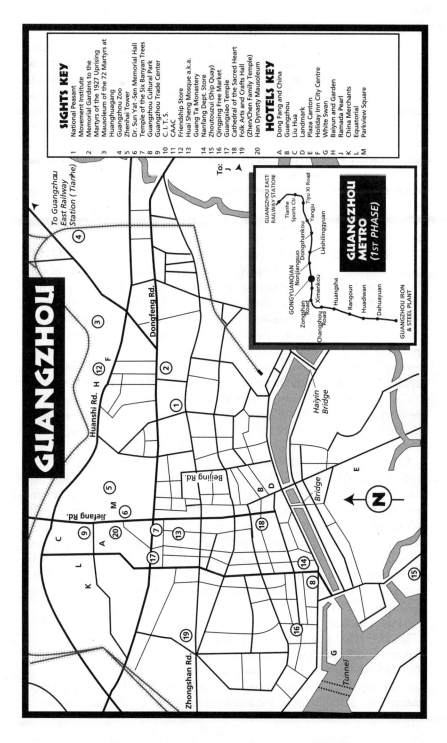

GUANGZHOU

SIGHTS KEY

1 National Peasant Movement Institute
2 Memorial Gardens to the Martyrs of the 1927 Uprising
3 Mausoleum of the 72 Martyrs at Huanghuagang
4 Guangzhou Zoo
5 Zhenhai Tower
6 Dr. Sun Yat-Sen Memorial Hall
7 Temple of the Six Banyan Trees
8 Guangzhou Cultural Park
9 Guangzhou Trade Center
10 C.I.T.S.
11 CAAC
12 Friendship Store
13 Huai Sheng Mosque a.k.a. Guang Ta Monastery
14 Nanfang Dept. Store
15 Zhoutouzui (Ship Quay)
16 Qingping Free Market
17 Guangxiao Temple
18 Cathedral of the Sacred Heart
19 Folk Arts and Crafts Hall (Zhen/Chen Family Temple)
20 Han Dynasty Mausoleum

HOTELS KEY

A Dong Fang and China
B Guangzhou
C Liu Hua
D Landmark
E Plaza Canton
F Holiday Inn City Centre
G White Swan
H Baiyun and Garden
J Ramada Pearl
K China Merchants
L Equatorial
M Parkview Square

To Guangzhou East Railway Station (Tianhe)

Dongfeng Rd.

Huanshi Rd.

Beijing Rd.

Jiefang Rd.

Zhongshan Rd.

Haiyin Bridge

Bridge

Tunnel

GUANGZHOU METRO (1ST PHASE)

GUANGZHOU EAST RAILWAY STATION
Tianhe Sports Ctr.
Tiyu Xi Road
Yangju
Dongshankou
Nonjiangsuo
GONGYUANQIAN
Zhongshan Road
Changshou Road
Ximenkou
Huangsha
Rangoun
Huadiwan
Dahuayuan
Lieshilingyuan
GUANGZHOU IRON & STEEL PLANT

N

To: J

If You Have More Time or Interest

Shamian (Shamien, Shameen) **Island**, in the Pearl River in central Guangzhou, became a British and French concession in 1859-60. It was then an 80-acre sandbank, later built into a European ghetto and much resented by the Chinese. The architecture reflects its European occupants, but, unfortunately, so many of the old buildings have been destroyed that its overall charm has almost disappeared. The island is joined to the mainland by bridges and now cars are allowed in. You can still find some of the old buildings, but it isn't the same as it was before the fancy White Swan Hotel was built in 1982. At the western tip of the island, this 31-story luxury hotel, built on reclaimed land, is among the top international-standard hotels in China. On Sundays, the English Corner is on Shamian Island (and at the Guangzhou Library on Zhongshan Road).

The **Guangdong Provincial Museum**, *Wenming Road, Tel. 83832195*, displays relics of local primitive society and is not as good as the Guangzhou Museum. The **Guangzhou Museum**, *Tel. 3330627*, is in the Zhenhai (Sea-dominating) Tower in Yuexiu Park and is better organized. The original tower itself was built in 1380 to assert the power of the Ming dynasty. It has been rebuilt several times since then. Located at one of the highest points in the city, it has been used as a pleasure palace for high-ranking imperial officials and as a Nationalist hospital. Starting with prehistory, on the second floor, to revolutionary history, on the fifth, the exhibits include some interesting old clocks, ceramics, and a painting of the burning of the 20,000 chests of opium. For a city of this size and wealth, however, you would expect a better, larger museum, especially one about Overseas Chinese.

The **Mausoleum of the Seventy-two Martyrs** at Huanghuagang (Yellow Flower) Hill (Xianlie Road) is past the Garden Hotel and the Friendship Store on the road to the zoo. This commemorates an unsuccessful attempt to overthrow the Qing in 1911, led by Dr. Sun Yat-sen. Of special interest to visitors of Chinese ancestry, this 260,000 square-meter park was built with donations from Chinese Nationalists' Leagues around the world. The stones in the main monument are inscribed in English with the names of the donors, among these Chicago, Illinois; Moose Jaw, Saskatchewan; and Lima, Peru. The miniature Statue of Liberty on top was replaced in 1987.

The **National Peasant Movement Institute**, *42 Zhongshan 4-Road, Tel. 83333936*, was a school for 327 peasant leaders from 20 provinces and regions. It was open only from May to September 1926 in an old temple. Mao Zedong was the director and Zhou Enlai a teacher.

The **Dr. Sun Yat-sen Memorial Hall**, *Tel. 83332430*, is a theater seating over 4,500, built in 1931 and expanded in 1975. This building is architecturally important because its huge hall is supported by four vertical concrete beams that branch out on top to form the octagonal roof. The modern technique and pure Chinese style, with its bright blue circus-tent-shaped ceramic roof, is unique. (For more on the life of Dr. Sun, see *Nanjing*.)

The ***Guangxiao Temple**, *109 Sheshi Road at Guangxiao Road; Tel. 83346775, 83358877,* has the longest history in the city. It was founded on the site of the residence of the King of the Southern Yue Kingdom. The temple was built in 397 A.D. to commemorate the visit of the Indian monk Dharmayasas, and is the largest temple in south China. An iron pagoda dated 967 A.D. stands inside, historic, well preserved, but not beautiful. The present buildings are from the Five Dynasties to the Ming. The attractive Sixth Patriarch's Hair-burying Pagoda is a miniature of the Flower Pagoda. See also *Shaoguan*.

The **Huaisheng** (Remember the Sage) **Mosque** and **Guangta** (Smooth) **Minaret**, *Guangta Lu; Tel. 83333593*, is only of historical value. It is not the least bit attractive. Considered the oldest mosque in China, it was built in 627 A.D. by Arab traders and is open daily. Visitors can climb its minaret, which has also been used as a lighthouse. The 26.3 meter minaret is said to be original. The tomb of the founding Moslem missionary, Sad Ibn Abu Waggas, is in the Orchid Garden.

The **Shishi** (Cathedral of the Sacred Heart), *Yide Road; Tel. 83336737,* was built in 1863-88. Its 57.95 meter Gothic spire was probably built deliberately taller than the pagoda nearby. Shishi means Stone House. It was closed as a church during the Cultural Revolution and used as a storehouse until 1979. Now it has been restored almost to its previous grandeur. Mass has been celebrated weekdays at 6 am and Sundays and festivals at 6, 7:30, and 8:30 am.

You can book the **Pearl River boat ride** with dinner through your hotels from April to October (about 7:30 pm, 30 Pier, Xiti) but its service needs work.

Gardens, Parks, & Zoos

Depending on the season, don't forget to bring your own insect repellent.

The **South China Botanical Garden** (Longyandong), in the north of the city; *Tel. 87705626, 87705693*, is a research institute of the Chinese Academy of Science. One of the world's largest botanical gardens, this 300-hectare garden is home to more than 2000 species of tropical and subtropical plants. Ask also about the Qinghui Garden in Shunde.

The **Orchid Garden**, *Dabei Road*, west of Yuexiu Park and behind the Foreign Trade Center; *Tel. 86677255*, is a delight for orchid lovers. It has over 100 species and 10,000 plants on five hectares.

The **Xi Yuan** (West Garden), *next to Dongfeng 1-Road; Tel. 81885867*, specializes in penjing, miniature trees and landscapes, of the Lingnan School.

The **Guangzhou Zoo**, *Xianli Road, Tel. 87752702*, is in the northeastern suburbs. It has 200 species, including pandas.

Yuexiu Park, *Jiefang Bei Road, Tel. 83346014*, within walking distance of the China Hotel, is the largest in the city, on 92.8 hectares. There you can find the sculpture of the five goats, symbol of Guangzhou. Or you can try **Liuhua Park**, *Xicun Gong Road, Tel. 86664095*, built in 1957-59, with more than 800,000 square meters.

Guangzhou Cultural Park, *near the Nanfang Department Store on Xiti 2-Ma Road, Tel. 81882488*, covers 8.3 hectares. More pavement and less sylvan than other parks, it is best avoided after 7 pm unless you want to mingle with masses of people enjoying Chinese opera, puppet shows, acrobats, exhibit halls, basketball games, and roller-skating. The annual Lantern Festival and flower shows are held here. A reproduction of a Han dynasty 'city' has wax figures in imperial period dress. (206 B.C. to 220 A.D.).

Fun & Games

You can rent **bicycles** near the back door of the White Swan Hotel, and from some other hotels. They are not allowed on some main streets during the day. A couple of **golf courses** have opened. And look on apartment building bulletin boards at the China and Garden Hotels, and Park 'N' Shop for announcements about the likes of the expatriate Hash House Harriers ("a drinking club with a running problem.")

Day Trips

Newly developed for tourism is **Lotus Flower Hill** (30 kilometers from Guangzhou), the **Yamen Fort** (50 kilometers toward Hong Kong) and **Dongguan**, where Lin Zexu burned the opium. The Huangpu Military Academy (1924) should be of interest to modern history buffs. It's on **Changzhou Island**, *Huangpu, Tel. 82201082*. The **Museum of Hong Xiuquan's Former Residence** (leader of the Taipings) is in Guanglubu Village, Huaxian County, 18 kilometers from the city.

Another escape from the city is a visit to a nearby village, many of which grow and preserve fruit and olives for export, an interesting as well as delicious process, as guests are frequently given samples. Lucky are those who go during the lichee season! (April to late June.)

The **Flying Dragon World Fun City** (Feilong Shi Jie), in Dashi Town about 10 kilometers from Guangzhou is supposed to be the largest theme park in China. Centered on snakes, it has a 53.8 meter-high pagoda with an elevator, the temple of the mythical White Snake, and a snake garden.

Here you can eat snakes, and buy medicines made from them and take in a show featuring women playing with snakes.

Festivals

There's a festival in the second lunar month, 10th to 13th day, at the Nanhai God Temple, Miaotou village, Huangpu, *Tel. 82270927*. The Happy Festival with performing arts groups is in the autumn. A fine food festival takes place during the autumn Trade Fair.

The **Canton Trade Fair** is held annually from April 15 to April 25, and October 15 to October 29 at the Foreign Trade Center. North Americans can make arrangements through the U.S. China Travel Service, San Francisco, *Tel. (415) 398-6627 or 1-800-332-2831. Fax 398-6669*. Pickpockets as well as traders visit Guangzhou for the event, so be careful. You can also apply for an invitation through a Chinese trading corporation or the China Foreign Trade Center Group, *117 Liu Hua Road, 510014. Fax 86665851*. During the fair, you can buy a pass in its Dong Fang Hotel office. In the early 1990s, over 40,000 traders attended each fair.

NIGHTLIFE & ENTERTAINMENT

Lucy's Bar on Shamien Island; the bars in the China, White Swan, and Garden Hotels; and the Holiday Inn are popular with foreigners. The **Adler** is a brew pub near the Landmark Hotel, *Hai Zhu Square*, and the **Hill Bar** is on *Huanshi Dong Road* between the Friendship Store and the GITIC International.

The **Viking Bar** is two blocks to the left out of the China Hotel.

SHOPPING

Locally made goods are carvings of ivory, jade, bamboo, and wood, painted porcelain (porcelain from Jingdezhen; handpainted here) and gold and silver jewelry. Shantou (Swatow) drawnworks and embroidery are famous, and are cheaper here.

The main shopping area is around **Zhongshan 5-Road** and **Beijing Road**. The **Guangzhou Department Store** is the best at *12 Xihu Road (and Beijing Road), Tel. 83331817*. Also good is the **Nan Fang Da Sha** department store at *49 Yian Jiang Xi Road, Tel. 81861261*.

China Hotel's stores are trying to become exclusive and upmarket. The shops in the World Trade Centre in front of the Friendship Store on Huanshi Dong Road are the most expensive in town.

The **Friendship Store** is at *369 Huanshi Dong Road, Tel. 83336628*, and open 8:30 am to 9 pm. It is moderately priced and is like most other big department stores in the city with imported name brands and locally manufactured goods. It is across from the Garden Hotel and next to the

Baiyun. The store in the Trade Fair Building is also a state shop with medium prices.

The **Qing Ping Free Market** mentioned above has been selling antiques like old coins, water pipes, and old porcelain, with many fakes and reproductions. Lots of fun is the **antique street market** at about *10 Da He Road near Qing Ping Road*. Across the street from the hospital is a lane with a red gate and curved gold Chinese roof. This **Da He Lu Market** has about 300 stalls and is open daily from about 9 am to about 5 pm. The goods are the usual "silver" jewelery, old ceramics, tea pots, reproductions and fakes, more fun than serious but you might find some treasures there. I did.

The stores at the **White Swan Hotel** have good quality and variety for silks, crafts and antiques. The **#Guangdong Cultural Relics Store**, is at *696 Renmin Bei Road, Tel. 86678608*. The **Guangzhou Antique Store** is at *170 Wende Bei Road, Tel. 83330175*.

The **Huanghua Free Market** and the **Xihu Night Market** (open from 7 to 10 pm) are good for casual clothes, mainly T-shirts, dresses, jackets, and trousers. Prices for Hong Kong-made items can be about three to five times Hong Kong prices, so beware. Some locally-made clothes, factory overruns, and seconds are reasonably priced there.

EXCURSIONS FROM GUANGZHOU
Foshan

Foshan (Fashan) is about 25 kilometers southwest of Guangzhou by expressway, with a population of 365,000. China United Airlines flies between Foshan and Beijing, Nanjing, and several other cities. It is a pleasant but not a world-class destination, interesting because of its prosperity, the Ancestral Temple, and Shiwan ceramics. You can also reach it by train. It is a good one-day excursion from Guangzhou.

Named 'Hill of Buddhas' because a mound of Buddhist statues were excavated here, this is one of the **Four Ancient Towns of China**. The city is over 1,300 years old and is famous for its handicrafts. In addition, it makes machines, electronics, chemicals, textiles, plastics, pharmaceuticals, and cement. It has a half-a-kilometers-long street of locally made ceramic and pottery stores.

The **Ancestral Temple**, now the **Foshan Municipal Museum**, was originally erected in the Song (Emperor Yuanfeng, 1078-1085) and rebuilt in 1372 after a disastrous fire. Expanded and rebuilt after Liberation, the temple contains sculptures, ancient relics, and a 2,500 kilogram bronze figure named Northern Emperor. Note the variety of decorations on the bases of the arches and the stone, wood, and brick carvings. Four of the statues are made of paper, the others of wood or clay.

The roof, decorated with Shiwan pottery figures, is one of the most elaborate in the country. A little gaudy, but artistically and culturally important.

Locally made are cuttlebone sculptures, brick carvings, silk, lanterns, paper-cuts, and of course the famous Shiwan ceramics. **Foshan Folk Art Institute** produces palace lanterns, T-shirts, and paper cuts. It is a training institute for master crafts people in all fields. The **Shiwan Artistic Ceramic Factory** is one of the most famous porcelain factories in China; some of its works adorn the tops of many temples in south China and Hong Kong. Its collection of maroon-robed lohan, with expressive, bulging eyes and unglazed faces, is well known. Its show room exhibits the work of many masters. Tours usually visit a silk factory too.

An air-conditioned bus with television goes from the station near the Foshan Hotel in Foshan to **Hai'an** (from where you can get a ferry to Haikou on Hainan Island). The trip takes about 10 hours.

The best food is in the hotels and the **CHANCHEN CITY RESTAURANT**, *107 Renmin Road, Tel. 2226733*. All of these hotels have Hong Kong television reception. The best hotel is the Golden City.

FOSHAN HOTEL *(Binguan), 75 Fenjiang Nan Rd., 528000. Three stars, Tel. 3335338. Fax 3352347. Dist.A.P. eight km. Dist.R.W. three km.*

Attractive downtown garden hotel. 1973. Eight stories. 214 rooms. Extension built in 1993-4. B.C. Outdoor pool. Gym. IDD. Japanese and Chaozhou food. CITS.

GOLDEN CITY HOTEL *(Jin Cheng Dajiudian), 48 Fenjiang Nan Rd., 528000. Three stars, Tel. 3357228. Fax 3353924. Dist. A.P. eight km. Dist.R.W. three km. Credit Cards.*

Downtown location across from Exhibition Center. Built 1989. 19 stories. 180 rooms. IDD. B.C. Outdoor pool and gym.

CITS is at *Foshan Hotel, Tel. 3353338, 2223338, Fax 2248944*; **CTS**, *Overseas Chinese Hotel, Tel. 2223828*; **Guangdong Nanhai Tourism Bureau**, 69, Shidong Xia Road, 528000, Tel. 6332401 X 2067, Fax 6337423. **Police** are at *Tel. 110* and the telephone code is *0757*.

BY BUS TO HONG KONG

Buses to Hong Kong from Guangzhou are cheaper but not faster than taking the train. After booking (preferably three days in advance) you only need to arrive at your hotel terminal fifteen minutes before departure. The Garden Hotel has the most buses. The double decker Citibus is less comfortable than GD-HK Bus Company, but it has connections to Admiralty on the Hong Kong side. The three to four hour trip means shorter lines but struggles with luggage at the two border points. Avoid arriving in Hong Kong during rush hours.

Jiangman

Jiangman (Kiangmen or Kongmoon in Cantonese) is about 100 kilometers south of Guangzhou. You can reach this old waterfront city by road or ship from Guangzhou or by daily non-stop four-hour ferry from Hong Kong and Macau. It is mainly for people of Chinese origin finding their roots. There isn't much to see except a charming old city but Jiangman City is made up of five counties: Xinhui, Heshan, Kaiping, Enping, and Taishan. Xinhui is 20 minutes away by road.

The small Ming dynasty **Chen Bai Sha Temple** was built in honor of a famous philosopher. Two-fifths of the people here are Overseas Chinese or have Overseas Chinese relatives and therefore receive remittances from abroad.

The newest, most modern hotel is the Crystal Palace. The East Lake is a good garden-style hotel. Both are close together in the suburbs, five kilometers from the port and two kilometers from the bus station. Good walks are in the neighborhood.

CRYSTAL PALACE *(Yin Jing Jiudian), 22 Guang Hou Rd., 529051. Four stars, Tel. 3373288. Fax 3373001. Credit Cards.*

Built 1990. Extension in 1994. 214 spacious rooms. B.C. Large pool. Good food. H.K.T.V. Gym. Bowling and tennis. Helipad. H.K.J.V.

EAST LAKE HOTEL *(Dong Hu Binguan), 15 Guang Hou Rd., 529051. Three stars, Tel. 3363611. Fax 3361010, 3351010. Credit Cards.*

Built 1973, ren. 1993. Three stories, 208 small rooms. 1990 Azalea Villa with only suites. B.C., H.K.T.V. IDD. Pool.

Travel information for Jiangman: **CITS,** *13 Nonglin Road, 529000. Tel. 3356562, 3353384;* **CTS,** *15 Gangkou Road, 529051. Tel. 3333611. Fax 3351010.* The telephone code is *07682.*

Shantou

Shantou (Chaoshan), a port city and Special Economic Zone in northeastern Guangdong province, is 350 kilometers by air north of Guangzhou, 10 hours by bus. It soon can also be reached by expressway from Shenzhen in three hours, and by ship from Hong Kong. Flights currently connect with Hong Kong, Singapore, Bangkok, Kuala Lumpur and 36 Chinese cities. Air connections are planned with Japan and train with Guangzhou.

Shantou is the ancestral home of innumerable Chinese emigrants to Southeast Asia, Japan, and Africa. Many Chinese were also kidnapped from here and sent to Cuba in the late 1800s. Today about 15% of the population receives remittances from overseas. With the two municipal areas of Shantou and Chaozhou, and 11 counties, it has a population of about 10 million. The weather is mild, with an annual rainfall of 1,400 to 2,000 millimeters, mainly in the summer.

Shantou is famous for its **port**. At one time Europeans used it for the importation of opium to China. The district is also famous for its drawnworks, lace and embroidery. It produces carpets, painted porcelain, jewelry, bamboo carvings, lacquer, and stone, shell, and gilded wood carvings.

Shantou is a 2,000-year-old town to which disgraced officers of the Tang were exiled, notably Han Yu, who objected to his emperor spending so much money on Buddhist structures. Ling Shan Temple (Tang) in Chaoyang County has a record of his dispute with the founder of the temple.

In Shantou city, 30 kilometers south of Chaozhou, are the **Arts and Crafts Exhibition** and **Zhong Shan Park**, with its 'gardens within gardens.' To the east of Shantou is tiny **Maya Islet**, seven kilometers by ferry with a temple to Sea Goddess Mazu and the old British Customs House. A globe at Shantou University marks the Tropic of Cancer.

Chaozhou is one of the traditional **Four Famous Ancient Towns**, and still has Tang and Song architecture. Among the attractions in Chaozhou City are: the **Kaiyuan Temple** from the Tang dynasty (with its rare set of Buddhist sutras presented by a Qing emperor), **West Lake Park**, the arts and crafts factory, and the embroidery factory. Across the Xiangzi Bridge is the Han Wen-gong Temple.

Both of the top hotels are in the Special Economic Zone within the main urban area.

GOLDEN GULF HOTEL *(Jin Hai Wan Da Jiudian)*, *Jinsha Dong Rd., Shantou, 515041. Five stars, Tel. 8263263. Fax 8265163.*

Built 1991. 28 stories, 300 units. Pool, sauna, tennis, and gym. Dong Fang (Guangzhou) Group management.

SHANTOU INTERNATIONAL HOTEL *(Guoji Da Jiudian)*, *Jin Sha Dong Rd., 515041. Four stars, Tel. 8263263. Fax 8451796, 8293678. Dist.A.P. 15 km. Credit Cards.*

Built 1988. 26 stories. 353 rooms. IDD. B.C. USTV. Revolving restaurant. Inhouse movies, 24-hr room service.

Travel information for Shantou: **CITS** is at *136 Yuejin Road, Shantou. Tel. 8295620, 8295621. Fax 8451796, 8293678.* The telephone code is *0754.*

Shaoguan

Shaoguan, the city, is not pretty enough to be worth the trip. The surrounding countryside, however, is a nice mix of anthropology and unusual mountain scenery. The area was settled 120,000 years ago! You can visit with some of the 130,000 Yao and Zhuang minority peoples. If you want to get off the beaten path, especially in winter, when other parts of China are too cold, you might consider Shaoguan.

Shaoguan is in northern Guangdong near the Hunan, Jiangxi, and Guangxi borders. A city of over 410,000 people on the Beijing-Guangzhou railway, 220 kilometers from Guangzhou, it should have a railway line from Shenzhen and an airport soon. It has 310 frost- free days, with an annual rainfall of up to 220 millimeters mainly in the summer. The hottest temperature in summer could be 40 degrees centigrade; the coldest in winter is an occasional minus four.

Archaeologists have found human skull fossils in Maba District, Qujiang County, dating from 120,000 years ago. You can visit the **Museum of Maba Man**, 19 kilometers south of Shaoguan, two kilometers from Maba town. You can also tour the one-kilometer-long cave where they found the bones. In summer you can go white-water rafting at Jiulong Shibatan (Nine Dragon Shoals) near Pinshi.

Tourists can also visit the 1,400-year-old **Nanhua** (South China) **Temple** in Qujiang County, 24 kilometers south of Shaoguan. This recently restored temple has a pagoda dating from the Ming and a statue of the Priest Huineng, the abbot in 677 A.D. who developed the Dhyana sect. During the Cultural Revolution, his bones were found inside the statue. Also in the temple are wooden arhats and a 5000-kg bronze bell (both Song). This, the largest temple in South China, is on 12,000 square meters of land.

Shaoguan city's Shaoguan Hotel is a centrally-located high-rise while the Green Lake is in the leafy outskirts. Both are three stars. Other hotels in the area are barely adequate.

GREEN LAKE VILLA HOTEL *(Bihu Shan Zhuang), Shahu Rd., 512028. Three stars, Tel. 774871. Fax 769930. Dist A.P. 35 km. Dist R.W. six km.*

Attractive, isolated setting. Built 1987-1988. Ren. 1990. Two stories, 128 rooms. IDD. Credit Cards., bicycles.

SHAOGUAN HOTEL, *162 Jiefang Rd., 512000. Tel. 8818870.*

For Shaoguan travel information: **CITS** is at *Tel. 8870982, Fax 8884601.* The telephone code is *0751.*

Taishan

Taishan (Cantonese, Toishan; Toishanese, Hoishan) should not be confused with Taishan, the mountain in Shandong farther north, listed in this guide under Tai'an. Taishan is a county on the southern coast of Guangdong province, 146 kilometers southwest of Guangzhou and about 80 kilometers as the crow flies, west of Aomen (Macau). You should reach Taicheng, the county seat, by public minibus from Guangzhou in about three hours. Check with China Travel Service in Guangzhou. Their buses have been leaving twice a day.

A fast way to go there from Hong Kong is the four-hour ferry to Guanghoi, and then bus or taxi to Taicheng.

Taishan is important because many natives left it and their families for the Chinatowns of North America, Southeast Asia and Australia. Many of these and their descendants visit to find their roots. For tourists, the attractions here are rural; you should find it a restful exposure to south China. It does not have magnificent temples and palaces but it still retains a lot of its old over-the-sidewalk architecture and charm. But things are changing so get there soon.

You can visit cottage industries like embroidery, artistic ceramics, bamboo weaving, etc.; or explore a village. Near the Overseas Chinese Hotel is a statue of Chen Yu Hi, a Chinese- American who returned to China to start in 1906 the first railway line by a private company in China. The 100 kilometer-long track was used from 1912 to 1942 when it was destroyed by the Japanese. The old railway station still standing nearby is patterned after one in Seattle at the time. There is also a small museum. The population of Taicheng is about 980,000.

On the outskirts of town is a seven-story Ming pagoda. **Stone Flower Mountain**, one of Taishan's eight scenic attractions, is about two kilometers northeast of the town with an artificial lake and weird rock formations. Its **Stone Flower Mountain Inn** (*Shihua Shan Lu Guan*), *Tel. 5525834*) has classes for foreigners and local people. Foreign students have taught English here. Write Mr. Feng Yuan Chao at the Taishan Tour Company.

Shang Chuan Island's **Fei Sa Beach** is about 64 kilometers south of Taicheng, plus a 40-minute boat ride. It has four kilometers of beach and clear water. The inns there are not up to standard but the new **Chuan Island Provincial Holiday Resort** is being built. *(For information, Tel. (750)5534218 or fax 5534218.)* Nearby are the **St. Francis Xavier Church** where the Jesuit died in 1552 (his body is on display in Goa), and a primeval forest inhabited by 3,000 monkeys. To the east is Zhongshan County, birthplace of Dr. Sun Yixian (Sun Yat-sen).

Taicheng has a unique festival on the ninth day of the ninth lunar month. During the Qing, a young scholar, angry that he could not get a state post, buried his poems and articles in a tomb on one of the mountains. Then he became sucessful. Ever since, people have been visiting the tomb for luck.

Taishan food is basically the same as Cantonese, but there are some dishes that are unique, like mud fish, steamed minced pork with salted egg, and peanuts fried with water chestnuts.

After the opening of a **Ramada Hotel** here with 244 rooms, the Ramada should be the best hotel until the Garden Hotel's new 150-room extension is finished in 1997.

GARDEN HOTEL *(Yuanlin Jiu Dian), 529200. Tel. 5525890 or fax 5531573. Three stars. Dist.bus station one kilometer. Credit Cards.*
Attractive garden-style hotel on the edge of a man-made lake at the base of a mountain. 108 rooms. Hot spring water in all rooms. CITS. IDD. H.K.J.V. KYZ Management.

TAISHAN HOTEL (Binguan), Orchard Village, Taicheng, 529200. Three stars. Tel. 526888. Fax 522683. Credit Cards.
Built 1989-91. 12 stories. 80 small rooms. H.K.T.V. IDD. B.C.

The **Taishan Bureau of Travel and Tourism** and **Taishan Tour Company** are at *19 Stone Flower Overseas Chinese Village, Huan Bei Street, 529200. Tel. 525847, 529999.*

Xinhui

Xinhui (Cantonese Hsinhui; local dialect Sunwai) is a county about 80 kilometers southwest of Guangzhou. It dates from the Sui dynasty, 581 A.D. and claims the death also of the last Song emperor, the child with his prime minister. From here, many Chinese emigrated to America and Australia. It is in the heart of fan-palm country; every spare inch seems to have these trees whose leaves are woven into baskets, fans, and mats.

The county seat, Huicheng, has a population of about 110,000 and is a two-hour journey by road from Guangzhou. It is also a three-hour boat ride from Hong Kong, or an overnight boat ride from Guangzhou. (First you go to Jiangmen, and then it's a half-hour by road to Xinhui.) It will be on the Guangzhou-Zhuhai railway line. Huicheng is about 118 kilometers from Zhuhai.

You can visit the **fan-palm factory** or relax on very pretty 422 meter high **Guifeng Mountain**, *Tel. 6640693*, on which is **Yuhu** (Jade) **Lake**. A Han dynasty temple, destroyed during the Japanese war, has been rebuilt on the mountain. In another direction from the city and seven kilometers away, a magnificent 500 year old banyan tree, believed to be the largest in the world and called **Birds' Paradise**, *Tel. 6671924*, is home at night to thousands of cranes and egrets and is best seen at dusk at the edge of the city. A small **museum**, *Tel. 6665906*, is across from the Guifeng Guest House in the old Confucian Temple, first built in 1044.

In the southeastern part of the county 40 kilometers away are the **Yamen Fort**, *Tel. 6288551*, a modest building constructed in 1809 and used during the Opium War; and the remains of **Ciyuan Temple**, *Tel. 6288300*, recently renovated, first built in the Ming by a famous poet. It commemorates the Song officials and generals who fought heroically to the death, and the queen mother's "tomb." None of the attractions here are world class and Xinhui is primarily for Overseas Chinese looking for their roots.

The **Overseas Chinese Association** in Xinhui has been organizing free 20 day summer camps for people with roots in the county. Classes are in calligraphy, history, traditional medicine, etc. Ask travel agents in the Chinatowns of America or the Xinhui Tourism Bureau.

Aside from the woven palm products, this county is noted for its dried Mandarin orange peel used in soups and congee. (The best smell strongly of oranges.)

Huicheng, Xinhui's county seat, has three three-star hotels: the **KANGZHOU HOTEL** on *Guifeng Road, 529100, Tel. (07656)6663788. Fax 612878.* There's also the **XINHUI HOTEL** *(Jiudian) on Zhi Zhen Bei Road Zhong, 529100. Tel. 6663700. Fax 6667621.* It has 21 stories and 150 rooms and a revolving restaurant. The new **ZHONGLI HOTEL** *(Jiu Dian)* run by CTS is best.

The **Xinhui Tourism Bureau** is at *36 Zhuzi Road, Tel. 6619035, 6617771. Fax 6612122.* **CTS** is *Tel. 6663419. Fax 6667489.* The telephone code is *0750.*

Xiqiao Mountain

Xiqiao Mountain, about 25 kilometers away from Foshan, is a resort area with the three-star **XIQIAO MOUNTAIN HOTEL** *(Dajiudian)* at the base of a 400-meter-high mountain. Primarily for hikers, the mountain has three lakes, 44 caves, 72 peaks, 207 springs, innumerable waterfalls and eight villages. At the base are a small Ming tower and Qing Taoist temple, an amusement park and a cable car.

CTS is at *White Cloud Cave, Nanhai County 528200; Tel. 6886799.*

Zhaoqing

Zhaoqing (Chaoching) is about 100 kilometers west of Guangzhou on the west bank of the Xijiang River. You should visit it for its Seven Star Crags, and its relatively tranquil atmosphere, a good town for walkers and bicycles. It is also famous for its Duan inkstones. It can be reached by ship, bus, or train from Hong Kong or Guangzhou, or by railway from Guangzhou and soon direct trains from Shenzhen. It is building an airport. The population is about 200,000. The weather is subtropical, with an annual precipitation of 1599 millimeters mainly from April to August.

Known since ancient times, Zhaoqing was the home for six years of the Italian Jesuit missionary **Matteo Ricci**. He lived in 'Shuihing' in the 1580s. While no one knows exactly where Ricci's house was, an educated guess places it between the boat landing and the Ming pagoda in the old city by the river. The district here has a Song dynasty gate with houses that look like they haven't changed since Ricci's time. An earthen wall circles the old city and you can walk or bicycle it for an interesting experience.

For good background, read *The Wise Man from the West – Matteo Ricci and His Mission to China* by Vincent Cronin.

Zhaoqing was also one of the starting points of the Northern Expedition in 1926, and was not really developed as a resort until 1955. Then, 460-hectare **Star Lake** was created for irrigation, fish breeding, and scenery. Walkways, bridges, and lights were set up in the caves.

Seven Star Crags, so named because they appear placed like the seven stars of the Big Dipper, is like a potted miniature garden. Its mountains are very much like those of Guilin. You can climb 130-meter Heavenly Pillar for the view.

The seven crags are named Langfeng (Lofty Wind), Yuping (Jade Screen), Shishi (Stone Chamber), Tianzhu (Heavenly Pillar), Chanchu (Toad), Shinzhang (Stone Palm), and Apo (Hill Slope). The biggest cave is at the foot of Apo Crag and you can enter it by boat. If you hit the rocks at **Musical Instrument Rock**, you get different musical notes.

Zhaoqing also boasts the **Baiyun** (White Cloud) **Temple**, built in the Tang (618-907) and the Chongxi, Wenming, and Xufeng pagodas. Qingyun Temple is at the middle of 1000-meter-high Dinghu (Tripod) mountain, 18 kilometers northeast of Zhaoqing. You could also look for the Yuejiang Tower, and the Water and Moon Palace, from the Ming. These were damaged during the Cultural Revolution but are now restored.

The mountain, which is a nature preserve, has a 30 meter-high water fall on its northwest side.

Area shopping, in addition to the famous inkstones, include ivory and bone carvings, sandalwood fans, paintings, straw products, umbrellas, and jewelry. Ginseng Beer is made here too. An interesting store is the **Guangdong Zhaoqing Duanxi Factory of Famous Ink Stones** on Gongnong Road. The **night market** with some clothes, antiques, and crafts is between the Overseas Hotel and the Star Lake Hotel.

The CTS-owned restaurant in Sam Sui on the road towards Guangzhou is very good, simple, and with very fresh vegetables.

The best hotel by the lake in town is the Star Lake. Second is the Overseas Hotel. If you want to be away from town beside the lake, there's the Songtao but it isn't as good. They are all 80 kilometers from the closest airport in Foshan.

SONGTAO HOTEL *(Binguan), Seven Star Lake Resort, 526040. Three stars Tel. and fax 2824412. Dist.bus station four kilometers by road, two kilometers by boat across the lake. Dist.river port six km. Credit Cards.*

Set in the park between two of the crags (one 90 meters high.) Built 1978. Three and four stories. 211 rooms. IDD. B.C. USTV.

OVERSEAS CHINESE HOTEL *(Huaqiao Dasha), 90 Tianning Bei Lu, 526040. Three stars, Tel. 2232952. Fax 2231197. Dist.R.W. four km. Credit Cards.*

Near bus station, stores, night market and lake. Built 1987, ren. 1993. 239 rooms. USTV. B.C. IDD.

STAR LAKE HOTEL *(Xing Hu Sing Dajuidian), 37, 4th Duan Zhou Road, Four stars. Tel. 2221188. Fax 2236688. Credit Cards.* This downtown hotel is quite good, but its windows were constantly fogged up. It's close to the lake, and well located for the interesting night market outside. 31 storeys. 400 rooms. Swimming pool, mini-golf, and gym.

For Zhaoqing travel information: **CTS**, *Tel. 2833699 or fax 2231197*; **CITS**, *Tel. 2826984. Fax 2234492.* The telephone code is *0758*.

Zhongshan

Close to Portuguese-administered Macau, and across the Pearl River delta south of Hong Kong, **Zhongshan** (Chungshan) can be directly reached by 1 1/2 hour hovercraft from Hong Kong at least five times a day, or via Macau. It is about two hours by six-lane expressway, southwest of Guangzhou. An expressway with Shenzhen should be open in 1997. You can obtain visas for the whole of China at the port about 10 kilometers from Shiqi in 15 to 20 minutes. An instant camera is available for visa photos if working.

Zhongshan is usually included in tours from Hong Kong because it has the **former residence of Dr. Sun Yat-sen** (Sun Yixian) *in Cuiheng village, 26 kilometers from Shiqi, Tel. 5501691.* The father of the Chinese republic himself designed the house, a blend of Spanish and local styles. The flossy Sun Yixian Memorial Middle School and an interesting folk culture museum are nearby. For more about Dr. Sun Yat-sen see *Nanjing*.

Tours are also taken to **Guang Feng village**, *Shalong Town, Tel. 8558683*, ten minutes away by road, where you get a one-kilometre boat ride along a canal through purple water hyacinths to a village set up for tourists. On display at the village are snakes, an old farm equipment exhibit, archery, pig races, and birds' nest and sharks fin factory. The experience is relaxing and pleasant.

Shiqi (Shekki, Shekket) is the cultural, economic, and political center of Zhongshan City, which has 25 urban and rural districts. The urban population of Shiqi is 220,000. It is in water country, full of intriguing waterways begging to be explored. It has a lot of activity, and new buildings. Yet the water, the age-old river boats, could remind you of a much smaller, older Bangkok. The **Zhongshan** (Chung Shan) **Hot Spring Golf Club** is close to the **Zhongshan Hot Spring Resort**, *Sanxiang Commune, Zhongshan City, Tel. 6683888. In Hong Kong, Tel. 28335666, 28335723.* The Palmer Course Design Company, named after Arnold Palmer, designed the 18-hole, par 72 course. The club can arrange visas.

The top hotels in Zhongshan District City are the Zhongshan International and the Fu Hua. Reservations are recommended weekends and Hong Kong holidays. The Fu Hua and Zhongshan International are close together at the bridge in the center of Shiqi near the night market and shops. They are about even in quality, though guests at the International Hotel might be more likely to be disturbed by unsolicited visitors. A new hotel opposite the Fu Hua should open soon. All hotels here receive Hong Kong television programs.

CUIHENG HOTEL *(Binguan), Cuiheng Village, 528454. Three stars, Tel. 5502668. Fax 5503333.*

About 29 kilometers southeast of Shiqi; 24 kilometers from Zhongshan ferry port. Across road from post office and bus station, and a couple hundred meters from the home of Dr. Sun Yat-sen. 1988. Very modern looking hotel, with hotel's Rolls Royce parked in front. Three stories, 242 rooms. Villas. Pool. Wax museum on hill behind hotel. Amusement park.

FU HUA HOTEL *(Jiudian), 1 Fuhua Rd., Shiqi, 528401. Four stars, Tel. 8866888. Fax 8861862.*

Located 15 kilometers from Zhongshan port. Built 1986, ren. 1995. 19 stories, 242 rooms. Smoke hoods and emergency flashlights. Revolving restaurant on roof. Bank of China, H.K.T.V., B.C. IDD. Bowling. Garden. Separate building for sports with large swimming pool, night club, 30-piece gym, six-lane bowling, and sauna. Chaozhou food. 15% service charge. Weekend rates subject to 10% surcharge during Hong Kong holidays.

ZHONGSHAN (CHUNGSHAN) HOT SPRING HOTEL *(Wenquan), Shanxiang Township, 528463. Three stars, Tel. 6683888. Fax 6683333. Credit Cards.*

Located 20 kilometers northwest of Macau, and 37 kilometers south of Shiqi. Built 1980. 15 villas. H.K.J.V. Isolated rural setting next to golf course. Attractive garden style. 400 rooms. Shooting gallery. Horses. Children's playground. Two swimming pools.

ZHONGSHAN INTERNATIONAL HOTEL *(Guoji Jiudian), 142 Zhongshan Road Section Number One, Shiqi 528401. Four stars, Tel. 8633388. Fax 8833368. Dist.A.P. 56 km. Dist.R.W. 85 km. Credit Cards.*

Built 1986. 22 stories. 369 rooms. First-class well-maintained modern hotel in the center of the city. Revolving restaurant. B.C. Good quality stores. IDD. Four bowling lanes. Sauna. Outdoor pool open all year but not heated. Gives 20% discount any time. 10% service charge.

For Zhongshan travel information: **CTS**, *Fuhua Hotel, Tel. 8866888. Fax 8861888 or 8822369;* **CITS**, *142 Zhongshan Road, First Section, Shiqi, 528401. Tel. 8811888. Fax 8611376;* Telephone code, *0760.* For **tourist complaints**, *38 Zhongshan Road, 2nd Section, Tel. 8805211 or Supervisory Bureau of Tourism Quality of Guangdong Province, 185 Huanshi Xi Road,*

510010, Tel. 6677422. Fax 6665039; **Tourist Hotline,** *8611888, 8806928;* **Zhongshan Tourism Bureau,** *38 Zhong Shan 2nd Road, 528400, Tel. 8805211, 8806928. Fax 8806615.*

Zhuhai

Zhuhai is adjacent to the Portuguese colony of Macau across the Pearl River delta southwest of Hong Kong. You can reach this Special Economic Zone directly by ferry from Hong Kong or Shekou, or by road via Macao. Zhuhai is a two-hour drive from Guangzhou if you're lucky. A 140 kilometer expressway from Guangzhou should be finished soon. Its airport has links with 18 other Chinese cities. A railway between Zhuhai and Guangzhou and connected with the rest of the country should also be finished soon.

There has been talk also about the world's longest bridge extending 50 kilometers from here to Hong Kong but so far there have been no signs of it. You can get a three-day visa upon arrival without photos. You can extend this visa in Zhuhai (photos needed).

Zhuhai is one of the five largest tourist destinations in China with visitors mainly from Hong Kong and Macao, business travelers and weekend vacationers. The best beach is at **Juizhou Islet,** an area now being developed with a two-kilometer-long cable car, and old style fishing village, bird garden, and motor boats. The sea water is generally very murky in this region.

There's also an 18-hole **golf course** and international trade and exhibition center. See *Zhongshan* just above. The urban population is 160,000. **Zhuhai International Golf Club/Pearl Land Amusement Park** are adjacent, over 30 minutes by road north of the city. The amusement park is huge and has an 1.8 kilometer roller coaster, and a 36- seat, four-abreast ferris wheel. The golf club has a restaurant, Japanese-style bath, visa service, and cheap pick-up at Zhuhai port on the border.

Zhuhai has at least 83 hotels and resorts. The top hotel is the Zhuhai Resort, followed by the Yindu (Silver Capital). Most tour groups stay at the Zhuhai Hotel because of the good service and garden, or the Zhuhai Resort by the sea. The Gongbei Palace is beautiful with its garden but the service is not as good. Opening soon is the Grand Bay Hotel managed by KYZ, a Cathay International Hotel.

Reservations are needed weekends, July-August and Hong Kong holidays.

GONGBEI PALACE HOTEL *(Gongbei Binguan), Shuiwan Rd., Gongbei District 519020. Tel. 8886833. Credit Cards.*

Ten minute walk from Customs House at Macau border. Built 1984. Very attractive garden-style hotel with villas. 290 rooms. B.C. Gym. pool and beach. H.K.J.V.

YINDO HOTEL, *Yuehai Road, Gongbei, 519020. Tel. 8883388. Fax 8883311, 8892896.*

Built 1989, four kilometers from the Customs House has the best lobby, pool and sports. 299 rooms. European style decor. B.C. Outdoor pool, tennis, bowling and miniature golf.

ZHUHAI RESORT *(Dujiachun Jiu Dian, or Zhuhai Holiday Resort), Shi Hua Shan, 519015. Four stars, Tel. 3332038. Fax 3332036. Credit Cards.*

On waterfront. Buit 1986, ren. 1991. 10 stories, 462 rooms, 87 villas. IDD. HKTV and USTV. B.C. Tennis, bowling, outdoor pool, roller skating, horses, archery, and go-karts.

ZHUHAI HOTEL *(Binguan), Jingshan Road, 519015. Four stars, Tel. 3333718. Fax 3332339, 3332339. Credit Cards.*

Built 1982. Extension 1994. Total 422 rooms. Hong Kong and Macau J.V. Attractive garden-style hotel with villas. Well maintained. Three stories, 283 rooms. IDD. USTV. There are 'Stop-smoking' and male-fertility clinics. B.C. Tennis, Pool.

For Zhuhai travel information: **CITS** and **Overseas Travel Corp.**, *2-3/F Xinhai Bldg., Yuanlin Road, Jida, 519015, Tel. 3333859, 3334546, 3336698. Fax 3332822, 3336718. Hong Kong office, Tel. 23686181;* **CTS**, *4 Shuiwan Road, Gongbei 519020; Tel. 8885777 or Binnan Road, Xingzhou, 519000; Tel. 8886849. Fax 8888456;* **Zhuhai Tourism Bureau**, *6/F, Yongfa Building, Jiuzhou Da Dao Ji Da, Tel. 3334697. Fax 3333360.*

PRACTICAL INFORMATION

• **Ambulance**, *Tel. 120*

Consulates

If you need help with passports and visas, or other kinds of assistance:

• **Australia**, *GITIC Plaza, Tel. 83312738, 83311888 X 1503*
• **Canada**, *China Hotel, Suite 1563-4, Tel. 86660569 or 86663388X1563, fax 86672401*
• **Japan**, *Garden Hotel, Tel. 83343090, 83343009*
• **Malayssia**, *Tel. 87372988*
• **Poland**, *63 Shamian Street, Tel. 81865009, 81861854*
• **Thailand**, *White Swan Hotel, Tel. 81886968 X 3310*
• **U.S.**, *White Swan Hotel, Tel. 81888911 X 256, 81862441, Fax 81862341. United States Information Agency, Garden Hotel, Tel. 83354269, 83338999 X 7351*
• **Vietnam**, *13 Tao Jing Bei Lu, Tel. 83580555 X 1001 or X 604*

Travel Agents & Tourism Information

• **CITS**, *Open daily 8,30 to 12 noon; 2 to 5 pm. 179 Huanshi Road, 510010 (next to main railway station), Tel. 86677881, 86677151. Fax 86678048. For tickets, tours and other services, 86677449, 86666273, 86666089. Fax 86682344*

- **CTS**, *Guangdong branch, 10 Qiaoguang Road, 510015 (Haizhu Square next to Hotel Landmark Canton. Tel. 83336888 X 5385. Fax 83336417*
- **CYTS Tours Corporation**, *third floor, Bao Shan Plaza, 509, Huan Shi Dong Road, 510075. Tel. 87784047. Fax 87765112*
- **Guangdong Tourism Administration**, *185 Huanshi Xi Road, 510010, Tel. 86677426, 86670695. Fax 86665039, 86677410.* Should have list of stores, restaurants and hotels approved for foreign tourists. For complaints and suggestions, contact: *Business Management Dept., Tel. 86677422*
- **Guangzhou Tourist Corporation**, *4 - 155 Huanshi Xi Road, 510010. Tel. 86665182, 86670695. Fax 86677563.* Class A. Organizes tours from abroad for foreigners and outbound for Chinese people.
- **Telephone Code**, *020*
- **Tourism Hotline**, *Tel. 86677422*

GUILIN

(Kweilin: City of Cassia Trees)

In northeast Guangxi, the first 'province' west of Guangdong, **Guilin** was founded as a prefecture in 214 B.C. Guilin is famous for its vertical limestone mountains rising above flat tree-lined streets, rice and water chestnut fields, and the meandering Li and Taohua (Peach Blossom) Rivers. It is also known for its caves. The **Li River cruise** is the main reason tourists flock here.

Guilin developed with the opening of the Ling Canal. It was the provincial capital until 1014 and a command post for the Northern Expedition in 1928. The Japanese war destroyed much of the city during which the Seven Star Cave alone sheltered 5,000 refugees from bombs.

The weather is subtropical, the hottest 36 degrees centigrade in August; the coldest minus three. The rainy season is February to May, the annual precipitation 1900 millimeters. The best time to visit is autumn or late spring, when it is warm enough to ignore the rain.

The scenery is best seen in the mist which inspired centuries of landscape painters, or when the sun and clouds conspire to give you constantly changing pictures. From November until the February rains, the water in the river may be low. It has been recently dredged, and with a reservoir controlling the flow, boats should be able to use it year-round.

ARRIVALS & DEPARTURES

Guilin is a 55-minute flight northwest of Guangzhou with air links with 22 other Chinese cities, and direct flights with Hong Kong. It is connected by tourist train with Nanning and Guangzhou (17 hours!). You can also reach it by rail from Beijing, Kunming, Shanghai and Zhanjiang, and by bus with Wuzhou (the port for the boat from Guangzhou and Hong Kong). A new international airport is due in 1997.

The **Guilin Airport** can be reached at *Tel. 2832826.*

ORIENTATION

Guilin has only one international-class tourist attraction, the **Li River cruise**. But Guilin is a small and beautiful city with a relaxing pace, clean air, and fun tourist shopping. The population is 400,000, nearly one in ten of whom are dependent on tourism. In the last few years, it has started to get livelier. The land is generally flat so bicycling and walking are great. The standard of English in the hotels is higher than other cities its size. You can spend a week here poking into alleys, hiking in the countryside, and taking side trips to investigate minorities around Nanning. From even quieter Yangshuo you can canoe on the Li River and also bicycle.

While many tours see the sights in Guilin in a fairly hectic pace (tour groups need at least two days), the city is wonderful for the resourceful individual traveler, a favorite of honeymooners. Best of all, prices here are among the cheapest in China.

Because one-third of the 10 million people living in Guangxi are of the Zhuang nationality, Guangxi is an 'autonomous region' rather than a 'province.' National guides may not understand the local dialect.

Guilin is one of the 24 historical cities protected by the State Council. Some of its houses are antiques and you should stroll through the past at your leisure. Taxis are plentiful and have meters that rarely get used.

WHERE TO STAY

The top hotel is the **Sheraton**, then the **Holiday Inn**. After that it's a toss-up between the **Royal Garden** and **Windsor Gui Shan** because of their less convenient but not impossible locations. The Garden is the most beautiful. The less luxurious **Universal** and **Fubo** are also good, especially for their location and Cantonese food. The Fubo is better than the Universal. The **Plaza** looked acceptable but is too far out to be considered except as a last resort. The Royal Garden and Holiday Inn have the widest twin beds.

The Ronghu is a "socialist" hotel. The noisy Osmanthus seems to be going downhill, and is in a crowded neighborhood. The English is poor.

The best location for business people are the Holiday Inn and the Ronghu on a lake, a short walk to CITS, city hall, and tourist shopping. The best location for tourists is the west bank of the Li River. This is also relatively central to CITS, city hall and tourist shopping because Guilin is a tiny city. The Sheraton, Fubo and Universal hotels are all within walking distance of the night tourist market, antique shops, cormorant fishing and the Sheraton's cheaper restaurants. A little further is the biggest department store.

On the east bank are the Royal Garden and the Gui Shan, less convenient to shops. The Park is pretty, but even further in the suburbs. The Hubin, Guilin and Taihu guest houses are for backpackers.

DISCOUNTS IN GUILIN HOTELS

Foreign tourism is down, so haggle on prices here all year round. Assuming they have the room, the **Fubo** *gives a 20 to 30% discount in peak season, and 50% in low season, making it the best buy in the city then. The* **Holiday Inn** *gives a 20% discount in low season December 1 to March 31 and 10% in high season May, September and October. The* **Sheraton** *gives a maximum 10% walk-in discount all year round and "sure-saver" rates if booked direct with the hotel weeks ahead of time. The* **Universal** *gives a 20% discount all year round.*

The following prices are subject to change, a 10% service charge and 5% government tax.

FUBO HOTEL *(Fubo San Zhuang), 121 Bin Jiang Rd., 541001. Three stars, Tel. 2829988. Fax 2822328. $70-$80. Dist.R.W. 8 km. Dist.A.P. 20 km.*

Excellent location next to Fubo Hill, with a great view of the mountains. Built 1992. Four stories. 150 rooms. USTV. Cantonese and Sichuan food. Generally good, but a bit scruffy. English was a problem. Managed by Vista International.

GUILIN PARK HOTEL *(Gui Hu Fandian), 1, Luosi Hill, Laoren Shan Qian, 541001. Three stars aiming for four. Tel. 2828899. Fax 2822296. $70-$90. Dist.A.P. 17 km. Dist.R.W. 5.5 km.*

Very pretty suburban setting in northwest part of town next to Laoren Hill with good feng-shui. Built 1990. Five stories, 268 rooms. USTV. Cantonese and Zhejiang food. Dim sum, gym, steam bath and sauna. Outdoor pool. Bit run down and English a problem. Managed by Merit International Hotels.

GUILIN PLAZA *(Guan Guang Jiudian), 20 Li Jiang Rd., 541004. Three stars. Tel. 5812488. Fax 5813323. $70-$80. Dist.A.P. 15 km. Dist.R.W. five km. Dist.Zhishan Bridge one kilometer.*

In suburbs near the International Exhibition Center one kilometer from the river on the east side of town, nowhere near good shopping. 1991. 13 stories, 288 rooms. European food. Cantonese and Sichuan restaurants. Bicycles. USTV but no CNN. Outdoor pool, gym, and sauna. Primarily for tour groups. H.K.J.V. Difficult to get a taxi. English a problem.

GUILIN ROYAL GARDEN HOTEL *(Di Yuan Jiudian), Yanjiang Rd., 541004. Four stars aiming for five. Tel. 5812411, 5813611. Fax 5815051. $85-$105. Dist.A.P. 17 km. Dist.R.W. six km.*

You can walk to ethnic village from here. Built 1987, some ren. 1995. Eight stories, 340 spacious rooms, wide beds, but smallish bathrooms. Good furniture and decor. Rooms could be a long walk from elevators. USTV. Huge atrium garden coffee shop. Japanese restaurant. 24-hour room service and coffee shop. Clinic. Outdoor pool and tennis. Has mountain bikes for rent.

HOLIDAY INN GUILIN *(Jia Ru Binguan), 14 Ronghu Nan Rd., 541002. Four stars, Tel. 2823950. Fax 2822101. In US, Tel. 1-800-HOLIDAY. $110-120. Dist.A.P. 14 km. Dist.R.W. 3.5 km.*

Built 1987. Ren. 1995. Nine stories, 259 rooms. Small, intimate atmosphere. Cathedral ceiling and balconies in top-floor rooms. Cantonese, Sichuan and Asian food. USTV but no CNN. Health club. Bicycles. Can provide lunch boxes for boat trip, or if groups book a whole boat, it can provide food and beverage service. It can also set up a barbecue on Yao mountain. Gym, steambath and outdoor pool.

HOTEL UNIVERSAL GUILIN *(Huan Qiu Dajiudian), 1 Jiefang Dong Rd., 541001. Three stars, Tel. 2828228. Fax 2823868. Dist.A.P. 14 km. Dist.R.W. seven km.*

Closest to Liberation Bridge. Fruit and vegetable market outside. Built 1988. Renovations due 1996. Seven stories, 230 rooms. USTV, no CNN. Cantonese and Italian restaurants. Disco. Macau CTS Management.

OSMANTHUS HOTEL *(Dangui Fandian), 451 Zhong Shan Nan Rd., 541002. Three stars, Tel. 3834300, 3832261. Fax 3835316. Three-star west wing $60-80; Dist.A.P.14 km. Dist.R.W. one km.*

Built 1986; west wing ren. 1992-93. 14 stories, 214 rooms. Even-numbered rooms have river view. Somewhat rundown. Soft beds. Outdoor pool. Cantonese dim sum. Rooms stuffy but should be okay with airconditioning turned on. Disco. Bicycles. Carpets and English are problems. Vista International Hotel management. Lower quality east wing not recommended.

RONGHU HOTEL *(Fandian), 17 Ronghu Bei Rd., 541001. Tel. 2823811. Fax 2825390. $65 and $70. Dist.R.W. four km. Dist.A.P. 14 km.*

Buildings Five and Six are three stars. Six is better and cleaner, built in 1990 and renovated in 1995. 200 rooms. Five was built in 1986 with smaller rooms and fewer services. Eight buildings on large hilly grounds, total 455 rooms. Japanese restaurant. Food not great. Gym, tennis court and conference service. Both buildings have USTV, no CNN. Other buildings are older, with high ceilings, old-fashioned decor and not as conveniently located. Bicycles for rent.

SHERATON GUILIN *(Wen Hua Fandian), Bing Jiang Nan Rd., 541001. Five stars, Tel. 2825588. Fax 2825598. In US, Tel. 1-800-325-3535. $105-$145. Dist.A.P. 25 km. Dist.R.W. five km. 1988. Possible renovations in 1996.*

Six stories. 430 large rooms, some non-smoking. USTV. 24-hour room service. CITS. Cantonese and Sichuan food. 20-metre outdoor pool. Sauna and gym. Bicycles. Beautiful atrium lobby and garden with waterfall. Reservations usually held until 4 pm the same day. Dragonair office.

WINDSOR GUI SHAN HOTEL *(Guishan Dajiudian), Chuan Shan Rd., 541004. Four stars, Tel. 5813388. Fax 5814851. $90-100. Dist.A.P.15 km. Dist.R.W. five km. Credit Cards.*

Suburban setting between two rivers near Seven Star Park. Built 1988. Five stories, four connecting buildings. Could be long walk to room. 607 rooms. Moslem rooms and restaurant. Outdoor pool. Gym. Steam room. Jacuzzi. Bowling. Clinic. Bicycles. USTV. Lots of shops. CAAC. Managed by Windsor Hotels International (H.K.)

WHERE TO EAT

Chinese food here is usually Guangxi or Cantonese. Food is served with chili sauce and fermented bean curd as condiments. You should like the bean curd if you like blue cheese. Mix a bit with your rice. The local rice wine, Sanhua, is made from a 200-year-old recipe.

The **SHERATON HOTEL** and **HOLIDAY INN** are the best for Chinese and western food. The **ROYAL GARDEN HOTEL** has Japanese food. For Cantonese, there's the **JIULONG RESTAURANT**, *Tel. 3835527*, on the road almost across from the Osmanthus Hotel.

Night food markets are outside the Osmanthus and the Seven Stars Hotels. The **SHERATON** has a fast food restaurant which serves hamburgers, pizza, gumbo, Chinese noodles and won ton. It has also opened a **Food Street** with local food and Sheraton standards. Both are on the southwest side of the hotel.

The **HONG DENG LONG (RED LANTERN) RESTAURANT**, behind the Holiday Inn on Xi Yin Road, *Tel. 2834949*, is good for Sichuan, Cantonese and Guilin food. It is cleaner and quieter than the Jiulong. The **TALIAN HOTEL** on the same street as the railway station has good Cantonese food. Outside of the hotels, there are no decent bars.

SEEING THE SIGHTS

For those in a hurry, one morning could be spent at Fubo Hill and Seven Star Park, and the afternoon at Reed Flute Cave, Diecai Hill and Elephant Hill. Tourist attractions usually open 8 am to 5 pm. The Li River boat trip could be enjoyed on a second day. The Ming Tomb Museum, the Guilin Museum, *at Xishan Park, Tel. 2822892,* Gao Shan for the view, a handicraft factory, shopping, just walking or cycling or the Ling Canal can complete your third or fourth day.

Diecai (Folded Brocade) **Hill,** *Tel. 2825817,* 3.6 kilometers from the Sheraton Hotel, is the tallest hill in town at 73 meters. The peaks are named Bright Moon, Crane, and Seeing Around the Hill. Partway up, past the ornamental arch, is the Wind Cave with Ming and Song poems and memorials on its walls. You can get a good view of the area from the top.

Fubo (Whirlpool) **Hill,** *Tel. 2823620,* a short walk north of the Sheraton Hotel, named after famous Han Marshal Ma Fubo, is 60 meters high. At the base is a 7.5 ton iron Qing bell belonging to the temple originally here. To the right is the **Cave of the Returned Pearl**, where guides might tell you a dragon left a gift of a pearl for a poor family, who returned it. 'This illustrates the honesty of working people.' Nearby is a rock where Ma Fubo tested his sword and a cliff with Tang Buddha's. Part way up on the east side is a pavilion with a view of the river.

Qixing (Seven Star) **Park,** *Tel. 5813546,* 2.7 kilometers from the Sheraton Hotel, is about 10 square kilometers. It contains a zoo, Camel Hill (with nearby miniature garden) and Seven Star Hill whose seven peaks are positioned like the stars in the Big Dipper. **Seven Star Cave** on the west side of Potaraka Hill has three levels; visitors enter the middle one. It is bigger than Reed Flute Cave, one kilometer long, 43 meters at its widest, and 27 meters at its highest. Colored lights highlight the grotesque limestone formations. With lots to see, you may want to return for a more leisurely look. Just think, you will be following in the footsteps of tourists from the Sui (581-618) dynasty!

A forest of cassia trees blossom in spring and a 700-year old stone replica of the Flower Bridge (Song) spans a stream. Originally built of wood but destroyed in a flood, the bridge was designed so that the water below reflects its arches to form a complete circle.

The 'Cave for Hiding a Dragon' looks like it could snugly fit a dinosaur. The most famous of the stone Song steles nearby lists people doomed for execution. The emperor sent copies around China (although paper was invented by then) and when the verdict was reversed, all but the stele in Guilin were destroyed. Also on the west side of Putuo (Potaraka) Hill is the Yuanfeng (Deep and Windy) Cave, and on top, the Putuo (Potaraka) Temple (good views) and Guanyin cave.

Ludi (Reed Flute) **Cave,** *Tel. 2822254,* is eight or nine kilometers from the Sheraton Hotel. One kilometer long, this cave takes about 40 minutes to explore. The temperature inside is a cool 20° C. The lighting is cleverly placed so that with a bit of imagination, the limestone resembles

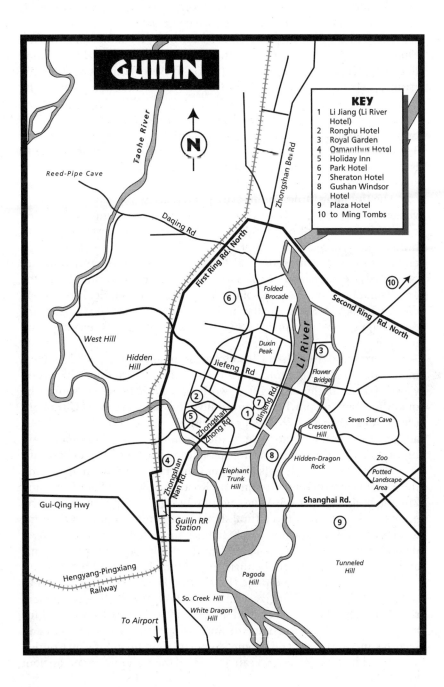

GUILIN

N

KEY
1 Li Jiang (Li River Hotel)
2 Ronghu Hotel
3 Royal Garden
4 Osmanthus Hotel
5 Holiday Inn
6 Park Hotel
7 Sheraton Hotel
8 Gushan Windsor Hotel
9 Plaza Hotel
10 to Ming Tombs

Taohe River

Reed-Pipe Cave

Zhongshan Bei Rd

Daqing Rd

First Ring Rd. North

Folded Brocade

Second Ring Rd. North

West Hill

Hidden Hill

Duxin Peak

Li River

Jiefeng Rd

Flower Bridge

Seven Star Cave

Crescent Hill

Binjeng Rd.

Zhongshan Zhong Rd

Elephant Trunk Hill

Hidden-Dragon Rock

Zoo

Potted Landscape Area

Zhongshan Nan Rd.

Gui-Qing Hwy

Shanghai Rd.

Guilin RR Station

Hengyang-Pingxiang Railway

Tunneled Hill

Pagoda Hill

So. Creek Hill

White Dragon Hill

To Airport

a giant goldfish, a Buddha, a wall of assorted vegetables, etc. The reeds that grow at the entrance gave this cave its name.

Xiangbi (Elephant Trunk) **Hill**, *Tel. 2825844*, 1.4 kilometers from the Sheraton Hotel, at the junction of the Li and Yang Rivers, really does look like an elephant drinking. Shuiyue (Moon-in-Water) Cave is between the trunk and front legs. Elephant Eye Cave is where you would expect. The Samantabhadra Pagoda tops the hill.

Duxiu (Unique Beauty) **Park** was the site of the mansion of Zhu Shouqian, grandson of Emperor Hongwu of the Ming, which dates from 1393. Destroyed during the Qing, and again during the Japanese war, it is now the teachers' college. Today, only the original wall, its gates and steps remain.

The **Jingjiang Ming Tombs** are a good place to bicycle. You pass old villages, water buffalo herds, mountains and several intriguing Ming cemeteries, a total of 320 tombs in 100 square kilometers. All persons buried here in relatively simple graves are descendants of the Ming emperor's family. A **museum**, *Tel. 5811430*, and several guardian statues of animals, servants and officials are at the unexcavated tumulus of the grandson Zhu Shou Qian Chi of the dynasty founder's older brother. He died in 1370 A.D. Much smaller and less elaborate than the Ming tombs near Beijing, they are worth a visit if you have the time. Open daily 9 am to 5 pm.

There's also **Yao Shan** (Broadcast Mountain), which is 300 meters high with a road to the top, but there's nothing more there than good views. To see if the chair lift is working, *call 5814592*. It should be operating 9 am to 4 pm. For the more adventurous, you can get **Ultra-light plane rides**, *Tel. 5816478*, at your own risk of course. If you're not THAT adventurous, you can hire one of the Royal Garden Hotel's **mountain bikes**, and take off between the rice paddies and fields of water chestnuts.

There is the **Li River Folk Customs Center** (Feng Qing Yuan) beyond the Royal Garden Hotel on Yanjiang Road. It now has Miao, Dong and Zhuang buildings, a lovely wind-and-rain bridge, Dong drum tower – all great for photographs. Its cultural shows have genuine minority dancers, a 450-seat indoor theater, cock fights, horse fights, minority food, demonstrations and sale of arts and crafts. But it's not very professional and the horse fights might be upsetting. Open 8 am to 10 pm daily.

You can still visit the **Lingqu** (Ling Canal, see above) dug in 214 B.C. to connect the Chang (Yangtze) and the Zhu (Pearl) rivers. It was an inland route to Guangzhou, used as such until the 1930s. It is still important for irrigation, of interest to engineers and history fans. It has 18 locks and sections and starts about 66 kilometers north of Guilin in Xing'an County. You can ride a small bamboo raft and enjoy the tranquillity and ancient bridge.

Li River Trips

You can book the **Li River boat trip** with a travel agent or your hotel. The price is about the same. If you want to try for a cheaper trip, you could shop around for boats for Chinese tourists. These leave near the Universal Hotel. Be aware that guides here speak only Chinese, the boats are not as clean, and there is no air conditioning.

Boats for foreigners leave from **Zhu Jiang wharf** about 20 kilometers from the city. Only some are air-conditioned and not all have protection from the rain or sun on the roof deck. The ride from Zhu Jiang to **Yangshuo** is 59 kilometers, and takes about four hours. Prices usually include lunch and the bus back to Guilin from Yangshuo. The tour south to Yangshuo usually returns by land about mid-afternoon.

For more information directly from the cruise folks, contact the **Guilin Tourism Motor Boat Co.**, *3 Fuxing Road, Tel. 5815595, 5813306.*

The Li River, normally 50 to 100 meters wide, winds its way between some incredible stone peaks, the highest about 80 meters. Pollution control has been upgraded, but you still notice dishes being washed in the river.

Look for **Crown Cave** (shaped like the British imperial crown), a cock with tail up bending down to pick up rice, followed shortly by the U-shaped **Ram's Hoof Mountain** on the right. On the right is **Conch Shell Hill**, then a temple on a cliff. You should complain if peddlers are blocking your view. If you're trying to save on camera film, the most beautiful area is between **Yangdi Village** and **Snail Hill**, that is, between Number Nine and Number 16 on the map they give you.

On the way, look for large cormorants (real birds, not stone), usually seen sitting on fishing boats. If you're lucky you might even watch them at work, fishing on behalf of people.

Yangshuo, the tiny town at the end of the boat ride, has a park, museum, good shopping and an old temple. If time allows, you could walk along the main street to the right of the landing. Behind Green Lotus Peak on the left of the landing is **Jian** (Mirror) **Hill**, so named because some of its cliffs are smooth. The museum has copies of famous paintings of galloping horses and Li River scenes by Xu Beihong who lived here between 1935 and 1938.

You might want to stay overnight, bike, hike or rent a canoe. The best hotel is the three-star **YANGSHUO HOTEL**. You can take a bus back the next day. You could also do the whole trip in a cheaper public bus giving you more time to shop. You can still look at some of the same lovely scenery but you are not on the water.

A variation is a two-day Li River cruise with stops at **Daxu village** and a minority cultural center. There is overnight camping at **Crown Cave** in tents, or a simple hotel. Twenty-nine kilometers south of Guilin at Cao

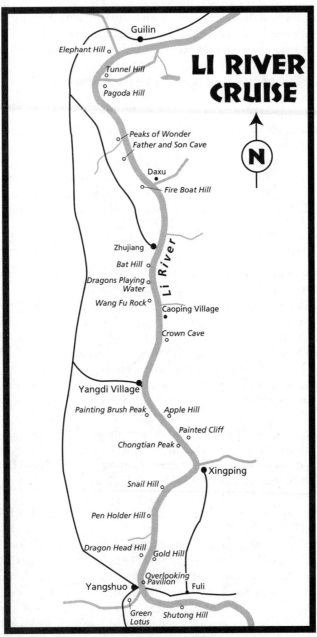

Ping village, Crown Cave has several levels and a cable car. It also has a subterranean river on which you can boat for three kilometers. Near Crown Cave is a small, clean two-star **inn** with a barbecue in the evening.

After caving, people can also swim, rent boats, sauna, get a massage and visit the nearby village. No bicycles. The only access seems to be by boat. The food and service are good though the furniture is simple and the rooms small. The setting is beautiful and gives photographers a chance to capture the river in a variety of different lights. For information, contact the **Guilin Huazhiguan Tourist Development Co.**, *Tel. 2835968, 2835989. Fax 2835988*

Festivals & Theme Parks

Festivals include the **Cassia Festival** in March, and the annual **Mountain and River Festival** is in October or November (you need three days for this festival). One night is spent in the mountains with the minorities. A Taiwan joint venture company has opened a 18-hole golf course 40 kilometers away. See also *Nanning* selection below for **Liuzhou**, 140 kilometers by highway from Guilin.

SHOPPING

You can buy locally-grown oranges, pomelo, and mangosteens (luohan guo) in season. Guilin also produces artistic pottery, bamboo, new and old-style wood carvings, redwood chopsticks, woven and plated bamboo, dough figures, stone exercise balls, tablecloths, embroidery, and proletarian items like bicycle bells and down jackets.

The main shopping area is along **Zhongshan Zhong Road** where you can find the **Guilin Department Store** and the **Arts and Crafts Center**. The largest department store is **Wang Chen Shan Sha**, *89 Jiefang Dong Road at Zhang Yang Road*, two blocks behind the Universal Hotel.

Haggling is imperative in the markets and antique store. Even the government **Guilin Antique Store**, *2 Shabu Bei Road, Tel. 2828172*, came down by half on one of my purchases. The **Myer Guilin Jewelry Manufacturing Company**, near the Holiday Inn at *211 Li Zhong Road, Tel. 2822525 or 2822547*, exports to the United States and Europe but does not usually sell in China. They give gifts to taxi drivers and guides who bring guests.

The **night tourist market** between the Universal and Sheraton hotels has 100 stalls and is full of jewelry, tea pots, old gilded wood carvings, silk shirts, table cloths, porcelain, wooden duck, 'opium pipes.' etc. Occasionally you can find something really valuable like 12" long, old, gilded wood carvings for Y100 a pair, circular crocheted table cloths six feet in diameter for Y80, and a fine child's silver necklace with bells (I bought one; they asked Y600 but gave in at Y140). Counter the first asking price with one-quarter the price and try to settle for a third.

The best shopping is in **Yangshuo** for cheaper 'antiques,' the same sort of things as the night market. There is no time between the boat and the bus; you usually get about 20 minutes. Serious shoppers should forget about the boat trip and go by bus earlier in the day. Avoid ethnic earrings because they have big stems requiring big ear holes. Prices are cheaper than Guilin because there is more competition.

NIGHTLIFE & ENTERTAINMENT

The **night boats** to watch the cormorants can take a minimum of 45 minutes from the Er Hao Mao Tou, Number Two Pier near the Universal Hotel. Cormorant fishing is traditionally done at night by men so their wives can take their catch to market the next morning. The process is fascinating, the light on the fisherman's bamboo raft attracting the tiny fish. The birds swim underwater and jump back on board the raft with fish tails sticking out of their beaks only to lose their catch to the fisherman.

There are 'ethnic' dance and song performances at the Gui Shan and Royal Garden Hotels. Both are entertaining, but the costumes, performers and dances are not really authentic.

The **Li River Folk Customs Center** and **Night Hoover Theater** near the Holiday Inn, *85 Jiefang Road, Tel. 2826925*, also have shows but the folk customs center's isn't good. The Night Hoover Theater is a combination of amateurish acrobats and folk dances with lively and charming performers. The food there isn't great but it's fun.

If you want a real minority show, it's best to go on a tour to real Yao and Miao villages, where performances are sometimes held.

The best disco is at the Sheraton; the best karaoke bars are at Holiday Inn and Universal, both with songs in English. Be forewarned of bars outside hotels that overcharge for the drinks of hostesses who invite themselves to sit with you.

PRACTICAL INFORMATION

- **Ambulance**, *Tel. 120*
- **CITS**, *14 Ronghu Bei Road, 541001, Tel. 2827254. North American Department, Tel. 2825759. Fax 2822936. FIT Department, Tel. 2822648, 2827254*
- **CTS**, *Tel. 3830271. Fax 3835621*
- **Guilin Municipal Tourism Bureau Inspection Station**, *Ground Floor, 14 North Ronghu Road, 541001. Tel. 2824344. Fax 2826230*
- **Guilin Tourism Administration**, *(information) Tel. 2826533, 2824344. Fax 2829111*
- **Police**, *Tel. 110*
- **Tourist Hotline**, *Tel. 3830265, 3830275*
- **Telephone Code**, *0773*

HAIKOU, HAINAN ISLAND

Haikou is the capital of Hainan, China's second largest island and its 31st and smallest province. Hainan is 30 kilometers off China's southern coast, and includes the **Xisha**, **Nansha** (Spratley), and **Zhongsha Islands**.

Han dynasty troops first colonized Hainan. From the Tang dynasty, disfavored scholars and officials were sent here to live in exile, a tropical Siberia. During the 1930s and 1940s, a Communist army detachment fought here, and after Mao's victory in 1949 part of the island became an autonomous region because a large percentage of the population are national minorities: mainly Li and Miao, but also Hui.

Hainan Island with 34,000 square kilometers is just about as big as Taiwan. The Chinese government is developing it as a very special economic zone with more flexibility and openness than other such zones so most visitors to Haikou are business people. The government has targetted Sanya and Yalong Bay in the south as resorts areas.

The weather is tropical, with 2000 millimeters of rain a year. October to April is the peak tourist season. You can get a visa to China upon arrival in Hainan. Mosquitos are a problem from late April and you should take precautions against malaria. May is the time for lichees, 23 varieties of mangoes and jackfruit. Typhoons usually hit July to September but have attacked the island other times as well.

ARRIVALS & DEPARTURES

You should be able to fly now or soon directly to Haikou from Bangkok, Hong Kong, Kuala Lumpur, Macau, and Singapore. It has air connections with 38 Chinese cities. You can also go by almost direct train in 52 hours from Beijing twice a week.

ORIENTATION

The island produces tea, coffee, rubber, fish, sugar, coconut and rice. The population is over seven million, of whom 1.2 million are minorities. Haikou itself has an urban population of 300,000 and who knows how many transients. It has traffic jams and can be hectic, with a frontier atmosphere. People are out to make a fast yuan, in a situation less controlled than that of the rest of China.

While prostitution is illegal, it is pretty obvious. Massage parlors with private clinics on the floor below blatantly advertise treatment for venereal diseases. You might get a call at night about 'special services.'

WHERE TO STAY

The best hotels now in Haikou are the Golden Coast Hotel (a four to five star good for business people and tourists), second the Haikou Hotel and International Financial Center Hotel. Then there's the Haikou Tower Hotel which is popular with tourists. SMI Hotels and Resorts is opening the five-star Hainan Mandarin Hotel on Seaside Avenue in 1997.

HAIKOU HOTEL *(Binguan), 4 Haifu Dado, 570001. Tel. 5350264, 5350266. Fax 5350232. Credit Cards.*

Built 1988. 10 stories. 184 rooms. IDD. B.C. Pool. Gym.

HAIKOU INTERNATIONAL FINANCIAL CENTER HOTEL *(Jinrong Da Sha), 33 Datong Rd., 570102. Four stars. Tel. 6773088. Fax 6774574. Dist.A.P. two km. Credit Cards.*

Built 1987, ren 1995. 22 stories, 241 rooms. B.C. IDD. Dragonair. Outdoor pool. Bowling. Gym. Eastwest Enterprise management.

HAIKOU TOWER HOTEL *(Tai Hua Jiudian), Binhai Rd., 570105. Three stars, Tel. 6772990, 6773962. Fax 6773966. Near bus station. Dist.A.P. three km. Credit Cards.*

Built 1986. Two-stories, 200 units. IDD. B.C. USTV. Tennis. Pools. Jogging trails. Bicycles. H.K.S.T.T. management.

WHERE TO EAT

Local specialties include Wenchang-style chicken, Jiaji duck, Hele crab, and Dongshan mutton. One of the best restaurants is the **CHAO JIANG CHUN RESTAURANT** *in the Haikou International Financial Centre Hotel, 33 Da Tong Road, Tel. 6773088, 6774099.* Specialties here are Cantonese and Chaozhou food and seafoods.

SEEING THE SIGHTS

In Haikou, you can visit the recently restored **Five Officials Memorial Temple**, originally built in 1889 in honor of its banished officials. Near this is the **Su Temple**, a memorial to the famous Song poet, Su Dong Po, who was banished to Hainan in 1097 at the age of 61. Travel agents will also send you to the **Hai Rui Tomb**; while mildly interesting, you can ignore all these if you want. The only important tourist attraction in Hainan are the **southern beaches**, but world class resorts and facilities were not ready at press time and aren't due until 1997. In the meantime, you can still relax on the beaches of **Sanya** (see below).

SHOPPING

Rubies and rose quartz are native to the area. Cultured pearls, fruit, and minority handicrafts are made locally.

EXCURSIONS FROM HAIKOU

You can fly direct to **Sanya** from Haikou, but you can also fly direct from 11 other Chinese cities. Flights have started or are planned with

Hong Kong, Macau, Singapore, Korea and Japan, with Chinese visas available also on arrival. An international airport is 15 kilometers from Sanya.

Three roads go from Haikou south to Sanya. If you take the 296 kilometer central road, you can stop at the Feng Mu Deer Farm and then visit a Miao village. There's a modest hotel and the Museum of Nationalities in Tongzha. If you go via the 321 kilometer eastern expressway route, you can visit the Monkey Peninsula, Overseas Chinese farm and Kangle Garden Resort at Xinlong, and stop at the Chao Yin Si Temple on Mount Dongshan. Non-stop this would be a 3 1/2 hour drive to Sanya. Air-conditioned buses go from the Overseas Chinese Hotel in Haikou to Sanya.

In the Sanya area itself, you can visit a Moslem fishing village, a pearl farm, a monkey island, and visit the rocky "Ends of the Earth." A dive shop should be next to the Sanya International Hotel. A golf course is due to open soon.

Aside from the hotels, a good place to eat fresh seafood are the restaurant stalls on Lu Hui To Beach, at the west side of the downtown area, two kilometers west of Da Dong Hai beach. The Haiwei Seafood Restaurant near Monkey Island is no longer good.

Yalong Bay is 20 kilometers southeast of Sanya, has a beautiful white sand beach backed by a line of mountains and is better than any beach in Sanya. Five-star resorts are being built here.

Until the new resorts and hotels open, the best in Sanya is the South China Hotel, then the Jinling Holiday Resort. Both are on or near Da Dong Hai beach.

JINLING HOLIDAY RESORT (*Do Jia Chang*), *Lu Ling Rd., Dadonghai, 572021. Four stars. Tel. 214081, 214088. Fax 214088. Above beach.*

Built 1989. 147 suites. B.C. Fresh water pool. Tennis. Due soon are apartments, offices, night club, water-cycling, parachuting, windsurfing, water skiing, and scuba diving. Qing Yu Tai Village, Lu Ling Road Tel. 213649, fax 212648.

SANYA INTERNATIONAL HOTEL (*Guoji Dajiudian*), *Yuya Rd., 572000. Three stars. Tel. 273068. Fax 232049. Dist.A.P. five km.*

On ocean and riverfront (but not beach).

SOUTH CHINA HOTEL (*Nan Zhong Hai*), *Dadonghai, 572021. Four stars. Tel. 213888. Fax 214005. Dist.bus station three km. Dist.pearl farm four km.*

On three kilometer-long Da Dong Hai Beach. 1992. H.K.J.V. sauna, massage, tennis courts, swimming pools, and water park.

The telephone code for Sanya is *0899*.

PRACTICAL INFORMATION

• **CTS**, *17 Datong Road, Haikou 570001, Tel. 6709393. Fax 6772095*
• **CITS**, *Haixi Lu, Sanjiaochi (next to Haikou Hotel), Haikou, Tel. 5354640, 5352117. Fax 5358187. Or third floor, H.T.S.O. Building, Sanjiaochi, Haikou. Tel. 5355284. Fax 5358187*
• **Hainan Provincial Tourism Bureau**, *Hainan Tourism Administration Building, 6 Haifu Road, Tel. 5358432. Fax 5353074. (Brochures)*
• **Hainan Tourist Corp.**, *5-6/F Hailu Building, Haifu Ave., Haikou, 570003. Tel. 5351679. Fax 5351679*
• **Store Hours**, *8 am to 10 pm.*
• **Tourist Complaints**, contact **Supervisory Bureau of Tourism Quality of Hainan Province**, *Room 606, Tel. 5358451. Fax 5353074*
• **Telephone Code**, *0898*

JINGDEZHEN

(Chingtechen)

In the northeast part of Jiangxi province, northeast of Nanchang, **Jingdezhen** is a must for porcelain lovers. It was from here that some of the best was shipped to Europe centuries ago, including the famous blue-and-white. It has been producing porcelain for over 2,200 years and imperial porcelain since the Northern Song, over 980 years ago.

Today Jingdezhen is still producing some of the best porcelain in China, a combination of the right clay, abundant pine wood for fuel, and easy transport (on the Yangtze). The city was founded in the Han and is considered one of China's Three Ancient Cities. The population is 400,000; the altitude 300 to 500 meters.

ARRIVALS & DEPARTURES

You can reach Jingdezhen by road, usually leaving Nanchang after breakfast and arriving about 4 pm. You can get there by rail from Nanchang or Nanjing.

WHERE TO STAY & EAT

JINGDEZHEN HOTEL *(Binguan), 60 Fengjing Rd., 333000. Three stars. Tel. 225015, 225950. Fax 226416. $47 to $60. Dist.A.P. seven km. Dist.R.W. two km. IDD. Credit Cards.*

SEEING THE SIGHTS

You can choose a factory to visit. Each has its own specialty. You can go to the site of the ***Hutian Porcelain Kiln**, dating from the Five Dynasties (white glazed) to the Song (celadon) and Yuan (blue-and-white).

They can also find where they mine the kaolin clay. **Pearl Hill** is the site of the Ming and Qing imperial kilns.

The town itself is surrounded by mountains and the **Chang River**. The town has a **Pottery and Porcelain Exhibition Hall**, and the **Pottery and Porcelain College**. The **Ceramic Museum** is at *21 North Lianshe Road, Tel. 228514, 229783*, and is open 8 to 11:30 am, 2 to 5:30 pm Monday to Friday. The annual porcelain festival is October 11 to 14.

SHOPPING

The **Friendship Store** is at *25 Zhushan Zhong Road, Tel. 223742* for porcelain. It will pack and ship. Another good place to shop is **Jingdezhen Antique and Curio Store**, *Tel. 224207, 224209*.

PRACTICAL INFORMATION

- **CTS** and **CITS**, *8 Lianhuatang Street, 333000. Tel. 222905 (CTS), 222573, 222939. Fax 222311 (CTS), 222937*
- **Tourism Bureau & Hotline,** *Tel. 222904, 222905. For complaints, 8 Lianhuatong Street, Tel. 222903*
- **Telephone Code**, *0798*

JIUJIANG

(Kiukiang, Chiuchiang, or Xunyang)

Jiujiang is in northern Jiangxi province on the south bank of the Yangtze River, where it bends south between Wuhan and Nanjing. It is bounded on the east by Poyang Lake and Mt. Lushan on the south. This 2000-year-old city has been used as a port for the porcelain city of Jingdezhen since ancient times. It was also a treaty port and currently is comprised of two urban districts, ten rural counties, and Mt. Lushan.

ARRIVALS & DEPARTURES

Jiujiang is ccessible by train from Nanchang, and by plane or by passenger boat along the Yangtze.

WHERE TO STAY & EAT

NANHU HOTEL, *28 Nanhu Rd., 332000, Two stars. Tel. 8222272, 8225041).*

Beside South Lake, with villas.

SEEING THE SIGHTS

Of interest to visitors are the **Yanshui Pavilion** in the middle of Lake Gantang, a 1,840-square-meter island covered with gardens, halls, and pavilions; and the causeway between Lake Gantang and Lake Nanmen, built in 821 A.D.

Also important are the **Dasheng Pagoda** in Nengren Temple and the Xunyanglou and Suojianglou Pagoda. Important also is the **Donglin Temple**, the birthplace of the 'Pure Earth' sect of Buddhism (founded 1,500 years ago), and **Poyang Lake Migrant Birds Preserve**, said to be the largest in the world (from October to March). It sees cranes, stocks, whistling swans, spoonbills and mandarin ducks.

PRACTICAL INFORMATION
· **CITS**, *28 Nanhu Road, 332000, Tel. 8223390. Fax 8221895*
· **Jiujiang Tourism Bureau**, *33 Xunyang Road, 330002. Tel. 8226191*

LUSHAN

Lushan is part of Jiujiang City, 40 kilometers south of the port of Jiujiang. It overlooks Poyang Lake and the Yangtze River. Primarily an old mountain resort, Lushan is highly recommended as an escape from the heat or as a rest stop near the end of a trip. It is great for hiking and is a beautiful place to visit, with enough religious, historical, and folkloric aspects to make it interesting.

A resort was developed here in the last half of the 1800s. About 100 hotel buildings and villas were completed and used by wealthy Chinese, government officials, and foreign missionaries. Most of these people were carried by sedan chair up a steep, nine-kilometer path. People still climb this path from the base in about two hours from Lianhuaden (Lotus Flower Hole). Chiang Kai-shek also visited Lushan when he wasn't campaigning against Mao Zedong at nearby Jinggang Shan. He lived in Building Number 180 in the East Valley.

The hottest weather is a rare 32 degrees centigrade at noon in July; the coldest, minus 16 degrees in January with snow from the end of November through February. The best time to visit is June through October. There's lots of mist and rain, especially April and May, great for mood photographs but not for view. The altitude is 1,094 to 1,400 meters; the annual precipitation: 1916 millimeters.

Lushan has a permanent population of about 9,000 in Gulin. The mountaintop tourist belt is about eight by four kilometers.

ARRIVALS & DEPARTURES
The closest airport is in Jiujiang (see above).

ORIENTATION

Lushan is divided into an East Valley and a West Valley, with a tunnel at Gulin. Taxis are available. A tourist bus leaves downtown Gulin near the entrance to the city park whenever full, *Tel. 8282037.*

WHERE TO STAY

Some of the buildings here are over 100 years old. Most are made of stone, with lots of space and high ceilings. All are modest with low standards.

The three-star **LUSHAN HOTEL** is best; *446 Hexi Road, 332900, Tel. 8282060. Fax 8282843.* The best hotel for business people is the two-star **VILLA VILLAGE HOTEL**, *179 Hedong Road, 332900.*

WHERE TO EAT

You'll want to eat in the local hotels here. The local delicacy is the Three Stones: stone frog, stone fish, and stone fungus.

SEEING THE SIGHTS

First stop should be the **Grotto of Taoist Immortal**. Beyond the moon gate to the right is a cave about 30 feet wide, deep, and high, where Lu Tungpin, a famous monk, studied Taoism so successfully that he became one of the Eight Taoist Immortals, the one with the supernatural sword. Note the formation over the mouth of the cave, shaped like Buddha's hand.

At the **Big Heavenly Pond**, the water in this pool maintains the same height (it is said) through rain or drought, and is thus said to be 'made in Heaven.' The pavilion behind the pond is on the site of a temple, built to commemorate the spider who saved the first Ming emperor Zhu Yuanzhang's life by spinning a web to cover him while Zhu was hiding in a well from his rival.

The monks who lived in this temple were Taoists who tried to achieve immortality through study and meditation. As a test, they jumped off **Dragon Head Cliff**. If you look down, you can probably guess why they were never seen again. The climb down to Dragon Head Cliff (by no means the bottom) is about 170 steps, but the view is worth it. On the way, look for a carved step that was probably part of the old temple.

Hanpokou ('the Mouth that Holds Poyang Lake') named after the shape of this pass in relation to the lake, is the best place for the rising sun. The lake is one of China's largest and is 20 kilometers away.

The **Lushan Botanical Garden** is a short walk from Hanpokou. Belonging to the Academy of Science, this garden has exchange programs with Britain's Royal Botanical Gardens and the National Arboretum in Washington, DC. Here are 3,700 varieties, including trees, flowers, grasses, and medicinal herbs on 740 acres of land. Started in 1934, it is the only subalpine garden of the ten botanical gardens in China. Tourists are free to wander through the green houses (tropical and subtropical plants), which are open daily from 7:30 am to 6 pm. Groups can get a guide.

The most exotic plant here is the metasequoia tree, a species thought to be extinct and seen only in fossils until one was found in a primitive forest in west China and propagated here. A large specimen stands labeled by the driveway near the parking lot.

SHOPPING

Gulin, the only shopping area, was destroyed by fire in 1947 and then rebuilt. The arts and crafts stores sell porcelain dishes and statues made in Jingdezhen, 180 kilometers away. Other good buys are cloud-mist green tea and watercolors of the mountain scenery. Locally made handicrafts are walking sticks and bamboo brush or pencil holders.

PRACTICAL INFORMATION

· **CITS**, *Lushan Hotel, 454 Hexi Road, 332900; Tel. 8282497. Fax 8282428*

NANNING

The capital of Guangxi Zhuang Autonomous Region, **Nanning** is in the southwestern part of Guangxi near the northeastern border of Vietnam. The urban population is one million.

Nanning has a subtropical climate, meaning great fruit, flowering trees, and mild, humid weather. Its hottest is 38 degrees centigrade; its coldest is five degrees. The annual precipitation of about 1300 millimeters is mostly May to September. Nanning is worth visiting because of its national minorities, its karst caves, medicinal herb garden, and as a gateway to Vietnam.

ARRIVALS & DEPARTURES

You can reach it in six hours by train from Guilin and by train or bus from the Vietnam border. The Nanning-Kunming railway should be completed in 1997. You can also get to Nanning by air from 16 Chinese cities, Hanoi (30 minutes) and Hong Kong (over one hour).

ORIENTATION

Founded in 214 B.C., Nanning was the provincial capital from 1912 to 1936, and after 1949. It has a few industries.

WHERE TO STAY

The top hotels are the Majestic (Mingyuan Fandian) and then the Yongjiang in the city centre and the Ming Yuan's three star section.
MAJESTIC HOTEL *(Mingyuan Xindu Fandian), 38 Xin Min Road, 530012. Tel. 2830808. Fax 2830811. Dist.A.P. 35 km. Dist.R.W. 3.5 km.*
New hotel aiming for five stars. In 100,000 square-meter park in commercial district. Built 1995. 300 rooms. USTV but no CNN. In-house movies. IDD. Call-waiting feature on telephones. In-room safes. 24-hour B.C. Executive floors. Cantonese, Asian and American restaurants. Deli. Gym and outdoor pool with jacuzzi, jogging, tennis, and golf. A Majestic International Hotel (related to the Furama in Hong Kong.)
MINGYUAN HOTEL (Fandian) 38 Xinmin Rd., 530012. Three stars, Tel. 2830808. Fax 2830811.
Eleven villas built from 1952 to 1985.
YONGJIANG HOTEL, *41 Jiangbin Dong Rd., 530012. Three stars, Tel. 2808123. Fax 2800535.*

WHERE TO EAT

The food here is much like neighboring Guangdong's: Cantonese. Please avoid eating endangered species. An interesting **night food market** is on Zhongshan Road behind the Yongjiang Hotel, but be careful of the hygiene. The restaurants in the top hotels are where you should eat.

SEEING THE SIGHTS

A tour from Nanning to the Vietnam border might be:
• **Day One**: arrive in Nanning with city tour of Green Hill Park, the Ethnic Culture Garden and Xiling Cave.
• **Day Two**: Bus to Chongzhuo (160 kilometers) for stone forest, slanting tower and lunch. Then bus to Ningming (67 kilometers) for boat trip along Zhuojiang River to see 2000-year old cliff paintings and overnight in Huashan Ethnic Culture Village.
• **Day Three**: Ningming to Youyiguan in Pingyiang (border city), a dozen kilometers from Lang Son in Vietnam.

The **Guangxi Museum**, *Minzu Road*, has botanical and zoological specimens, historical relics, and Taiping history. It also boasts the largest collection of bronze drums (over 300) in China. The 126.5 hectare Nanhu (South Lake) Park in the southeast has 1200 varieties of medicinal herbs, plus orchids and bonsai. The **Guangxi Botanical Garden of Medicinal Plants**, eight kilometers from the city in the eastern suburbs, has 2100 kinds on 200 hectares. It also raises animals for medicinal purposes.

The **Yiling Cave**, 32 kilometers north in Wuming County, is much like a Guilin cave, with colored lights to highlight weird rock formations here that look like lions, a hen, and vegetables. Visitors usually walk 1100 meters. Outside is a pavilion built in the elaborate style of the Zhuang people.

For those interested in the customs of national minorities, visit a **Zhuang village** in Wuming County, and in Nanning, the **Guangxi Minority Nationality College**. The **Guangxi Art College** teaches the art, music, and dances of the minorities. The Ethnic Garden displays real houses of the Zhuang, Yao, Miao, and Dong nationalities and a Dong bridge and drum tower. Arts and crafts are demonstrated and sold.

Twelve different nationalities live in the region, of which the Zhuang form over one-third. They are somewhat similar to the hill people of northern Thailand. The colorful Miao and Yao live here also. This makes Nanning a good place to look for handicrafts to study and buy.

The Taiping Heavenly Kingdom originated from **Jintian village*, 272 kilometers northeast of the city. This was the most extensive peasant uprising in Chinese history. It started in 1851 and took over a large portion of the country with a capital in Nanjing. Its disruptions were largely responsible for the immigration of Chinese people from south China to America, Australia, and other parts of Asia. At the home of Wei Changhui, one of the leaders, revolutionists made weapons.

SHOPPING

Locally made are Zhuang brocade, ethnic embroidery, bamboo, and pottery ware. The province also sells artistic shell, horn, and feather products, and stone carvings. Also produced are Xishan tea and Milky Spring Wine. You can visit the silk factory. Locally grown are jack fruit, mango, almond, and longan.

You might want to check out the following stores: **Arts and Crafts Service**, *Xinhua Road, Tel. 2822779*; **Foreign Languages Bookstore**, *Minsheng Road, Tel. 2827033*; **Friendship Store**, *Renmin Road, Tel. 2823480*; **Nanning Antique Store**, *19-2 Gucheng Road, Tel. 2807810*; and **Guangxi Tourist Produce Market**, *Tel. 2803019*.

EXCURSIONS FROM NANNING

Beihai is Guangxi's sea port, and one of the 14 Open Coastal Cities. A tourist train from Guilin connects it with Nanning. It has a good beach and the largest holiday resort in Asia is being built there.

The best hotel, when open, is probably the **SHANGRI-LA HOTEL**, *33, Chating Road. New and aiming for four stars. Dist.A.P. 20 km. Dist.R.W. seven km. 425 rooms. B.C. Outdoor pool, two tennis courts, gym and sauna. USTV.* It's not on a beach, though.

There's also the three-star **FURAMA** *(Fuli Hua), 31 Beibu Gulf Chating Road, 536000. Tel. 2050080. Fax 2050085.*

CITS is at *6 Beibu Gulf Dong Road, 536000. Tel. 3033038 X 702. Fax 3054477.* Beihai's telephone code is *0779.* Business hours are 8 am to 12 noon; 2:30 to 5:30 pm; store hours are 9 am to 9 pm.

Liuzhou is toward and closer to Guilin, with many Dong, Hui, Miao, Yao, and Zhuang nationalities and festivals. It has the **Liuhou Temple** and tomb of the famous Tang writer who worked to free women from being bond slaves. There are also the **Dule Caves** (much like Guilin's) and the Bai Lain Cave where Liujiang (Liuchiang) Man lived 20,000 to 30,000 years ago. Open now is the **Longshen Minority Area** with Yao, Zhuang and Dong minorities. You need an extra one or two days for the visit.

If you want to stay in the area, try the **LIUZHOU GRAND HOTEL** (Fandian), *2 Longcheng Road, 545001,* with IDD and pool. **CITS** and the **Liuzhou Tourist Bureau** are in the *Liuzhou Hotel, Tel. (772)285669.*

A good time to visit is during the **Dragon Boat Festival** (5th day of the 5th month), the Zhuang Song Festival (3rd day of the 3rd month), Lantern Festival (15th day of the 1st month), and Mid-Autumn Festival (15th day of the 8th month) ' all on the lunar calendar. At the Song Festival, small groups of male and small groups of female singers compete with each other in wit, knowledge, and vocal quality. Then the boys chase the girls they like in order to continue the contest with more privacy. The festival also includes throwing embroidered balls, and dragon and buffalo dances.

The **Zuojiang Huashan Tourist Area** has the **Mount Hua Rock Paintings** which are found along the **Ming River**, 180 kilometers away from Nanning near the Vietnam border. Here you can take a boat trip to wonder at primitive riverside rock paintings and dances inspired by the paintings. You can also watch local people pan for gold and visit the **Longrui Nature Reserve**, the only place in the world inhabited by rare white-headed langur monkeys and golden camellias.

You can also travel to **Guilin** from here; see separate listing above in this chapter.

GOING TO VIETNAM

*If you have a valid Vietnam visa, you can fly from Nanning to **Hanoi** any Monday, or take the train from Nanning straight to Hanoi. A boat goes from Fangcheng in China to Haiphong in Vietnam. Be sure you have all necessary documents for Vietnam; border guards in Vietnam looking for bribes have been hassling travelers.*

PRACTICAL INFORMATION

- **BusinessHours**, Offices 8 am to 12 noon; 2:30 to 5:30 pm; Stores, 9 am to 10 pm.
- **Guangxi CITS**, *40 Xinmin Road, Nanning, 530012. Tel. 2804960. Fax 2801041*
- **Guangxi CTS**, *7 Xinhua Street, 530012. Tel. 2828711. Fax 2827829*
- **Guangxi Tourist Corporation**, *Ms. Chen Ying, F.I.T. Dept. Manager, 40 Xinmin Road, 530012. Tel. 2816197. Fax 2804105.*
- **Tourist Complaints**, contact **Supervisory Bureau of Tourism Quality**, *Tel. 2802312. Fax 2801041*
- **Telephone Code**, *0771*
- **Tourism Administration**, *Tel. 2805859, 2807774. Fax 2801041.* Fax for a list of interesting tour possibilities including forest preserves, Zhuang Nationality traditional medicine, hot sand treatment, and dates of festivals.

SHENZHEN

(Shumchun)

On the Hong Kong border, this Special Economic Zone has been the wealthiest and the fastest growing in China. In 1979, it had 20,000 people. Today, urban and rural, it has at least 2.3 million. Aspiring to become the next Hong Kong by the year 2010, it has its own stock exchange and a tightly-packed garden of skyscrapers. Fifty percent of all "foreign" arrivals into China pass through its Customs Houses. Most are Hong Kong commuters. Shenzhen has the highest cost of living in China, but it is still considerably cheaper than Hong Kong.

Shenzhen is not just for business people. It is Hong Kong's weekend playground. It has theme parks, amusement parks, and resorts. Some of these are world class. One of its golf and country clubs was designed for the 1995 World Cup.

ARRIVALS & DEPARTURES

A high-speed train line connecting Beijing to Shenzhen is due in 1997. It is reached by air from at least 48 Chinese cities, Bangkok, Jakarta, Singapore, and soon perhaps Seoul, Moscow, Amsterdam, Kuala Lumpur and Khabarovsk. **Huangtian Airport** is 40 kilometers west of the city. There is also a six-lane expressway.

From Hong Kong's Kowloon Railway Station in Hung Hom, there are fast and frequent electric trains. It takes less than one hour. Only travelers on the through-express trains to Guangzhou now cross the famous old covered bridge at Shenzhen. The rest might have to endure long lineups in two Customs Houses. Trains are the fastest and most convenient way to get to downtown Shenzhen from downtown Kowloon because of heavy road traffic.

There are also city and hotel buses between the two cities, and direct buses from Hong Kong to Splendid China and some of the hotels and resorts. (Some buses do not have signs in English.) No Hong Kong taxis are allowed into Shenzhen. Ferries with Macau are planned if they haven't already started.

Citibus 500, *Tel. Hong Kong (852) 27458888 or fax 27865876,* goes from China Hong Kong City (Canton Road) with stops at City One Shatin, Sha Tau Koh border point, Shenzhen City, Honey Lake, Shenzhen Bay (for Splendid China theme park), Xili Lake and Hot Spring Lake. Departures are at least eight times a day. The last bus returns from Shenzhen Bay to Hong Kong at 5:30 pm, too early alas, for the parade at Folk Cultures Village. Aside from rush hours and weekends, going by bus avoids queues at the border points.

Ferries also go from Hong Kong to Shenzhen's Shekou. From here you can also get a taxi or bus to Splendid China.

Formalities

You can enter China at Shenzhen with the usual China visa, but you can also enter Shenzhen and Shekou without a visa for 72 hours if you make your bookings through China Travel Service or any other designated Hong Kong travel agent. You can start the procedure through China Travel Service in North America or elsewhere before you go. You have to be in a group of at least three people.

You can obtain a five-day visa for Shenzhen at the Shenzhen Customs House if you enter from the Hong Kong border by train between 7:30 am and 10 pm. The border is open from 6 am to 11 pm daily. To avoid the lineups, leave Kowloon station at 8:45 pm so you can cross the border about 10 pm. Later than that, you run the risk of Chinese border officials being unavailable to grant visas. Another good time to cross is early morning before the rush.

ORIENTATION

Shenzhen is about seven by 10 kilometers spreading mainly east and west from the railway station. A 39.5 kilometer subway is planned from the main railway station to Shenzhen airport.

The main resorts are in the suburbs, or toward Shekou, which is 29 kilometers west. At least two resorts have amusement park rides, the biggest at the **Honey Lake Country Club** (eight kilometers from the train station), boasting the longest roller coaster ride (two kilometers) in the world. Its monorail is 4.5 kilometers long. One of the biggest resorts is being built towards the Daya Bay Nuclear Power Station, 30 kilometers to the northeast.

WHERE TO STAY

Hotels and food in Shenzhen are cheaper than in Hong Kong for the same quality. The English is generally not as good as Hong Kong's. This city has over 100 hotels for foreigners. The ones listed here receive television from Hong Kong.

The top hotel is the **Shangri-La**, then the **Sunshine** and **Landmark**. The Forum is the best four star. The best for business people depends on where you are doing business. Shekou, 30 kilometers west of the Shenzhen railway station, is near the science park with its many factories and is about 10 kilometers from Splendid China. Here are the lovely five- star Nanhai and the cheaper but adequate Marina Ming Wah. The Nanhai is on the waterfront; the Ming Wah on a mountain.

In Shenzhen itself, on the east side of the railway station closer to the International Trade Centre is the top-rated Shangri-La Hotel. On the west side is the Forum, cheaper and good. Closer to the downtown area which is not all that far away is the very good Sunshine.

The Shenzhen Bay and the Nanhai have the most garden space and would be best for children, but are far from good shopping. Until the new five-star hotel opens close to Splendid China in 1997. The best and most convenient to three of the theme parks is the Shenzhen Bay Hotel, comfortable and basic with good restaurants.

There are other cheaper hotels in this neighbourhood. Many of the Shenzhen Bay's rooms overlook the Folk Culture Village, and you can usually spy flocks of egrets in nearby mangroves, and the skyscrapers of Hong Kong's New Territories across the bay.

From the higher floors of the railway station hotels downtown, you can make out Hong Kong's Sheung Shui, a neat switch after decades of tourists getting a peek at China from Hong Kong. I haven't found any three-star hotel I really like in downtown Shenzhen. The Guangdong is downtown, mediocre with poor maintenance, but should do in a pinch. It has little if any English and takes credit cards. Look also at the Shenzhen International.

Prices listed here are subject to change, negociation and a 15% service charge. Hotels usually quote their prices in Hong Kong dollars (about HK$7.70 = US$1). All have IDD and services expected of international standard hotels.

FORUM HOTEL SHENZHEN (*Fulin Jiudian*), *67 Heping Road, 518010. Four stars, Tel. 5586333. Fax 5561700. In US, Tel. 1-800-327-1177. US$146 to $166. West side of railway station. Dist.A.P. 40 km. Credit Cards.*

Built 1990, ren. 1996. 25 stories, 541 rooms. Wide twins. In-room safes. B.C. Sichuan, Japanese and international food. Deli. Executive and non-smoking floors. Outdoor pool. Gym. 24-hr room service and coffee shop. USTV. Claims largest ballroom in city. Inter-Continental Hotels.

GUANGDONG HOTEL *(Yue Hai Jiudian), 130 Shennan Dong Road, 518001. Three stars. Tel. 2228339. Fax 2234560. HK$430-$600. Dist.R.W. two km. Dist A.P. 30 km.*

There are 208 rooms, with narrow twin beds. HKTV. Narrow halls with low ceiling. B.C. Tours eat here. Japanese restaurant. Gym. Steam bath.

LANDMARK HOTEL SHENZHEN, *2 Nanhu Road, 518001. Five stars. Tel. 2172288. Fax 2290473, 2290479. HK$1000 to $1391. Dist.A.P. 40 km. Dist.R.W. three km. Credit Cards.*

Built 1994. 351 rooms. IDD. In-room safe. USTV. Executive and non-smoking floors. B.C. Gym. Chao Zhou restaurant. A Cathay International Hotel.

SHANGRI-LA SHENZHEN HOTEL *(Shang Gorilla), East Side, Railway Station, Jianshe Rd., 518001. Five stars, Tel. 2330888. Fax 2339878, 2330470. In US, Tel. 1-800-942-5050. US$155. Dist.A.P. 42 km. 200 metres from entrance to railway station. Credit Cards.*

Built 1992. Ren.1995. 31 stories, 523 large rooms. In-room safes and voice-messaging system due soon. Executive and non- smoking floors. B.C., USTV. Revolving restaurant. 24-hour room service. Clinic. Gym. Jacuzzi, sauna, steambath. Outdoor pool.

SHENZHEN BAY HOTEL, *Overseas Chinese Town, 518053. Four stars, Tel. 6600111. Fax 6600139.*

There are 308 rooms with narrow twin beds. Many rooms with balconies. Sign in English says "Please dress properly," otherwise English and Cantonese (yes Cantonese!) need work. Beautiful outdoor pool. Tennis. Gym. Night Club.

SHENZHEN INTERNATIONAL HOTEL, *1 Dongmen Bei Rd., 518001. Tel. 2222763. Three stars.*

SUNSHINE HOTEL *(Yanguang Jiu Dian), 1 Jiabin Road, 518005. Five stars, Tel. 2338888. Fax 2226719. In North America, Tel. 1-800-44UTELL.*

Across plaza from Seibu Department Store. Free shuttle for guests from downtown Hong Kong once a day or from railway station. Built 1991. Two-story lobby. 10 floors. 307 rooms and 20 suites. Wide halls with low ceilings. No CNN. 24-hour B.C. 16th floor has male-only library and bar; no unescorted women. It also should have an indoor pool, gym, minigolf, and two executive floors. 24-hour buffet and 24-hour room service. Japanese food. Chaozhou restaurants. McDonald's.

Outside Shenzhen City

Shekou is 30 kilometers from downtown Shenzhen and has 50-minute hovercraft service with Hong Kong four times a day. It is 20 nautical miles away from Hong Kong's Central, and is close to the Sea World Amusement Park. A retired cruise ship, the Minghua/Sea- World, is now moored in the bay, providing 239 small and claustrophobic hotel rooms. There is also an exhibit of the Qin Dynasty Terracotta Warriors.

MARINA MING WAH, *Gui Shan Rd., Shekou, 518067. Three-star standard, Tel. 6689968. Fax 6686668. Dist.A.P.25 km. Dist.R.W.30 km. Two kilometers from Hong Kong ferry port (free shuttle bus). Credit Cards.*

Built 1992. Six stories, 113 rooms. Small bathrooms. IDD. B.C. Clinic. USTV, no CNN. Atmosphere like pleasant college dormitory. Due soon is a gym, pool, tennis, service apartments, and offices. Swiss-Belhotel Management H.K.

NAN HAI HOTEL *(Da Jiudian), Shekou, Shenzhen, 518069. Five stars, Tel. 6692888. Fax 6692440, 6679476. Dist.A.P. 28 km. Dist.R.W. 30 km. Credit Cards.*

In residential area near town close to Hong Kong ferry pier. Built 1985, ren. 1995. 11 stories. 396 rooms. In-room safes. USTV, B.C. Tennis. Mini-golf, pool, disco. Bicycles. 24-hour room service. Small gym. 27-metre outdoor year-round pool. Bus once a day from Hong Kong. Shuttle bus to Splendid China. Free shuttle to railway station. Ideal for honeymooners. Managed by Miramar International Hotels Management Group (H.K.).

WHERE TO EAT

Food at the theme parks is interesting but basic. We couldn't find any international class restaurants in them. At the **TUJIA PAVILION** in the Folk Culture Village, you can buy sticky rice wrapped and steamed in lotus leaves, and near the entrance is a restaurant serving knife-cut noodles, a specialty of Shanxi province. But the Chinese restaurants in the nearby **SHENZHEN BAY HOTEL** are international class.

McDONALD'S is outside the gate of Windows on the World. You won't starve there. In town, food in the top hotels is very good, especially the Cantonese.

SEEING THE SIGHTS

The day trippers can view China's greatest concentration of skyscrapers. They might note the reservoir that supplies half of Hong Kong's water supply. Greater Shenzhen has no historical monuments save the modest grave in Shekou of the last Song emperor, who fled here to escape the Mongols.

Three theme parks are together around the Shenzhen Bay Hotel, about a 20 minutes' drive west towards Shekou: Splendid China, Folk Cultures Village, and Windows on the World.

Splendid China (Jinxiu Zhong Hua) is on 29 hectares with over 80 of China's top tourist attractions in 15:1 miniature, including a part of the Great Wall, a Suzhou garden, the Terracotta Warriors, and three Yangtze gorges. It is highly recommended (but not in the rain). Take a guide as no explanations are in English.

Thousands of tiny ceramic people, each different, in period or ethnic dress, and in scale, add liveliness. They include Mongolian wrestlers in their leather vests and baggy pants, emperors paying homage at the temple of Confucius, and the Yangtze Gorges. Open 8 am to 5:30 pm daily.

The **Folk Culture Village** is next to the miniatures. This is a 180,000 square meter exhibition of 24 different life-size minority buildings, with demonstrations of handicrafts, cooking, and three shows a day of dances and songs of all 56 nationalities. Evenings have a parade with perhaps a costume show, wedding processions, and carnival.

It is a lot more interesting than Splendid China because it has real people. With samples of full-scale Tujia, Uygur and Wa architecture, and of course real Miao, Jinuo and Tibetan people in ethnic dress, you can really get a good introduction to China's 55 minorities. These ethnically diverse peoples total 8% of the population. They live on over 50% of the land.

If you want to do more than just shoot photos, take an interpretor so you can ask questions. There is only one small sign with a limited amount of information in English beside each exhibit.

While the dirt, poverty, and the variety within cultures are missing in each exhibit, there are enough farm implements, hanging husks of corn, and weaving looms to show how these people differ from the Han majority. In some cases, you can get ethnic food. And the toilets are clean!

You can spend six hours at Folk Culture Village but it can be done quickly in two plus the parade. The 7:30 pm daily parade is lively and professional with visiting groups, permanent floats and show-biz adaptions of minority dances. In case you missed it the first time, the parade goes through its routine twice. Its happy-happy atmosphere with 300 performers should not be missed. Photo opportunities abound and attendants willingly pose. No one runs shyly away nor asks for money. For lazy tourists, this can be a substitute for the real thing.

You can go there even as late as 4 pm by taxi, snack on the grounds, and explore until the 7:30 pm parade.

On the other side of the Shenzhen Bay Hotel is **Windows of the World**, a 480,000 square meter theme park with miniatures of monuments from all over the world like the Golden Gate Bridge and Eiffel Tower.

Safari Park, a wild animal park with 15,000 animals is in another part of the city, is at *Xi Li Lake, 518055, Tel. 6622888*. It takes at least two hours to tour it plus at 4 pm its parade of animals and clowns. You take buses through the various habitats. Among the 150 species are pandas, golden monkeys, Asian elephants, red- crested cranes, and Asian tigers.

If you have to choose, go to Splendid China and Folk Culture Village because they are uniquely Chinese. There are parks similiar to Windows of the World in Beijing.

Shenzhen also has a museum, botanical garden and pearl farm. One of its several golf courses is open 24 hours. A marine world is being planned. The best beach is east of the city at **Xiao Mei Sha** with a three-star hotel.

Festivals
During the summertime litchi (lichee) season, tourists come here to pick this sweet fruit. The tour price usually includes all-you-can eat and 2.5 kilograms to take home. A **Lichee and Fine Food Festival** takes place the end of June and early July.

SHOPPING
At the theme parks, there's the usual tourist stuff, mostly poor quality. In town, however, there's the fancy **Seibu Department Store** near the Sunshine Hotel with brand names such as Givenchy, Salvatore Ferragamo, and Chanel. A **shopping mall** with a branch of Dickson's, the Hong Kong department store, is in the *Tian An International Building, Ren Min Nan Road, Tel. 2296161* with such names as Ralph Loren, Via Roma, and Harvey Nichols.

Although Shenzhen makes many international name brand clothing, I couldn't find any stores with factory overruns. Things are cheaper in Guangzhou. The closest Shenzhen has to factory shopping is "Lao Jie" or "Gao Guy," old street or Nanqing Jie near Jiefang Road in the eastern part of the city. There you might find locally- made export-quality clothing, Reeboks, carpets, bags, bedding and toys. Clothing sizes are small. This is a tiny street near McDonald's. (Go out the front door of McDonald's, cross the street to the left, turn right until you come to an narrow archway over a narrow street. That's it. Don't expect Hong Kong.) China's first Wal-Mart should be open here by now in Luohu District.

PRACTICAL INFORMATION
· **Business Hours**, 8,30 or 9 am to 5,30 pm, mostly five days a week for offices; 9 am or 10 am to 10 pm for stores daily.

- **Shenzhen China International Service,** *2 Chuan Bu Street, Heping Road, 518001. Tel. 2338822, 5588411. Fax 5572151, 2329832; also 6 Yan He Nan Road, 518005*
- **Shenzhen CTS,** *5th Floor, China Travel Service Building, 40 Renmin Nan Road, 518001. Tel. 2258447. Fax 2235576*
- **Shenzhen Tourist Association,** *18th floor, Grand Skylight Hotel, 68 Shennan Zhong Road, 518041, for information.*
- **Telephone Code,** *0755*

22. SOUTHWEST CHINA

CHENGDU

(Chengtu)

Located in central Sichuan province of which it is the capital, **Chengdu** has a history of over 2,000 years. In the fourth century B.C., the King of Shu moved his capital here and named it Chengdu ('Becoming a Capital'). In the Han, after brocade weaving became successfully established, it was called the Brocade City. During the Three Kingdoms, it was the capital of Shu. Many American, Canadian, and British missionaries and teachers lived here before 1949.

With an altitude of 500 meters, its hottest temperature is 37 degrees centigrade in July and its coldest may be minus three degrees centigrade in January. The tourist season is April to November, with July and August uncomfortably hot. Annual precipitation is about 1000 millimeters, mainly in July and August.

The population is 9.2 million, both urban and rural. Minorities in the province include Naxi, Qiong, Yi, Jingpo, Mao and Tibetan.

ARRIVALS & DEPARTURES

Chengdu is slightly over two hours by air southwest of Beijing. There are direct flights from 52 other cities in China, Singapore, Hong Kong and soon Japan. It can also be reached by a 25-hour train from Kunming through 250 kilometers of tunnels.

A four-lane, five to six-hour, 340 kilometer expressway trip from Chongqing should now be available.

ORIENTATION

Today it is the provincial capital and an educational and industrial center. Its industries include metallurgy, electronics, and textiles. The area grows rice, wheat, canola, chilis, and sweet potatoes. It also grows medicinal plants and herbs that are sold all over the country.

Chengdu has so much to offer, you need at least three days to cover the city, preferably more for nearby excursions. You might consider the following schedule if you have three days:

- **Day One**: Du Fus Cottage, the Temple of Marquis Wu, Tomb of Wang Jian, brocade, bamboo-weaving, jade-carving or lacquerware factory, or provincial museum.
- **Day Two**: Zoo, Divine Light Monastery, and the River-Viewing Pavilion
- **Day Three**: Dujiangyuan and Green City Mountain

GETTING AROUND TOWN

This city is bustling with chronic traffic jams. Its downtown areas are crowded especially around the Jin Jiang and Minshan Hotels and north towards one of the few remaining statues of Chairman Mao, and the big department stores. A trip to the zoo could take five hours. Use the ring road around the city. A 46 kilometer subway is being built.

WHERE TO STAY

The top hotels are the **Jin Jiang**, the **Minshan**, and then the **Chengdu**. The Dynasty and Sichuan Hotels were too new to review but they should also be among the top. The Jin Jiang and Minshan are both near the Jinjiang River have the CAAC and CITS offices conveniently closeby. From the Dynasty and Sichuan Hotels, you can walk to the department stores. The Chengdu Hotel is further away but still central.

The Golden River and the Tibet Hotel are okay for budget travelers. Many foreign backpackers stay at the Jiaotong Hotel near the bus station to Leshan. Prices are subject to 10% service charge.

CHENGDU HOTEL *(Fandian), Dongyiduan, Shudu Road, 610066. Four stars, Tel. 4444888. Fax 4441603, 4432083. Dist.A.P. 18 km. Dist.R.W. eight km. Credit Cards.*

In industrial area, far from anywhere. Built 1984, Renovations 1995 and 1996. 12 stories, 310 small rooms. IDD and B.C. Indoor pool, gym, and clinic. USTV. Korean and Japanese restaurants. Executive floors. Haggle for discount. Member of China Friendship Tourist Hotel Group. Adequate but not classy.

YINHE DYNASTY HOTEL *(Yin He Wang Cao Fandian), 99 Xia Xi Shun Cheng St., 610016. Aiming for five stars. Tel. 6618888. Fax 6243131 or 6748837. Dist.A.P. 22 km.*

Located downtown close to the Sichuan Exhibition Centre and near Maos statue. Next to the three-story underground shopping mall, said to be the biggest in Asia. Built 1995. Six and 26 stories. 380 rooms. Hairdryers. IDD. USTV. Executive floors. One non-smoking floor. Hong Kong management. Mexican, Thai, Cantonese, Chaozhou and continental food. Sushi bar. American barbecue and teppanyaki. Gym, outdoor pool, bowling, steam bath, and sauna.

GOLDEN RIVER HOTEL *(Jinhe Dajiudian), 18 Jin He St., 610031. Three stars, Tel. 6642888. Fax 6632037. Dist.A.P. 18 km. Dist.R.W. four km.*

Built 1988. 17 stories, 900 beds (best on seventh to ninth floors). Narrow hallways. Warm friendly hotel. Budget travelers only.

JIN JIANG HOTEL, *80, Section 2, Ren Min Nan Ave., 610012. Five stars, Tel. 5582222. Fax 5581849. Dist.A.P. 17 km. Dist.R.W. eight km. Credit Cards.*

Ren. 1993. Nine stories. 523 rooms with three telephone jacks, in-room safes. B.C., IDD. H.K.J.V. Film developing. Post office. Cantonese and Korean cuisine. Bicycles. USTV. Gym. Outdoor pool. Bowling. Tennis. Clinic with dentist. Post office. Good air ticket office. A five-star VIP Building, the **YIDONG HOTEL** at the back, has its own white marble lobby, fine furniture, chandeliered hallways, and two floors of executive suites. The South Wing has good standards. The East Wing is cheapest. Y690 to Y1700. Price should include breakfast.

MINSHAN HOTEL, *55 Section 2, Ren Min Nan Road, 610021. Four stars, Tel. 5583333, 5554924, Fax 5582154. Dist. A.P. 17 km. Dist. R.W. seven km.*

Ren. 1994. 21 stories. 327 rooms. USTV. IDD. B.C. Cantonese and Japanese food. Health food. Clinic. Gym and outdoor pool.

TIBET HOTEL, *10 Renmin Road, 610081. Three stars, Tel. 3334001. Fax 3333526.*

WHERE TO EAT

This is one of the best cities for Sichuan food. Flower petals and herbs are used in such specialties as fried lotus flower, governors chicken, diced chicken with hot pepper and peanuts, and smoked duck with tea fragrance. Try also the dumplings and Dan Dan noodles. See Chapter 11, *Food & Drink*.

If you don't like hot spices, ask the restaurant to tone them down. The food is still good without chilis. If you want more hot spices, order a dish of *la jiu*. For local snacks, ask for *lai tong yuan* dumplings or *long tao* dumplings.

Aside from restaurants in hotels – which are very good – restaurants used to tourists are the **QI YUN-LOU**, *251 Wuhouci Street, Tel. 5541851* (almost at the entrance to the Zhuge Liang Memorial Hall) – ask for the crispy rice, the dan-dan noodles and wonton soup – and the **BOYAYUAN RESTAURANT**, *3, 4th section, Renmin Nan Da Jie. Tel. 5581007*, which is on the grounds of the Sichuan Provincial Museum. The bean curd, chili peppers, and bean sprouts are all good.

The **NU LICAN RESTAURANT**, *1 Jinhe Street, Tel. 6633382, 6635181,* has traditional peasant food. Ask for the beef simmered in soy sauce and five-star annis, the shoe-string potatoes, and egg custard. Ignore the dirty floor and the karaoke flashing on 16 television monitors showing women in bathing suits reminiscent of the 1940s. The staff is attentive.

The restaurant at the **TRADITIONAL MEDICINE UNIVERSITY** serves "healthy food," *Tel. 7762134, or 7769241 X 493.* The famous 18th century MA PO DOU FU RESTAURANT, *197 Xi Yu Long Street, Tel. 6674512,* is still there but with mixed reviews. It originated the well-known spicy hot bean-curd dish and still offers 30 kinds of bean-curd dishes.

The ninth floor Chinese restaurant at the **JIN JIANG HOTEL** is especially good. Try the tea-flavoured duck.

For western food, stick with the hotels.

SEEING THE SIGHTS

***Du Fu's** (Tu Fu) **Thatched Roof Cottage** is a 20-hectare park with a replica of the modest residence of the famous Tang poet who lived here and wrote 240 poems for four years from 759 A.D. A temple and garden were first built as a memorial in the Northern Song. The pavilions here are from the Qing era. Among the exhibitions are some translations of his poems in 15 foreign languages which might help you understand his importance. Open daily.

The **Temple of Marquis Wu**, *at 231 Wuhouci Avenue* in the southern part of the city, was originally built in the sixth century in memory of Zhuge Liang (Chuke Liang), a famous strategist, statesman, and prime minister of Shu during the Three Kingdoms (220-265 A.D.). Here are tablets written during the Tang, larger than life-size statues, and the still unexcavated Tomb of Liu Bei, the King of Shu. The current buildings are Qing. The ***Zhuge Liang Memorial Hall** is a historical site under State Council protection.

The **Wangjianglou** (River-Viewing Pavilion) in the southeastern part of the city was once the residence of a Tang dynasty woman poet, Xue Tao. The park has over 100 varieties of bamboo. Sit in the Pavilion for Poem Reciting or the Chamber to Relieve Your Resentment. Sit in them quietly for half an hour, breathe deeply and see if they inspire you, too, to poetry. Open daily.

The **Sichuan Provincial Museum** is about two kilometers south of the Jin Jiang Hotel. It has an amazing display of bronzes from the Ba Culture that developed in the Yangtze valley to the east. These are the people whose coffins you look for in the hills on the side trips from the Yangtze cruises. Unique to the Ba culture are these incredible humanoid figures.

The 25-hectare **Chengdu Zoo** is six kilometers north of the city and boasts over 12 giant pandas, the largest collection of this endangered species in captivity anywhere in the world. Only a few might be on display however. The zoo also has rare golden-hair monkeys among 2,000 animals of over 200 varieties. Open daily.

Try to see the *Tomb of Wang Jian (847-918 A.D.), *5 Fuqin Dong Road*, the emperor of Shu in the 10th century, if you are interested in history. Wang Jian captured not just Sichuan, but parts of three other provinces, and proclaimed himself emperor in 907. The 23.4 meter-long tomb is elaborate with double stone arches and carved musicians. Open daily.

The Baoguangsi (Divine Light Monastery) should not be missed. It is 18 kilometers north of the city at Xindu, and famous. Originally founded during the Eastern Han, about 2000 years ago, it became the site of a palace ordered built by Tang Emperor Li Huan. During the Ming, war destroyed the monastery but it was reconstructed on its original foundation during the Qing in 1671. Pagodas, five halls, and 16 courtyards make it most impressive. The Tang Pagoda is 30 meters high, 13 stories with a glazed gold top. The 500 arhats are from the Qing in 1851, each about two meters high, unique and vivid. Look for the 175-centimeters-high stone Thousand Buddha Tablet, carved on four sides in 450 A.D. and for the Buddhist scriptures written on palm leaves from India. Open daily.

If you dig museums, the Sichuan Provincial Museum, *3, Section 4, Renmin Nan Road*, is at your disposal. Learn more about the Long March through Sichuan and local history. Open daily.

There's another Buddhist monastery, the Wenshu (God of Wisdom) Monastery, *15 Wenshuyuan Street, Beimen*. Founded in the Tang and reconstructed in 1691, this temple has ancient paintings and a white jade statue from Burma, gilded Japanese scripture containers (Tang), and other treasures. Open daily.

The *Dujiangyan Irrigation System, a one-hour drive northwest (57 kilometers) in Guanxian county, usually takes a full day. It was originally built in 256 B.C., the oldest such project in the country. Impressive because of its age and scope, it controlled floods and diverted half of the Minjiang River to irrigate the fertile Sichuan plain. This area has old temples with murals. It has a 240-meter long swinging bridge first built before the Song, but most recently rebuilt in 1974, so don't be afraid to walk on it. The Fu Long Kuan (Dragon Subduing Temple) houses a statue of Li Bing, the mastermind of the project. The Erwang (Two Kings) Temple is a memorial to Li Bing and his son.

Near Dujiangyan is a deer farm where you can buy Pilose Antler Juice for an aching back, impotence, and premature ejaculation. Also near Dujiangyan and 90 kilometers from Chengdu is Qingcheng (Green City) Mountain, one of the birthplaces of Taoism and still a Taoist center, with 38 buildings left of its 70 original temples, shrines, and grottoes. There's a cable car now at Qingcheng Mountain, but you have to hike a way first.

With some of its cliffs shaped like city walls (hence the name), this strikingly beautiful mountain rises up to 1,600 meters. It was also a base for a peasant insurgency led by Zhang Xianzhong (Chang Hsien-chung), who captured Chongqing in 1644 and occupied Chengdu. Visitors can reach the Jian Fu Temple (Tang) by road. There are guesthouses midway up and on top.

One of the founders of Taoism, Zhang Daolin, put up an altar here for preaching. The **Cavern of Taoist Master Temple** was founded in 617 to 605 B.C. The building is from the Tang and contains a portrait of Zhang Daolin, stone carvings of the Three Emperors, Ming woodwork, and murals of the Eight Taoist Fairies. The mountain is full of legends.

SHOPPING

Of the factories that can be visited, the following are most interesting to visitors: make bamboo weavings, brocade, Shu embroidery, filigree crafts, and lacquerware. Chengdu is one of the largest and cheapest source of Chinese medicines, with prices about one-twentieth Hong Kong's. The main shopping is on Renmin Road, Yanshikou, and Chunxi Road. A big department store is the **You Yi Guan Chang** (Friendship Store) near Qing Shi Qiao on Chun Xi Road.

The **Chengdu Bamboo Weaving Factory** is at *12 Jie Fang Road, Section 1,* and **Number Two Shu Embroidery Factory** is at *11 Heping Street.*

In the evening, the street between the Jin Jiang and Minshan Hotels and Chairman Mao is a half-kilometer-long sidewalk art gallery of ethnic crafts and paintings, stuffed animals, and "antiques." On the Jin Jiang Hotel side is a line of antique and craft shops that also sell tourist junk but some genuine relics from Tibet that look like parts of human skulls (carved!), ceremonial daggers, scriptures and *tankgas*. Try **Yue Gu Tang**, *72, 2 Section, Renmin Nan Road, Tel. 6692311.*

EXCURSIONS FROM CHENGDU
Wildlife Preserve

Baoxing County, 350 kilometers west of Chengdu, has a wildlife preserve that is bigger than Wolong with 100 pandas, but park officials cannot guarantee you'll see any here either. Baoxing has Yi and Yao minorities, with traditions stronger than at Jiuzhaigou.

Emei Shan Mountain

Emei Shan Mountain is 170 kilometers southwest of Chengdu and 37 kilometers from Leshan. Together with the **Sansu Shrine**, they make an interesting trip of at least three days, but either Emei or Leshan can be a quick one-day or overnight trip if you don't climb.

Emei Shan is one of China's four great Buddhist mountains. You can reach the base by tourist train from the North Railway Station in Chengdu in less than two hours. The climb to the summit of Emei Shan and back can be done on foot in one day if you're energetic, or two days for the less agile. Along the 60-kilometer stone paths are 23 monasteries, intriguing caves, gushing waterfalls, magnificent views, and birds. Be careful of monkeys; they are known to steal food, scratch, and bite.

Land Rovers drive within six kilometers of the peak at Jioyin Hall, at 2,670 meters. At that height, it can be very chilly, about -20°C at the top in January. Hostels are at the base of and on the 3,100-meter-high summit and there are restaurants along the way. Guides are available.

The best time to climb is from April to June, and September to November. It may be too cold and slippery for climbing from December to March, but the mountain is beautiful. The rainy season is July and August.

Baoguo Temple, at the base, has a scale-model map of the mountain with lights. The temple originates from the Ming. **Wannian Monastery** (Samantabhadra Monastery) on the slope dates from the fourth century. Its bronze and iron buddhas are Song to Ming. The bronze Samantabhdra on a white elephant is 7.4 meters high and weighs 62 tons. The beamless brick hall, its roof, and square walls, are said to be typically Ming.

The best place to stay is the **RED SPIDER MOUNTAIN HOTEL** (*Hong Zhu Shan Binguan*), *614201. Tel. 233888. Fax 233788. Dist.A.P. 130 km. Dist.R.W. 10 km. Credit Cards.* It is near the Baoguo Temple. Built 1935. Three stories. 180 rooms. 10 buildings. Its three-star Number Eight V.I.P. building was opened in 1992. IDD, B.C. Bicycles. CITS. It is the largest hotel in the city. There's also the **EMEI SHAN GRAND HOTEL**, *Baogao Temple, 614201. Two stars. Tel. 522579. Fax 522061.* It's near the main street up the mountain with 340 rooms.

And the **XIONGXIU HOTEL**, *Emei Shan, 614201 with two stars, Tel. 523888. Fax 522406.* The telephone code is *0833*.

Jiuzhaigou

You'll need five days to visit this beautiful wilderness area, which was the setting for the Hollywood movie *The Little Panda*, about two children saving a panda from poachers. The road here is not good.

Jiuzhaigou is a nature preserve about 500 kilometers from Chengdu in Nanping county, a one-and-a-half day drive. You can stay in the two-star **JIUZHAIGOU HOTEL** that now has a 100 three-star rooms with 24-hour hot water, but no credit card service nor IDD. An airport is being built.

The preserve comprises 60,000 hectares of primitive forest with species earlier thought to be extinct. Naturalists should go wild with excitement here. Expect exotic animals, forested hills, carpets of flowers, lakes and waterfalls. Jiuzhaigou means *nine stockades can* which are about 2500 meters above sea level. Tibetan and Qio. ties live in the area. The best time to visit is September and early ~   ~er.

Leshan

Leshan is about 170 kilometers southwest of Chengdu (the closest airport and three and a half hours by road) and 40 kilometers from Emei Mountain. The long trip by road is an opportunity to see the Sichuan countryside, the architecture of the farmhouses, and the obnoxious truck drivers. A new 175 kilometers expressway should open in 1998.

Leshan is 35 kilometers from a railway station. Warm rains from April to June add to the mystical atmosphere. It is a small 1,300-year-old town of 200,000 people, a good place for pedicab rides. It is the home of the ***Dafu** (Great Buddha) **Temple**. Here sits a Buddha (either 58.7 or 70 meters in height, depending on sources) started in 713 A.D. and completed 90 years later. It is believed to be the second largest Buddha in the world. From Leshan city across the river, visitors can take a public bus to the front gate, or arrive by ferry. The view from the water is better; otherwise you can't see the temple guardians. From the water, you should see an even bigger, more virile, reclining Buddha, head to the right, formed accidentally by the shape of the hills and a pagoda. At the confluence of three rivers (Min, Dadu, and Qingyi), the monastery buildings stand at Buddhas eye level.

THE GREAT BUDDHA, LESHAN

This huge statue was built to offset the large number of serious accidents on the river. Since statistics were probably kept before and after, it would be enlightening to know if the statue was worth it. You can reach the **Wuyou** (Black) **Temple** in 15 minutes by footpath from the Dafu Temple. It has a good museum for its tiny size.

The **Oriental Buddhist Capital theme park** is 10 kilometers from the Jia Zhou Hotel with reproductions of famous buddhas. There is also the 2,000 year old **Mahao Cliff Tomb,** south foot of Lingyun Mountain.

The best hotel is the **JIA ZHOU HOTEL** *(Binguan), 19 Bai Ta Road, 614000. Three stars. Tel. 2134415, 2139888. Fax 2133233. Y450. Credit Cards.* Good location on a main street across the river from the Great Buddha. Built 1953 with a second building in 1987. 13 stories, 296 rooms. B.C., bicycles. IDD. On the site of a former Canadian mission near shopping, a park, and boat to Great Buddha Temple.

The **GODDEST HOTEL,** *96 Haitang Road, 614004. Three stars, Tel. 2132022. Fax 2133358. Y350. Credit Cards.* Guests have to walk 20 minutes downhill to stores. It also has six storeys but no elevators. IDD.

Two small guest houses fringe the head of the Buddha with caves, bare floors, and Chinese beds.

Leshan CITS is at *129 Renmin Nan Road, Changchen Building, 614000. Tel. 2124570, 2133198. Fax 2132154.* The tourist hotline is *Tel. 2124570.*

Contact the **Leshan Tourist Bureau,** *23 Boshui Street, Leshan, 614000, Tel. 2131968* if you have any complaints. The telephone code is *0833.*

Sansu Shrine

Sansu Shrine is in Meishan County 89 kilometers south of Chengdu. It was the residence of three famous literary men of the Northern Song and became a shrine during the Ming (1368-98). The current structures are Qing. If you have no time, you can miss it.

Tibet

Tibet is most easily reached from Chengdu with twice-a-day flights leaving early morning. You can book flights and tours from most large travel agencies in China, but Chengdu (and Beijing) have branches of Tibetan travel agencies.

Try **CITS,** *Tibet Shigatse Branch, Jiao Tong (Traffic) Hotel, 77 Linjiang Road, 640041. Tel. 5551017 X 115 or 5591124. Fax 5582777.* It should only take two days to get permission.

The **Tibet Travel Bureau** is at *Tibet Hotel, 10 Renmin Bei Road, 610081. Tel. 3334001. Fax 3333526. See Tibet.*

Wolong Nature Preserve

Wolong Nature Preserve is about 150 kilometers by bumpy, narrow road from Chengdu. The scenery is great and there are hiking trails with maps. It gets cold at night because of the altitude. There are many pandas in the wild, but you might not see any except in cages; there are usually about six around. Some can be seen only on video monitors. Recent visitors found they had to pay to take photos. Some refused the offer to pat these wild creatures not wishing to disturb them. (You might see more pandas in the Chengdu Zoo.)

There's a panda museum here. Read *The Last Panda* by George B. Schaller. Naturalists estimate that there are now about 1,000 pandas in the wild. Ask about the **September Panda Festival**.

You can stay in the very modest **FORESTRY BUREAU HOSTEL**, *Tel. (08489) 443404*, which has heaters in every room, lots of blankets and adequate meals. 10 suites with baths. Travel agencies can book rooms for you. There's lots of room for hiking. In 1994, a hotel at Wolong opened with a karaoke bar. Chengdu is building a breeding facility with help from abroad.

Xichang

China's satellite launching center is in Xichang and tourists are welcome. From Chengdu, it is an overnight train ride on the Chengdu-Kunming railway line. Be sure you get permission before you go if you want to see a launch, arranged through any travel agent. Xichang has an airport. It also has the **Museum of Liangshan Yi Slave Society** on Qionghai Lake in a southeast suburb. It was a stop on the southern Silk Road and claims a visit by Marco Polo. It is the home of the largest community of the Yi nationality in China. There's also the renovated **Nyingma Longchen Nyingtik** (Maiwa) **Tibetan Temple** in Hong Yuan County in northwest Sichuan, originally built in 1646.

The **Xichang Travel Company** and **CITS** are at *2 North Lane, Xiyanjing South, Shengli Road, 615000. Tel. and fax 223061*. Telephone code for the area is *0834*.

Zigong

Zigong (240 kilometers from Chengdu and Chongqing), is noted for its locally-found dinosaurs and giant lanterns. There's a daily train from Chengdu. It has a **dinosaur museum** (built at the site with over 100 specimens), a **salt museum** (showing 2,000 years of the industry), and a **Chinese lantern museum**. The city makes those huge spectacular lanterns decorating Beijing's Beihai Park in summer. A good time to visit is the **Lantern Festival** which lasts for about 20 days before and after the spring festival. The very fancy ***Shaanxi Guild Hall** houses the salt museum. The hall was first built in 1736 A.D.

The best hotel is the three-star **SHAWAN**, *1 Binjiang Road, 643000. Tel. 228888, 221168. Fax 221168. Dist.A.P.107 km. Dist.R.W.one km. IDD, Credit Cards. $40.* It is more centrally located than the two-star **TAN MU LIN GUEST HOUSE**, *2, Tangkan Shang Road, 643000. Tel. 224121. Fax 226257.*

CITS Zigong is at *2 Tangkan Shang Road, Zigong 643000. Tel. 229006. Fax 227313.*

The **Control Department**, *Zigong Tourism Bureau, Number Three Building, Tan Mulin Hotel, 643000. Tel. 222141,* should be contacted if you have any complaints. The telephone code is *0813.*

PRACTICAL INFORMATION
- **Business Hours**, Stores open 9 am to 9 or 10 pm.
- **CTS Sichuan**, *Tel. 6632630, Fax 6639304*
- **CYTS Tours**, *99 Dong San Duan Yi Huan Road, 610061, 4438971, Fax 4449911; seventh floor, Bai Yun Hotel, 6 San Duan, Renmin Nan Road, 610041, Tel. 5585064, Fax 5583854.*
- **Jin Da Travel Agency**, *Jin Jiang Hotel, Tel. 5582222 extension 59. Fax 5589955*
- **Sichuan Overseas Tourist Corporation** and **Sichuan China International Travel Service**, *65 Renmin Nan Road, Tel. 6650780, 6672369, 6628731. Fax 6672970*
- **Sichuan Provincial Tourism Bureau**, *19 Section 2 Renmin Nan Road, 610016. Tel 6671647. Fax 6671042.* For complaints and brochures.
- **Telephone Code**, *028*
- **Tourist Complaints**, contact **Supervisory Bureau of Tourism Quality of Sichuan Province**, *65 Section 2, Renmin Nan Road, 610012, Tel. 6657478. Fax 6671042.*
- **U.S. Consulate**, *4, Lingshiguan Road, Section 4, Renmin Nan Road, Tel. 5589642. Fax 5583520*

CHONGQING
(Chungking)

Chongqing in southeastern Sichuan province is located on mountainsides between the Changjiang (Yangtze) and Jialing Rivers.

Chongqing is over 3,000 years old. It was the capital of the Kingdom of Ba in the 12th century B.C. During the Song, it was named Chongqing, which means double celebration. During the Qing, a 10 meter-high, seven-kilometer wall was built around the city. In the 19th century, Chongqing was one of the treaty ports open to foreigners, and foreign missionaries and teachers worked here before 1949. Innumerable books have been written in English about this area.

In the late 1930s, during the Sino-Japanese War, the Nationalist government moved its capital here, and Han Suyin's book *Destination Chungking* reflects that period. Unfortunately, Japanese bombs destroyed much of the city, and few ancient relics survived the war. Zhou Enlai (Chou En-lai) lived here as he tried to work with the Nationalists against the Japanese. American (Stillwell, Hurley, Marshall, Wedmeyer) missions attempted unsuccessfully to get the Nationalists to work with the Communists. Read Theodore H. White's *In Search of History* for more information on that period in the 1940s. The Communists took over the city in November 1949.

The highest temperature in summer is 40°C; the lowest in winter, 6°C. The annual precipitation is 1000 millimeters. Chongqing is one of the three furnaces of China. There are clear skies only in summer, and fog between November and March. The urban population is about 4.1 million.

ARRIVALS & DEPARTURES

Chongqing is a little more than a two-hour flight southwest of Beijing, or an overnight train ride from Chengdu. There are flights from Hong Kong, Macau, and 42 Chinese cities including Lhasa (thrice a week). **Jiangbei Airport** is 30 kilometers from downtown. When departing by air, give yourself at least one hour from downtown to the airport.

A new highway connecting Wuhan with Chongqing should be finished about 1998, and a new highway between Dazu and Chongqing cutting the distance from 175 to 130 kilometers should be finished soon as well.

ORIENTATION

Today, Chongqing is crowded and industrial. It has very few bicycles because of the narrow, winding, and hilly roads. The houses clinging to the hillsides are fascinating. But the hills make for lots of traffic congestion (and air pollution) especially downtown and near the Jialing Bridge, the only bridge to the airport. The city has started constructing a subway, due about 2000. Parts of the new city road along the shore in downtown Chongqing should be in use now to relieve some of the congestion.

Chongqing is now primarily of interest to students of modern history. It is also the place where you can get a two-day trip to the Dazu sculptures, and take a ship down the Yangtze through the gorges. See *Yangtze Gorges*.

WHERE TO STAY

The best hotel is the **Holiday Inn Yangtze**, then the **Chongqing Guest House** (Binguan). The **Renmin** is next, isolated on the top of a hill, its former Nationalist congress hall an impressive Temple of Heaven clone.

The Chongqing Hotel (Fandian) follows a long way behind in fourth place with a staff that tries hard, but the place smelled of coal gas and who knows what else. Use it only as a last resort. It does have a crowded downtown location from which you can walk downhill to the cruise ships at San Ma Tou pier in five minutes. The Holiday Inn is the furthest from the docks on the south bank of the Yangtze close to corporate offices.

The closest to the congested downtown shopping core around Liberation Monument (Jiefang Bei) are the two Chongqing hotels, the Binguan is in a less congested area. None have bicycles for rent. The Holiday Inn and the Chongqing Hotel have the best western food. Most have dirty carpets in public areas.

You can usually get around the downtown area for about Y10 in a cheap taxi, but not from the Holiday Inn whose only taxis are expensive. The airport is about 30 kilometers from the hotels, the train station about three to five kilometers

CHONGQING GUEST HOUSE *(Binguan), 235 Minsheng Road, 630010. Four stars, Tel. 3845888. Fax 3830643.*

Built 1949. Eight stories, 265 rooms. Executive floor. Cantonese restaurant, Korean barbecue and hot pot restaurant. USTV. Somewhat glitzy lobby. Large recreation center with karaoke, disco, night club, billiards, games and mini-golf. Sauna and massage, clinic and indoor pool.

CHONGQING HOTEL *(Fandian), 41-43 Xin Hua Road, 630011. Three stars, Tel. 3849301. Fax 3843085.*

On a congested street with post office around the corner. Built 1987. 200 rooms, sauna, business center, clinic. Cantonese food. Hong Kong joint venture.

HOLIDAY INN YANGTZE *(Yangzi Jiang Jia Ri Fandian), 15 Nan Ping Bei Rd., 630060. Four stars. Tel. 2803380. Fax 2800884. In uS, Tel. 1-800-HOLIDAY.*

Built 1989. Ren. 1995. USTV. 21 stories, 379 rooms. Non-smoking floor. Executive floor. Local snack restaurant, German beer house, coffee house and grill room. 24-hour room service. Outdoor pool, steam bath, tennis, and putting green. No downtown shuttle bus.

RENMIN (PEOPLE'S) HOTEL, *173 Renmin Rd., 630015. Three stars, Tel. 3851421. Fax 3852076. Credit Cards.*

Across street from city hall and near museum and park. Built 1953. Ren. East Wing 1994. Seven stories. About 248 rooms. Big twins. USTV. No real western restaurants, just a coffee shop. Currently hosts mainly

Asian tour groups and individual travelers. 214 rooms. 24-hour B.C. (no English-language newspapers). This hotel now has a branch in Moscow.

WHERE TO EAT

Sichuan food is famous. Not all of it is chili hot. See Sichuan Dishes in Chapter 11, *Food & Drink*. The restaurants in the hotels are best.

The **SICHUAN HOT POT RESTAURANT** on Jiao Chang Ko Street is famous and privately run. The **LE YUAN (PARADISE) RESTAU-RANT**, *Tel. 2812321, 2812322, at Nan Qiao Tou Ke Pu Zhongxin,* is across the superhighway from the Holiday Inn beside the big Buddha in the amusement park.

The **WEIYUAN RESTAURANT**, *Tel. 3833592,* near Liberation Monument on Zhou Rong Road has local Sichuan food. And the **NAN KONG QUE**, *Tel. 3851250,* on Mei Zhuan Xiao Street, has Dai minority style food.

SEEING THE SIGHTS

Closer to Chongqing, you can learn a bit about China's version of modern history at the **Hong-yan Cun Revolutionary Memorial Hall** (Red Crag Village) at *13 Hongyang Village.* This was the office of the Communist Party and the Eighth Route Army between 1939 and 1946. It was also the residence for Chou En-lai and other revolutionary leaders including, briefly, Mao Tse-tung. This office was opened as a result of the kidnapping of Nationalist leader Chiang Kai-shek in Xi'an in 1936.

The prison used by the Nationalists for Communist prisoners is at **Zhazi Cave**, at the base of Golo Mountain in the northwestern suburbs. Today, it holds an exhibition on the infamous Sino-American Special Technical Cooperation, allegedly responsible for the tortured deaths of many people who fell afoul of Nationalist government officials. Open daily. For less recent history, there's the **Chongqing Museum**, *Pipashan Zheng Street*, near Loquat Park, open daily, with a display of Ba relics and ship burials. If you want to go back farther than that, try the **Chongqing Museum of Natural History**, *Beibei District*, 43 kilometers northwest of the city. Dinosaur bones were found in this region and some are on view here. Open daily.

For art lovers, the **Sichuan Fine Arts Institute** in Huang Kuo Piing District is well worth a visit. The institute is one of the best in China, with a teacher-student ratio of 1:2. It has an excellent three-story gallery with art for sale. Open daily. There is also a good **zoo** here, with a panda house. You can now pet a panda in this zoo for a fee, but don't do it. These are wild, endangered creatures.

For those who just want to pass the time relaxing while waiting for boats, there's **Eling** (Goose Neck) **Park**, between the two rivers. It has pleasant pavilions, ponds, and gardens. Open daily, 6:30 am to 8 pm. **Pipashan** (Loquat Hill) **Park** is the highest point in the city and was a former warlord's residence. There's a good view of the two rivers and the city. You can probably see monkeys and birds. Open daily, 6:30 am to 10 pm.

Nanshan (South Mountain) **Park** on the south bank of the river is where General George C. Marshall, the American mediator, and Chiang Kai-shek lived. The Nationalist leader lived in Yun Xiu, now renovated and open to tourists. The **General Joseph Stillwell Museum** is open with exhibits from the Japanese war. Close by is **Laojun Cave**, where Lao Tzu, the founder of Taoism, lived.

An 800-meter-long cable car goes across the Jialing River from Cangbailu Station to Jinshajie Station for a birds-eye view of the area. It operates 6 am to 11 pm. Another cable car goes across the Yangtze. A funicular tram is at the main pier so people do not have to climb up from the cruise boats to the street. The tram, however, is very dirty.

TRADITIONAL MEDICINE AT WORK!

Visitors can go to the Traditional Medicine Hospital (Chongqing Chang Hang Yiyuan, San Xia Men Zhen), even though it is extremely dirty and the English of the head doctor who gives the briefing is not good. Dr. Wen Da Qi Gong Shi is easier to understand. He entranced our group with an impressive demonstration of "bio-energy" or "bio-electricity," whereby a human head helped power a 200-watt light bulb.

Three people in our group tried qi gong treatment: those with arthritis or back pain felt some relief after a short free demonstration. The arthritic could raise his arm afterwards and he couldn't before! The tourist who paid Y100 for a full body massage didn't feel any different afterwards.

Qi gong, or Chinese yoga, is effective in solving some medical problems but it is not a one-shot miracle cure. Most ailments need several treatments over a period of time, but a short demonstration can indicate a possible treatment plan. Yes, there are qi gong clinics in North America too. Besides, you have nothing to lose here except a small fee, if that, for trying. Qi gong treatment is not invasive, nor does it involve drugs. You are subjected only to a vigorous massage and the Buddhist chant "Om mani padme hum."

In Chongqing also, we found a self-styled healer in the "Temple of Heaven" building of the Ren Min Hotel who only charged Y50 for a good 20 minute workout that gave a little temporary relief for ringing-in-the-ears. Then we paid Y100 for some herbs he recommended. Who knows? Maybe it will work for you!

SHOPPING

Chongqing is a miserable place to shop because it's so crowded. The main shopping area with department stores and the Friendship Store is around Liberation Monument (Jiefeng Bei). The biggest department store is the **Chongqing Bai Hou Gong Si**. Made in the province are umbrellas, silk, satin, bambooware, glassware, jewelry, knitting wool, and carpets. There are also tiny flash lights.

The **Painters Village** is at *24 Hwa-Cun, Hualongqiao, 630043*, and has woodblock prints and paintings. It is a good place to shop or just to enjoy good art because you can meet the artists and see them working. Some of the artists have exhibited abroad. No crowds are around here nor are there any at the Chongqing Museum's good gift and antique shops.

EXCURSIONS FROM CHONGQING

Stone Buddhist Sculptures at Dazu

Dazu is the home of the **Stone Buddhist Sculptures** and is about 105 kilometers northwest of Chongqing. These ancient outdoor sculptures are also three hours or 240 kilometers southeast of Chengdu. The population is about 780,000. The altitude is 380 meters.

Some connoisseurs consider these sculptures better preserved and of finer quality than those in Luoyang, Datong, or Dunhuang. Decide for yourself. About 50,000 of them are located in 43 places in Dazu County, most not readily accessible by car. Under State Council protection are ***Guangdashan**, ***Longtan**, and ***Linsongpo**.

To see both Beishan and Baodingshan, where many sculptures are located takes about a day and a half. Since the carvings are in hilly surroundings, take time to enjoy the natural scenery and the nearby water reservoir too. Study details. Look for the mother sleeping next to a bed-wetting child, the village girl tending ducks, the funeral rites, the wedding, etc.

The largest concentration of sculptures are at ***Beishan** (Northern Hill) (Tang to Song), two kilometers north of the Dazu Guest House. From the car park, you have to climb nearly 400 stairs. However, the 25-minute climb (10 minutes downhill) is spread out along pleasant, shady trails and is much easier than expected.

The sculptures at ***Fowan** are grouped together like beehives. A couple of chambers are fenced with iron gates and locks. Although some of the sculptures have been damaged, the arrangement and the preservation of others are excellent. Take special note of the enchanting Goddess of Mercy of Number 125, and Number 113. Number 155 and Number 136 are worth careful inspection. The pagoda, about one kilometer away, is also full of sculptures and is a popular picnic spot with local students.

The first statue was carved here in 892 A.D. by Wei Junjing. It was then a military camp.

Also worth seeing with a large number of sculptures is *Baodingshan (Song dynasty), 15 kilometers northeast of the Dazu Guest House. The ones here were basically done by one monk, Zhou Zhifeng, from 1179 to 1249, and centered on the theme Life is Vanity. The daily life of people is well-illustrated with vivid facial expressions and body language. The work here is largely intact and the sculptures are huge. The Sleeping Buddha is 31 meters long, and some of the standing figures are seven meters high. It is essential that you obtain a tour guide to explain highlights to you. To see this grouping takes only a few minutes.

The sculptures at *Xiaofowan are in the Shengshao Temple near the entrance of *Dafowan. Many tourists are only shown Dafowan, but other sculptures are close by. If you want to see more, insist on it. Another group of sculptures, carved in the Song dynasty, are at Shimenshan, 23 kilometers from the Dazu Guest House. Also under State Council protection here are *Guangdashan, *Longtan, and *Linsongpo.

An excellent book on Dazu has been published by the Sichuan Provincial Academy of Social Sciences in English and Chinese that you can pick up while there.

You might be able to tell roughly when the sculptures were created because the Tang figures are simple, smooth, and more alluring. The Five Dynasty statues are meticulously carved with details. The Song statues are rather reserved but distinctive in personality and expression.

The largest statue is the Sleeping Buddha and the most famous a 1000-armed Goddess of Mercy, both at Baoding Hill. The face of the Hen Wife is particularly beautiful. You may notice that many of the larger statues are bigger at the top and lean forward to make viewing easier from below.

The only place to stay is the DAZU GUEST HOUSE (Binguan), 47 Gongnong Street, Longganzhen, 632360, Tel. 721888. Fax 722827. It has been rated one or two stars, but it was recently renovated and upgraded with 132 rooms. CITS and CTS are at 47 Gonglong Street, 632360 Tel. 722474, 722085. Fax 722827. Dazu's telephone code is 08227.

Fengdu

Fengdu, 170 kilometers east of Chongqing on the Yangtze, can be reached by an overnight boat ride. It has a restored seventh-century city based on an ancient legend, a gathering place for ghosts. It has crude statues of demons and is considered Hell, with unique celebrations of the Qing Ming festival.

Diaoyu Castle

At **Hochou/Hechuan**, about 100 kilometers north of Chongqing is a fortress which changed the history of Europe. At **Diaoyu Castle** in 1259, five kilometers southeast of Hochou, the Mongolian King Mangu/Mongke, elder brother of Kublai Khan, was killed while personally trying to take this castle with an army of 70,000. His death stopped the invasion of Europe as Mongol leaders in the field withdrew to war among themselves for the leadership of the Mongol empire. Only the walls and a few structures remain. See also "Yangtze Gorges" and "Chengdu" for other places of interest in this area.

PRACTICAL INFORMATION

- **Changjiang Cruise Overseas Travel Corporation**, *4-12 Datong Street, Tel. 3849664, 3834201. Fax 3844170*
- **China International Travel Service**, *Chongqing Branch, 175 Renmin Road, 630015. Tel. 3850806, 3850188. Fax 3850095, 3850196. Liaison office for information about cruise ship movements, Tel. 3850280, 3850280*
- **CYTS Tours**, *6, 125 Ren Min Road, Shi Zhong District, 630015. Tel. 3862910. Fax 3850951*
- **Sunshine Tourism Group**, *Chongqing Sunshine Travel Company, Chongqing Binguan, 235 Minsheng Road, Chongqing 630010. Tel. 3845888 extension 4502, 3816942.*
- **Regal Cruises**, *Tel. 3830507 X 5282, 3818661*
- **Telephone Code**, *0811*

GUIYANG

(Kweiyang)

Guiyang, the capital of Guizhou (Kweichow) province, is due south of Chongqing. Guizhou is a landlocked region known for its minorities, many of whom still wear their unique costumes even in the fields. It has some of the best ethnic embroidery and batik in China. It also has beautiful mountains, and China's largest waterfall.

The city is at an altitude of 800 meters. The western part of the province reaches a height of 2,100 meters. The terrain is rugged with karst formations, underground rivers, jagged peaks, dramatic valleys, and terraced rice fields. The scenery around Anshun is better than the Stone Forest outside of Kunming, and is easier to photograph.

The annual precipitation is 900-1500 millimeters, mainly in June to August. The coldest January temperature averages 4.6° C. The warmest is June at about 27°C. We suggest visiting in February because of the festivals, and the terraces of yellow canola blossoms. But be warned; there is little or no heat in the hotels, even in the capital, and it can be cold.

The province is rich in minerals like aluminum, coal, iron, lead, gold, silver, and zinc. It has China's largest mercury deposit. They grow rice, corn, tobacco, cork, raw lacquer, and timber. The urban population is about 800,000.

ARRIVALS & DEPARTURES

Guiyang has direct flights with Hong Kong and air links with at least 24 other Chinese cities. The new Long Dong Bao Airport, big enough for 747s, is due soon and is eight kilometers from Guiyang, closer to the city than the current airport. Guiyang is also at the hub of railway lines with Chengdu, Nanning, Kunming, and Changsha.

ORIENTATION

Guizhou is one of my favorite areas. It has been a part of recorded history since the Shang dynasty about 3,000 years ago. The high percentage of ethnic groups is due to its hard-to-cultivate land and karst mountains. The dominant Han people did not want it and the minorities had no choice. Today, out of a total population of 30 million, 36.5% are minorities: Miao, Bouyei, Dong, Yi, Shi, Hui, Gelo, Zhuang, Yao. They contribute to the fascinating architecture and more than 100 lively festivals a year, many unlike those in other parts of China. These include bullfights, horse races, and lusheng (bamboo pipes) dancing.

Because this province has only recently been opened to tourists, people will find the unusual here but don't expect private baths and hot water anywhere outside of Guiyang and Kaili. You'll be lucky to get a clean, functioning hotel room. Think of your accommodations as camping, and you'll be okay. New hotels are being built however, but with more tourists, do not expect the minorities to remain unchanged.

You can still find some villages untouched by tourists, still with warm hospitality, a brilliant bouquet of ethnic clothing, elaborate welcoming ceremonies, totem worship, a coffin on a back porch to make its future inhabitants happy, and unusual music. Miao music reflects their mountain home. I suggest you take a tape recorder as well as lots of film. Each village has different costumes and women's hairstyles.

During festivals, Miao women might also wear 15 kilograms of silver jewelry on their heads, around their necks and waists. The **Dragon Boat races** are around July and the weather is best in September and October (but no festivals).

Most tourist attractions open daily from 9 am to 6 pm. Office hours are 8:30 am to 6 pm, five days a week. Store hours are 8:30 am to 7 pm.

WHERE TO STAY

The only hotels in the province that have 24-hour hot water and IDD are the **Plaza** and **Park**. They and the Huaxi are the only hotels that can change money but the hours might not be convenient.

The best hotels in Guizhou are the Park and the Plaza, but don't expect much. They do try to keep higher floors relatively clean for fussy foreign tourists. They are passable if you don't mind dirty carpets. The Park has bigger rooms. Both are in downtown Guiyang. The Huaxi is in the suburbs within walking distance of some Sinocized Miao villages and the large Huaxi Park. These three take major credit cards, have money change, business center, IDD, etc. A four star hotel should open soon.

HUAXI HOTEL *(Binguan), Wei Zhai, Huaxi 550024. Two stars, Tel. 3851129. Dist.A.P. 14 km. Dist. City center 17 km.*

Built 1952. Ren. 1992. 22 buildings on 3.6 square kilometers of park. Small shop. Some rooms have high ceilings and are the biggest in town.

PARK HOTEL *(Guizhou Fandian), 66 Beijing Rd., 560001. Three stars, Tel. 6822888, Fax 6824397. Dist A.P. 39 km. Dist.R.W. four km.*

The Park has 410 rooms. Some USTV.

PLAZA HOTEL *(Jin Zhu Dajiudian), 2 Yanan Dong Rd., 550001. Three stars, Tel. 6825888. Fax 6822994. Dist.A.P. 34 km. Dist.R.W. two km.*

Built 1989-90. 26 stories. 175 rooms. Gym and sauna. Clinic. Stuffy. Smaller rooms than Park, narrow corridors, and karaoke.

WHERE TO EAT

Local food is frequently chili hot, but you can get bland, cook-it-yourself hot pot. Dog is a favorite, especially in Pan Jiang town, 60 kilometers from Guiyang towards Kaili where there are at least 60 dog restaurants. Please note that the giant salamander is an endangered species. Roasted bean curd and roasted corn are typical snack foods.

It is safest to eat in tourist hotels. There's also the very modest **XIAO JIANG NAN RESTAURANT** in Chonganjiang town (between Kaili and Huangping) with its lovely setting beside a river. It has an exhibit of Gejia batik. There are also many tiny food stalls with questionable hygiene but delicious food. You can arrange to eat minority food in homes.

SEEING THE SIGHTS

Guiyang itself has little to see beyond karst caves, wild monkeys, some temples, and visits to Sinocized Bouyei and Miao villages. It is an ordinary city, dirtied by coal dust. You have to get out of it.

Outside of town, however, is another story. Strolling from village to village and just dropping in is great especially on market days when you can walk with the people. There are few if any bicycles and motor vehicles.

I came across a one-man coal mine once! Great scenery and friendly natives.

NIGHTLIFE & ENTERTAINMENT

There is not much to do in the evenings, but you can take in an ethnic song and dance show or go for a walk.

SHOPPING

Guiyang has stores with embroidery but the place to buy is in the countryside where women will sell their grandmother's baby carrier to you. There's a tiny one-man silver jewelry factory in the village of **Tang Bai** near Zhenyuan (Shidong), but not much silver on sale unless you order it; and an **embroidery factory** (seeded by UNICEF) is in *Taijiang at 444 Heping Street*. Both are within a few hours drive of Kaili.

Each village sells only its own unique styles. Expect to be surrounded by a lot of competing women peddlers. Look for embroidered or batik pieces and silk or cotton jackets, but check collars. They are not well-tailored and tend to slip back. Also look out for fancy baby carriers, silk funeral boots, caps, purses and sleeve pieces. Be aware that pleats will wash out of skirts and that handicrafts are getting mass produced and commercial. Look for quality, fine workmanship, and muted dyes.

The cheapest embroidery shopping in Kaili is from the peddlers who wait at the gate of the hotel. **Kaili** has good shopping in the museum but stores on the street and inside the hotel are expensive. I found great shopping in the Gejia village of **Matang** near Kaili which expected our tour group. Goods were well laid out for our selection.

Please note that some of the costumes on sale are worn only for weddings, funerals, and religious ceremonies. If you grow tired of them, offer them to a museum in your own country.

There are also large commercial batik factories in **Anshun**, one of which has a fashion show of sorts with poor designs. Also produced in the province are Mao tai (the most famous and most potent Chinese liquor), pears, persimmons, oranges, kiwi fruit, and tangerines.

EXCURSIONS FROM GUIYANG
Anshun

Anshun can be reached by a 1 1/2 hour tourist train from Guiyang once a day, or an 11-hour train ride from Kunming. Public tour buses are at the Anshun station. Tourists can also do a hurried day trip by bus from Guiyang or stay overnight in Anshun.

The only real tourist attraction is **Huangguoshu Falls**, China's biggest waterfall, 96 kilometers from Anshun and near Zhenning. It is 150 kilometers from Guiyang and is best seen after the rains from June to early October, when the falls can be 74 meters wide and 81 meters high, In April, they can be just a trickle. You can walk behind them. Some world-class views of the countryside are near the waterfall.

A trip here can be combined with the **Dragon Cave**, which has an 840-meter relaxing boat trip inside the cave, *Tel. (0853) 22615*. You can also visit Bouyei villages. Especially interesting is the **Shi Tou Zhai** or Stone Village, constructed completely of stone. The people there have been very poor, and are desperate to sell their excellent traditional batik.

Among the groups near Anshun are the **Old Han**, whose ancestors were sent by the first Ming emperor to fight a Miao rebellion 600 years ago. They won and to this day, the style of their clothing has not changed. The women still wear a white headband in mourning for the soldiers who died. About 100,000 of them seem to live in a time warp. Also in the area are a batik factory and **Chaiguan** village, with its masked peasant opera.

None of the hotels here are good, but the Hongshan is the best.

HONGSHAN HOTEL *(Binguan), Baihuang Road, 561000, two stars, near a small lake. Tel. 222088, 223101.*

Built 1982. 39 rooms for foreigners. Thin walls and generally grubby. Air conditioning.

NATIONALITIES HOTEL *(Minzu Fandian), 69 Ta Dong Rd., 561000. Two stars. Tel. 222500. Dist.A.P. 11 km. Dist.R.W. three km.*

Built 1986. Over 70 rooms for foreigners. Renovating as soon as money available. Ethnic and Han food. Generally grubby.

For travel information: **CITS**, *Tel. 5554403. Fax 5554403*; the telephone code is *0412*.

Ethnic Villages

Kaili, capital of Qiandongnan, the Miao and Dong Autonomous Prefecture, is 300 kilometers east of Anshun in the eastern part of the "province." It is a 196 kilometer, 4 1/2 hour drive east of Guiyang. From a base in Kaili, you can make day trips to **Miao** and **Gejia villages**. Most roads are paved. More roads will be improved and hotels built in the distant future.

In the villages, you can see women laden with silver jewelry (during festivals or on request) and hear antiphonal courtship singing. Expected guests are greeted with a drink of wine out of a buffalo horn, and dances of welcome.

The **Museum of National Minorities** in Kaili is good, and though it lacks titles in English, is well worth visiting. The huge **Sunday Market** is for local people to shop and is good to see. Open 11 am to 4 pm, it is located near the Ying Pong Po Nationalities Hotel.

CITS, *second floor of the Kaili Hotel. Tel. 222547, Fax 222547. Ask for Mr. Pan Xin Xiong.* This office covers the whole Southeast Guizhou region

Taijiang, 50 kilometers from Kaili, is the center of Miao culture with a 97% Miao population. You can visit many Miao villages here too. These include Qinman, Wengxiang, Xijiang, and Upper Langde. In **Baiying** village (Majiang County), the pattern of the cloth looks Scottish and they can give a bull-fighting demonstration (but not to the death).

The Gejia village of **Matang**, 23 kilometers from Kaili, has been extremely well organized for tourists and the dances are good. The official costume of Gejia women is of male military origins because of the bravery of the women who fought Han soldiers during the Qing dynasty. The skirt is short for riding horses. Though the Gejia say they are a separate group, the government classifies them as Miao. Their founder General Da Sa was probably Manchu. He was a general married to a Miao woman and forced to flee to the mountains. The Gejia worship water buffalos.

Huangping County, east of Kaili has a **Museum of Minority Festivals** in the Feiyun Temple. **Zhenyuan**, about 140 kilometers east of Kaili, is near the **Black Dragon Cave and Temple** in Miao style. The Miao and Dong are descendants of dragons or water buffaloes who believe these animals were born of butterflies. If you are prepared to rough it, the **WUYANG GUEST HOUSE** in Zhenyuan has a very pretty river setting.

There is also a **Museum on Marriage Customs** in Xinyi, a bird sanctuary at Grassy Lake in Weining County, its black neck swans seen in winter and early spring. From Kaili, you can actually drive to Guilin.

The **KAILI HOTEL** *(Binguan) is at 3, Guangchang Road, 556000. Two stars. (Tel. 0855)221658 or Tel. and Fax 222547. Dist.A.P. 198 km. Dist.R.W. five km. No credit cards.* This is the only tolerable hotel in the area and is next to the museum and should have heat and air conditioning.

PRACTICAL INFORMATION

- **CITS**, *20 Yan'an Zhong Road, 550011. Tel. 5825873, 5825292, 5861911. Fax 5824222.*
- **CYTS Tours**, *8th floor, 334 Wei Qing Road, 550003. Tel. 6833474. Fax 6825024.*
- **Guiyang Plaza Holiday Travel Service**, *2 Yan'an Dong Road, Tel. 6827048, 6825888 X 0288. Fax 6822994.*
- **Guizhou Provincial Tourism Administration**, *5 Yan'an Zhong Road, 550001, Tel. 6892357, 6892434, 6892360. Fax 689f2309, 6832574. (Brochures)*
- **Tourist Complaints**, contact **Supervisory Bureau of Tourism Quality of Guizhou Province**, *346–5 Zhonghua Bei Road, 550001, Tel. 6892360. Fax 6892309*
- **Telephone Code for Guizhou**, *0851*

KUNMING

(Kunnanfu)

Kunming is the capital of Yunnan province, which borders Vietnam, Laos, and Burma. Kunming is beautifully situated on the 330 square-kilometers Dianchi Lake, China's sixth largest. Because of its altitude (1894 meters) and its subtropical location, it is blessed with the best weather in China, spring all year round. (Snow, however, fell in 1991.) The hottest temperature is 29 degrees centigrade in May and the coldest is minus one degree centigrade in January. Precipitation is 1,500 millimeters, mainly from May to August.

One of the loveliest times to visit is February when the camellias are in bloom. The best times to visit are February to May and August to November. The urban population is 1.3 million.

ARRIVALS & DEPARTURES

You can reach Kunming by train from Chengdu, Changsha, and Vietnam (24 hours). It has airlinks with 30 Chinese cities, Rangoon, Bangkok, Chiang Mai, Singapore, Hong Kong and Vientiane. More routes are expected in the future.

ORIENTATION

Yunnan province is the third most desirable tourist destination in China. You could easily spend two weeks here. It is important to see because of its mountain scenery, its national minorities, the artistry and history of its temples, architecture, the Burma Road and the Stone Forest.

In the province are several unusual sights. These range from almost year-round snow-capped mountains to tropical jungles where elephants and monkeys roam freely. One third of its over 34 million people belong to 25 national minorities. Many of the groups, especially the women, still wear their distinctive clothes, even while working in the fields and practice old customs like the Dai Water-Splashing Festival.

The city is completely surrounded by mountains. Sightseeing here can be a little rugged. The Dragon Gate necessitates a climb of 200 stairs, but the effort is well worth it.

WHERE TO STAY

A new four-star hotel, the Stanford, a Hong Kong joint venture, is going up near Green Lake. Until this is finished, other hotels get renovated, and the new five-star hotel opens at the Kunming International Trade Building on the way into town from the airport, the classiest hotel is the four-star section of the **Green Lake**. The King World is a worn-looking second.

Regarding location, the Holiday Inn and Kunming are nearest to the fancy Sakura department store, the City Hall and main square. The Golden Dragon and King World are around the corner and a couple blocks down the street and closer to the railway station. These four are slightly more convenient for travelers. But the Green Lake has a park, and is walking distance to the Bird and Flower Market and many shops.

The following recently published prices are subject to change, 10 to 15% surcharge and negotiation. Prices might be cheaper if you go through a travel agent.

CAMELLIA HOTEL *(Cha Huan Binguan), 154 East Section Dongfeng Rd., 650041. One-star, Tel. 3163000, 3162918. Y120-Y230; Dorms Y30 a bed. No Credit Cards.*

A favorite of budget travelers. IDD. Built 1985. Ren. 1989. 13 stories. Bus to Dali, etc. Tours to Stone Forest. Don't expect much English or service. Has message board. One of its two buildings has USTV.

GOLDEN DRAGON *(Jinglong Fandian), 575 Beijing Rd., 650011. Four stars, Tel. 3133104, 3133015. Fax 3131082. Dist.A.P. seven km. Dist.R.W. 450 meters Credit Cards.*

Built 1988-89. Ren. 1995. 18 stories, 302 rooms, small bathrooms. IDD. In-room safes due soon. Executive floor. In-house movies. B.C., USTV. CAAC domestic. Dragonair. Gym, bicycles. Tennis and outdoor hot spring pool. Clinic. Low season September to March 31.

GREEN LAKE HOTEL *(Cuihui Binguan), No 6 Cui Hu Nan Rd., 650031. Tel. 5158888, 5155788. Fax 5153286. $90-$150 (new wing). Dist.A.P.15 km. Dist.R.W. eight km. Credit Cards.*

Four-star standard in the 1993 section, with 17 stories and 306 deluxe rooms. USTV. IDD. B.C. CAAC domestic. Its 1946 two to three star section, reconstructed in 1980, has five stories, 142 spacious rooms with high ceiling and dirty carpets. Good for budget travelers until it gets rebuilt. A Hong Kong joint venture Cantonese restaurant is outside the lakeside door. High season during the Spring Festival, Nationalities Festival about April 12, and Trade Fair about August 8.

HOLIDAY INN KUNMING *(Yinghua Binguan), 25 Dong Feng Dong Lu, 650011. Four stars. Tel. 3165888. Fax 3135189. In US, Tel. 1-800-HOLIDAY. $98-$155. Dist.A.P. five km. Dist.R.W. two km. Credit Cards.*

Built 1993. 18 stories, 180 rooms. Small bathrooms. Widest twins in town. Executive floors. 24-hour B.C. Gym. Year-round indoor pool. Clinic, Italian, Cantonese and Sichuan food. Silkair, 16-lane bowling alley. Breakfast buffet Y85 plus 15%.

KING WORLD HOTEL *(Jinhua Dajiudian), 28 Beijing Nan Road, 650011. Four stars, Tel. 3138888, 3138656. Fax 3131910. $80 to $108 includes buffet breakfast and free aiport shuttle. Dist.R.W. 400 m. Dist.A.P. five km. Credit Cards.*

Near Yunnan Foreign Trade Building in busy commercial area. Built 1992-93. 22 stories. 320 rooms. USTV, IDD. Gym, massage, chess and mahjong. Clinic. Bake shop. French, Italian, Sichuan, Yangzhou and Cantonese cuisines. Yunnan Airlines. Managed by Jin Jiang Hotels. Low season November-December.

KUNMING HOTEL *(Fandian), 145 Dong Feng Dong Rd., 650051. Tel. 3162172, 3162063. Fax 3163784, 3138220. Dist.A.P. five km. Dist.R.W. three km. Credit Cards.*

Next to CAAC. Built 1982, three-star South Building ren. 1992. 122 rooms. Better 1989 four-star back section North Building ren.1992. 248 rooms. B.C. Gym. Indoor pool. Garden. USTV but no CNN. 24-hour coffee shop, room service. Yunnan Airlines next door. Clinic. Tour desk.

WHERE TO EAT

Specialties include Rice Noodles Crossing the Bridge, Yunnan ham and crispy, deep-fried goat's cheese. The adventurous could try snake, deep-fried bees, or congealed blood. Dai food includes grasshoppers. Try the cook-it-yourself hotpot. The best dinner and minority dance restaurant is the **JIXING YUNNAN FLAVOR FOOD CITY** see *Nightlife* section below for this dinner show and for the **NANYUAN FOLK SONG AND DANCE RESTAURANT**.

For Yunnan cuisine, there's the **KUNMING HOTEL** and the **YUNNAN CROSSING-THE-BRIDGE RICE NOODLES RESTAURANT**, *39 Nan Hua Street, Tel. 3131453.*

Do not consider the popular state-run Grand Restaurant on Nanhua Road near the Noodles Over the Bridge Restaurant. At the Grand, I found water on the dishes, chipped drinking glasses and at 1 pm no food on the buffet table. When food finally did arrive, pushy crowds from other rooms rushed and quickly grabbed it all. A manager realized our American group was not about to fight for food too, and arranged to have some brought to our table. What we did manage to eat was delicious, but it's not worth it. Another place to avoid is the Hong Fang Zi Restaurant.

The **HOLIDAY INN** has had the only western chef in the city. Not to be considered the same quality, but also serving western food is the modest **YUE LAI RESTAURANT** on North Beijing Road between the Guangdong Hotel and the Kunhu Hotel. A **donkey restaurant** is northeast of the Green Lake Hotel by the lake usually with a couple of live donkeys outside. It serves rat and snake too. (Several other donkey restaurants are near Yunnan University.)

Southwest of the Green Lake Hotel, by the lake, is a tiny much-recommended, no-name restaurant with very low stools. No signs in English; the place is usually full with a queue outside. The food is quite good.

SEEING THE SIGHTS

If you only have one day, you have to choose between a tour of the city or going to the Stone Forest. It is better that you stay at least two days, preferably more. Important in the city are the Western Hills, Golden Temple, Black Dragon Pool, Bamboo Temple, Yuantong Temple, Daguan Park and Green Lake.

Xishan (Western Hills), *Tel. 8182211*, is about 26 kilometers from the Kunming Hotel. The 14th-century Huating Temple is the largest in the city. South of here is the **Taihua Temple** (Yuan) with the best view of the sunrise over the lake. The **Sanqing Tower**, two kilometers farther south, was the summer resort of Emperor Liang of the Yuan. It has nine tiers each about 30 meters above the other. On the top is the **Long Men** (Dragon Gate) with another great view of the lake. The stone corridors, chambers, paths, and intricate carving of the Dragon Gate were cut from 1609 to 1681.

The coppercast *****Golden Temple**, *Tel. 5154306*, 11 kilometers northeast of the city, is 300 years old, 6.5 meters high and weighs 200 tons. The **Qiong Zhu** (Bamboo) **Temple**, 18 kilometers northwest of the Kunming Hotel has 500 life-size arhats carved in the Qing. These are very expressive and well worth a visit. The temple was founded in 1280.

The **Daguan Lou Pavilion**, *Tel. 4142335*, across the lake from Xishan Hill (seven kilometers from the Kunming Hotel), has a 180- character couplet at its entrance, the longest ever found in China. Composed by a Qing scholar, the first half praises the landscape while the second deals with Yunnan history. Also important is the **Black Dragon Pool**, *Tel. 5150395*, with its Ming temple and tomb. The Heishui Shrine here may be from the Han. Nearby are the Botanical Gardens. **Yuan Tong Si**, the only Tang temple in town, is a little over one kilometer from the Green Lake Hotel.

The **Yunnan Ethnic Group Village** on Dian Chi Road is worth a visit for the architecture (Bai, Dai) and an introduction to Yunnan's minorities. It is 12 kilometers from the Holiday Inn. There are dance demonstrations and a sampling of the water-splashing. But unless you are there during these demonstrations, you can find very few people in minority costume to photograph. If you are going to real minority villages, skip this. But if you are shopping for minority crafts, go for a look.

The Stone Forest

The **Stone Forest of Lunan**, one of the highlights of a Kunming visit, is 80 kilometers southeast of the city. It can be a day trip or an overnight in the adjacent two-star **STONE FOREST HOTEL** *(Binguan), Lunan County, 652211, Tel. 7795401*. On the way to the Stone Forest is a new golf course and a lake, which is usually a stop for tourists. Singapore money is developing a 34-square-kilometer tourist resort with casino and villas. Many tourist buses now stop at a huge store owned by a collective under the Yunnan Provincial Tourism Administration so it should be okay. It sells jade and other stones, and all manner of tourist goods. You can watch them carve jadeite from nearby Burma.

If you want to visit a real Sani village, this is not the place; the village here at Stone Forest is highly touristy.

About 270 million years ago this area was covered with water. The limestone pushed its way out of the receding sea and rain continued to corrode the stone into these artistic pinacles. One-fifth of its 64,000 acres is open to visitors. Here too are many steps. The shortest of the two routes is 2 1/2 hours long, but you can get the picture in much less time.

Near the hotel is a Sani ethnic village with minority-type handicrafts for sale. While much is machine-made, you should be able to find some museum-quality pieces here. Peddlers can be a real nuisance. Groups of local dancers in ethnic costume have entertained hotel guests in the evening. The Stone Forest is very commercialized with fake zebras and even a camel. The blandness of the Stone Forest makes it difficult to photograph. You can hire a local guide in Sani costume to take you around.

The trip between Kunming and the Stone Forest is remarkable because of the hilly scenery and the eucalyptus trees. A fascinating cave 100 meters straight down is located 93 kilometers from Kunming and 24 kilometers from the Stone Forest at Jiuxiang in Yiliang county. A word of warning: one of our group was overcome by the humidity, particularly towards the bottom. He spent an hour negotiating the stairs back up, a few at a time. The waterfall there was pretty however, but not worth that experience.

Other Attractions

If you have more time, take a two-hour boat cruise on 340-square-kilometer **Lake Dianchi** but go only for the rest, as not much can be seen (except for Daguan Lou, fish farms and people fishing with large triangular nets). The **Provincial Museum**, *Tel. 3163694,* is towards the Green Lake Hotel. Open daily except Sundays from 9 am to 4:30 pm, it has a worthwhile exhibit of minority costumes. The **Institute for Nationalities** also has a good exhibit of minority costumes but you have to make arrangements through a travel agent well in advance as it is not generally open.

Along the west shore of the lake is **Sleeping Beauty Hill** and a series of swordlike peaks. On the southern tip of the lake is Jinning county town, the birthplace of the famous Ming navigator Zheng He, who sailed to East

Africa half a century before Vasco da Gama. The Memorial Hall to Zheng He is on a hill above the town.

Festivals & Markets

Festivals and markets are worth experiencing: in addition to the **Water-splashing Festival** in Jing Hong in April, there's the **Yi Torch Festival** (in late July or early August) in the Stone Forest and Chuxiong, the **Third Moon Market** (usually April, sometimes May) in Dali, and the **Horse and Mule Market** (about early April in Lijiang).

Ask about other minority markets. **Lijiang** is especially mind-boggling. An **arts festival** with performances by most of China's national minorities has been held mid-February to early March.

A good detailed regional guide with photos is Patrick R. Booz's *Yunnan*.

Walks

There are nice walks in the **Western Hills**, around **Green Lake Park**, and behind the **Green Lake Hotel** (for old architecture). Kunming is otherwise a bustling, modern city with traffic jams.

NIGHTLIFE & ENTERTAINMENT

The best dinner and minority dance restaurant is the **Jinxing Yunnan Flavor Food City**, *inside the gate of the Camellia Hotel*. Attendants are dressed in ethnic costumes.

Groups usually go to the **Nanyuan Folk Song & Dance Restaurant**, *260 Shuang Long Qiao, Luosiwan. Tel. 3137225, 3135742*. Adventurous eaters there can try the pigs ears, eels, and duck web but it has more conventional fare, too, including dried and fried beancurd, deep-fried duck, and the sweetest snow peas ever. The dance show inspired by Yunnan's national minorities, is professional and fast paced, romanticized and not necessarily authentic. But it's fun and there's a program guide in English.

The best **disco** is at the Holiday Inn. Also good are the dance halls at the Kunming and the Golden Dragon Hotels. The **Golden Peacock**, *beside Daguan Park on Daguan Road, Tel. 4145558*, is an incredible dive with a great show. The **Kunming Hotel** also has good entertainment. The **Kunming Ice House** near the Kunming Hotel has cold beer. The **Blue Sky Bar**, *Tel. 3167666, Baita Road at number 12*, (west side of street, between the Camellia and Holiday Inn), is okay with no hassles and no hostesses, but it's dumpy.

No place is free of prostitutes unless there is a current campaign against them. Be wary of bars outside of hotels because you might have to buy drinks at high prices for the girls who sit with you. At least one of these bars has been known to give a guest an incredibly high bill at the end of an evening and threatened him with violence unless paid.

SHOPPING

Look for batik, feather products, minority handicrafts, embroidery (especially shoulder bags and clothes), tin and spotted copperware. You can get minority crafts at the **Yunnan Ethnic Group Village**, though the cheapest handicrafts are from peddlers at the gate of every hotel. The cross-stitching is an excellent buy.

A cheap batik store is southwest of the Green Lake Hotel by the end of the lake. The **Yunnan Antique Store**, *Qingnian and Dongfeng Road, Tel. 3161198*, open 9 am to 7 pm, is worth a look. Try the **Bird and Flower Market** about five blocks behind the Green Lake Hotel where antique jewelry and porcelain, real and fake, share space with live gold fish and budgies. In this area too are a growing number of real antique stores.

The **Friendship Store** is on the *third floor of the Kunming Department Store, 99 Dong Fang Xi Road, Tel. 3164698, 3169971*; an **arts and crafts store** is at *162 Qingnian Road, Tel. 3163277* on the same street as the Holiday Inn but beyond the square. The **Sakura Department Store** is beside the Holiday Inn. The **Southwest Plaza** (Xi Nan Da Xia), on *Chaochang Street at Qing Nian Street* is the largest department store.

EXCURSIONS FROM KUNMING

Jing Hong

Jing Hong is the place to visit minorities and their villages. It is southwest of Kunming in Xishuang Banna region (pronounced She-Schwan-Ban-NA), about a 740-kilometer, 24-hour drive on paved roads. Planes fly the 45-minute flight daily. Air connections between Jing Hong, Bangkok and Chiangmai (Thailand) should start any day now.

At an altitude of 550 meters, Jing Hong is humid but not overly hot in May. This area rises up to 2,300 meters, and grows rubber and tea. There are 1,200 to 2,000 millimeters of rain annually. Take precautions against malaria. Jing Hong's population is about 30,000 people.

Thirteen minorities inhabit this region. The ethnic cultures here are similar to those of the northern Thailand and Laotian hill tribes, but the standard of living is higher. Just outside the **Dai Village** is a park with a replica of a beautiful white stupa or pagoda next to a genuine Buddhist monastery with a friendly abbot. A museum of Dai costumes will open in Jing Hong soon.

You can take a steamer on the **Lancang River** (which becomes the Mekong 30 kilometers away in Laos). In Yunnan this river falls 1,780 meters and 14 power stations, one already opened at Manwan, will eventually harness it for electrical power.

You can visit **Aini** and **Jinuo** villages in the mountains. Guides tend to just drop you off at villages allowing you to wander around on your own. Dont be afraid to knock on doors. You can even ask them to don their costumes for photos. (Tip them five yuan or buy something.)

Interested visitors should go armed with questions about life styles, unique customs, technology, child rearing, courtship rituals and the percentage of women on village councils.

A visit to a Dai village can include songs, dances and a demonstration of the Water-Splashing Festival (below) any time of the year if the village is expecting you. Some of these villages can also provide good meals in a Dai home. The temples are similar to some in neighboring Laos. You can take an organized tour or you rent a bicycle or car and go off on your own. You could also take public buses, but they are infrequent.

The **Water-Splashing Festival** marks the Dai New Year. If it's well-organized, there will be minority dances and demonstrations, dance dramas, and bamboo rocket competitions. Wa tribesmen, former head-hunters, may sacrifice a bull. CITS has a boat for you to watch the dragon boat races. The water-splashing is confined to certain areas between 10 am and 4 pm on one designated day. Take a water pistol and shower cap. Guides loan you basins. Local youths attack you gleefully. It is a lot of fun, but keep your mouth closed. Keep your valuables at the hotel and your camera in a plastic bag.

Shopping is best at the various tourist attractions or factories: silver jewelry, embroidered purses, natural marble pictures and tie-dyed cotton. You can buy handicrafts directly from villagers. It is cheaper, but more frantic if you're in a group. In Jing Hong, there's the **early morning food market** to see and craft stores outside the gate of the Xishuangbanna Hotel.

The **Botanical Garden**, 75 kilometers west of Jing Hong is badly maintained, but the drive there through intensely exotic and lovely countryside is worth the trip. Nearby **Simao** with an airport is the mother of all the world's tea; 23 kinds of tea still grow wild there. There is also the wild life reserve with wild elephants at **San Cha He**, 30 kilometers from Jing Hong. 250 Asian elephants lived here in 1994 but poachers, now executed, have killed many. Visitors can see only a small part of the reserve. There is a simple restaurant but no hotel.

Hotels are modest, but the Crown is the best and should be comfortable. The Banna Hotel is adequate. The hostels in the Dai village (Manjinglan) are just barely recommended for backpackers. But many backpackers stay there and like them. No hotel has IDD.

JING HONG CROWN HOTEL, *666100. Three star standards. Tel. 2128888. Fax 2127270. 1994. Credit Cards.*

You can change money here, and there is USTV.

BANNA HOTEL *(Binguan), 11 Galan Zhong Rd., 666100. Two stars. Tel. 2123679. Fax 2123368. Dist.A.P. seven km. Dist. bus station two km.* Built 1956. Ren. 1992. 230 airconditioned rooms. Mosquito nets. Dorm for backpackers. Bicycles. No money exchange. Poor management. Beautiful spacious garden and river view. Great location in town. Power cuts throughout the day, however, and hot water in evenings only. No western food. CITS.

When you get hungry, try the Dai-style **YIN BING DAI WEI CANTING RESTAURANT, NAN FENG RESTAURANT** (Sichuan food), and the restaurant in the **JINCHONG HOTEL** (Di Er Jiao Dai So). In some Dai restaurants, there are minority dances and guests are asked to contribute a song. The **YIN BING** and **XING GUANG** were the best of the 27 or so restaurants in the Dai village as of my last visit, but ask around first. Unless things have improved, the food in the Banna Hotel is terrible. But food at the **CROWN HOTEL** is fine.

For local travel information: **CITS Xishuangbanna Sub-branch,** *Banna Hotel, 12 Ga Lan Zhong Road, Jing Hong, 666100. Tel. 2122032. Fax 2125980,* can arrange day trips to villages. **Jin Man Lan Tourist and Leisure District,** *Jing Hong 666100. Tel. 2124910, 2124811 X 3040. Fax 2127270.* The telephone code is *0691 or 08838.*

Xiaguan & Dali

You can now fly from Kunming to Lijiang (one hour) and probably to Dali, but that would be cheating you of a long road trip through fascinating countryside. Part of the fun and adventure is getting there. Public air-conditioned buses are crowded and can be booked at the Camellia Hotel in Kunming. The best view is the side behind the driver. A railway should be completed before the year 2000.

About three-hours' drive west of Kunming along the **Burma Road** is **Chuxiong**. During festivals, the Yi people sing and dance all night in the center of town, courting and conversing socially through music. The rhythms and energy level are amazing. A minorities' fashion festival has also been held here. Chuxiong's tourist hotel can be a lunch stop for trips to Dali.

If you take precautions about hygiene, the stalls along this road can also provide memorable meals with congealed blood, pork kidneys, squirming eels and hot chilis, cooked before your very eyes.

Xiaguan is at an altitude of 1,000 meters, the capital of **Dali Bai Autonomous Prefecture**. About a 12-hour 400-kilometer drive from Kunming, it is at the southern tip of 41-kilometer-long **Lake Erhai**. The highest temperature here is 29° C in June. The coldest is -3° C in December. Annual rainfall is 1,200 millimeters mainly May to August. Its windy all year round but the strongest winds are from November to

March. There is a tea brick factory and a temple to the Tang general who failed to conquer Xiaguan.

You can take boat trips on the 2,000-year-old man-made lake to see 3,800-meter-high **Cangshan Mountain**, snow-capped most of the year. Have you ever heard of an antique lake before?

Public buses in Xiaguan stop running after 7 pm, but you can usually hitch a ride on a horse cart. The one-star **ERHAI HOTEL**, *140 Renmin Street, 671000, Tel. (872) 22186*, is adequate but it is more interesting to stay in Dali.

Be aware that there is a tendency to confuse the names Dali and Xiaguan. Xiaguan was the old term for greater Dali, and the name is still used. **Dali** is 10 kilometers north of Xiaguan, an old walled town with marble factories and some of the best marble in China. Some houses are made of marble. Look for a large obelisk erected by conqueror Kublai Khan. It is a good place for hiking around, generally flat in the valley, with inviting mountains.

Dali was the capital of the Nanzhao and Dali kingdoms. The Tang emperors never conquered the Nanzhou empire but the Mongols subdued it in the 13th century and Marco Polo visited. It has the **Sanyuejie** (Third-Moon market), the 15th to 20th day of the third lunar month, with caravans of horses and mules, and containers of traditional medicines arriving to be traded. About 30,000 people take part in the market which is enlivened by races and perhaps gambling. The site west of Dali at the foot of the mountain is a former Nationalist execution grounds.

The **San Ta Si** (Three Pagoda Temple) on the west shore of Lake Erhai, four kilometers outside the northwest gate of Dali, was built in the Nanzhao/Tang period over a thousand years ago, and was recently renovated. The view of the lake, the three towers (70 and 43 meters tall) and the mountains behind are famous.

Butterfly Pool on the northern tip of the lake is a natural spring with one huge tree covering it. In May, strings of different kinds of butterflies appear. **Xizhou**, just north of Dali, has especially remarkable Bai architecture, incorporating marble, white-washed walls and black trim. The much-decorated houses are courtyard style. The women's dress is basically white with red or black vests and a colorful bonnet. The **TIAN ZHUAN HOTEL** (Binguan) is built in the Bai style and is charming but basic.

You'll see an abundance of signs in English advertising tours, trips, food and accommodations. Contact Edward He for tours, *19 Guang Wu Road, Dali 671003. Tel. (0872) 70275*.

For hotels in Dali, the new one-star **MINZU YUAN** (Minority Court) is the best. The others are the **DALI HOTEL** *(Binguan), 245 Fuxing Road, Gucheng, 671003. Tel. (0872)70387* and the **RED CAMELLIA NUMBER TWO**. A three-star hotel should be ready soon.

For food, try the **LA LA CAFE, JIMMYS PEACE CAFE,** and the **TIBETAN CAFE,** all popular with backpackers. Also interesting is **MR. CHINA'S SON CAFE,** *67–5 Bo Ai Road, 671003.* The owner He Li Yi is the author of two books in English, including his autobiography *Mr. China's Son* published in the United States.

From Dali, you can travel on to **Shizhong Shan** near Jianchuan (a long, one-day excursion north), which has a unique Buddhist grotto reached by a steep 45-minute climb. Women there rub a one-meter-high female genitalia for fertility and boys rub it for courage. It also has some of the earliest Buddhist carvings in China, several styles, including some humans with long curly hair, foreigners perhaps. At the base of this mountain lies an exotic old monastery.

Shibao Shan nearby also has temples and an annual singing contest in late August or early September by young people of many minorities. During the festival, thousands sleep under the trees or in temples. Courtship here also is by song. Fish is the local specialty, but the cooking is not outstanding.

Lijiang & Zhongdian to Tibet

Lijiang is further north, about 600 kilometers from Kunming, where the **Yu Long** (Jade Dragon) **Mountain** rises spectacularly 6000 meters above sea level. Lijiang's airport at **Diqing** is north of town. In Lijiang the Naxi people still use hieroglyphic writing and wear sheepskin capes on their backs for warmth and to cushion heavy baskets. On the sheepskin are seven small embroidered moons to show how hard they work (until the moon and stars appear).

Some of the Naxi are matriarchal with walk-in marriages. At age 14, the boys are put out of their homes and have to find girlfriends to sleep with. Without a girlfriend, a male sleeps with the dogs. There are no marriages. Men eat breakfast with their mothers. Children are supported by all the males in the community. Joserf F. Rock, Peter Goullart, Li Lingcan, and Yang Fuquan are scholars who have written books on the Naxi people.

Lijiang is an old town with winding streets and old bridges, considered the best place to visit in China by some adventurous travelers. It is a good place for walks. Also important to see are the **Liuli Temple** and **Dading Temple,** both in Ming architecture. **Basha,** 10 kilometers from Lijiang, was the political and economic center of the Naxi during the Ming. The **Dabaoji Temple** has Ming and Qing murals, a combination of Lamaism, Taoism, and Buddhism.

The **LIJIANG GUESTHOUSE** (60 rooms) is in the Naxi style. Its 1993 extension and service are better than the **GULU WAN HOTEL,** and it's near the bus station. There should be a three-star hotel here soon.

THE BURMA ROAD

*The fabled **Burma Road** goes from Kunming as far as Xiaguan, and instead of going north to Lijiang it runs south to the Burmese (Myanmar) border. From Xiaguan onward, the hotels are barely adequate. Do not expect air conditioning, heat, IDD, money exchange, credit cards, carpets, coffee shops, bars, 24-hour electricity or hot tap water. Take cash for buying from villagers and lots of small change. Dali/Xiaguan is usually an overnight stop on the Burma Road, first used as part of the southern silk route from Sichuan to India in the fourth and fifth century B.C.*

*The Burma Road was built from 1937 to 1939 by 160,000 Chinese and Burmese laborers. The United States financed it to supply China in her fight against the Japanese. It was used by the Allies until 1942 when it was closed by the Japanese capture of Burma. It was extended and reopened between India and Kunming in 1945 and renamed the **Stillwell Road** after the American general.*

Unfortunately, there is nothing in Yunnan to mark this Sino-U.S. achievement except for a small, hard-to-find pillar in Kunming. Local people seem to know nothing about it. There is a monument to the Chinese soldiers who fought in the Japanese war (near historic Tengchong).

Along the road live Yi, Dai, Bai, Lisu, Deang, and Achang minorities. Ask about the famous bronze drums. There are also neolithic sites and takins, pheasants, camphor trees, coffee and pepper, all indigenous to this area.

*The drive south from Dali is also paved and takes about nine hours through the mountains, the highest elevation reaching 4,000 meters. Many World War II battles took place here. **Tengchong** sits near extinct volcanoes and hot springs with geysers. It has a huge rhododendron forest, with the biggest tree 16 meters high.*

Flights go between Kunming and Baoshan City, 176 kilometers from the border, and between Kunming and Dehong at the border. At Dehong, you should be able to see the barter trade between the two countries and pigs sniffing for heroin. The urban population is 920,000. Manshi, also on the Burmese border, has an airport.

Tours into Burma, Laos, and Thailand have generally been for Chinese nationals only, but travel agents should be able to get permission to take foreign travelers to these countries.

Zhongdian is north of Lijiang toward the Tibet border at an altitude of 3,000 meters. Considerably off the tourist path, you can visit a once prosperous Tibetan Buddhist temple, **Guihua Si**, on a hilltop. During the Cultural Revolution, the Red Guards almost totally destroyed it. The main hall has been reconstructed and a visit to this remote area is rewarding. The temple has a simple inn.

The scenery from Dali to Zhongdian is especially great for bird watchers from March to September. It is full of lakes, forests, and mountain views. I recommend C.P. Fitzgerald's *Tower of Five Glories* about his experiences in this area in the 1930s.

Tibet requires a permit which could take two to three months to process so don't expect to enter from Zhongdian immediately. It is possible but not easy to go from Kunming to Lhasa by land. From Zhongdian it can be another 11 days by land cruiser, camping overnight in snowy mountain passes or in the gorges of the upper Lancang (or Mekong) Rivers.

Before you go to this area, try to contact several travel agents and the **Yunnan Exploration and Amusement Travel Service**, *73 Renmin Xi Road, North Section of Building B in Kunming. Tel. 5312283, 5310278 X 2208. Fax 5312324, 5310923*, which has organized such trips.

PRACTICAL INFORMATION

• **CITS** and **CTS**, *8 Heping Xincun, Huangcheng Nan Road, Kunming, 650011. CITS Tel. 3132895, 3131671. Fax 3169240; CTS Tel. 3326370. Fax 3333446.* CITS Kunming *(Tel. 3138888, X 3104 and 3105. Fax 3148988, 3165895)* and Thai Airways have offices next to and north of the King World Hotel. At CITS, a one-day city tour by Panda Bus with lunch and guide, costs Y200, and to the Stone Forest Y220.

• **CYTS Tours**, *23 Lao Hai Geng Road, 650034. Tel. 4141037. Fax 4167841*

• **Telephone Code**, *0871*

• **Tourist Hotline**, *Tel. 3135412*

• **Yunnan Overseas Travel Corporation**, *154 Dong Feng Dong Road, 650041. Tel. 3163018, 3188833. Fax 3132512, 3132508*

• **Yunnan Travel and Tourism Bureau**, *218 Huan Cheng Road, Kunming, 650011. Tel. 3134560, 3134019. Fax 3135204, 3169240*, for brochures and information. For complaints, *Tel. 3139197 or Fax 3174343*.

The **Thai Consulate** is at the King World Hotel. The **Laotian** and **Burmese Consulates** are at the Camellia Hotel. A Vietnamese consulate should open soon.

WUHAN

Wuhan, the capital of Hubei, is really three cities: **Hankou** (Hankow), **Hanyang**, and **Wuchang**, separated from each other by the Yangtze and Hanshui Rivers, and joined by bridges. It is the most important site of the republican revolution, and is noted for its industries, its ancient chime bells, and as a gateway to the Wudang Mountains and Yangtze Gorges. It has been an important port for at least 2,000 years.

Several foreign nations forced concessions here after the Opium War, and some of the architecture in Hankou still reflects old Europe. Wuchang is especially famous because on October 10, 1911, the first victory of the Sun Yat-sen revolution against the Manchus took place here, although Sun himself was absent. Wuhan became the headquarters of the left wing of the Nationalist party. In 1923, the Communists led a successful railway workers strike.

The Communists took the city in May 1949. The three cities merged administratively shortly afterward. During the Cultural Revolution, it experienced some of the heaviest fighting between factions.

The weather is hottest in July and August at 42°C, and coldest in January and February at 5°C. The annual precipitation is 1,200 millimeters, mainly February to May. The population is 6.3 million, the fifth largest city in China.

ARRIVALS & DEPARTURES

Wuhan is 18 hours by train south of Beijing and 18 hours north of Guangzhou. The capital of Hubei province can also be reached by ship, or by air from 44 cities and Hong Kong. The new airport is in Hankou 20 kilometers from the city and it might have flights soon with Singapore, Japan and Korea.

ORIENTATION

Wuhan is the home of the huge Wuhan Iron and Steel Works. Other industries include automobiles, electronics, textiles, and computer software, and it is booming. It has recently opened a circular beltway around the city, alleviating somewhat the traffic jams downtown. The city itself dates from the 11th century B.C. (Shang).

The city wall in Hanyang, no longer standing, was first built in the Han, almost 2000 years ago. The Wuchang wall was built during the Three Kingdoms (220-265), by Sun Quan, King of Wu, and can still be seen at the Small East Gate. Hankou and Hanyang were originally one city, but in the 15th century, the Hanshui River changed its course.

Students of modern Chinese history must visit the site of the first victory of the republican revolution, on Shouyi Road in Wuchang. There, revolutionists accidentally exploded some ammunition, and this point of no return started the lightning that led to the takeover of the city. A statue of Dr. Sun Yat-sen dominates the front of the Hubei Military Government Building, now the 1911 Revolution Memorial Hall. Republican troops broke through the Qiyi Men (Uprising Gate) and seized Wuchang.

Originally named Zhonghe Gate, the Qiyi Gate is one of the 10 original gates of Wuchang.

WHERE TO STAY

The best hotels are the **Holiday Inn** and the **Wuhan Asia Hotel**. The best three-star is the Ramada. Good three star hotels include the Lakeview Garden, Yangtze, and Jiang Han. The four- and five-star Shangri-La Hotel is due in 1998 with 750 rooms.

High season is April to June, September and October. Prices listed below are subject to change, negotiations, and 15% surcharge.

LAKEVIEW GARDEN, *115 Luoyu Road, Wuchang, 430070. Three Stars, Tel. 7800858. Fax 7800896.*

YANGTZE, *539 Jiefang Road, 430030. Three Stars, Tel. 5862828. Fax 5854110.*

JIANG HAN, *245 Shengli Road, 430014, Three Stars, Tel. 2811600. Fax 2814342.*

HOLIDAY INN WUHAN, *868 Jie Fang Da Dao Ave., 430022. Four stars. Tel. 5867888, 5845484. Fax 5845353. In North America, Tel. 1-800-HOLIDAY. $100 to $145. Dist.A.P. 27 km. Dist.harbor two km. Dist.R.W. five km. Credit Cards.*

Built 1996. 407 rooms. Bowling, pool, and health center. 27 floors, 394 rooms. IDD. USTV. Executive floors. Non-smoking rooms. Cantonese and Asian cuisine. Revolving restaurant. 24-hour room service. B.C. Gym, outdoor pool and tennis court. Offices.

QING CHUAN HOTEL, *88 Xi Ma Chang St., Hanyang, 430050. Three stars, Tel. 484-6688. Fax 5864964. Credit Cards.*

This basic hotel near the Yangtze River Bridge and Yellow Crane Tower is convenient if your cruise ship docks at its pier but it is a long way from downtown and the main cruise ship pier there. Built 1984; ren. 1991. 24 stories. 300 rooms. B.C. Gym, sauna, tennis, and beauty salon. Casino, IDD, USTV and Sichuan food.

RAMADA HOTEL, *9 Taibei Yi Rd., Hankou, 430015. Three stars, Tel. 5787968. Fax 5803581, 5789171. Tel. 1-800-8547854. $75 to $110. Dist.A.P.25 km. from international airport. Dist.Hankou R.W. five km. Dist. 14 km. from Yangtze River cruise ship pier. Credit Cards.*

Adjacent to Fountain Amusement Park in business and commercial district. 1994. 162 rooms, some with only showers. USTV. Cantonese and Asian food. IDD. In-house movies. B.C. Shuttle bus. Gym. Tennis. Cheaper rooms with shower only.

WUHAN ASIA HOTEL *(Yazhou Da Jiudian), Wuhan International Convention Centre, 616 Jiefang Rd., Wuhan 430030. Four stars. Tel. 3897777. Fax 3808080, 4807878. $110 to $125. Dist.A.P.60 km. Dist.R.W.15 km. Credit Cards.*

Renovations 1996. 265 rooms. Good reputation. B.C., USTV, 24-hour room service. Revolving restaurant. About 15-minutes drive from main pier. Cantonese and Sichuan food. Disco and private karaoke rooms. Outdoor pool and gym.

WHERE TO EAT

Among the well-known Hubei dishes are: mianyang three steamings of fish, pork, and chicken; grilled meats of five kinds of poultry; fish balls soup with egg white in the shape of the Three Gorges; stir-fried sliced pork kidney in phoenix-tail shape; fried boneless eel; braised wild duck in brown sauce; steamed catfish; lotus seeds with white fungus in sweet soup.

Food is good in the hotels, and at the **YINZUO RESTAURANT**, *109 Yan Jiang Da Dao in Hankou, Tel. 2836657* and the **LAOTONGCHENG RESTAURANT**, *1 Dazi Road, Hankou, Tel. 2814966*, both for Wuhan food. The **JADE COURT RESTAURANT**, *245 Shengli Street in Hankou, Tel. 2811600* is good for Cantonese.

SEEING THE SIGHTS

The **Museum of Hubei Province**, *188 Dong Hu Road, Wuchang, Tel. 6813171*; open 8 am to noon; 3 to 5 pm daily, displays some of the world's most exciting recent archaeological discoveries. In 1978, 20,000 articles were excavated from the Zenghouyi Tomb, just outside of Suizhou city. Dating from the Warring States period 2,400 years ago, the tomb of Marquis Yi of Zeng contained bronzes, weapons, lacquer, musical instruments, gold, and jade. The contents were found in water in which oxidized copper was accidentally dissolved. This saved most of the pieces from decay. Some of the lacquer is still preserved in water that shows the original brilliant red at its best.

Most important in the find is a complete set of 65 ritual bells of different sizes. When struck, they emit a perfect 12-tone system covering five octaves. Each bell also has two tones depending on where it is struck, a quality that has not yet been found in any other bell anywhere else in the world. In addition, the name of the tone and the date were inscribed on each bell in both the Zeng and Chu scripts. The two languages side by side here are as valuable to linguists as the Rosetta stone.

The bells were a gift from the King of Chu. Since the reigns of the donor and the recipient overlapped by only a few years, the technology to produce them must have been at an astoundingly high level. Not only are their tones precise, they were probably cast in a short length of time. The heaviest is 203.6 kilograms and 1 1/2 meters high. Imagine pouring hot metal into a mold that size! And of the exact amount to produce the prescribed tone!

Ritual bells were only played for ceremonies, not for pleasure. Only aristocrats and royalty were allowed to possess them, and only in certain numbers. Reproductions have been played for tour groups who have heard Jingle Bells as well as ancient Chinese music.

The five-story, 51 meter-high, **Huang He Lou** (Yellow Crane Tower), *Tel. 8877330*, in Wuchang is a symbol of the city and has a good view. Open 7:30 am to 5:30 pm. It was first built in 223 A.D. on top of the Yellow Swan riverside rock and inspired many famous poets, including Li Bai. It was destroyed by nature or war and rebuilt several times. It was reconstructed and expanded on its present site on Snake Hill in 1981. The design is based largely on the Qing version that lasted from 1868 to 1984, but is 20 meters taller. It also has elements of the previous versions, pictures of which are inside. The tower gives a good view of the Yangtze and the city; there's an elevator.

The legend of the wine shop on the original site inspired the poets. Here, the owner used to give free wine to an old man who drew a picture of a yellow crane on the wall in gratitude. After the old man left, the crane came to life and danced for the customers, and the owner became rich. When the old man returned decades later, he mounted the crane and flew off into the sky. Nearby are the White Tower, the Tablet Corridor, and gardens. Wuhan will be rebuilding 20 historical buildings in the vicinity.

If you're looking for other things to do while you wait for your ship, the **Minority Museum** is at *13 Hong Xiang, Wuchang, Tel. 8873616*, open daily 8 to 11:30 am; 2 to 4:30 pm. The 45-meter-high, seven-story **Hongshan Pagoda**, *Wuluo Road, Wuchang, Tel. 7884539*, dates from the Yuan (1279). Open 7 am to 5 pm. The **Guiyuan Temple**, *20 Cuiwei Heng Road, Hanyang, Tel. 4841367*; open 8 am to 4 pm, started at the end of the Ming over 300 years ago, is the most important Buddhist temple in the city, and is one of the 10 biggest in China. It contains 500 clay arhats, each life-size, distinctive, and 250 years old.

You can also take a half-day trip to the museum at the ***Ancient Copper Mine** in Tonglushan Daye county, described by a Canadian metallurgist as incredible. One hour by road from Wuhan, it takes another half-hour to explore. It is now an open pit with mining tools, shaft, ropes, and baskets, started in the Zhou about 3,000 years ago. Nowhere else in the world at the time was mining technology so far advanced.

NIGHTLIFE & ENTERTAINMENT

Noteworthy cultural events include the **Wuhan Acrobatic Troupe**, **Beijing Opera Troupe of Wuhan**, the **Wuhan Song and Dance Drama Troupe**; and, of course, the **Zenghouyi Chime Bells**. All of these have performed abroad. For fun, there's **J.J.'s Disco**.

SHOPPING

Local products are gold and silver jewelry, lacquerware, carpets, shell carvings, carved turquoise, boxwood carving, feather fans, colored pottery, jadeware, and paintings.

Try the **Wuhan Department Store**, *358 Jie Fang Da Dao, Hankou, Tel. 5864821*. Open 8:30 am to 8:30 pm; the **Wuhan Antique Store**, *169 Zhongshan Da Dao, Hankou, Tel. 3786538*. Open 9 am to 5 pm; **Hubei Antique Shop** *(Provincial Museum); Wuhan Antiques and Curios Store, 1039 Zhongshan Avenue, Hankou*; **Wuhan Carpet Weaving Mill**, *14 Hankou Ruixiang Road*; **Wuhan Friendship Store**, *Jiefang Da Dao Avenue, Hankou*; **Wuhan Service Department of Arts and Crafts**, *Minshen Road, Zhongshan Avenue, Hankou*.

EXCURSIONS FROM WUHAN

Shennonjia Prime Forest Scenic Spot in the west of the province adjacent to Sichuan is 3,250 square kilometers of forests, mountains, minority villages, and the home of the Chinese "big foot." The government will probably be opening this to tourism in the near future. See *Yangtze Gorges* below.

Shishou, 300 kilometers west of Wuhan near the Yangtze, is for animal lovers. Here is a reserve where the government with the help of Hong Kong's Ocean Park is trying to save fresh-water dolphins or *baiji* from extinction. There could be eighteen dolphins resident by now. Scientists estimate that only 100 of these mammals are left in the wild. One named Qiqi is at the Institute of Hydrobiology in Wuhan. No one is allowed to kill dolphins or speed on a 135 kilometer section of the river west of Wuhan and cruise ship passengers have seen dolphins swimming between Wuhan and Jingsha.

The **Wudang Mountain** is about 200 kilometers northwest of Wuhan and needs at least five days. It is the home of the Wudang style of martial arts. This important Taoist center has an impressive collection of religious buildings. Mostly built in the Ming, it includes eight palaces, two temples, 36 nunneries, and 62 grotto temples, all along a 30 kilometer-or-so mountain path. The highest of its 72 peaks, Tianzhu, is over 1600 meters. On top is the *Golden Hall (Yuan and Ming), made of gilded copper. Wudang is not as strenuous as other mountains. New hotels are at the foot.

Wulingyuan is a national scenic spot in the south of the province, about 300 kilometers southwest of Wuhan and accessible by air. See *Changsha*.

For the **Yangtze Gorges**, keep reading. From Wuhan, you can take a regular ferry or one of the luxury cruise ships through the Yangtze Gorges to Chongqing. Give yourself plenty of time to find your ship. The CITS

Liaison office should know where it is docked but the quays are not always marked in English. Most ships leave from Number 19 Pier (Shih Jiu Hao Ma Tou) across from the Formosa Hotel in Hankou but this may no longer be the case. Ask your hotel or CITS exactly how to get there The ships *Yangzi Jiang, Yangtze Paradise, Yangtze President* and *Splendid China* have docked near the Qing Chuan Hotel. Check with the Cruise Booking Department, Yangtze International Travel.

PRACTICAL INFORMATION

- **Business Hours**, 8:30 or 9 am to 5 or 5:30 pm for offices; 8:30 or 9 am to 7 or 8:30 pm for stores. Five days a week. 9 am to 12 noon; 1:30 to 4:30 pm for Bank of China.
- **Changjiang Cruise Overseas Travel Corporation,** *55 Yanjiang Avenue, 430014. Tel. 2814005, 5858125. Fax 2811049, 5893340*
- **CITS**, *Room 303, 1365 Zhongshan Avenue, 430014, Tel. 2842331, or 48 Jianghan Yi Road, Hankou; Tel. 2816356, 2833505. Fax 2811891, 2811706. For cruise ship information, Tel. 2816553, Wu Dan Dan.*
- **CTS**, *1365 Zhongshan Avenue, Hankou 4300314, Tel. 3821666. Fax 5811074, Yangtze Cruise Branch, Tel. 3821161 or 3856721.*
- **Hubei CITS** and the **Hubei Overseas Travel Corporation,** *7-8/F, Xiaoanhu Building, 26 Taibei Yi Road, 430015. Tel. 5784100, 5784125. Fax 5784089, 5784109*
- **Hubei Yangtze International Travel Service**, *21 Chezhan Road, 430017. Tel. 2809939, 2811706. Fax 2818738.* The Cruise Department here should know about ship movements.
- **Telephone Code,** *027*
- **Tourist Complaints**, contact **Supervisory Bureau of Tourism Quality of Hubei Province**, *Building 2, Qingshiqiao Area, Hanyang, 430050. Tel. 4818760. Fax 4822513*
- **Tourist Hotline**, *Tel. 2832914*
- **Wuhan Tourist Administration**, *17 Hezuo Street, Hankou, 430014. Tel. 2832389, 2833107. Fax 2177868, 2817868.* For information.

YANGTZE GORGES

(also known as Yangzi or Changjiang River Gorges)

The boat trip through the gorges and on the great river itself between **Chongqing** and **Yichang** or **Wuhan** is highly recommended, not just for its spectacular scenery but also for its history. Bring binoculars, a telephoto lens if you're a camera bug, and some books.

The scenery includes sheer cliffs and mountains rising up to 1,000 meters on both sides of narrow, rushing water, old towns cut by slender lines of stone steps, and a mountain almost lined from top to bottom with a pagoda. You can hear reproductions of ancient chime bells, and see a 2,000-year old gentleman. You can race a dragon boat, hear the old songs of the boatmen, and look for wild monkeys and hanging coffins.

You will see social history: ships still unloaded by strings of men carrying loads on their backs. If you go up the Daning River or Shennonjia Stream, you might see Tujia men pulling boats upstream with shoulder harnesses and chanting in the old way. Some work nude if they don't expect tourists.

The Yangtze River is a busy highway. Except for a few short sections, there has been no other road along the river between Yichang and Chongqing. (There is one being built now.)

When To Go

The best time to visit is **September** and **October**. The rainy season is May to August. There are landslides due to heavy rains and floods in July and August disrupting land excursions. The winter is cold, the hotels and ferries inadequately heated. A padded jacket or sweater and windbreaker is necessary for the wind in the gorges even in mid-October. Expect delays by fog from early November into March. Also expect delays waiting for berths at ports especially Chongqing and Wuhan. Most cruise ships for foreign tourists have air-conditioning.

Interesting Reading & Background

Guides will tell you stories of the Three Kingdoms, but bring your own books along: a copy of Richard McKenna's *The Sand Pebbles*, John A. Hersey's *A Single Pebble* or Caroline Walker et al's *On Leaving Bai Di Cheng, the Cultures of China's Yangzi Gorges*. Probe International's *Damming the Three Gorges* is an environmental group's readable critique of the feasibility study of the proposed dam. Van Slyke's *Yangtze, Nature, History and the River* also describes the foreigners who lived here. *The Romance of the Three Kingdoms*, a historical novel, has been translated into English, and the names of the heroes of this great military story, their statues and temples, will keep coming up almost anywhere you go in the Yangtze valley: Liu Bei, Zhang Fei, Guan Yu, and Zhuge Liang. There's also their arch enemy Cao Cao.

If you don't have a guide with you, maybe the steward or cook on your ferry or fellow passengers can point out landmarks. You might want to get a detailed color tourist map.

The highlights of the archaeology and history in this area are largely the **Ba culture**, a little known group who lived here from about the 16th century B.C. to the third century B.C. and had capitals in Chongqing and Jingzhou. They were worshippers of white tigers and left behind some very distinctive and impressive bronzes in humanoid forms. (Visit the

THE DAM

A controversial dam is currently being built that will displace over a million people, raise the water level about 110 meters, and lessen the dramatic effect of the gorges. It will help control floods, and provide irrigation and hydroelectric power. You should be able to see the furious construction activities at the **Three Gorges** *dam site, unless you sleep through it.*

The largest civil engineering project in the world, plans call for submerging 632 square kilometers of land, creating a lake at Chongqing, and bringing the area into the 21st century. The Yangtze valley around the gorges is now about 40 years behind Beijing. The project hopes to improve travel logistics in this area with new bridges, more flights, airports, easier navigation and better hotels.

You will see towns and temples that will be covered by water and new buildings on doomed land completed by resilient people out to take advantage of the government's promises to compensate them for buildings destroyed due to the dam project. While construction of the dam has now started, cruise ships could be affected as early as 1997 or as late as 2002. At that time, ships will either be diverted to a canal, or passengers will have to transfer from a downstream to an upstream ship. Otherwise the cruises will continue as before.

Critics argue that sedimentation will destroy the dam's turbines in less than 10 years, that it will affect the ecology, and destroy historical sites. They say that the costs far outweigh the benefits, especially in terms of disrupted lives. If you get the chance, ask local people how they feel about it.

provincial museum in Chengdu.) These are the people whose hanging coffins you look at in the Three Lesser Gorges and elsewhere in the valley.

The state of Chu dominated the area from about 770 B.C. until it was taken over by the King of Qin, the first emperor of China in 221 B.C. This was the period of the poet-statesman Quyuan, whose death inspired the first dragon boat races. The Three Kingdom's period started about 220 A.D. with an oath in a peach orchard, and ended in 265 A.D. during which battles were fought between contending kingdoms, the Wei, Shu and Wu. Ask about the famous Battle of the Red Cliffs west of Wuhan.

The Yangtze was also the focus of foreign merchants, gunboats, and missionaries in the late 1800s and early 1900s, but guides will not give you much information about this embarrassing period. This is the time of the novel and move, *The Sand Pebbles*.

SAILING THE GORGES

Passenger ferries are the cheapest way to travel the Gorges. They operate all year round. Here the top second-class accommodations come with a lounge and the best view if you can get one of the cabins. This class has bunks for four people to a cabin, soap, toothbrushes, towels and tea. The public bathrooms might have a tub, shower, western toilet and lots of water all over the floor. Try for an outside cabin. The inside ones can get pretty stuffy in summer, and you might find other passengers gambling noisily on the floor outside your room all night.

In second, third, fourth, or fifth class, you share a room with an increasing number of people, get suffocated by cigarette smoke, worry about thieves, or sleep in hallways. At the same time, you will probably meet some of the sweetest, most generous people in the world.

Below second class, you need your own towel, mug, soap, etc. Steaming hot water is available. Fourth class has 12 bunks to a cabin. Hope for a spot near the door. To get a place to sit indoors you have to book a berth. This is essential in cold weather. No one gets private toilets, baths, or air-conditioners.

Stops are short and not necessarily at tourist sites. Nor can you be sure your ship will get close enough to take a photo of the lovely 11-story pagoda at Shibaozhai unless you have a lens at least 200 millimeters long. But you only pay for passage to where you get off. And by ferry you can get closer to Chinese people and experience with them the loudspeakers blaring announcements at 6 am and queues for showers. After all, didn't you come here to meet the people?

As for the food, it is usually edible but with little variety. You usually have to line up and maybe will get pushed and shoved. Or find a Chinese friend who knows about self-preservation to help you. There is a crude basic dining hall with chairs and tables.

You can book ferries all the way between Chongqing and Wuhan or Yichang through travel agencies in these cities, or directly at the pier three days ahead of time. You can book shorter runs in each city of departure, at the pier or town booking office. It is better to ride from Chongqing only to Yichang or Yueyang because the stretch between Yichang and Wuhan, a whole days ride, isn't all that interesting (though you might like the rest, and the search for wild dolphins).

The river is relatively safe between Wuhan and Chongqing. In no place is it over three kilometers wide and in some places only 100 meters. River traffic controllers are strict. Ships have fire alarms, smoke detectors, life boats and jackets. Traffic is heavy so if there is trouble, help is close by. Ships have radar and captains are in radio contact with control towers along the way.

Town Hopping

It is possible to go along the Yangtze by ferry spending the nights on land. It has been done successfully but not without problems. Only the adventurous few travel this way. Most hotels or county guest houses are terrible: no toilet seats, no workable plumbing, thin curtains, no air-conditioning, no 24-hour hot running water, few rooms with private baths, and lots of dirt. There's also no television in English, and no *China Daily*.

Most hotels are high on a mountain; you have to climb with your luggage. Few towns have porters and English-speaking travel agents. While every major community has ferry service at least once and some-time three times a day, it can be canceled because of fog and bad weather. Taxis are hard to find. Few people speak English and few restaurants are good. You should take precautions about dirty eating utensils and inadequately cooked food. Only banks can change money and no one accepts credit cards. Except for tourist towns, no town has IDD yet.

The only real hotel between Chongqing and Yichang is at Wanxian. But things are changing and you might be all right.

Town hopping means you can do a lot of hiking and climbing, spend time seeing monuments and views that ship tourists can't. The Yangtze from a mountain top is glorious. The scenery away from the river is also marvelous.

As on the ferries, you need a translator to get the most out of such travel and you might not find one. If you don't speak Chinese, think how you will make your wishes known. How will you buy a ticket? And get a berth assignment once on board? How long will it be before you see the Gorges? How long will the ship stop in each port?

Cruise Ships

Currently over 60 much more expensive air-conditioned tourist ships ply the Yangtze from mid-March to late November. About 20 of these meet standards expected by foreigners. These should be booked through travel agents in North America or China at least six months ahead to fit your schedule, or if you're flexible, you can try at the last moment. You are isolated from Chinese people but you can expect more comfort than ferries and few if any of the hassles. The government has started to regulate these ships and their safety, and rate them with stars the same way it rates hotels. Five stars are at the top.

You can expect an English-speaking tour guide to be on ships two stars and up but the level of the guide's ability improves with the number of stars. On one-star ships half the cabins should have private baths, and all get twelve hours of hot water a day. On three stars and up, you get international direct dial telephone service, a gym, and 24 hours a day hot and cold water in your cabin. On four stars and up you get Star Television satellite reception. On five stars you could have a swimming pool.

Itineraries differ depending on which way you are going, up or down river, and which ship you book. Most people go between Chongqing and Yichang downstream but upstream is cheaper and longer with fewer passengers. Upstream is all right too if you have the time. Some downstream passengers go on to Wuhan thus avoiding the stress of making transfers and bookings out of Yichang.

If you have a particular site you must visit, make sure you take a ship that will stop there. If you are going upstream, make sure that your ship will stop for all announced sightseeing spots. They don't always. Some ships stop either at Badong for the Shennonjia Stream or at Wushan for the Three Lesser Gorges, but not both.

The highlight for many tourists is the day trip on the **Three Lesser Gorges** on the **Daning River**, or the similar **Shennonjia Stream** at **Badong**. These are on smaller boats through narrower canyons with hanging coffins, wild monkeys and Tujia villages. The water is crystal clear when not white and bubbly. The better trip is the Shennonjia Stream which is more like rafting with no diesel fumes and no engine vibrations.

Stops usually include climbing a lot of stairs, part of the Yangtze lifestyle. Ships themselves also require climbing. None have elevators. Most have four or five stories. Chongqing has an elevator now from shipside to the street.

The best ships are frequently, but not always, the newest because ships age quickly here. The older Victorias and Regals (*Princesses Sheena, Jeannie,* and *Elaine*) are also top of the line for service. All but the Regals are made in China and look slapdash. The Victorias have been tops for food and entertainment (but it depends on the staff, each ship is different). Victoria I has a classier Mediterranean lobby. The cabins on the Regals are small and on the *Sheena* they have stinted on the food. (I had to request rice with my Chinese meal and it arrived cold.) The Regal's ships were built in Germany and are the best made, but they were designed for tourists on the Volga River.

The Holiday Inn stopped managing ships on the Yangtze in 1995 and I don't know what this means for the lovely Scandinavian-style *East King* and *East Queen*. These two ships have dining rooms too small for their guests, bigger cabins than the Regals and Victorias, smaller televisions, but a room safe and refrigerator. Avoid the Ping Hu 2000 with its poor service and design. Avoid small ships that cater only to Chinese passengers; they don't know how to serve foreigners.

The *Yangtze President* should be good. The *Yangtze Pearl* and *Yangtze Princess* should be acceptable. The *Shenzhou* was a state guest house with waterfall, and two-story dance hall. The *Qiao Feng* has large cabins but a

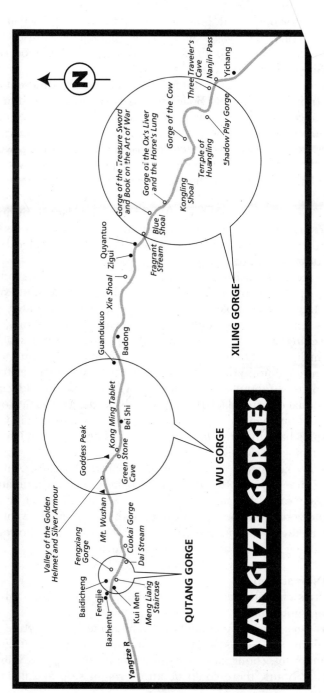

YANGTZE GORGES

reputation for poor food, poor service, and no planned activities. The *Blue Whale* and the *Yangtze Spirit* of the Changjiang Cruise Overseas Travel Corporation are both new. See *Chongqing*. Also good is China Travel Service's *Splendid China*.

The quality of the ships differ; they are owned by different companies. Do not expect the Love Boat. There is usually a captain's dinner, and a final dance (to ancient music, so bring your own cassettes). Some ships have smelly toilets. The newer ones have picture windows so you can enjoy the view from your cabin and televisions. Few have working swimming pools. Some have been delayed by repairs. Most have thin walls. Some have no laundry service on the next-to-last day.

All ships are regulated through the gorges by the navigation authorities and some have to go through the gorges after dark or during meal times. Expect to get up at one or four in the morning if you don't want to miss these. Expect queues of ships waiting to get through each gorge or the locks at Yichang.

The more expensive cruise ships have guide-interpreters but not all announce points of interest along the way in English. The most expensive cruise ships have double rooms with private baths, laundry, doctor, currency exchange, post and telegraph, beauty salon, library, lounge (with evening movies), pool (rarely working), a bar, western snack food, and a small store. There could be a gym and mah jong room. Fax and telephone communications from ships have to bounce off satellites so are very expensive (about $15 a minute). CITS in Fengdu and Zigui has international direct dial (IDD) service at dockside. The quality of television reception changes as the ships progress and is usually in Chinese. Some ships have in-house movies, maybe in English. Some have dance parties, mah-jong classes and karaoke.

Fellow passengers can be any nationality: Germans, Americans, British, Chinese, Hong Kong, Taiwan, Japanese and Singaporean. Dress is generally casual but most ships have a captain's banquet or cocktail party and your crew could be dressed in white. You might want to take something dressy (but not too dressy) for that occasion. Do however take good walking shoes or boots for shore excursions.

Ferry Downstream

Here's a sample itinerary. Schedules differ, of course, but this should give you a good idea:.

Day One: Leave Chongqing early (about 7 am). Note **white pagoda** and **Buddha** on north bank. At about three hours out, you pass Fuling; at 8 1/2 hours out, Zhongxian. At about 10 hours out, you pass **Shibaozhai**. At 12 1/2 hours, there could be an overnight stop at 2,000-year-old **Wanxian**.

Day Two: The ship leaves early (about 2:30 am), depending on the current, to reach the first gorge 4 1/2 hours later at daylight. Just before Qutang Gorge are **Fengjie** and **Baidicheng**, or White King City. Near the entrance of the gorge on the north bank is a two- story pavilion with red lacquer columns, which marks the beginning of the gorges. On the south side of **Kui Men Gate** are two stone towers and five Chinese characters, which mean The Kui Men Gate is an unmatched pass.

The **Qutang** (Chutang) **Gorge** is eight kilometers long and takes about an hour to pass through. It is the most imposing of the gorges, only 100-150 meters wide. Prepare for a very windy passage, as the wind as well as the water, is tunneled between the cliffs.

The **Wuxia** (Wuhsia), or Wu Gorge, starts 30 minutes after you leave the Qutang. It is 44 kilometers long and takes about 1 1/2 hours (upsteam 3 1/2 hours) to pass through. Look for the **Twelve Peaks Enshrouded in Rain and Mist**, of which you can see six on the north bank and three on the south. Of these the **Peak of the Goddess** is the highest, at over 1,000 meters. It has a tall stone column on top that looks like a strongly built young woman gazing from high up in the sky at the waterway down below. Look for a table-shaped rock with six Chinese characters meaning The Wu Gorge boasts craggy cliffs, said to be written by a prime minister of the Shu Kingdom in the third century.

The town of **Wushan** is between the Wu and the Qutang Gorges. From here cruise ships stop for a shore excursion on the **Daning River** through the **Lesser Three Gorges**. Twenty minutes after leaving the Wu Gorge is the town of Badong which could have pomelos, oranges, and persimmons for sale on shore if in season. Look for an old pavilion high on a hill. You are now in Hubei province.

About one hour from Badong shortly after Zigui is **Xiang Xi** (Fragrant Stream) on the north side, where the lovely imperial concubine Wang Zhaojun accidentally dropped her pearls 2,000 years ago. The water here is said to be limpid and fragrant as a result. There's more about this woman, who is considered one of the four most beautiful women in Chinese history, in Chapter 17, *North China*, section on Hohhot.

Shortly after Xiang Xi is the 75 kilometer-long **Xiling** (Hsiling) **Gorge**, which takes about 1 1/2 hours (upstream two hours) to pass through. It is the longest and has been the most treacherous of the three. Thirty minutes beyond the entrance, on the south side, is **Kuang Ming village**, with a large temple, Huang Ling Miao, then comes **Five Sisters Peaks**, **Three Brothers Rocks**, and the **Needle**. While still in the Xiling Gorge, you'll see **Zhongbao Island** and **Sandouping**, about 65 kilometers before Yichang, is the site of the largest dam in the world and a new bridge across the Yangtze.

The end of the Xiling Gorge is marked by a large **Buddha**, and a statue of **Zhang Fei of The Three Kingdoms**.

In the east part of Yichang, you go through the locks of the 1988-built 70-meter-high **Gezhouba Dam**. If you stay on board onward to Wuhan, you arrive late afternoon the next day and avoid the hassle of getting transportation out of Yichang.

Important Stops Along the Way

Some ferries and most cruise ships make stops in Badong, Fengjie, Fengdu, Jingsha, Shibaozhai, Wanxian, Wushan, Yichang, Yueyang and Zigui. Below are brief descriptions of each stop:

Badong is where you get off to see the **Shennonjia Stream** – about a six-hour trip by bus and boat from here. This is a very difficult excursion to do on your own and the tourism office organizes a tourist bus. The village in the Gaolin Scenic Area where you get an 18-passenger boat that is about 47 kilometers, by dirt road, from the ferry pier on the north side of the Yangtze, at a point about three kilometers west of Badong.

You drift three and a half hours with a lunch stop down the stream, helped by three boatmen. No noisy engines disturbs the tranquility. The scenery here is very beautiful and the air clear. There is a restaurant stop along the way.

In Badong itself, the crude **COUNTY GUEST HOUSE** is on the hill a few meters off the main street. High on the hillside, an enlightened governor built a pavilion in the Song to meet with his subjects. The current one is Qing.

Fengjie, at the western end of the Qutang Gorge, was the capital of the state of Wei during the Spring and Autumn Period (722-481 B.C.), the time of Confucius. The tomb of Liu Bei's wife is here. Here on a hill top, reached by a ferry and 300 steps, is Baidicheng or White King City with it great view of the river. Wax statues show you how Liu Bei entrusted his son to Zhuge Liang.

Fengdu (170 kilometers east of Chongqing on the north bank) has been regarded as hell and a gathering place for ghosts since the seventh century. Here believers built 48 Taoist and Buddhist temples, all destroyed in the 1960s by Red Guards. Rebuilt recently by Fengdu townspeople, it now has tacky statues of demons and hell, of no artistic merit. These will, however, give you an idea of the folk concept of the after-life, and the role of religion in their lives. Guides here make you go through various tests of agility and strength, all of which you can probably pass, and make it to heaven (instead of hell). The **Qing Ming Festival** celebrated here is special.

The ghost city is on a 288 meter-high hill reached by stairs or a cable car. It often remains open after hours (7 am to 5:30 pm) to accommodate

cruise ships. While well lit, you should take a flash light after dark. C.
puts on a ghostly show at its store in town which can be missed. A re.
village is nearby that will be moved across the river to a new site. The ghost
city will remain here.

Jingsha is between Wuhan and Yichang about ten hours east of
Yichang by ship. It is a recent union of the cities of **Jingzhou** (the capital
of the State of Chu), and **Shashi** (a 2000-year old trans-shipment port),
opened to foreign trade in 1895. It is one of the best places to stop. It has
a good museum where if you're lucky, you can hear the ancient chime
bells played (See *Wuhan.)* They were found nearby. This museum is also
the home of the 2000-year-old gentleman, his silks and hemp shoes.

In another part of the city is an ancient gate and walls from the Three
Kingdoms period (220-265 A.D.), so well preserved that costume movies
are made here. **CITS** in Jingzhou is at *Jiangling, 434100. Tel. 467999, Fax
466429.* The telephone code is 0716. Shashi has an airport and links with
Guangzhou and Shenzhen. **CITS** here is *Tel. 212325. Fax 217499.* The
telephone code is also *0716.*

Shibaozhai (Precious Stone Village), or Shibao Block on the north
bank about 10 hours downstream from Chongqing, has an 11-story Qing
pagoda. It is built on a limestone rock hill that rises to 160 meters above
the river. The smaller ships can stop here. The Regals and Victorias
cannot either until someone builds larger facilities.

In the main temple here are statues of Liu Bei, Zhuge Liang, Guan Yu,
and Zhang Fei, historical personages. Three of these swore oaths in a
peach orchard to support each other. They are immortalized in *The
Romance of the Three Kingdoms* novel. Emperor Liu Bei, who led an
unsuccessful army to avenge the death of Guan Yu, retreated here and
died in sorrow.

Wanxian is a 2,000-year old city and became a treaty port in the 1890s
when its biggest crop was opium. It is the largest town between Chongqing
and Yichang. In 1926, the British accused the Chinese of interfering with
a foreign steamship company here. Two British gunboats started shooting and over 3000 people were killed. Some historians consider this one
of the first successful assertions of Chinese power against the imperialists.

You have to climb about 85 steps to get to this town of 700,000 for a
silk factory and the Zhang Fei Temple (to be relocated because of the
dam). New here will be a bridge across the Yangtze, a Three Gorges
museum, and an airport.

The **TAIBAI HOTEL** has been alright in the past, at *30 Baiyan Road,
634000. Tel. 223976.* About 80 rooms. No money change, but it is near the
Bank of China (closed Sundays). **CITS** is *Tel. 226704. Fax 224163.* The
telephone code is *0819.*

you disembark to a small boat for about three and
_____aning River through the 50 kilometer-long **Lesser**
_____. This is between the Wu and Qutang gorges. If the water
_____ow, you might have to climb up a steep slope to get to the bus for
_ne short ride to the boat pier. You should however be able to get a sedan
chair ride (don't pay more than Y20) if you can't handle the climb. If the
water level is high, you will be able to get on the motor boats right from
your ship, and avoid the aggressive peddlers trying to sell you fruit. This
should be a five-hour excursion, not to be attempted if diesel fumes
bother you. Seats are best in the front of the boat, and photographers
should sit directly behind the boatmen who will push it with poles to help
the engine climb up the foamy white rapids. You might have to queue up
behind other such boats or get out and walk for a few meters around the
most difficult parts.

Look for the square holes made in rock walls for horizontal posts for
the plank roads. If you're lucky, you can go past the restaurant in
Shuanglong/Double Dragon village to an attempted reproduction of
such a plank road, and more chances of finding wild monkeys. Downstream of Double Dragon village, look up near the sky in two narrow
horizontal caves for the old coffins of the Ba people. Enjoy the clarity of
the water, and the vertical cliffs. Much will disappear with the completion
of the Three Gorges Dam.

Yichang is a 2,400-year old settlement became a treaty port in 1876
and was almost leveled by Japanese bombs during World War II. It grew
dramatically with the building of the 2,605 meter-wide **Gezhouba Dam** in
the late 1980s. You can visit this dam and study a model of the new Three
Gorges Dam. Your ship will probably take a 12 minute, 30-meter high
water-borne elevator ride in its locks. In Yichang itself, you can visit by
land the eastern end of **Xiling Gorge** at Nanjin Pass with its statue of
Zhang Fei of The Three Kingdoms, a giant welcoming **Buddha**, and the
Three Travelers Cave.

It is worth a visit for the scenery high above the river. In the city also,
the **Sturgeon Research Institute** is good for ecologists and those who
want to look at a couple of live specimens of this huge, ugly fish from the
dinosaur era, an endangered species.

On the Yangtze near the Three Gorges Hotel you'll find the **Zhenjiang
Ge**, which is two pagodas, one from the early Qing. These are dedicated
to Li Bing, builder of the Dujiangyan Irrigation system in 256 B.C.

From Yichang, there are flights a couple of times a week with
Guangzhou and Changsha and three times with Wuhan. An international
airport is being built. A direct express train has been leaving Beijing every
other day at midnight and arriving in Yichang about 3 am on the second
morning. A highway is being built between Yichang and Beijing. The train

between Wuhan and Yichang takes 11hours. The bus is faster and more direct and runs on an express highway.

Yichang has adequate but scruffy three-star hotels: the Three Gorges Hotel is nicely located on the waterfront near the wharves. It is relatively new but looks run down.

PING HU HOTEL *(Ping Hu Dajiudian), 87 Dong Shan Rd., Tel. 225011. Fax 224223. Dist.R.W. about two km. Dist.ferry pier 3 1/2 km.*
Built 1989. 12 stories. B.C. Sauna and gym.

THREE GORGES HOTEL, *Yanjiang Road. Three stars, Tel. 221911, 221944. Fax 442025. Dist A.P. 18 km. Dist.Gezhouba Dam two km. Some Credit Cards.*
Built 1986, ren. 1992. 11 stories, 132 rooms. Bar, foreign exchange service, beauty salon, clinic, and B.C. USTV. CITS is on the grounds of the Three Gorges Hotel, *Tel. 442192, Fax 447064.*

CYTS Tours is at *218 Yan Jiang Da Road, 443000. Tel. 223453. Fax 223177.* Yichang's telephone code is *0717.*

For the town of **Yueyang**, see separate listing in Chapter 21, *South China.*

Zigui, west of Yichang, can be reached from Yichang in six hours by road or one hour by ship. The **ZIGUI CHENG JIAO DAI SUO** (Zigui City Guest House), *Tel. (07278) 22555,* is uphill about two kilometers from the pier and is next to the bus station, main street market and stores. It's a new, good-looking building with bad plumbing.

The **Quyuan Temple** here was built in 1976-85 and will be moved again. The original ninth century Tang site was flooded because of the Gezhouba dam. Quyuan was the poet/statesman who drowned himself because the King of Chu did not heed his correct advice about the threats from the state of Qin. You can pay respects at his tomb which contains some of his clothes. The temple has 1976-made slate tablets of his poetry based on Qing designs, a painting of Quyuan by Yang Chu, and a 400-year old statue of Quyang. He was born in this county.

Cruise ship passengers can usually race fellow tourists in dragon boats here. This is the traditional way to honor Quyuan (and save him from the fish). Boat men also perform a powerful boat dance at a dockside theatre right beside your ship in the evening and CITS provides a convenient store.

PRACTICAL INFORMATION

If you're looking for a cruise ship with a US office, try **Regal China Cruises**, *57 West 38th Street, New York, NY 10018, Tel. (212) 768-3388, or 1-800-808-3388. Fax (212)768-4939.*

You can also contact **China Travel Service** in the U.S. for its *Splendid China* ship.

"LI SAO" BY THE POET QUYUAN

Quyuan,poet and statesman, in whose memory dragon boats are raced once a year all over the world, tried unsuccessfully to save the Kingdom of Chu from the first emperor of China:

The conspirators steal their heedless pleasures;
Their road is dark and leads to danger.
What do I care of the peril to myself?
I fear only the wreck of my lord's carriage.
I hastened to his side in attendance
To lead him in the steps of the ancient kings,
But the Fragrant One would not look into my heart;
Instead, heeding slander, he turned on me in rage.

Reprinted from **China Tourism**, translator unknown.

COME BACK SOON!

23. RECOMMENDED READING

If you know nothing about China, start out with a general history like Brian Catchpole's *A Map History of Modern China*, an easy read (high-school level) with half maps and diagrams. You can graduate from that to *China, Yesterday and Today*, a paperback that you might want to take with you for background. This covers the history of China, its political life, agricultural policy, etc.

Good bedside reading and very informative are the *Wise Man from the West*, about Matteo Ricci's unsuccessful attempts to convert China to Christianity 400 years ago, and *Son of the Revolution*, an autobiography of a young Chinese who grew up on the wrong side of the political fence and married his American teacher. *Son of the Revolution* is imperative for anyone wanting to get an insider's look at today's system, how the various campaigns since 1949 have affected the kind of people that you will be meeting, and how some Chinese circumvent the rules and stifling bureaucracy.

Sterling Seagrave's *Soong Dynasty* is fascinating, about the Chinese Christian who was educated in America, and whose children controlled China's economy for several decades.

There' also Jung Chang's *Wild Swans*, an excellent story of three generations of women in one family in China and the U.S. And of course Amy Tan's *Joy Luck Club*.

For dynastic history, Raymond Dawson's *Imperial China* is another book to carry along –a good index and lots of juicy gossip about the likes of Tang Empress Wu and her boyfriends. For Beijing, read any biography of the Ming or Qing emperors and that of Empress Dowager Cixi (Tzu Hsi) and her boy friend. For Tibet, read Heinrich Herrar's classic *Seven Years in Tibet* or John Avedon's more recent *In Exile From the Land of Snows*, about the current Dalai Lama's life. Behr's *The Last Emperor* gives more background than the movie.

For British involvement in China, there's George Woodcock's *The British in the Far East*, about the bad, old, but interesting imperialists like

Captain Charles 'Chinese' Gordon. For U.S. involvement, there's John Fairbank's *The United States and China*. If you're interested in missionaries, try Pat Barr's *To China with Love* or Alvyn J. Austin's *Saving China-Canadian Missionaries in the Middle Kingdom, 1888-1959*.

For more recent history, Edgar Snow's *Red Star Over China*, not only relates the history of the Long March but has the only autobiography dictated by Mao. Also recommended is Jonathan D. Spence's *The Search for Modern China*. If you are concerned about human rights, get reports from Amnesty International, and since you might be arguing about Tiananmen Square, do read the Chinese versions obtained from Chinese missions abroad, as well as Western sources like Simmie and Nixon's *Tiananmen Square* or Gargan's *China's Fate*.

For the Cultural Revolution, the classic is Jean Daubier's *A History of the Chinese Cultural Revolution* and Roxanne Witke's *Comrade Chiang Ching*, one of the best books about Chairman Mao's widow. A best-seller in the late 1980s was Nien Cheng's *Life and Death in Shanghai* about the Cultural Revolution.

Among the modern Western novels, a lot of old China flavor is in Pearl S. Buck's *The Good Earth* and *Pavilion of Women*. Or try a Chinese novel. Gu Hua's *A Small Town Called Hibiscus* is very good as a book and movie.

If you're interested in Chinese arts and crafts, I would take along Margaret Medley's *A Handbook of Chinese Art*, Michael Sullivan's *The Arts of China*, or C.A.S. Williams's *Outlines of Chinese Symbolism and Art Motives*. These are all excellent reference books, profusely illustrated, that will help you appreciate the architecture, symbols, mythology, and customs of China. But do keep in mind that Williams's was written before 1949.

The authority on foot binding is Howard S. Levy's *The Lotus Lovers*. You can still find these shoes in antique markets and women with bound feet if you look.

Chinese periodicals can usually be found in bookstores in many Chinatowns. In San Francisco, the best-stocked store for China books is **China Books and Periodicals** *(Tel. 415-282-2994)*.

Many western periodicals now have their own correspondents in Beijing, and you should keep your eyes open for news reports about China before you go. *China Daily*, Beijing's English language newspaper, is printed also in New York City, San Francisco, and Hong Kong. Hong Kong's *South China Morning Post* has especially good China coverage.

If you are looking for Jewish roots in Shanghai, contact the **Sino-Judaic Institute** in Menlo, California.

You can pick up the very good Cartographic Department maps and China City Guides after you get there. One exists for every major city.

RECOMMENDED READING 613

READING LIST

Austin, Alvyn J. *Saving China – Canadian Missionaries in the Middle Kingdom, 1888-1959.* Toronto; University of Toronto Pres, 1986.

Barr, Pat. *To China with Love –The Lives and Times of Protestant Missionaries in China, 1860-1900.* New York: Doubleday & Co., Inc., 1973.

Behr, Edward. *The Last Emperor,* Toronto: General Paperbacks, 1987.

Booz, Elizabeth, B. *Tibet.* Hong Kong: Shangri-la Press, 1986. Lincolnwood, IL: Passport Books.

Coonay, Eleanor and Alteri, Daniel. *The Court of the Lion.* New York: Avon Books, 1989.

Coye, Molly Joel, etc., editor. *China, Yesterday and Today.* New York: Bantam Books, 1984.

Dalrymple, William. *In Xanadu, A Quest.* William Collins Sons & Co., London. Toronto, 1989.

Daubier, Jean. *A History of the Chinese Cultural Revolution.* New York, Toronto: Vintage Books, 1974.

Fairbank, John K. *The United States and China.* Cambridge: Harvard University Press, 1983.

Fitzgerald, C.P. *The Tower of Five Glories –A Study of the Min Chia of Ta Li, Yunnan.* West Point, CT: Hyperion Press, 1973.

Gargan, Edward A. *China's Fate –A People's Turbulent Struggle with Reform and Repression, 1980-1990.*

Gu Hua. *A Small Town Called Hibiscus.* Beijing: Panda Books, 1983.

Guisso, R.W.L. and Pagani, Catherine. *The First Emperor of China.* Toronto. Stoddart Publishing, 1989. In the U.S. Birch Lane Press, New York.

Haldane, Charlotte. *The Last Great Empress of China.* New York: Bobbs-Merrill, 1965.

Hopkirk, Peter. *Foreign Devils on the Silk Road.* New York: Oxford University Press, 1989.

Levy, Howard S. *The Lotus Lovers, The Complete History of the Curious Erotic Custom of Footbinding in China.* Prometheus Books, Buffalo, N.Y. 1992.

Li Nianpei, *Old Tales of China – a tourist guidebook to better understanding of China's stage, cinema, arts and crafts.* Beijing: China Travel and Tourism Press, 1981.

Liang Heng and Shapiro, Judith. *Son of the Revolution.* New York: Vintage Books, 1984.

Lo Kuan-chung. *Three Kingdoms.* Robert Moss, translator and editor. New York: Pantheon, 1976.

McCawley, James D. *The Eater's Guide to Chinese Characters.* Chicago and London: The University of Chicago Press, 1984.

Richardson, Hugh E. *Tibet and Its History*, Boston and London: Shambala, 1984, Random House distributor.

Ryder, G., ed., *Damming the Three Gorges*, Toronto: Probe International, 1990.

Snow, Edgar. *Red Star Over China*. New York: Penguin, 1977 (first published 1937).

Spence, Jonathan. *To Change China; Western Advisers in China, 1620-1960*. Boston, Toronto: Little, Brown, 1969.

Tsao Hsueh-Chin. *The Dream of the Red Chamber (Hung Lou Meng)*, New York: The Universal Library, Grosset & Dunlop, 1973.

Turner-Gottschang, Karen, etc. *China Bound –A Guide to Academic Life and Work in the PRC*. Washington, DC: National Academy Press, 1987.

Van Slyke, Lyman P. *Yangtze: Nature, History and the River*. Reading, MA: Addison-Wesley: 1989.

Walker, Carol et al. *On Leaving Bai Di Cheng, the Culture of China's Yangzi Gorges*. NC Press, Toronto, 1993.

Warner, Marina. *The Dragon Empress: The Life and Times of Tz'u- Hsi, Empress Dowager of China, 1835-1908*. New York: Macmillan, 1972.

Wiens, Herold J. *China's March Towards the Tropics*. The Shoe String Press, Hamden, Conn. 1954.

Wu Zuguang. *Peking Opera and Mei Lanfang*. Beijing: New World Press, 1981.

Wu Zuguang. *Doing Business in Today's China*. The American Chamber of Commerce in Hong Kong.

24. CHINESE CHARACTERS

I have listed below as many Chinese characters or pinyin romanization as I could get for the names of restaurants, stores, and tourist attractions. You can communicate by pointing to them so non-English speakers will know where you want to go.

Each city is arranged alphabetically within its region. Within each area itself, I've alphabetized the listings for easy reference.

SECTION	PAGE
Regional Food	*616*
Beijing	*618*
East China/Shanghai	*619*
North China	*624*
Northeast China	*627*
Northwest & Central China	*628*
Tibet	*632*
Southwest China	*632*
South China	*634*

SOME IMPORTANT AGENCY LISTINGS

CITS 国际旅行社
CTS 中旅社
CAAC 中国民航

REGIONAL & SPECIAL FOOD

BEIJING DISHES (aka Peking or Northern) 北京
- Smoked chicken/duck 熏鸡／鸭
- Crispy duck 香酥鸭
- Peking duck 北京烤鸭
- Sweet-sour fish/pork 糖醋鱼／肉
- Deep-fried shrimp toast 炸虾托
- Chicken and cucumber salad 凉拌三丝
- Stir-fried pork with bean sprouts (served with pancakes) 京酱肉丝
- Chinese cabbage with black mushrooms 冬菇白菜
- Pan-fried onion cake 葱油饼
- Hot and sour soup 酸辣汤
- Pan-fried dumplings with minced pork 生煎小包子
- Steamed bread rolls 银丝卷
- Assorted meat soup in casserole 什锦砂锅
- Shrimp with popped rice 虾仁锅巴
- Apple/banana fritter 拔丝苹果／香蕉

CANTONESE DISHES (aka Guangdong or Southern) 粤菜
- Crisp-skinned roasted goose/pork 烧鹅／烤乳猪
- Steamed chicken with green onion 葱油鸡
- Stir-fried diced fish/filet 松子鱼／炒鱼片
- Shark's fin in chicken and ham soup 鱼翅羹
- Steamed live fish 清蒸鱼
- Quick-boiled fresh shrimp 白灼虾
- Stir-fried beef in oyster sauce 蚝油牛肉
- Cantonese stuffed bean curd 酿豆腐
- Sauteed fresh Chinese vegetable 炒新鲜蔬菜
- Assorted meats in winter melon 冬瓜盅
- Bird's nest in coconut milk 椰奶燕窝羹

DIM SUM DISHES 点心
- *Har gau*: smoothly wrapped shrimp dumpling 虾饺
- *Shui mai*: minced pork and shrimp dumpling 烧卖
- *Cha shiu bau*: barbecued pork buns 叉烧包
- *Tsun guen*: deep-fried spring roll with pork, mushrooms, chicken, bamboo shoots, and bean sprouts 春卷
- *Ho yip fan*: steamed fried rice wrapped in lotus leaf 荷叶饭
- *Pai gwat*: steamed pork spareribs 排骨
- *Gai chuk*: steamed chicken in bean curd wrapping 腐竹包鸡
- *Daan tart*: egg custard tart 蛋挞

FUJIAN DISHES 福建菜
- Five spices roll 五香卷
- Fried fish slices 炒鱼片
- Fried pig's kidneys 炒腰片
- Spareribs in sweet-sour sauce 糖醋排骨
- Fish with brown sauce 红烧全鱼

- Fried straw mushrooms with pork 草菇肉片
- Fried shrimps in sweet-sour sauce 糖醋虾
- Fried razor clams in sweet-sour sauce 糖醋鲜蚌

SHANDONG DISHES 山东菜
- Abalone with green vegetables on shell 鲍鱼青菜
- Fresh scallops with shell 鲜带壳干贝
- Roast prawns 烤大虾
- Conch with fire 火螺
- Steamed sea bream 馒头
- Sweet and sour croaker 酸甜黄花鱼
- Three Delicacies Soup 三鲜汤
- Toffee apples 拔丝苹果

SHANGHAI DISHES 沪菜
- Smoked fish 熏鱼
- Deep-fried shrimp balls 炸虾球
- Vegetarian vegetables 素什锦
- Sauteed fresh bamboo shoots 红烧冬笋
- West Lake fish 西湖醋鱼
- Chicken with cashew nuts 西湖醋鱼
- Scallops with turnip balls 干贝萝卜球
- Won-ton (dumplings) in soup 虾仁馄饨
- Beggar's chicken 叫化鸡
- Sauteed egg plant 红烧茄子
- Lion's head casserole 红烧狮子头
- Sweet sesame dumplings 芝麻汤园

SICHUAN (SZECHUAN) DISHES 川菜
- Smoked duck with camphor and tea flavor (not spicy hot) 樟茶鸭
- Stir-fried chicken with hot pepper 宫爆鸡丁
- Spicy stir-fried prawns 干烧明虾
- Stir-fried shrimp with peas 碗豆炒虾仁
- Stir-fried squid with/without hot pepper 金钓鱿鱼
- Bon-bon chicken 棒棒鸡
- Dry-fried string beans 干煸四季豆
- Steamed spareribs (or pork) coated with rice powder 粉蒸排骨
- Steamed fish with fermented black beans 豆豉鱼
- Ma-po bean curd 麻婆豆腐

SUZHOU DISHES 京菜
- Sauteed shrimp meat 清炒虾仁
- Squirrel Mandarin fish 松鼠桂鱼
- Stewed turtle 清蒸元鱼
- Stir-fried eel 生炒鳝贝
- Fried crisp duck 香酥肥鸭
- Water-shield soup with floating Mandarin duck 鸳鸯莼菜汤
- Snow-white crab in shell 白雪蟹斗
- Pickled duck 苏州酱鸭

BEIJING 北 京

Airport 北京机场
Baita Shan (White Dagoba Hill) 白塔山
Baiyunguan (Temple of White Clouds) 白云寺
Baohedian (Hall of Preserving Harmony) 保和殿
Beihai (North Sea Park) 北海公园
Beijing Arts and Crafts 北京工艺美术公司
Beijing Department Store 北京百货公司
Beijing Gu Guanxiangtai (Ancient astronomical observatory) 古天文台
Biyunsi (Temple of Azure Clouds) 白云寺
Chairman Mao Memorial Hall 毛主席纪念堂
Chang Ling 乾陵
China Art Gallery 中国美术馆
Confucius Temple 孔庙
Cultural Palace of the Nationalities 民族文化宫
Dazalan 颐和园
Diamond Throne (Vajra Throne) Pagoda 金钢宝座塔
Ding Ling 定陵
Dragon King Temple 龙王庙

Fang Shan Restaurant 仿膳
Fire 火警
Friendship Store 友谊商店
Gu Gong (Imperial Palace) 故宫
Hall of Dispelling Clouds 排云殿
Hall of Five Hundred Arhats 五百罗汉堂
Hall of Jade Ripples 玉栏堂

Jiaotaidian (Hall of Union) 交泰殿
Jingshan (Coal Hill) 景山
Jueshengsi (Temple of Awareness of Life) aka Temple of the Great Bell 大钟寺
Kunninggong (Palace of Earthly Tranquility) 坤宁宫
Liulichang 兆龙饭店
Lugouqiao (Reed Valley Bridge) aka Marco Polo Bridge 芦沟
Marco Polo Shop 懋隆商店
Monument to the People's Heroes 人民英雄纪念碑
Museum of Chinese History 中国历史博物馆
Museum of the Chinese Revolution 中国革命博物馆
Niujiu Mosque 牛街回民区
Overseas Chinese Hotel 第二华侨饭店
Peking Roast-Duck Restaurant 北京烤鸭店
Police 燚舠
Qianmen Gate 天安门
Qianqingong (Hall of Heavenly Purity) 乾 清
Quanjude Peking Duck Restaurant 前门烤鸭店
Railway Station 火车站
Renshoudian (Hall of Longevity and Benevolence) 大戏楼
Shisan Ling (Ming Tombs) 十三陵

Shudian (Capital Museum) 首都博物馆
Sichuan Fan Dian 四川饭店
Taihedian (Tai Ho Tien; Hall of Supreme Harmony) 太和殿
Tan Zhe Si 潭拓寺
Temple of the Sea of Wisdom 智慧海
Temple of the Sleeping Buddha (Temple of Universal Spiritual Awakening) 卧佛寺
Tiananmen Square 前门城门
Tiantan (Temple of Heaven) 天坛
Tingliguan (Pavilion for Listening to Orioles) 听鹂馆
Tower of Buddhist Incense 佛香阁
Wangfujing Ave. 王府井
White Dagoba Monastery 白塔寺
Xiang Shan (Fragrant Hill) Hotel 香山饭店
Xiang Shan (Fragrant Hill) Park 香山公园
Xiequyuan (Garden of Harmonious Interests) 谐趣园
Xinhua Book Store 新华书店
Yiheyuan (Garden of Cultivating Peace) 仁寿殿
Yonghegong (Lama Temple) 雍和宫
Yuanmingyuan Ruins 圆明园
Zhonghedian (Hall of Complete Harmony) 中和殿
Zhongnanhai 中南海
Zhoukoudian 周口店

Embassies
Australia 澳大利亚大使馆
Britain 英国大使馆
Canada 加拿大大使馆

France 法国大使馆
Japan 日本大使馆
Mongolia 蒙古共和国大使馆
New Zealand 纽西兰大使馆
Philippines 菲律宾大使馆
Poland 波兰大使馆
U.nited States 美国大使馆

EAST CHINA

FUZHOU 福州
Baita (White Pagoda) 白塔
Friendship Store 友谊商店
Fujian Antique General Store 省文物总店
Gushan (Drum Hill) 鼓山
Hualin (Gold Mountain) Temple 华林寺
Lingyuan Dong (Spirit Source Cave) 灵源洞
Memorial Hall of Lin Zexu 林则徐祠堂
Qianfo Taota (Thousand Buddha Pottery Pagodas) 千佛陶塔

Shuiyun Ting (Water and Cloud Pavilion) 水云亭
Wuta (Black Pagoda) 乌塔
Wuyi Mountain 武夷山
Yongquan Si (Surging Spring Temple) 涌泉寺

HANGZHOU 杭州

Tomb and Temple of Yue Fei 岳飞庙　岳坟
Baidi Causeway 白堤
Beigao Feng (North Peak) 北高峰
Cable Car 缆车
Feilaifeng (Peak that Flew from Afar) 飞来峰
Gu Shan (Solitary Hill) 孤山
Hangzhou Botanical Garden 杭州植物园
Hangzhou Silk Printing and Dyeing Complex 杭州丝织厂
Huagang Park 花岗公园
Hupao (Tiger) Spring 虎跑
Jade Spring 玉泉
Liuhe Ta (Pagoda of Six Harmonies) 六和塔
Longjing (Dragon Well) 龙井
Longjingcun (Dragon Well Village) 龙井村
Meijiawu Tea Garden 梅家坞茶园
Mogan Mountain 莫干山
Pinghuqiuyue (Autumn Moon on Calm Lake Pavilion) 平湖秋月
Tidal Bore of the Qiantang River 钱塘江观潮
Wenlan Ge (Pavilion for Storing Imperial Books) 御书楼
Wuling Guesthouse 武陵宾馆
Xi hu (West Lake) 西
Xiaoyingzhou (Three Pools Mirroring the Moon) 小瀛州
Yan'an Road 延安路
Yaoling Cave 瑶琳仙洞
Zhang Xiaoquan Scissors Shop 张小泉剪刀店

Zhejiang Hospital 浙江医院

HEFEI (HOFEI) 合肥

Cured Mandarin Fish 腌鲜桂鱼
Filizi Braised Chicken 符离集烧鸡
Huangshan (Mount Huangshan) 黄山
Jiuhuashan (Mt. Jiuhua) 九华山
Lecturing Rostrum/Archery Training Terrace 教弩台
Ma'anshan (Horse Saddle Mountain) 马鞍山
Stewed Turtle 清炖马蹄
Temple to Lord Baozheng 包公祠
Wenzhenshan bamboo shoots and sesame cakes 向政山笋和芝麻糕
Wuhu 芜湖
Xiaoyaojin 逍遥津

HUANGSHAN MOUNTAIN 黄山

Cable Car 缆车
Jade Screen Tower 玉屏楼
Lian Hua (Lotus Flower) 莲花峰
Tian Du (Heavenly Capital Peak) 天都峰

NANJING

Arts & Crafts Service 工艺美术服务部
Bamboo Garden 竹海
Botanical Garden 植物园
Dasanyuan Restaurant 大三元
Foreign Languages Bookstore 外文书店
Friendship Store 友谊商店
Gulou Drum Tower 鼓楼
Jiangsu Provincial Musuem aka Nanjing Museum 江苏省博物馆

Linggu (Valley of the Soul) Temple 灵谷寺
Maxiangxing Moslem Restaurant 马祥兴菜馆
Meiyuan Xincun (Plum Blossom Villa) 梅园新村
Ming Palace 明宫遗址
Mochou (Sorrow-Free) Lake Park 莫愁湖
Nanjing City Wall 南京城墙
Nanjing Municpal Museum 南京市博物馆
Shanjuan Cave 善卷洞
Shitoucheng (Stone City) of the Wu Dynasty 石头城
Sichuan Restaurant 四川饭店
Southern Tang Tombs 南唐二陵
Stone Engravings of the Southern Dynasties
Sun Yixian (Sun Yat-sen) Mausoleum 中山陵
Taiping Museum 太平天国历史博物馆
Tea Plantation 阳彡茶园

Xiaoling Mausoleum (Ming Tomb) 明陵
Xuanwu Lake 玄武湖
Xuzhou 徐州
Yuhuatai (Rain-Flower) People's Revolutionary Martyr's Memorial Park
Zhonggong Cave 张公洞   雨花台烈士陵园
Zhonghua Gate 中华门
Zijinshan (Purple Mountain) aka Bell Mountain 紫金山

NINGBO 宁波

Ayuwang (King Asoka) Temple 育王寺
Bao Guo Temple 保国寺
Putuo Shan 普陀山
Tiantong Temples 天童寺
Tianyige Library 天一阁

QUANZHOU 泉州
Heavenly Princess Palace 天妃官
Islamic Tombs 圣墓

Old God Rock 老君岩
Overseas Chinese University 华侨大学
Qingjing (Grand Mosque) 清净寺
Tomb of Zheng Chenggong 郑成功墓
Tower of the Two Sisters in-law 姑嫂塔
Wind-Shaking Rock 风动石

SHANGHAI 上 汝
Australia Consulate 澳大利亚领事馆
Botanical Gardens 植物园
Confucius Temple 孔子庙　　　　中国共产党第一次全国代表大会会址
First National Congress of the Communist Party of China Site
Foreign Language Book Store 外文书店
Friendship Branch (Antiques and Curio Branch) 友谊商店古玩部
Hong Qiao Airport 虹桥机场
Huangpu Park 黄浦公园
Huangpu River boat trip 黄浦江游船
Jade Buddha Temple 玉佛寺
Jiading County 嘉定
Longhua Pagoda and Temple 龙华塔　寺
Railway Station 火车站
Renmin (People's) Square 人民广场
Residence of Chou En-lai 周恩来故居
Shanghai Antique Store 上海古玩商店
Shanghai Arts and Crafts Store 上海工艺美术商店
Shanghai Arts and Crafts Trading Corp. 上海工艺美术交易所
Shanghai Friendship Store 上海友谊商店
Shanghai Industrial Exhibition Hall 上海工业展览馆
Shanghai Municipal Museum 上海市博物馆
Shanghai Municipal Tourism Administration 上海旅游局
Shanghai Zoo 上海动物园
Songjiang County 松江
Square Pagoda 方塔
Statue and Tomb of Song Qingling (Soong Ching-ling) 宋庆龄墓
Tang stone pillar 唐朝
U.S. Consulate 美国领事馆
Yu Yuan Garden 豫园
Zuibai Ci (Pond for Enjoying Bai's Drunkenness) Garden 醉白池

SHAOXING 绍兴
East Lake 东湖
Jianhu Lake 鉴湖
Luxun Memorial Hall 鲁迅纪念馆

Orchid Pavilion 兰亭
Second Hospital 第二医院
Shen Family garden 沈园

SUZHOU 苏州

Changlang Ting Yuan (Gentle Wave or Surging Wave) Pavilion 沧浪
Confucius Temple 孔庙
Grand Canal Boat Tours 大运河游船
Han Shan (Cold Mountain) Temple 寒山寺
Hu Qiu (Tiger Hill) Garden 虎丘
Lingyan (Divine Cliff) Hill 灵岩
Liu (Lingering) Garden 留园
Shizilin (Shih Tzu Lin; Lion Forest) Garden 狮子林
Twin Pagodas 双塔寺
Wangshi (Master of Nets) Garden 网师园
Xiyuan (West Garden) Temple 西园
Yi (Joyous) Garden 怡园
Zhuozheng (Humble Administrator's) Garden 拙政园

WUXI 无锡

Grand Canal 大运河
Hui Shan Clay Figures Factory 惠山泥人厂
Huzhou 湖州
Jiangyin 江阴
Jichang (Garden to Entrust One's Happiness) Garden 寄畅
Lake Tai 太湖
Liyuan (Li Garden) 蠡园
Longguang (Dragon Light) Pagoda 龙光塔
Meiyuan (Plum Garden) 梅园
Tianxia Di'er Quan (Heavenly Second Spring) 天下第二泉
Xihui Park 锡惠公园
Yuantouzhu (Turtle Head) Islet 鼋头渚

XIAMEN

Arts and Crafts Factory 工艺美术厂
Botanical Gardens 万石植物园
Ferry Quay 轮渡码头
Friendship Store 友谊商店
Gulangyu (Drum Wave) Island 鼓浪屿
Lacquer Thread Sculpture Factory 漆绒雕厂

Museum of Anthropology 人类博物馆
Nan Putuo (South Putuo) Temple 南普院
No. 1 Hospital of Xiamen 厦门第一医院
Overseas Chinese Museum 华侨博物馆
Riguang Yan (Sunlight Rock) 日光岩

Turtle Garden 鳖园
Xiamen Antiques and Curious Store 厦门文物店
Xiamen International Airport 厦门国际机场
Xiamen Railway Station 火车站
Xiamen University 厦门大学
Zheng Chenggong Memorial Hall 郑成功纪念馆

YANGZHOU 揚州
Shouxi (Slender West) Lake 瘦西湖
Daming Temple 大明寺
Jian Zhen Memorial Hall 鉴真纪念堂
Yangzhou Museum 扬州博物馆
Geyuan Garden 个园
Heyuan Garden 何园

ZHENJIANG 湛江
Dashikou 大市口
Jiao Hill 焦山
Jinshan (Golden Hill) 金山
Tongxinglou Restaurant 同兴楼饭店

NORTH CHINA

BAOTOU 包头
Baotou Carpet Factory 包头地毯厂
Kongdulung Reservoir 昆都仑水库风景区
Nanhaizi Water Park 南海子水上公园
Tomb of Genghis Khan 成吉思汗陵墓
Wudangzhao Temple 五当召

BEIDAIHE 北戴河
Guanyin Temple 观音祠
Pigeon's Nest 鹰角石
Tiger Stone 老虎石

CHENGDE 承德
Anyuan Temple 安远庙
Changlang Islet 沧浪屿
Club Stone 磬锤峰
Friendship Store 友谊商店
Hall of No Worldly Lust but True Faith aka Nanmu Hall 楠木殿
Imperial Library 文津阁
Imperial Summer Resort 避暑山庄
Jinshan Pavilion 金山亭
Mahayana Hall 大乘之阁
Outer Temples 外八庙
Pule 普乐寺

Puning Temple 普宁寺
Putuozongcheng Temple 甲乙并兴剡景
Qing Dynasty-Style Street 清朝一条街
Xumifushou (Longevity and Happiness) Temple 须弥福寿
Yanyulou (Misty-Rain Tower) 烟雨楼

DATONG 大同

Brass Products Factory 铜器工厂
Friendship Store 友谊商店
Great Wall 长城
Huayan Si (Huayan Monastery) 华严寺
Nanchan Temple 南禅寺
Nine Dragon Screen 九龙壁
Sakyamuni Wooden Pagoda at Foguang Temple 佛宫寺释迦塔
Shanhua Monastery 善化寺
Wutai Mountain 五台山
Xiantong Temple 佛光寺

HOHHOT 呼和浩特

Dazhao Temple 大召庙
Great Mosque 清真大寺
Provincial Museum 内蒙古博物馆
Tomb of Wang Zhaojun 王昭君坟
White Pagoda 白塔
Wutasi (Five Dagoba Temple) 五塔寺
Xiaozhao Temple 灵隐寺

JINAN 济南

Baotu Quan 豹突泉
Five-Dragon Pool 五龙潭
Heihu Quan (Black Tiger Spring Park) 黑虎泉
Jiuding (Temple of the Nine Pagodas) 九鼎寺
Lingyan Temple 灵岩寺
Liubu 柳阜
Qianfo (Thousand-Buddha Hill) 千佛山
Shandong Provincial Museum 山东省博物馆
Simen (Four Door Tower) 四门塔
Xingguo Si (Revive the Nation Temple) 兴国寺
Yellowstone Cliff 黄茅岗
Yilan Ting (Pavilion of Panoramic View) 一览亭
Zhenshu Quan (Pearl Spring) 珍珠泉

QINGDAO

Badaguan Area 八达关
Jimo Hot Spring 即墨温泉
Laoshan Mountains 崂山
Luxun park 鲁迅公园

No. 1 Huiquan Pearl Spring Beach 汇泉第一海水浴场
Passenger Quay 客运码头
Pier 栈桥
Pu Songling Home 蒲松龄旧址
Qingdao Antique Store 青岛文物商店
Qingdao Arts and Crafts Shop 工艺美术商店
Qingdao Museum 青岛博物馆
Qingdao Museum of Marine Products 青岛水族馆
Railway Station 火车站
Shilaoren 石老人海滩
Taiping (Great Peace) Taoist Temple 太清宫
Taiqing Taoist Temple 太平宫
Xiaoyu Shan (Little Fish Hill) 小鱼山
Xiaqingdao (LIttle Qingdao Island) 小青岛
Zhongshan park 中山公园

QINHUANGDAO 秦皇岛

Dong Shan (East Mountain) 东山

QUFU 曲阜

Confucian Temple 孔庙
Kong Family Mansion 孔府

SHIJIAZHUANG 石家庄

North China Revolutionary Martyrs' Cemetery 华北军区烈士陵园
Cangyan Hill 苍岩山
Hebei Provincial Exhibition Hall and Museum 省展览馆
Longxing Buddhist Temple 隆兴寺
Xibaipo Village 西柏坡
Zhaozhou Anji Bridge 赵州安济桥

TAI'AN 泰安

Daimiao (Temple to the God of Taishan) 岱庙
Mt. Tai (Taishan) 泰山
Nantian (Southern Celestial) Gate 南天门
Tian Kuang Hall 天贶殿
Tianzhu Feng (Heavenly Pillar Peak) 天柱峰
Tomb of Feng Yuxiang (Feng Yu-hsiang) 冯玉祥墓
Zhongtian (Middle Celestial) Gate 中天门

TAIYUAN 太原

Chongshan Monastery 崇善寺
Dingcun 丁村
Jinci Temple 晋祠
Pingyao 平遥
Shanxi Provincial Museum 山西省博物馆

Shengmu (Sacred Lady Hall) 圣母殿

Yong Le Palace 永乐宫

TIANJIN 天津
Ancient Culture Street 古文化街
Dule (Temple of Solitary Joy) 独乐寺
Friendship Club 友谊俱乐部
Panshan (Screen of Green) Mountain 盘山
Tianjin History Museum 天津厂史博物馆
Tianjin Museum of Natural History 自然博物馆
Zhou Enlai (Chou En-lai) Museum 周恩来纪念馆

YANTAI 烟台
Dengzhou 登州
Kongtong Isle 崆峒岛
Museum 烟台博物馆
No. 1 Bathing Beach 海水浴场
Penglai Pavilion 蓬莱阁

Xiguan Village 西关村
Zhang Yu Wine Company 张裕葡萄酒厂

NORTHEAST CHINA

ANSHAN 鞍山
Mt. Qianshan 千山风景区
Tanggangzi Hot Spring Sanatorium 汤岗子温泉

CHANGCHUN 长春
Changchun Film Studio 长春电影制片厂
Changchun Fur Factory 长春市皮毛厂
Changchun No. 1 Motor Vehicle Plant 长春第一汽车制造厂
Changchun Wood Carving Factory 长春木雕工艺厂
Chunyi Hotel Restaurant 春谊饭店
Friendship Store 友谊商店
Frog oil soup 哈什蚂油汤
Ginseng chicken 人参鸡
Houtou (golden orchid monkey head) mushrooms 猴头菇
Jilin Provincial Antique and Curio Store 吉林省文物店
Nanhu Park 南湖公园
Provincial Chunyi Hotel 省春谊宾馆
Songhua Lake 松花湖
Thick deer antler soup 鹿茸羹
Xinlicheng Reservoir 新立城水库

DALIAN 大连
Natural History Museum 自然博物馆
Ornamental Glass Factory 玻璃制品厂
Passenger Quay 客运码头
Railway Station 火车站
Tiger Park Beach 老虎滩公园
White Clouds Mountain Park 白 云山公园

HARBIN 哈尔滨
Ice Sculpture Festival 冰灯游园会
Miniature Railway 儿童铁路
Zhalong Nature Preserve 扎龙自然保护区

JILIN 吉林
Jilin Exhibition Hall 吉林展览馆
Songhua Lake 松花湖

SHENYANG 沈阳
Beiling North Tombs (aka Zhaoling) 北陵
Dongling East Tombs (aka Fuling) 东陵
Imperial Palace 阳故宫
Laobian Dumpling Restaurant 辽宁大厦
Qianshan Mountain Park 千山公园
Shenyang Steam Locomotives Museum 沈阳火车博物馆

NORTHWEST CHINA

ANYANG 安阳
Azure-Cloud Palace Temple 碧霞宫和大石佛
Mausoleum of Yuan Shi Kai 袁林
Red Flad Canal 红旗渠
Wen Feng Pagoda 灵谷寺
Yin Ruins 殷墟
Yuefei's Temple 岳飞庙

DUNHUANG 敦煌
Cangjing (Preserving Buddhist Scriptures) Cave 藏经洞
Carpet Factory 地毯厂
Mingsha (Singing Sand) Hill 鸣沙山
Mogao Grottoes 莫高窟
White Horse Pagoda 白马塔
Yangguan Pass 阳关
Yumen (Jade Gate) Pass 玉门关

JIAYUGUAN
Bell and Drum Tower 鼓楼
Jiuguan County Museum 酒泉博物馆
Jiuquan 酒泉
Luminous Jade Cup Factory 玉杯厂
Wei and Jin Tombs 魏晋墓群

KAIFENG 开封
Guild Hall of Three Provinces 山陕甘会馆
Longtime (Dragon Pavilion) 龙亭
Pota Pagoda 繁塔
Tie Ta (Iron Pagoda) 铁塔
Xiangguo Temple 相国寺
Yanqing Taoist Temple 延庆观
Yuwang Miao (King Yu's Temple) 禹王台

KASHI 喀什（喀什噶尔）
Abakhojia Tomb 阿巴克和加麻扎
Hanoi 罕诺依
Mt. Kongur 公格尔冰山
Mt. Muztagta 穆士塔格山
San Xian (Three Immortals) Buddhist Caves 三仙洞
South Lake 南湖

LANZHOU 兰州
Baita (White Pagoda Park) 白塔
Bingling Temple Caves 炳灵寺石窟
Maiji Grottoes 麦积山石窟
Tainshui 天水
Wuquan (Five-Fountain) Hill 五泉山

LUOYANG 洛阳
Arts and Crafts Store 美术／工艺商店
Baima Si (White Horse) Temple 白马寺
Fengxian Temple 奉先寺

Longmen (Lungmen) Grottoes 龙门石窟
Luoyang Municipal Museum 洛阳博物馆
Qiyun (Cloud Touching) Pagoda 齐云塔
Tomb of Guan Yu (Kuan Yu) 关林庙

TURPAN 吐鲁番
Astana Tombs 阿斯塔娜古墓
Flaming Mountains 火焰山
Gaochang 高昌故城
Hui 回族

Imim Minaret 额敏塔
Jiahoe (Yarkhoto, Yaerhu) 交河故城
Karez wells 坎儿井
Pazikelik (Baziklic, Bazeklik) Thousand-Buddha Caves 柏孜克里克千佛洞
Uygur (Uighur) 维吾尔族

URUMQI 乌鲁木齐
Baicheng 拜城
Free Market/Bazaar 自由市场
glacier 冰山
Hong Ding Shan Ta (Red Hill Pagoda) 江顶山塔
Lake Tianzi (Heavenly Lake) 天池
Nanshan Pasture 南山草原
National Minorities Palace 少数民族宫
Tianshan (Heaven Mountain) 天山
Urumqi General Carpet Rug Factory 乌鲁木齐地毯厂
Xinjiang Museum 新疆博物馆

XI'AN 西安
Banpo (Panpo) Museum 半坡博物馆
Binxian County 彬县
Caotang Temple 草堂室
Dayan (Big Wild Goose) Pagoda 大雁塔
Famen Temple 法门寺
Great Mosque 大清真寺
Horse and Chariot Pit 车马坑
Huaqing Hot Springs 华清池
Huashan Mountain 华山
Huxian County Town 户县
Museum of Emperor Qin's Terracotta Army 秦俑坑博物馆
Museum of the Eighth Route Army 八路军西安办事处博物馆
Qianling 乾陵
Small Wild Goose Pagoda 小雁塔
Tomb of Emperor Qinshihuang (Chin Shih Huang-ti) 秦陵
Tomb of Yang Guifei 杨贵妃墓
Ximen (West) Gate 西城门
Zhaoling 昭陵

XINING 西宁
Bird Island 鸟岛
Dongguan Mosque 东关　清真寺
Golmud 格尔木市
North Mountain Temple 北禅寺
Qinghai Lake 青海湖

Taer Monastery 塔尔寺

YAN'AN 延安
Baota (Precious Pagoda) 宝塔（延安宝塔）
Huangling County 黄陵
Residences of Chairman Mao 毛主席旧居
Wangfo Dong (Cave of the 10,000 Buddhas) 万佛洞
Yan'an Revolutionary Memorial Hall 延安革命纪念馆

YINCHUAN 银川
Chengtian Monastery Pagoda 承天寺宝塔
Drum and Bell Tower 钟鼓楼
Great Wall 长城
Haibo (Sea Treasure) Pagoda (aka North Pagoda) 海宝塔
Hanyan Canal 汉延古渠
Helan Mountain 贺兰山古石画
Jade Emperor Pavilion 玉皇阁
Mt. Xumi 须弥山
Museum 博物馆
Qingtongxia 青铜峡
South Gate Mosque 南关清真寺
Tanglai Canal 唐徕古渠
Tongxin Mosque 同心清真寺
Twin Pagodas at Baizi Pass on Mt. Helan 拜寺口双塔
Western Xia Mausoleum 西夏王陵
Zhongda Mosque 中大寺

ZHENGZHOU 郑州
Astronomical Observatory 观星台
Dahecun Village 大河村
Dengfeng County 登封层
Fawang Temple 法王寺
Gaocheng 告城
Han Tombs at Dahuting (Tiger-hunting) Pavilion 打虎亭村汉墓
Mangshan Mountain 邙山
Mixian County 密县
Qimu Tower 启母阙
Shaolin Monastery 少林寺
Shaoshi Tower 少室阙
Songshan Mountain 嵩山
Songyang Shuyuan (Songyang Academy of Classical Learning) 嵩阳书院
Songyue Pagoda 嵩岳寺塔
Ta Lin (Forest of Pagodas) 塔林
Taishi Tower 太室阙
Wangcheng Gang (Royal City Mound) 皇城岗
Zhongyue Miao (Central Mountain Temple) 中岳庙

TIBET

Drepung Monastery 哲蚌寺

Jokhang Temple 大昭寺
Norbulinka Park 罗布林卡
Potala Palace 布达拉宫

Sera Monastery 色拉寺
Tashilhunpo (Zhasilhunbu) Monastery 扎什伦布寺

SOUTHWEST

CHENGDU 成都
Baoguangsi (Divine Light Monastery) 宝光寺
Chengdu Arts and Crafts Shop
Chengdu Zoo 成都动物园

Cultural Park 文化公园
Deer Farm 养鹿场
Du Fu's (Tu Fu) Thatched Roof Cottage 杜甫草堂
Dujiangyan Irrigation System 都江堰灌溉系统（灌溉工程）
Erwang (Two Kings) Temple 二王庙
Fu Long Kuan (Dragon Subduing Temple) 伏龙观
Guanxian County 沃县（灌县）
Meishan County 眉山县
Qingcheng (Green City) Mountain 青城山
Renmin Road 人民路
Sansu Shrine 三苏祠
Sichuan Provincial Museum 四川省博物馆
The Temple of Marquis Wu 武候祠
Tomb of Liu Bei 刘备墓
Tomb of Wang Jian 王建墓
Wangjianglou River-Viewing Pavilion 望江楼
Wenshu (God of Wisdom) Monastery 文殊院
Wolong Nature Preserve 卧龙自然保护区
Xindu 新都
Yanshikou 盐市口
Zhuge Liang Memorial Hall 诸葛亮殿

CHONGQING 重庆
Cable Car 缆车
Chongqing Arts & Crafts Service 重庆二艺美术服务
Chongqing Department Store 重庆百货公司
Chongqing Gallery 重庆美术馆
Chongqing Museum of Natural History 重庆自然博物馆
Eling (Goose Neck) Park 鹅岭公园

Friendship Store 友谊商店
Hong-yancun Revolutionary Memorial Hall (Red Crag Village) 村革命纪念馆
Sino-American Special Technical Cooperation 中美合作所集中营展览馆

DAZU 大足

1,000-armed Goddess of Mercy 千手观音
Baodingshan 宝顶山
Dafowan 大佛湾
Xiaofowan 小佛湾

EMEI SHAN 峨眉

Baoguo Temple 报国寺
Jieyan Hall 接引殿
Wannian Monastery 万年

KUNMING 昆明

Black Dragon Pool 黑龙潭
Butterfly Pool 蝴蝶泉
Daguan Lou Pavilion 大观楼
Golden Temple 金殿
Huating Temple 华亭寺
Institute for Nationalities 少数民族学院
Lijiang 丽江
Long Men (Dragon Gate) 龙门
Memorial Hall to Zheng He 郑和纪念馆
Provincial Museum 博物馆
Qiong Zhu (Bamboo) Temple 筇竹寺
Rice Noodles Crossing the Bridge 过桥米泉
Sani Nationality Village 撒尼族
Sanyuejie (Third-Month Market) 三月街
Shibao Shan 石宝山
Shizhong Shan 石钟山　石窟
Sun Ta Si 三塔寺
Taihua Temple 太华寺
The Stone Forest of Lunan 路南石林
Xishan (Western Hills) 西山
Yu Long (Jade Dragon) Mountain 玉龙山
Yuan Tong Si 园通寺

LESHAN 乐山

Dafu (Great Buddha) Temple 大佛
Wuyou (Black) Temple 乌尤寺

WUHAN

Ancient Copper Mine in Tonglushan 古铜矿铜绿山
Guiyang Temple (of Original Purity) 归元禅寺

Hankou (Hankow) 汉口
Hanyang 汉阳
Hongshan Pagoda 洪山宝塔
Huang He Lu (Yellow Crane Tower) 黄鹤楼
Hubei Antique Shop 武汉古玩店
Hubei Military Government Building 武昌起义军政府旧址（红楼）
Museum of Hubei Province 湖北省博物馆
No. 1 Hospital, Wuhan Medical College 武汉医学院附一院
No. 2 Hospital, Wuhan Medical College 武汉医学院附二院
Qiyi Men (Uprising Gate) 起义门
Small East Gate 小东门
Wuchang 武昌
Wudang Mountain 武当山
Wuhan Antiques and Curious Store 汉古玩店
Wuhan Friendship Store 友谊商店
Wuhan Port Passenger Transport Station 武汉港客运站
Wuhan Service Department of Arts and Crafts 工艺美术店

SOUTH CHINA

CHANGSHA 長沙
Aiwan Pavilion 爱晚亭
Fire 火警
Han Tomb Site 墓址
Hunan Antique Store 湖南省博物馆文物商店
Hunan Arts and Crafts Shop 湖南工艺品商
Hunan Provincial Embroidery Factory 湖南省湘绣厂
Hunan Provincial Museum 湖南省博物馆
Juzi Orange Island 橘子岛
Lushan Temple 麓山寺
Police 警察
Yuelu Academy 岳麓书院
Yuelu Hill 岳麓山
Zhongshan Rd. Department Store 韶山路百货商店

FOSHAN 佛山
Foshan Folk Art Institute 佛山民间艺术研究社
Foshan Municipal Museum 祖庙博物馆
Shiwan Artistic Ceramic Factory 石湾美术陶瓷厂
Silk Factory 丝织厂

GUANGZHOU 廣州
Bank of China 中国银行
Banxi (Pan Hsi) Restaurant 泮溪酒家
Beijing Road 北京路
Colored Painted Porcelain Factory 广州织金彩瓷工厂

Daxin Ivory Carving Factory 广州大新象牙工艺厂
Dr. Sun Yat-sen Memorial Hall 中山纪念堂
First Hospital/Zhongshan Medical College 学院第一附属医院
Foreign Trade Center 外贸中心
Friendship Store 友谊商店
Guangdong Arts and Crafts Service 广东工艺美术服务部
Guangdong People's Hospital 广东人民医院
Guangdong Provincial Museum 广东省博物馆
Guangxiao Temple 光孝寺
Guangzhou Antique Store 广州文物商店
Guangzhou Cultural Park 广州文化公园
Guangzhou First People's Hospital 广州第一人民医院
Guangzhou Gold and Silver Jewelry Center 广州市金银首饰总汇
Guangzhou Museum 广州市博物馆
Guangzhou Porcelain and Pottery Shop 广州陶瓷
Guangzhou Restaurant 广州酒家
Guangzhou Zoo 广州动物园
Huaisheng (Remember the Sage) Mosque and Guangta Smooth Minaret 光塔寺
Liu Rong (Six Banyan Trees) Temple 六榕寺
Liuhua Park 流花公园
Mausoleum of the Seventy-two Martyrs 黄花岗七十二烈士墓
Nanfang Dept. Store 南方大厦商店
Nanyuan Restaurant 南园酒家
National Peasant Movement Institute 广州农民运动讲习厅
Orchid Garden 兰圃
Passenger Pier for Hong Kong 洲头咀客运码头（往香港）
Pearl River Boat Ride 珠江游船
Qing Ping Ziyou Shi Chang 清平路自由市场
Railway Station 火车站
Second Hospital/Zhongshan Medical College 医学院第二附属医院
Shamian (Shamien, Shameen) Island 沙面
Shishi (Cathedral of the Sacred Heart) 石室
South China Botanical Garden 华南植物园
U.S.Consulate 澳洲航空公司
Xi Yuan (West Garden) 西园
Yuexiu Park 越秀公园
Zhen (Chen) Family Temple 陈氏书院（陈家祠）
Zhongshan 5-Road 中山五路

GUILIN 桂林

Cave for Hiding a Dragon 龙隐洞
Diecai (Folded Brocade) Hill 叠彩山
Fubo (Whirlpool) Hill 伏波山
Guilin Airport 桂林机场
Ludi (Reed Flute) Cave 芦笛岩
Qixing (Seven Star) Park 七星岩
Xiangbi (Elephant Trunk) Hill 象鼻山
Yangshuo 阳朔

HAINAN ISLAND 海南岛

Dongshan Mutton 东山羊肉
Ends of the Earth 天涯海角
Five Officials Memorial Temple 五公祠
Hai Rui Tomb 海瑞墓
Haikou 海口
Hele Crab 和乐蟹
Jiaji Duck 加积鸭
Monkey Peninsula 衡山
Overseas Chinese Farm/Xinlong 华侨
Pearl Farm 珍珠场
Wengchang-Style Chicken 文昌鸡

JIUJIANG

Causeway between Lake Gantang and Lake Nanmen 甘棠湖和南门湖之间的长堤
Dasheng Pagoda 大胜塔
Yanshui Pavilion 烟水亭

LUSHAN 庐山

Big Heavenly Pond 大天池
Grotto of Taoist Immortal 仙人洞
Guilin (Shopping Area) 牯岭
Hanpokou (the Mouth that Holds Poyang Lake) 含鄱口
Lushan Botanical Garden 庐山植物园
Pavilion for Viewing the Yangtze 望江亭

NANNING 南宁

Arts and Crafts Service 工艺美术服务部
Foreign Languages Bookstore 外文书店
Friendship Store 友谊商店
Guangxi Art College 广西艺术学院
Guangxi Botanical Garden of Medicinal Plants 广西药用植物园
Guangxi Museum 广西博物馆
Institute of Nationalities 广西民族学院
Nanhu (South Lake) Park 南湖公园
Nanning Antique Store 南宁古物店
Yiling Cave 伊岭岩

SHANTOU 汕头

Arts and Crafts Exhibition 工艺展览馆
Chaoyang County 潮阳县
Chaozhou City 潮州市
Embroidery Factory 潮绣厂
Gourd Hill 文尖塔
Han Wen-gong Temple 韩祠

Jiaoshi Scenic Spot 岩石风景区
Kaiyuan Temple 开元寺
Ling Shan Temple 灵山寺
Maya Islet 妈屿海滨浴场
Shantou City 汕头市
Wenguang Tower 葫芦山
West Lake Park 西湖
Zhong Shan Park 中山公园

TAISHAN 台山

Fei Sa Beach 飞沙里
St. Francis Xavier Church 沙勿略墓
Stone Flower Mountain 石花山

ZHAOQING 肇庆

Mateo Ricci Home 利玛窦
Seven Star Crags 七星岩

ZHONGSHAN 中山

Cuiheng Village 翠亨村
Dr. Sun Yixian (Sun Yat-sen) Home 孙中山故居
Shiqi 石岐
Zhongshan (Chung Shan) Hot Spring Golf Club 中山温泉高尔夫球会

ZHUHAI 珠海

Juizhou Islet 九洲岛
Pearl Land Amusement Park 教育街自由市场
Zhuhai International Golf Club 珠海高尔夫球场

INDEX

*Look under **Destinations** in this index for specific cities,
counties, towns, and villages.*

Accidents: see Emergencies
Acrobats 130-131, 167, 269, 305, 404, 595
Acupuncture: see Where to Stay in each Destination for clinics; see also Health
Air travel: airline codes 147; CAAC 147; Chinese airlines 89, 146-150; flight times from Beijing 149; taxes 97, 147; flying standby 88, 148; luggage allowances 64, 150; refunds 149; regulations 68-69; smoking 147; tickets and reconfirming reservations 97, 146-148
Alien travel permit 70-71
Altitude Sickness 480
Amity Foundation 56-57
Ancestor Worship 51
Ancestral Temples: see Temples
Anthropology: see Ethnic Minorities
Antiques 160; see Shopping under each Destination
Applause 133-134
Archaeological sites: see Museums; Horse and chariot pits 488; Terracotta Warriors 441-442
Art, favorite subjects of 163-164
Arts and Crafts: available everywhere; see Shopping in each Destination
Astronomical observatories 234, 302, 469
Automobile travel: Self-Drive cars 156-157

Backpacking: see also Hitchhiking and, in most Destinations, some cheaper hotels
Banks 121-122; some are listed under Practical Information in major Destinations
Beaches: Beidaihe 367-368; Dalian 407-408; Qingdao 359-365; Qinhuangdao 365-367; Sanya 538-539; Shantou 514-515; Taishan 375; Yalong Bay 539; Yantai 390-395; Zhuhai 523-525
Beer: see Beverages
Beggars 99
Beijing Man: see Peking Man
Bell Towers: see Towers
Bethune, Dr. Norman 34, 373
Beverages 172-173, 176, 188, 363; ice 176
Bicycle rickshaws 154-155
Bicycles 153-154, 510
Birds 403, 518; Cormorant fishing 536
Boat trips 156, 267, 322, 335-336, 340, 509; see also Cruises
Books: see Recommended Reading
Bookstores 99
Border formalities 96; Immunization 69-70; Customs Regulations 68-69; Passports 70; Visas 70-71
Botanical Gardens: see Gardens
Bridges 234, 316
Bronzes 123-124

Buck, Pearl S. 338
Buddhism 51-55
Buddhist Sites: Monasteries and Temples in most Destinations; see also Cave Temples; Guan Yin; Zen Buddhism. Among the more important ones: Chengdu 559, 560, 561; Datong 348-349; Emei Shan 561-562; Guangzhou 509; Hengshan 497; Jinan 357; Kaifeng 461; Kunming 582; Lanzhou 420; Leshan 563; Mid-air 349; Putuo Shan 310; Shaolin Temple 468; Songshan 468; Tai'an 376; Taiyuan 401-402; Tianjin 384, 386; Wuxi 327; Xiamen 331; Xi'an 443-444, 447, 449; Yangzhou 335
Bund (in Shanghai) 263
Bus travel: to China 92; shuttle buses 156. See individual hotel's tour buses 145, 156; within China 153, 156
Business basics 99-100
Business travel tips 66, 77-78

CAAC: see Air travel
Calendar, lunar 119
Calligraphy: see Painting and calligraphy
Camels 167; Dunhuang 433; Kashi 416
Cancellations 146; see also Travel Agents

Cathedrals: see Churches and cathedrals
Cave Homes: Sanmenxia 475
Cave Temples 54-55, 289, 307; Baicheng 433; Bingling 420-421; Binxian 451; Dali 589; Dazu 571; Dunhuang 54, 467; Kashi 449; Kuqa 433; Luoyang 55, 473; Maiji 420-421; Turfan 429; Yungang (Datong) 55, 348
Celsius-Farhenheit Conversion 119
Ceramic Army: see Terracotta Army
Ceramics: see Pottery and ceramics
Checks personal: see Currencies
Chefoo Schools Assoc. 77
Cheng Cheng-Kung: see Koxinga
Chiang Kai-shek/Jiang Jieshi and sites associated with 33, 305, 308-309, 435, 443, 570
Children 126-127; babysitters 101; books for 164; 'Children's palaces' 265; traveling with 101
China Friendship Associations 77, 116
China International Sports Travel Company: see Travel Agents
China International Travel Service (CITS) see Travel Agents; China Youth Travel Service (CYTS); see Travel Agents
Chinese ancestry: see Overseas Chinese
Chinese citizens, looking up specific 118-119; socializing with 132-135;
Chinese language 21-22; learning 113-115, 116-117; pronunciation 114
Chinese missions abroad 71-72
Chou En-lai 33, 36, 55, 219,

220-221, 226, 316, 384
Christianity and missionaries 55-57, 381, 388, 391, 482, 517, 519-520, 566-567; Nestorian sect 51, 312, 446
Churches and cathedrals 57, 274, 278, 385, 455, 509
City Walls and gates: Beijing 221; Kaifeng 459; Lugouqiao 234; Nanjing 303; Xi'an 445-446
Cixi/Tsu Hsi, Empress Dowager and sites associated with ø22, 224, 227-228, 342, 395-396, 435
Clay figures 328
Climbing: see Hiking, Mountains
Cloisonne, Where to Buy 238, 270, 450
CNN 64-65; see also USTV listed under hotels in each Destination
Confucius, Confucianism, and sites associated with 29, 57, 275, 304, 323, 369, 370-373;
Consulates 102, 275-276, 410, 524, 566
Cosmetics and toiletries: see Packing
Courier: see Mail Service
Courtesy and manners: see Local Customs
Crime by Foreigners 103-104, 106
Crime against Foreigners 105, 132, 136
Cruises 75, 533-535, 597-610
Cultural Minorities: see Ethnic Minorities
Cultural Revolution 35, 37, 46-47, 56, 219
Currency 67, 96, 97-98, 104-105, 121; credit cards 103, 121; exchange rate 121; travelers' checks 105, 121;
Customs regulations 68-69, 96, 97-98

Dalai Lama 38, 39, 41, 54,

476-485, 487-489, 489-491
Dance parties and discos 130-131; see Entertainment in each Destination
Daoism; see Taoism
Deer 107, 345, 400, 539, 560
Democracy 37-41
Demonstrations 103
Deng Xiao-Ping 36, 37-40
Design motifs traditional 137-142; dragons 137
Destinations:
Anshan 407
Anshun 576-577
Anyang 465-467
Badaling 243-244
Badong 606
Baicheng 399, 433
Baoshan 590
Baotou 353-354
Beidaihe 367-369
Beihai 546-547
Beijing 193-245
Bengbu 292
Binxian County 451
Burma Road 587, 590
Changbai Shan Mtns. 400
Changchun 397-400
Changjiang River: see Yangtze
Changsha 493-497
Changzhou 306
Chaozhou: see Shantou
Chengde 342-347
Chengdu 556-566
Chongqing 566-573
Chuxiong 587
Cuiheng 521-522
Dali 587-589
Dalian (Port Arthur) 407-409
Dandong 409
Daning River: see Three Small Gorges
Datong 347-350
Dazu 567, 571-572
Dehong 590
Dengfeng County 468-470
Dunhuang 411-414
Dujiangyan 560
Emei Shan 561

640 CHINA GUIDE

Everest Mountain:
see Qomolangma
Fengdu 572
Fengjie 606
Foshan 512-513
Fushun 409
Fuzhou 278-281
Ganden Monastery 492
Golmud 458
Gongxian 467
Grand Canal 281
Great Wall 243-245
Guangzhou 497-524;
arriving from Hong
Kong 499, 513
Guilin 525-535
Guiyang 573-578
Gulangyu 331-332
Gyantse 490
Haikou 537-540
Hainan Island 537
Hangzhou 281-290
Hankou: see Wuhan
Hanyang: see Wuhan
Harbin 401-404
Hefei 290-294
Heihe 403
Hengshan Mt. 349, 497
Hohhot 350-355
Hongdong 380
Huangguoshu Falls
576-577
Huangling County 451
Huangping County 578
Huangshan Mt. and
Huangshan City 289,
292, 294-297
Huangzhong 457
Huashan Mt. 451-452
Huaxi 328
Huxian, Guangdong
510
Huxian, Shaanxi 448
Jiangman 514
Jiangyin 328
Jiayuguan 414-416
Jilin 400
Jimei 330
Jinan 355-359
Jing Hong 585-587
Jingdezhen 540-541
Jingzhou 607
Jintian village 546
Jiuzhaigou 557, 562-563

Jiuhua Shan Mt. 292-293
Jiujiang 541-542
Jixian County 245, 386
Kaifeng 459-463
Kailash 491
Kaili 577
Karakoram Highway 94
Kashi 416-418
Keqiao 316
Kunjirap Pass 94
Kunming 579-591
Kuqa 433
Lake Yamdrok Yamsto
491
Lanzhou 418-422
Laoshan 364
Leshan 563-564
Lhasa 476-492, 564, 591
Li River 533-535
Lianyungang 306-307
Lijiang 584, 589
Linfen 380
Linxia 420
Liuzhou 547
Lokha 491
Lunan 582-583
Luoyang 470-475
Lushan Mt. 542-544
Ma'anshan Mt. 293
Mangshan 465
Matang 578
Mogan Shan Mt. 289
Mudanjiang 403
Mutianyu 244
Nanjing 297-308
Nanning 544-548
Nantong 307
Ningbo 308-311
Omei Shan:
see Emei Shan
Putian City Fujian 280
Putuo Shan 310-311
Qangtang Grasslands
491
Qingdao 359-365
Qinghai 458
Qinhuangdao 365-367
Qintong 336
Qiqihar 403
Qomolangma Mt.
(Mt. Everest) 93, 491
Quanzhou 311-314
Qufu 369-373
Qujiang County 516

Rongbuk 491
Ruicheng County 380
Samye 492
Sanmenxia 465
Sanya 538-539
Shanghai 246-277
Shanhaiguan 366-367
Shannon 491
Shantou 514-515
Shaoguan 515-516
Shaoshan 493, 496
Shaoxing 315-317
Shashi 607
Shekou 552
Shennonjia Stream 602,
606
Shenyang 404-410
Shenzhen 548-555
Shibaozhai 607
Shigatse 489-490
Shijiazhuang 373-375
Shiqi 521
Silk Road 29, 422-426
Simatai 244
Siziwang 353
Songshan 468
Stone Forest: see Lunan
Suzhou 317-325
Tai'an 375-377
Taijiang 578
Taishan, Guangdong
516-518
Taishan, Shandong 375
Taiyuan 377-380
Tangshan 381
Taxkorgan 94
Thousand Island Lake
289-290
Three Lesser Gorges
602, 608
Tianjin 381-387
Tian'shui 421
Tiantai 290
Tibet 476-492, 564,
591
Tongchuan City 452
Tonglu County 289
Tsedang 491
Tsurpu 491
Turpan 426-429
Urumqi 429-434
Wanxian 607
Weifang 387-389
Weihai 389-390

Wolong Nature
Preserve 565
Wuchang: see Wuhan
Wudang Mt. 596
Wuhan 591-597
Wuhu 293
Wulingyuan 496
Wuxi 326-329
Wuyi Mt. 280
Wuzhou 526
Xiaguan 587-588
Xiahe 421
Xiamen 329-333
Xi'an 434-453
Xianfen County 380
Xichang 565
Xigaze: see Shigatse
Xihu 282, 284-285
Xilinhot 353
Xinhui 518-519
Xining 456-459
Xizhou 588
Xuzhou 307
Yalong Bay 539
Yan'an 451, 452
Yangshuo 533, 536
Yangtze Gorges 592,
597-610
Yangzhou 333-336
Yantai 390-395
Yichang 608
Yinchuan 453-456
Yixian 396
Yixing 307
Yueyang 496-497
Yuncheng County 380
Zedang 491
Zhangmu 491
Zhaoqing 519-521
Zhengzhou 463-470
Zhenjiang 336-341
Zhenyuan 578
Zhongbao Island 605
Zhongdian 590-591
Zhongshan 521-523
Zhoukoudian 234
Zhuhai 523-525
Zigong 565-566
Zigui 609
Zunhua 395-396
Dinosaurs 565, 569
Dragons: see Design Motives
Drinking water:
see Beverages

Driving (by yourself) 105,
156-157
Drum towers: see Towers
Du Fu (Tu Fu) sites associ-
ated with 467, 559
Dynasties 22, 41-43; see also
History (28-32) and
Emperors

Earthquakes: see
Emergencies
Economy 47-49, 248-249
Electricity 102
Embassies 102, 241-242
Embroidery 317, 495, 561
Emergencies (Earthquakes,
Typhoons, lost passports,
money accidents)
102-106, 242-243, 276
Emperors: see also Genghis
and Kubulai Khan; Cixi;
Pu Yi, Last Em-peror;
and sites associated with
32, 33, 382, 385, 398,
407, 409; Qin First
Emperor 365, 366,434,
441-443, 599; Yellow
Emperor 451
Employment for foreigners:
see Work
Endangered Species 68-69,
106-107, 608
English Corners: see various
Destinations
Entertainment, Nightlife
and Recreation 107, 111-
112, 122-124, 124-126,
130-131, 166-168;
see also Sports.
Ethnic Minorities 44-45, 60,
161, 223, 430, 515,
532, 536, 544, 546, 547,
553, 587; see also
Burma Road 590;
Chuxiong 587; Dali
587-588; Guizhou 574;
Jing Hong 585;
Kunming 582, 583,
585-586;Lhasa 476-
492; Lijiang 589;
Wuhan 595
Exchange students and
programs 78-79
Experts, foreign: see Work

Families, home stays 388,
390, 392; visiting
relatives 76-77, 129-130
Fang Lizhi 39
Feather pictures 367
Ferries 90-91, 92, 146, 156;
from Hong Kong 91;
see also Boat Trips
and cruises.
Festivals 61-62, 111-112;
also listed in many
Destinations
Film studios: see Theme
Parks and Movie Sets
Flirting 135
Floods
Food and Restaurants 169-
179; Tipping 177;
Banquets 171, 175;
Breakfasts 173, 183-184;
Buffets 170-171;Cautions
176-177; Courtesies
174; Desserts 172;
Dog 178, 575; Euro-
pean and Western food
173-179; Fast Food and
Food Streets 176;
Health restaurants 178;
How to eat some
foods 177; Ice, see
Beverages; Inviting
Chinese to 175;
Kosher 172; Mono-
sodium glutamate
(MSG) 177, 179;
Ordering 170-171;
Special diets 171-172;
Regional dishes 178-179;
Forbidden City: see Palaces
Foreign experts: see Work
Forests: see Wildlife and
Nature Parks
Forts 338-339,393,415,518,
573
Free Markets: see Shopping
and Antiques
Frescoes: see Murals
Friendship Stores 161; also
listed under Shopping
in most Destinations.

Gang of Four 36, 37, 219,
221
Gardens, including

Botanical gardens and Parks 107; Beijing 222, 227, 229, 230; Chengde 344-345; Chongqing 570; Guangzhou 509-510; Guilin 530; Hangzhou 287; how to visit 107; Jing Hong 586; Lushan 543-544; Nanjing 302, 305; Nanning 545; Shanghai 263, 267, 274, 275; Suzhou 320-321; Wuxi 327-328; Xiamen 332; Yangzhou 335

Gates: Beijing 221, 222; Kunming 582; Nanjing 303; Xi'an 448

Genghis Khan and sites associated with 227, 350, 412, 453

Gifts 66, 134; to take to China 66; to buy in China, see Shopping

Glaciers 431

Glass, artistic Dalian 407

Gliding 415, 466, 467, 458

Gold 391, 402, 418

Golf courses: Beijing 232; Shenzhen 554; Tianjin 382; Zhongshan 521; Zhuhai 523

Government 49

Grand Canal 281; Changzhou 274; Hangzhou 281; Suzhou 322; Tianjin 381; Wuxi 326; Yangzhou 333

Great Leap Forward 35

Great Wall 29, 219, 243-245, 366; Beijing 198; Chengde 342; Datong 349; Jiayuguan 415; Shanhaiguan 365-367; Silk Road 423; Tianjin 386; Yinchuan 455

Group Tours and Prepaid Travel 73-75;

Special Tours 76

Guan Yin, Goddest of Mercy 52, 54, 59, 310, 331, 345, 368, 379, 386; Statues found in most Buddhist temples.

Guanxi 135

Guest, visiting as 81

Guesthouses: see Hotels

Guides: see Travel Agents

Guild Halls 322, 384-385, 394, 461

Hair Dryers: see Packing.

Handicapped Travelers: see Wheelchair

Health 65, 69-70, 104, 109-111

Health insurance: see Insurance

Helicopter service 150, 410

Herbs and herbal medicine 110; available in many hotels, Chinese pharmacies and Friendship Stores

Hiking, Walking, and Climbing 154, 166, 168; walks listed in many Destinations; see also Mountains

History 32-43

Hitchhiking 128, 153

Holidays 111-112

Home-stay programs: see Families

Hong Kong, traveling via 90; Travel Agents 86-88

Hot-air ballooning 166, 466

Hot springs: Anshan 407; Fuzhou 278; Tianjin 384; Weihai 390; Xi'an 443; Zhongshan 521

Hotels and Guest Houses 127, 180-189, 190-192; chains 73, 188; checkout 158; toll-free phone numbers 73; prices 188-189; reservations 72-73; star-ratings and room classifications 183-186; individual hotels listed in each Destination.

Hu Yao-bang 37, 38

Hunting 168

I Ching (Book of Changes) 466

Ice sculpture festival, Harbin 402

Illness: see Health

Immigration: see Border Formalities;Passports; Visas

Immunizations 69

Imperial Palace: see Palaces

Individual or Independent Travel 73, 75-76

Islam, sites associated with 60, 234, 313, 335-336, 352, 357, 384, 417-418, 428, 432, 444-445, 454, 457, 509

Ivory 511; Regulations 68-69

Jade factory 433; see also Antiques

Jews: Kaifeng 462; Shanghai 267-268; see also Food, Kosher

Jiang Zemin 49

Karakoram Highway 94

Kazakhstan, traveling via 89-90

Kirghizia, traveling via 89-90

Kites and kite festivals: Nantong 307; Weifang 387

Korea, traveling via 92, 382, 389

Korean War 34-35

Koxinga (Cheng Cheng-Kung) 31, 280, 313, 314, 329, 332

Kublai Khan 31, 282, 482, 588

Kung fu 166

Lamaism and Lama temples (same as Buddhism and Buddhist temples) 54, 232, 345-346, 352, 421, 457, 481-484, 487-489, 489-491, 588, 589

Languages 113-115
Lao Tzu 57-59; see Taoism
Laundry 64, 115, 128-129; prices 67; see every tourist hotel in Destinations
Law: see Crime, Emergencies
Leaders, Chinese 32-40
Li Bai, poet 293
Liberation 34
Libraries, ancient and modern 309, 345
Liddell, Eric 380
Limestone formations and caves: Anshun 576-577; Guilin 525, 533-534; Kunming 582-583; Nanning 545, 547; Zhaoqing 519, 520
Lin Zexu, sites associated with 280, 510
Local Customs 63, 132-135; 136, 137
Local Time 143
Locomotive Museums: see Steam Locomotives
Long March 33
Lu Xun, sites associated with 315, 331

Maba Man (in Shaoguan) 516
Macau, traveling via 92-93
Magic shows: Beijing 236 Shanghai 269
Mail service and post offices 117, 131-132; couriers 132; fax 132, 143; telexes 132; see also hotels in various destinations
Malaria 65, 69, 109
Manchukuo 33, 397
Manichaeanism 313-314
Mansions: Beijing 234; Taiyuan 379; Tianjin 384
Mao tai 175, 576
Mao Zedong (Mao Tse-tung) 33, 34-37, 46, 55, 452, 493, 495, 496
Marathons 167, 288
Marble 588
Marble Boat 229

Marco Polo 31, 282, 337
Maritime history 313
Markets: see Antiques and street markets, listed in many Destinations
Marriage 119
Marshall, George C. 570
Martial arts 468, 596
May Fourth Movement 32
Medicine: see Health; also Practical Information in Destinations for hospitals and ambulances
Memorial Halls: see Temples
Mile-Kilometer Conversion 120
Mines and mining 347
Mirages: Yantai 393
Missionaries: see Christianity
Monasteries: see Buddhist and Taoist sites and temples
Money: see Currencies
Mongolia, traveling via 93
Monkey King 306
Moslems: see Islam
Mosques and minarets: see Islam
Mosquitoes: see Malaria
Motorcycles and Scooters 154
Mountains 76, 279, 289, 292, 293, 294-296; Emei 561-562; Hengshan 497; Huashan 451-452; Lushan 542; Taishan 427, 431; Urumqi 431-432; Wutai 349
Movie sets: see Theme Parks
Movies and videos with Chinese themes 68
Mummies: Changsha 494; Jinzhou 607; Jiuhua 292-293; Turpan 428-429; Urumqi 432
Murals 415, 429, 444, 448; see also cave temples
Museums 122-129, 223-234, 290, 300, 302-303, 304, 313, 331, 351, 374, 384, 388, 390, 398, 406, 408,

409, 421, 441-443, 445, 452, 465, 466, 474, 494, 505-506, 508, 510, 513, 545, 565, 569, 577, 583; see also Palaces, Tombs, Temples, Memorial Halls and major Destinations
Music, including Opera 124-126, 316, 595; see also Nightlife & Entertainment in each Destination
Musical Instruments 124, 317, 433, 595-596
Myth of the White Snake and Blue Snake 339; see also Taoism

Names (how to refer to and address people) 135
Neolithic sites: see Museums
Nepal, traveling via 93-94
Nestorianism: see Christianity
News 64-65. See hotel lists in each city for USTV
Newspapers and periodicals 64-65, 184
Nightlife: see Entertainment
Nunneries, 323, 332

Opera: see Music
Oracle bones 466
Overseas Chinese, Ancestral villages of 130; Chinese relatives 129-130; customs rules for 76-77; Travel tips for 76-77, 519

Packing 62-67; see Air Travel for luggage allowances
Pagodas: most destinations have at least one
Paintings and calligraphy: on sale everywhere; see Shopping in each Destination; see also Tombs for Frescoes; Rock paintings; Peasant paintings 448; Stele Museum, Xi'an 446
Pakistan, traveling via 94-95
Palaces: Beijing, Imperial 222-225; Summer, 228-229

Manchurian 398;
Shenyang 405-406;
Tibetan 487, 488, 491;
see also Taiping
Pandas 559-560, 565, 569
Parks: see Gardens
Passports 70, 104-105
Peking Duck 392
Peking Man 28, 225, 234, 302-307
Phoenix: see Design Motives
Photography and videocameras 65, 127
Ping Pong 166
Pinyin spellings 21, 41-43, 136-137
Plants, buying 165
Politics, asking questions or joking about 135
Population 48-50; see also each destination
Porcelain: see Pottery
Post Office: see Mail Services
Pottery, ceramics and porcelain 540
Prepaid tours: see Group Tours
Pu Yi, Last Emperor: see Emperors

Quyuan, poet 610

Radios, shortwave 64-65
Rafting, white water 167, 399, 516
Recommended Reading 611-614 and in various destinations
Recreation 166-167
Red Guards 36
Religion 50-60; see also specific religions and topics
Renminbi (RMB): see Currency
Reservations: see Travel Agents and Arrangements, and Air Travel
Restaurants: see Food
Rickshaws: see Bicycle Rickshaws
Rock Paintings 455, 545
Romanization of Chinese: see Pinyin
Rugby 167
Russia, traveling via 95-96

Safe Deposit boxes 181, 184
Safety, personal 101, 132, 136, 187
Sail-boarding/Windsurfing 332
Sandalwood fans and soap 324
Sandstorms 350, 413, 426, 453
Satellite launch 565
Scholarly visits: see Students
Schools, visiting 126
Scientists 76
Scuba Diving 167, 408
Shang dynasty sites 463, 466
Shell art, Where to Buy 367
Shenzen airport 91-92
Shopping 158-165; antiques 240-241, 273-274; Certificates of origin 69; Department stores 161, 239; Factories 160; Free Markets 162, 239, 512; Friendship Stores 161, 239; Haggling 162; see each destination's Shopping section
Silk and silk industry 271, 288, 290, 298, 324-325, 328
Silk Road: see Destinations
Skiing, Alpine 166-167, 400, 403
Sky-diving 467
Smoking 136, 176; see also individual hotels for non-smoking areas
Snakes 408, 510
Soccer 166
Song and dance troupes: see Nightlife & Entertainment in each Destination
Song festivals: see Ethnic minorities
Soong Ching-ling/Song Qingling 233-234, 265, 266
Southeast Asia, traveling via 95

Splendid China 553
Sports 166-168, 187; see also specific sports sections in many destinations; China International Sports Travel 167; competitions 167
Springs, Jinan 355-357; see also Hot Springs and pools; Statuary and carvings; see also Caves, Temples, and Tombs.
Steam Locomotives 399, 403, 406, 407
Stillwell, Gen. J. 570
Stillwell Road: see Burma Road
Students foreign, in China 78-79
Subways 156; Beijing 196-198; Guangzhou 505; Shanghai 250
Sun Yat-sen 32, 55, 229, 265-266, 300, 508-509, 521, 592
Swimming: see Beaches
Symbols traditional: see Design Motifs

Tailors 105
Taiping Rebellion 304, 546;
Taiwan, traveling via 96
Taoism 50-51, 57-59; sites associated with: Beijing 234; Chengdu 560-561; Chongqing 570; Lushan 543; Qingdao 364; Quanzhou 313; Suzhou 323-324; Xi'an 449; Yantai 393; Yueyang 496-497; Zhengzhou 468
Taxes and Surcharges 187
Taxis 96-97, 155-156, 198, 250
Tea and tea production 282, 287, 586; see also Food
Teaching 79-80, 317
Telecommunications 142-143;
Telephoning prices 142; in hotels 142, 187-188;

telephone codes 143;
see also Mail services.
Tennis 167
Temples: see also Buddhist
sites and temples;
Confucian temples;
Lamaism and
Lama temples; Taoism
sites associated with;
Temple of Heaven 226;
God of Taishan 377;
Ancestral 505, 512-513;
Bigan Miao 467;
Memorial Halls: God
of War 443, 474;
King Yu 461; Lama
Temple 232; Lin
Zexu 280; Liuhou 547;
Lord Bao 461;Meng
Jiang-nu 366; Sea
Goddess 366, 384, 393,
394, 515; Shuimu,
Mother of Water 378;
Sansu 561; Sun Yat-sen
508-509; Yan'an
Revolutionary Memorial
Hall 452; Yue Fei 286-
287, 466; Zheng He 304,
584; Zhuge Liang 559;
Terracotta Army 441
Theme parks, movie sets,
and reproduced ancient
streets 233, 399, 448,
462, 510, 532, 553-559, 570
Tiananmen Square 38-39,
219-220
Tibet and Tibetan Buddhism
35, 54-55, 65, 103, 476-492
Tidal bores 290
Time Zones 143
Tipping 144
Toiletries 64
Toilets 134, 144, 146, 181
Tombs: tomb museum 474;
Abakhojia 418; Astana
428-429; Gen. Feng
Yuxiang 377; Genghis
Khan 354; Good Wife
321; Guan Yu, God of
War 479; Han (imperial)
447-448, 474; Han 467,
495; Hu Mulan 452;
Islamic 313; Jade
Emperor 394;

Koxinga 332; Manchu
409; Mao Tzedong 222;
Marquis Yi of Zeng 607;
Ming 231-232, 292, 302,
532; Mohamed Kashgari
418; Nanyue 505, 506;
Puhaddin 335-336;
Qing (imperial) 395-396;
Quyuan 609; Martyrs
508; Royal Tibetan 491;
Shang/Yin 466; Song
(imperial) 305, 467, 552;
Wang Zhaojun 352;
Wei and Jin 415; Western
Xia 454-455; Yellow
Emperor 451; Yuan
Shi Kai 466
Tours: see Travel agents
and arrangements
Tow paths 316
Towers: Bell 415, 444;
Drum 303, 415, 444;
Misc. 314, 366, 497;
Yellow Crane 595
Train travel 88, 90, 91,
146, 150-153; Trans-
Siberian Railroad 95;
see each destination
under Arrivals &
Departures
Travel agents, organizers,
and arrangements
67-68, 81-88, 112-113,
243; Guides 109
Travelers' checks: see
Currency
Tribal weaving, where to
buy: see Ethnic Minorities
Tsingtao Beer 359
Typhoons 105-106

Uzbekistan, traveling via
89-90

Videos: see Movies and
Videos
Vietnam, traveling via 95
Visas 70-71, 97, 103, 195;
transit visas 70
Voltage 102

Wade-Giles 114, 136-137;
see also Pinyin spelling
Walks 154; see Hiking and

Walks in many
Destinations
Water, potable 188
Waterfalls, largest 576-577
Water Sports: see Beaches;
Rafting; Scuba diving;
Sports; Swimming
Weather 61-62, 63
Weddings 134
Weight and Measures
119-120
Wheelchair Travelers 157
Wildlife and Nature Parks
399, 457, 491, 547, 554,
561, 562-563, 565, 596
Wine 173; see also Food
Work, for foreigners 77,
79-81, 278
Wushi martial arts 468;
see also Entertainment
in a few Destinations

Xi'an Incident 33

Yang Guifei 443, 448
Yuan Shih-kai 32
Yurts 343, 351

Zen Buddhism 309-310
Zhou En Lai: see Chou En-la
Zoos 218, 266, 402, 407,
510, 557, 559-560, 569

FROM THE PUBLISHER

Our goal is to provide you with a guide book second to none. Please bear in mind, however, that things change: phone numbers, admission price, addresses, etc. Should you come across any new information, we'd appreciate hearing from you. No item is too small for us, so if you have a great recommendation, find an error, see that some place has gone out of business, or just plain disagree with our recommendations, write to:

Ruth Lor Malloy
Open Road Publishing
P.O. Box 20226
Columbus Circle Station, New York, NY 10023

OPEN ROAD PUBLISHING
Your Passport to Great Travel!

*Going abroad? Our books have been praised by **Travel & Leisure, Booklist, US News & World Report, Endless Vacation, American Bookseller**, and many other magazines and newspapers!*

Don't leave home without an Open Road travel guide to one of these great destinations:

France Guide, $16.95   **Central America Guide**, $17.95
Italy Guide, $17.95   **Costa Rica Guide**, $16.95
Paris Guide, $12.95   **Belize Guide**, $14.95
Portugal Guide, $16.95   **Honduras & Bay Islands Guide**, $14.95
Spain Guide, $17.95   **Guatemala Guide**, $16.95
London Guide, $13.95   **Southern Mexico & Yucatan Guide**, $14.95
Holland Guide, $14.95   **Bermuda Guide**, $14.95
Austria Guide, $15.95   **Hong Kong & Macau Guide**, $13.95
Israel Guide, $16.95   **China Guide**, $18.95

<u>Forthcoming foreign guides in 1996 and 1997</u>: Greece, Turkey, Ireland, Czech & Slovak Republics, Moscow, India, Vietnam, Japan, Mexico, Kenya, Bahamas, and more!

Open Road's American Vacationland travel series includes:
Las Vegas Guide, $12.95
Disney World & Orlando Theme Parks, $13.95
America's Most Charming Towns & Villages, $16.95
Florida Golf Guide, $16.95

<u>Forthcoming US guides in 1996 and 1997</u>: Colorado, San Francisco, California Wine Country, Arizona, New Mexico, and more!

PLEASE USE ORDER FORM ON THE NEXT PAGE

ORDER FORM

Name and Address: _____

_____

_____

_____ Zip Code: _____

Quantity	Title	Price

Total Before Shipping _____

Shipping/Handling _____

TOTAL _____

Orders must include price of book <u>plus</u> shipping and handling. For shipping and handling, please add $3.00 for the first book, and $1.00 for each book thereafter.

Ask about our discounts for special order bulk purchases.

ORDER FROM: **OPEN ROAD PUBLISHING**
P.O. Box 20226, Columbus Circle Station, New York, NY 10023